JAMES BOSWELL

The Later Years
1769–1795

James Boswell (1740–1795). Painted by Reynolds, 1785.

JAMES BOSWELL

The Later Years
1769–1795

FRANK BRADY

HEINEMANN: LONDON

William Heinemann Ltd

10 Upper Grosvenor Street, London W1X 9PA

LONDON   MELBOURNE   TORONTO

JOHANNESBURG   AUCKLAND

First published 1984

ISBN 0 434 08530 8
Copyright © 1984 by Frank Brady

Printed in the United States of America.

FOR JIM

PREFACE

THIS BOOK GOT its start in 1965. Professor Frederick A. Pottle was just about to publish *James Boswell: The Earlier Years* (1966), the first volume of a two-volume biography, and he asked me to collaborate with him on the second volume. Though my name would appear first on the title-page, this was to be a joint and equal enterprise. We decided that I would write drafts of each chapter, Mr. Pottle would review and revise them, and then we would shape the final version together. This was the method which had worked smoothly when we co-edited *Boswell on the Grand Tour: Italy, Corsica, and France* and *Boswell in Search of a Wife*.

Mr. Pottle made detailed, helpful comments on my drafts of the first two chapters, and read the fourth without supplying suggestions. Then, up to the ninth chapter he was too busy even to read the drafts, nor did he have time to revise the chapters he had read. As I was finishing the ninth chapter he withdrew from collaboration because of his heavy commitments to other projects: in particular, he was in the midst of writing *Pride and Negligence*, his lucid, authoritative history of the Boswell Papers. After I finished, he read this entire volume in typescript and galley proof, again providing most useful corrections and suggestions. Mr. Pottle's work has been the inspiration for this volume, and I have made constant demands on his time, knowledge, and advice throughout its composition. But I alone am responsible for its opinions and its errors.

One problem was left over from collaboration. We had agreed to avoid the pedantry of giving references to our own (that is, mainly his) previously published work. For fear of overlooking important passages, I have made no systematic effort to identify borrowings in the first nine chapters from Mr. Pottle's writings. I can only acknowledge here that my great obligation to him includes phrases, sentences, and perhaps even paragraphs that will have a familiar sound to those acquainted with his publications. In case I have borrowed from their work without acknowledgement, I wish also to thank Mr. Pottle's co-editors in the reading edition of Boswell's private papers: the late William K. Wimsatt, Charles Ryskamp, Charles McC. Weis, Joseph W. Reed, and Irma S. Lustig.

Inevitably, as I wrote this book, I had to consider the purposes and problems of biography in general. Much of what I have to say about them appears in the text, especially in the discussion of the *Life of Johnson* (ch. 17), but it seems appropriate to repeat some points here. The life of a writer, like that of a tailor or anyone else, may be of considerable interest in itself, but the crucial concern of literary biography must be to show, as clearly as the inherent difficulties in the process allow, the connections between a writer's life and his work. A biography can never account for the work, but it can create a context that illuminates it, just as generic and historical contexts do. We need, for example, to know something about the characteristics of epic as a genre as well as something about 17th-century conditions to understand *Paradise Lost*; but also, to grasp it as fully as possible, we need to know something about Milton the individual. Still, the connections between the life and the work seem often best left implicit. The kind of crude pointing, for instance, that identifies a fictional character with some real prototype confuses more than it clarifies.

Though his contract with the reader requires the biographer to stick to his documents and to give his sources, he must be allowed to draw inferences to fill out his presentation, just as we all depend on inferences in our dealings with each other. At the same time, the biographer must refrain from assimilating his subject to himself. Biographers also should restrain the impulse to keep a "sorecard" (as the typo has it), by which they demonstrate their superiority to their subjects, and

> Compound for sins they are inclined to
> By damning those they have no mind to.

Or those they are inclined to, but happily can conceal. "Tell me all your honest heart," Johnson wrote,[1] and Boswell confided in detail in him, in others, and especially in his own journal. Because of this revelation of infirmities, Boswell offers special temptation to a display of high moral tone that is both disagreeable and unnecessary. Moral judgement may be left to the reader.

These obvious infirmities have also misled certain of Boswell's biographers and critics into a condescension towards his literary genius, all the more ludicrous when it is clear that, as writers, they weren't good enough to tie his shoe-laces. In contrast, it is a real problem for Boswell's biographer to know from the start that no matter how fine his performance it will never rival the *Life of Johnson*. As Boswell himself said to Fanny

---

[1] 30 Aug. 1773 (*Life*, ii. 384).

Burney, "There's nothing like it; there never was; and there never will be!" [1]

Boswell lends himself to quotation, and though his easy, natural style puts the defects of his biographer's into relief, I have used direct quotation extensively. To avoid stiffness, short phrases from Boswell and others are sometimes included without quotation marks. Their sources are given in the endnotes.

While I have assumed that the reader has a general knowledge of Mr. Pottle's *James Boswell: The Earlier Years*, which this volume is intended to complement, I have occasionally inserted brief reminders to place certain figures.

---

[1] Madame d'Arblay (Fanny Burney), *Memoirs of Dr. Burney*, 1832, iii. 115 (cited in Collins, p. 37).

ACKNOWLEDGEMENTS

I HAVE LEARNED what Dr. Johnson meant when he said, "Of the caution necessary in adjusting narratives there is no end." [1]   A great many people have helped me write this book, and I have not kept an adequate record of their names.   I hope those not specifically mentioned below will realize how grateful I am to them.   And it is sad that so many of those listed have not lived to receive recognition.

First let me thank the staff of the Boswell Office at Yale over the past seventeen years, especially Irene Adams, Harriet Chidester, Tulin Duda, Benjamin F. Houston, Caterina Kazemzadeh, Marcia W. Levinson, Christopher R. Myers, and Marion S. Pottle.   I have drawn frequently and with confidence on the great mass of annotation to Boswell's journal compiled by Charles H. Bennett.

Many Scots provided hospitality and assistance as I traced Boswell in Ayrshire and Edinburgh, and through the Highlands and Hebrides: Patricia Boswell, Sir Ivar and Lady Colquhoun of Luss, the 28th Earl and Countess of Crawford, the 10th Earl and Countess of Elgin, Flora Lady Eliott of Stobs, Sir James Fergusson of Kilkerran, R. S. M. Milne, Nicholas T. Phillipson, Robert Campbell Preston, and Major and Mrs. Patrick Telfer Smollett.   I remember with special gratitude and affection that grand old lady, Dame Flora MacLeod of MacLeod, and her daughter, Joan Wolrige Gordon.

For assistance of various kinds I wish to thank Marque A. Bagshaw, Peter S. Baker, G. W. S. Barrow, Mark Bitensky, Ian T. Boswell, John R. D. Boswell, Anthony E. Brown, Mary E. Burkett, Margaret Christian, Thomas Crawford, A. Dwight Culler, Richard M. Dunn, Sir Arthur Boswell Eliott of Stobs, Frank H. Ellis, Lillian Feder, Dick Hamilton, Nellie P. Hankins, Catherine Jestin, Ruth Lord, Will Le Moy, Bernard Lytton, Andrew McClellan, Ruth McClure, Allen Mandelbaum, Rosalind K. Marshall, Edwine M. Martz, Georges May, Kay Mowland, Jean Munro, Duncan Mutch, Alison R. Opyrchal, Martin Price, Rufus Reiberg, John C. Riely, Fred C. Robinson, Margaret Ross, Henry W. Sams, Antony P. Shearman, Francis W. H. Sheppard, Warren H. Smith, John Strawhorn, Joan H. Sussler, Valerie

---

[1]Johnson to Dr. Burney, 1 Nov. 1784 (*Life*, iv. 361).

Vaughan, Edward A. Weller, Mark Wollaeger and Nancy Wright.   My graduate students in a 1967 seminar in biography at the City University of New York started me thinking seriously about the problems biography involves, and my colleagues in a 1979 NEH Summer Seminar in biography tested and extended that thinking very helpfully.

Several manuscript collections have been of essential value, and I am grateful to the libraries and private owners who have generously allowed me to use and quote from them.   I have drawn most heavily on documents belonging to or in the possession of Mary Hyde, the Trustees of the National Library of Scotland, the Pierpont Morgan Library, Rear-Admiral P. F. Powlett, the Scottish Record Office, and of course Beinecke Library at Yale.   I wish also to thank the Berg Collection, the British Library, the Cumbria County Record Office, the Edinburgh Central Library, the Fondazione Sella, Arthur A. Houghton, the Houghton Library, the Huntington Library, the Lewis Walpole Library, the Osborn Collection, the Rosenbach Museum, and the Director of the Sheffield City Libraries and the Trustees of the Fitzwilliam Estate.

The help given me by the following organizations and institutions has made it possible for me to write this book.   I wish to thank the John Simon Guggenheim Memorial Foundation (fellowship, 1966–67), the American Council of Learned Societies (summer grant, 1969), the National Endowment for the Humanities (senior research fellowship, 1976–77), the administration and staff of Yale University for their cooperation; and, especially, administrators and colleagues at the Graduate School and Hunter College of the City University of New York, who awarded me several research grants and made my work much easier in many ways.

Eric Mendelsohn, Gale Sigal, and Gordon Turnbull checked references, and Mr. Turnbull, an astute and thorough critic, made suggestions on style and content throughout.   Marshall Waingrow kindly reviewed ch. 17.   Rachel McClellan deserves special mention: she was tireless in locating material, checking references, making suggestions on style and content, proofreading, and in particular helping to choose, gather, and get permissions to reproduce illustrations.   Also, she largely carried through the laborious task of compiling the index.   Dan Lacy and Thomas H. Quinn of McGraw-Hill have been encouraging and patient.   Anita R. Jones typed the manuscript with unusual care and accuracy.

My greatest debt, as always, is to Fred Pottle.

F. B.

New Haven and New York
10 December 1983

CONTENTS

ILLUSTRATIONS

Frontispiece
James Boswell, painting by Sir Joshua Reynolds. Reproduced by permission of the National Portrait Gallery, London.

Following page 200
John Stuart, Viscount Mountstuart, painting by Sir Joshua Reynolds. Reproduced by permission of the Earl of Wharncliffe.

Samuel Johnson, LL.D., painting by Sir Joshua Reynolds. Reproduced by permission of the Quaker Collection, Haverford College Library.

Henry Dundas, painting by Sir Joshua Reynolds. Now in a private Scottish Collection.

Sir William Forbes of Pitsligo, Bt., painting by Sir Joshua Reynolds. Reproduced by permission of Sotheby Parke Bernet and Company.

Pasquale Paoli, painting by Richard Cosway. Reproduced by permission of the Uffizi Gallery, Florence.

Edmond Malone, painting by Sir Joshua Reynolds. Reproduced by permission of the National Portrait Gallery, London.

John Courtenay, etching by James Sayer. Reproduced by permission of the Trustees of the British Museum.

James Lowther, first Earl of Lonsdale, painting by Thomas Hudson. Reproduced by permission of the Lonsdale Estate Trust.

"The Pacific Entrance of Earl-Wolf, into Blackhaven," engraving by James Gillray. Reproduced by permission of the Trustees of the British Museum.

Sir Alexander Boswell, Bt., painting by Sir Martin Archer Shee, present whereabouts unknown. Photograph reproduced by permission of the National Portrait Gallery, London.

xv

CHRONOLOGY

25 November 1769 Marries his first cousin, Margaret Montgomerie, at Lainshaw, Ayrshire. On the same day Lord Auchinleck marries his first cousin, Elizabeth Boswell, at Edinburgh

End of *James Boswell: The Earlier Years*

1771	Paoli visits Scotland
1772	Revisits London for the first time since marriage
1772	*Reflections on the Late Alarming Bankruptcies*
1773	Veronica born
1773	Elected to The Club
1773	Tours Highlands and Hebrides with Johnson
1774	Euphemia born
1774	Defends John Reid, sheep-stealer
1775	Alexander born
September 1777	Meets Johnson for ten days at Ashbourne, Derbyshire
1777–83	*The Hypochondriack*
1778	James Jr. born
1780	*Letter to Lord Braxfield*
1780	Elizabeth born
30 August 1782	Lord Auchinleck dies. Succeeds as Laird of Auchinleck
1783	First *Letter to the People of Scotland* (on Fox's East India Bill)
13 December 1784	Johnson dies
1785	Second *Letter to the People of Scotland* (on the Bill to diminish the number of Lords of Session)
1785	*Journal of a Tour to the Hebrides*
1785	Meets Lonsdale
13 February 1786	Called to the English bar
1788	Recorder of Carlisle
1788	*Ode by Dr. Samuel Johnson to Mrs. Thrale*
4 June 1789	Margaret dies
1790	Breaks with Lonsdale, and resigns Recordership
1791	*No Abolition of Slavery*
16 May 1791	*Life of Samuel Johnson, LL.D.*
1793	Second edition of *Life*
19 May 1795	Dies in London

PROLOGUE

[This Prologue offers a brief summary of the first twenty-nine years of Boswell's life together with a few comments on Scotland and the times for the benefit of readers unfamiliar with F. A. Pottle's *James Boswell: The Earlier Years*, the first volume of this biography. Some points made here are repeated in later chapters.]

I

JAMES BOSWELL WAS BORN in Edinburgh on 29 October 1740, the eldest son of Alexander Boswell, a rising advocate of 33, and his wife Euphemia (Erskine). Two brothers also survived childhood: John (b. 1743) and David (b. 1748). Like his father "Old James," Alexander combined his Edinburgh legal practice with a deep devotion to Auchinleck, the family estate in Ayrshire, to which he succeeded in 1749. In 1754 he was appointed one of the fifteen members of the Court of Session, the highest civil court in Scotland, assuming the non-hereditary judicial style of Lord Auchinleck. A year later he became "a judge of the double robe" when he was appointed one of the six members of the Court of Justiciary, the highest criminal court in Scotland. Lord Auchinleck exhibited those virtues most esteemed in a Presbyterian, Whig society: he was upright, hardworking, shrewd, practical, and totally unimaginative. A noted teller of anecdotes, he directed his sarcasm at all that was flighty, fanciful, or unusual in any way. Euphemia, ten years younger than her husband, was gentle, timid, and pious.

The family lived in Blair's Land (a "land" was a tall building with a number of flats), Parliament Close, in the heart of Edinburgh. Boswell was educated first at Mundell's School and then at home by the family chaplains, until at thirteen, a common age for matriculation, he entered the University of Edinburgh. A pampered, fearful, stingy child, kept

1

overdependent on his parents and allowed no will of his own, he early displayed the family tendency to sink into periods of melancholy.   The University provided a respectable if socially limited education and Boswell, according to his own account, was praised for intellectual distinction.   There he met two lifelong friends: John Johnston of Grange, afterwards a "writer" (solicitor) in Edinburgh, and William Johnson Temple, son of the sometime mayor of Berwick upon Tweed, afterwards an Anglican clergyman.

At sixteen Boswell was sent to Moffat, a spa north of Dumfries, to recover from a nervous crisis of some kind, and was briefly converted to Methodism.   But about this time (to quote Mr. Pottle), he discovered "he had a natural power of inspiring affection," and his personality underwent a remarkable change: "the timid, priggish, prematurely grave youngster was replaced outwardly by a vain, noisy, bouncing, odd, comical, good-humoured youth of manly features and masculine bearing whom many men and most women found immediately attractive."   In periods of stress, however, his lack of basic self-confidence was liable to manifest itself again.

After going through the four-year Arts course at the University Boswell began, as his father had planned for him, the study of Civil Law there. But he was far more interested in the theatre, both because it was fascinating in itself and because it served his adolescent need to distance himself from his parents.   He also took to scribbling: paraphrases of the Psalms, odes, eclogues, verse epistles, songs, and comical ballads.   His first prose piece of any length was a pamphlet, *A View of the Edinburgh Theatre during the Summer Season, 1759 . . . by a Society of Gentlemen*, published in February 1760, which singled out for praise a Roman Catholic actress, Mrs. Cowper, with whom he was vainly in love.

But Lord Auchinleck, alarmed at his son's stage-struck progress, had already (autumn 1759) transferred the scene of his activities to the University of Glasgow, where Boswell attended Adam Smith's lectures on moral philosophy (ranging from ethics to economics) and rhetoric.   And from Glasgow Boswell eloped (his word) to London in March 1760 with the notion—presumably under Mrs. Cowper's influence—of becoming a monk. Though very briefly becoming a Catholic, he almost immediately abandoned religion for what he called "the melting and transporting rites of love" as well as other delights of the metropolis; and under the guidance of Alexander, Earl of Eglinton, an Ayrshire neighbour, he was introduced "into the circles of the great, the gay, and the ingenious."   These circles included David Garrick, the most famous of English actors; Laurence Sterne, the season's sensation as the author of *Tristram Shandy*; and even Edward,

Duke of York, younger brother of the future George III, to whom Boswell read his Shandean autobiographical poem, *The Cub at Newmarket.*

After three wonderful months, Lord Auchinleck fetched Boswell home to parental tutelage and the Civil Law once more.   Or rather to a conflict of wills, for having experienced London Boswell's aim was now a commission in the Guards.   Matters came to a crisis in the spring of 1762: in exchange for a guaranteed allowance of £100 a year Boswell signed a document, which he later referred to as a renunciation of his birthright, giving his father the power to vest the estate in trustees after his death. As part of this bargain, no doubt, he was permitted to return to London to pursue a commission.

The story of the next year is told in Boswell's celebrated London Journal (November 1762–August 1763): his efforts to get a commission in the Guards failed; his hope for "at least a winter's safe copulation" with an actress, Louisa, ended in satiety and gonorrhoea.   But also he enjoyed himself by publishing his indiscreet correspondence with his friend Andrew Erskine, and by becoming acquainted with prominent people like Oliver Goldsmith and John Wilkes.   Still, his varying moods darkened into depression as he vacillated about his career.   Then on Monday 16 May 1763 in the back parlour of Thomas Davies's bookshop in Russell St., Covent Garden, he met Samuel Johnson.   This acquaintance, which Boswell soon cultivated, was to assure his fame; his immediate future was determined by another bargain with his father: he would study law at Utrecht for a winter, be allowed to visit Paris and some German courts, and then take up his father's profession in Edinburgh.

Boswell was bored, chaste, and deeply unhappy for much of his stay in Utrecht, but he weathered it out and revived as soon as he started (June 1764) on a Grand Tour that was to extend far beyond his father's original plan.   First the German courts, followed by interviews with Rousseau and Voltaire *en route* to a jaunt through Italy: Turin, Milan, Naples where he consorted with Wilkes, Rome during Holy Week, Venice with his new friend Lord Mountstuart (eldest son of the former Prime Minister, the Earl of Bute), Florence, and sweet Siena where Giroloma Piccolomini (Moma), wife of a leading citizen, fell deeply in love with him.   But what made this Grand Tour unique was Boswell's visit to primitive Corsica, where Pasquale Paoli was leading Corsican rebels first against the Genoese and later the French.   On the way home (January 1766), Boswell learned from a newspaper at Paris that his mother had died, and he hurried back to Scotland, taking in his charge Rousseau's mistress, Thérèse Le Vasseur, with whom he conducted a casual affair.   He stopped just long enough in London to deposit Thérèse, to renew his friendship with Johnson, and to have an interview on the subject of Corsica with the great William Pitt, who called Paoli a hero out of Plutarch's *Lives*.

It was time to settle down.   Having submitted the required Latin thesis in Civil Law (dedicated to Mountstuart), Boswell passed advocate on 26 July 1766 and quickly built a respectable practice, though he did arouse some comment by his zeal in defending poor criminal clients, including a sheep-stealer named John Reid, whom he got off in the teeth of the evidence.   But his most significant role as a young lawyer was as a volunteer in the Douglas Cause, the greatest lawsuit of eighteenth-century Scotland. The orphaned Archibald Douglas claimed the huge estates of his uncle, the Duke of Douglas, as the son of the Duke's sister, Lady Jane Douglas. But he had been born in very obscure circumstances in Paris when his mother was fifty, and other claimants, notably the guardians of the young Duke of Hamilton, claimed that Douglas was a supposititious child and actually the son of Parisians.

The circumstantial evidence in the case clearly favoured the Hamiltonian argument but Boswell, who felt his own filiation was often metaphorically in question, warmly supported Douglas in a series of anonymous publications.   The first was *Dorando, a Spanish Tale*, a transparent allegory which slandered the Hamiltonians under the name of the Arvidoso party, and predicted Douglas's victory in the Court of Session.   (When the newspaper publishers of Edinburgh were cited for contempt of court for spelling out *Dorando's* application to the Cause, Boswell calmly acted as counsel for one of them.)

Contrary to his prediction, the Hamiltonians triumphed in the Court of Session by one vote (July 1767), the case being immediately appealed to the House of Lords.   That November Boswell published two short but effective pamphlets, *The Essence of the Douglas Cause*, which compressed the immense record of evidence in the case into a lucid presentation of the Douglas argument; and *Letters of Lady Jane Douglas*, which showed her belief in her son's genuineness and made a powerful appeal to tender feelings. In February 1769 the House of Lords reversed the decision of the Court of Session, and Boswell led the Edinburgh mob that broke his father's windows for failing to illuminate them in honour of Douglas's victory.

Enthusiastic as he was for Douglas, Boswell was even more deeply devoted to the Corsican cause.   As soon as he returned to the Continent from Corsica Boswell became its propagandist, contributing a series of what he privately distinguished as "facts" and "inventions" to the newspapers to rouse support for Paoli.   And the Corsican cause provided the incentive for his first major work, *An Account of Corsica, The Journal of a Tour to That Island, and Memoirs of Pascal Paoli*, published in February 1768.   A best seller, translated into Dutch, German, Italian, and twice into French, it mobilized widespread British sympathy for the Corsicans.   Boswell also raised money to buy arms for them, and edited a volume called *British Essays in Favour of the Brave Corsicans* (1769).   But the British government was reluctant to risk war with France by openly helping Paoli, and superior French force drove him into exile in England (June 1769).   Johnson accurately summarized the *Account of Corsica* itself: "Your History is like other histories, but your Journal is in a very high degree curious and delightful." Though much slighter than his later *Tour to the Hebrides* and *Life of Johnson*, this work already evinces Boswell's supreme ability both to depict character through select detail and to utilize his own personality as part of his presentation. And the *Account of Corsica* made him famous at twenty-seven. As he remarked to Paoli many years later, "I had got upon a rock in Corsica and jumped into the middle of life."

Amid this whirl of public activity, Boswell also sustained an intense private existence centred on his search for a wife.   Marital possibilities ranged from the completely unsuitable gardener's daughter to the equally unsuitable—for almost opposite reasons—brilliant bluestocking, Belle de Zuylen (Zélide), whom Boswell had met during his stay in Holland and was still courting, by post, in a most tentative manner.   Other prospects included Elizabeth Diana Bosville, daughter of Godfrey Bosville, his wealthy Yorkshire "chief"; Catherine Blair ("the Princess"), highly favoured by Lord Auchinleck as the heiress of a nearby estate; and sixteen-year-old Mary Ann Boyd, an Irish cousin.   Not that Boswell lacked for immediate pleasure while he delighted in this not wholly serious round of lovemaking: he had established a connection with a Mrs. Dodds ("Circe"), a lively grass widow.

Nor had Boswell's travels ended.   After the publication of *Corsica* he had gone to London in spring 1768 to keep up his friendship with Johnson and to enjoy fame as an author; though he was confined for several weeks with a venereal infection, London's hold on his imagination grew still stronger. In spring 1769 he set off for Ireland to renew his suit for Miss Boyd, accompanied by his first cousin and confidante from childhood, Margaret Montgomerie.   His new reputation made him a great social success in Dublin, but poor Mary Ann was dismissed as too young.   In fact it was Margaret with whom he was in love.   That July they became engaged, much to the displeasure of Lord Auchinleck, who could not sneer at the ancestry of his own niece but who could and did object vigorously to her lack of fortune. Again he and Boswell found themselves on very strained terms.   Boswell remained determined to marry Margaret, but convinced himself that first he must go to London to find a cure for a serious, persistent case of gonorrhoea.   Once there, he could not resist the lure of one of the great public shows of the time, the three-day Shakespeare jubilee at Stratford, presided over by Garrick, where he made a highly satisfactory appearance at the masquerade ball as an armed Corsican chief.   It was his last bachelor fling.   On 25 November 1769 he and Margaret were married at her family home, Lainshaw, in Ayrshire.   On the same day Lord Auchinleck married *his* first cousin, Elizabeth Boswell, in Edinburgh.

I I

OUR CONCEPTION OF eighteenth-century Scotland is largely formed by that great series of novels in which Sir Walter Scott constructed a usable national history: *Old Mortality* (laid in 1679), *Rob Roy* (1715), *The Heart of Midlothian* (1736), *Waverley* (1745), *Redgauntlet* (1766), *Guy Mannering* (1781), and *The Antiquary* (1790s).   Scott relied on the dramatic possibilities inherent in the connections and contrasts of time (past/present), locale (Highlands/Lowlands), politics (Jacobites/Whigs), religion (Covenanters/moderates), and class (gentry/common folk).   What emerges is a composite of the Scottish character: independent, proud of family and country, highly aware of rights and dignity, often narrow-minded and fiercely prejudiced, but admirably honest, shrewd, articulate, tenaciously loyal to conscience, and capable of a fine generosity of spirit.

Scott's narratives are animated by the competing claims of romance and realism, and take place in an atmosphere marked by resonance and depth. The actual Scotland of Boswell's time was both flatter and more complex than that depicted in this series of portraits.   To the Lowlander, the Highlands and Hebrides remained as unknown, in Dr. Johnson's phrase, "as Borneo or Sumatra."   Their significance also steadily diminished as Scotland made the transition into a commercial age.   It was taken for granted that society's interests were more important than the individual's, and few except radicals questioned the legitimacy of subordination, the theory that the proper arrangement of society was a hierarchical order— still visible in institutions like the army or the Anglican church. Subordination was upheld in practice by restricting the franchise to about 4,000 voters in a population of 1,500,000, and these voters were largely controlled by local magnates, great and small. In other matters, well-to-do merchants dominated the few burghs of any size, and the gentry ruled the rural areas with little dispute. Manufacturing grew (first linen, then cotton), the Glasgow tobacco trade flourished until the American War, and a few mines were worked. But the Lowlands were primarily agricultural and, despite recurrent periods of suffering when the crops failed, both land and farming methods were much improved during the eighteenth century. Roads were wretched until late in the period, and goods of any weight were shipped by sea. For recreation the common people had, as usual, sex and drink, to which Presbyterians of the various denominations added a passionate attachment to religion, theological hair-splitting being a welcome intellectual diversion.

Edinburgh, the ancient capital, lost its political importance with the Union of 1707, but it remained the largest city in Scotland (pop. 80,000 in 1790) and its unquestioned legal and intellectual centre. Starting in the late 1760s, the New Town was laid out in its pleasing rectangular pattern of Georgian houses. Boswell stayed faithful to the Old Town, built around the Royal Mile as it runs downhill from the Castle to the Palace of Holyroodhouse. The Courts of Session and Justiciary sat in Edinburgh—though justiciary judges also went on circuit—and the profession of choice for the middle and upper classes, as throughout Scotland, was the law. What gave Edinburgh its name as the "Athens of the North" was the remarkable group of thinkers who gathered there: Adam Smith, David Hume, the historian William Robertson, the political scientist Adam Ferguson, the chemist Joseph Black, Lord Monboddo who wrote on anthropology and language, Lord Kames who wrote on every topic, a dozen more writers of stature but less permanent interest, and the finest medical faculty in Europe. It was also a small enough place so that everyone knew everyone.

Boswell belonged to this distinguished society by birth and upbringing, but he was far more proud that he was of the line of Boswell of Auchinleck, where the family had been established since the beginning of the sixteenth century. Though never politically notable—they had a talent for lining up with the losing cause—Boswell's ancestors married well, establishing many connections with the noble and powerful. But their sense of dignity rested on their own consequence as landed gentry.

By the late seventeenth century, reverses had diminished the family fortunes considerably, but Boswell's grandfather and father restored and extended the estate. Lord Auchinleck, in particular, was assiduous in buying land and pruning the trees he himself had planted. Boswell boasted of the new house in the Adam style that his father had built, of the size of the estate (it ran east to west for almost fifteen miles), of the 600 tenants. Like Milton's Eden, it was "a happy rural seat of various view," at least for those temperamentally suited to country life. And it was remote. Though only 70 miles from Edinburgh as the crow flies, the primitive roads made it an overnight journey for most of Boswell's life.

In 1769 Lord Auchinleck's rent-roll amounted to a comfortable £1,000–1,200 a year, to which he added his salaries as a Lord of Session (£700 a year) and (Justiciary £200 a year). It can be confidently assumed that he lived well within his income. Boswell's troubles in later life were emotional rather than economic in origin; still, a comparable income would have eased the burdens of existence. At the time our story opens, however, every prospect pleased.

CHAPTER

1

IN APRIL 1772, Boswell met John Wilkes for the first time in six years. When Wilkes teased him for not coming to see an old friend in gaol, Boswell was prompt to defend himself: "I do assure you I am glad to meet with you, but I cannot come to see you. I am a Scotch laird and a Scotch lawyer and a Scotch married man. It would not be decent."

Decency—discretion, propriety—Boswell had struck a new note. In most people it is the disreputable that remains hidden; in his case, it is the respectable elements of his character that became submerged or forgotten. Marriage had focused his goals. He had taken on responsibility and put away childish things. Not merely the drinking and raking that contemporaries expected in any high-spirited young man. Boswell had put behind him all those exceptional desires and excursions that had given his bachelor life its unusual colouring. In 1760, at the age of nineteen, he had run off to London, become a Catholic briefly, and spent three eye-opening months before being hauled home. Since then, a will and energy both imperfectly under control had hurried him into a series of similar enthusiastic indiscretions. He had insisted on trying to obtain a commission in the Guards. He and his friend Andrew Erskine had amused themselves by printing their gossipy correspondence. A violent partisan of Douglas in the great Douglas Cause, he had published anonymously a transparent allegory, *Dorando*, libelling not only the Hamiltonians on the other side, but attributing a judgement on the Cause to his father's good friend and colleague, Robert Dundas, Lord President of the Court of Session, that was the opposite of his real one. And when his father refused

to illuminate his windows in honour of Douglas's victory, Boswell led the
mob that broke them.   No wonder David Hume had described him not
only as "very good humoured, very agreeable," but also as "very mad."

Equally this will and energy had been put to more generally acceptable
purposes.   Willing to risk rejection, Boswell had talked his way around the
Grand Tour, negotiating interviews with some of his most important contemporaries—Rousseau, Voltaire, and Pitt.   He had also made two outstanding friends: Samuel Johnson and the great Corsican general, Pasquale
Paoli.   Boswell's trip to Corsica, far off the usual track of the Grand Tour,
had led to his becoming both useful and conspicuous in the Corsican struggle for liberty against the French; and it inspired his first major work, the
highly successful *Account of Corsica*.   Now that past also lay behind him:
the Corsican cause was dead, and for a time anyway there would be no
more jaunts to London to see Johnson.

The enduring motif of Boswell's life had been his struggle with his
father.   Alexander Boswell, styled Lord Auchinleck, wore the double gown
of the Courts of Session and Justiciary, the highest civil and criminal courts
in Scotland.   He was also a prosperous landowner, dedicated to improving
and extending Auchinleck, his estate in Ayrshire.   "Give Your Son His
Will" was the title of Boswell's early attempt at a comedy—he was seldom
subtle about his desires—but Lord Auchinleck had no patience with this
foolish notion, and his reactions to Boswell's eccentric activities ranged from
shock and dismay to outrage.   They had lost their natural intermediary
when Boswell's mother died in 1766, and though, the same year, Boswell
passed advocate at his father's insistence, their relationship remained full
of strains.

Boswell's most serious indiscretion was to marry his penniless first
cousin and friend from childhood, Margaret Montgomerie, on 25 November 1769, at her family home, Lainshaw, in Ayrshire.   His father under-
scored his strong objection to this financially disastrous marriage by marrying
his own middle-aged first cousin, Elizabeth Boswell, on the same day in
Edinburgh.   Still, Boswell's marriage committed him to his father's mode
of life, to being sober, practical, and responsible, to taking his place among
his hard-working fellow advocates, as the new couple settled in Edinburgh.

And marvellous to say, Boswell was happy.   Not through that agitation
of mind or intensification of consciousness with which he had always identified happiness, but through a calm contentment he had never experienced
before.   His growth in self-discipline showed itself in his circumspect behaviour towards his father and stepmother.   Whether it was a tingling in
Lord Auchinleck's veins, as Erskine joked, or merely a need for companion-

ship that led him to remarry, Boswell hid his anger at what he felt was his
father's folly and betrayal of him, and the two families stayed at least on
visiting terms.   Yet as a supporter of Douglas, who was supposed to have
been born to a mother of fifty, Boswell could hardly have been soothed
when the Rev. W. J. Temple observed that "women at forty seldom conceive; if they do, it is often fatal to them."   Boswell took consolation in his
present good relations with his father, reassuring himself that "honest man,
he really is, I believe, very fond of me."

Marriage was the basis of his happiness.   He and Margaret were first
separated two months after their wedding by the death of her brother-in-
law, Capt. Alexander Montgomerie-Cuninghame.   After they attended the
funeral she stayed on in Ayrshire, and their letters crossed in the post.
Margaret wrote:

> How much am I indebted to my kindest, dearest friend for the
> relief his friendly letter[1] gave me.   I dare say you can figure my
> distress and may therefore judge how agreeable it was to receive
> good accounts when I was so apprehensive of the contrary. . . .
> May the Almighty bless and preserve you to your ever faithful
> friend.   I am sorry your father has been indisposed.   Is it the
> cold or his old complaint?[2]

Boswell showed equal concern:

> I am anxious on account of the cold which you had when I left
> you.   I am afraid your rising so early and taking so kind a charge
> of me when setting out may have done you harm.   Pray take care
> of yourself.   You have always been my steady friend.   Consider
> that your being well and happy is absolutely necessary to make
> me so.   I think in that manner in order to direct my conduct.
> Believe me, my dearest, the short absence which I have now suf-
> fered has convinced me still more feelingly than before how much
> I love you, what real happiness it is to me to enjoy your company,
> and how ill I can do without you.   Indeed it is a great comfort
> that we have an entire confidence in each other's affection, which
> no doubt alleviates the pain of separation.   It is a common ob-
> servation that we never value sufficiently any happiness till we are
> deprived of it.   It is lucky if a short separation has the same effect
> on both our minds that the long and melancholy parting by death
> has on the survivor.   I declare to you, my dear Peggie, that my
> strong imagination is so much affected just now that I can form,
> I dare say, a tolerably just idea of what I should feel if you was

[1]Not recovered.
[2]A stoppage of urine.

taken from me, for this life. I pray fervently to God for your
preservation.... You see I am very serious just now.

Very much in love, very dependent on one another, but Boswell's
attitude is the more self-conscious. He is counting his blessings. Already
he is brooding over Margaret's possible illness or death, as he was always
to do when separated from her, though on this occasion he must have been
particularly concerned because of her pregnancy. In May they were pleased
to move from their temporary accommodations in the Cowgate to an admirable "house" (flat) in Chessel's Buildings in the Canongate.

As well as realigning Boswell's relationship with his father, marriage
inevitably had its impact on his friends. Some brides like their husbands
to seal devotion by sacrificing old friendships, or at least demand to "new-
mint"—as Charles Lamb puts it—such relics before they pass current. Fortunately, Margaret accepted John Johnston of Grange, Boswell's closest
Edinburgh confidant, at once as "a real, comfortable friend," and Grange
(as Boswell always calls him) over the years came to act as family guardian
when Boswell was on his travels.

But in faraway Devon, Temple, Boswell's "old and most intimate friend,"
showed some weakening of confidence. Not openly connected to Margaret; though Temple had never met her, he felt able, on the basis of
Boswell's accounts, to praise her "easiness of temper and equal flow of
spirits," and in his "sacerdotal character" to offer his blessing. It was rather
sensitivity about the situation in general. In late February 1770, his alarm
burst forth:

> I am uneasy at not hearing from you. I wrote to you and Mrs.
> Boswell some time in December last. I cannot conceive the mean-
> ing of your silence. Pray deliver me from this anxiety and write
> by the return of the post.

Temple's uneasiness was fed by other sources. Living on an annual
stipend of £80 and a steadily decreasing private income, heartily sick of
his own profession and bored with the mindless society of a rural parish,
he fumbled his way towards some profitable pursuit. Over the next few
years various possibilities entertained him: the study of medicine; translations of Bruckerus, Della Valle, Fra Paolo, or almost anyone; a history
of Florence or Venice. But, though industrious, Temple lacked books
and self-confidence. Hume had greatly impressed him in his early Edinburgh days, and now his refrain was, "Ask Mr. Hume what I should read,
what I should do." Meanwhile, Mrs. Temple was multiplying inexorably.

A not wholly satisfactory letter from Boswell in May led Temple into some teasing questions:

> Does Mrs. Boswell engross you entirely?   Can the gay, the volatile Boswell, whom hardly variety itself could satiate, confine himself to one object?   Have you no expedition in your head, no essay in prose, no epistle in verse?   Or do you begin to think it your chief merit to be a good husband and a good lawyer?

The answer to Temple's last question was yes.   Marriage had freed Boswell to concentrate his energies on the law in its various branches: civil, criminal, and ecclesiastical.   In winter (November 1769 to March 1770) and summer (June to August 1770) terms of the Court of Session, Boswell appeared in over forty causes and made 115 guineas.   This busy, if not unusually profitable, practice continued to benefit from his father's position on the Bench, some fifteen of Boswell's causes being argued before him. Naturally enough Boswell was ordinarily engaged as junior counsel.   But Lord Auchinleck's £300 yearly allowance provided the most substantial part of his income; it was a family tether to Scotland and the law.

Boswell found, as most readers do, criminal cases more compelling than civil, and one of his most flamboyant drew to a close in the spring of 1770.   His client, William Harris, merchant in Ayr, had been arrested in August 1768 for forging and uttering banknotes of the Thistle Bank of Glasgow on a grand scale.   In November 1769 he escaped from the Edinburgh Tolbooth; after recapture he badly slashed a keeper's head with a bottle, and pretended insanity.   (On a smaller felonious scale, a fellow prisoner accused him of using a marked deck at cards.) Although his defence was headed by Alexander Lockhart, Dean of the Faculty of Advocates and a master of pathos, Harris had no chance.   He tried to strangle himself with his handkerchief and garters on 6 February 1770, was found guilty by the Court of Justiciary on 24 April, and was hanged in the Grassmarket on 30 May.

The plentiful evidence scattered through the papers connected with his case suggests that Harris was rash, greedy, and stupid.   Yet James Neill, "writer" (solicitor) in Ayr, thought him a "poor, distressed man," and after Harris was retaken Boswell, with his customary generosity to the friendless criminal, gave him a guinea.   But charity was mixed with Boswell's unassuageable curiosity about the impact of visibly approaching death.   Would the condemned man (criminals were the handiest experimental subjects) abandon worldly considerations to fit himself for eternity?   The evening before Harris's execution, Boswell insisted on knowing "from him as a dying man the truth as to his accomplices." Harris persisted in his previous account, whatever that was, leaving Boswell incredulous. At the end, Harris "seemed very penitent and not at all frightened. He suffered great pain to all appearance." His hanging threw Boswell into shock, followed by gloom.

Criminal cases, like Harris's, mainly provided excitement and a chance to be prominent; civil law was the advocate's staple. Practice at the bar of the General Assembly, the leading body of the (Presbyterian) Church of Scotland, which met for two weeks in the spring, might be considered the advocate's *bonne bouche.* To argue cases before an impressionable jury of over 350 ministers and elders was very different from pleading before the Lord Ordinary in the Court of Session or the six judges of the Court of Justiciary, though the latter court also offered a jury as audience. The General Assembly was the only great debating school left in Scotland. But practice there, though lucrative, was not quite the thing, as Boswell's friend and fellow-advocate John Maclaurin observed in *The Moderator's*[1] *Advice to James Boswell, Esq.* (to the tune of "A Bumper, Squire Jones"):

> Sure great is the folly
> In him whom Paoli
> His friendship permitted to share,
> To go for a guinea
> (Dear Boswell, what mean ye?)
> To plead at so scurvy a bar. . . .

Briefed by Walter Scott, W.S.[2] (the novelist's father), Boswell took his first case there late in May. It was one of the most celebrated cases of the time, the Patron of St. Ninians v. the People of the Parish, bearing directly on the split in the Church of Scotland between the Popular or Highflying party, led by Boswell's grand-uncle Dr. Alexander Webster, and the more liberal Moderate party, led by Principal William Robertson. The focus of their differences was the right of the patron, upheld by the Moderates, to present a minister to the parish whether or not the people concurred.

This issue roused something close to class struggle. In politics and in daily life, the Scottish people submitted with some docility to the nobility and gentry who ruled them. They rendered unto Caesar. But religious independence was their passionate inheritance from John Knox and the

---

[1]The Moderator was the presiding officer of the General Assembly.
[2]Writer to the Signet, the highest class of "writer."

Covenanters, and the ministry was the traditional route by which the bright poor boy moved upwards in society.   The people clung with such feeling to their own choice of minister that they sometimes resisted presentations by force or seceded to form a new church.

The Moderates argued that popular elections caused division and tumult, that the patron was likely to make a wiser choice than the people, and that patronage tended to raise the intellectual and social level of the ministry.   Further, Robertson and his friends skilfully appealed to the General Assembly's assertion of supremacy over the lower courts: kirk-session, presbytery, and synod.

St. Ninians was a model case.   The patron, Sir John Steuart of Allan-bank, presented David Thomson to this extensive and populous parish in 1766.   Fifty-five years old and hampered by "a weak voice and delicacy of constitution," Thomson was repeatedly rejected by the lower courts, which were as repeatedly overruled by the General Assembly.   The case dragged on until 1773—Boswell appearing each year on behalf of the patron—and when Thomson was finally admitted to the parish, the presiding minister was so rude that he was severely rebuked by the General Assembly.   Most of the congregation seceded.

As well as being Edinburgh's major business, the law provided much of its entertainment.   United in what was termed technically "The College of Justice," the bench and bar formed in effect a large men's club of social equals, ready on occasion to laugh at themselves or at least at each other. A repeated target for wit was the extraordinary collection of bright, self-willed, and often eccentric judges which made up the Court of Session ("the Fifteen").   They have come down to us stuck over with picturesque-ness, but they were a sturdy and original lot who compelled respect as much as they invited laughter.   In any case, no one is funnier than a superior. Boswell parodies their reactions to an unidentified case in his *Court of Session Garland*.   (Maclaurin "used to sing it frequently," Robert Chambers wrote much later, "in the slow, drawling, *naïf* style, which added so much to its value in the estimation of a last-century hearer.")

> The judgement Lord Alemoor as illegal blames;
> 'Tis equity, ye bitch, replies my Lord Kames.
> This question, quoth Hailes, to judge we can't pretend
> For justice, I observe, wants an "e" at the end,
> An "e" at the end, etc. . . .
>
> Lord Coalston expresses his doubts and his fears,
> And Strichen throws in his "well, wells" and "oh, dears."

This very much resembles the case of McHarg
And should go the same way, says Lordie Barjarg,[1]
Lordie Barjarg, etc.

Says Pitfour, with a wink and his hat set a-jee,[2]
I remember a case in the year twenty-three:
The Bailies of Banff against Robert Karr,
I remember it well, I was then at the bar,
Then at the bar, etc. . . .

Then up spoke the President, and an angry man was he,
To alter this judgement I never can agree.
The east side cried "yes," and the west side cried "not,"[3]
But it carried "adhere"[4] by his casting vote,
Casting vote, etc.

As this piece shows, marriage had not completely silenced Boswell the writer. Besides poetic squibs, he acted as the *London Chronicle*'s occasional correspondent in Edinburgh, and for years also favoured the *Public Advertiser* in London with a series of letters signed "Rampager," "to rampage" meaning "to indulge in joyous, extravagant merriment, free of all care and all malice." Free of all thought, anyway, these "lively essays" (Boswell's estimate) usually offered frothy comment on political affairs, but they also rampaged over a range of topics from Dr. Molineux's Smelling Medicine to book titles applied to events of the American War.

Seeing his name or even his anonymous opinions in print aggrandized Boswell's sense of self, and he did not distinguish between excellent reporting and indifferent attempts to entertain. What mattered was that his writing had an effect on others. But what was the self he was nurturing?

It was a puzzle he approached indirectly through an anonymous essay, "On the Profession of a Player," spread over three issues of the *London Magazine* (August–October 1770). Boswell was fascinated by "that mysterious power by which a player really is the character which he represents." Representation is achieved through "a kind of double feeling": the emotions appropriate to the role "must take full possession, as it were, of the antechamber of [the actor's] mind, while his own character remains in the innermost recess." The transition to Boswell's own profession was easy:

[1]Called "Lordie" because of his small size.
[2]Pitfour wore a hat on the bench to shade his weak eyes.
[3]The Court sat in a semicircle, with the President in the middle.
[4]"Adhere" and "alter" are the equivalents of "sustain" and "reverse."

> This is experienced in some measure by the barrister who enters
> warmly into the cause of his client, while at the same time when
> he examines himself coolly he knows that he is much in the wrong,
> and does not even wish to prevail.

Similarly, in society we pretend to care more about others than we do, and
in many a scene of social life a man has "to work himself into a state of
feeling which he would not naturally have had."

The actor, sustaining two characters simultaneously, is the extreme
case of the ordinary person, who has to co-ordinate inner and social selves.
(Boswell's own ability, and need, to take on the tone of his company was
unusual, but it reflected his youthful search for models and his uncertain
sense of identity.)   And the actor, he goes on, becomes someone else
"without the intervention of any cause whatever, but a voluntary operation
of his own mind."

"How does one do that?" is the implied question.   Boswell seeks refuge
in simile: some minds take "a colour from the objects around them, like
the effects of sunbeams playing through a prism; and others, like the
chameleon, having no colours of their own, take just the colours of what
chances to be nearest them."   He concludes that the more "artificial feeling" an individual assumes, the less character of his own he retains "unless
indeed he is born of an uncommon degree of firmness."   Certain men—
he quotes Hume—" 'are nothing but a bundle of perceptions.' "

Was he prism, chameleon, or just a bundle of perceptions?   Beneath
this question lurks, grim as Grendel's mother, the old unsettling problem
of free will vs. determinism (or as Boswell likes to phrase it, Liberty vs.
Necessity).   If he had free will, supposedly he could make himself whatever
he wanted to be, or at least what one part of him wanted to be.   Indeed
a few years earlier he had bravely announced to Temple, "I will be myself."
The self he was now trying to create and sustain was the social being: he
was becoming the respectable lawyer that his father, wife, friends, all saw
as his proper social role.   And he had, he said, a comfortable life as a
married man.   Yet somewhere there was a strain; an inner voice protested.
When Temple complained about his situation, Boswell replied, "Well do I
know that I have the seeds of the same discontent.   But I strive to bury
them."   Not that he had yet experienced any real dissatisfaction.   On the
contrary, marriage and his law practice seemed to buoy as well as steady
him.   Perhaps only because they did, was he able to turn his attention to
the struggle between the clamours of the self and the compulsions of society.

If balancing internal against external demands causes the self as a
whole to fluctuate, it is not surprising that its superficial manifestations can

flicker and vanish.   In the same essay, Boswell reflects on the imperma-
nence of representation, on the loss of intonation, gesture, and attitude.
Implicitly he both looks back to *Tristram Shandy* and forward to the *Life of
Johnson* in generalizing the point:

> The appearance of our ancestors . . . would be still more lively if
> every little article of manners in every character were preserved;
> and, if not preserved by writing, many characteristical minutiae
> must fade away with the age that gave them birth.

Yet however any individual shifts about, he faces the same inflexible
end; and Boswell, obsessed with the fact and significance of death, fantasizes
about the passing both of the actor's personality and his impersonations
into rigidity:

> . . . when those features which have been so often employed to
> express the vanities of human emotion and passion must be con-
> vulsed with the agonies of dissolution . . . when those who have
> animated such a multiplicity of characters must sink into cold
> insensibility. . . .

This is Boswell in the graveyard mode but, sadly, abstract meditation
had acquired a concrete meaning.   After a dangerous two days of labour,
Margaret gave birth on 28 August 1770 to a son, who lived less than two
hours.   Boswell appealed to his friends.   To Grange: "It was not kind in
you to leave me alone yesterday.   I had a terrible day. . . .   Pray come to
me directly."   And to Temple, now in Northumberland to look after his
property: "You may imagine my feelings. . . .   I have much need of your
comfort."   Temple offered philosophic consolation on infant mortality,
and an account of a dream: "I thought you told me you had been unfaithful
to your wife, and I heard it with tears.   I must see Mrs. Boswell."   And
then, "Is Mr. Hume now at Edinburgh?"   Faithful as always to his immediate responses, Boswell rejected consolation:

> Nature has given us such an instinctive fondness that being de-
> prived of an infant gives us real distress.   I have experienced this,
> and there is no arguing against it. . . .   [Mr. Hume] will be here
> again in ten days.

Temple's visit, soon after this exchange, was a great success.   "How
can I express with what regret I parted from you!   I had not passed a
week so happily a long time," he wrote.   And, too, there was "the sensible,
the lively conversation of Mrs. Boswell (let me call her your *excellent wife*)
and her tender attention about me. . . .   Never did I see such a command
of temper, such amiable sensibility."   That triangle had resolved itself as

much as such triangles do.   Temple and Margaret had recognized that
they were not threats to each other.

Boswell's answer illuminates his first year of marriage:

> I am fully sensible of my happiness in being married to so excellent
> a woman, so sensible a mistress of a family,[1] so agreeable a com-
> panion, and above all so affectionate and peculiarly proper help-
> mate for me.   I own I am not so much on my guard against fits
> of passion and gloom as I ought to be, but that is really owing to
> her great goodness.   There is something childish in it, I confess.
> I ought not to indulge in such fits.   It is like a child that lets itself
> fall purposely, to have the pleasure of being tenderly raised up
> again by those who are fond of it.   I shall endeavour to be better.
> Upon the whole I do believe I make her very happy.

Margaret having recovered, the Boswells left for Ayrshire in early
October 1770, staying first with her relations at Lainshaw and Treesbank
and then moving on to Auchinleck.   Here or later, something went very
wrong between Margaret and her in-laws.   Whatever happened, it was an
incident that required Margaret, in Temple's view, "to learn a little dissimulation or, to give it a more honourable name, a little Christian charity
and forgiveness." But Margaret had pride as well as common sense, and
she never returned to Auchinleck during her father-in-law's lifetime. It is
quite likely she was never asked.

The routine of existence continued.   Boswell's old friend at Rome,
Andrew Lumisden, envisaged him "at the bar pleading the cause of the
widow and orphan," but the winter term (1770–71) of the Court of Session
was more prosaic and profitable: 56 causes, 83 fees, 140½ guineas.   (Advocates might receive several fees in the same cause, and the unusual extra
half-guinea belonged to Boswell's share of expenses in a suit.)   One case
concerned the demands of love and fortune.   Boswell was among the
counsel for Anthony Philip Miller, noted German oculist in the Canongate,
who sued Anthony Angelo Malevolti Tremamondo ("Mr. Angelo"), the
equally noted Italian master of the Royal Academy for Teaching Exercises
(riding academy), for non-payment of dowry.   Miller had removed a small
piece of steel from Angelo's eye, and as payment together with the hand
of Angelo's daughter was generously promised various goods: a diamond
ring worth 50 gs., a gold snuff-box worth 30 gs., lace worth 30 gs., and
half the furniture in Angelo's house.   But the Academy was never far from
insolvency, and Angelo failed to pay.   The suit hinged on whether oral

[1]Household.

witnesses were sufficient to substantiate the specifics of a dowry in the absence of a written agreement; and the Court ruled, 7–6, that they did not.   The lady in question, caught between husband and father, reportedly died of a broken heart.

Absorbed by domesticity and his practice, Boswell did not turn his attention south until the end of the term.   Meanwhile, Godfrey Bosville, his "Yorkshire chief," sent news of an old friend in London:

> Wilkes and Liberty are forgot; I believe they will be separated by his creditors.   A sudden fit of piety has come upon him; he is purging his ward of Farringdon Without: without common whores, I suppose.   It is a sign the beggar's blessing has left him, or he never would be so cruel to his old associates.[1]

Immured in Mamhead, Temple contributed more complaints:

> My wife's questions, indeed, and the petulance and squalls of my children often interrupt me and distract my attention.   I then shut my book and think of the quiet life of a bachelor, but soon resume my good humour again and endeavour not to make worse by a tormenting repentance what cannot now be remedied.

One voice is missing.   What Boswell writes to Johnson (18 April 1771) indicates how much of a break marriage had made in his life:

> I can now fully understand those intervals of silence in your correspondence with me which have so often given me anxiety and uneasiness; for although I am conscious that my veneration and love for Mr. Johnson have never in the least abated, yet I have deferred for almost a year and a half to write to him.

Veneration and love persist but need is, at most, dormant.   Nor has the possibility, or perhaps the thought, of returning to London yet occurred to Boswell; he had recently invited David Garrick to Scotland and now he invites Johnson, offering as inducement their old project of touring the Highlands and Hebrides.   Johnson's reply, two months later, showed he was unchanged:

> I never was so much pleased as now with your account of yourself; and sincerely hope that between public business, improving studies, and domestic pleasures, neither melancholy nor caprice will find any place for entrance. . . .   My dear Sir, mind your studies, mind your business, make your lady happy, and be a good Chris-

---

[1]One version of the beggar's blessing runs, "May your prick and your purse never fail you."

tian. . . . I hope the time will come when we may try our powers both with cliffs and water.

That May Boswell was again immersed in General Assembly causes. A ministerial member sketched him: "Boswell, the advocate, with a heavy eye, full of wit, industry amidst a love of pleasure, and attentive though dissipated." Attentive he had to be for he was involved in six causes, fees 28 guineas. St. Ninians came into view again, and Boswell's substantial doubts about the rights of patrons must have been reinforced when an opponent remarked, "I did not expect that a people struggling for liberty would be attacked by the friend of Paoli." Boswell also defended the Rev. William McMaster, accused of fornication and called a "whoremonger" by a vehement member of the Assembly. This charge elicited Johnson's lexicographical precision: "As you don't call a man an ironmonger for buying and selling a penknife, so you don't call a man a whoremonger for getting one wench with child." Nevertheless, McMaster lost his case at the next year's meeting of the Assembly.

In the same month the Boswells moved again, this time to David Hume's flat in James's Court on the north side of the Lawnmarket between the Castle and Parliament Square. James's Court contained one of the most elegant and exclusive buildings in the Old Town, though the flats consisted only of four or five rooms and a kitchen. The inhabitants had their own "parliament" for police purposes and their own scavenger; they gave parties and balls restricted to themselves, a custom Boswell disliked. But the house was "large enough . . . very convenient, and exceedingly healthful and pleasant." Margaret was much taken with it, obviously a crucial consideration. Also, it was just up the street from the law courts in the Parliament House and cheaper than their Canongate house. Some time later, Grange moved in below them.

The law was Boswell's profession, but writing was as necessary to him as breathing and almost as natural. Edinburgh lawyers, fortunately, were expected to be literate. "A lawyer without history or literature is a mechanic, a mere working mason," says Paulus Pleydell in *Guy Mannering*. "If he possesses some knowledge of [books], he may venture to call himself an architect." Several judges and lawyers explored subjects apart from the law, and even a sample of their productions shows their versatility: Hailes's *Annals of Scotland*, Monboddo's *Of the Origin and Progress of Language*, Sir John Dalrymple's *Memoirs of Great Britain and Ireland*. Kames, as was well known, wrote on everything. But then it seemed as if everyone in Edinburgh wrote on something or other: Hume, Hugh Blair, Robertson, Adam Ferguson, and any number of minor figures.

His *Account of Corsica* had made Boswell better known as an author than any of his fellow lawyers; he hardly needed precedent when he cast about for a literary avocation.   For some time Hailes had been urging him to undertake a glossary of old Scots law terms; now Temple wrote, "I long to see your Observations during your Travels." [1]   Boswell was often to return to this project.   But at the moment, presumably inspired by the reception of *Corsica*, he talked of writing a history of Sweden.   Clearly he was picking the wrong part from *Corsica*, the "History" rather than the "Memoirs of Paoli," as an object of imitation.

In any case, Sweden had to wait.   First came the summer session, and then a tour with Margaret into Northumberland and Durham.   It was the only jaunt outside of Scotland that they ever took as a married couple, and they enjoyed it thoroughly.   Margaret "was delighted with the quick, lively motion of driving post."   (Post-chaise was to stage-coach what the private car is to the bus.)   And the sightseeing lived up to expectations: Flodden Field, where the first Boswell of Auchinleck fell in battle beside his king in 1513; Durham, with its "grand cathedral . . . truly a noble Gothic structure"—the modern eye, of course, differentiates it as Norman; Alnwick, where they sat an hour with the Rev. Thomas Percy and were shown round the feudal stronghold of the Percys of Northumberland.

They hurried back to Edinburgh to greet a distinguished visitor: Paoli. The "authentic account" of his tour which Boswell wrote for the *London Magazine* presents it as developing into a quasi-royal progress.   Accompanied by the young, spirited Count Burzynski (Polish envoy extraordinary), Paoli arrives incognito on 3 September at Peter Ramsay's Inn, Cowgate Port.   Dined and entertained, they set out for Glasgow two days later with Boswell as guide, stopping at the Carron Ironworks from which cannon and "warlike stores" had been shipped to the aid of the brave Corsicans. In Glasgow Paoli is recognized, and the streets and windows fill with spectators.   At Auchinleck, Boswell's father is "extremely happy to receive such guests" for two days.   (It is said he later described the exiled Paoli as a "land-louping [2] scoundrel of a Corsican.")   They are escorted to the march of Ayrshire by the Sheriff-Substitute of Ayrshire, the Sheriff-Depute of Renfrewshire, several local gentlemen, and a detachment of the tenants of Auchinleck.   They view Loch Lomond, receive the freedom of Glasgow and Dumbarton, and are feasted by the magistrates of Glasgow—fifty-two at table at the Saracen's Head Inn.   Another day at Edinburgh completes

[1] On the Continent, 1763–66.
[2] Land-roving.

the expedition, with the Boswells accompanying their guests as far as Haddington.

Paoli's presence in Edinburgh was a magnet for the notable: Blair, Hume, Robertson, and the rising politician Henry Dundas, all came to dinner or supper.   And he was given a taste of local entertainment. Dr. Gregory Grant, known for his musical suppers, was host one afternoon upstairs in the same entry: Nancy and Betsy Ord, the Lord Chief Baron's daughters, sang; Annie Cuninghame, Margaret's niece, played while Boswell danced a reel with the two little Grants, Miss Dolly Gregory, and the Miss Ords.

Paoli was impressive: years later he was remembered, passing through Kilmarnock, as "a tall, buirdly,[1] military man, about fifty, with tied hair." He detested small talk; his character, both shrewd and open, and the independence of his judgement shine through the remarks Boswell recorded on a wide range of topics—from beauty, poetry, and metaphysics to comments on his new acquaintances:

> Robertson lacks sensitivity.   People who write take on the feelings
> of others, and lose the habit of having feelings of their own.   Hume
> is an Epicurean.   He is fond of a good table and of quiet pleasures;
> he has no delicious ones for they would draw him away from his
> impassivity, just as those who work in the   [2] are allowed only
> pleasures consonant with their condition.

But it is Paoli's noble self-consciousness that still rings out, in a handful of remarks worthy to be put beside those sayings in the *Account of Corsica* that had inspired many throughout Europe.   He never forgot who he had been or still was.   The hills around Loch Lomond were "little tame children" compared with those in Corsica yet, he said, "They make me remember I am no longer worth anything."   A little later, "Ah, how happy could I be here if my people were free or hated me."   Then a series of observations that open up his grand view of existence:

> True glory is a light which spreads out from us to all times and
> ages, and so is independent of us. . . .   One must think of the people
> as of a child with affection, but not boast of their praise.   They
> know nothing.   When, upon consideration, a gentleman disap-
> proves of me, I am displeased not because he holds such an opinion
> but because I am afraid he may be right.   But if it is a matter of

[1]Large and well-made, stately.
[2]Manuscript defective.

common opinion, I don't get upset if I myself don't agree with
it. . . . The French have no imagination.   It is impossible for
those slaves to have any.

Paoli felt ashamed of having been conquered even by the French, but
disaster could not subdue his spirit.   "Like a lion," he said, "I retire into
myself."

The presence of greatness reminded Boswell of his part in making
Corsica and Paoli famous.   Once more he realized, as he later put it, "I
had got upon a rock in Corsica and jumped into the middle of life."   And
once more he had started to journalize.   The gap from 28 October 1769
to 4 September 1771 is the longest in Boswell's surviving journal from its
inception in 1761 until his death in 1795.   Paoli's visit had shaken him out
of his pleasant routine; it forced him to recall the roles he had played in
a large, exhilarating world beyond the limitations of Edinburgh.   He needed
his journal for such a *memorable* visit.

In the realm of the happy, the journal is a discordant if hidden voice.
Even if restricted to recording external events, it necessitates a point of
view: this is what I see and how I see it.   It leads towards self-definition,
and is the quickest and sharpest way to emphasize one's individuality.   But
the price of uniqueness is to stand apart from one's fellows.   The re-
sumption of the journal promised that, whatever Boswell said, he would
never be content to dwindle into a Scots laird, lawyer, and married man.

2

I

THE DRUMS AND TRUMPETS of Paoli's tour died away, and the proud companion to a hero reverted to dutiful son and pupil. Auchinleck, Boswell declared, was his great object, and he spent October there being instructed by his father in pruning and the complicated election law of Scotland. Together with domesticity and the law, Auchinleck in future years would be the third great factor in his life. This was the happy rural scene which held in balance physical labour, mental occupation, and emotional ease—an ideal of stability and usefulness that went back to Roman times. Boswell rampaged about it: he was "digging deep for antiquities, planting out the thorns of law, weeding a crop of poetry, or making hay of human existence while the sun of cheerfulness shines." Only Margaret's absence disturbed him. Without her, he said, his heart fluttered like a bird in a cage.

One immediate and unpleasant aftermath of Paoli's visit Boswell incited himself. John Dalrymple, Lord Provost of Edinburgh, had failed to entertain or confer the freedom of the city on its distinguished visitor. Taking what must have been simple inadvertence as a conscious slight, Boswell characterized Dalrymple in two anonymous letters to the *London Chronicle* as a fat, servile Luckenbooths draper, interested only in profit. When Lord Hailes, Dalrymple's brother, charged him with the letters, Boswell's response was silence; but Hailes endorsed the copy of his protest with the words, "He visited me no longer." Although Johnson's visit was to restore casual contact and Hailes and Boswell continued to correspond, they seldom met. One filial thread had been broken.

The long-term consequence of Paoli's visit was that it catalysed Boswell's desire to return to London.   In the same "Rampager" in which he had praised the pleasures of bucolic existence, Boswell confessed nostalgia for

> that great emporium of men and manners, news and nonsense, politics and playhouses, and all other subjects of entertainment, while I live at a great distance from you and move in a narrow sphere little diversified with enlivening objects.

Then he added stoutly, "I do however as well as I can."

What he was doing at the moment was taking part in Burnett v. Clark, the celebrated case of Lord Monboddo's horse.   In treating the horse, the farrier Clark had added treacle to the prescribed mixture.   The horse died, and Monboddo (James Burnett) sued for violation of instructions. Boswell represented his Lordship and Maclaurin the defendant; the Bench quoted Roman law at length; and, when he lost, Monboddo became so angry that he refused to sit any longer with his brethren, preferring the seat within the bar reserved for eminent guests.

But mostly the law was a grinding routine: "home, paper writing," "home, close," "hard, Candacraig," "hard work," "hard, hard work."   In January 1772, Wilson v. Smith and Armour was tried, the case of vicious intromission on which Johnson was to deliver, by request, an extended opinion.   In February, Boswell defended George McDonald, accused of stealing an ox and seventeen sheep.   Feeling manly and calm and bold, Boswell attacked the death penalty for theft, and praised McDonald for procreating "young, hardy Highlanders, who will soon be up and ready to carry the arms of Britain into the distant quarters of the globe."   The jury convicted him on the sheep-stealing charge only, and McDonald anticipated the travels of his progeny by being transported for life.

Still, London.   Boswell had been laying up his reward.   He had the favourite excuse of Scottish lawyers—cases appealed from the Court of Session to the House of Lords—for combining business with pleasure.   The legal exodus to London that spring was numerous: James William Montgomery (Lord Advocate), Henry Dundas (Solicitor-General), Andrew Crosbie, David Rae, Sir John Dalrymple, Samuel Mitchelson, Jr., Alexander Wight, Sandy Fergusson of Craigdarroch.   Boswell was to defend John Hastie, schoolmaster of Campbeltown, Argyll, who had been dismissed from his £20-a-year job for brutality and irregular attendance.   Hastie had won his case in the Court of Session and the Campbeltown magistrates appealed.

One appeal was a slender basis for a two-months' jaunt, but Boswell had also laid up his reasons:

My views in coming to London this spring were: to refresh my
mind by the variety and spirit of the metropolis, the conversation
of my revered friend Mr. Samuel Johnson and that of other men
of genius and learning; to try if I could get something for myself
or be of service to any of my friends by means of the Duke of
Queensberry, Lord Mountstuart, or Douglas, all of whom had
given me reason to expect their assistance; to be employed in
Scotch appeals in the House of Lords, and also see how the land
might lie for me at the English bar; and to endeavour to get my
brother David well settled as a merchant in London.   There is
business enough.

More reasons than necessary.   Of course Boswell was a reformed man,
but even the reformed deserve occasional relief from the daily round.
Boswell needed to get away for a while from Scotland, the law, his father,
Auchinleck.   Possibly even from Margaret; short absence would make
sweet return, and he was to miss her very much.   On the night before he
left they had a serious quarrel, perhaps their first.   Home from dining
with his father (he writes in his journal),

and romping like to have been fatal.   π [Peggie] to part.   I looked
it in the face calm a little, but soon grew uneasy.

"Romping" was contemporary idiom for sexual fooling about.   Margaret
had miscarried ten days earlier; what happened, at a guess, was that Boswell
insisted on sexual relations, and she started to bleed.   Frightened and
angry, she threatened to leave a man so selfishly intent on his own pleasure.
This covered a deeper uneasiness: Boswell was about to take an extended
trip while her health was still delicate.   She hated to see him go; she would
leave him instead.   They made it up again.

The next entry in Boswell's journal (14 March 1772) is fully written,
for the first time since October 1769.   London meant liberation, and liberation demanded extended notice.   Boswell is no less honest than he had
been, but the tone changes: he is re-entering the world and what he writes
is for the record.   He explains, as to a reader, his feelings about the journey:

I was in a flutter to a certain degree at the thoughts of setting out
for London, for which I have always had an enthusiastic fondness.
I was at the same time seriously concerned at parting with my
wife. . . .   To part with a valuable friend and constant companion
and go four hundred miles from her, though but for two months,
is something considerable to a domestic man who has any turn to
anxiety of mind.

All true, but it was up and away, and anxiety vanished.   Boswell and
his companion, William Wilson, W.S., who had given him his first fee, read

law papers and sang and argued about *The Beggar's Opera*. At Grantham
he was instantaneously affected by the comely figures of the Rev. Mr.
Palmer's wife and daughter. The English inns were admirable and driving
in a post-chaise a pleasure. After a comfortable five-day trip they rolled
over Highgate Hill, with London hidden in thick fog below, and disem-
barked at the familiar Lemon Tree Inn at the top of the Haymarket.

Immediately Boswell touched bases. He called first on Paoli; next on
Johnson, who was with his great friends the Thrales in Southwark; and
then, uneasy about where to spend the night, proceeded to the Dillys', his
publishers, in the Poultry, where he received his usual hearty welcome,
substantiated by cold fowl and ham and tarts and a basin of excellent soup.
The next day he found very good lodgings, centrally located, in Conduit
Street. Even the maid pleased him when he retired, by asking in a sweet
English voice, "Do you want anything more tonight, Sir?"

Since his last excursion to London in 1769 Boswell had changed, or
so he insisted. Repeatedly this spring he contrasts his present firmness
and cheerfulness of mind, his steady, composed character, with his former
idle, weak, dissipated self. Still, as his responsiveness to the maid indicates,
desire was quick to revive. His ideas, he says, naturally ran "into their old
channels, which were pretty deeply worn," and from the start of this holiday he had to resist his favourite rationalization: if the Old Testament
patriarchs could keep concubines, why could he not contract "temporary
likings unconnected with mental attachment"? This excuse came to him as
he walked up the Strand "and passed through a variety of fine girls, genteelly dressed, all wearing Venus's girdle." It was real temptation, but he
withstood it.

Two of his projects died in conversation. Brother David had put
down roots as a merchant in Valencia, and it would take a war and hard
times to force his return to England. For Boswell himself, the English bar
remained a desirable goal but he could find neither logical reasons nor
practical means for attempting it. Among his potential patrons, Queensberry offered least: Boswell called upon arrival in London, was politely
received, and that was that. Mountstuart, Lord Bute's son, greeted him
as if they had never parted, and not having changed himself he assumed
that Boswell was still the very odd and extravagant person (so Boswell puts
it) he had known in Italy. He could provide no immediate help; even a
survivancy—the promise of being next in line for some office—was impossible to procure. Daydreaming was free, though, and Mountstuart
could grandly guarantee a seat on the Court of Session which it would
never be in his power to bestow. And Boswell could continue to believe

that Mountstuart was "truly an amiable young nobleman with very good parts, and is only too indolent and cool till pushed."

If Mountstuart was indolent and cool, Archibald Douglas of Douglas was a cold fish. In the battle for survival, he must have learned early not to question who he was; an identity crisis was a luxury he could not have afforded. A prudent selfishness sufficed. He married well: his first wife, Lucy, was the daughter of the Duke of Montrose; his second, Frances, the sister of the Duke of Buccleuch. Though still harassed by Hamiltonian lawsuits, he had acquired a truly magnificent town house in Pall Mall. And he aspired to nobility.

Monboddo's exertions in the Douglas Cause may well have earned him his seat on the Court of Session, and Edward Thurlow's handling of its English phase was to prove an important step on his road to the Chancellorship. Boswell had done Douglas at least equal, if less formal, service, and he expected treatment accordingly. It was a spectacular mistake for one who prided himself on his understanding of others. When Lady Lucy behaved at first meeting with fashionable English reserve, Boswell "made way" for himself by eating a plentiful breakfast and forcing her to answer questions. (He had forgotten for once his dislike of Scots familiarity.) On one occasion when Douglas was entertaining elegantly, Boswell told him it would do him good to look back on the Cause. His way of persuading Douglas to spend some time in Scotland was to remind Douglas of how much trouble it had cost to make him a Scotsman.

On earlier visits Boswell had been content to enjoy himself in London; now he was a man of business, looking forward to his first appearance in the House of Lords, and he attended regularly to familiarize himself with procedure, before Campbell v. Hastie came on. Lord Apsley, the Lord Chancellor, was a nonentity; but Lord Mansfield, Chief Justice of King's Bench, was the greatest British judge of the century. It was a feast to hear him, Boswell thought, and naturally something of an ordeal to speak before him. On the great day, 14 April 1772, Boswell's friends gathered round: General Oglethorpe, active and warm-hearted, appeared early in the morning; Sir Alexander Macdonald sent his coach for him. Two large bumpers of wine confused rather than inspirited, and the occasion seemed a little unreal:

> I amused my mind sometimes with the idea of my being an English counsellor, sometimes with the idea of my being a Scots lawyer come up to plead one of the appeals from the court of his country [here Boswell wakes up] which was the truth.

A hurry of spirits, and Boswell found himself mounting the little platform where he was to speak. His friends there included Lords Lyttelton

and Mountstuart, Garrick, the faithful Edward Dilly, the elder and younger
Strahans (both printers); and, from professional interest, Samuel Smith,
headmaster of Westminster School.   Boswell started in a very low voice
and warmed up gradually; throughout he was careful to speak slowly and
distinctly.   ("They would be expecting to see the bold Boswell," said Garrick
the next day, "and so you restrained yourself.")   Garrick thought he could
have been more animated—he himself certainly would have been—but
Mansfield, Boswell heard later, said he spoke very well.   Even so, Mansfield
summed up dead against Hastie, and the Court of Session was reversed.
Duty accomplished, Boswell stopped at his lodgings to change his wig, and
was off to dine with Elizabeth Montagu, the grandest of bluestocking
hostesses.

The Boswell who had raked all around London before marriage was
muted; his amusements, like his character, had become respectable.
The city glittered as ever, but somehow it seemed larger and less manage-
able.   A visitor there, Boswell felt, was like "one at a great table who is
unaccustomed to it and whose attention is distracted by the variety of
dishes."   The comparison is appropriate both in terms of his unfailingly
physical temperament and in suggesting the central fact about London
social life, that it was organized around meals.

Breakfast, taken about 10 a.m., was very light, usually just tea and
bread and butter, though it could rise to the splendour of Lord Eglinton's,
the best in town: "bread and butter and honey and marmalade of oranges
and currant jelly and muffins, well buttered and comfortably toasted."
People dropped in without invitation, and sometimes a little business got
done.   Breakfast acquaintances overlapped supper ones, but supper, perhaps around 10 p.m., was quieter and more intimate; oysters and port with
Macdonald at Boswell's lodgings; or punch and some biscuits with Sir John
Pringle, his father's best friend and sympathetic to Boswell within the conventional rules.   Once in a while supper made part of an elaborate occasion,
as when Mansfield, legs stretched before him and heels knocking together,
held court, with his distinguished company speaking little and low and, in
Boswell's opinion, too obsequiously.   Most prized, supper meant tea at
Johnson's house with its long-time inmate, the blind Anna Williams, where
Johnson talked not for victory but from the heart, where (as in Johnson's
definition of friendship) there was an exchange of intimate thoughts.

Dinner, ordinarily eaten at 4 p.m., was the full measure of sociability.
When Boswell, at 22, had come to London to pursue a commission in the
Guards, he had prudently engaged to eat dinner at his landlord's—*prix fixe*,
a shilling—if unengaged.   And he had taken many of his meals alone in

taverns.   No need now to fall back on such humble resources.   During his fifty-three days in London this spring, Boswell missed dinner twice, dined alone at a tavern twice, dined with Johnson and others half a dozen times at a tavern, and ate his remaining dinners as someone's guest.

Many meals, to be sure, were taken with the equivalent of family: Paoli, Godfrey Bosville, Bosville's son-in-law Macdonald, and Pringle, with whom he ate Easter dinner.   Others were plain, comfortable meals, often with Scottish hosts.   He walked out to Kensington to dine with James Elphinston, schoolmaster and advocate of phonetic spelling.   (Elphinston so mangled Martial's epigrams that his brother-in-law offered to pay him not to publish his translation.)   He took beefsteaks, porter, and port with young Strahan, while waiting for the respondent's case in Campbell v. Hastie to be run off.   He dined with other Scottish lawyers at the Lord Advocate's, with his wife's closest friend the Hon. Mrs. Stuart, with the antiquary John Claxton, with the biographer John Campbell, with the banker Robert Herries.   Quite "curious" was dinner with "Royal" Ross, patentee of the Theatre Royal in Edinburgh, where Boswell contemplated the now most proper Mrs. Ross, once the notorious courtesan Fanny Murray, heroine of the Potter-Wilkes *Essay on Woman*:

> Awake, my Fanny! leave all meaner things;
> This morn shall prove what rapture swiving brings!

Boswell enjoyed these dinners, but it was the great occasions that heightened his sense of being.   Really good company meant Mrs. Montagu's with Paoli, Lyttelton, and the Archbishop of York.   He owed this invitation to his links with Paoli and Corsica; and it was also as "Corsica" Boswell that he attended the "Honest Whigs" Club at the London Coffeehouse, which he had joined, his head full of Corsica and Liberty, several years earlier.   A sounding-board for Benjamin Franklin, this group included Joseph Priestley: Unitarian minister, materialist, necessitarian, and great scientist.   In later years Boswell would grow indignant at the mention of his name, but now he must have felt pleased with himself when Priestley read aloud Anna Letitia Aikin's poem, *Corsica*, with its praise of Boswell.

Among entertainments, most to Boswell's taste was the grand crush at the Lord Mayor's annual dinner and ball.   Edward Dilly procured the tickets, and Paoli lent his coach, with coachman and Swiss footman in silver-laced liveries; Boswell's servant Joseph was also "mounted behind, for the sake of grandeur."   There was a terrible struggle to get into the Egyptian Hall of the Mansion House, though it seated over 300 people: more tickets had been issued than there were places, and Boswell was afraid he would

lose the very small Dilly.   But it was worth it.   "Foreigners of distinction . . .
ices in perfection."   Burgundy and champagne at call, and Boswell annexed a bottle of each.   The band played and toasts were proposed.   It
was all vulgar show and wonderful fun.

Of course a person might encounter anyone at such a gathering, and
Boswell took the opportunity to run into Wilkes accidentally, and resume
their old badinage:

> BOSWELL (so that Wilkes can overhear).   "This is excellent; this is
> like ourselves; quite Scotland." . . .   WILKES.   "Don't sit by me or
> it will be in the *Public Advertiser* tomorrow." . . .   BOSWELL.   "Upon
> my word, you had a grand entertainment here today."   WILKES.
> "You did not see the sheep's head.   You did not see the haggis."

Public roles in public places.

A small private gathering at the dramatist and actor Samuel Foote's
villa was a miniature triumph of ostentation.   A dinner to invite a man to,
it was served on a set of plate worth £1,200 and, as the height of luxury,
Foote

> did not say, "Gentlemen, there's madeira and port and claret."
> But, "Gentlemen, there's *all* sorts of wine.   You'll call for what
> you choose."   He gave us noble old hock . . . sparkling cham-
> pagne, constantia, and tokay.   When the latter was served round
> he said, "Now you're going to drink the best wine in England";
> and it was indeed exquisite.   His claret flowed of course.

I I

THESE WERE PLEASURES.   The deep sustaining tie to London was his
relationship with Johnson, whom Boswell had not seen for two and a half
years.   Before leaving Edinburgh, he wrote to prepare the way:

> I fairly own that after an absence from you for any length of time
> I feel that I require a renewal of that spirit which your presence
> always gives me, and which makes me a better and a happier man
> than I imagined I could be, before I was introduced to your
> acquaintance.

Johnson responded generously: "Whether to love you be right or wrong,
I have many on my side: Mrs. Thrale loves you, and Mrs. Williams loves
you."   Then, alluding to their projected jaunt to the Hebrides, he added,
"Let us try to make each other happy when we meet, and not refer our
pleasure to distant times or distant places."

Their first meeting instantly renewed the connection.   Sitting in Johnson's study, Boswell heard his weighty step coming up the timber stairs. "He had on an old purple cloth suit and a large whitish wig.   He embraced me with a robust sincerity of friendship, saying, 'I am glad to see thee, I am glad to see thee.' "   The conversation had its old comfortable sweep: Hastie the schoolmaster; Johnson's political pamphlets, *The False Alarm* and *Thoughts . . . Respecting Falkland's Islands*; the naturalists Banks and Solander; that ever interesting topic, ghosts; old families; life after death; mimicry; and a subject which was increasingly to exacerbate Boswell's relations with his father, the Auchinleck entail.   (Lord Auchinleck wanted to entail the estate on heirs, male and female, of his own body; Boswell, with "Gothic, Salic" enthusiasm, wanted it restricted to males, and extended to all male descendants of the family founder Thomas Boswell.)   It is a subject we will hear much more of.

If their acquaintance in 1763 makes up the first phase of Boswell's relationship with Johnson, and their encounters between 1766 and 1769 comprise the second, then their reunion this spring opens the third and final phase: as a lawyer and settled married man, Boswell was as near Johnson's equal as he would become.   In ceremonial renewal of their friendship, they dined at the Mitre in the room where they had first supped nine years earlier.   This spring they were often together, varied settings and varying moods eliciting, as always, from Johnson unpredictable, memorable utterances, while Boswell kept his record of apparently disjointed particulars that would some day yield underlying continuities.

One day will serve as a slight example: in the midst of a small, happy dinner-party at Paoli's, Johnson, with his willingness to face what others preferred to gloss over, declared,

> It is so far from being easy and natural for a man and woman to live in a state of marriage that we find all the restraints and motives in civilized society are hardly sufficient to keep them together.

(Yet he always argued, and it was not a paradox, that "even ill-assorted marriages were preferable to cheerless celibacy.")   And when they wandered that night through the newly opened pleasure dome, the Pantheon, Johnson, very loud and violent, perceived that Sir Adam Fergusson was "a vile Whig."

Dinner at Macdonald's on 6 April provided a false omen to a swelling scene.   Johnson, much taken with Lady Macdonald, announced, "I will go to Skye with this lady.   I'll go anywhere under this lady's protection."   She responded that *Rasselas* was the finest novel she had ever read.   Johnson differentiated Richardson and Fielding: "There is more knowledge of the heart in one letter of Richardson's than in all *Tom Jones*." When that "very pretty lad," Thomas Erskine (later Lord Chancellor), objected to Richardson as tedious, Johnson replied, "Why, Sir, if you were to read Richardson for the story, your impatience would be so much fretted that you'd hang yourself. But you must read him for the sentiment." They also discussed the merits of the feudal system, a subject to become crucial the next year: Boswell pro, Macdonald con, Johnson judiciously in the middle.

Recording Johnson took time, and he was demanding in other ways. Yet when Boswell once missed dinner on his account, he gave credit to virtue: "A man is always pleased with himself when he finds his intellectual inclinations predominate." The conversation between a hungry Boswell and a gloomy Johnson dwelt on ghosts, witches, and the efficacy of prayer.

Then there was Johnson's rough side. One night they supped with Bennet Langton and a few others at the Crown and Anchor. With Johnson in a bad humour and the others afraid to venture, Boswell "as usual risked boldly in order to get him to speak." In fact, he went so far as to uphold the maxim, *in vino veritas*.

> "Would not you, Sir, now, allow a man oppressed with care to drink and make himself merry?" JOHNSON. "Yes, if he sat next you." This was one of his great broadsides. I know Mr. Johnson so well and delight in his grand explosions, even when directed against myself, so much that I am not at all hurt.

It must have been difficult to maintain such detachment at all times. Much later, Boswell commented perceptively:

> Johnson's harsh attacks on his friends arise from uneasiness within. There is an insurrection aboard. His loud explosions are guns of distress.

Despite such momentary checks, Boswell was carried along on a wave of happiness and excitement that spring, whose crest came on 10 April with dinner at General Oglethorpe's, Johnson and Goldsmith present. Johnson argued fluently and forcibly for the lawfulness of duelling in defence of one's honour, a question of distressingly practical interest. Oglethorpe re-created the Turkish siege of Belgrade in 1717, where he had served as a young man, on the table with a finger dipped in wine, Johnson listening with the closest attention. Johnson and Goldsmith debated whether two persons with differing views could be friends, a discussion which prompted Johnson to say the next day that Goldsmith talked just so others would not forget he was present. BOSWELL. "I like very well to hear honest Goldsmith talk away carelessly." JOHNSON. "Why yes, Sir, but he should not like to hear himself."

Boswell comments on this dinner at Oglethorpe's:

> I had a full relish of life today.   It was somehow like being in London in the last age.   I felt myself of some real personal consequence while I made one of such a company; and nothing was wanting but my dearest wife to go home to, and a better fortune in the mean time to make her live as she deserves.

He went on to complain, "Words cannot describe our feelings.   The finer parts are lost, as the down upon a plum."   But he could catch his mood in a sentence: "I just sat and hugged myself in my own mind."

Living much together developed a "companionable ease and familiarity," which Johnson and Boswell would share for the rest of their lives. On Good Friday, Boswell found him with a folio Greek New Testament reading "a little with a solemn hum," and went away to avoid interruption. After the splendour—music, wax lights, frankincense—of Easter mass at the Sardinian Minister's chapel, he called again, this time accompanied by Paoli.   They discussed whether the blind could distinguish colours by touch, and the respective merits of plain and elaborate literary styles.   Near the end of Boswell's stay, he and Johnson passed some very good days with the hospitable Thrales in Streatham.

In the midst of his account of these relaxed, congenial visits, dinners, and evenings, Boswell casually interpolates a remark of basic importance. Johnson commented (31 March) on Goldsmith's *Life of Parnell* that "nobody could furnish the life of a man but those who had eat and drank and lived in social intercourse with him."   In his journal, Boswell continues:

> I have a constant plan to write the life of Mr. Johnson.   I have not told him of it yet, nor do I know if I should tell him.   I said that if it was not troublesome and presuming too much, I would beg of him to tell me all the little circumstances of his life, what schools he attended, when he came to Oxford, when he came to London, etc. etc.   He did not disapprove of my curiosity as to these particulars, but said, "They'll come out by degrees."

Superficially, Boswell had found the literary avocation that would complement his legal career.   Actually, as we know, he had decided to take on immortality.   It was not his goal; the goals he could visualize were those of a prosperous landowner, successful advocate, and well-known politician: for those, his ambitions were high.   But here is the far greater goal he could achieve.   Hints of his plan had appeared earlier.   In 1764, on his travels through Germany, he had written to Johnson "from the tomb of Melanchthon"—literal-mindedly lying flat on top of it—in "solemn enthusiasm of mind" to say that if Johnson died before him, he would endeavour to do honour to his memory; but that letter he did not dare to send until many years later. In 1768, he had ventured to ask Johnson whether it would be improper to publish his letters after his death, Johnson replying that he could do with them what he wished.

Now Boswell announces a constant plan, as a matter determined upon perhaps for some time. He wonders about Johnson's reaction to the idea, but not at all about his ability to carry it out. He has the material: he has been recording Johnson's conversations fully since they first met in 1763. He has the necessary experience: the unique merit of his *Account of Corsica* lay in his conversations with Paoli. Above all, as Boswell remarked just two weeks later, he has "really a genius for particular history, for biography." He does not mean that he is an especially gifted biographer, but that his innate ability takes this direction.

From the beginning of their acquaintance, Boswell had taken Johnson as Mentor; from now on, Johnson was openly also Subject. He measures Johnson with the cool detachment of the professional appraising the work in front of him. Later, in writing the *Life of Johnson*, Boswell often complained about how long and tedious a task he had undertaken. Very seldom does he show any fear that he is unequal to its performance.

Boswell's last days in London went by in a rush. His separation from Margaret was causing him a good deal of anxiety. They corresponded regularly, and she wanted him home. "Hipped [1] black" on 30 April with guilt for his long absence, he was revived by a good letter the next day. But he also responded to pressure in a different way by going "with bad women a *little*."

There was so much happening in London that it was hard to leave. Dinner with Sir Joshua Reynolds on 6 May effectively initiated one of the most satisfying intimacies of his life. (Goldsmith by introducing them, he later said, had given him "a jewel of the finest water.") Here he also met Topham Beauclerk and Edmund Burke for the first time. When Boswell spoke of "Liberty and Necessity" being tried at law, Burke replied, in the first of his many plays on words Boswell was to set down, "I should be for Necessity, as Necessity has no law." Boswell was moving into the circle of The Club, having supper at Goldsmith's the next night with Reynolds and

---

[1] Afflicted with hypochondria.

Langton; here, still a collector of lions, he announced that the Prime Minister, Lord North, had granted his request for an interview, and Goldsmith commented, with blundering vividness, that he would no more have expected an answer from Lord North than he would have from Jesus Christ. The interview went off well, if mysteriously to posterity: "Father's joke as to juries on rebels."

One triumph remained.   Next to Johnson, Boswell's great object that spring was Garrick.   He had been very kind to Boswell on his early trips to London, and perhaps Boswell had lost interest in him a bit after meeting Johnson.   Not that Garrick would have much noticed.   As George Dempster said, next to the King he was the best-known man in Great Britain.   Lord Camden, sometime Lord Chancellor, was his intimate; the great Lord Chatham flattered him in verse.   Only Johnson's affection and approval, which Garrick valued more than anyone else's, was carefully measured.   From Scotland, Boswell had revived their acquaintance assiduously in letters, with praise in "On the Profession of a Player," and in writing the Dedication to him of Donaldson's Edinburgh edition of Shakespeare.

Early on this jaunt, Boswell found Garrick holding court like a little minister of state in his flat in the fashionable Adelphi, and did not feel encouraged to stay.   (Among Garrick's entourage that morning was that "fine, sly malcontent," John Cleland, author in his youth, as Boswell remarks, of "that most licentious and inflaming book," *Fanny Hill*.)   But as the spring went on, they grew more friendly and a high point came on 8 May when Garrick called very early, announcing himself as Rantum-Scantum (harum-scarum); while they walked in St. James's Park, Garrick took off Johnson's view of himself: "Davy has some convivial pleasantry about him, but 'tis a foolish fellow." As they neared the Thames, Garrick recited Macbeth's "Canst thou not minister to a mind diseased," a performance Boswell never forgot.   The next night Boswell supped at Garrick's, "all elegance, burgundy, etc.," and Garrick gave the company Fielding, Johnson, and Tetty (Johnson's long-dead wife), perhaps including the famous scene of Johnson's connubial ardour, which as a schoolboy Garrick had absorbed through the keyhole.

After such delights, what temptation could hold Boswell further?   On 11 May, Paoli's coach took him to say farewell to Mrs. Thrale, who urged him to bring his wife next year.   The following day he was up before 5 a.m. and off to Edinburgh by the west route: Leicester, Manchester, Carlisle.   Materially he had accomplished little, but he had enjoyed "admirable health, fine spirits, the conversation of the first geniuses." It was a time, he said, of almost complete felicity. What may have lingered longest with him was Johnson's parting comment. Percy, Johnson had heard, intended to write his life; Johnson himself thought fifty people would attempt it. He hoped, Johnson said, that Boswell would live to write all their lives.

CHAPTER

3

I

LONDON WAS SOCIETY, freedom, and an intensified sense of being; Edinburgh was family, home, and work. Boswell found the transition difficult to manage after this marvellous spring. Home again, he was irritated by Scots vulgarity, and dull in spirits. A sure sign of returning depression was his picking once more at the problem of free will. It led to a tête-à-tête with the Rev. Thomas Reid, whose *Inquiry into the Human Mind on the Principles of Common Sense* (1764) had quieted his metaphysical anxieties in the past. A "close evening of philosophy," Boswell noted, "yet not quite clear." It never would be. Early in June he came down with a bad cold.

But guineas were guineas, so he descended as before into the noisy bustle of the General Assembly, where he was becoming a prominent advocate. Nine causes in a crowded two weeks provided 35 guineas (house rent for the year and five guineas extra). The legal issues that came before the General Assembly were easy to grasp if not to resolve, and Boswell could be counted on to present them clearly, vigorously, and with those sarcastic touches congenial to the Scottish mind.

In his outstanding case this spring, Boswell represented the People of Marykirk, Kincardineshire, in a nice question of nepotism. King's College, Aberdeen, had auctioned the presentation of sixteen churches in 1766, and John Brymer, an innkeeper, had bought Marykirk's. Brymer had paid only £200 instead of the £300 asked because the incumbent appeared so healthy, but he died in 1771 and Brymer presented his son to the parish. In short, his purchase turned out to be a profitable speculation even though his parishioners resented being considered as party to a familial investment.

Boswell urged the obvious objection of simony, but as Bannatyne MacLeod, the opposing counsel, argued, the younger Brymer had not paid his father for the presentation, and a patron could be guided by affection if his choice was otherwise qualified. The Assembly affirmed the presentation without a vote.

Trouble with Lord Auchinleck recurred in August, at the end of the Court of Session's summer term. Boswell had now been married for almost three years, and an advocate in busy practice for twice that long. He had proved his steadiness, and he wanted his father to acknowledge it by re-turning the "renunciation" of his birthright that Boswell had signed in 1762: for a mess of pottage (an allowance of £100 a year), Boswell had agreed that his father, if he chose, could vest the estate in trustees after his death. Nor was Margaret provided for, in case Boswell predeceased her. But Lord Auchinleck was not yet satisfied that Boswell had acquired a solid grounding in the law, and they disagreed sharply over the entail.

These ostensible causes of dispute focused much deeper feelings of resentment. Each felt cheated in a tacit bargain. A lonely man, Lord Auchinleck thought Boswell selfishly insensitive to his need for compan-ionship after Boswell's mother's death, especially since he had made every allowance for youthful follies. But Boswell, having with great unwilling-ness taken up the profession his father had forced on him, having tried again and again to adapt himself to his father's uncongenial habits and rigid assertion of authority, found himself little respected or loved. Yet he retained for his father, he said, much of the tenderness of a child, and he repeatedly reached out for his affection and esteem: he needed them to establish his own independence. But his volatility and flights of fancy— in general, a lack of ballast—grated on the old man, who responded with coldness or sarcasm.

The situation was poisoned by worsening relations between the second Lady Auchinleck and her stepsons. Lieutenant John, always difficult and intermittently insane, had quarrelled with her and removed to board again with Dr. Wilson in Newcastle. And Boswell thought her ill-disposed to-wards himself. Surely she was aware that he and Margaret regarded her as an interloper who had married an old man for money, security, and position, and to escape being an old maid, which Defoe's Roxana, speaking for the century, terms "the worst of nature's curses." The two women, both touchy about their marriages, must have disliked each other strongly. Margaret, anyway, showed her distaste for her mother-in-law in looks if not in words, and in return Lord Auchinleck virtually ignored her. Caught up in these complicated ill-feelings, Boswell announced to his father that he could not accompany him to Auchinleck for the autumn recess. "Parted, having the advantage of him," Boswell declared, but cooler heads took a different view. Temple scolded, and Sir John Pringle pressed him to hurry—cheerful, attentive, and studious—to Auchinleck. Boswell stayed in Edinburgh.

Autumn was a listless period, and his spirits were often bad. Since Margaret was pregnant, they worried that sexual relations might be harmful: "Night quite Cytherean, misch[ief? or ance?]. Uneasy as if real wrong." Boswell began to indulge in fits of temper, and finally makes an ominous disclosure to his journal: "You drank too much port. Night, sallied forth to New Bridge, etc." Some kind of sexual contact, which was followed, a week or so later, apparently by a genital problem: "Still very uneasy. My valuable π made me send for Lamplighter.[1] She is my best friend and the most generous heart. He could not say yet." A few days later, "Declared safe."

Listlessness alternated with restlessness. Boswell neglected the law— so much for his father's lengthened, sage advices—turning to literary projects to take up his time. He found a hobby in extracting curious material from old records of the Scottish Privy Council, which he intended eventually to publish. He also persuaded his fellow proprietors of the *London Magazine* to let him contribute a series of informal essays, called *The Hypochondriack*. But he couldn't get more than a start on them, perhaps discouraged that neither Margaret nor Temple approved of this attempt to gain, as Temple put it, "the admiration of hucksters and pedlars!"

Visitors were a more acceptable distraction: Thomas Pennant, the traveller, appeared in September, a "neat, little man"; a week later Langton arrived in Edinburgh for an extended stay. The wonder of the season was the appearance of Banks and Solander—celebrated for having accompanied Captain Cook on the *Endeavour* to Tahiti, New Zealand, and Australia—now just returning from Iceland. Monboddo, who thought that the orang-utan and man belonged to the same species, and that somewhere there were men with tails, was displeased to learn that the travellers had nowhere encountered that appendage; and Boswell turned Banks and Solander to use by publishing their Icelandic anecdotes in the *London Magazine*.

Essentially the motor was idling. Boswell was as compulsive about journalizing in public as about keeping a diary in private, but he badly needed an occasion. It blossomed in the collapse of the Ayr Bank (Douglas, Heron, and Co.), the most spectacular Scottish economic failure of the

---

[1]Presumably a nickname for a surgeon, most likely Alexander Wood.

century.   Scotland in the 1760s was an underdeveloped country: its agricultural improvers were busy, its linen industry and tobacco trade prospered, but its supply of capital was limited and uncertain.   A group of wealthy landed gentlemen, including the Dukes of Buccleuch and Queensberry and the Earl of Dumfries, decided to remedy this condition by establishing the Ayr Bank, to the benefit of the country and some 225 eager partners.

From its start in 1769, the Ayr Bank was managed on principles so reckless as to border on criminal negligence.   The directors made loans with abandon—many of them to themselves—on land and other non-convertible security, and attempted to replenish their supply of capital by borrowing money at high interest rates and by issuing their own banknotes. In Adam Smith's homely analogy, the Bank was like a pond feeding a continuous stream, which its owners proposed to keep full by carrying buckets of water from a well some miles away.   A chain reaction of failures starting in London closed the Bank temporarily in 1772, but the directors threw good money after bad until it finally went out of business a year later.   The stockholders lost over £660,000 on capital of £130,000, and many landowners in the west of Scotland, particularly in Ayrshire, were ruined, forcing the sale of a great number of estates over the next twenty years.

The Industrial Revolution was to make its way slowly in Ayrshire in the latter half of the eighteenth century, though in the year of the Ayr Bank's founding, a Glasgow instrument-maker, James Watt, patented his steam engine, and in 1776 Smith's *Wealth of Nations* was to provide the clear, influential rationale for an industrial, capitalistic society based on specialization of labour.   The Ayr Bank was a disastrous experiment in capitalism by amateurs.   Industrialization hardly impinged on the Auchinleck estate during Boswell's lifetime, though when his near neighbour, Sir John Whitefoord, was forced to sell his estate, Ballochmyle, in 1786 to pay off his losses in the Ayr Bank scheme, the new owner, Claud Alexander, established a large cotton mill and model industrial village at Catrine, two miles from Auchinleck House.

Boswell had no stake himself in the Ayr Bank, and his reaction to its failure had little to do with the practical situation.   Rather his 25-page pamphlet, *Reflections on the Late Alarming Bankruptcies in Scotland*, rapidly produced in early November, was intended to serve "not only for immediate admonition," as he wrote in his presentation copy to Lord Kames, "but as a sketch of the present manners in Scotland so much altered to the worse from what his Lordship remembers."

Immediate admonition consisted in exhorting fraudulent bankrupts not to weasel on their debts, but principally the *Reflections* presents Boswell as *censor Scotorum*. Moral decay set in with the Union of 1707, and since that date Scotland had advanced in riches and barbarity. People are extravagant and too eager to get rich quickly; they entertain indiscriminately and drink too much; they spend too little on dress. An abominable spirit of levelling is abroad. Boswell quotes approvingly an unnamed French writer who divides society into two classes: the nobility, whose duty is to defend it; and the plebeians, whose duty is to work and not aspire above their station. In such a society, one might ask, what is the function of the lawyer? But in this mood of philosophic feudalism Boswell was unconcerned with present if necessary imperfections in the system. Directly, the *Reflections* eulogizes subordination; tangentially, it touches on the rise of capitalism and the transformation of the landed gentry. To make sure his pamphlet was not ignored, Boswell reviewed it favourably in the *Edinburgh Advertiser*.

After the psychic release provided by the *Reflections*, Boswell's energies became fully and happily absorbed by the routine of business that winter. One week set a record in fees—23 guineas. And now he was sufficiently established in his profession to be made one of the examiners of the Faculty of Advocates.

But Boswell's career as an advocate is hard to animate since most of his cases present boring arguments about property or breach of contract, sometimes involving such small amounts of money that no one would litigate them today. Fullarton v. Dalrymple stands out somewhat from the usual humdrum. Nabob Fullarton, Boswell's old rival in pursuit of Catherine Blair, had competed successfully in 1770 against Charles Dalrymple of Orangefield for the post of chancellor (provost) of the ancient burgh of Prestwick. But during an election-eve riot, Fullarton struck one John Crawfurd a severe blow, for which he was arrested by Crawfurd's brother, a constable, detained for three hours and ill-treated. Fullarton sued various and sundry, but his chief complaint was that Orangefield, as a J.P., should have travelled a mile to Prestwick in the middle of the night to extricate him. It was all a political plot, Fullarton asserted. The Court of Session found Constable Crawfurd's zeal excessive, and Fullarton's other claims little more than acts of malicious vexation. So far the record, but Boswell's condensed notes of the judges' remarks show that girls somehow triggered the brawl. "Casual commotion," said Lord Gardenstone, "all owing to advent of girls. The other people under apprehension prudery of one of the girls." Given the prevailing state of morals, accurately reflected in Burns's poems, girlish prudery could not have been a common failing in Ayrshire.

If the issues lawyers dealt with were often trifling, the customs of the profession seem strangely convivial.   Advocates did not maintain offices, but invited clients to their homes, or met them in the Parliament House or other public places.   Boswell one evening gathered with two of Orangefield's agents at Walker's Tavern:

> Orangefield, our client, was held as entertainer.   We drank champagne, played at whist, supped, drank champagne, and played at cards again till five in the morning.   I *lost*.

Boswell shows no scruples about amusing himself at his client's expense, but for the next day he adds:

> I had not drank much, but being now in a sober, regular habit want of sleep had hurt me.   I could not get up till twelve.

Whist-playing had become a steady diversion, and early in the next year— easy the descent to Avernus—for the first time Boswell held a whist-party in his own home.

On rare occasions, Edinburgh also reached towards high life, like the masquerade given by Sir Alexander and Lady Macdonald.   Denounced from the pulpit as "the encourager of intrigue, of libertinism, of debauchery," it encouraged, in fact, no more than fashionable, decorous insipidity. Boswell appeared as a dumb conjurer, not an inspired role.   A more common recreation was family gatherings, one of which had unfortunate consequences:

> Lord Dundonald's and Sir George's families, Dr. Webster and Dr. Boswell dined.   It was a jolly meeting of friends, but I drank too much and was greatly heated.   We played a rubber at whist, and Lord and Lady Dundonald went away.   I had been in the morning for a little at the trial of Murdison and Miller for sheep-stealing. I went out to go again to it for a little.   In my way—complete— for the first and I fancy last time—trial a few minutes.

Since the Parliament House is less than a five-minute walk down the Lawnmarket from James's Court, Boswell had not let opportunity pass him by. This first lapse from fidelity also marked a return to the drinking-whoring sequence which had characterized his bachelor existence.

If, by modern standards, an advocate met his clients casually, so too the manners of the Court of Session seem personal and informal, as this exchange shows; it comes from Boswell's notes on Grieve v. Borland, one of the small civil causes that were the advocate's bread and butter:

COALSTON.   I wish they would write with more temper.   There
are several strong expressions in the Answers.[1]
AUCHINLECK.   There are so.
(I maintained that I was only answering the severe insinuation
in the Petition.   I was right and stood to it.   But the President
still shook his head to me, patting with his forefinger upon
his nose.)
KAMES.   You're a good-natured fellow, Boswell.
PRESIDENT.   Ay, but has a wicked pen (smiling).

As usual, Boswell's heart was in his criminal cases, one of which that
spring sharply illustrates not only his lasting sympathy for the unfortunate
but some of the conditions that produced them.   Linen manufacture had
gone into a slump in the early 1770s; at the same time a series of bad
harvests led to a scarcity of grain.   The price of bread rose to nearly
twopence a pound, at a time when the wages of a Dundee weaver had
dropped to eight or nine shillings a week.   (Many women supplemented
their husbands' wages by spinning yarn at home for another four or
five pence a day.)   Mutton and beef, at six or seven pence a pound, were
out of the question.   The inevitable outcome of the situation was predicted
in the *Scots Magazine* for March 1772:

> The poor cannot long continue to purchase the necessaries of life
> at these prices, and they must and will be fed.   If they cannot
> procure food by the produce of their labour, they will grow des-
> perate and seize it by force.

In the following December and January, large mobs gathered in Perth,
Cupar, Dundee, and some neighbouring towns, carried off or spoiled grain
being loaded for shipment out of the area, and advancing into the countryside plundered the farms of grain dealers, always "the objects of public
execration."   The country dwellers—gentry, farmers, and tenants—fought
back vigorously, and a few straggling rioters were committed to prison.
But even the conservative *Scots Magazine* acknowledged

> the total want of meal in the market in Perth for eight or ten days
> and the neglect of the police to provide against this, beside a
> scarcity of that sort of provision for a long time past, so that the
> poor were hard put to it for subsistence.

With the customary wisdom of newspapers, this account asserts that the
poor should have appealed to the magistrates.
As might be expected it was the courts, not the magistrates, that were

[1]Drawn by Boswell.

invoked, and on 15 March 1773 Boswell defended a Dundee sailor, Richard
Robertson, who was charged with taking part in the mob that had destroyed
the house of Thomas Mylne of Mylnefield.   The jury found unanimously
that Robertson had indeed been part of the mob, but also that he had not
been involved in sacking the house.   That evening Boswell, also heavily
engaged in the similar case of Cameron and Tosh, hurried home to discover
that Margaret, who had been in labour since the previous evening, had
given birth to Veronica, a "fine little thing."   It was the effective start of
his long-desired family.   On the 17th the prosecution and defence argued
the equivocal import of the verdict against Robertson: Boswell urged that
since the jury had not found Robertson guilty of a criminal act he might
have intended to warn or aid Mylne, an ingenious assertion based on two
recent similar incidents.   But the Court of Session "painted in very lively
colours the fatal and dangerous consequences which must ever attend the
licentious practice of mobbing," and sentenced Robertson to transportation
for life, unmoved by his claim of innocence and passionate plea to be
hanged rather than separated from his family forever.

The jury had sympathized as far as it dared with the rioters, while the
Court of Session enforced the interests of the propertied.   Still, riot, then
as now, was a powerful means for securing the attention of Government.
After the riots a new corn-law was enacted to provide municipal granaries,
a society was established in Edinburgh for the Relief of the Honest and
Industrious Poor, and police forces were strengthened throughout Scotland.

I I

BOSWELL'S JAUNT to London in 1772 had at first seemed an unusual
break in his settled life, but London experienced again was irresistible and
he had decided on the spot to return every spring.   Some things have to
be done only once to turn into a habit.   He had no excuse this year, except
that common to all the *literati* who travelled on occasion to London: James
Beattie, whose *Essay on the Nature and Immutability of Truth* was held by the
converted to have demolished Hume; Hugh Blair, well paid for his widely
read sermons; William Robertson, at the moment Hume's only rival as an
historian; Adam Smith; Lord Monboddo, riding horseback all the way until
he was over 80 because he disdained the carriage as an effete innovation
of the Moderns.   All wanted to refresh themselves at the centre of intel-

lectual life. (It must be admitted that Boswell never instanced any of them as examples.)

This year he intended to honour the claims of domestic affection by bringing Margaret with him, a solution equally easy and impractical. Margaret disliked travel; she was to have a young, increasing family to take care of; she was shy with strangers or the great, and content with her homely life in Edinburgh. Nor could she have fitted into Boswell's strenuous and erratic London existence. She would stay at home, taking advantage of Boswell's absence this spring to prepare their move downstairs to larger quarters, a duplex; Boswell would make the journey by himself.

Far from altering Boswell's plans, the birth of Veronica provided him with a fine excuse to prepare for his arrival in London, while adding to his future archives at Auchinleck. On 29 March he wrote eleven letters, the most notable to Goldsmith:

> You must know my wife was safely delivered of a daughter the very evening that *She Stoops to Conquer* first appeared. I am fond of the coincidence. My little daughter is a fine, healthy, lively child, and I flatter myself shall be blessed with the cheerfulness of your comic muse. She has nothing of that wretched whining and crying which we see children so often have; nothing of the *comédie larmoyante* [the genre of sentimental comedy which *She Stoops to Conquer* did so much to displace].

But instead of mentioning his departure for London the next day, Boswell added, "Pray write directly. Write as if in repartee."

If not an exercise in repartee, Goldsmith's reply showed him—half-indignant, half-amused at himself—as London's "only *poet militant*." In the midst of deserved, unexpected, and flattering success, Goldsmith, always as "irascible as a hornet," had been stirred up by a letter in the *London Packet* signed "Tom Tickle" (generally taken to be that busy, scurrilous hack, William Kenrick), which imagined "the *great* Goldsmith" as standing for hours "surveying his grotesque orang-utan's figure in a pier glass"; and followed this compliment with, "Was but the lovely H—k as much enamoured, you would not sigh, my gentle swain, in vain." Especially resenting, he said, the reference to his friend Miss Horneck, Goldsmith on 26 March had attacked the *Packet*'s publisher, Thomas Evans, in his office, and the combatants had had to be separated, reportedly by Kenrick himself. Evans sued for assault and the newspapers screamed freedom of the press, while Goldsmith defended himself in a statement arguing that the laws were inadequate to protect individuals from libel. "I don't care how it is," he told Boswell; "come up to town, and we shall laugh [Evans's suit] off whether it goes for or against me."   The suit was settled by Goldsmith's donating £50 to a Welsh charity.

Arriving in London two days before Goldsmith wrote this letter, Boswell settled in Piccadilly, and immediately entered on the subject of the day with Johnson:

> BOSWELL.   "I fancy, Sir, this is the first time that [Goldsmith]
>   has been engaged in such an adventure."
> JOHNSON.   "Why, Sir, I believe it is the first time he has *beat*; he
>   may have *been beaten* before.   This, Sir, is a new plume to
>   him."

Boswell had thought Goldsmith on first meeting, at Tom Davies's on Christmas Day 1762, "a curious, odd, pedantic fellow with some genius," and the conversation seems to have been strenuously literary since the company "talked entirely in the way of geniuses."   Later, Boswell had been irritated that Goldsmith was more intimate with Johnson than he was, but as the occasion for envy wore away Boswell developed a high esteem for him, and by 1773 they were on easy and cordial, if not intimate, terms. Boswell's record this spring expands when he comes to their discussions with Johnson, at Oglethorpe's on 13 April (does luxury enfeeble?); at Paoli's two days later (the King's projected visit to *She Stoops to Conquer*); and at Oglethorpe's again on 29 April, where Johnson paid his famous, simple compliment to the play:

> I know of no comedy for many years that has so much exhilarated
> an audience, that has answered so much the great end of comedy—
> making an audience merry.

If, on many occasions, Goldsmith appears blundering, forward, envious, and—above all—ridiculous, this was the Goldsmith everyone knew. He seems to have suffered from that kind of uneasiness which manifests itself not as bashfulness but in increasingly desperate attempts in company to attract favourable notice, or notice of any kind.   Yet Goldsmith must have found his own behaviour exquisitely vexatious.   To describe him merely as versatile underrates his talents; few writers have demonstrated such smooth ability in so many genres: poem, essay, play, and novel. With the shrewdest eye for human affections and follies, he commanded an elusive but unmistakably individual mixture of irony and sentiment, most conspicuously displayed in *The Deserted Village* and *The Vicar of Wakefield*.   Apart from Johnson, Goldsmith was the ablest writer in England, yet except for a few happy moments he was unable to capitalize in society on his talents.   And he knew it, as his description of himself in *Retaliation* shows: "magnanimous Goldsmith, a gooseberry fool . . . with chaos and blunders encircling my head."   Self-conscious, absurd, irritating, but also warm, lovable, and—as Boswell remarked—"the most generous-hearted man that exists."

Boswell's retrospective summary of Goldsmith as a writer offers an example of fine discrimination:

> His mind resembled a fertile but thin soil.   There was a quick, but not a strong, vegetation of whatever chanced to be thrown upon it.   No deep root could be struck.   The oak of the forest did not grow there; but the elegant shrubbery and fragrant parterre appeared in gay succession.

Goldsmith, playing Dr. Minor to Johnson's Dr. Major, is the most vivid member of this spring's cast, but Boswell instinctively sketched any promising subject.   In particular he claimed that having become "a kind of enthusiast" in his profession he enjoyed collecting specimens of it.   The enthusiasm was fitful, but the specimen-collecting was an insistent drive whose select example was Lord Mansfield.   Mansfield was compelling, to begin with, because of his power; if he were to take a liking to Boswell, he could be the most influential of patrons.   And in himself he was a study in contrasts: Boswell greatly admired his public performance, his "full, easy, and choice expression," but tête-à-tête Mansfield seemed artful and reserved.   Boswell could not resist poking his specimen by bringing up Andrew Stuart's violent assertions, in his *Letters to Lord Mansfield*, of Mansfield's bias in favour of Douglas in the great Cause.   Mansfield brushed Stuart aside; that case was closed.   Boswell could never grasp the character of a professional jurist like Mansfield, entirely secure in his ability.   Vanity cannot assess pride, it can only register its manifestations: talking to Mansfield "was like being cut with a very, very cold instrument."

In contrast to the impression Mansfield made on him, Boswell remarks three weeks after a dinner at Paoli's:

> Situation has a great share in the production of every character. While I was with the General at the head of his nation in Corsica, I could collect many memorabilia.   Now I cannot recollect anything that passed this day.

But power and situation were not the only factors to govern Boswell's memory.   A variety of experiences could command attention.   Naturally enough, an event like hearing Burke for the first time in the House of Commons, when he pelted the Ministry with figures of speech: an admirable performer, Boswell thought, rather than a persuasive advocate. But also some simple pleasure, like the snug monthly meeting of the proprietors of the *London Magazine*: "a good supper . . . madeira . . . excellent old port at half a crown a bottle." Or an uplifting spectacle, like the orphans of Christ's Hospital at "their wholesome frugal supper, bread and butter and beer," walking in procession and bowing to the governors. (A comparable sight evoked the ambivalences of Blake's *Holy Thursday* in *Songs of Innocence*.)

Goldsmith was allowed to score at least once that spring, when he told Johnson, "If you were to make little fishes talk, they would talk like WHALES." It was true Johnson lacked Goldsmith's literary flexibility; instead he was the oak of the forest, in life as well as in his writings, and as such he dominates this jaunt and journal. He even provided advice on keeping a journal:

> The great thing . . . is the state of your own mind; and you ought to write down everything that you can, for you cannot judge at first what is good or bad; and write immediately while the impression is fresh.

(As a modern critic comments, it was like Aristotle instructing Menander on how to get a laugh. Yet there is something irreducibly mysterious in that choice of detail—Boswell couldn't have explained the process of selection himself—which enables him to put a scene directly in front of the reader.) In return, Boswell again pressed Johnson for details of his early life, and Johnson promised them all for twopence, though adding characteristically, "I hope you shall know a great deal more of me, before you write my life."

Boswell was to learn a great deal more on their long-discussed expedition to the Hebrides, to which Johnson was now committed. Meanwhile, he collected from various sources all he could, including Johnson's own, often sharp, opinions of others: Garrick had no ear, Burke sacrificed everything to wit, Percy's ballads drove him to parody. Boswell himself, Johnson said during a dispute, talked like one just hatched. (All these remarks were softened or omitted in the *Life of Johnson*.) And Johnson provided a valuable lesson in authenticity when he annihilated the well-known story that Lord Chesterfield had kept him waiting in the antechamber while he talked to Colley Cibber.

Boswell also busily discussed Johnson's past and present with their friends: with Garrick, Johnson's admirable conversation; with Beauclerk, his growing good nature and supposed Jacobitism; with Goldsmith, an absurd newspaper scandal about his relationship with Mrs. Thrale. And not only did he spend part of Good Friday with Johnson, an event which became a devout habit, but to his astonishment Johnson invited him to Easter dinner:

> Very good soup, a boiled leg of lamb and spinach, a veal pie, an excellent rice pudding, pickled walnuts and onions, porter and port wine.

Boswell had hardly expected knives and forks.

Still, Johnson was not the only beast in view that spring, though Boswell in his journal covered the tracks of his other pursuit. He wanted very much to become a member of The Club, and certain names—Goldsmith, Beauclerk, Langton, Percy, Reynolds, and (the very recently elected) Garrick—appear in the journal as retrospective clues. (The lack of explicit references to electioneering warns us that Boswell could suppress delicate matters when he chose to.) He was frank enough later about his aim; where he reports Johnson in the *Hebrides* as saying, "Sir, you got into our club by doing what a man can do," Boswell added a footnote in the second edition:

> This, I find, is considered as obscure. I suppose Dr. Johnson meant that I assiduously and earnestly recommended myself to some of the members, as in a canvass for an election into parliament.

His ambition was nothing to be ashamed of, but Boswell's election was no forgone matter. The day of decision arrived on 30 April 1773. Boswell was left after dinner at Beauclerk's while the other gentlemen went off to The Club to ballot on him. Several members opposed his election, Burke for one objecting that Boswell had so much natural good humour it was scarcely a virtue; and one blackball was sufficient to exclude. But as Johnson, his sponsor, later told him, "Sir, they knew that if they refused you they'd probably never have got in another. I'd have kept them all out." Boswell passed some moments in deep anxiety until Beauclerk's coach returned to fetch him to the Turk's Head, Gerrard St., Soho ("in flutter—prayed in coach"). Johnson, leaning over a pulpit-like chair, charged him with his duties as a member.

Years afterwards Boswell wrote, "I question if any election now would give me a higher sensation." It meant acceptance. Not into the Johnsonian circle—he had been a full member of that for some time—but into the most select intellectual group in London. Besides those named, it already included the dramatist George Colman, and the young William Jones, later the first great British scholar of Sanskrit. During Boswell's lifetime it was to add, among others, Charles James Fox, Edward Gibbon,

Adam Smith, Richard Brinsley Sheridan, George Steevens, Joseph and Thomas Warton, Charles Burney, Edmond Malone, John Courtenay, and William Windham. Writers and scholars predominated: the only two English authors of any eminence in this period who did not belong to it were William Cowper and Horace Walpole. (At Garrick's funeral it acquired the well-known but temporary designation of The Literary Club.)

The Club's purpose was general conversation, that interchange of ideas among eminent men which constituted the highest of social pleasures, and its members were already so noted for their range of interests and achievements that Boswell and Johnson amused themselves on their tour of the Hebrides by making up a faculty for an imaginary university from their number. And Boswell was a fit choice. His mind lacked the amplitude of Burke's or the versatility of Goldsmith's; he would never be able to match Smith's capacity for abstract thought or Gibbon's learning and power of historical generalization. But he had paid his dues. His *Account of Corsica* had made him famous, as much on the Continent as at home. And he was a desirable companion not merely for that sociability and good humour of which we shall hear so much, but for intelligence. Like Johnson, he made acute observations about others because he relentlessly observed himself. In their writings, Johnson had the unusual power of raising observation to convincing, if often gloomy, generalization; Boswell was strong in his discrimination of particulars. Johnson makes the reader absorb the force of a maxim; Boswell involves him fully in a situation.

But admission to The Club meant far more to Boswell than social or intellectual acceptance by his peers. He was a Scot who found the high road to England otherwise blocked: he had failed to obtain a commission in the Guards; he would never reach high political or legal office like Mansfield or Wedderburn or Dundas; he would never even become an M.P. like Dempster. But his election, an unusual honour for a Scot, was a rite of passage by which Boswell was assimilated to the English intellectual establishment. This assimilation sealed his emotional transference to London.

Boswell and Johnson solemnized the event by dining tête-à-tête the next day at the Mitre, where Johnson stressed Boswell's cosmopolitan nature in remarking that he was "the most *unscottified*" of his countrymen. And, as if instinctively returning to the source of his literary strength, Boswell sat up on the night of his election and journalized: "not able as formerly, but wrote 26 pages." (Almost half the fully written journal of this year's jaunt was composed at this one sitting.)

The rest is coda. Boswell's final ten days in London were distinguished

by the first of a great series of dinners at the Dillys'.   It was on this occasion
that as Johnson hammered the anvil-like Dr. Mayo on the subject of toleration, Goldsmith was so overborne in his attempts to "shine" by Johnson's
loud voice that "in a passion [he] threw down his hat . . . exclaiming in a
bitter tone, 'take it.' "   Finally he grew so outrageous that Johnson called
him impertinent (apologizing later).   Meanwhile Langton, with unchar-
acteristic imprudence, ventured to suggest that heretical opinions might
be tolerated in speculations on the nature of the Trinity, and Johnson
tossed and gored him for introducing so delicate a subject in the company
of Dissenters.   So often tossed himself, Boswell said he found it a rich
sight to see Langton's long legs high in the air.

Langton was also inspiration for the last significant moment of
Boswell's stay in London.   Boswell learned, to his feudal displeasure, that
Langton had instructed their legal friend and fellow Club member, Robert
Chambers, to draw up a will leaving his estate to his three sisters in pref-
erence to a remote male relation.   Johnson joined strongly in dispraise of
folly:

> An ancient estate should always go to males.   It is mighty foolish
> to let a stranger have it because he marries your daughter and
> takes your name.   I would not let a rascal take my name.   As for
> an estate newly acquired by trade, you may give it, if you will, to
> the dog *Towser* and let him keep his *own* name.

But something else in Langton's solemn will-making touched off Johnson's sense of the grotesque: he called Langton the "testator" and mimicked
him reading his will to the first innkeeper on the road, "after a suitable
preface upon mortality and the uncertainty of life."   And then to Chambers, "I hope you have had more conscience than to make him say, 'being
of sound understanding.'   Ha, ha, ha!   I hope he has left me a legacy.
He should leave hatbands and gloves to all The Club.   I'd have his will
turned into verse like a ballad."

Chambers showing some impatience, they left his rooms in the Temple
while Boswell encouraged Johnson's remarkable mood, calling out, "Langton the testator, Langton Longshanks."

> This tickled [Johnson's] fancy so much that he roared out, "I
> wonder to whom he'll leave his legs?"   And then burst into such
> a fit of laughter that he appeared to be almost in a convulsion;
> and in order to support himself laid hold of one of the posts which
> were at that time at the side of the pavement, and sent forth peals
> so loud that in the silence of the night his voice seemed to resound
> from Temple Bar to Fleet Ditch.

CHAPTER

4

THE NEXT CONVERSATION between Johnson and Boswell took place several months later when Johnson, having overcome his habitual inertia, had travelled north. In the evening of 14 August 1773, they strolled up the High Street of Edinburgh towards Boswell's flat in James's Court. As the stench of the open running sewers struck Johnson, he grumbled in Boswell's ear, "I smell you in the dark!" At once sounds the keynote of Boswell's journal of their tour to the Hebrides, its concentration on the presentness of each moment, immediate and inescapable. When Boswell complained a few days later that the kind attentions of their hosts tired him, Johnson generalized the point: no matter how one ought to react, "sensation is sensation."

This stress on sensation, the feel and impact of daily life, was deeply rooted in Boswell's temperament. More than most people he lived each day, and he lacked some of the ordinary adult's ability to distance or deaden feeling. Sensation for him included sensuality, the strong operation of the senses; sensibility, the willingness to be moved, even to weep when he heard Highland music or an account of the battle of Culloden; and, at base, simply an eager openness to experience. And conviction reinforced temperament. The *savoir vivre*, he said, is "to multiply pleasurable sensations as much as possible—not merely animal sensations, but those of the fine arts, of knowledge, and of reasoning."

Travelling slows down time while it quickens the mind and emotions. "Incidents upon a journey," Boswell wrote a few years later, "are recollected with peculiar pleasure; they are preserved in brisk spirits." Robust and flexible at thirty-two, Boswell showed himself a remarkably good traveller:

eager, responsive, cheerful, managing with tact and good humour the petty discomforts and uncertainties that poison travel for the less resilient.

Travelling is also notorious for intensifying the power of recall, but in Boswell's case the tour to the Hebrides evoked a consciousness so heightened that except for its lack of distorted perception it might seem abnormal. Boswell the journalist had been provided with a special stimulus. He had often observed Johnson at rest in the familiar surroundings of London. Now Johnson was in motion, to react to and reflect upon new, unexpected, and sometimes unsettling situations, against the rapidly changing and sharply contrasted background of Scotland.

It is impossible to disentangle Johnson and Boswell's daily experience from Boswell's accounts of it in the *Tour* and the *Hebrides*,[1] though other sources add further perspectives: detached anecdotes clinging along the route, Johnson's letters to Mrs. Thrale, and especially Johnson's *Journey to the Western Islands of Scotland*. But the *Journey*, though including much that Boswell omits, aims at a different effect. Johnson insisted that "our business was with life and manners," but his business was with man, not men; apart from polite acknowledgements of hospitality, he seldom mentions individuals except to illustrate general points. His powerful mind—fixed in attitude, settled in opinion—works like a great mill (in Boswell's phrase) on the material furnished it. "Diminutive observations" give a factual basis to the abstractions and generalizations he found congenial, and he presents a more coherent overall description of the Highlands than Boswell does. But fundamentally Johnson reflects on the flow of history, on the transformation of a part-pastoral, part-feudal society into a commercial one. Johnson the traveller paid attention to small inconveniences and petty pleasures. Johnson the writer, though acknowledging the "local" effect of Iona, characteristically rises beyond "sensation" in defining it:

> Whatever withdraws us from the power of our senses; whatever makes the past, the distant, or the future predominate over the present, advances us in the dignity of thinking beings.

Boswell, in contrast, seems immersed in sensation, in the rough and tumble of daily events, but this is an aspect of his unusual method as a journalist and biographer. Earlier English biographers, such as Cavendish in his *Life of Wolsey* and Walton in his *Life of Donne*, say little about them-

---

[1] *Tour* designates Boswell's original journal, first published from the manuscript in 1936. *Hebrides* designates the first edition of the journal as Boswell published it in 1785. *Life*, v. designates the third edition of *Hebrides*, published in 1786, and constituting the fifth volume of the Hill-Powell edition of the *Life* (1934–64); see the Textual Note.

selves.   And even though much of his *Life of Savage* emerged from personal
and deeply felt observation, Johnson keeps his role as narrator subordinate.
Boswell, as some readers have persistently complained, puts himself forward all the time.   Since so much of his material came from his journals,
it would have been difficult to excise himself from it.   Far more important,
Boswell saw how to use himself artistically in juxtaposition to his subject,
as the significant other character in the biography.

The simplest example of Boswell's strategy is the earliest.   The "Memoirs of Pascal Paoli" section of the *Account of Corsica* revolves around a giant
and a dwarf star, the mature Paoli and the naïve Boswell, who exists to ask
the innocent, revealing question, to evoke the grand response, to highlight
the hero.   In the process Boswell exaggerates his own limitations: "Never
was I so thoroughly sensible of my own defects as while I was in Corsica.
I felt how small were my abilities and how little I knew."   Boswell in
miniature mirrors Paoli: he play-acts the ruler, riding out on Paoli's horse
accompanied by Paoli's guards; real state and distinction, real power, rest
in Paoli.

The other important element in this depiction is the background.   In
the Benbridge portrait of Paoli commissioned by Boswell, the background
consists of some stylized rocks, trees, and hills; and Boswell treats his background, Corsica and the Corsicans, in the same generalizing fashion: a
rugged country inhabited by a brave, unspoiled, and simple people, who
throw Paoli's stern and active virtues into sharp relief.

The tour to the Hebrides offered Boswell the possibility of a more
complex and exciting arrangement.   Scotland becomes an active entity,
initially set in uneasy opposition to Johnson, their hostility well publicized.
In this ready-made scenario, Boswell casts Johnson as John Bull, true-born
Englishman.   Boswell, guide and journalist, also acts as mediator, coming
to Scotland's defence when necessary; though now, while preserving the
naïf, Boswell takes on the additional gloss of a detached citizen of the world.

To emphasize this triangulation, Boswell begins the *Hebrides* with the
block characterization of his subject with which he will end the *Life of
Johnson*.   It is too long to reproduce in full, though omissions weaken its
subtlety and impair its rhythm.   But partial quotation can suggest its flavour:

> . . . a sincere and zealous Christian, of high Church-of-England
> and monarchical principles, which he would not tamely suffer to
> be questioned . . . impetuous and irritable in his temper, but of a
> most humane and benevolent heart. . . .   He united a most logical

head with a most fertile imagination, which gave him an extraordinary advantage in arguing, for he could reason close or wide as
he saw best for the moment. . . .   He was conscious of his superiority. . . .   He was somewhat susceptible of flattery.   His mind
was so full of imagery that he might have been perpetually a
poet. . . .   He had a constitutional melancholy, the clouds of which
darkened the brightness of his fancy and gave a gloomy cast to
his whole course of thinking. . . .   He was prone to superstition
but not to credulity. . . .   He had a loud voice and a slow deliberate
utterance. . . .

His person was large, robust, I may say approaching to the
gigantic, and grown unwieldy from corpulency. . . .   He was now
in his sixty-fourth year, and was become a little dull of hearing. . . .
His head and sometimes also his body shook with a kind of motion
like the effect of a palsy. . . .   He wore a full suit of plain brown
clothes . . . a large, bushy, greyish wig . . . boots, and a very wide
brown cloth greatcoat . . . and he carried in his hand a large English oak stick.

Let me not be censured for mentioning such minute particulars.
Everything relative to so great a man is worth observing.

Minute particulars are, of course, the constituents of the Boswellian
mode, and contemporary taste officially preferred Johnson's grandeur of
generality.   But if Boswell's mode is accepted as suitable, a perceptive
reader of this or any era would recognize in the clarity, resonance, and
fine discrimination of this sketch alone the signs of a great writer.

Boswell holds back his own self-portrait until the moment of their departure from Edinburgh.   Though much slighter than his sketch of Johnson, it shows the same precision in what he selects to say about himself:

. . . a gentleman of ancient blood, the pride of which was his
predominant passion. . . .   He had thought more than anybody
supposed, and had a pretty good stock of general learning and
knowledge.   He had all Dr. Johnson's principles, with some degree of relaxation.   He had rather too little than too much prudence, and his imagination being lively, he often said things of
which the effect was very different from the intention.   He resembled sometimes

The best good man, with the worst-natured muse.

(Rochester's line was an admirable excuse for those moments when Boswell's
apparent ingenuousness cut too close to the bone.)

Even before their departure from Edinburgh, Boswell has established
his triangular plot.   In the laigh (under) Parliament House, the sight of

the Treaty of Union between England and Scotland aroused Boswell's "*old Scottish* sentiments" about loss of independence. Johnson, taking the bait, responded with one of the traditional sneers at the Scots, their failure to rescue Mary, Queen of Scots, from her English prison. Boswell then expands the scene dramatically:

> [JOHNSON.] " . . . And such a Queen, too!—as every man of any gallantry of spirit would have sacrificed his life for." Worthy MR. JAMES KER, *Keeper of the Records*. "Half our nation was bribed with English money." JOHNSON. "Sir, that is no defence; that makes you worse." Good MR. BROWN, *Keeper of the Advocates' Library*. "We had better say nothing about it." BOSWELL. "You would have been glad, however, to have had us last war, Sir, to fight your battles!" JOHNSON. "We should have had you for the same price though there had been no Union, as we might have had Swiss or other troops. No, no. I shall agree to a separation. You have only to *go home*."

This gibe at the notorious population drift to England, to the milk and honey of jobs and preferment, glances at the unexpectedness of Johnson's own journey to Scotland. It was a journey in time as well as in space, back first to Martin Martin's *Description of the Western Islands of Scotland* (1703), which had fascinated him as a child. Martin's account mingles several layers of culture: remnants of the pagan Celts; the earliest Christian influence radiating from Iona; the medieval period, in widespread survival of feudal customs and other reminders of pre-Reformation Christianity. "Of browneis and of bogillis full this buke." But prosaic details interwoven with the marvellous give Martin's *Description* its eighteenth-century value of being, or passing for, factual. The combination can be curious enough. When fowlers land in the Flannan Islands, for example,

> they fasten the boat to the sides of a rock, and then fix a wooden ladder, by laying a stone at the foot of it, to prevent its falling into the sea; and when they are got up into the island, all of them uncover their heads, and make a turn sun-ways round, thanking God for their safety. The first injunction given after landing is not to ease nature in that place where the boat lies, for that they reckon a crime of the highest nature, and of dangerous consequence to all their crew. . . .

The ordinary Grand Tourist travelled back in time to the sources and monuments of Western culture, especially to the Rome of the first centuries, the golden age of civilization. To visit the semi-barbarous Scottish outlands inverted the Grand Tour and brought Johnson and Boswell into touch with an opposed vision of the past.   This vision, now loosely and misleadingly called Rousseauistic, asserted that the savage was superior to the civilized man, and that the groves of Eden might be approximated in the islands of the South Pacific or some other unspoiled region.   Both a work like Diderot's *Supplément au voyage de Bougainville*, or an actual example like Omai, the South Seas native whose gentlemanly bearing so impressed the British upper class, sustained this shimmering possibility.

As might be expected, Johnson was sceptical that Nature's plan was anywhere near this simple or, if it was, that art did not improve upon it considerably.   But it would be exciting to observe a society in an earlier stage of culture.   Not that Johnson and Boswell anticipated modern anthropological interest in primitive psychology or social organization; it never occurred to them that the basic structures of the mind or the tribe might be elucidated by primitive belief and custom.   Their main interest was in the present conformation of society or, as Boswell puts it simply, in "a system of life almost totally different from what we had been accustomed to see."

And it lay at the other end of their own island.   The Union of 1707 had gradually brought the Lowlands into closer relationship with England, though Lowlanders held to their own law, often to broad Scots—Lord Auchinleck never spoke anything else—and above all to their sense of national identity.   The Gaelic-speaking Highlands were even more resistant to change.   But after the Rebellion of 1715 was suppressed, the Government established garrisons and built military roads; and when Prince Charles Edward landed in 1745 important Highland chiefs, like the great Duke of Argyll, remained loyal to George II, while others, like MacLeod of MacLeod and Macdonald of Sleat, shifted with the wind.   The Hanoverian victory gave the final blow to the Highland feudal system: the rebels' estates were forfeited, though often to return eventually to their former owners; military tenures and heritable jurisdictions, two basic means by which the chiefs and principal landowners controlled their tenants, were abolished; and it was forbidden to carry arms or wear Highland dress. The British ministry encouraged loyalty by recruiting Highland regiments to fight in the Seven Years' War.   These political developments had social and economic counterparts that led to a fairly rapid erosion of the traditional patterns of Highland life.   Still, in 1773, as Johnson remarks, "to the southern inhabitants of Scotland, the state of the mountains and the islands" was "equally unknown with that of Borneo or Sumatra."

Unknown, despised, and feared.   Juxtapose a tribal, warlike society with an agricultural one, and the results are predictable.   For centuries the Highlanders had considered Lowland cattle their natural prey, the Black Watch regiment being incorporated in 1739 to suppress their "liftings." As late as 1755 an observer could praise one ragtag group of Highlanders for not having stolen a single beast for the past two years. In war they were notably fierce soldiers, who overran much of the country in the '45. At Prestonpans, the impetuosity of the Highland charge so panicked the British dragoons and infantry that the battle lasted only a few minutes. Even after the slaughter of Culloden imposed peace on the Highlands and violence became uncommon, many Lowlanders would have echoed the prudent suspicions of Bailie Nicol Jarvie of Glasgow, "Ye maunna expect me to gang ower the Highland line—I'll gae behind the line at no rate."

Johnson and Boswell were not to cross the line until they reached Inverness, and the early part of their tour was uneventful. First came a few days in Edinburgh. The *literati* gathered warily, not even Principal Robertson venturing to grapple at close quarters, and Johnson later approved his caution: "Robertson is a man of eminence, and the head of a college at Edinburgh. He had a character to maintain and did well not to risk its being lessened." Hume, the arch-enemy, remained across the North Loch in St. David Street, contenting himself with whist and cookery. Johnson, who thought you should strike hard in battle, savaged him heart and head: "I know not indeed whether he has first been a blockhead and that has made him a rogue, or first been a rogue and that has made him a blockhead." There was some sightseeing: though he considered Boswell's new rooms handsome and spacious, Johnson found the buildings of the Old Town very mean, rather like the old part of Birmingham. Edinburgh was, in short, provincial. Nor did matters improve as they started their progress on 18 August. Fife seemed a remote and backward region. The decay of St. Andrews and its university was mournful, and the harvest plains of Angus as they roll towards the blue and glittering sea seemed notable chiefly for their lack of trees and hedges.

If nature failed, there was always the refreshment of staging Johnson in a new scene. So they turned aside to Monboddo, "a wretched place, wild and naked, with a poor old house." Though Johnson and he did not like each other, Lord Monboddo received them politely in his role of Farmer Burnett, complete with rustic suit and little round hat. From the merit of Homer's shield of Achilles—a companionable topic—the conversation drifted to history:

MONBODDO.   "The history of manners[1] is the most valuable.   I
never set a high value on any other history."   JOHNSON.   "Nor I;
and therefore I esteem biography, as giving us what comes near
to ourselves, what we can turn to use."   BOSWELL.   "But in the
course of general history, we find manners.   In wars, we see the
dispositions of people, their degrees of humanity, and other particulars."   JOHNSON.   "Yes, but then you must take all the facts
to get this, and it is but a little you get."   MONBODDO.   "And it is
that little which makes history valuable."   Bravo! thought I; they
agree like two brothers.

Biography is what we can turn to use.   This is the principle, ethical
rather than utilitarian, on which Johnson and Boswell based their biographical work.   But the passage also illustrates certain characteristics of
Boswell's writing: stylistically, the clear concision of the phrasing.   Dramatically, the confrontation between Johnson and an opponent, with
Boswell as middleman, here with its unexpected issue in agreement.   Nar-
ratively, Boswell's ability to move in and out of the scene, to act both as
participant and observer.

Soon came a touchier subject, the relative happiness of the savage
(Monboddo, advocate) and the London shopkeeper (Johnson, advocate).
We might wish some details of the discussion were preserved, since this
reflected the central question (the respective merits of a semi-feudal and
a commercial society) posed by the tour itself.   But in this last oblique
transposition of the quarrel between the Ancients and the Moderns the
positions had become frozen, and Johnson was to admit he could have
argued equally well on behalf of the savage.   Perhaps this is why the
argument remained amiable, and nothing was said, pro or con, about tails.
Yet eighteenth-century common sense found eccentricity its prime target,
Johnson remarking later he was sorry Monboddo spoiled sense and learning with such theories:

> Other people have strange notions, but they conceal them.   If
> they have tails, they hide them; but Monboddo is as jealous of his
> tail as a squirrel.

Aberdeen, their next stop, turned into a bore.   But Slains Castle, seat
of the Earl of Erroll, was an outpost of aristocratic elegance.   Slains rose
sheer from the sea cliff, and Johnson thought the prospect across the North
Sea towards Denmark the noblest he had ever seen.   Boswell was "ex-

[1]Social behaviour in general.

ceedingly pleased" by the affable stateliness of Lord Erroll, hereditary
Constable of Scotland. A title tended to impress him, especially that of
an old family when represented by one of the tallest and handsomest men
in Britain. Still, sensation remained sensation: the fire in Boswell's bedroom blazed, the sea roared, and the pillows smelled disagreeably of sea-
fowl feathers. Erroll's father, Lord Kilmarnock, had been beheaded on
Tower Hill in 1746, and Boswell feared his ghost might appear. He slept
badly.

Strichen offered the first remains of the pagan past, a Druid temple—
or four stones, anyway, parading as a Druid temple. The ruins of one
Druid temple, they soon discovered, were very much like those of the next.
And the same could be said of caves and other natural curiosities. To the
heath near Forres they brought their own powers of imagination as Johnson, a remarkable declaimer, repeated Macbeth's speech on first seeing the
witches, in a "grand and affecting" manner. Suddenly they are glimpsed
from another source. Carruthers, who published a fine edition of the
Hebrides in 1852, picked up a tradition that Johnson at Inverness had
imitated the newly discovered kangaroo:

> He stood erect, put out his hands like feelers, and, gathering up
> the tails of his huge brown coat, so as to resemble the pouch of
> the animal, made two or three vigorous bounds across the room.

"The great thing is to bring objects together," Boswell was to remark
on seeing Johnson at Iona, and as they entered the Highlands the opportunities for contrast increased and intensified. But the transition itself
from Lowlands to Highlands was hardly perceptible, and their preparations
minimal. Johnson had brought pistols to Scotland, which Boswell persuaded him were unnecessary. Boswell suggested lemons, which Johnson
thought would be insulting to their hosts. The most serious change was
from post-chaises to horses and Highland ponies, on which Johnson sat
like a sack. When they left Inverness for Fort Augustus on 30 August, they
had three horses for themselves and Joseph, Boswell's giant Bohemian
servant, with a fourth for their portmanteaus. Two Highland guides walked
with them. Their route, casually laid out a few days earlier, was Fort
Augustus, Glenelg, Skye, Mull, Iona, Oban, Inveraray, which they followed
closely, with the involuntary addition of Coll.

Loch Ness was lovely enough to rouse a feeble interest in landscape,
also stimulated no doubt by their consciousness of being in the Highlands.
"On the left," says Johnson,

> were high and steep rocks shaded with birch, the hardy native
> of the North, and covered with fern or heath. On the right

the limpid waters of Loch Ness were beating their bank, and waving their surface by a gentle agitation. Beyond them were rocks sometimes covered with verdure, and sometimes towering in horrid nakedness. Now and then we espied a little corn-field, which served to impress more strongly the general barrenness.

Unusual in itself as a Johnsonian description of nature, the passage also reminds us that Johnson was a city dweller, whose jaunts had been confined mainly to the cultivated regions of the Midlands. To the modern traveller he seems to over-emphasize wildness and barrenness, as he discovers around him "the gloom and grandeur of Siberian solitude" or a "wide extent of hopeless sterility." It is true that the motorist can now condense Johnson and Boswell's three-day journey from Inverness to Glenelg into three or four hours, but other than being embellished with a few dams as well as a great many sheep the landscape has changed little. The strength of Johnson's feelings is pointed up by his later reaction to a wide sweep of sand-dunes in Coll. Boswell says,

> Mr. Johnson was like to be angry with me for being pleased with them. I said I saw only dryness and cleanliness. He said he never had had the image before. It was horrible, if barrenness and danger could be so.

It was as if the vacuity of mind he feared became mirrored in the landscape.

Yet Johnson had come to Scotland to see "wild objects—mountains—waterfalls—peculiar manners." Of mountains he was very soon to have more than enough. The Fall of Foyers, reached that day after some irksome clambering, was steep and almost dry; imagination had to fill its streams. But an old woman in a hut provided a fine specimen of local manners, as well as one of those scenes in which Boswell delighted to observe Johnson. The differences between Johnson's account and Boswell's are typical and revealing. After describing the construction of the hut in some detail, Johnson summarizes the old woman's "system of economy": family, goats, potatoes, and barley. It was a modern Highland pastoral: she offered some whisky and told of attending the kirk eight miles away each Sunday; they responded with a shilling (sixpence each, Boswell notes); she begged some snuff, the Highland luxury.

Boswell, on the other hand, picks out a few details about the hut, "a fire of peat, the smoke going out at a hole in the roof . . . a pot upon it with goat's flesh boiling." Then he focuses on the human:

> Mr. Johnson asked me where she slept. I asked one of the guides, who asked her in Erse. She spoke with a kind of high tone. He

told us she was afraid we wanted to go to bed to her.   This
coquetry, or whatever it may be called, of so wretched a like being
was truly ludicrous.   Mr. Johnson and I afterwards made merry
upon it.   I said it was he who alarmed the poor woman's virtue.
"No, Sir," said he.   "She'll say, 'There came a wicked young fellow,
a wild young dog, who I believe would have ravished me had there
not been with him a grave old gentleman who repressed him.
But when he gets out of the sight of his tutor, I'll warrant you
he'll spare no woman he meets, young or old.' "   "No," said I.
"She'll say, 'There was a terrible ruffian who would have forced
me, had it not been for a gentle, mild-looking youth, who, I take
it, was an angel.' "

Mr. Johnson would not hurt her delicacy by insisting to "see
her bedchamber," like Archer in *The Beaux' Stratagem*. . . .

The allusion to *The Beaux' Stratagem* supplies the key to the interview.
Boswell treats the scene as comedy, not in Farquhar's light-hearted, slightly
sentimentalized Restoration mode, but with Farquhar as a sophisticated,
even artificial, contrast to rustic coquetry.   The scene is Farquhar reduced
to essentials.   But its fun lies in the comic masks Johnson and Boswell
assign to themselves and each other.   How do they look to the old woman,
they ask.   And how, by implication, to each other?

Something close to a contradiction lies at the heart of Boswell's journal.
He presents each day's events and impressions as an easy, spontaneous
record of the normal flow of experience.   At the same time, the journal
is highly self-conscious, an account intended for Johnson, who read and
occasionally corrected it.   It was explicit preparation for the biography of
Johnson Boswell intended to write.   Johnson himself called it "a very exact
picture of a portion of his life," and wished it were twice as long.
And it raised his opinion of Boswell.

As the tour proceeded, the journal took on a shadow existence of its
own that affected the relationship between the two men.   It became a
supplementary means of communication, Boswell using it to convey criticism, or continue an argument that Johnson then answered.   Boswell even
had the boldness to record some of Johnson's peculiarities, such as talking
to himself and "uttering pious ejaculations," hoping that Johnson would
explain them.   Johnson passed over these remarks without comment.   The
journal could also get in the way.   When Johnson complained at one point
that they saw little of each other, Boswell blamed it on the need to post his
journal.   Elsewhere he confesses, "I did not exert myself to get Dr. Johnson
to talk, that I might not have the labour of writing down his conversation."

In the journal, Boswell gave solidity to the moment and the day; it embodied the present.   It also provided a version of "instant replay," as he and Johnson read it over and talked about what had happened.   Finally, the journal was a nexus unifying past, present, and future.   As they sailed to Iona, Johnson remarked, "This is roving among the Hebrides, or nothing is," and Boswell reflects,

> A man has a pleasure in applying things to words, and comparing the reality with the picture of fancy.   We had long talked of "roving among the Hebrides."   It was curious to repeat the words previously used, and which had impressed our imaginations by frequent use; and then to feel how the immediate impression from actually roving differed from the one in fancy, or agreed with it. It will be curious, too, to perceive how the impression made by reading this my journal some years after our roving will affect the mind, when compared with the recollection of what was felt at the time.

Johnson was also journalizing.   He had started early to take "wonderfully minute" notes, and somewhere near Loch Cluanie, on the road from Fort Augustus to Glenelg (1 September), he conceived of his *Journey to the Western Islands*.   His description of the moment brings out some of the differences between his habits of mind and Boswell's:

> I sat down on a bank, such as a writer of romance might have delighted to feign.   I had indeed no trees to whisper over my head, but a clear rivulet streamed at my feet.   The day was calm, the air soft, and all was rudeness, silence, and solitude.   Before me and on either side were high hills which, by hindering the eye from ranging, forced the mind to find entertainment for itself. Whether I spent the hour well I know not; for here I first conceived the thought of this narration.

"The use of travelling is to regulate imagination by reality and instead of thinking how things may be, to see them as they are."   So Johnson told Mrs. Thrale.   Boswell would have added that how things "are" depends on how they are looked at in the perspectives of past, present, and future. He associates the Highlands, if faintly, with his Corsican experiences. Johnson, here and elsewhere, assimilates the life of the mountains and the islands into the patterns of the chivalric romance.   As in these works, so now "the adventurer might very suddenly pass from the gloom of woods, or the ruggedness of moors, to seats of plenty, gaiety, and magnificence." As he looks back he thinks that "the fictions of romantic chivalry had for their basis the real manners of the feudal times."   At other moments he is reminded of the simple life Homer describes, and the Rambler recalls Odysseus in his wanderings among remote lands and peoples. The unmediated vision is rare; forced in upon itself, the mind sees through what it knows.

Arcadia rapidly gave way to Boeotia. On the same day, while resting at the hamlet of Auchnashiel, they were surrounded by an unnerving circle of the wild and wretched Macraes, in effect Gaelic-speaking Indians who were gratified by a liberal distribution of snuff, tobacco, and halfpennies. The riding turned rough, and as they crossed the formidable pass of Maam-Ratagain Johnson's horse stumbled and for the only time in the tour he felt the touch of real danger. One of the guides tried to divert him by whistling at the pretty goats and making them jump. When they neared Glenelg, Boswell without explanation started to ride ahead to prepare for their reception at the inn. Johnson panicked and recalled him with a tremendous shout. In tranquillity, he would recollect that

> the imaginations excited by the view of an unknown and untravelled wilderness are not such as arise in the artificial solitude of parks and gardens. . . . The phantoms which haunt a desert are want and misery and danger; the evils of dereliction[1] rush upon the thoughts; man is made unwillingly acquainted with his own weakness, and meditation shows him only how little he can sustain, and how little he can perform.

Boswell failed to sense the depth of Johnson's fear and they came close to a serious quarrel, Johnson declaring the same evening that if Boswell had gone on without him he would never have spoken to Boswell again after their return to Edinburgh. To complete their discontent, the inn was squalid and unprovisioned. They were shown into a greasy, stinking room where from a miserable bed sprang a man whom Johnson called "black as a Cyclops from the forge," and Boswell compared to Poor Tom in *Lear*. Boswell ate a bit of broiled hen, and drank some rum and sugar supplied by a neighbouring gentleman; Johnson limited himself to lemonade and a piece of bread. They slept in hay, though Boswell spread out sheets and, says Johnson, "lay in linen like a gentleman."

Their introduction to the Hebrides was equally inauspicious. Boswell's only good friend in Skye was Sir Alexander Macdonald, one of its two great chiefs and landowners. Sometime officer in the Coldstream Guards, Sir Alexander had succeeded his brother Sir James (known as the Scottish Marcellus for his exceptional promise) on his early death in 1766. Sir

[1]Desertion.

James was one of the few men of his own age whom Boswell greatly admired; in Sir Alexander he found a pedantic, remorselessly facetious companion, almost morbidly addicted to puns and rhymes, but nonetheless
congenial and helpful.   His wife was that beautiful Elizabeth Diana Bosville, daughter of Boswell's "chief," who at one time had figured away on
Boswell's matrimonial list, and who had impressed Johnson in London the
previous year.   They had promised a cordial welcome.

Macdonald was to maintain that he had expected the travellers in July
or August at Monkstadt, his seat in the northern tip of Skye.   When they
failed to appear, he and his wife, six months pregnant, set off for Armadale
on the southern coast *en route* to Edinburgh.   Here they were accommodated at the house of one of his tenants.   He sent his boat to the mainland
for the travellers, but after several days his men ran out of provisions and
returned just a few hours before Johnson and Boswell arrived at Glenelg.
They had to find a boat themselves to carry them to Skye.

Boswell records that Lady Macdonald met them with "a kind of jumping for joy," while Macdonald, a proper Etonian, celebrated Johnson's
arrival in alcaics.   Materially, their entertainment was mean.   The Macdonalds were travelling light, without cook or lady's-maid.   Dinner was ill-
dressed and, what was worse, unconvivial.   At tea, for lack of the common
decencies of the tea-table, they had to pick up the sugar with their fingers,
which Johnson found peculiarly repulsive.

What Johnson and Boswell chose to criticize seems trivial, but their
irritation in part had sources which had nothing to do with Macdonald:
the upsetting events and fatigue of the previous day, a turn in the weather
to rain, even their commitment to their expedition now that they had landed
in Skye.   They had reached the "verge of European life."   But also they
were now totally dependent on the hospitality of their hosts, and from the
chief of the Macdonalds they had expected a princely reception.   Instead
he lived, said Johnson, like someone in a London lodging-house.   Boswell,
as a modern scholar suggests, may have been especially angry since he was
in some sense Johnson's host throughout their tour, and he reacted to
Macdonald's lack of cordiality as if shamed in his own house.   They certainly suspected Macdonald of having left Monkstadt early to avoid entertaining them at home.

Their complaints were quickly generalized.   Macdonald's basic fault
was that he showed none of that generosity of spirit which was the hallmark
of a Highland chief.   Though he claimed to have established confidence
between himself and his people, they testified otherwise.   Boswell wanted
to leave the next day (Friday 3 September), but Johnson insisted they

weather it out until Monday. They charged Macdonald head on with lacking the proper feudal outlook, and Johnson undertook to sketch the appropriate emblems for a chief: a magazine of arms and whole roasted oxen, with a flag out to invite all the Macdonalds to beef and whisky. Macdonald kept raising objections but avoided the essential point: he was a new-model chief, one of those educated in the Lowlands or England who had taken on the values and ways of the dominant culture. A chief no longer maintained large numbers of tenants and retainers to display his power and dignity; what counted now was rents and profits. His guests thought Macdonald had the rapacious soul of an attorney. Emigration was epidemic; later the sight of the emigrant ship *Nestor* in the harbour of Portree led Boswell to think that it made a short settlement of the differences between a chief and his clan. Even Lady Macdonald turned out, at close quarters, to be insipid and dull—heavy enough to sink a ninety-gun ship. Boswell describes Johnson's later mimicry of her, " ' "Thomson, some wine and water," ' with her mouth full; adding, 'People are generally taught to empty their mouths of meat before they call for drink. She wants to be whipped in a nursery.' "

It was a bad weekend. Boswell retreated into hypochondria, no doubt aroused or aggravated by his recent quarrel with Johnson, yet the sight of Johnson calmed him, he said, as a rock does a man whose head is turning at sea. Johnson endured with patience, writing Latin odes in the next few days to Skye and Mrs. Thrale. His mind was much at home with his *Thralia dulcis*. They escaped on Monday to the cheerful tacksman's farm of Mackinnon of Coirechatachan, on horses unwillingly provided by Macdonald, and which they were unwillingly to return, late and thoroughly lame. Macdonald remained their butt throughout the tour, as in this characteristic exchange about the story that Macdonald, meeting a sergeant with twenty men at work on the road, gave the sergeant all of sixpence for the men for drink:

> JOHNSON. "There is much want of sense in all this. He had no business to speak with the sergeant. He might have been in haste and trotted on. He has not learnt to be a miser; I believe we must take him apprentice." BOSWELL. "He would grudge giving half a guinea to be taught." JOHNSON. "Nay, Sir, you must teach him gratis. You must give him an opportunity to practise your precepts."

From time to time Boswell provides Views of Dr. Johnson. At Aberdeen it is Johnson as giant, telling a little girl "in a hollow voice that he lived in a cave and had a bed in the rock, and she should have a little bed cut opposite to it!"   Or he is the gallant buck, who says, when a pretty young lady on his lap kisses him, "Do it again . . . and let us see who will tire first."   Less distinctly, he is the philosophic Rambler or Orpheus enchanting the barbarians.   The noblest of all such views occurs in the passage from Skye to Raasay:

> We got into Raasay's *carriage*, which was a good stout open boat made in Norway.   The wind had now risen pretty much.   But we had four stout rowers, particularly a MacLeod, a fellow half-naked, with a bare black head, robust and spirited, something half-wild Indian, half-English tar.   Mr. Johnson sat high on the stern like a magnificent Triton.   Malcolm [MacLeod] raised an Erse song, *Hatyin foam foam eri*, to which he gave Jacobite words of his own.   The tune was "O'er the moor among the heather," Highlandized.   The boatmen and Mr. Macqueen chorused, and all went well. . . .   Here again I was strongly struck with the long-projected scheme of Mr. Johnson's and my visiting the Hebrides being realized.   I called to him, "We are contending with seas," which I think were the words of one of his letters to me.   "Not much," said he; and though the wind made the sea lash considerably upon us, he was not discomposed.

At the little "court" of Raasay, they were deep in the world of the Hebrides.   It was not the land of ancient pastoral but a region of mountains, streams, and storms, where walking was difficult and even horseback riding uncomfortable.   Yet the civilized flourished in this primitive setting. MacLeod of Raasay, representative of the MacLeods of Lewis, was a gentleman with a fine gentleman's house, who entertained with a combination of easiness and elegance they were to come upon elsewhere among the Hebridean gentry.   On the evening they arrived (8 September) a fiddler played for an impromptu ball, and thirty gathered for supper.   Again Boswell contrasts Johnson with his surroundings:

> It entertained me to observe him sitting by while we danced, sometimes in deep meditation—sometimes smiling complacently— sometimes looking upon Hooke's *Roman History*—and sometimes talking a little amidst the noise of the ball to Mr. Donald Macqueen, who anxiously gathered knowledge from him.

It was an intensely physical world which Boswell, full of energy, enjoyed tremendously.   One day he walked to the top of Dun Caan (1,456 ft.) with a party that included sturdy old Malcolm MacLeod, Prince Charles's one-time guide during his wanderings after Culloden.   There, Boswell says, we ate "cold mutton and bread and cheese and drank brandy and punch. Then we had a Highland song from Malcolm; then we danced a reel to which he and Donald [and] Macqueen sang." [1] It was only the beginning of a 24-mile tour of the island.

"This is truly the patriarchal life: this is what we came to find," announced Johnson. Actually, as he says elsewhere, they had come too late to see what they had expected, "a people of peculiar appearance, and a system of antiquated life." Farming methods remained laborious and feeble, but Skye cattle were driven south in large numbers to be fattened and sold. (The ferrying of the cattle to the mainland reminded one pious observer of the departure of the children of Israel from Egypt.) Kelp was collected to be burnt for alkali, a profitable operation; otherwise there was little trade. Oatmeal was the principal import, and the potato had taken hold. The chiefs and tacksmen lived usually in pleasant, small, crowded houses; the common people in primitive cabins where, in Johnson's phrase, they rejoiced in the comforts of smoke. Nearly everyone used peat for fuel. At the worst under this transitional system, the tyrannical chief turned into the grasping landlord. At its best, as at Raasay, the travellers found plenty, civility, and cheerfulness.

Besides recording the present, Boswell and Johnson explored the past. Boswell, who enjoyed moods of sentimental Jacobitism, became engrossed by stories of Charles Edward's narrow escapes from British troops in the Hebrides. His most important source was the famous Flora Macdonald, whom the Prince had accompanied, awkwardly disguised as her maidservant Betty Bourke, in his journey across Skye. The whole history of the "Wanderer's" escape was grandly romantic, and Boswell's clear, extended account of it appears in his *Hebrides* as fine counterpoint to their own journey.

Johnson investigated the more remote past, the antiquities, customs, and literature of the Highlands. It was a frustrating process for, like more recent anthropologists, Johnson discovered that the natives told him either what they wanted to believe or what they thought he wanted to hear. Their vagueness was most irritating. His principal informant was the Rev. Donald Macqueen, already mentioned, minister of Kilmuir in Skye, an intelligent, enthusiastic, but overconfident antiquarian. Johnson made short work of a number of Macqueen's discoveries, particularly of the supposed remains of a temple of the goddess Annait (probably the ruins of an early Christian church or monastic community). Yet they reversed roles when it came to belief in the second sight, the ability to see at a distance or into the future. Martin had credited the second sight fully, and Johnson found

---

[1]Donald MacLeod of Canna and John Macqueen, son of the Rev. Donald Macqueen.

belief in it still common in Skye though the ministers unanimously denied its existence. Johnson's intelligence questioned strongly what his imagination wanted to accept, and he concludes his discussion of the second sight by saying, "I never could advance my curiosity to conviction, but came away at last only willing to believe." Other legends he swept aside:

> Of Brownie, mentioned by Martin, nothing has been heard for many years. Brownie was a sturdy fairy who, if he was fed and kindly treated, would, as they said, do a great deal of work. They now pay him no wages, and are content to labour for themselves.

As Boswell remarks, Johnson was superstitious but not credulous.

Brownie was small game compared to the pursuit and destruction of the dragon Ossian. James Macpherson, a young Scottish tutor in a private family, had spectacularly satisfied the contemporary hunger for primitive poetry by "translating" the works of a supposed third-century Gaelic bard named Ossian, including two epic poems, *Fingal* (1762) and *Temora* (1763), into fluently cadenced prose. The popularity and influence of Ossian were enormous. Goethe inserted an affecting passage from Ossian into his *Sorrows of Young Werther*; Coleridge and Byron imitated him in their youth; Napoleon declared that Ossian—*hélas*, for want of better—was to him what Homer was to Alexander and Virgil to Augustus. Hazlitt, an acute critic, declared that the world's four principal works of poetry were Homer, the Bible, Dante, and, not least, Ossian. And Ossian's influence was to achieve permanence in the poetry of Walt Whitman.

The success of Ossian, the most startling phenomenon in the history of British literature, did not extinguish doubt of his authenticity. Today, compared with the convincing version of Scottish history that Scott was to construct, Ossian seems no more than a fancily cloudy string of children's adventure stories, but at the time he filled the need to give the country an heroic past. Scots *literati* had discovered Ossian, or Macpherson anyway, and Scots *literati* defended them both vigorously and stubbornly. Others, including Johnson, were sceptical from the start. Fond of romances but jealous for truth, he hated Ossian all the more because it was romance parading as history; and he insisted that Macpherson produce the manuscripts on which his translations were based. Macpherson blustered and shuffled: he would not produce the manuscripts on demand, or he had already exhibited them at a bookseller's, or he was preparing an edition of the originals (unfinished at his death in 1796). Still it is fair to say that when Johnson went north in 1773 he was prepared to recant if manuscripts or even extensive oral originals could be produced.

On this point he and Macqueen, a true believer in Macpherson, changed

sides again, and a sporadic debate about Ossian occupied them on the
journey through Skye. Macqueen alleged that he could repeat passages
in the original and that he had heard his grandfather owned a copy of
Fingal, but brought to the test of comparing Gaelic original and English
translation he was unable to persuade his audience they were similar. Yet
his belief, like the supple willow, Boswell said, was no sooner pressed down
than it rose again. Johnson's incredulity rested in part on his critical sense
that Ossian was "a mere unconnected rhapsody": "Sir, a man might write
such stuff for ever, if he would *abandon* his mind to it." Wordsworth was
to back Johnson's brutal and amusing assertion with detail:

> Having had the good fortune to be born and reared in a moun-
> tainous country, from my very childhood I have felt the falsehood
> that pervades the volumes imposed upon the world under the
> name of Ossian. From what I saw with my own eyes, I knew that
> the imagery was spurious. In nature everything is distinct, yet
> nothing defined into absolute, independent singleness. In Mac-
> pherson's work, it is exactly the reverse; everything (that is not
> stolen) is in this manner defined, insulated, dislocated, deadened—
> yet nothing distinct. It will always be so when words are substi-
> tuted for things. . . .

Wordsworth's argument reflects his own mode of vision, of course, but it
is telling. Johnson simply concluded that the works of Macpherson "never
existed in any other form than that which we have seen," which led into
his *obiter dictum*, "a Scotchman must be a very sturdy moralist, who does
not love Scotland better than truth." No remark in his *Journey* was more
bitterly resented.

On the return crossing from Raasay to Portree in Skye, Johnson dis-
coursed on the fear of death: "Nay, no wise man will be contented to die
if he thinks he is to fall into annihilation. . . . No, there is no rational
principle by which a man can be contented, but a trust in the mercy of
GOD, through the merits of Jesus Christ." Boswell thought it worth any
sermon, "delivered with manly eloquence in a boat upon the sea, upon a
fine, calm Sunday morning, while everyone listened with a comfortable air
of satisfaction and complacency." From Portree to Kingsburgh and then
the travellers scrambled across the swampy moor of northern Skye, which
afforded "all the possible transpositions of bog, rock, and rivulet," to Dunvegan, seat of the MacLeods of MacLeod. The MacLeods divided the rule
of Skye with the Macdonalds, and Dunvegan remains the oldest continuously inhabited castle in the Hebrides. Johnson and Boswell decided they
had entered Skye at the wrong end, so striking was the contrast between
their reception here and at Armadale. Young Norman MacLeod, quick,

intelligent, "very elegant of manners, and very graceful in his person," realized their idea of a feudal chief. Though immensely in debt, he and his people preserved their old interdependence; typically, he told Boswell, "I would rather drink punch in one of their houses . . . than be enabled, by their hardships, to have claret in my own." (Later, feeling confined in Skye, he became an army officer, served with distinction in India, rose to the rank of major-general, and spent his money as fast as he got it.) His mother's management of the household united economy and good living.

Though suffering from a cold which made him miserably deaf, Johnson expanded in these congenial surroundings. Boswell records more memorable Johnsoniana at Dunvegan than anywhere else in Scotland:

> On chastity. "I have much more reverence for a common prostitute than for a woman who conceals her guilt. The prostitute is known. She cannot deceive. . . .
> On theory and practice. "No man practises so well as he writes. I have, all my life long, been lying till noon. Yet I tell all young men, and tell them with great sincerity, that nobody who does not rise early will ever do any good."
> On innate evil. "Lady MacLeod asked, if no man was naturally good. JOHNSON. 'No, Madam, no more than a wolf.' BOSWELL. 'Nor no woman, Sir?' JOHNSON. 'No, Sir.' Lady MacLeod started at this, saying in a low voice, 'This is worse than Swift.' "
> On drinking. "He has great virtue in not drinking wine or any fermented liquor, because . . . he could not do it in moderation. . . . Lady MacLeod would hardly believe him, and said, 'I'm sure, Sir, you would not carry it too far.' JOHNSON. 'Nay, Madam, it carried me.' "
> On his melancholy. " 'I inherited . . . a vile melancholy from my father, which has made me mad all my life, at least not sober.' Lady MacLeod wondered he should tell this. 'Madam,' said I, 'he knows that with that madness he is superior to other men.' "

Conversation was interspersed with mild walks through the grounds and an "abundance of good things genteelly served up." Boswell compared himself to a dog with a bone: he had run away with Johnson to Skye so that he and their hosts could feed upon Johnson undisturbed. One night Johnson relaxed a little too much and talked of how he had "often thought" if he kept a seraglio he would clothe the ladies in linen or cotton, which showed dirt better than silk. Boswell "laughed immoderately" at the idea of Johnson fantasizing about a seraglio, and Johnson took immediate revenge: "properly prepared," he said, Boswell would make a very good eunuch in his establishment. Stung, Boswell replied that he would play his part better than Johnson.   But Johnson was a master at infighting, and he expatiated on Boswell's role with such fluency that for the moment, Boswell says, "he made me quite contemptible" and felt really hurt, so hurt indeed that he records no details and wished he could wipe the incident from his memory. It was the old bull vs. the young bull, apparently the only record of overt sexual competitiveness between them.

Dunvegan's warm hospitality and picturesqueness, "sea—islands—rocks—hills—a noble cascade," made it very attractive to its guests.   Their hosts were more aware of its inconveniences.   When Lady MacLeod talked of moving to a nearby farm where she could keep a garden, she called forth a burst of feudal enthusiasm.   Johnson told her "with a strong voice and most determined manner: 'Madam, rather than quit the old rock, Boswell would live in the pit.   He would make his bed in the dungeon.' " MacLeod offered Johnson a beautiful little island in Loch Dunvegan called Isay if he would live on it for a month a year, and Johnson filled his imagination with it wonderfully.   He talked of "how he would build a house there—how he would fortify it—how he would have cannon—how he would plant—how he would sally out and *take* the Isle of Muck; and then he laughed with uncommon glee, and could hardly leave off."   After that, the company drank to him as "Island Isay."

"At Dunvegan," says Johnson, "I had tasted lotus, and was in danger of forgetting that I was ever to depart, till Mr. Boswell sagely reproached me with my sluggishness and softness."   In fact, the weather was steadily getting worse, and it was necessary to seize any break in it to get away. They left on 21 September, going by way of the headland farm of Ullinish, and Talisker on its inlet deep between the hills, past the Cuillin range where snow had already fallen, back to Coirechatachan.   There Boswell drank with the jovial company until nearly five in the morning, and required brandy for his hangover.   It was the first time he had drunk too much on the journey, and Johnson treated this slip with what Boswell was content to call "good-humoured *English* pleasantry":

Ay . . . fill him drunk again.   Do it in the morning that we may laugh at him all day.   It is a poor thing for a fellow to get drunk at night and skulk to bed, and let his friends have no sport.

They were now under the guidance of Donald Maclean, the young laird of Coll, who had kindly offered to conduct them to the other islands.   But the weather held them back at Armadale, where Macdonald's bailie was much more hospitable than his master had been.

By now Johnson and Boswell were experienced travelling companions.

It was a copartnership in which Boswell provided "gaiety of conversation and civility of manners" (Johnson's later praise) and Johnson an "immense fund of knowledge and wit."   Johnson was all integrity, Boswell all adaptability. Everywhere they went, Boswell looked out for Johnson's comfort; interpreted him when necessary to their hosts; and "led" him into conversation, not like an orchestra conductor, he said, but like a lawyer leading a witness.

No activity invites friction more than travelling together, but they got along remarkably well.   Johnson put up with Boswell's occasional moments of troublesome kindness and family pride; he mocked Boswell gently once as they passed some barren rock by saying, "This shall be your island, and it shall be called Inch Boswell," laughing, says the bewildered Boswell, "with a strange appearance of triumph."   Boswell endured Johnson's outbursts of irritability and sarcasm, erupting from a temperament so thin-skinned that its dissatisfaction with itself could tinge everything around it.   For the most part Johnson concealed this disposition from the Scots, who found his superiority of mind quite astonishing: "Stay till Dr. Johnson comes. Say that to *him*!" became their watchword in arguments.   He was, said one man, "just a *hogshead* of sense."   The Scots responded also to his fundamental good will.   Boswell remarks that "the Scottish phrase of 'honest man,' which signifies kindness and regard, was often and often repeated by many" of the people they met.   Johnson reacted warmly to their cordiality and respect, and to himself with a little amazement: "I cannot but laugh to think of myself roving among the Hebrides at sixty.   I wonder where I shall rove at fourscore."

They took passage (3 October) for Mull on a small boat.   Boswell, proud of being a sound sailor, ate bread and cheese and drank whisky, rum, and brandy on deck.   On this he piled a dinner of boiled mutton, boiled salt herring, beer, and punch.   Sickness followed fast, the wind blew, the rain came down hard.   Mull was in sight when the storm grew stronger, and they were forced to run before the wind to Coll.   On a dark night a harbour there was easy to miss, and they might well go aground on its rocky shore.   Boswell took to prayer though "disturbed by the objections . . . against a particular providence," and then begged to be made useful.   Young Coll put a rope, tied to the top of a mast, in his hand and told him to hold fast until called to pull on it.   "If I had considered the matter," Boswell says,

> I might have seen that this could not be of the least service; but his object was to keep me out of the way of those who were busy working the vessel, and at the same time to divert my fear by employing me, and making me think that I was of use.   Thus did

I stand firm to my post, while the wind and rain beat upon me,
always expecting a call to pull my rope.

Meanwhile, Johnson lay below in philosophic tranquillity, a greyhound of
Coll's at his back keeping him warm.

The description of the storm shows to particular advantage Boswell's
ability to shift perspective, in this case to combine the immediacy of the
scene with his later view of it.   It also illustrates a typical narrative stance
and its implications.   The reader takes his cue from the author.   Though
the phrasing here, for example, has all the economical directness of Swift,
it shows none of Swift's satiric attitude towards his narrators, with its hint
that if the reader does not recognize the narrator as a fool he is one himself.
Fielding, in contrast, invites the reader to share a sceptical urbanity about
the world of his characters.   But Boswell's narrative recalls Goldsmith's
definition of the comic character: "that natural portrait of human folly and
frailty, of which all are judges because all have sat for the picture."   This
is the riskiest method of the three: where the readers of Swift and Fielding
share their authors' superiority to their characters, Boswell's readers must
identify, in part anyway, with his character, with human folly and frailty.
The alternative is to confuse Boswell the narrator with Boswell the character, and despise both.

Coll, safely reached, turned out to be one extended low-lying rock,
covered with sand and heath.   Persistent bad weather kept them there ten
days.   Fortunately, they took to young Coll, a Highland chief of the best
new kind.   He was small, brisk, and shockingly informal with his people.
He was also determined to import the new crops and farming methods he
had learned in England.   Already he had introduced turnips, despite local
scepticism, and the natives had learned, as Johnson puts it, "that turnips
will really grow, and that hungry sheep and cows will really eat them."
Johnson and Boswell found him independent, good-humoured, and unfailingly helpful.   His island was less attractive.   They quickly exhausted
its antiquities and curiosities, not overlooking two rocks which a giant and
his mistress had thrown at each other.   Another definite drawback was
that it lacked "that very essential particular," a proper "little house" (privy).
Boswell and Johnson pondered the matter:

Mr. Johnson said I had that much at heart.   He said if ever a
man thinks at all, it is there.   He generally thinks then with great
intentness.   He sets himself down as quite alone, in the first place.
I said a man was always happy there too.   Mr. Johnson said he
did not know that.

Reduced to entertaining themselves, one night Johnson "strutted about the room with a broadsword and target . . . and another night," says Boswell,

> I took the liberty to put a large blue bonnet on his head. His age, his size, and his bushy grey wig with this covering on it, presented the image of a venerable shanachie;[1] and, however un-favourable to the Lowland Scots, he seemed much pleased to assume the appearance of an ancient Caledonian.

It was Johnson's most unexpected role, this transformation in which Boswell suggests the momentary reconciliation of opposites.

The fact was that they were tired of travelling. It rained constantly. Johnson longed to return to the mainland and, as he said, go on with existence. But luckily for the reader they determined for Iona, landing at Tobermory for the trip across Mull. It was very rough going, "a most dolorous country." Johnson's little Mull horse hardly supported his weight, and the large oak stick he had carried all the way from London disappeared. The Hebrides had lost their novelty; like his own abducted Pekuah in *Rasselas*, Johnson had anticipated romance, grandeurs, and miseries, and had arrived at boredom. He became very irritable, and persisted in claiming that his oak stick had been stolen. At least it allowed him a final joke at the treelessness of Scotland. "No, no, my friend," he said to Boswell, "it is not to be expected that any man in Mull who has got it will part from it. Consider, Sir, the value of such a *piece of timber* here!"

That night (16 October) they stopped at Ulva with the chief of the small but ancient clan of MacGuarie. In true Highland contrast they were shown to fine beds in a room where broken windows had let in rain to muddy the clay floor. Next came the pretty, fertile little island of Inchkenneth, where Coll turned them over to his chief, Sir Allan Maclean. Boswell wandered into the night to pray at an outdoor cross to St. Columba, but hastened back for fear of ghosts. Their good-byes to Coll were affectionate and final; the next year he drowned in the passage between Ulva and Mull. They looked at the last of what seems an endless series of caves, and were rowed along the shore with Sir Allan to Iona. There they slept manfully in a barn.

If Dunvegan is the secular climax to the tour, the place which most completely fulfilled their vision of patriarchal Highland culture, Iona (Icolmkill) stands as its religious counterpart. From here, with the landing

[1]Gaelic oral historian.

of St. Columba in the sixth century, Christianity first spread among the
Picts and Scots, and Iona became the traditional resting-place for many of
their kings.   The ruins Johnson and Boswell saw (now much restored)
date mainly from the Benedictine community of the thirteenth century
and later.   Iona remains the most sacred place in Scotland, and its antiquity
and remoteness deeply moved both travellers.   In the ruined cathedral,
Boswell says,

> I warmed my soul with religious resolutions.   I felt a kind of
> exultation in thinking that the solemn scenes of piety ever remain
> the same, though the cares and follies of life may prevent us from
> visiting them, or may even make us fancy that their effects were
> only "as yesterday when it is past," and never again to be perceived.
> I hoped that ever after having been in this holy place, I should
> maintain an exemplary conduct.   One has a strange propensity
> to fix upon some point from whence a better course of life may
> be said to begin.   I read with an audible voice the fifth chapter
> of St. James, and Dr. Ogden's tenth sermon.   I suppose there has
> not been a sermon preached in this church since the Reformation.
> I had a serious joy in hearing my voice, while it was filled with
> Ogden's admirable eloquence, resounding in the ancient cathedral
> of Icolmkill.

Johnson is less personal and more grand:

> That man is little to be envied, whose patriotism would not gain
> force upon the plain of Marathon, or whose piety would not grow
> warmer among the ruins of Iona!

Back to Mull, and after solemnity a moment of farce and folly.   Sir
Allan's sister was married to John Maclean of Lochbuie, fabled as a Fal-
staffian throwback of a laird: perhaps under the impression that he retained
his heritable jurisdiction, Lochbuie had briefly imprisoned two men a few
years earlier in his old castle at Moy.   (When this feudal gesture came to
the attention of the Court of Session, it cost him £200.)   Closer examination
showed Lochbuie to be only "a bluff, hearty, rosy old gentleman, who
greeted Johnson by bawling out, "Are you of the Johnstons of Glencoe or
of Ardnamurchan?"   Supper was poor, everything having to be stewed in
one pot.   Lochbuie was hospitable, however, and after supper he, Boswell,
and Sir Allan each drank a bottle of port.   Then came a social bowl of
punch.   Johnson, at this time an abstainer, went off to bed admonishing
Boswell, "Don't drink any more *poonch*."   But Boswell, who must have been
feeling the strain of the journey, reports, "I was seized with an avidity for
drinking" and "slunk away from him, with a consciousness of my being

brutish and yet a determination to go somewhat deeper." (This is the journal as confession.)   Before they could start on the second bowl Boswell's stomach rescued him: he threw up.   It was a disheartening experience so soon after his holy resolutions at Iona.

And so to Oban (22 October) and the security of the mainland.   Johnson and Boswell had dreaded being "shut up for months upon some little protuberance of earth" in the Hebrides, but beneath this realistic consideration one can perhaps sense a fear of confinement, such as made Johnson repeatedly equate a ship with a gaol.   To Mrs. Thrale he quoted the song,

> Every island is a prison
> Strongly guarded by the sea.

When Boswell wondered at his calmness on Skye, Johnson remarked, "When a man retires into an island, he is to turn his thoughts entirely on another world.   He has done with this."   Now they were alive again, like Antaeus restored to contact with the earth.

The return to Edinburgh proceeds in a series of brilliant vignettes, which Boswell reconstructed years later from the briefest notes.   Their last day of Highland travelling, through the hills to Inveraray, was also the roughest.   Wind, rain, blasts, showers, cataracts, torrents, says Johnson in his *Journey*, "made a nobler chorus of the rough music of nature than it had ever been my chance to hear before."   He hated being thought an old man and endured uncomplainingly.   On arrival at their excellent inn he even had a gill of whisky to discover "what it is that makes a Scotchman happy."   Inveraray presented a problem.   Boswell wanted to call on the Duke of Argyll but the Duchess, sometime Duchess of Hamilton, hated him for his support of Douglas in the Cause.   Johnson swept aside this objection as the Duke's affair, and Boswell's call procured an invitation to dinner.   Operating by the maxim that nothing succeeds like excess, Boswell broke custom and toasted her Grace's health.   She got her revenge.   When Boswell said something about believing in the second sight, the Duchess recalled his credulity about Douglas with "I fancy . . . you will be a Methodist."   Johnson, cordially received, was gentle, complaisant, and "so entertaining that Lady Betty Hamilton went and placed her chair next his, leaned upon it, and listened eagerly."   Boswell once more stands back to relish the scene:

> It would have made a fine picture to have drawn the sage and her
> at this time in their several attitudes.   He did not know all the
> while that it was a princess of the blood who thus listened to him.

Loch Lomond was next: Rossdhu (the Colquhouns of Luss) and Cameron (Commissary Smollett), where Johnson lectured to general satisfaction

on the origin of evil.   They were in civilized country once again and
enjoying it, ready to laugh heartily "at the ravings of those absurd visionaries who have attempted to persuade us of the superior advantages of a
state of nature."   They had seen it; they knew otherwise.   At Glasgow the
professors were as reticent as their Aberdeen brethren; Johnson never got
the opportunity to dispute his way through Scotland.   With his desire for
long life, he was cheered by dinner with the Earl of Loudoun, a well-known
general, and his mother, who in her nineties preserved all her faculties.
She must have been a formidable old lady.   Johnson wrote to Mrs. Thrale:
"She had lately a daughter, Lady Betty, whom at seventy she used to send
after supper early to bed, for girls must not use late hours, while she sat
up to entertain the company."   A visit to another old lady, the Dowager
Countess of Eglinton, was a great success.   The patroness of the poet Allan
Ramsay and one of the most beautiful women of her day, she was still
majestic in figure and elegant in conversation.   Discovering that she had
been married the year before Johnson was born, she proclaimed she would
adopt him and embraced him on leaving with "My dear son, farewell!"
On 2 November they arrived at Auchinleck for a week's visit.

The quarrel between Johnson and Lord Auchinleck is the great un-
written scene in Boswell's journal.   It would have made an extraordinary
climax to his account of the tour, this confrontation between his spiritual
and physical fathers, who embodied as well some of the deepest traits and
most strongly held prejudices of Englishman and Scot.   At first it looks as
if Boswell is leading up to the scene, by providing a contrast to Johnson
in an incisive sketch of his father: a conscientious judge now somewhat
failed; always even-spirited, a fine, poker-faced teller of stories; accustomed
to great attention; above all, a sanguine Whig and Presbyterian.   And a
despiser of Johnson as "a *Jacobite fellow.*"   (According to Sir Walter Scott
he sneered at Johnson as "a *dominie*,[1] mon—an auld dominie; he keeped a
schŭle, and cau'd it an acaadamy.")

Boswell also maintains suspense.   Before arriving, he begged Johnson
to avoid three topics: Whiggism, Presbyterianism—and Sir John Pringle.[2]
Johnson replied politely, if with insufficient recollection of past behaviour,
that he would certainly not bring up subjects disagreeable to his host,
especially when that host was Boswell's father.   The first day went smoothly;
Lord Auchinleck showed Johnson his fine collection of Greek and Roman
classics, which was housed in his forty-foot-long library.   The second day
it rained as usual, and Johnson disposed of a visitor who asked him how

[1]Schoolmaster.
[2]Johnson and Pringle disliked each other.

he liked the Highlands with, "Who *can* like the Highlands?—I like the inhabitants very well."   The third and fourth days Boswell was able to show Johnson the Place (the cultivated area around Auchinleck House) and the romantic rocks and woods of his ancestors.   The woods were largely the work of Lord Auchinleck, but Johnson also admired the Old Castle whose ruins, "striking images of ancient life," stand high above the Lugar Water.   Boswell chose this setting for a lecture on the antiquity and honourable alliances of his family, including inevitably his distant but genuine connection to a Royal Personage.   On seeing Johnson at Iona he had remarked that landscapes or views were defective without human figures to give them animation.   That animation was mainly psychological: to see Johnson *here*, to recount to the Rambler—certainly not for the first time— the glories of the Boswells of Auchinleck, was to fulfil a project he had dreamed of scarcely two months after they had met in 1763.   It was a high point of satisfaction.

It was probably on the following day—Boswell is not quite sure—that the explosion occurred.   Perhaps like Mr. Dick's recollection of King Charles's head it was irrepressible; in any case it was introduced by something similar.   Lord Auchinleck was showing Johnson his collection of medals, and Cromwell's head introduced Charles I and Toryism.   "They became exceedingly warm and violent," says Boswell, "and I was very much distressed by being present at such an altercation between two men, both of whom I reverenced; yet I durst not interfere."   Granting Boswell's reverence, it is possible to wonder how much he wanted to interfere.   Any dramatic confrontation greatly interested him.   But to see the two men who dominated his life at each other's throats may also have induced an understandable trace of *schadenfreude*.   Whatever his reaction, he continues,

> It would certainly be very unbecoming in me to exhibit my honoured father and my respected friend as intellectual gladiators ["intellectual" was an afterthought] for the entertainment of the public; and therefore I suppress what would, I dare say, make an interesting scene in this dramatic sketch.

"A very capital scene" is what he first wrote, and he cannot bear to let it all vanish.   So he includes one morsel:

> Dr. Johnson challenged him . . . to point out any theological works of merit written by Presbyterian ministers in Scotland.   My father, whose studies did not lie much in that way, owned to me afterwards that he was somewhat at a loss how to answer, but that luckily he recollected having read in catalogues the title of *Durham on the Galatians*; upon which he boldly said, "Pray, Sir, have you read

Mr. Durham's excellent commentary on the Galatians?"—"No, Sir,"
said Dr. Johnson.   By this lucky thought my father kept him at
bay, and for some time enjoyed his triumph; but his antagonist
soon made a retort which I forbear to mention.

Originally Boswell had included this reply, the manuscript continuing after
Johnson's "No, Sir": "My father then had him before the wind, and went
on, 'How came you, then, to speak with such contempt of the writings
of . . .' " (the rest of the leaf is torn off).   But Malone recalled later, "At
Auchinleck, when old Mr. Boswell pretended to recommend *Durham on the
Galatians*, he concluded, 'You may buy it any time for half a crown or three
shillings.' JOHNSON.   'Sir, it must be better recommended before I give
half the money for it.' "   The rest of Boswell's account is discreet summary:

> In the course of their altercation, Whiggism and Presbyterianism,
> Toryism and Episcopacy, were terribly buffeted.   My worthy he-
> reditary friend, Sir John Pringle, never having been mentioned,
> happily escaped without a bruise.[1]

The next day, the sabbath, they rested.   Boswell diverted himself with
time and perspective:

> I had a pleasing satisfaction in reading some of Dr. Johnson's
> works in the library, looking up to him as at a great distance as I
> formerly used to do, and then running into his room and chatting
> with him as friend and companion.

On Monday 8 November, Lord Auchinleck, with "the dignified courtesy
of an old Baron," waited on Johnson to the post-chaise that took him and
Boswell to Edinburgh.

For ten days Johnson played the lion.   While Boswell returned to his
duties in the Court of Session, Johnson held his levee.   Margaret was in
attendance to pour endless cups of tea, though she shared Lord Auchinleck's opinion that he influenced Boswell too much; also he let candle grease
drip on the carpet.   Boswell and Johnson complained of being harassed
with invitations but thought harassment better than neglect.   Johnson visited the Court of Session, where he found the pleadings too vehement—
"This . . . is not the Areopagus"—while Lord Auchinleck pointed him out
to a brother on the bench as Ursa Major.   At Prestonfield there was a
gleam from Lady Anne Lindsay, who wrote the ballad, *Auld Robin Gray*.

---

[1]One further, and perhaps apocryphal, scrap of the conversation derives from Sir Walter
Scott.   When Johnson challenged Lord Auchinleck to say what good Cromwell had ever
done for his country, the old judge replied, " 'God, Doctor! he gart kings ken that they had
a *lith* in their neck'—he taught kings they had a *joint* in their necks."

In recounting Lady Eglinton's "adoption" of Johnson, Boswell blunderingly said that she was married the year after Johnson's birth; this would have made him illegitimate, as Johnson quickly pointed out. Lady Anne saved the moment, "Would not the *son* have excused the *sin?*"

The last episode of the tour was the most amusing. Sir John Dalrymple, the eccentric author of *Memoirs of Great Britain and Ireland*, pressed Johnson to visit him at Cranston, which lay on Johnson's road to London. Dalrymple, says Boswell, had been attacking them behind their backs, and they accepted the invitation reluctantly. After a slow start from Edinburgh, they dallied at Rosslyn and then saw Hawthornden by moonlight, which echoed for Boswell "rare" Ben Jonson's visit to Drummond. By now they were very late for the promised feast on a seven-year-old sheep, but Johnson refused to hurry and improved the journey by parodying Dalrymple's mannered style:

> Dinner being ready, he wondered that his guests were not yet come. His wonder was soon succeeded by impatience. He walked about the room in anxious agitation; sometimes he looked at his watch, sometimes he looked out at the window with an eager gaze of expectation, and revolved in his mind the various accidents of human life. His family beheld him with mute concern. "Surely," said he with a sigh, "they will not fail me."—The mind of man can bear a certain pressure; but there is a point when it can bear no more. A rope was in his view, and he died a Roman death.

On their arrival they found a draughty house and a cold reception. Boswell describes breakfast the next day with suave malice. Dalrymple asked the company whether they preferred the sheep's shoulder or leg for dinner: Lady Dalrymple voted "shoulder" and Johnson "leg." Boswell continues:

> He was certain of my vote and Sir John, who could not in decency deny his guest what he liked best, was obliged to join. Poor Lady Dalrymple appeared much disconcerted, and was an innocent victim to the censure of Dr. Johnson, who supposed she was unwilling to give us what was best. He said to me afterwards, "Sir, this is an odious woman. Were I Dalrymple, I'd go and entertain my friends at Edinburgh and leave her to herself. Did you observe her when we voted 'leg'? Sir, she looked as if we had voted for roasting one of her children." The truth, as I afterwards discovered, was that Sir John was not accurate in his information. There was no seven-year-old sheep killed, and no leg in the house. Accordingly none appeared, for which some foolish excuse was made.

That evening in search of comfort, Johnson and Boswell moved to the nearby inn at Blackshiels, and on the following day (22 November) Johnson took coach for London.

When the memories of hard travelling, bad accommodations, boredom, and loneliness faded, Johnson came to look back on the time spent in the tour as "the pleasantest part of his life." Most diversified, most unusual, seem more appropriate superlatives. What he remembered was the surge of new impressions, "new scenes of nature and new modes of life." It says a good deal for his flexibility of mind that he was able to assimilate so much at his age that was strange and even disagreeable, to produce in his *Journey* not only the best contemporary account of the Highlands but the finest conventional travel book, in English at any rate, of the eighteenth century. It is a pity that he and Boswell never undertook the other jaunts they talked of from time to time, to Sweden and the Baltic, or even—in one fanciful moment—to see the Great Wall of China.

Standing back from the tour, Boswell spoke of it as "the transit of Johnson over the Caledonian hemisphere." It must have seemed at some later periods important and wonderful but also remote, like a dream. What gave it solidity, what authenticated it, was his extended narrative, a grand segment of his vision of Johnson, more even in texture and more brilliant in finish than any portion of equal length in the *Life of Johnson*. It is different also in form from the *Life*, which is an important reason why Boswell chose to publish it separately. Boswell may be unique among biographers in constructing both a narrative (the *Tour*) and a portrait (the *Life*) of the same subject, and the narrative has its special effect. We recall the tour, in either the manuscript or published version, as a string of sharply defined episodes that accumulate to form a picture in depth, a dynamic pattern in which Johnson and Boswell, very much in the foreground, move across a landscape densely populated with figures.

CHAPTER

————————◆◆◆————————

5

I

THE BIOGRAPHER OF Boswell continually hears in the background a persistent grey murmur of sound, which pours forth advice, remonstrances, cries for help, and expressions of deep, unchanging affection. It is, of course, Temple's voice, strident, monotonous, yet almost soothing in its repetitiousness over the years, like the sound of katydids in a New England August. Yet it is easy to wonder why Boswell not only endured Temple's querulousness but returned his affection. The difference in their political views—for most of his life Temple was a rampant Whig—could be passed over, but their characters had diverged deeply since their early acquaintance. Temple developed the temperament of a scholar: regular, high-minded, timid, and complaining. He was shy and stiff in company. Boswell became sensual, gregarious, and, in Temple's opinion, loud.

What they visibly shared was a love of literature, a susceptibility to depression, and a recurrent conviction that life and the world had cheated them. But their friendship rested on a much more solid, and indeed unshakeable, basis: they had overcome that opposition between love and respect which the eighteenth-century mind found so troublesome. Kant generalized the point: love attracts, respect repels, and "*attraction* and *repulsion* bind together rational beings." Love seeks openness and trust; respect urges dignity and reserve. Our need for love makes us search for a confidant, but no man is a hero to the friend who knows his weaknesses.

The opposition between love and respect was no theoretical point; it presented a concrete problem to Boswell and his contemporaries. Eighteenth-century manners were formal and shades of deference demanded exact observance; when honour was at stake tempers were touchy, and quarrels led with dangerous quickness to duels. The self-contained person could live comfortably within the prescribed rules, but Boswell could never make up his mind about behaviour:

> Without reserve there cannot be dignity, and my warmth and gaiety, which procure immediate small applause, counteract the wish which my pride forms for respect in general.

But this wavering does not even take into account the Boswell whose deeper impulse was to keep nothing secret about himself. In his early days Boswell had often insisted that he must be *retenu*: "I am too open," he wrote, "and have a desire to let all my affairs be known. This I must endeavour to correct." If he did so endeavour, it was in vain.

The intimacy between Boswell and Temple had developed in the plasticity of adolescence, when emotions were warm and manners had not yet stiffened into adult restraint. "The inexpressible satisfaction of opening all our thoughts to one another," as Temple put it, gave their friendship its enduring value and, as they grew older and less tolerant of their differences in temperament, made their correspondence more enjoyable than their occasional meetings. Boswell was *coeur mis à nu*. He made Temple his mentor, confessed his ambitions and failings, his amorous adventures and other sins of the flesh, sure to be listened to, scolded, and pardoned. In return, Temple asked for advice, consolation, and love. In later years, their correspondence—by far the longest and most significant of Boswell's life—can become depressing in its tone of dejection and record of disappointment. But we are likely to read these letters one on top of another rather than at the long intervals at which they were received and, in any case, complaint is a privilege and gratification of close friendship.

Temple's complaints have already been illustrated and do not bear repetition in detail: his shrewish wife and quiverful of children were an encumbrance, and his relations a financial abscess; his literary ambitions wavered; his nerves were bad. One outburst epitomizes a steady state of melancholy:

> I am already dead; I am buried alive. . . . My letters contain the dreams and visions of a mere breathing animal, not the plans and occupations of a living agent.

In this "solitary, cheerless, anxious situation," he recurs in every letter to their mutual affection, praises Boswell's "sympathizing, benevolent, candid [1] nature," and declares, "your affection for me, my dearest Boswell, is the

---

[1]"Warm-hearted" rather than "frank."

greatest consolation I have in life." Once, provoked by the long intervals in their correspondence, Temple even threatened to die before Boswell got around to writing his next letter.

Most of all Temple wanted to be with Boswell again, and this wish was fulfilled in London at the beginning of May 1773, with Temple and his wife *en route* to Berwick to attend to family business. Boswell, who had not seen them since 1769, was "hurt a little" by their appearance (shabby country friends?), but they travelled north together with apparent success, and especially enjoyed an unrestrained evening at Wooler Haugh Head on the Scottish border. Just as they were to part the next morning, however, Boswell reduced Mrs. Temple to tears. She had always kept up social pretensions and Boswell told her roughly—under provocation, no doubt, and with a cold coming on—that her sons could not be expected to amount to anything more than clerks, stewards to noblemen, and such. He and Mrs. Temple had never liked each other, and this surge of plain speaking caused a breach only papered over by his apologies and her assurances of regard.

Boswell returned to the drudgery of the law, the one exception to legal tedium that summer being Hinton v. Donaldson on copyright. According to the existing Copyright Act (8 Anne, c. 19), copyright held for fourteen years and, if the author was still alive at the end of that period, could be extended for another fourteen. The London booksellers (publishers) maintained, however, that under common law they held copyright in perpetuity. (This much-debated right was obscure to the point that William Warburton, who delivered opinions on all matters, could write first on one side of the subject and then, after a decent interval, on the other.) In 1769, the Court of King's Bench determined the dispute in favour of the booksellers (Millar v. Taylor). But Boswell's early publisher Alexander Donaldson, specializing in cheap reprints in London and Edinburgh, ignored the decision, and the booksellers, pushing their luck, brought both an action in Chancery and a suit against him in the Court of Session. The case aroused great interest in Edinburgh, an important printing centre, and both sides retained distinguished counsel: David Rae, Alexander Murray, and Allan Maconochie for Hinton; John Maclaurin, Ilay Campbell, and Boswell for Donaldson. In an unusual procedure, the Lord Ordinary (Coalston) called for oral arguments, which took four days. (Boswell thought he spoke well, but it was Campbell who was singled out for his performance.) Coalston ruled in favour of Donaldson, and on appeal the full bench affirmed his decision, 11–1 (28 July).

Now Donaldson took the offensive by appealing the Chancery decision, which had gone against him, to the House of Lords (Donaldson v. Becket). Remembering the significant effect of his propaganda in the Douglas Cause, Boswell wanted to make his special kind of contribution, but as Donaldson's counsel and with a sedate reputation to maintain, he could hardly risk another defamatory allegory like *Dorando*. Instead, the *Letters of Lady Jane Douglas*, so effective in their appeal to the more tender feelings, provided a kind of model; as in that work, he could print some of the "documents" in the case. And what more favourable material than the opinions of the judges themselves? Before and after his tour with Johnson to the Hebrides, Boswell worked up his notes, persuading several of the judges to revise their opinions freely for the benefit of peers and posterity. Then a rush to the printers, and *The Decision of the Court of Session upon the Question of Literary Property . . . Published by James Boswell, Esq., Advocate, One of the Counsel in the Cause* appeared almost simultaneously in London and Edinburgh—"elegantly printed, and covered with marbled paper"—just in time to be distributed to the peers before debate began on 4 February 1774. Since the appeal before the Lords was based on the Chancery decision, it was conducted by English counsel, and Boswell's only, though perhaps important, contribution was his pamphlet. After extensive argument Donaldson's right to reprint was upheld, and as in the Douglas Cause the decision set off bonfires and illuminations in Edinburgh, this time urged on by a mob with a drum and two pipes. Donaldson v. Becket remains the basis of British and American copyright law, the only case in which Boswell participated to retain legal significance.

The Literary Property case roused a flurry of excitement, whose immediate impact brought Boswell alive. A criminal trial in the summer of 1773 also provided a break, pathetic this time, in deadening routine. Boswell appeared, as usual, for the defence. On 11 January 1773, Thomas Gray, a soldier living on pension in Musselburgh, quarrelled with his wife and got drunk. On his way home, he was harassed by a youthful mob, who pursued him to his house, broke a hole in the roof, and threw down sticks and stones through hole and chimney. Gray, of "weak intellects" and driven into a frenzy, rushed into the street and killed a passer-by, James Niven, who happened to be a good friend. When he was brought to trial in July, Boswell let the case go forward, hoping that lack of premeditation would exculpate him. But a unanimous jury found Gray guilty, and at that late point Boswell and his co-counsel Charles Hay, pleading that they had not found Gray insane until after their previous defence, asked for a delay in sentencing. (Perhaps Boswell thought he could always rescue Gray on grounds of insanity, and wanted to try the other line of argument first.)   The Court agreed to postpone sentence until November. (Gray's fate is unknown, but a search in the Register House in Edinburgh turned up the papers in the process tied together, and stuck among them the knife used to kill Niven.)

Otherwise, summer provided a placid flow of visitors: Charles Dilly, Pringle, Percy, and Andrew Lumisden, sometime secretary to the Old Pretender, who had just returned from exile. Most important, Temple.   Mrs. Temple contributed to the gaiety of the occasion by remaining in Berwick, and Boswell and Temple passed a happy week, whose high point—for Temple, at least—was tea with David Hume. In June Boswell was elected Master of Lodge Canongate Kilwinning No. 2 (Masons), and later in the year Joint Grand Warden for Scotland.   His interest in the Masons was convivial, as attested by the minutes in his hand of a meeting held the following summer: "The Lodge having met, although there were very few brethren present . . . the evening was passed in social glee, every brother having sung, though not as a precedent."   The minutes are countersigned by a large splash of wine.

I I

WHAT MOST SUSTAINED Boswell's spirits during the summer of 1773 was the noble prospect of observing Johnson as they traversed the Highlands and Hebrides.   And he was correspondingly let down after Johnson's return to London.   Legal business was sparse during the winter session of 1773–74, and even when he was busy Boswell felt exhausted and indolent. In practical terms, London was out of reach that spring: money was scarce and Margaret pregnant.   But Boswell tried anyway; he hoped to gain Johnson's help by invoking his piety of place, urging the spiritual exhilaration of celebrating Easter in St. Paul's.   Johnson's reply was unarguable: since Mrs. Boswell "permitted you to ramble last year, you must permit her now to keep you at home."

In this situation even Temple might appear an object of envy, since he was caught up in authorship.   Temple had put together *An Essay Concerning the Clergy*, a manual of education, behaviour, and attitudes appropriate to the aspiring minister.   Perversely enough he was most anxious to get Hume's opinion of his project, and when Hume then defined a clergyman as "a person appropriated to teach hypocrisy and inculcate vice," Temple could only respond, "how ungenerous, how unhandsome!"   The *Essay* is an exercise in feebleness (or, in eighteenth-century idiom, imbecility), with here and there a venture at an opinion: Temple finds Plato overrated; prefers the sermons of Bourdaloue and Massillon (John Wesley spoke contemptuously of their "pretty, elegant sentences") to those of his countrymen Tillotson, Barrow, and Clarke; and thinks farming a useful defence against "that listlessness and languor to which a sedentary life is unavoidably subject." That existence would have been languid indeed to which a reading of the *Essay* imparted a keener relish, but Temple thought it had done him good in ecclesiastical circles and he began to hope for translation to some less poverty-stricken parish.

While Boswell was both commenting on Temple's *Essay* and exerting pressure on the Dillys to publish it, he was also providing stray information for a far more important work, Johnson's *Journey to the Western Islands of Scotland*. The travel book rivalled the sermon as the most popular literary genre of the day, and Johnson had pondered its nature, as he had pondered most subjects. In *Idler*, No. 97, he had mocked those "sons of enterprise" who dragged their readers over an indistinguishable succession of rocks and streams, mountains and ruins. "The great object of remark is human life," Johnson had insisted to the aspiring travel writer, and his grandly panoramic survey of Hebridean manners and customs was faithful to his own advice. The *Journey to the Western Islands* appeared in January 1775 to great applause (Macpherson and many other Scots dissenting), and Boswell was touched to find Johnson had described him in the first paragraph as

> a companion whose acuteness would help my inquiry, and whose gaiety of conversation and civility of manners are sufficient to counteract the inconveniencies of travel in countries less hospitable than we have passed.

This was gratifying praise, but Boswell was sitting on a book, his own journal of the tour, which also remarked on human life, in a very particular, vivid, and, for the time, unique manner. Edward Dilly, alert to the potential of another *Corsica*, urged Boswell to bring his "observations" on his tour with Johnson, as well as his "remarks" on his earlier tour of Holland and Germany, to London in the spring of 1775 for possible publication.

Johnson would then be the immediate impediment, though he felt warmly about the journal. When Boswell lent it to Mrs. Thrale, Johnson remarked to her, "I am not sorry that you read Boswell's journal. Is it not a merry piece?" And, amused, "One would think the man had been hired to be a spy upon me." And later,

> He moralized and found my faults, and laid them up to reproach me. Boswell's narrative is very natural and therefore very en-

tertaining; he never made any scruple of showing it to me.   He is a very fine fellow.

But given the manners of the period, the manners of most periods, Boswell's Hebridean journal was far too personal to publish in full during Johnson's lifetime, and though he agreed to look over any sections taken from it for publication Boswell sensed a lack of enthusiasm.   For a moment he thought of putting something together behind Johnson's back, but that wild notion subsided and he laid the journal away for eventual publication.

Johnson's reluctance was unlikely to stem either from fear of competition or of revelation, though he may have wondered whether Boswell's book might be a distracting gloss on his own.   But his sense of the genre was very different from Boswell's.   Earlier Johnson, having alternately encouraged and discouraged him about *Corsica*, rested finally in praise; but when Boswell later mentioned a book of Continental travels Johnson said he would lessen himself by it: what could he say that was new?   Boswell protested: "But I can give an entertaining narrative, with many incidents, anecdotes, *jeux d'esprit*, and remarks, so as to make very pleasant reading." Entertainment wasn't enough, Johnson told him; readers wanted to learn something from a book of travels.

For the time being, Boswell kept his hand in with more periodical contributions: a review of the Edinburgh Theatre's 1773–74 winter season; Goldsmith's song, "Ah me! when shall I marry me?" otherwise unpreserved, which he had dropped from *She Stoops to Conquer*; and a fine, brief account of travels in exotic Abyssinia extracted "as from a flinty rock with pickaxes" from an ill-tempered Bruce of Kinnaird, who thought he had discovered the source of the Nile.

Literary small change, and Boswell had, in any case, concentrated his attention on local politics.   Not that he considered writing and politics as alternatives: though early in life he had looked up to an author as someone mysterious and wonderful, and spoke of literary fame as the most valuable of possessions, he never regarded himself *primarily* as an author.   He was a gentleman of ancient family, heir to an extensive estate, who practised law and who had every right to aspire to political office.   As early as 1763 Lord Auchinleck had proposed a seat in Parliament as a worthy objective for Boswell the future advocate, and whatever mistakes he made at other times in dealing with his son, here he struck the mark.   Fantasies of high political attainment are common in young men, but Boswell endearingly wrote his down: James Boswell, M.P., would prove a better speaker than Pitt and become a principal Secretary of State.   And, like many another Scot, he was ambitious to aggrandize the Family.

Looking back on Boswell's impulsive, abortive, and finally heartbreaking political ventures, the biographer sees all as vanity, vanity. Looking forward in 1774, Boswell seemed to have a decent chance for a modest political career. He had a good family interest, and he had made a national name for himself from his spectacular efforts to help Paoli and the Corsican cause. But the average M.P. did not make a name for himself, he did not take up causes; already Boswell fails to fit the pattern. And if a man, like William Wilberforce, took up a cause he needed solid backing. Boswell had no such support; further, with the French conquest of Corsica his cause disappeared. Still, ambition whispered that since he had become a member of London's most eminent literary circle, why should he not take his place in its most select political club? Burke provided a dazzling model.

Whatever led Boswell to involve himself in the General Election of 1774, it was certainly time for him to start building a political career if he was interested in one. The Ayrshire situation had the advantage of being particularly unsettled. The incumbent M.P., elected in 1768, was David Kennedy, a good, honest, merry fellow, according to Boswell, but essentially a "joker" incapable of public business. Kennedy, however, had a qualification which outweighed his intellectual limitations: he was the brother of the Earl of Cassillis and had been elected with the support of the Earl of Loudoun, it being understood that Loudoun could name the candidate at the election of 1774. This alliance effectively excluded the nominee of the Earl of Eglinton, the most influential of Ayrshire peers and landowners. (Loudoun and Eglinton were the chief rivals in the county, with Cassillis at the moment holding the balance of power.) But this aristocratic *pas de trois* was threatened by a group of the landed gentry who had memories of electoral success in the 1740s, and angry at being ignored in these cosy arrangements they nominated Sir Adam Fergusson of Kilkerran. Faced with this threat to their squabbling hegemony, Cassillis, Eglinton, and Loudoun united behind Kennedy.

The Scottish franchise was a tangled relic of feudalism but, when untampered with, supposedly reflected the enshrined maxim that influence should ever be in proportion to property. Electors were expected to be substantial property owners; these were called "real" voters, and made up a large majority of the 128 on the Ayrshire freeholders' roll of 1774. But through common, shady manoeuvres the roll could be swollen by creating "nominal and fictitious" votes and, when the stakes were high enough, it was. Possibly the Ayrshire election of 1774 had a faint ideological dimension: the peers inclined to a strict interpretation of the property-influence ratio, while their opponents argued for independence from the peers and their pernicious, unconstitutional control of the House of Commons.   In effect, the gentry supported something resembling a one-property owner, one-vote position, which is why Boswell called them "a kind of democratical coalition."   ("Democratical" has no relation to any modern British conception of democracy, dreamed of then only by radicals.)   But whatever theories peers and gentry may have held, the struggle for power was not limited by principle.   Kennedy's party sought the backing of the gentlemen of the county, while Fergusson's coalition acquired two essential blocs of votes controlled by the Earls of Dumfries and Glencairn.

Boswell's political outlook involved such an inconsistent though genuine mixture of attitudes that it might have been hard to predict which side he would support.   "Liberty" had been the key word of *Corsica*; in 1768 he supported, with reservations, Wilkes's right to sit for Middlesex; and after initial hesitation he remained steadily pro-American during the American Revolution.   At the same time, he always thought of himself as a Tory, he admired strong leaders like Chatham and Paoli, and his veneration for George III was to grow almost oriental.   One commentator has remarked shrewdly on "the peculiar turn of Boswell's mind at whatever age . . . the same liberal point of view coupled with conservative principles." As party distinctions eroded, Boswell himself found a resemblance between his basic political attitudes and Burke's.   Like Burke, Boswell attached himself to a small, aristocratic group, but where Burke had presented a reasoned, theoretical basis for the existence of the Rockingham Whigs in his *Thoughts on the Cause of the Present Discontents* (1770), Boswell acted only from strong, unformulated emotion when he became a warm supporter of the Ayrshire peers.   True, for some quasi-feudal reason he regarded Archibald Montgomerie, Earl of Eglinton, as his political chief; true, Margaret called cousins with Eglinton, in a country where kinship meant much. On the other hand, self-interest would have suggested he join the gentry if he hoped ever to represent Ayrshire in the House of Commons; he must have noticed that in his lifetime the peers had always nominated one of their close relations.

In the background, also, was a serious joker, Lord Auchinleck.   When Boswell threw his support to the peers, what was he throwing?   According to his own later account, his father told him he would take no part in the election, and Boswell started on his political career confident that he could dispose of the family interest, only to discover that the Lord President had persuaded his father, after twenty years of political inactivity, not only to support Fergusson but to create ten nominal votes.   The Dundases of Arniston had long been a powerful force in Scottish legal and political affairs, and the President's younger half-brother, Henry Dundas, was starting to put together that web of connections which was to make him the political ruler of Scotland for the rest of the century. Fergusson was only one strand in the web, and Lord Auchinleck's votes, which in any case failed to "mature" in time for the election, a minor element in Fergusson's coalition; but naturally Boswell was furious. He must have promised backing he could not supply; he looked like a fool.

Apparently Temple thought Boswell had taken silence for approval and, always eager to do the correct thing, criticized him for it: "Was ever anything so imprudent, so disrespectful as to engage your interest without your father's approbation?" (Boswell's reply is missing, but in his next letter Temple begged pardon for his "mistake about Lord Auchinleck.") There seemed to be other mistakes: Lord Auchinleck had backed Kennedy in the election of 1768, and must have been genuinely persuaded that the success of the "triple alliance" would mean, in his words, "the annihilation of the gentlemen's interest."

Still the election focused deeper issues. Though the Ayrshire contest was a local struggle which had little to do with Whig and Tory, certainly a man who had been called "the greatest Whig in Britain" could hardly have looked with pleasure on the political aspirations of a son who described himself as "a High Tory of the school of Johnson," especially with his own argument with Johnson so fresh in mind. And political differences gathered intensity from personal ones. The entail question festered, and this was only the most prominent feature of the estrangement in the family. Lord Auchinleck must have been constantly encouraged not only by his wife but by her elder sister Margaret, who lived much of the time with them, in his inclination to rebuff this eccentric and undutiful son, who was so boldly anticipating his demise. Hadn't this son abandoned his respectable example to trail after an English dominie? For Boswell and Margaret, Sunday dinner at his father's was a penitential exercise, described on one occasion as "the usual constraint joined with the usual small conversation." Boswell was inclined to attribute his father's creation of nominal votes (which, earlier, Lord Auchinleck had strongly condemned) to a gradual mental failure which the Dundases had taken unscrupulous advantage of. Their intervention, he remarked, had rendered Boswell a cipher in his own county; in August 1774 he refused to dine with the Lord President and by the next February they were no longer on speaking terms. Nor did the election, held in October 1774, prove promising in itself. Kennedy expected to win, but some of his nominal voters refused to take the "trust oath" that they were real proprietors, while Fergusson's nominal voters,

including a parson, swore without scruple.   Fergusson was elected by a
vote of 60 to 47.

Frustrated as author and politician, Boswell found some compensation
in the satisfying continuity of family life: Veronica survived the tricky
procedure of inoculation, and Euphemia, the longest-lived and most difficult of Boswell's children, was born on 20 May 1774.

Equally important to Boswell's stability was his law practice, though his
attitude towards it veered constantly.   Business was thin during the winter
of 1774 but he made his way as best he could and, significantly, began at
least to think himself more and more successful as a lawyer.   And the
following summer he had never been so busy.   Not that he would ever
become one of the leaders at the bar; he did not pretend to rival Lockhart's
command of oratorical flourish and circumstantial detail, or the combined
acuteness and industry of the two busiest counsel, Ilay Campbell and Robert
Macqueen.   Even his friend Maclaurin, who had got off to a poor start,
was in more demand.

But Boswell had advantages as a lawyer besides that of being Lord
Auchinleck's son.   As he often remarks, he spoke well in court, and his
many surviving papers show, as could be expected, that he wrote clearly
and effectively.   He admitted his father was right in saying that his legal
knowledge was shaky, and made a sustained effort to improve it: in the
spring and summer of 1774 he and his friend Charles Hay held a "law
college," agreeably interspersed with lawn bowls, in which they went through
John Erskine's recently published, authoritative *Institute of the Law of
Scotland*.

Boswell, however, lacked the instincts of a lawyer.   Faced with an
obscure point he went from colleague to colleague seeking opinions, until
Macqueen sensibly told him to consult the law books.   "Had I at first *read*,"
Boswell concedes, "instead of *thinking* and *asking*, I might at once have been
made certain."   Boswell the writer would never have run around in circles.
Even more damaging was his tentativeness; he wrote in his journal: "An
important part of my life should be my practice as a lawyer."   The conditional mood tells all.

Yet his business grew.   Hay, who was to ascend the Bench as Lord
Newton and become fabulous as a drinker in an age of drinkers, put Boswell
in the way of some profitable cases, which Boswell summarizes as "Earl
Fife's politics": this was a complex of lawsuits involving nominal votes in
the counties of Elgin and Banff, where Fife was struggling with the Duke
of Gordon for political control.   Boswell was unimportant among Fife's
lawyers, the consultations involved were tedious, and Gordon won most of

the cases anyway. But it was money in his pocket, and learning of Camp-bell's and Macqueen's annual incomes (about £1,500 to 2,000) excited "solid, coarse ambition."

Still, he often felt that either the bar or Scotland by itself was a burden; and the combination of the two seemed at times more than any able, im-aginative person could bear. The pull of London was insistent, and the most reasonable avenue of escape remained the English bar. In *Boswelli-ana*, his collection of consciously entertaining anecdotes and clever sayings, he wrote *circa* June 1774: "I always wished to go to the English bar. When I found I could labour, I said it was pity to dig in a lead mine when I could get to a gold one." As Burke was an influential model in politics, so Mansfield and Alexander Wedderburn (now English Solicitor-General, later Lord Chancellor and Earl of Rosslyn) were almost irresistible examples of Scots who had made their way to high legal position in England. Mans-field's education and legal experience were completely English, but he had had to contend constantly against the innuendo that he was a Jacobite like his brother James, Earl of Dunbar in the Jacobite peerage; Wedderburn had begun his career at the Scots bar but had transplanted himself after having insulted the Lord President of the time in open court. Of course, Boswell's motive for wanting to change his sphere of practice was temper-amental rather than professional.

Goldsmith's death in April 1774, an obtrusive reminder of mortality, touched off an anxious round of letters reminding Boswell's English friends of his existence. Only in London were his talents and personality appre-ciated at their full value; only in London did mere existence blossom into life: that was the nub of it. The scales balanced between duty and desire. Scotland presented a dull, secure, and known future—as knowable as fu-tures can be—which would honour his career and family position; in Lon-don, he would be weighed down by his ignorance of English law, his fear of disinheritance, and Margaret's reluctance to leave home ground. But the move offered an excitingly vague vision of a glorious future.

Boswell's conflict of emotions about his legal career was more obscure and more uneven in its development than appears in this retrospective summary, but it came to an unexpected focus in the John Reid trial of 1774, which converted conflict into crisis, and in the root sense of "crisis" became a turning point in his feelings about the law. Charged with sheep-stealing, Reid had been Boswell's first criminal client eight years before, and in the teeth of the evidence Boswell had persuaded the jury to bring in a verdict of "not proven," an unpleasant shock to the order of things as perceived by the High Court of Justiciary. The Lord Justice Clerk "Tam"

Miller especially cherished his indignation and shortly after, when delivering his opinion in the Douglas Cause, indulged in an *obiter dictum* attacking Reid's acquittal.

Now Reid was again charged with sheep-stealing, though on a much smaller scale: only 19 sheep as against 120 in 1766. Experience, one might think, would have taught Reid a lesson but perhaps it taught the wrong one: if once you get away with it, try again. In any case, John Reid, flesher (butcher), of Hillend, in the parish of Muiravonside, and shire of Stirling, was charged with theft and/or reset of theft, i.e., receiving stolen sheep and feloniously disposing of them, "crimes of a heinous nature and severely punishable, especially when committed by a person of bad fame, habit and repute to be a thief, or sheep-stealer."

Few of the facts were in question. Someone in October 1773 had stolen 19 sheep from Alexander Gray, at Lyne in Peeblesshire, some thirty miles from Hillend. Gray's herdsman, Robert Paterson, suspected Reid, and a few days later found three of the sheep grazing in a meadow near Reid's house, with two more, skinned but identifiable from the marks on their heads, hanging in his flesh-house. When Reid heard Paterson was looking for him, he panicked and ran away to England. Apprehended when he was so "infatuate" (his own term) as to return home, he made a "declaration" before the Sheriff-Depute of Edinburghshire in March 1774 sufficient to keep him in the Edinburgh Tolbooth until the law turned at its leisure to deal with him. And having caught up with Reid, the law had no intention of letting him go. The prosecution team was formidable: James Montgomery (Lord Advocate), Henry Dundas (Solicitor-General), and two experienced Crown Advocates-Depute, William Nairne and Robert Sinclair. Boswell alone represented the prisoner though backed, at Boswell's request, by Michael Nasmith, W.S., as agent (solicitor). Even Crosbie, co-counsel for Reid in 1766, refused to take public part in his trial, having warned Reid then that Reid could not expect his help if he got into trouble again. About to take its revenge, society withdrew, leaving the prisoner isolated.

The grim scene before Reid at eight o'clock on the morning of 1 August 1774 would have intimidated a braver man. On the bench sat the Lord Justice Clerk presiding and Lords Auchinleck, Coalston, and Kames (Lords Kennet and Pitfour were late). Boswell argued that since Reid had been acquitted in 1766 his reputation should not be held against him, and apparently the Court agreed to restrict that charge to the period thereafter. The evidence as to Reid's possession of the sheep was damning, Paterson's circumstantial account being sufficient to convict in itself. But the pros-

ecution was leaving no loophole.   A second herdsman was called, followed
by Paterson's son.   Boswell, fighting hard, objected to the boy's being
allowed to testify since he had been scarcely over twelve at the time of the
theft, and cited an eminent legal authority, Mackenzie of Rosehaugh.   Sinclair replied that the boy was to be examined "only in the way of declaration"
and, whatever Mackenzie had said, such declarations were received by
established practice.   The reaction from the Bench was macabre:

AUCHINLECK.   I remember in the first trial I was on, which was
    for a murder, a little girl swore to having seen the panel [1] mix
    a powder, which clenched the evidence of poison.
COALSTON.   There is a great difference between civil and criminal
    questions.   In the first, people have the choice of their wit-
    nesses.In the other, they have not.

The boy was called.   Boswell's trial notes continue:

JUSTICE CLERK.   Boy, do you go to the Church?—to the Kirk?
BOY.   No. I gang to the meeting-house.[2]
AUCHINLECK.   You know that God made you?
BOY.   (stupid).
AUCHINLECK.   Wha made you?
BOY.   (with shrill voice).   God!
AUCHINLECK.   You ken it's a sin to lie?
BOY.   Ay.
PITFOUR.   You know you are always in the presence of God, and
    that an overruling Providence superintends us all, and that
    you will be severely punished both in this world and the next
    if you say what is not true?

In spite of this pious opening, even Pitfour's expansion of the question
into mellifluous English idiom, the boy's evidence provided only trifles.
But the next two witnesses, Reid's neighbours, William Black and Robert
Shaw, were deadly in backing up the charge of theft and in testifying to
Reid's "habit and repute" as a sheep-stealer.

The prosecution now introduced Reid's "declaration" of the previous
March, in which he asserted he had bought the sheep from one William
Gardner, but refused to explain why he had run away from the neighbourhood.   Gardner was in Stirling prison, sentenced to transportation
for stealing a piece of cloth, but Boswell did not call him, arguing in-
geniously that a man convicted of housebreaking was "infamous and intestable."

[1]Defendant.
[2]The boy means that he belongs to a congregation of Seceders, not to the Church of
Scotland.

Instead, he offered to prove the bargain through the hearsay evidence of Andrew Auld.   The Lord Advocate felt sure enough of his ground not to object to Auld's testimony, despite Kames's mutterings that to admit hearsay evidence would wound the law.   In the event, Auld proved distressingly vague, being only able to testify to Gardner's telling him about some bargain or other between him and Reid more than a year earlier. Boswell at this point offered to show by two of the jury at Reid's trial in 1766 that the judges were strongly prejudiced against Reid, but to save time the Lord Advocate agreed to this fact.

Both the Advocate's and Boswell's summaries turned on the elimination of the reset of theft charge.   The Advocate wanted to convict Reid of the more heinous crime of theft, while Boswell evidently hoped that the jury, faced with clear alternatives of innocence or guilt, would be too unsure about the theft itself to convict Reid.   (The Advocate seems overcautious since the Court, a hanging court always, was quite capable of hanging any man, and especially this man, for receiving and disposing of stolen sheep, which was capital if "habit and repute" was also proved.)   The Advocate also stressed Boswell's charge of prejudice, not because it was malicious or untrue, but in order to remind the jury that the Court thought Reid was guilty before.   According to what may have been his own account in the *Edinburgh Advertiser*, Boswell summed up for his client "in a very masterly and pathetic manner, which did him great honour both as a lawyer and as one who wished for a free and impartial trial by jury," the last phrase alluding to Boswell's view that the judges brutally overawed juries, which were inclined to a lenity inconsistent with the law.   On his part, the Justice Clerk "complained loudly to the jury he and the Court had been arraigned."

Enclosed at five o'clock that afternoon, the jury almost immediately found Reid guilty of theft, and though it would not be revealed officially until the next afternoon the verdict leaked at once.   As was customary, Boswell then met the jury at Walker's Tavern where everyone got drunk at the Crown's expense and Boswell enjoyed the jurors' appreciation of his fine courtroom showing and general importance.   When the party broke up at midnight, Boswell "much in liquor" strolled the streets for a while no doubt looking, though in vain, for a vigorous climax to his strenuous day.

The Lords of Justiciary also had their habit and repute: justice was their duty and mercy a dubious option.   On announcement of the verdict, Boswell moved to postpone sentence for a few days "as he would endeavour to show that a capital punishment should not be inflicted."   The judges argued the point in open court, all except Kames being in favour of immediate sentence.   There was no hesitation about the sentence itself: they agreed with warm unanimity that theft of a *grex* (flock) was a capital crime. The Justice Clerk declared in good eighteenth-century idiom, it "would hurt my mind to think that a *grex* should not be capital."   Auchinleck urged the question of numbers: if stealing 19 sheep was not capital, why should stealing 100 be?   Kames ran the argument the other way; not only was the theft of 19 capital but so would be the theft of 9, though his opinion had a medieval flavour: he would prefer reparation to hanging.   But sheep-stealing was carried on by low people who could not make reparation, and if they were not hanged the law would be in the dismal position of being unable to repress such crime.   Finally, Coalston contributed another example of his bizarre logic: while one act of theft "as of a small thing, as one sheep" *need* not be a capital crime, it *could* be capital; and in fact sheep-stealers were *always* hanged.   (Coalston gives the impression of a mind in search of a principle, but content enough if it does not find one.)

The scene unavoidably suggests Daumier: the judges croaking in sadistic malevolence, the advocates preening themselves on their display of professional skill, the prisoner at the bar trembling in guilt and wretchedness.   Of course that is not how the participants saw themselves.   The judges' harshness, especially, indicates the gap between eighteenth- and twentieth-century social views.   Modern society is correctly called materialistic, but in respect to unquestioned, hard-bitten materialism we cannot compare with our ancestors of two hundred years ago.   Labour and lives were cheap.   Property was not a status symbol but the reality of status, and its scarcity increased its sanctity.   Adam Smith said, quite without irony,

> Civil government, so far as it is instituted for the security of property, is in reality instituted for the defence of the rich against the poor, or of those who have some property against those who have none at all.

Boswell's political and social views were solidly conventional, and it would be anachronistic to regard him as a zealous defender of the theoretical rights of the poor.   But he had a strong sense of justice; it even stuck in his throat to defend a guilty client, though more than once in Boswell's career Johnson told him to leave the question of guilt to the court. Conversely, he was willing to go to almost any length to defend an innocent one.   But was Reid innocent?   In the next few weeks, Boswell questioned him closely and often, and though Reid admitted stealing sheep on other occasions—more instances came back to him as time went on—he steadfastly maintained his innocence of the present charge.   Boswell also pursued Reid's story that Gardner was responsible for the theft, but Gardner, his

trail fading as he departed involuntarily for America, denied any involvement.

If justice failed, mercy might save Reid.   Boswell petitioned the King
through Lord Suffolk (one of the three Secretaries of State) for commu-
tation of sentence to transportation, and began to call on influential
noblemen to intervene in Reid's favour.   Lord Erroll (Reid's father-in-law
had been one of his long-time tenants) refused coolly, but Lord Pembroke
made at least a token gesture of help.   On 2 September came a fortnight's
reprieve from Lord Rochford, another Secretary of State, while Government waited for a report on the case from the Justice Clerk.

As caught up as he was in saving Reid's life, Boswell kept, if rather
unevenly, a sense of detachment—not the lawyer's professional detachment
but the detachment which he seldom lost in any drawn-out situation.   Intense involvement, extraordinary detachment: the combination may be
unusual but it is characteristic.   He stood back and looked at Reid: he
thought of having his career depicted, à la Hogarth, in "The Sheep-Stealer's
Progress," and he persuaded Reid to have his portrait done "while under
sentence of death."   Boswell was so attached to this last circumstance that
he hoped the reprieve would not arrive until the portrait was finished.
Happily it did not.

Yet Boswell increasingly identified with Reid's situation, if not with the
man himself.   His mind reverberated to a series of linked ideas and questions: "We are all condemned to die.   But what is it like to know the hour
of one's death?   How does a man die?   What is it to pass from the known
to the unknown?   How will I die?"   A few years earlier he had asked
Johnson whether the fear of death was not natural to man and Johnson
had replied, "So much so, Sir, that the whole of life is but keeping away
the thoughts of it."   Yet a man should prepare to meet his Maker, prepare
by confessing and repenting his sins.

All these thoughts, mingled with his immediate feelings about Reid,
seem to lie behind the scene Boswell put on with him in prison on 7
September, the day originally scheduled for Reid's execution.   Boswell had
arrived a little before two o'clock, thinking that Reid had lied to him about
Gardner's participation in the theft:

> I had wrought myself into a passion against John for deceiving
> me and spoke violently to him, not feeling for him at the time.
> I had chosen my time so as to be with him when two o'clock struck.
> "John," said I, "you hear that clock strike.   You hear that bell.
> If this does not move you, nothing will.   That you are to consider
> as your last bell.   You remember your sentence.   On Wednesday

the 7 of September. This is the day. Between the hours of two
and four in the afternoon; this is that very time. After this day
you are to look upon yourself as a dead man; as a man in the
middle state between the two worlds. . . . You are to look on this
fortnight as so much time allowed to you to repent of all your
wickedness, and particularly of your lying to me in such a way as
you have done. . . . I think it your duty to own your being guilty
on this occasion if you be really so, which I cannot but think is the
case. By doing so you will make all the atonement in your power
to society. But at any rate I beseech you not to deny your guilt
contrary to truth."

Then Boswell steps back to comment:

This was as vehement and solemn a harangue as could be made
upon any occasion. The circumstance of the clock striking and
the two o'clock bell ringing were finely adapted to touch the imagination.[1] But John seemed to be very unfeeling today. He persisted in his tale. There was something approaching to the ludicrous
when, in the middle of my speech to him about his not being
properly alive, he said very gravely, "Ay, I'm dead in law."

Boswell's exercise in the sublime and pathetic has come unstuck. Reid
will not play his part or, when he tries to, botches it. Worse was to come:

I was too violent with him. I said, "With what face can you go
to the other world?" And, "If your ghost should come and tell
me this, I would not believe it." This last sentence made me
frightened, as I have faith in apparitions, and had a kind of idea
that perhaps his ghost might come and tell me I had been unjust
to him.

Boswell realizes that the scene is stagy and the reversal comic, but he wanted
to enact a moment of self-realization in which a man faces his fate directly—
"Be absolute for death"—and he uses the only modes he knows. What
response would have satisfied him? Perhaps only the one he devised

---

[1]The effect Boswell wants is illustrated by a passage from his favourite poet, Edward
Young:
    The bell strikes one. We take no note of time
    But from its loss: to give it then a tongue
    Is wise in man. As if an angel spoke,
    I feel the solemn sound. If heard aright
    It is the knell of my departed hours.
    Where are they? With the years beyond the Flood.
                                        (*The Complaint; or, Night Thoughts*, i. 55–60)

Johnson's crictictaster Dick Minim counted among his triumphs that "by his contrivance
the bell was rung twice in *Barbarossa*" (*Idler*, No. 60).

himself, a Boswell-written "mournful case of poor, misfortunate, and un-happy John Reid," dated the same night:

> This is the very day on which I was doomed to die. . . .   Oh! listen then unto me, while I am yet in the land of the living, and think that it is my GHOST speaking unto you!

This melodramatic plea for mercy was printed and distributed "to conciliate the lower populace," and the printer added, "taken from his own mouth." Reid was angered by this fraud, but Boswell thought the "case" could do no harm.

Boswell was still concerned to save the body as well as the soul.   On 3 September he wrote to the Duke of Queensberry, on 5 September to Lord Cornwallis and again to Pembroke; and on 10 September twice to Lord Rochford, in one letter enclosing a notarized statement from Reid's wife stating that Reid had spent the night of the theft in bed with her, and in the other reminding Rochford of their common interest in the oppressed Corsicans.   Characteristically, he also published a letter in the *London Chronicle* (20 September), signed "A Royalist," attacking the Justice Clerk for his prejudice against Reid.   As Nasmith, thoroughly caught up in the case, informed a friend (6 September), "We fear the Lord Justice Clerk.   The battle is betwixt Boswell and the Court.   He is opposing all his interest. He is all humanity."

The ruffling of official feathers accomplished nothing.   The King's decision had been taken by 9 September, before any of Boswell's recent appeals, even the one directed through Queensberry, is likely to have reached him.   Miller's report had been final, Suffolk remarking that all this fuss could have been avoided if Boswell had consulted with the Justice Clerk before petitioning for a respite.   Pembroke reported that the King was inclined to commute the sentence to transportation, but that Miller's version of the case had been so violent he would have had to resign if it had been ignored.   Boswell, of course, had anticipated that it would be a "bloody opinion."   On the night the bad news came, Boswell got "monstrously drunk" and blacked out, to be told by his wife the next day that he had cursed her in a shocking manner and even thrown a candlestick with a lighted candle at her.   His repentance was immediate and total.

Boswell nourished one last, fantastic hope—that Reid could be res-urrected after hanging.   Nothing could display his commitment to the case more clearly.   The idea was inspired by contemporary interest in reviving the apparently dead, but to revive Reid involved more than humanitarian considerations: it would be direct defiance of the Court's order.   Prudence and Margaret argued against such an outrageous act.   Still, that Boswell could find conspirators in this project shows how much the cruelty of the law was resented.   Even the name of the Marchese di Beccaria, the great penal reformer, came up in the discussion of the case.   Boswell persuaded Sandy Wood to enlist two other medical men to help, and prevailed on a former client, Andrew Bennet, to let him use his stable for the attempt. But as the time of Reid's execution approached, it brought second thoughts with it.   Though agreeing to go through with the experiment, Wood argued that Boswell might be doing Reid a disservice by recalling him from eternity: "He may curse you for bringing him back.   He may tell you that you kept him from heaven."   Boswell gave up.

The day of execution came and—as Boswell was to spread all over the newspapers—that

> forenoon in particular every effort was used to make [Reid] confess
> if he really was guilty.   He was again and again told in the most
> solemn manner that he could not hope for mercy if he went into
> the other world with a lie in his mouth, but he still declared his
> innocence.

At 2 p.m., dressed in white linen death clothes with black ribbons and tall nightcap, he said goodbye to his wife in the Tolbooth and marched, arms pinioned and rope around his neck, through the Lawnmarket, down the West Bow, and onto the scaffold in the Grassmarket.   His white hairs spread over his face, said an observer, made his appearance still more pitiable.   His final words were, "Take warning.   Mine is an unjust sentence."   Boswell and Nasmith stayed till the end, and paid the porters to carry the body away.   Deeply shaken, as usual, by an execution, Boswell sat dismally by his fireside that night, so paralysed with fear that he hardly dared rise from his chair.

CHAPTER

6

I

BOSWELL'S DEFENCE OF John Reid was a trial of his own ability to affect events, and Reid's execution was a naked demonstration of his powerlessness in a struggle with public authority. He had exerted himself fully, and the Establishment had put him aside as a strong man puts aside a boy. The effect on him was decisive. A more detached advocate might have taken the outcome as a matter of professional routine, a more persistent one might have pressed forward to the next cause; but Boswell was always uncertain in his attitude towards his profession, and this defeat destroyed his momentum as a lawyer. Though his practice would remain stable for several years and he would even feel enthusiastic about it at times, Reid's trial crystallized his distaste for the Scottish bar; from now on he would seldom think of a seat on the Court of Session, the honourable goal of many advocates, as more than at best a dignified retreat from his great hopes for himself. Ambition would seek other channels.

The direction of Boswell's thinking showed up sharply this autumn, when he made an apparently minor but significant choice about his career. It occurred to him very sensibly that he might apply to take on the work of the Sheriff-Depute of Ayrshire, its chief law officer, while leaving the incumbent, as was customary, the income for life. It was a demanding job and would involve him heavily in the county, but it was a very helpful step towards the bench, and for one who wished to represent Ayrshire in the House of Commons it offered a fine chance to make himself known and useful. But Lord Loudoun refused his backing and, more important, the fantasy of London employment distracted him; he wanted to keep himself free from Scottish engagements.

On a deeper level, the Reid trial was also a ritualized though desperate skirmish in the prolonged struggle between Boswell and his father.   In one of life's overdone ironies—fiction would not dare so far—Boswell practised as a civil and criminal lawyer in the courts where his father sat. No one worried about conflict of interest; on the contrary it was taken for granted that Lord Auchinleck would view his son's clients sympathetically, and Boswell's business jumped when his father sat in the Outer House in his customary week's turn as Lord Ordinary.   Lord Auchinleck seems, in fact, to have maintained an admirable impartiality on the bench, but Boswell's position was understandably difficult.   Most children think of their parents as judges, but few have the misfortune to face their fathers shrouded in authority, the literal judges of their professional skill, as they plead a client's cause.   As suggested earlier, the enforced intimacy of bar and bench was lightened by their informal mingling: judges and lawyers dined and drank together, respected and jeered at each other.   But manners were not that easy between Boswell and his father; their confrontations in court must have reinforced those swings between dependence and independence which characterized Boswell's reaction to paternal supervision.   Their difficult relationship was to reach its crisis in the quarrel about the entail that stretched over the next two years.

A visit to Valleyfield, Sir George and Lady Preston's place in Fife across the Forth from Edinburgh, provided a few days' comfortable interlude after Reid's execution.   With the occasional exception of Auchinleck, Valleyfield was the only country house where Boswell felt content for more than a day or two at a time.   The Prestons had been like parents to him and Margaret since their marriage, and Boswell associated Valleyfield with his gentle, anxious, pious mother, who had grown up in nearby Culross. Except when it was tied to the terrors of Presbyterianism, the memory of his mother always consoled Boswell, and in turn he was to bring his children to Valleyfield to cherish this connection with her family.

But Valleyfield was only a respite; Boswell returned to Edinburgh to an unexpected, unpleasant echo of the Reid trial.   It will be recalled that Boswell published a letter in the *London Chronicle*, signed "A Royalist," which attacked the Lord Justice Clerk for prejudice against Reid.   The letter was useless—it could not arrive for insertion in the newspaper until the day before Reid's execution—so it served merely as an outlet for Boswell's anger and frustration.   The Justice Clerk ignored it "as calculated for the meridian of London," but his son William, in a defiant letter, demanded that Boswell acknowledge he was "A Royalist" and publicly apologize for false and scandalous aspersions on his father.   The affair was embarrassing: Reid's trial was finished business, and William was a youth of nineteen, slight and effeminate looking, little more than a boy. Sure that Boswell would be killed in a duel, the ordinarily sensible Margaret in panic suggested flight to another country. Boswell himself was anxious but resolute; he wrote to William admitting authorship but, as he summarizes his letter,

> assuring him, as I truly could, that he was in a mistake in supposing that I attacked either his father's honour or honesty. That I meant no injury and if I had used any expressions which had been misunderstood I was sorry for it. That if after this candid explanation any disagreeable consequences should ensue, I should have the comfort to think I was not to blame.

Having been advised by two of his more strong-minded relations that this letter did not violate the delicate bounds of honour, Boswell sent it off (7 October 1774) and waited.

Meanwhile, Col. Archibald Campbell, parliamentary candidate for the Stirling burghs, asked Boswell to be his counsel and a delegate for Culross, one of the five burghs included in this electoral group. Boswell, much pleased, jaunted off to electioneer in Fife. When he returned on 17 October, William was close to a challenge: he demanded that Boswell meet him at Paxton's Inn and bring a friend. Margaret was "like one in a kind of delirium." But Boswell's cousin, Capt. Robert Preston, and the young man's uncle intervened to bring the matter to ceremonious resolution, William having (Boswell decided), "spirited ideas of honour and the regard he owed to his father's character, but not clearly knowing how he should proceed." A few weeks later, Boswell called on the Justice Clerk, who had known nothing of the possible encounter, to tell him the whole story, and the Justice Clerk offered some kindly advice: a man like Boswell with a character to support should not splash about publishing squibs in the newspapers. (It was a common enough practice.) "I am resolved," Boswell wrote in his journal, "to restrain myself and attend more to decorum."

Forty-eight years later, Boswell's eldest son Alexander was to indulge in precisely the same kind of anonymous newspaper attack; having refused to apologize, he was called out and killed by his opponent, James Stuart of Dunearn, who said he had aimed at random. The jury acquitted Stuart after his counsel read passages from Boswell's *Life of Johnson* which admitted the necessity of duels.

Through what he called delicate conscientiousness, Boswell's appointment as a delegate for Campbell also threatened trouble. Voters at an election, Boswell remembered too late, might be required to subscribe to the Formula, an oath intended to weed out Roman Catholics.   The oath was now very seldom put but, if it was, Boswell could not swear that he abhorred the doctrines of purgatory and the invocation of angels and saints. Yet if he did not swear to the Formula he was barred from ever voting at an election, and it would mean a complete breach with his father.   In fact, he thought he might as well leave Scotland since he would have no future there.   (It is characteristic of Boswell and perhaps to his credit that it never occurred to him to justify swearing falsely on the ground that his vote as a delegate was a formality.)   He considered excusing himself from attendance at the election or arranging secretly with the opposition not to put the Formula, but decided in the end to take his chances.   When 31 October, the day of the poll, came and no one suggested the Formula, Boswell felt "like a man relieved from hanging over a precipice by a slight rope."   Celebration followed victory, and he retired to bed at nine that night, fully intoxicated.

The Eatanswill kind of electioneering Boswell had been engaged in was sufficient excuse for drinking, but the election faded into the past and the drinking went on.   Early one night in November Boswell, drunk, fell heavily down the steep, narrow steps of Advocates' Close, escaping with a badly bruised heel.   On the day before Christmas (ostentatiously not a holiday in contemporary Scotland), he got drunk with two Irish army officers and wandered into the mean lodgings of two whores, though he was not drunk enough to "venture" with them.   He admitted to himself that he loved drams like a savage, and told others that of all human arts he valued distilling the most.   People, in turn, were beginning to say that he drank hard pretty often.

It can be stated at this point that Boswell never would become an alcoholic nor even a solitary drinker, and though drinking sometimes interfered with his daily practice it never impeded his legal career.   Nor was he unusual: Edinburgh was full of hard-drinking advocates, the circulation of the bottle ranking with the cultivation of the soil as the two favourite pastimes of the Scottish gentry.   Nor would drinking keep him from finishing his two greatest books, with the extended daily labour they required.

But Boswell, to apply Johnson's phrase, was a man "without skill in inebriation."   He tended to get drunk quickly and then stay at the same level of intoxication for some time; if he went on for too long he either lost all control or blacked out.   Aware that he was using liquor more and more as a release from his boredom with daily life, Boswell reacted by swearing reform and reprobating his conduct in his journal.   But these gestures did not satisfy him.   His common but unfortunate mistake was to take drinking as a cause rather than a symptom of malaise, and while his concern about it was serious, his treatment was characteristic: he began to keep tabs on himself by noting each day how much he drank and what effect it had on him.

Still, Boswell's mood and prospects were generally good.   He had suffered a brief recurrence of the free will-determinism impasse—"the subject," he wrote, "which most of all has perplexed and distressed me at different periods of my life"—and a twinge of long-absent hypochondria, but his spirits rose as the winter went on.   His practice was respectable, bringing in £300 a year, and the Lord President, to whom he refused to speak, praised his pleading in open court.   Also, as noted, Johnson had described him exactly as he could wish in his just published *Journey to the Western Islands of Scotland*.   Their names were now publicly and indissolubly linked.

One night that February Boswell summarized his situation.   The setting was a performance of *The Beggar's Opera*, his great early favourite, but Macheath's blackguard elegance no longer provided a fascinating model; instead, Boswell said of himself:

> I was cheerful and happy, having no pretensions, being very well established as an agreeable companion, and being a married man. . . .   I could not help indulging Asiatic ideas as I viewed such a number of pretty women, some of them young gay creatures with their hair dressed with flowers.   But thoughts of mortality and change came upon me, and then I was glad to feel indifference.

Jeunes filles en fleurs, and then admonitions of brief mortality.   "Asiatic ideas" is Boswell's shorthand for sexual variety in imitation of the Old Testament patriarchs, and these pleasing fantasies were pushing more and more to be put into practice.   Years of marriage had led to plain speaking. Margaret complained that he talked only childish nonsense to her, and he retorted that they were not temperamentally congenial.   As he wrote in his journal, "She has excellent sense and a cheerful temper . . . [but] no superstition, no enthusiasm, no vanity; so that to be free of a disagreeable contrariety, I may be glad to keep good humour in my mind by foolish sport."

Disparity in sexual drive was an even more basic cause of dispute. When Boswell finally told Margaret he must have a "concubine," she replied that he could go to whomever he pleased.   This was hardly a considered answer, and unsatisfactory in any case from Boswell's moral standpoint.

But the subject had been broached and he continued it in his journal, where he characterized himself as having "an exuberance of amorous faculties, quite corporeal and unconnected with affection and regard," while Margaret was "moderate and averse to much dalliance." He turned to Temple, his "priest":

> I am *too many*, as the phrase is, for one woman; and a certain transient connection, I am persuaded, does not interfere with that attachment which a man has for a *wife*, and which I have as much as any man that ever lived; though *some* of my qualifications are not valued by her as they have been by other women—ay, and well-educated women too. Concubinage is almost universal. If it was *morally* wrong, why was it permitted to the most pious men under the Old Testament? Why did our Saviour never say a word against it?

So much by way of preparation for this spring's jaunt to London, the letter to Temple just cited being written *en route*. London offered an abundance of lodgings: Paoli's mansion, which he declined in favour of a flat in Gerrard Street, Soho; a bed at the Dillys' in the Poultry when he was in the City; and later this spring for the first time a room in Johnson's house in Johnson's Court, Fleet Street, when he stayed late. He was invited to more dinners than he could eat, and caught up in delicious bustle.

Possibly because of his recent and much-discussed tilt with Macpherson over the authenticity of Ossian, Johnson was in a particularly contentious mood. From that quarrel which revealed a "Scotch conspiracy in national falsehood," he had turned to trample on the Americans. In his vehement pamphlet, *Taxation No Tyranny*, he united (so Boswell was to remark in the *Life*) "positive assertion, sarcastical severity, and extravagant ridicule, which he himself reprobated as a test of truth." He ran down *Gulliver's Travels*, dismissed Gray ("dull in a new way"), was even ingenious in attacking that easy target, Colley Cibber:

> It is wonderful that a man who for forty years had lived with the great and the witty should have acquired so ill the talents of conversation; and he had but half to furnish, for one half of what he said was oaths.

Nor did the Hanoverians escape: "George the First knew nothing, and desired to know nothing; did nothing, and desired to do nothing." When Reynolds remarked on "the extraordinary promptitude with which Johnson flew upon an argument," Boswell responded in one of his happier figures of speech: "Yes . . . he has no formal preparation, no flourishing with his sword; he is through your body in an instant."

All this, of course, was only one side of Johnson. He could also be generous in his praise of Garrick's prologues, secretive about his dried orange peel, blunt (according to the dramatist Arthur Murphy) in declaring that the greatest pleasure in life was fucking. Meanwhile Boswell continued to observe him closely. It is in the account for this year that Boswell makes his most famous remark about biographical method:

> I am so nice in recording him that every trifle must be authentic.
> I draw him in the style of a Flemish painter. I am not satisfied
> with hitting the large features. I must be exact as to every hair,
> or even every spot on his countenance.

The grandeur of generality is necessary but not sufficient; character must emerge from detailed reporting, especially of conversation. Yet even Boswell realized that "it is impossible to put down an exact transcript of conversation with all its little particulars. It is impossible to clap the mind upon paper as one does an engraved plate, and to leave the full, vivid impression." But he can preserve impressions that rise into characterization, such as Davies's remark that Johnson laughed like a rhinoceros. And he can hit off "the large features," the broad strokes of character— Johnson's "deliberate and strong utterance," his lack of physical fear—and worries much less about them.

Boswell's skill at moving back and forth between detail and generalization, between presentation and comment, shows in a vignette of Johnson in conversation with a protégé, a printer's apprentice, better narrated in the journal than in the *Life*. Johnson intends to give the boy a guinea, and has him called down to the backyard of the establishment. "There," says Boswell,

> I had an example of what I have heard Mr. Johnson profess, that
> he talks alike to all. "Some people," said he, "tell you that they
> let themselves down to the capacity of their hearers. I never do
> that, Sir. Let a man speak intelligibly and uniformly." . . . "Well,
> my boy," said he, "how do you go on?" "Pretty well, Sir. But
> they are afraid I an't strong enough for some parts of the work."
> johnson. "Why, I shall be sorry for it; for when you consider
> with how little mental power and corporeal labour a printer can
> get a guinea a week, it is a very desirable business for you." (The
> words were pretty exactly these; and the little, short, thick-legged,
> snivelling urchin, as one may say, was shaking himself and rubbing
> his pockets, while Johnson rolled superb.) "Do you hear—take

all the pains you can; and if this does not do, we must think of some other way of life for you.   There's a guinea."

As Boswell's ideas of representing Johnson come more clearly into focus, he starts to reach out for other views of him.   Johnson stimulated figurative description: to Davies's remark about his rhinoceros-like laugh, Boswell later added Orme's comment that Johnson's mind rolled and polished thoughts as the ocean polishes pebbles, and Pembroke's that "Johnson's sayings would not appear so extraordinary were it not for his *bow-wow way*."   The Thrales were collecting anecdotes of Johnson, and Boswell told himself,

> I must try to get this *Thralian* miscellany to assist me in writing Mr. Johnson's life if Mrs. Thrale does not intend to do it herself. I suppose there will be many written.

This prize he would never be able to secure, but he could record Garrick's wonderful mimicry of his old master, "repeating with pauses and half-whistlings interjected,

> Os homini sublime dedit—caelumque tueri
> Jussit—et erectos ad sidera—tollere vultus;[1]

looking downwards all the time and, while pronouncing the four last words, absolutely touching the ground with a kind of contorted gesticulation." Sometimes his investigation of Johnson past and present met the subject's resentment; "When Boswell gets wine," Johnson told Langton, "his conversation consists all of questions."

Boswell asked questions on his own account also, in his pursuit of happiness (to use a contemporary phrase).   He longed for a system to counterbalance his temperament: "I am a being very much consisting of feelings.   I have some fixed principles.   But my existence is chiefly conducted by the powers of fancy and sensation."   Obsessed with Pope's "Man never is, but always to be, blest," he asked Johnson, "Is a man *never* happy for the present?" and was told, "Never but when he's drunk."   Boswell had been busy testing that road to happiness.   On one occasion late in March, Garrick told him he was "drunk as *muck*," and a few days later he went drunk to The Club, attacked Johnson boisterously for attending a play he could neither see nor hear, and harassed Charles James Fox with "vinous compliments" until Fox moved to another part of the table.

Bacchus had his usual companion, whom Boswell calls here "*vaga Venus*"

---

[1]"He gave man an uplifted face, made him look at the sky, and hold his countenance erect towards the stars" (Ovid, *Metamorphoses*, i. 85–86, "tueri" for "videre").

(roving Venus), the ladies of the town.   He told Temple that desire rose only when he had "too much claret, and then there is a *furor brevis* as dangerous as anger" (an enlightening analogy); he asked Temple unsuccessfully to give him "a plenary indulgence . . . for Asiatic multiplicity." Restrained by fear of disease, he ordinarily did not risk completion.   One hungover morning he wanted Venus to come to the aid of Bacchus: he sallied forth in vain search of a beautiful Devonshire wench he had recently been lasciviously fond of (his phrase), hoping, as many have, that "by dalliance" he "might divert the uneasiness of yesterday's debauch."

These pleasures are picturesque, but they were largely divagations in Boswell's busy round; he lived at a much faster pace in London than in Edinburgh, filled with a "heat of blood, vigour of nerves, and fever of spirits," seized with an avidity to put as much as possible into a day until it burst.   Nor did this highly social existence keep him from business: his fees covered all but £20 of this year's jaunt.   His main occupation, though, was reminding his princely friends, Queensberry, Mountstuart, and Douglas of his need for a government post or sinecure.   As well, he started to eat the set number of meals at the Inner Temple necessary to qualify him for admission to the English bar.

Another ardently cultivated princely friend was Henry Herbert, tenth Earl of Pembroke—charming, easy, clever, the authority on manège, and a completely unscrupulous gallant—who finally took some persistent hints and invited Boswell with Paoli to Wilton.   But lack of anticipated grandeur accentuated Boswell's usual distaste for the country, and after a day or two he was so gloomy he could hardly speak.   He pressed on, however, to Temple's vicarage at Mamhead, Devon, where bread and milk, with warm water to wash his feet, restored him so that he slept placidly under Temple's rather humble roof.   Here, beneath a venerable yew, he pledged sobriety (not more than six glasses of wine at a time).

Back in London a week later—we are now at the beginning of May— he shifted to Paoli's house, which was to remain his London headquarters over the years until he acquired a house of his own.   Another fine two weeks, including visits to the Thrales at Streatham and a little excursion to Beauclerk's splendid country place near Highgate, and he was on his way back to Edinburgh in almost as good spirits as on his way down.   Prompted by Margaret and Johnson, he took a present for his stepmother. He also took with him Johnson's advice: read more and drink less.

But Edinburgh was beyond any such feeble remedy.   It was a physical shock, which brought out Boswell's every weakness and anxiety.   The summer session of the Court (12 June to 12 August 1775) was the flattest two months of existence he could remember.   It was worse than that.   The immediate causes of distress, he told Temple, were "the unpleasing tone, the rude familiarity, the barren conversation of those whom I found here, in comparison with what I had left"; he was reduced to "a coarse labourer in an obscure corner."   But Boswell summarizes his complaints better than a biographer can:

> My father's coldness to me, the unsettled state of our family affairs, and the poor opinion which I had of the profession of a lawyer in Scotland, which consumed my life in the mean time, sunk my spirits woefully; and for some of the last weeks of the session I was depressed with black melancholy.   Gloomy doubts of a future existence harassed me.   I thought myself disordered in mind.

Another letter to Temple expands the last points:

> While afflicted with melancholy, all the doubts which have ever disturbed thinking men come upon me.   I awake in the night, dreading annihilation or being thrown into some horrible state of being.

These letters to Temple are pleas for support, as Boswell is unable to focus the sources of his deep depression, to get beyond the symptoms.   Yet he toiled on, his fees amounting that summer to a prosperous £125, and in what must have been an attempt to relieve gloom he embarked on a dangerous flirtation with a handsome, gay widow, Elizabeth Grant of Ballindalloch.   His comment needs no gloss:

> My notions of intercourse between the two sexes are perhaps too licentious.   I am somewhat of a Solomon in that.   But, without any argument, it is clearly wrong for me to let my *affection* be at all carried away from my wife and children.

Fortunately the Widow Grant's ill-breeding revealed itself and disgusted him.

Boswell tried other remedies for melancholy: medicine, in case he was suffering from a physical disorder; and a set of chemistry lectures by the great Joseph Black, which bored him and served to revive an old feeling of inadequacy: "I have never been properly disposed to acquire any regular stock of knowledge."   One lapse into intoxication led to his prim comment, "the drunken manners of this country are very bad."   But on the whole he stuck to sobriety.

His father and the law remained too much for him.   Lord Auchinleck was highly dissatisfied with Boswell for "wandering" to London, as well as with Margaret for having encouraged (so he maintained) Boswell's idle and

extravagant conduct, and he started to exert financial pressure by withholding one-third of Boswell's £300 allowance.   When the Court of Session
rose, the clouds immediately began to recede, but the respite was brief.
A dismal week in late summer at Auchinleck is again plainly summarized
in a letter to Temple:

> It is hardly credible how difficult it is for a man of my sensibility
> to support existence in the family where I now am.   My father . . .
> has a method of treating me which makes me *feel* myself like a
> *timid boy*, which to *Boswell* (comprehending all that my character
> does, in my own imagination and in that of a wonderful number
> of mankind) is intolerable.   His wife too . . . is so narrow-minded,
> and . . . so set upon keeping him totally under her own manage-
> ment, and so suspicious and so sourishly tempered, that it requires
> the utmost exertion of practical philosophy to keep myself quiet.
> I, however, have done so all this week to admiration, nay, I have
> appeared good-humoured; but it has cost me drinking a consid-
> erable quantity of strong beer to dull my faculties.

Still, the Place was really princely, and Boswell believed, or hoped, that he
perceived some dawning of pleasure in the country; at worst, he would
force a taste for rural beauties.   But he was at a stalemate with his father;
though "I am doing beyond his utmost hopes," Boswell said, Lord
Auchinleck declined to restore Boswell's renunciation of his birthright; in
return, Boswell refused to yield in the matter of the entail:

> There is a kind of heroism in it, but I have severe paroxysms of
> anxiety; and how unhappy it is for a man to have no security for
> what is dear to him but his father's death.

No wonder Boswell felt anxious.

I I

THEN THE BEGINNING of a new era.   Alexander, Boswell's first surviving
son and eventual heir, was born on 9 October 1775, being named according
to Scots custom after his paternal grandfather.   No event could be more
significant for the Family of Auchinleck which, Boswell needlessly reminded Temple, "is my supreme object in this world."   The congratulations poured in: Oglethorpe—what warm blood the old man had in him!—
wrote, "I rejoice to hear you have a son, and hope he was got with such a
gust of joy as may continue your spirit to the succeeding age"; Pringle
commented with amusement that Sandy's birth would preserve Auchinleck

from "saltatorian pollution."[1]   Since one child out of two died before the age of six mortality was a serious threat, but for the moment the continuity of the Family was secured.   It followed inevitably that the dispute over the entail—with its long history and extensive cast of characters—would come squarely to the front.   It will help to summarize this tangled dispute before its last stages are recounted.

Lord Auchinleck wanted to entail the estate, both the lands he had inherited and those he had acquired, on heirs whatsoever of his own body. To entail the inherited lands he needed Boswell's consent.   Theory and history, however, led Boswell to refuse.   He believed in the principle of male succession—he was to claim that he imbibed his fervour for it from his father—and he pointed to the example of David Boswell, the fifth laird, who had passed over his four daughters to leave an embarrassed estate to his nephew, Lord Auchinleck's grandfather.   Boswell wanted to reach back to entail the estate on heirs male of the founder of the Family, Thomas Boswell.   The dispute between him and his father was chronic and passionate.   Boswell had sworn a solemn oath (and oaths were not lightly taken) to his father in 1767 that if the estate were left to heirs whatsoever he would cut his own throat.   Two years later, his anger had turned outward: holding a piece of the Old Castle in his hands, he knelt upon its ruins and swore that if any but the rightful heir should hold the estate "this stone should swim in his heart's blood."   And he kept the stone.

Why entail the estate at all? The reason was shamefully obvious: Lord Auchinleck did not trust Boswell with it, and did not care if the world knew he did not trust him.   To repeat: in 1762, in exchange for an inalienable allowance of £100 a year (part of the £300 allowance he was now receiving), Boswell had signed an agreement which permitted his father to vest the estate in trustees after his death, Boswell to receive half the free rents and the right to reside at Auchinleck, but with no say in the management of the property.   This was the renunciation of his birthright that he was determined to repossess.   Presumably Lord Auchinleck intended the estate to descend to Boswell's sons or daughters, assuming that any survived him; one of his grandchildren might show the intelligence and prudence Lord Auchinleck despaired of finding in his own sons.

On the other hand, why did Boswell insist on balking his father's sensible arrangements?   Lord Auchinleck held almost all the cards, and he sat grim and poker-faced behind them.   Without question, he could

[1]Lord Auchinleck's version of the entail was meant to exclude a poor relation, David Boswell of Leith, who was a dancing-master.

do what he pleased with the extensive lands he himself had acquired, but over the years he had talked of selling off all the lands of Auchinleck or of disinheriting Boswell.   Better to snuff out a candle, he said, than to let it stink in its socket.   The vagueness of the threat did not make it less menacing; it increased the basic uneasiness Boswell felt every time he defied his father.   In particular he feared that if he tried a permanent move to London, his father would sell off the estate.   At the moment, as already mentioned, Lord Auchinleck was withholding one-third of his £300 allowance, which in turn was half his annual income; even with his full allowance Boswell could hardly make ends meet, and a financial crisis would soon be upon him.   Nor had his father yet agreed to make a settlement on Margaret and the children in case Boswell predeceased them.

The struggle drew in other members of the family.   The preceding winter, Commissioner Cochrane, Boswell's maternal grand-uncle and an old friend of Lord Auchinleck's, told Boswell rather confusingly that his father had entailed the old estate on heirs male of Boswell's great-grandfather, and these heirs would forfeit Lord Auchinleck's own acquisitions if any of them challenged this arrangement.   Boswell, though shaken, "remained firm for the support of the male succession . . . the only true representation of an ancient barony."   Alexander's birth roused him to seek support from the next heir male, his brother David (now Thomas David—or T.D.—in deference to the Spanish prejudice against Old Testament names): would he provide generously for Margaret and the children in case he succeeded to the estate through Boswell's firmness?   But T.D., ever prudent, was cautious about committing himself, and Boswell had to fight back the feeling that T.D. was too anxious about his own interest. When Boswell consulted his cousin Claud, for whose theoretical rights he thought he was fighting, he was advised without hesitation to give in to his father.   Claud, who was not too strong in the head, could be disregarded. But Margaret could not be, and she was violent: how could he subject his family to such awful financial risk for the sake of an abstract scruple?   It was plain she had not a spark of feudal enthusiasm.   Among his relations only his uncle, Dr. John, showed any sympathy and that hardly involved principle; he said that Lord Auchinleck "from his youth had been set on wealth and on his own personal consequence."

But how *could* he endanger his inheritance for a scruple?   Grant Boswell's pride of family, grant his patriarchal logic, and a zeal and energy still overflow on the question which could only have been aroused by his feelings about his father.   The root of Boswell's lack of self-confidence was his father's contempt and harshness.   That contempt showed itself most painfully in Lord Auchinleck's version of the entail. The son admires his father and looks for his love, yet needs to displace him; the most kindly way these desires can be reconciled is for the son to succeed naturally to his father's position. Sons today, we know, seldom follow their fathers' occupations as a matter of course, nor do many inherit large landed estates: succession tends to be a much more indirect affair. But Boswell was expected to step directly into his father's place as Laird of Auchinleck, and would quite likely, if he stuck to Scotland, become a Lord of Session in his turn. Now he was threatened with what was, in effect, castration.

Boswell's recourse was to appeal from the representative of the Family to the principle of Family. He often linked his melancholy temperament to that of his paternal grandfather (who, like himself, had not always been on good terms with Lord Auchinleck); at this crucial point he was reaching back to Thomas Boswell, the "very honourable founder" of the Family itself. His father was successful, formidable, cold, domineering; he could do what he wanted with his own acquisitions. But by entailing the estate on heirs whatsoever of his own body, he identified the Family with himself. This Boswell could not allow. His maleness, his integrity, his independence, and his inheritance were one to him. Whatever his father said or did, Boswell was himself a Boswell of Auchinleck and he must hold to the principle that male succession was impersonal.

Naturally the birth of Alexander shifted the perspectives of both grandfather and father. For Lord Auchinleck this promise of continuity must have made Boswell's argument for heirs male seem even more foolish than it had before. At the same time, Alexander's birth increased Boswell's importance, since it strongly suggested that the line of Boswell of Auchinleck would pass through him. For Boswell, Alexander's birth made the principle of male succession seem more speculative, though not less significant.

A financial crisis brought the dispute to a confrontation. Though Boswell's practice was going on satisfactorily, it could never bring in enough money to pay the £1,300 he still owed towards the purchase of the marshland of Dalblair in 1767, for which his father had co-signed. In November 1775 the Dalblair creditors asked for their principal. Lord Auchinleck offered to take over the property himself but Boswell demurred, wishing to figure in Family annals as having added to the estate. After a good deal of discussion Lord Auchinleck agreed to supply £1,000 at Candlemas (2 February 1776) towards payment, with an additional £200 to come out of Boswell's allowance.

This generous action provided an irresistible opportunity for whole-some admonition.   Lord Auchinleck began with Boswell's extravagance and then took him back over the Ayrshire election of 1774, blaming him for forsaking family connections, especially the Lord President.   Boswell saved his defence for his journal, where he rehearsed the shameful way in which his father had made him seem insignificant.   He could hardly have failed to contrast the backing the Lord President gave to his half-brother Henry Dundas with his father's treatment of him.   Inevitably a discussion of the entail followed.   For the first time Boswell learned directly from his father that he proposed to settle the estate on heirs whatsoever of his own body.   "Confounded," Boswell spoke a few words calmly in favour of male succession.

Clearly now Lord Auchinleck alternated between intervals of weakness, illness, sometimes forgetfulness—what Boswell calls "failure"—in which Boswell often found him "milder and more affectionate" than usual, and longer periods of comparative vigour in which for the most part Lord Auchinleck was chillingly indifferent to him.   On this occasion Boswell thought him gentler than usual, but when the subject of the entail was resumed on 27 December, Lord Auchinleck's chronic irritation erupted. First he threatened to cut Boswell's allowance to the minimum £100 a year, and second to have a trustee take over the debt for Dalblair, with Boswell thrown in gaol for non-payment.   Then the quarrel escalated:

> I was quite calm; told him that I had pursued the very plan of life[1] which he was anxious I should follow, though it was dis-agreeable to me; that I was doing very well, and that I did not expect such usage from him.   That if he would entail the estate on heirs male without stopping short and cutting off the descend-ants of Craigston[2] I would join with him; but that as he told me that he went no farther than the heirs male descending from my grandfather[3] and then went to heirs female, I thought the entail unjust and could not agree to it.   I unluckily mentioned something that Maclaurin had said.   This made my father worse.   He said, "I see you have been consulting lawyers.   I will guard against you."   And then he said, in a diabolical-like passion, "I shall put an end to it at once.   I shall sell it off and do with the money what I please."   He also threw out some morose, contemptuous[4] reflections: as if I thought myself a very wise man, and was the

[1]As an advocate.
[2]The dancing-master's line.
[3]Evidently something of a concession.
[4]As usual Boswell spells this word "contemptous," which presumably indicates his pro-nunciation of it.

reverse, and how I went to London among the *geniuses* who despised me.   He abused Dr. Johnson, and when I mentioned keeping up a connection with Lord Mountstuart treated him with contempt.   In short he was as bad as possible.   I told him he no doubt had it in his power to do as he threatened, but I wished he would think seriously if he could do so with a good conscience, and that there was a Father in Heaven to whom both of us were answerable.   He said that he himself would have settled the estate on my daughters, failing my sons, but that he had taken a race of heirs male to please me; that he believed I was the only man in Edinburgh who would insist to have his own children disinherited, but that I had no natural affection.   I was a good deal agitated inwardly.   He appeared truly odious as an unjust and tyrannical man.   I recollected Dr. Johnson's saying that he would as soon hang himself as sell his estate, but yet I could not be sure what he might do.   I however considered that I ought not to be accessory to injustice, to cutting off any of my brethren,[1] and that if he should even sell the estate, I could reflect that I had been firm in what I thought honest and honourable.   I pleased myself too with thinking that I might purchase the estate by the intervention of a friend, and so disappoint him totally.

"It was," Boswell concludes, "an abominable altercation," and feeling the strain he got drunk, followed women in the streets, fell and badly sprained his ankle.   Two days later he uttered a "wild speech" at Grange's which, as Grange predicted, he later repented.   He began to waver.   Investigation revealed that the estate handed over to his great-grandfather as heir male had been virtually bankrupt, and Boswell himself was floundering in embarrassed circumstances.   Margaret cleverly suggested that he could entail his own Dalblair on heirs male forever.   Now he decided that Johnson, the inevitable court of appeal, must be consulted; Margaret seized on the idea and wrote to him herself.   When the oracle replied that Boswell was under no moral obligation to preserve strict male succession, she shed tears of joy.   Lord Hailes concurred with Johnson.   Further investigation showed that Thomas Boswell had left his estate to heirs general, though Boswell found a precedent for his position in his great-grandfather's having left the estate to heirs male.   Pringle, asked to intervene, replied:

It is not in my power nor, I believe, in that of any third person's to mediate between you.   Who unasked by a father, and such a one of yours (used to direct, and not to be directed, and justly conscious of his own good intellects), will take upon them to tell

[1]All heirs male (*Life*, ii. 417 n.—2–3 Feb. 1776).

him that he ought to give his son a larger allowance; that he ought to love him more; show him more countenance; and indulge him with his approbation in leaving his wife and family to spend his time more agreeably in the metropolis for two months every year; much less in quitting his country to live here upon an uncertain prospect of subsistence.

Boswell's feudal enthusiasm continued essentially undiminished, and as theory it would never diminish.   Still, three men whose opinions he highly respected had told him that his scruples were unnecessary and even silly.   He dodged a bit more: when the Dalblair creditors pressed for payment in February, he asked their trustee, John McAdam of Craigengillan, a wealthy friend of the family, to interpose, but he was catching at a straw.   Quite apart from the practical situation, since Boswell claimed he was basing his position on a "sacred trust" for which the evidence looked increasingly shaky, and his feelings were inadmissible evidence, he began to reconcile himself to what seemed immediately desirable as well as unavoidable.

Under this trial, Boswell's actions and moods were more or less predictable.   Another outbreak of gambling, one night playing whist until Lawrie, his clerk, found the group "sitting like wizards" at seven in the morning; they played on until nine when Boswell had to appear in court. Occasional drunkenness with unfortunate results:

> . . . when I got into the street I grew very drunk and miserably sick, so that I had to stop in many closes in my way home, and when I got home I was shockingly affected, being so furious that I took up the chairs in the dining-room and threw them about and broke some of them, and beat about my walking-stick till I had it in pieces, and then put it into the fire and burnt it.   I have scarcely any recollection of this horrid scene, but my wife informed me of it.   She was in great danger, for it seems I had aimed at her both with chairs and stick.   What a monstrous account of a man!   She got me to bed, where I was excessively sick.

So much for the pledge taken under the venerable yew at Mamhead.   But rather less drinking than might be anticipated, and what Boswell drank upset him:

> I found that my constitution was quite unfit for the least excess in wine, for although I had but the smallest share of three bottles of claret among four, I was feverish and even sick.

The drinking and fits of rage naturally caused marital stress.   Margaret could be very critical of Boswell's drinking in low company and gambling till late hours, though she seems not to have cherished any exalted notions of reforming him; indeed Boswell remarks, "she is wonderfully easy in forgetting my bad conduct." She would, however, insist on staying up anxiously all night when he was out, which occasioned a good deal of self-reproach.   But Boswell devised a more severe test of her devotion to him: she came across his journal with its record of renewed philandering (perhaps with Sandy's nurse), which was easily decipherable in spite of its use of Greek letters (e.g., προμισεδ for "promised").   "She spoke to me of it," says Boswell,

> with so much reason and spirit that, as I candidly owned my folly, so I was impressed with proper feelings; and, without more argument than that it was disagreeable to so excellent a spouse, resolved firmly to keep clear.

He thought himself lucky to have been caught before proceeding further in mischief, and had taken care he would be caught.

To have so excellent a spouse is in itself a problem.   Boswell was so aware of Margaret's virtues—common sense, forthrightness, cheerfulness, forbearance—and of her love for him that he found it difficult to let himself criticize her in return.   At most he could accuse her of being insufficiently respectful or of not paying enough attention to his moods.   Clearly these complaints were inadequate to express the depth of resentment he sometimes felt towards her, and at his worst he took to tantrums: one night after a trifling dispute, he "started up and threw an egg in the fire and some beer after it"; he said he felt like breaking and destroying everything. She supports him emotionally against his father but she doesn't *see*—who can?—why he is so set against the proposed entail.   In turn, unable to blame her except when drunk or in a sudden moment of anger, he almost always feels himself in the wrong.   It is not surprising he thought himself unfit to be a married man:

> My good practice is never of sufficiently long continuance to have a stable consistency.   It is shaken loose by occasional repetitions of licentiousness.   The wounds of vice break out afresh.

In every direction, Boswell burst out in self-denunciation:

> I am sensible that I am deficient in judgement, in good common sense.   I ought therefore to be diffident and cautious.   For some time past I have indulged coarse raillery and abuse by far too much.

> There is an imperfection, a superficialness, in all my notions.

I understand nothing clearly, nothing to the bottom.   I pick up
fragments, but never have in my memory a mass of any size.   I
wonder really if it be possible for me to acquire any one part of
knowledge fully.   I am a lawyer.   I have no system of law.   I
write verses.   I know nothing of the art of poetry.

One can be sure that Boswell was a better lawyer than poet, but even
if he is responding to a puritanical conscience, no man who records such
opinions of himself needs anyone else to write him down.   He is expressing,
of course, his father's view of him, and he feels particularly shaky as a
lawyer where the contrast between them is most naked.   In spite of his
busy practice, better than last winter's, and occasional moments when he
recognizes he has done a good job, his dominant mood is one of incapacity:
"I had a poor opinion of my own qualifications as an advocate, but reproached myself inwardly with want of application to the study of the law."
Mea culpa.   Yet the same day he expresses this gloomy view of his abilities,
he received eight guineas in fees.

And his law practice went on amidst the *sturm und drang*.   At the time
of Reid's trial he had taken a few moments to try to rescue Henry
McGraugh, an Irish vagrant who was given to ordering food and drink in
taverns without being able to pay.   Twice he had been haled before the
Town Council and twice expelled from Edinburgh, but McGraugh could
not change his *modus operandi*.   On his third offence, the public prosecutor
asked that McGraugh be whipped through the city and imprisoned; Boswell
submitted a bill of suspension, the prosecutor reclaimed (replied), Crosbie
answered; and McGraugh stayed in the Edinburgh Tolbooth where, according to the aptly named turnkey, Richard Lock, he was a terror not
only to the other prisoners but also to the keepers.   Because of his long
confinement he was released at the beginning of February 1775, and dis-
appears from the scene, to be recalled only in Henry Erskine's *Patrick
O'Connor's Advice to Henry McGraugh* in which he is enjoined to become
counsellor, deacon, or bailie:

> Then each day you may guzzle, at the city's expense,
> Without Crosbie or Boswell to plead your defence.
> If you can't, my dear creature, to Ireland be gone;
> For the magistrates here hate all rogues but their own.

Most of Boswell's cases, of course, involved the predictable litigation
of landlords and tenants, debtors and creditors, family or business disputes.
Occasionally the issues become slightly more unusual: what are the per-
quisites of army officers (Rickson v. Bird); could a man ten-and-a-half
months dead have fathered an infant (Jack v. Copland); is a smuggler

entitled to relief for imprisonment for debt (Dick v. His Creditors)?   Three good burghers of Stirling were foolish enough to put in writing their agreement to divide the spoils of the Town Council (Paterson v. Alexander). The minister of Dunfermline was sued by parishioners whom he had attacked, under provocation, from the pulpit; one of them rose after the sermon to ask "what bribe he had received for telling so many lies from the chair of verity?" (Scotlands v. Thomson).   Poor Dr. Memis sued the managers of the Aberdeen Infirmary because, in a translation of their charter, they had called him "doctor of medicine" instead of "physician" like everyone else.   Some vanished nuance of medical malice was involved, but Memis's case was found trifling and he had to pay £40 expenses.   In the summer session of 1776, there would be Hope v. Tweedie.   Plaintiff and defendant had bet a pipe (105 gallons) of port, worth £40, as to which could walk to Edinburgh first from Tweedsmuir in Peeblesshire, a distance of thirty-six miles.   Tweedie, a large man, started well but gave up within five miles and said the bet was a joke, while Hope walked the distance and demanded payment.   The Court of Session thought the case irritatingly frivolous, Kames snarling that the next time there was a dispute at whist and Hoyle failed, would the Bench be called upon to decide it? Hope lost.

On 4 March 1776, for the first time since Reid's trial eighteen months earlier, Boswell defended a client in the Court of Justiciary.   Andrew Gibson, merchant (smuggler), *et al.* were accused of assaulting an excise officer, James Lawson, while in the performance of his duty the previous May.   Lawson had chased down the highway, imprudently single-handed, after Gibson and his friends, attempting to examine and confiscate smuggled goods.   Then the chase turned around; a number of the gang caught up with Lawson and beat him into insensibility.   None of numerous witnesses, however, could swear as to exactly who had struck Lawson, and the prosecution admitted that the chief suspect was still at large.   Excise officers were highly unpopular, as Robert Burns, himself one, made plain in his song, *The De'il's Awa wi' th' Exciseman*, and though human agency admittedly was involved in this instance, the panels were acquitted.   That evening at Princes Street Coffee-house the three advocates for the defence (Boswell, Crosbie, and Maclaurin) celebrated by sketching songs for a work to become known as *The Justiciary Opera*, which looks back to Gay's *Beggar's Opera* and forward to Gilbert and Sullivan.   Much altered and extended it was to be sung by generations of Edinburgh advocates.   A sample will give the idea (one must imagine the stage business, the judges holding up their gowns as they caper about):

Caliendrosus Maximus (*chief judge*):
> A plague o' such juries, they make such a pother,
> And thus, by their folly, let panels go free;
> And still on some silly pretext or another,
> Nothing is left for your Lordships and me.

[*Chorus:*]
> Our duty, believe us,
> Was not quite so grievous,
> While yet we had hopes for to hang 'em up all;
> But now they're acquitted,
> O how we're outwitted;
> We've sat eighteen hours here for nothing at all.

This evening of high spirits may seem an isolated spark in the midst of the frustration, anger, and self-misgiving which pervaded Boswell's life that winter, but such an impression derives from the necessity of imposing some narrative coherence on his career.   Even so, it comes as a surprise to find him remarking (14 January 1776) on a review of his journal that he is pleased on the whole with his existence.   It is the biographer's despair that Boswell's fluctuations in mood so faithfully resemble those found in many other lives.   The novelist can depict his protagonist as habitually strong or yielding, animated with heroism or descending with even steps the road to ruin; the biographer is at the mercy of his subject.

For all his self-doubt, Boswell was remarkably resilient.   He resists despair, cheering himself with various schemes of improvement: he will study chemistry while "at stool"; he and Harry Erskine will correct grammatical errors and Scotticisms in each other's law papers.   Especially he will write.   The previous winter he had suggested to Lords Covington and Kames that he write their lives; now he was meditating biographies of Hume and of his long-time friend, Sir Alexander Dick.   (What a wonderful series Boswell's *Lives of Old Men* would have been!)

But his projects were not all biographical: if only in passing, he entertained the idea of writing an essay on the law.   (That it so seldom occurred to him to write on the law shows how he felt about his profession.) He also suggested to himself histories of Ayrshire and of the Isle of Man. That winter he considered a didactic novel to be called "Memoirs of a Practical Metaphysician," demonstrating the extravagant variations of a life led according to abstract rather than practical principles.   The projects tumble out but, except for the one great scene he was to record in his journal for his "Life of Hume," they produced nothing; as he had told Temple the previous year, he could not "fix."

Throughout these years, then, Boswell restricted himself to occasional periodical contributions.   He versified his strongly pro-American feelings in *The Boston Bill: A Ballad*, and in *The Long Island Prisoners: An Irregular Ode*—newspaper fillers.   The metaphorical terms in which he saw this struggle reveal his outlook: Britain and its Colonies, he told Temple, were like father and son; and he wrote in a "Rampager" that the Americans could not be reduced to *"infantine dependence* on their mother."   He also contributed to the *London Chronicle* a fine, if unprophetic, account of Joseph Brant (Thayendanegea), the Mohawk chief, then being wooed in London to attack the Colonists: "His manners are gentle and quiet. . . .   He affords a very convincing proof of the tameness which education can produce upon the wildest race."   Brant was to lead the Indian contingent in the Cherry Valley (New York) massacre of 1778.

But Boswell's spirits sank as he came under increasing pressure to agree to his father's version of the entail.   One night he dreamt that his father had died; he woke up crying, but his father's indifference to him in court the next day froze his affection.   A few days later, distressed by the demands for payment of the Dalblair creditors, he even swore at Margaret, a sure sign (he said) that his mind was much disturbed.   Of course he could get angry at her; she would continue to love him.   Another time, in a temper, he threw a guinea note into the fire, but had sense enough to retrieve it.   His complaints became general: "Law business consumes my time, and indolence wastes it."   He went so far as to tell his father that he had freed himself from his scruples about remote heirs male, but told himself that the signing of the entail could wait until after he got back from London and the fuss that trip would cause.

A sudden political commotion put Boswell's relationship with his father in a new perspective.   Henry Dundas's influence had spread into Fife where a by-election was being held.   Its outcome hinged on the validity, now at issue in the Court of Session, of the vote of a Captain Dalrymple, who supported the anti-Dundas candidate.   Lord Auchinleck, who held the casting vote on the Bench, seemed to say in his opinion that Dalrymple's qualification was inadequate, but voted to sustain it.   Dundas, now Lord Advocate (the highest law officer in Scotland), "was indecently extravagant in his gestures," and told Boswell how sorry he was he would have to tell the House of Commons that Lord Auchinleck had spoken in one way and voted in another.   Lord Auchinleck pooh-poohed the dispute, but Boswell, who must have remembered young William Miller's behaviour, felt promptings to challenge Dundas to a duel, especially since there was a good deal of talk about his father's inconsistency.   The gain in the situation was evident: Boswell was forced to defend his father's honour against the assault of his father's great friends, the Dundases.   But there was also a concrete possibility of loss, and Boswell went sleepless one night in fear of exposing his life and perhaps leaving his wife and children in a disconsolate situation.

I I I

EVEN AT THAT, Boswell could more easily challenge Dundas than Lord Auchinleck, in particular when it was a question of his spring jaunt to London.   This year he tried a new tack; surprisingly but shrewdly, he asked Lady Auchinleck to intervene for him.   In a long tête-à-tête they had what today would be called a frank exchange of views, which momentarily dispelled mutual suspicion, and she agreed to prepare her husband for the news of Boswell's departure.   But Boswell's nerve failed him, and instead of calling on his father he wrote a note to him urging his usual reasons (legal practice, the need for keeping in touch with friends in high places) and a return of melancholy requiring relaxation (not a motive to impress his father) as his excuses for going to London.   Early the next morning (11 March 1776) he sneaked off, berating himself for timidity and declaring, "What misery does a man of sensibility suffer!"

And what pleasures does he enjoy!   Sunshine broke in upon his mind— as Johnson had predicted—as soon as he left Edinburgh.   London was more than a vacation, a reprieve from signing the entail; it was "happiness without alloy."   Pringle, a man of the world, assured him that a duel with Dundas would be quixotic, and Johnson concurred, so the major worry Boswell had brought with him melted away.   For the moment he had given up his English bar scheme, convinced of its impracticability by Pringle's cold calculations of what it would cost him financially to settle in London, but he had real hopes of obtaining something through Mountstuart's "noble Tory interest."   Mountstuart was making his bid as a statesman: he was pushing a popular issue, a Scots Militia Bill (for fear of Jacobite sympathizers the Scots were not allowed to maintain a militia), and, if he could unify all the politicians who disliked Dundas and his set, would have a strong chance to become an important leader in Scotland.

Casting Mountstuart in his old involuntary role of Maecenas—"You know how I delight in patronage," he told Temple—Boswell threw himself into the cause, took down Mountstuart's speech on the Bill from his dictation, and sat up all night copying it (as he finished he could see coaches from a masquerade rolling home in the early morning light).   Earlier, he had thought of writing a pamphlet on the Militia Bill; now he considered a pro-Mountstuart pamphlet to be called "The Present Political State of Scotland."

It was essential for Boswell to get an independency, a post paying a few hundred a year, while Lord Auchinleck was still alive, not merely because he wanted to get free from his father but because once he inherited Auchinleck he could not claim a pressing need for money. And Maecenas did make gestures, talked to the Duke of Queensberry, who was to talk to the Prime Minister, Lord North. As in 1775 there was discussion of a specific sinecure, Baron Maule's place as Clerk to the Register of Sasines, which brought in a useful £200 a year. But this discussion seems to have taken place in a vacuum. Boswell had been waiting all his adult life for Queensberry to do something for him, and the Duke had never done anything but be civil. Now Boswell found him "cold and indifferent and unmeaning." He did not bother to speak to North; nor was there any reason to believe that Maule would resign without a *quid pro quo*.

Yet at the same time Boswell was pursuing his sinecure he felt impelled to condemn such aspirations in a letter to the *London Chronicle* signed "Borax":

> I will venture to say that the expectation of a paltry office of a hundred a year is sufficient to limit the views of a man of this country,[1] who has received the best university education which it can afford.

But Boswell saw no contradiction: as will appear later, he would not behave like these other gentlemen; he would take the sinecure as his due and maintain his independence.

Boswell's best remaining hope was that Mountstuart would be successful in his political ambitions; that could open up a number of possibilities. Brought up to believe that a brilliant career was his for the asking, Mountstuart was wealthy, handsome, and reasonably intelligent; but he was also narcissistic, snobbish, and by his own admission indolent. Boswell had early noted his love of looking at himself in the mirror; an observer many years afterwards, remarking on his stately deportment and polished manners, went on to comment: "His sense of heraldic glories was acute and exquisite; they formed one of his principal studies and were almost his dearest delight." There was something of Baron Thunder-ten-tronckh in him. The intense pleasures of contemplating person and ancestry did not leave much time for playing the politician. Speaking "quite in the

[1]Scotland.

style of a prince," he told Boswell that he did not consult the Scottish M.P.'s about alterations in the Militia Bill; he summoned them to his house and told them what the alterations were to be.   Boswell was all admiration and Dundas must have laughed; that was no way to manage these gentlemen. The Bill failed, and Mountstuart became Baron Cardiff in the peerage of Great Britain with a seat in the House of Lords, whose dignity was much more appropriate to his character and station in life than the hurly-burly of the House of Commons.   Boswell begged his portrait, which was kindly bestowed on him.

The only solid consequence of Boswell's attempts to advance himself this spring was that Douglas himself suggested that he be made one of his counsel in the protracted litigation, now before the House of Lords, on the Douglas estate.   "Much in liquor," Boswell called to thank him, "or rather," he continues, "I believe, praised it as what was due to me."

Boswell's connections with the Great were invigorating, but they did not constitute what he called "pleasure."   That meant sex, and Boswell recurred to the topic compulsively in conversation with Johnson: the "mechanical reason" for marriage, debauchery, adultery.   He continued to talk to himself about casual whoring ("occasional transient connections with loose women") and, advised by Johnson to occupy his mind by taking an interesting course in some subject—chemistry, rope-dancing, whatever— thought of a course in concubinage.   That idea he was afraid to mention, but when he ventured Dr. John Boswell's antinomian opinion that the Christian religion prescribed no fixed rules for intercourse between the sexes, Johnson replied, "There is no trusting to that crazy piety."   Boswell, humbled, made up for it the same night by kissing a pretty servant in the garret of Johnson's own house in Lichfield.

As this example suggests, Boswell's conduct varied with situation and opportunity.   With Mrs. Stuart, his confidante on such delicious subjects as adultery, he continued an open and archly self-conscious flirtation; with the nineteen-year-old Countess of Eglinton (her husband was thirty years her senior), a furtive but still innocent one under the pretext of warning her against Lord Pembroke.   She seems to have been naïve, sentimental, and pretty; Boswell gave her a lock of his hair in exchange for a kiss.   As soon as he arrived in London he renewed sexual relations with an unnamed lady, who may be the No. 36 (a street number?) mentioned in his 1778 journal, who perhaps in turn was his old flame Mrs. Love.   Whoever she was, she gave solid satisfaction.   He dallied with some whores and lay with others; he even indulged in "a kind of license I never had" (the nature of which has been deleted by recent censorship).

Yet desire outran possibility; the will is infinite but the act a slave to limit. There were bad moments when he was "cold and disturbed and dreary and vexed, with remorse rising like a black cloud without any distinct form," when he appeared one of those whom St. Paul represents "as working all uncleanness with greediness." But the main consequences of pleasure were that he "began again to imagine that irregularity of commerce between the sexes was a trivial offence," and a *morbus* (venereal disease).

At the same time, Boswell was drinking so much that Paoli lectured him "genteelly" about it; he promised to give up liquor for a year and managed it for a month: plagued by Garrick and others to drink—Garrick told him he looked so ghastly that the crows would follow him—he got a dispensation to drink three glasses of wine at a time. "I was really growing a drunkard," he told Temple.

Since Boswell himself makes so much of his drinking and sexual roaming about, it is easy to over-emphasize them in discussing his character. Victorian biographers euphemized their subjects' weaknesses; modern biographers often seem discontented unless they can condescend to the vices and follies of the persons they are discussing. Yet a commentary that attacked Byron, for example, for his sexual activities (so much more piquant than Boswell's) would be thought foolish and irrelevant; as a Satanic hero, Byron sinned on a grand scale. One might as well blame Napoleon for being a lover of war. And Burns's rabbiting around seems merely the play of a free spirit. What opens Boswell to condemnation are his fits of repentance, his attempts and failures at lasting reform, the gaps between his theory and practice. We can blame him, if we must, because he blames himself. But Boswell's behaviour, his drinking and womanizing, was as commonplace in his time as it is today. Anyone, of course, can confer a moral mark on Boswell, but it seems more useful to consider what parts alcohol and sex played in his psychic economy.

London made Boswell hyperactive. "Every time I have been in London," he says, "I have insensibly overheated my mind by the rapidity of amusement." Release, both imaginative and physical, was essential after long months of repression in Scotland under the supervision of his formidable father and loving wife. His life is fluid; he responds with verve to his broken-up days in London, which were in such contrast to the routine that he needed to sustain him in Edinburgh and which, sooner or later, he always found disgusting. As well, he is taken far more at his own estimate in London, and as his self-confidence grows his moral scruples

weaken.   Yet he does not find this change in image totally convincing.
He writes:

> It is hard that the difference between my father and me checks
> my aspiring and extending spirit. . . .   I should not wonder so
> much at being well treated, for although educated very narrowly,
> and still depressed by my father from mistake, I ought to remem-
> ber that my character as a man of parts and extensive acquaintance
> makes people fond of my attention.

But he does sometimes wonder, he does not always remember: he has
something to prove to himself.   Part of the proof comes in explosions of
energy, fuelled by the release of desire in its triumph over restraint; and
the resulting fullness and intensity of sensation make Boswell feel alive.
To give this feeling permanence he is driven to writing down his experiences:

> I should live no more than I can record, as one should not have
> more corn growing than one can get in.   There is a waste of good
> if it be not preserved.

An odd remark perhaps, but it states Boswell's ruling passion.   Sober and
chaste he might have led, on balance, a happier life; he would certainly
have reproached himself much less and caused much less pain to others,
especially Margaret.   But he would have paid a high price in depression,
and might well have lacked the vitality to write the *Life of Johnson*.
    And Johnson is one of the principal keys to Boswell's exuberance,
because their love for each other allowed Boswell to approve of and love
himself.   Boswell's reaction on first meeting Johnson this spring is characteristic.   Johnson was with the Thrales in Southwark, and Boswell hastened to breakfast there:

> I was kindly welcomed.   In a moment he was in a full glow of
> conversation, and I felt myself elevated as if brought into another
> state of being.   Mrs. Thrale and I looked to each other while he
> talked, and our looks expressed our congenial admiration and
> affection for him. . . .   I exclaimed to her, "I am now, intellec-
> tually, *Hermippus redivivus*;[1] I am quite restored by him, by trans-
> fusion of *mind*."   "There are many (she replied) who admire and
> respect Mr. Johnson; but you and I *love* him."

Johnson was not merely to be respected, admired, loved, but to be
observed, tested, manipulated.   Boswell observed him on two jaunts that

---

[1]"Hermippus revived."   Boswell alludes to a work which argued that a man's life might
be lengthened to 115 years by inhaling the breath of healthy young women (*Life*, ii. 427 n. 4).

spring, one to the Midlands (Oxford, Birmingham, Lichfield, and Ash-bourne), where Johnson moved in silhouette against his native background; and the other a quick visit to Bath and Bristol, where, shown relics of the recently dead Chatterton, Johnson pronounced him the most extraordinary young man that he had ever heard of. He was exposed, both sponta-neously and deliberately, to various emotional and intellectual stimuli to see how he would react: hearing of young Harry Thrale's death, Boswell writes, "I was . . . affected with sincere concern, and was curious to see how Dr. Johnson would feel." Or, apropos of Aristotle's *Poetics*, " 'But how are the passions to be purged by terror and pity?' (said I, with an assumed air of ignorance, to incite him to talk, for which it was often necessary to employ some address)." Sometimes Johnson grew surly under this prodding: "Sir, you have but two topics, yourself and me. I am sick of both." More often he let himself be carried along the current of Boswell's interest and good humour.

The marvel of manipulation came in "the most famous of all dinner-parties," the Dillys' dinner on 15 May 1776, at which Boswell, driven by an "irresistible wish," arranged for the unsuspecting Johnson to encounter Wilkes, with whom he had carried on a public feud. Years later Boswell was to write that "a nice knowledge of character" was necessary to select the proper company for dinner; especially nice, he might have added, when the dinner's purpose was forceful confrontation. But he had had plenty of experience. As Mrs. Thrale commented:

> Curiosity carried Boswell farther than it ever carried any mortal breathing. He cared not what he provoked so as he saw what *such a one* would say or do.

Sometimes he was impelled by mere "mischievous love of sport," as when in the Hebrides he let Lady Lochbuie offer cold sheep's-head to Johnson for breakfast; on more significant occasions, he could not resist an oppor-tunity to see not only how Johnson but how his antagonist would react in an unanticipated situation. He could be sure that Johnson, at least, would react in a memorable way. Moreover, he tended to regard temptation of this kind as its own justification.

Boswell's account of this grand meeting is too well known to allow extended recapitulation, but his precise sense of arrangement, both in life and in narrative, deserves comment: he convinces Johnson that he has no right to find fault with the Dillys' company; with "solicitations, which were certainly as earnest as most entreaties to ladies on any occasion," he per-suades Mrs. Williams to allow Johnson to keep his engagement; he watches triumphantly as good food and Wilkes's polite helpfulness soothe Johnson's sullen virtue, underlined by Johnson's story of how he could not resist Foote's humour at a previous dinner: "The dog was so very comical that I was obliged to lay down my knife and fork, throw myself back upon my chair, and fairly laugh it out." Knowing that Johnson will not allow anyone to criticize Garrick except himself, Boswell intervenes when Wilkes mentions Garrick's penny-pinching. Johnson and Wilkes find common ground in discussion of an ambiguous phrase in Horace and in their easy dislike of Scotland, Boswell playing along with the joke. But having developed the scene from near-disaster to festive harmony, Boswell permits himself the final smile:

> Mr. Wilkes held a candle to show a fine print of a beautiful female figure which hung in the room, and pointed out the elegant contour of the bosom with the finger of an arch-connoisseur. He afterwards, in a conversation with me, waggishly insisted that all the time Johnson showed *visible signs* of a fervent admiration of the corresponding charms of the fair Quaker.[1]

Wilkes and Johnson were brothers in the flesh.

Both Wilkes and Johnson were too shrewd not to be aware of Boswell's manoeuvering, and they were content to play their parts. But in his interviews with Margaret Caroline Rudd, Boswell met his equal in manipulation. Apart from the Duchess of Kingston, convicted of bigamy (Boswell of course attended her trial), Mrs. Rudd was the feminine sensation of the year. Like Becky Sharp, she had to make her own way in the world and, like Becky, she was not fastidious about the means she used. The daughter of an Irish surgeon, she had married and separated early from a Lt. Valentine Rudd, and embarked on the career of a woman of pleasure. Apparently she specialized in wealthy men whom she later blackmailed. In 1770 she accepted the protection of Daniel Perreau, who introduced her as his wife, and to whom she bore three children. Perreau was a man of expensive tastes and uncertain occupation who, having been three times a bankrupt, started to play the dangerous game of speculation on the Exchange. His twin brother Robert, an apothecary, became involved in his risky affairs, and the two, presumably with the help of Mrs. Rudd, started to forge promissory notes. (In the eighteenth century, forgery, as a crime against property, was regarded virtually as a crime against nature.) When they were caught, the Perreaus accused her of duping them, and she retorted by turning Crown's evidence. The brothers were found guilty and

---

[1] Another guest, Mrs. Mary Knowles.

sentenced to be hanged; Mrs. Rudd was tried separately (8 December 1775). Dressed in second mourning and emphasizing her smallness, fragility, and helplessness, she so softened those present that the jury, after deliberating only thirty minutes, returned a verdict of "not guilty" to loud applause.

Boswell could not resist coming to grips with a woman of such extraordinary address and insinuation, and the interview gave high satisfaction. Though identifying himself only as a friend of Macqueen the advocate, an acquaintance of Mrs. Rudd's, Boswell was graciously received and immediately told the whole story. Then, no, she could never marry again even if her husband were dead, unless to a man of rank and fortune who could sustain her in her adversity. Boswell now found his opening:

> I said she was reckoned quite a sorceress, possessed of enchantment. She smiled and did not contradict me as to the past, but said she could enchant nobody. I begged her pardon and, with exquisite flattery said, "My dear Mrs. Rudd, don't talk so. Everything you have said to me till now has been truth and candour"; and I told her I was convinced she could enchant, but I begged she would not enchant me too much, not change me into any other creature, but allow me to continue to be a man with some degree of reason. I was as cautious as if I had been opposite to that snake which fascinates with its eyes. Her language was choice and fluent and her voice melodious. The peculiar characteristic of her enchantment seemed to be its delicate imperceptible power. She perfectly concealed her design to charm.

Like Garrick on stage, Mrs. Rudd was "natural, simple, affecting," and though Boswell tried her with silence and unpleasant gossip about her relations with two noblemen, she never lost her poise. "During all this interview," Boswell continues,

> I was quite calm and possessed myself fully, snuffed the candles and stirred the fire as one does who is at home, sat easy upon my chair, and felt no confusion when her eyes and mine met. Indeed her eyes did not flash defiance but attracted with sweetness, and *there* was the reason of the difference of effect between her eyes and those of more insolent or less experienced charmers. . . . I wished her good night with a kiss which she received without affection of any kind. . . . I concluded from every *circumstance* that she was now upon the town, though her conversation was so superior to that of common women. But I might be mistaken, for I never hinted at an intrigue. I wondered what she thought of me. I imagined I was very agreeable. . . . I would not for a good deal have missed this scene. We crowd to see those who excel in any art, and surely the highest excellence of art is the art of pleasing, the art of attracting admiration and fondness.

Boswell was an adept in the art of pleasing, yet it is characteristic of him that he wrote up this account of Mrs. Rudd in a letter to his wife. Luckily he had sense enough to send it to Temple instead.

One visit to his new Circe only roused the appetite. Boswell called several times, and the day after the Dillys' dinner appeared for a farewell interview. He sang "The Snake," a song he had composed in her honour, and seized for the first time with "delirium," he asked whether a pretty ankle was among her perfections, then eyes, then mouth, snatched several passionate kisses, and found it hard to take himself away. His final impression of her was that "like water corrupted and grown fresh again, her art is become purest simplicity." Temple had to discourage him from thoughts of corresponding with her. But Mrs. Rudd will reappear in this story.

Boswell's other farewells were more restrained. Paoli told him that he occupied himself with little things and that he must never let his character become ridiculous. Johnson had welcomed him to an assigned bedroom in his new house a few days earlier with "Nobody will come to it more welcome than you. Nobody loves you more or would do more for you." Now, as he once again urged Boswell not to drink, he broke through to one of those generalizations that make him a moralist worth listening to: "Every man is to take existence on the terms on which it is given to him. Yours is given to you on condition of your not using liberties which other people may." Further advice followed:

> Don't talk of yourself or of me. . . . Don't make yourself and me a proverb. Have no one topic that people can say, "We'll hear him upon it." BOSWELL. "Thank you for all your kindness." JOHNSON. "You are very welcome. Nobody repays it with more."

Boswell left well-satisfied with his visit, according to Johnson, who told Mrs. Thrale: "Some great men have promised to obtain him a place, and then a fig for my father and his new wife."

But whatever his expectations, after this richness Edinburgh seemed poor indeed, and as so often when Boswell returned from London he fell ill, this time with a persistent headache. "Black and indifferent" on a visit to Auchinleck, he was momentarily calmed and entertained by his father's stories. But his general mood remained bleak. As anticipated, Lord Auchinleck was angry over the jaunt to London, and unreasonable about the debt for Dalblair; Boswell picked up enough spirit to say, "You think too ill of me," but his melancholy deepened to thoughts of suicide. The entail could not be avoided. His relations and friends, natural affection, and common sense itself, told him that his attitude towards it was untenable. As the entail was finally made out, the estate was settled on heirs male of

Boswell's great-grandfather followed by heirs whatsoever, precisely the line
of inheritance agreed upon in his parents' marriage contract.

The day before the crucial interview on the subject, Boswell got drunk,
followed whores, fell and bruised his knee.   The next morning he was too
ill to attend to his practice.   That afternoon Stobie, his father's clerk, called
to say that if he did not sign the entail now his father would never ask him
again and would withhold his allowance.   At the last moment, Boswell had
veered once more and asked that his daughters be called in the entail after
heirs male of Lord Auchinleck's body.   His father "in a very bad frame . . .
would not alter an iota."   On the following day (7 August 1776) the entail
was signed, Boswell comforting himself that the succession was "secured
to *the sons of Auchinleck.*"   It was the dutiful, proper, practical decision, and
it was a crushing psychic defeat from which Boswell would never recover.

CHAPTER

7

I

THE SIGNING OF the entail forced Boswell to accept his father's version of Family continuity; at the same time, an interview (7 July 1776) with the dying Hume shook, as never before, his faith in individual immortality. While to the believer religion remains, as Johnson said, the most important of subjects, and "the reasonable hope of a happy futurity" the "one solid basis of happiness," it seems hardly possible for even the most devout today to share the literal-minded immediacy with which the hereafter was regarded in the eighteenth century.   Either at the moment of death or at the Last Judgement the soul, if qualified, entered into a state of bliss which amply compensated for its sufferings below.   The details were hidden—Boswell thought that hard—but many anticipated a state enough like an ideal intensification of our happiness in this world so that the Rev. Hugh Blair wondered at having to leave his house, study, and books; while Boswell understandably was made uneasy by the thought of even temporary separation from his spouse.   Johnson warned against too anthropomorphic a view of the afterlife, but Boswell could please himself by playfully looking forward to the gift of an elegant copy of Shakespeare on arrival, or assert seriously that there was no room for Whiggism in Heaven.

To pass from time to eternity seemed, to the confident, almost like stepping from one room into the next.   Equally, the fearful, like Johnson, lived in dread of stepping from this world into the abyss.   Most horrifying of all was the possibility that there was no next world—the possibility of annihilation, of nothingness.   Johnson could be overheard muttering to himself,

> For who would lose,
> Though full of pain, this intellectual being,
> Those thoughts that wander through Eternity,
> To perish rather, swallowed up and lost
> In the wide womb of uncreated night,
> Devoid of sense and motion?

But what proofs were there of another world? The Bible provides a convincing historical foundation for belief, reinforced by the enduring presence and reassuring ritual of the Church, the faith of millions, the demonstration of miracles. Quite satisfactory evidence, excellent even, and ample for those of a religious temperament. But for the unwillingly sceptical, like Johnson and Boswell, there was lamentably little direct, first-hand evidence. They snatched if warily, those doubting Thomases, at every tale of supernatural interposition in earthly affairs. There might well be good evidence of the spiritual world but, as Johnson said, "I like to have more." His was a particularly unhinging state of mind, caught between the fear of an afterlife in which he might be damned to eternity and the terror that the afterlife did not exist at all.

But damnation, as Belial argues in the passage above, is preferable to annihilation; "the great article of Christianity," Boswell said, "is the revelation of immortality." He identified the soul with consciousness, the core of self whose extinction would be far worse than an eternity of punishment, a punishment he had doubts about anyway. Every attack, then, on Christianity was to be bitterly repelled, since the existence of even one disbeliever weakened faith. How could one smother recurrent misgivings if others were allowed to assert arrogant free-thinking views openly and cogently? Boswell mortally hated Gibbon because Gibbon supported his attack on Christianity with the kind of evidence a lawyer was bound to respect.

Still, it was notorious that atheism amounted to little more than an affectation adopted to impress oneself or others: there were no deathbed atheists, or at least there shouldn't be. (All Europe was to watch for signs of anguished repentance when Voltaire died two years later.) For this reason the behaviour of Hume, the Great Infidel, would be crucial. His amiable disbelief had offered Boswell positive temptation. In a recent confused moment Boswell, though happy "in having pious faith," thought of asking him for arguments to support his spirits in case he became an infidel. Now it was urgent to observe whether Hume could maintain his usual serenity under the threat of imminent death and annihilation. Boswell had no thought of saving Hume as that formidable divine, Gilbert

Burnet, had converted the wicked Lord Rochester on his deathbed; it would be enough to see him tremble in the face of extinction.

> Hume was lean, ghastly, and quite of an earthy appearance. He was dressed in a suit of grey cloth with white metal buttons, and a kind of scratch-wig. He was quite different from the plump figure he used to present. He had before him Dr. Campbell's *Philosophy of Rhetoric.* . . . He said he was just approaching to his end.

Boswell got quickly to his first question: what did Hume think of religion? Hume answered he had given it up early in life after reading Locke and the Arian, Samuel Clarke, and had remained steady in disbelief for forty years. And religion's relation to morality? "He . . . said flatly that the morality of every religion was bad . . . that when he heard a man was religious he concluded he was a rascal, though he had known some instances of very good men being religious." Boswell now focused on his central topic, immortality. Was it not possible that there might be a future state?

> He answered it was possible that a piece of coal put upon the fire would not burn, and he added that it was a most unreasonable fancy that we should exist for ever. . . . I asked him if the thought of annihilation never gave him any uneasiness. He said not the least; no more than the thought that he had not been.

When they met in a future state, Boswell responded, he hoped to triumph over Hume, who was not to pretend that his infidelity had been a joke. "No, no," replied Hume. "But I shall have been so long there before you come that it will be nothing new."

Later Boswell would reflect:

> In this style of good humour and levity did I conduct the conversation. Perhaps it was wrong on so awful a subject. But as nobody was present I thought it could have no bad effect. I however felt a degree of horror, mixed with a sort of wild, strange, hurrying recollection of my excellent mother's pious instructions, of Dr. Johnson's noble lessons, and of my religious sentiments and affections during the course of my life. I was like a man in sudden danger eagerly seeking his defensive arms; and I could not but be assailed by momentary doubts while I had actually before me a man of such strong abilities and extensive inquiry dying in the persuasion of being annihilated. But I maintained my faith. I told him that I believed the Christian religion as I believed history. Said he: "You do not believe it as you believe the Revolution."[1]

_____
[1] Of 1688.

"Yes," said I, "but the difference is that I am not so much interested in the truth of the Revolution; otherwise I should have anxious doubts about it.   A man who is in love has doubts of the affection of his mistress, without cause."

Boswell's analogy gives his basis of belief away.   He wants to regard revelation as fact of an historical order like the Glorious Revolution; actually he is afraid it is fact of an imaginative order, like being in love.

Nor was Hume properly apprehensive: he spoke with "his usual grunting pleasantry, with that thick breath which fatness had rendered habitual to him, and that smile of simplicity which his good humour constantly produced."   In fact, he was "indecently and impolitely positive in incredulity"—dying men should be complaisant to their unsought visitors—and in defence of the afterlife, the most precious of beliefs, Boswell was hurried into speaking, like Johnson, brutally, irrelevantly, and *ad hominem*.   (Like Johnson, he felt attacks on religious belief were *ad hominem*.)   When Hume remarked that Johnson at least must have liked his Tory *History of England*, Boswell repeated Johnson's comment, "Sir, the fellow is a Tory by chance." Later, Boswell says that while he objects on principle to treating an infidel with civility,

> I am sorry that I mentioned this at such a time.   I was off my guard, for the truth is that Mr. Hume's pleasantry was such that there was no solemnity in the scene; and death for the time did not seem dismal.

Hume died in great tranquillity on 25 August.   His unshakeable composure had deeply upset Boswell, who tormented himself further by reading Hume's "worst" essays.   He rationalized Hume's lack of belief, as best he could, in a letter to Mrs. Thrale:

> Hume had certainly considerable abilities.   My notion is that he had, by long study in one view, brought a *stupor* upon his mind as to futurity.   He had pored upon the earth till he could not look up to heaven.

Still, Boswell's doubts lingered.   A year later when he pressed Johnson to explain Hume's apparent indifference to death, Johnson's answer was simple and sensible:

> He lied. . . .   He had a vanity in being thought easy.   It is more probable that he lied than that so very improbable a thing should be as a man not afraid of death; of going into an unknown state and not being uneasy at leaving all that he knew.   And you are

to consider that upon his own principle of annihilation he had no motive not to lie.

In spite of this reassurance, Boswell continued to feel uneasy in the company of sceptics and supported by that of the pious.   His most comforting responses to Hume, however, emerged on other levels.   Four days before Hume's death, Boswell had paid him a visit, "wishing," he says, "to converse with him while I was elevated with liquor, but was told he was very ill." As a substitute he "then ranged awhile in the Old Town after strumpets." The day before Hume's funeral he had a whore on Castle Hill.   (Sex, it is obvious, was Boswell's habitual solace for unhappy events.)   Six months later he took a whore to a mason's shed just by Hume's house, uniting the convenient with the symbolic.   And seven years afterwards he set all right by dreaming that he found a diary of Hume's which showed that his publication of sceptical treatises had sprung from vanity, and that he was really not only a Christian but a very pious man.   Boswell even dreamed some beautiful religious passages Hume had written.

The hold of the dead was persistent, but the grip of the living was pressing more powerfully.   In signing the entail, Boswell had not cleared his account with his father; instead, he had taken on, so to speak, a mortgage that would run as long as his father lived.   He had not even retained the portion of autonomy which his "renunciation" and guaranteed £100 a year of 1762 had provided; he had bought back his birthright by surrendering the essentials of his freedom.   Lord Auchinleck states in the entail that he acted "in the hopes and belief that I have fallen on a method of preventing children from being independent of their parents," and he was right. Boswell would now live under the shadow of his father's rules and desires. As a dependent, obedient son, he went off that autumn to Auchinleck for six weeks, leaving as usual his wife and children behind him, though Margaret had been ill during the summer with what she feared was the onset of consumption, the executioner of her family.

Just a year earlier only a considerable quantity of strong beer had made a week at Auchinleck bearable, and since then Boswell had fought and lost the battle of the entail.   He should have been miserable; instead, when he left on 20 October he reported that he had really been very happy. How is this possible?   Further, he went so far as to hope that

> in a little . . . I shall be fully convinced that happiness is rather in a sedate than in a flashy life, and shall never think it necessary for the entertainment of company, as I now habitually do, to have high merriment or brisk vivacity.

The pace at Auchinleck was sedate enough, since his father kept the management of the estate tightly in his own hands, invited few visitors, and did not encourage those who called to linger.   Boswell had no serious occupation.   He walked and rode round the estate, and played cards with his father, stepmother, and her elder sister Margaret, a high-powered nuisance.   He paid visits, not all of which were pleasant.   His cousin and good friend, James Campbell of Treesbank, was afflicted with "a monstrous incurable cancer eating away the right side of his throat and mouth."   Boswell goes on:

> He was in violent pain, and the putrid smell was shocking.   I could with difficulty support being in the room with him.   But I was comforted to find him most piously resigned to the will of GOD.

There was great need for resignation, since Mrs. Campbell, Margaret's sister, was seriously ill with consumption.   Treesbank himself died within six weeks.

Boswell also visited Lainshaw, a place tender to him as Margaret's family home, where they had been married.   The people from the neighbouring village of Stewarton flocked in, he was told, "as joyous on my being there as if it were the King," and he felt "vastly well" though he knew that Lainshaw's owner, Sir Walter Montgomerie-Cuninghame, must sell it to pay debts.   Boswell's response to this distressing problem was to take refuge in fantasy: he would buy the property so that Margaret would be called "Lady Lainshaw" and Veronica become its heiress.

Another excursion took him over the hills to Galloway on legal business. A flash of the old fretfulness showed itself on the return journey: he got very drunk one night, and to prove he was sober insisted on walking across a narrow bridge without rails over the rapid, deep Doon Water.   "Deep drowned in Doon" was the fate his wife would prophesy for Tam o' Shanter. The god of drunkards equally protected Boswell, but he knew he had had a lucky escape.

That autumn at Auchinleck was happy because Boswell carried out his purpose: to please his father by "insensible attentions" and by doing his duty as his father saw it.   "*Duty* in every department," he wrote, "is a cordial to the mind."   Submission had the advantage of protecting Boswell from his own impulses:

> Felt more agreeably when under parental awe than when unrestrained.   It put a lid on my mind and kept it from boiling vehemently.   Being thus kept quiet, I was happier than when agitated with ebullitions.

In this subdued role, Boswell cultivated the image of Auchinleck as "the romantic seat" of his ancestors.   No doubt mollified by "attentions" and the signing of the entail, his father kept his word and paid over £1,200 (including the £200 withheld from Boswell's allowance) to the creditors for Dalblair, telling Boswell to sin no more.   Laying out money on land, even when necessitated by his son's extravagance, was one expense Lord Auchinleck must always have approved.

But there were serious disadvantages in Boswell's regression to the role of young laird.   He could not show his resentment at his father's treatment of Margaret and the children; and when he noticed, as he often did, further signs of his father's failure, it revived his old fear that he would be unequal to succeeding him as Head of the Family.

It may seem surprising that Boswell so seldom thought of earning his independence by his own exertions as a lawyer.   He never got tired of telling people—he even told George III—that though his father had pressed him into the law he did as well as a volunteer.   This was no longer true, if it ever had been.   Though he enjoyed speaking in court, he found it difficult to put his mind to the daily routine.   The law in itself now meant little to him; it was a living, and possibly a means to advancement.   Yet even when he thought of making money, he identified the law so closely with his father that any protracted attempt to achieve success as a lawyer met very strong inner resistance, all the harder to cope with because Boswell was unwilling to recognize its character.   Instead, as time went on, he told himself that the effort wasn't worthwhile: grubbing at the law wasn't genteel; he might fail.

Independence would have to wait for that long-desired sinecure which would help to support him until he succeeded to the substantial estate of Auchinleck.   But his father did not die and in the meantime Boswell was tied, financially and emotionally, to him:

> My father bid me farewell with affection.   He had now quite forgotten his displeasure for my going to London in the spring without acquainting him.   He is really a good-natured man.

But Boswell would never be sure of salvation, either divine or paternal. Lord Auchinleck could have responded to, or at least respected, a son who made and took his own way, if he preserved an appearance of regard for him.   But, as already suggested, Boswell's alternations of defiance and dependence, his enthusiasms, his taste for London and odd people like Johnson, his excitability, his deplorable habit of scribbling about everything and publishing in the newspapers, in short his complete and unpredictable volatility, made the old man think him a strange bird.

I I

AND BOSWELL WAS far more unusual than even his father realized: he was compiling the most remarkable of English journals.   For a year after his return to Edinburgh in October 1776 little eventful occurred in his life, except that the journal, his most extended achievement, continued to accumulate.   This pause in his career offers a convenient opportunity to consider it.   While Boswell was unique in being both a great journalist and a great biographer, the journal, as well as providing much of the biographical material, embodies the deeper urge of his nature.   But journals are not self-explanatory, and we need to consider why Boswell wrote it, what it consists in, and how it holds a reader's attention.

A major motive among the cluster that impelled Boswell to keep a journal for much of his adult life was the need for objectification.   "A man loves to review his own mind," Johnson said; "that is the use of a diary or journal."   But much more was involved in Boswell's case.   Boswell stands outside himself, peering in at what he feels and says and does, to see what the record tells him he is.   In the process of recording, the journal comes to serve varied purposes from confessional to a balancing of the moral books to a source of later entertainment.   And in the tradition of Calvinistic self-examination Boswell also calls it an instrument of self-improvement: "As a lady adjusts her dress before a mirror, a man adjusts his character by looking at his journal."

This remark, to adapt what Johnson said about certain second marriages, relied more on hope than experience.   Though on going back to the famous London Journal of his youth, Boswell wrote that he felt "sickened in mind by reviewing my own sickly weakness," he never seems to have profited from his past.   Instead the journal acted as a buffer between him and the life around him, which negated his hopes for change.   Boswell's schemes for reform substitute for the actual effort, or as Geoffrey Scott summarized this process, "Boswell kept his good resolutions by writing them down and redressed his backsliding by copying them out."

But the mirror analogy, though conventional, is useful.   Most diarists, in fact, soften their mirrored reflections a good deal, perhaps out of consideration for others and surely for their own sakes.   "No man ever dared

to depict himself as he is," Camus said, or to cite Johnson on the same
point:

> Very few can boast of hearts which they dare lay open to them-
> selves and of which, by whatever accident exposed, they do not
> shun a distinct and continued view.

Boswell comes out better than most in this respect: if his journal failed
to improve him, it is at least exceptionally honest.   From early on he admits,
or asserts, that he wants to tell people everything about himself, and the
journal becomes his confidant of first and last resort.   He could allow
himself to register almost any thought or action (crossing out some later),
and loves, as he says, "to mark real feelings."   In the journal he claims
correctly, "I put down a fair transcript of the phases of my mind."

Apart from our unfathomable opacity, what limits Boswell is his unwillingness to go deeper than the mirror image.   Speaking of a moment
in the country when he had "got into a comfortable Auchinleck frame,"
he goes on, "It is in vain to investigate ideas and feelings of this kind.   They
are as immediate as the tastes of different substances."   But as well as being
useless, investigation could be disturbing.   "Few characters," he wrote,

> will bear the examination of reason.   You may examine them for
> curiosity as you examine bodies with a microscope.   But you will
> be as much disgusted with their gross qualities.   You will see them
> as Swift makes Gulliver see the skins of the ladies of Brobdingnag.

Boswell was tirelessly observant, as his biographies show.   And the
journal, of course, reveals constant reflection about himself.   Still, he is
shrewd rather than penetrating.   As an adolescent he had been terribly
afraid of ghosts, but got rid of his fear (so he said) "by a habit of not
thinking, not by reasoning about it."   Prolonged introspection only increased his uneasiness: "I am lost," he wrote in his journal, "when I think
too intensely of the course of things, and especially of the operations of
my own mind."   Yet he was always in danger of being sucked into his self-
consciousness:

> I am too concave a being.   My thoughts go inwards too much
> instead of being carried out to external objects.   I wish I had a
> more convex mind.   And yet the happiness of a rational being is
> reflection.   But I am too minute.   I am continually putting the
> Roman praetor's question, "*Cui bono?*" [1] to every incident of life,
> to each part of a whole.

---

[1] Literally, "Who stood to profit?" (Cicero, *For Milo*, xii. 32), but more generally, "What
purpose does this serve?"

Also he studied the characters of others too closely.   To probe into substance reveals the nothingness of which it is composed, the nothingness of this world he feared as he did the nothingness of the next.   He wrote once on the Justiciary Circuit, "Saw all things—judges, chaises—men and horses—all analysed, all vain."   Better to skim pleasingly along the surface.

Ex nihilo nihil fit.   Nothing will come of nothing.   But of course there is something within to which Boswell hopes his journal will give a shape and identity.   The early journal is an exercise in conscious self-creation. He says of his 1762–63 Journal that he wants it to present "a consistent picture of a young fellow eagerly pushing through life."   Still,

> Let me consider that the hero of a romance or novel must not go uniformly along in bliss, but the story must be chequered with bad fortune.   Aeneas met with many disasters in his voyage to Italy, and must not Boswell have his rubs?

To use one's journal to focus identity may not be unusual; what is extraordinary is the extent to which the journal itself becomes the *realization* of experience.   To quote Geoffrey Scott again:

> It is no exaggeration to say that Boswell regarded his journal as the principal duty and aim of his existence; life unrecorded was not life. . . .   Boswell did not feel he *possessed* an experience till it was written down: the *res gestae*[1] were mere preliminaries.

Scott does exaggerate, but he exaggerates in the right direction.   Recall the most singular remark Boswell ever made about his journal:

> I should live no more than I can record, as one should not have more corn growing than one can get in.   There is a waste of good if it be not preserved.   And yet perhaps if it serve the purpose of immediate felicity, that is enough.   The world would not hold pictures of all the pretty women who have lived in it and gladdened mankind; nor would it hold a register of all the agreeable conversations which have passed.   But I mean to record only what is excellent.

At the simplest level, the journal meant preservation.   A day unrecorded seemed to disappear; when Boswell lost his Dutch journal he said he felt as if part of his vitals had been separated from him.   "It is unpleasing," he wrote later, "to observe how imperfect a picture of my life this journal presents.   Yet I have certainly much more of *myself* thus preserved than most people have."   Still, he was puzzled that recollection gave

[1]Actions.

him more satisfaction than immediate experience, though he need not have been.   He collected experiences the way others collect furniture or coins. In recollection they were complete, and he could "replay" them as often as he wished.   He thought his ability to bring together impressions from widely separated periods was an "exceedingly rare" gift.   For such a person, the permanence of a record was "a multiplication of felicity."

More deeply, the fear of nothingness within generates not only the dread of eventual annihilation but also the terror of a present life without material substance.   It is in reaction to the threat of an earthly void that Boswell, in his journal and biographies, builds scenes notable for solidity and fullness.   They gave the world, and himself, body.

But Boswell ran the danger that art would absorb life.   He says, "[I] will go through almost anything with a degree of satisfaction if I am to put an account of it in writing," and Temple early accused him of looking for adventures so that he could adorn his journal with them.   If not going quite so far, Boswell does tend to blur life and journal: after a reconciliation with the late Lord Eglinton in 1763, Boswell writes, "Here now is a very material period in my journal" rather than "in my life."   Or he equates dulness of life with dulness of journal.   Or he celebrates Sandy's birth as the beginning of a new era—any event could signal a new era—by resuming his journal with a resolve to record something of every day.

A fantasy offers the most startling identification of journal and life:

> I had lately a thought that appeared new to me: that by burning
> all my journal and all my written traces of former life, I should
> be like a new being. . . .   Were I just now to go and take up house
> in any country town in England, it would be just a different ex-
> istence.

The continuity of self that others find in consciousness and memory Boswell assigns to his written records.

Though Boswell's honesty about himself was exceptional, his early journal is skewed somewhat by being a conscious record for others as well as himself.   His 1762–63 London Journal Boswell sent to Grange, and so organizes his experiences as he might have in a letter to the same trusted friend.   It makes a wonderful story and is intended to be honest within its limits: it tells the truth but not the whole truth.   And for the next few years on the Continent, Boswell wants to construct an entertaining narrative as well as register private feelings.   But travel journals were expected to serve as snapshot albums do today.   Nor is the record complete; Boswell continued to supplement the journal with memoranda telling himself what to do.   Boswell the actor struts on stage having been cued by Boswell the director, though behaviour often fails to accord with instruction. Then on his trip to Corsica in 1765 Boswell gained enough confidence in himself to discontinue these constant directives and became content to let the journal tell his story.

Apart from the Hebridean and Ashbourne Journals, evidently composed from the beginning with some thought of a larger audience, Boswell's journal after Corsica also became mainly a private record. It would be a terrible blow, he thought, to see it published during his lifetime. But his feelings about its posthumous fate were less definite. Shortly after Sandy was born, Boswell projected himself into the future:

> I thought that my son would perhaps read this journal and be grateful to me for my attention about him, for I was twice out speaking to his nurse.[1] My wife, who does not like journalizing, said it was leaving myself embowelled to posterity—a good, strong figure. But I think it is rather leaving myself embalmed. It is certainly preserving myself.

"Ev'n from the tomb the voice of nature cries." He had no doubt that, whether embowelled or embalmed, what would be preserved was the genuine James Boswell, so far as he could be known: he would be emBoswelled. And by rescuing him from annihilation day by day, the journal has contributed to an immortality in this world that he hoped for in the next.

Yet any attempt to reproduce life in art must adapt itself to the limitations and opportunities of the medium. The controlling shape of the journal is the daily entry, in which time moves "at the pace of natural life, set by the rhythm of waking and sleeping." Or it can move at that pace; it can move at any pace the journalist pleases. What is essential is the structure of dailiness, for once a journalist begins to group entries in what Boswell calls a "review" the journal edges towards autobiography. The pure journal cannot anticipate; it cannot achieve form beyond its mechanical format (though one can revise entries as Pepys did or, when writing some time after the event, cheat a little as Boswell does in the Louisa episode of the 1762–63 London Journal). So it seems shapeless and disorganized compared to the novel or even other types of personal non-fiction. And it is the only open-ended literary genre: its conclusion must always be accidental.

Still, the honest journal offers strong compensations. It is "realistic" at every level because it records what actually happened, at least as perceived through one mind. It has no problems with plausibility or coher-

---

[1]She had been newly hired.

ence.   Events are always credible and character consistent: the "inconsistent" simply constitutes a mode of narrative or plot development.   Detail may be dull but cannot be irrelevant, since it is what the journalist selected as relevant at the time.   The journal's format accommodates any subject, any point of view ("he thought" or "one might respond" as well as "I said"), and any tone.   Transitions are unnecessary.   Given its complete flexibility, it is not surprising that Boswell's only recurrent worry is whether he is being too circumstantial—in effect either that he is wasting time or boring a possible reader.

Boswell usually wrote up his journal from notes, of which a good many survive.   Fully written journal entries range from a sentence or two to accounts of considerable length: the entry for 16 March 1776, for example, runs to about 3,000 words.   Length depends on what Boswell thought worth recording, the time available, and his mood.   Short entries usually indicate that he is busy or depressed; medium-length ones (a dozen sentences or less) that life is just jogging along; long ones, that something highly pleasurable or significant is occurring.   At such points the journal competes with other activities for his time; then, as life once more becomes dull, the journal dwindles.   Content also is determined by interest: Boswell's law practice during this period (1776–77) is routine and he gives it little space; his attention is turned towards his family and inwards, along with the usual recording of social life and the daily round.

Boswell's brief notes are of no interest as journal, though they could be sufficient clues for elaborate reconstructions of events years after they occurred.   But as soon as the entries begin to extend themselves at all they can convey a great deal, as in this one for 22 August 1777:

> Visited Lord Kames.   Bayle's Manicheans fine.   Dined Lord Dundonald's.   Drank little, but had great desire for it.   Strolled in streets to find companion.   Luckily escaped.   Called Crosbie. Home with wife.   Had tea and read *Rasselas* from first to last. Was delighted.

Apart from an occasional obscure person or reference, Boswell's journal is easy to follow.   Here the reader needs to recall Kames, Dundonald, and Crosbie, and perhaps to be told that "Bayle's Manicheans fine" presumably means that Kames praised the article on Manicheism in Pierre Bayle's *Critical and Historical Dictionary*, that contemporary monument of sceptical learning.   Otherwise the day reconstructs itself.   Boswell's typical framework is one of events interspersed with reflections, a framework which can enfold, as it does here, widely varying activities and moods.   And let Boswell experience internal agitation or external motion and the journal, with its indefinitely expansible format, comes completely alive.

It is not possible to exemplify the journal with a really long entry but, to go back to 21 December 1776, here is a good part of an extended one:

> Was very ill in the morning,[1] but went to the court and pleaded well enough. Had dictated more law this week than any during this session, which comforted me. This day a petition from my father and me for recording our entail was moved to the court, and the registration authorized. I felt a slight twinge at being fettered, but instantly acquiesced in the family settlement being rendered stable and my father's mind being made quiet. I was a little melancholy this day on finding him failed when I sat awhile with him. It distressed me to apprehend that if he were gone, the dignity of the Family of Auchinleck would not be properly maintained. I had strange romantic projects of keeping myself in the most retired state, that my weaknesses might not appear. But then I considered that my vivacity and love of immediate personal distinction would hurry me at times into all kinds of social meetings and make me exhibit all my powers of jocularity, so that there would be an absurd inconsistency of conduct. I hoped however that I might by habits of restraint form a decent, settled character enlivened with moderate pleasantry. And, when I compare myself at present with what I was some years ago, I have good reason to be well satisfied. My present fault is having no elevated views, no great ambition. I see no dignity in the Court of Session, my present sphere. I think that if I were one of the judges I should feel myself but a little man in a narrow sphere, and I fear it is too late for me to try a more enlarged sphere in England. Yet why not try, if I can contrive to live there on as little or not much more than in Scotland? And though I should fail myself, I may get my heir forward, taking care, however, to keep him sufficiently fond of Auchinleck. Such speculations please me. . . .

The style is clear, plain, rapid, without sense of strain; and Boswell covers page after page in this manner, hardly crossing out a phrase. He is uneasy with abstractions; on the other hand, he is circumstantial without providing many particularized details: he sticks close to what theorists call the "substantive level" of diction ("spade"), as contrasted to either abstract or extra-concrete levels ("agricultural implement" or "dirty garden spade"). The syntax is simple, the phrase length modulated to suggest the rise and fall of the voice, and the statement of facts precise. Every sentence is immediately understandable.

[1]With a hangover.

Boswell's style shares the flexibility of the journal form: it can accommodate a wide range of material and a high degree of complexity. Here Boswell plays himself off against his father and, as he moves to within his own mind, his actual character against the one he hopes, perhaps, to attain; the present against the future; the probable against the possible. His attitude is both highly engaged (he is really thinking about his future) and yet detached (he is clear-sighted about his character and behaviour, if unwilling to give up his fantasies). The smoothness of transition from event to reflection, or from one reflection to another, makes his exceedingly mixed attitudes towards his father, as well as his reactions to the complications of his own temperament, easy to follow. All the while his thoughts move within the framework of Family, Edinburgh, Court of Session, Auchinleck, and his English goal. Not every entry in the journal, of course, falls so felicitously into patterns, but since they all emerge from the same mind the same thematic interweaving often recurs.

Boswell kept his journal compulsively, and it makes compulsive reading. The reader of journals is greedy for the actual: how do other people live, think, and feel? Of all literary forms, the journal comes closest to answering these questions directly: at its best, it realizes dramatically for the reader events and feelings in a way that seems spontaneous and true to immediate experience. Characters shift and shade off into obscurity; events are discontinuous, become prominent and disappear: even the form of the journal is comparable to living, as a day-to-day process whose outcome is unknown. But, unlike life, the journal is a written record, which in Boswell's case strings together all the unpredictable sequences of an important career, full of sharply portrayed incidents and dramatic reversals. Its length in itself draws the reader into an increasingly familiar group of figures, and a narrative which may extend a theme over many years or tell a tiny story in one or two entries.

Subjectivity is both the prime value and the limitation of the journal; interest and credibility are its crucial issues. Biography interposes the biographer between reader and subject; autobiography is liable to the corrective pull of hindsight. The journal draws the reader into another's mind without mediation or distortion. Prejudices, conscious or unconscious, the reader allows for as automatically as he does for the prejudices of the actual people he knows; whatever theoretical issues it may raise, bias is seldom a problem in practice.

But there are problems. It is at least a superficial paradox that the journal, apparently the most artless of literary forms, requires great skill to hold the reader's attention over a long stretch. It must compensate for lack of coherent narrative and character presentation by descriptive or thematic interest that depends directly on the writer's having an interesting, unusual, or powerful mind and some sense of what will entertain or involve a reader.   At the same time, skill must never diminish the effect of credibility.   The reader may enjoy the tall tales of Casanova more than the sober accounts of a reliable narrator, but he discounts Casanova's memoirs as in part fiction masquerading as fact.

It is possible to take the sophisticated attitude that whatever the journalist says, true or false, is revealing; but a reader is more likely to feel comfortable if he thinks he is reading a true story.   And if the narrative is based on verifiable fact he is apt to think better of it; like Johnson he believes that "the value of every story depends on its being true."   Boswell emphasizes circumstantial accuracy, the literal truth of matter-of-fact detail; and the credibility this gives his journal carries over to his attempts to register exact states of mind.   Here inconsistency plays its part: it would be difficult to invent such vivid variations of character.

The journalist's final advantage is that, other factors being equal, the reader tends to empathize more quickly and fully with real than with fictional characters simply because they are real.   For the same reason, the reader's attitude may shift sharply against a journalist, especially when, as in Boswell's case, he is extending the limits of what is permissible to say. On reading Boswell's journal after his death, his respectable executor Sir William Forbes repeatedly wrote "reprehensible passage."   Often true enough, but is this the comment of inherent decorum or protective hypocrisy?   Or both?   Johnson paraphrases an observation in William Law's *Serious Call to a Devout and Holy Life* as, "Every man knows something worse of himself than he is sure of in others."   And it is obvious that the reader who says, "Thank God, I am not like him," may be suppressing the unwelcome insight that they have a good deal in common.

But even the most sympathetically disposed can get impatient with vanity or self-pity, very likely elements in a journal since the writer so often uses it as a vent for the feelings he must repress in social life.   And the unremitting subjectivity of the journal may in itself become stifling.   Finally, the journalist runs the likely risk that the reader will see something in his story other than what he sees himself.

In the end, to recur to Johnson, the only way to determine literary merit is "length of duration and continuance of esteem."   Like his biographies, Boswell's journal shows every sign that it will stand the test of time. But its extent and brilliance necessarily distort our perception of him because of the way in which they situate the reader within what Amiel de-

scribed as "that molecular whirlwind which we call individual existence."
We apprehend Boswell from inside, as we do ourselves.   He is diffusive
as we are; he lacks the solidity we attribute to others.   The gain in intimacy
is enormous, but it is easy to lose a grasp on how his contemporaries
perceived him.

I I I

BOSWELL'S SECOND SON David, born on 15 November 1776, was a
moaning, sickly child, whose health improved gradually.   His arrival did
not much interrupt the routine existence that Boswell could seldom endure
for very long.   Feeling physically lazy and mentally barren, he had recourse
to his usual expedients, and one opportunity for amusing himself was
unfortunately near at hand.   Annie Cuninghame, his wife's niece, had
lived off and on with the Boswells for several years.   Though her age is
uncertain, she had evidently reached the point where, as Mr. Doolittle says
of his daughter Eliza, she was interesting to gentlemen, and Boswell took
an ungentlemanly interest in her, snatching "a little romping pleasure"
when he could, in spite of her reluctance.   The situation was uneasy:
Margaret had some notion of what was going on, and even the three-year-
old Veronica complained that Annie was "Papa's datie[1] now."   Finally
Margaret insisted on reading Boswell's journal, and was sufficiently shaken
not only by the extent of his interest in Annie but by several extramarital
escapades that she resolved, she said, to consider herself a wife no longer;
though for the sake of the children and to preserve appearances, she would
continue to live with Boswell as a friend.   Boswell's account of the sequel
will cover several such episodes:

> When I saw her in great uneasiness, and dreaded somewhat—
> though not with much apprehension—her resolution, I was awaked
> from my dream of licentiousness, and saw my bad conduct in a
> shocking light.   I was really agitated and in a degree of despair.
> She comforted me with hopes of my amendment. . . .   At night
> I calmly meditated to reform.

At least he left Annie alone after that, though once later he was "shockingly
harsh" to her when drunk.

It is easy to feel sorry for Margaret—Boswell himself often did—but
she would not have welcomed anyone's pity.   A woman of sense and spirit,

[1]Pet.

she was old enough to know her own mind when she married Boswell, and she was fully acquainted with his character. His drinking, gambling, and whoring irritated and alarmed her, and she was well aware of further defects, like his sporadic lack of consideration for others. But she loved him. He was "the man of her heart."

It seems pointless to give an extended recital of Boswell's routine sexual wanderings during the next year. Descriptions and names slide by: "a young slender slut with a red cloak," Peggy Grant, Peggy Dundas, "a big fat whore," "an old dallying companion now married," "Rubra," Dolly. Sometimes he ventured all lengths, or, to use his word, "embarked" on a quick trip to Cythera; at other times he restricted himself to "lesser lascivious sport." Betty Montgomerie, a natural daughter of Lord Eglinton, stands out a bit from the crowd. She had sufficient social position to be invited to dine with the Boswells, and of one such occasion Boswell writes:

> My fancy was pleased with Miss Montgomerie having noble blood in her veins. She was not sixteen, and was fresh, plump, and comely. Before dinner she allowed me luscious liberties with kindly frankness. I repeated them so often in my eagerness that my wife saw me and was offended. She agreed to meet me some evening in the Meadow.

But that relationship never progressed beyond dalliance and Betty was married off.

Collected in summary, these episodes of dissipation may seem to occur at random, but they do not. The first fit of whoring coincided with Margaret's lying-in with David, and when she was sufficiently recovered for Boswell to return to the conjugal bed, he remarks:

> It was very comfortable to get back to my good bed, and I told her what was true: that I really felt an indifference come upon me by living in a sort of separation from her, and that affectionate endearments were required to remove it.

That autumn and winter (1776–77), dulness deepened into hypochondria, not usually as the black depression Boswell sometimes felt, but as a state of indifference to everything, which modulated into

> a kind of *faintness of mind*, a total indifference as to all objects of whatever kind, united with a melancholy dejection. I saw death so staringly waiting for all the human race, and had such a cloudy and dark prospect beyond it, that I was miserable as far as I had animation. Either this morning or yesterday I awaked in terrible melancholy. I found however immediate relief by instantaneously praying to GOD with earnestness; and I felt the comfort

of piety. I absolutely was reduced to so wretched a state by my mental disease that I had right and wrong and every distinction confounded in my view. I loved my wife with extraordinary affection, but I had distinctly before me the time which *must* come when we shall be separated by death. I was fond of my children. But I unhappily saw beyond them; saw the time when they too shall be dead and, seeing that, I could not value them properly at present.

In this mood he fled from thought to sensation and Peggy Dundas. And, as often as not, came home and confessed. But greed of sensation, desire for sexual multiplicity, or even the child-adult relation he established with Margaret when he confessed are not enough to account for the compulsiveness with which Boswell pursued women, mainly those, like prostitutes, who could be had easily. He felt the need to assert himself against the blank situation he was in, a situation which he had in part consciously chosen. He laboured at a profession that interested him at best intermittently, where he could see and dislike his future: a judge of the Court of Session, "a little man in a narrow sphere." As already remarked, he had put himself at his father's mercy. If Boswell could never admit to himself the extent of his dependence on his father, even less could he allow himself to realize what intensity of resentment his father aroused. Instead he tries to behave dutifully, laments his father's indifference to him, blames Lady Auchinleck for alienating her husband from him. And remains depressed and anxious. He has cultivated his vivacity, his lack of reticence, his "happy insinuation, or the art of gaining upon a man"; he can and needs to be the life of every company. On the other hand, he repeatedly finds it surprising that not everyone likes him; he is too open, which is why his father fails to confide in him; he repeats things to people which he knows they will dislike; he is prone to childish buffoonery; and, in fact, many people consider him malevolent. He almost despairs of acting properly. How could he? Unable to stand up to his father, he cannot exert the authority of a good father over his own children.

Suddenly, but understandably, in mid-February 1777 Boswell's depression began to lift. Margaret had forgiven his most recent sexual indiscretions and, following an evening of a good deal of claret, he says, "I was in remarkable vigour of health and spirits, as I have sometimes been after drinking freely." The rising of the Court of Session was a definite number of weeks away and Boswell, the schoolboy, was looking forward to the holidays, perhaps even a trip to London. This had to be managed, however, since he had promised his father not to go without his consent.

At the beginning of March, Mary Campbell (Treesbank's widow) died,

and Boswell went west for the funeral.   It was a grisly affair: in preparing
the grave the diggers threw up the skulls of Treesbank's first wife and
younger brother.   But such mementoes did not spoil Boswell's enlivening
round of visits, in which he fancied himself quite a man of fashion, and
enjoyed "philosophic calm" and *"aisance du monde."*   The natives were
impressed, Lady Crawford (mother of the flirtatious Lady Eglinton) telling
him that his continued presence would help to invigorate the dull countryside.

Even Auchinleck seemed less burdensome than usual, since he was to
make only a short stay.   In fact, he "loved the country after the labour of
a Winter Session, and . . . had solid notions as a country gentleman," a state
of mind he wanted to preserve as a talisman against future perturbations.
And he attended his father "with pious duty."   When he finally got up
nerve to mention the prospect of London to Lady Auchinleck, she replied
sensibly that at his age he should decide such matters for himself and that
his father would not object to any reasonable proposal.   Authority himself
said that the trip was all nonsense but did not forbid it.   "After breakfast,
when I took leave of him," Boswell says, "he embraced me with a cordiality
which I valued more than the fond embrace of the finest woman."   As
Johnson said about Boswell's relationship with his father, "We all live upon
the hope of pleasing somebody."   And he was right: Boswell hoped to
please his father.

Back to Edinburgh *en route* south, when almost without warning David
died on 29 March 1777.   High infant mortality necessarily inured parents
to such losses; Johnson's consolation was "to keep three out of four is more
than your share."   Still, Margaret felt the baby's death acutely, and the
other children reacted without benefit of calm reflection.   Boswell records:

> This morning Veronica and Effie would see their little brother.
> Veronica calmly kissed him.   But Effie was violently affected,
> kissed him over and over again, cried bitterly, "O my poor billy[1]
> Davie," and run to his nurse who had also been hers, and clung
> about her, blubbering and calling to her, "O come and take him
> off the table.   Waken him, waken him, and put him in his cradle."
> With much difficulty we got her pacified.

Boswell's feelings were equally fervent in his own way:

> I was tenderer today than I imagined, for I cried over my little
> son and shed many tears.   At the same time I had really a pious
> delight in praying with the room locked, and leaning my hands

[1]Brother.

on his alabaster frame as I knelt.   I prayed *for* his spirit, but chiefly
to it as in the region of felicity, looking to a beautiful sky.

These scenes had an echo a few weeks later when Boswell, while instructing Veronica (now four) in the joys of heaven, found her afraid at
first of death, she saying, "I hope I'll be spared to you."   But when told
how Christ had opened its gates for us, she was so pleased she said, "Oh,
I'll kiss him."   Then Boswell fell to a favourite trick of testing people's
affection for him:

> "Suppose," said I, "Veronica, when you come to heaven, you do
> not find me there.   What would you do?"   Said she: "I would
> cry, 'Angels! where's my Papa?'"   She said this with such an en-
> chanting, earnest vivacity, as if she had really been addressing
> herself to the *celestial ministers*, that I was quite happy.   "But," said
> I, "suppose they should let you see me walking upon wild moun-
> tains and shut out because I had not been good enough?"   Said
> she: "I would speak to GOD to let you come in."   I kissed her with
> the finest fondness.

(A few years later he so vividly evoked the horrors of hell that the children
roared out and ran to him for protection.)

David's death persuaded Boswell to give up his jaunt.   Margaret needed
him, the Douglas case before the House of Lords had been put off, and
he would show his father he could do without the pleasures of London.
In fact, he was less keen to go now that his father had given him leave.
At the end of April he returned to Auchinleck and "a kind of negative
existence, being just a dutiful attendance" upon his father.   Lord Auchinleck seemed again to be failing, and Boswell thought he and Margaret
should take a lead; since he recorded "a kindly letter, very comfortable,"
from his father a month later, it is apparent that he never made this
suggestion to the person most immediately concerned.   On 8 May Boswell
wrote,

> I really think that this dull, uninteresting journal is not worth the
> trouble of writing.   But it is a register of my life, such as it has
> passed.

With that remark the journal fails, and interest turns outwards to
Boswell's most pathetic-comic case: Rule v. Smith, Hamilton, and Christie.
The case itself provides the pathos; Rule's "doer" or legal agent, James
Gilkie, the comedy.   On 23 September 1772, George Smith, a merchant,
seized two cows, two steers, and a heifer in payment of a debt from the
farm of 70-year-old Archibald Rule in Graystonlees, Berwickshire.   The

next day Smith reappeared with Robert Hamilton, a sheriff's officer, and Alexander Christie, an attorney of almost 70, to seize more of the stock. They were resisted by the actual debtor, Rule's youthful son Alexander, accounts differing as to what occurred. Smith's version was that Alexander, though ill with jaundice, wantonly assaulted him and his colleagues, but in the ensuing scuffle was so gently resisted that he cooled down, helped them gather some of the sheep for payment, and invited them to his father's house. Here he was said to remark that "if he had been then as well as he had been or used to be, he would not have allowed them all to have proceeded in the business." But later he "sent for a vomit from Berwick, which did him much harm; his fever increased; and on the third day after the scuffle he died."

Rule's version of these events was that Smith and his friends violently attacked Alexander with whips and sticks, got him down on the ground, and beat him till he vomited, while repeatedly calling out, " 'Kill him! Knock him in the head, and not let him live a minute longer!' or words to that effect." After Alexander's death, his father applied to the Sheriff for an inquiry, but the ensuing testimony convinced the Lord Advocate that the affair was "merely a scuffle in which the young man was the aggressor; and that there was no foundation for a trial for murder." Archibald Rule was so appeased, or so threatened, that shortly afterwards he agreed to sell his goods privately and hand over the proceeds to Smith rather than take the chance of a public auction.

There the matter rested, until James Gilkie "reawakened" it four years later. Gilkie was a small-time attorney who spent much of his energy litigating his own lawsuits, a loud, shrill purveyor of his wrongs in the press, and an occasional but tiresome thorn in the Establishment side. He owed Smith money, which was the reason (some said) that he incited Rule to charge Smith and the others with murder, it being possible under Scots law for a private prosecutor to bring charges if the Crown failed to do so. But presumably he had some encouragement from Rule. Gilkie, as agent, presented a memorial of the case to Boswell, as counsel, and "criminal letters" (the indictment) were drawn up. But when Gilkie returned to Berwickshire to execute the indictment, Smith had him thrown into gaol for debt and, to make matters worse, Rule's landlord persuaded, deceived, or intimidated Rule into disclaiming the criminal letters. Gilkie emerged unshaken, however, from gaol, hurried Rule before a J.P. to disclaim his disclaimer, and on 16–17 May 1777 trial proceeded before Lord Gardenstone at Jedburgh on the Justiciary Circuit, Boswell speaking "lively and well." Actually the trial centred not on the murder charge but on whether such a charge could be preferred in view of Rule's disclaimer of the criminal letters.   Gardenstone, heretically for the century, remarked that "life is the first object of our attention, property only secondary," but passed the case on to the wisdom of the entire High Court of Justiciary in Edinburgh. (Private comments of judge and counsel are instructive: Gardenstone said that Gilkie was of a "constitution to be unhappy, discontented, and turbulent, and confused, with twinkling of parts," and Boswell admitted that Gilkie had a jack-o'-lantern in his head.)   The High Court convened on 23 June and decided unanimously that Rule's disclaimer voided the indictment, though he was free to have a new one drawn up.   The Court then turned its attention to Gilkie, who had been issuing irresponsible attacks on the defendants in the press, and sentenced him to a month in the Canongate Tolbooth (more comfortable than the Edinburgh one), and longer if he could not find caution for proper behaviour.   So ended round one of Rule v. Smith.

The change from fully written journal to the mostly condensed notes in which Boswell registered his existence from mid-May to mid-September is like the shift from a peaceful major to an agitated minor key.   He accompanied his father to the Justiciary Circuit at Glasgow (10 May 1777) where he undutifully got very drunk, and his father angrily told him that such behaviour hurt Boswell's reputation.   Boswell records restraint: "I had presence of mind or rather of *heart* to be *kindly* with him."   (The kindness was wasted.)   He was always on the fret, irritated, for example, that on return to Edinburgh he could not have sexual relations with Margaret right then during the day.   After the Smith trial at Jedburgh, he made a brief show of business at the General Assembly, that "*vulgar and rascally* court" as he now called it, but by the time the Court of Session sat down for its summer term on 12 June, he was ready to give up practice altogether from low spirits.   That was impossible, of course; how otherwise could he support his family?   They were installed for the summer in a pleasant country house in the Meadows, less than a mile south of James's Court and near to Lord Auchinleck's new residence.   But if proximity was intended to promote kindliness between the two households it failed.

The two months of the summer term passed in a swirl of wretchedness. "Laboured" and "sunk" report continued drudgery and depression; and, thrashing about for relief, Boswell solaced himself with those usual snatches at pleasure, drinking and whoring.   He called himself "a depraved creature," and it did no good; he knew what was right but his behaviour was out of control.   And he had other causes for unhappiness.   Mountstuart, arriving in Edinburgh in all the glory of his usual nonchalance, announced that it would be a waste of influence to get Boswell a sinecure, since his father would soon die and he would not need it.

Then, in the middle of the summer, Margaret had a serious recurrence of consumptive symptoms, and Boswell realized for the first time that she might die in the near future. Characteristically, he "wandered evening and embarked. Wife waiting at entry. Sad vexation." The next day: "sunk and ill. . . . Called Nabob.[1] Comely maid. Even *now* dallied. . . . Wife justly not reconciled." At the end of July, Margaret had a miscarriage.

Boswell was miserable. He woke one morning saying to himself, "Oh, must I rise and endure another day?" But as the term came to its end, his spirits grew somewhat better: "Rising of session rather pleased me today, to have feeling of ease." Curiously, Boswell never seems to have connected his recurrent depression to his return from London and the court's summer term. He could say that he felt "a sort of lightness" when his father left for Auchinleck, even though (or because) no mention had been made of his paying a visit. But consciousness could not admit how much he hated his situation; if it had, he might have been forced to take action to correct it.

Instead, Boswell improved the summer by continuing to wander, and records—a glimmer of comic relief—that much intoxicated at a funeral he kissed a young girl in open day in the churchyard. Grange saw him, and the bare word "Methodists" suggests that some of those pious folk saw him too. The relief is the reader's; Boswell remained depressed. Godfrey Bosville brought part of his family to visit his son-in-law Lord (formerly Sir Alexander) Macdonald; and Boswell, though feeling guilty about it, excused himself from accompanying them to Auchinleck. He had a more attractive prospect: he was to meet Johnson at Dr. John Taylor's at Ashbourne, Derbyshire.

As soon as the jaunt began, Boswell became a new man. His journal (posted from a week to a month late) takes on a completely different character: it is fully written, easy, smooth, flowing. *En route* to and from Ashbourne he takes time to expatiate on any topic that strikes him: fellow passengers, sightseeing, inconveniences, chambermaids. Once arrived, he consciously focuses on Johnson, warning himself to make haste to record his sayings. The journal becomes semi-public: minor indiscretions—hardly a chambermaid goes by unfondled—can be edited out; near the end of his

---

[1] Alexander Boswall of Blackadder.

stay at Ashbourne he is promising Grange, "You shall hear me read excellent wisdom and wit from my journal."

Does the shift in Boswell's mood, close to a transformation of character, account for the style and content of the journal, or does the semi-public function of the journal impose a role on Boswell?   The word "role" suggests an answer.   In Johnson's presence and under his influence, Boswell can become a different person.   On Sunday, he reflects:

> While I sat in an *English Church*, and saw *Dr. Samuel Johnson* in the seat with me, and had my imagination filled with all the circumstances of learning, genius, worth, and literary distinction which that name conveys, and considered that he was my *intimate friend*, I was as serenely and steadily happy as I suppose man can be.

Fortunately, Boswell's unusual capacity for misery was equalled by his gift for happiness.

Boswell's detractors sometimes suggest that Johnson must often have found his company a great nuisance, but Mrs. Thrale knew better.   While he was awaiting Boswell's arrival, she wrote to Johnson: "Mr. Boswell will make Ashbourne alive better than three hautboys and the harpsichord." It is easy to forget how much he relied on Boswell's quickness of mind, good humour, and vitality, for satisfying company; and on Boswell's never-failing interest in him, fidelity, and love, for the deeper, more sustaining reassurance of his worthwhileness.

In return Johnson gave Boswell that enormous affection with which he could respond to so many people and which made him loved, as his extraordinary intellectual powers made him respected.   He wrote to Boswell at the time: "I set a very high value upon your friendship, and count your kindness as one of the chief felicities of my life."   And Boswell had earlier told him:

> My affection and reverence for you are exalted and steady.   I do not believe that a more perfect attachment ever existed in the history of mankind.

But Boswell's anxious temperament made him again and again demand assurances that Johnson cared for him; wasn't he uncertain of his father's love?   And Johnson, in reply, could grumble, "You always seem to call for tenderness."   Boswell's affection for and dependence on him could be embarrassing.   At Ashbourne, Johnson told him,

> My regard for you is greater almost than I have words to express, but I do not choose to be always repeating it; write it down in the first leaf of your pocket-book, and never doubt of it again.

Boswell, who could be very literal-minded, did just that: wrote it down in the little notebook he kept for details about Johnson's past life.

Equally important, Boswell stood in awe of Johnson, as he did of his father, but his father's harsh indifference humiliated him while Johnson's affectionate firmness, as before, freed him to be his best self. Boswell elaborated this point at Ashbourne:

> I really feel myself happier in the company of those of whom I stand in awe than in any other company, except when I have a temporary elevation of mind and delight in being with my inferiors, or a temporary gay, easy, pleasurable frame and wish to be with a friend upon an equal footing or a mistress. To be with those of whom I stand in awe composes the uneasy tumult of my spirits, and gives me the pleasure of contemplating something at least comparatively great. I have often and often experienced this, though I cannot clearly explain or account for it.

Just like Lord Auchinleck, Johnson provided a control for that uneasy tumult of spirits which ordinarily Boswell could only repress; in Johnson's beneficent presence, this psychic energy could flow into conversation and reflection.

Taylor, one of Johnson's oldest friends, was a rich, jolly clergyman of determined opinions—Johnson could rouse him to "a pitch of bellowing"— and no strong religious bent. His chief interest was his livestock, and his talk, naturally, was of bullocks. Taylor left them much to themselves, and Boswell had more of Johnson's company alone than ever again. The conversation centred on Boswell's basic topics: his love and fear of wine; his melancholy; his eagerness to try the English bar; and, an equally sensitive topic for Johnson, death and immortality. "His dread of death," Boswell writes,

> has sometimes shocked me, as I thought it a most gloomy and desponding consideration that his vigorous mind and exalted knowledge and moral excellence could not overcome the dread of what must certainly come to us all.

Comparison was natural:

> How terrible then must death be to me. Yet I really have at times no great horror at it. Perhaps such minds as his may be assailed with more violent terrors than feebler and more confined ones, as oaks are torn by blasts which shrubs escape from their lowliness.

Their tête-à-tête brought Johnson and Boswell very close in the interchange of intimate thoughts. The night before his departure, Boswell was afraid that he was keeping Johnson up too late but Johnson told him, "I don't care though I sit up *all night* with you." Human nature being what it is, they got into an argument over the American War and Parliamentary corruption, and were glad to part at 3 a.m. Boswell was firm in his views on this occasion, but at other times his attitude has traces of conscious submissiveness and unconscious resentment. He arrived at Ashbourne hoping that Johnson would not say a single harsh word to him during the visit, and then irritated Johnson by mentioning his birthday, as he knew mention would. A few days later he "unguardedly" said to Johnson, "I wish I saw you and Mrs. Macaulay together." [1] The storm burst: "You would not see us quarrel to make you sport. Don't you see that it is very uncivil to pit two people against one another?" And constantly Boswell links his deep attachment to Johnson to the thought (fear, he calls it sincerely) of Johnson's death, but he never doubts that he will outlive Johnson and write his biography.

These are lesser currents in the relationship. Boswell had almost never seen Johnson more uniformly social, cheerful, and alert, and he sparkled with some of his best-remembered opinions and sayings: whether a biographer should mention his subject's vices as well as peculiarities (questionable); the lugubriousness of Tom Warton's ballad style (parodied); how the prospect of hanging concentrates the mind wonderfully; the pleasure of driving briskly in a post-chaise with a pretty woman; if a man is tired of London, he is tired of life. As the two sit basking in the sun, they discuss the inadequate stipend of curates; later they argue whether actors have merit ("I was *sure*, for once," says the pro-theatrical Boswell, "that I had the best side of the argument"); they clear the waterfall of branches and a large dead cat; they stand "in calm conference . . . at a pretty late hour in a serene autumn night, looking up to the heavens." A lively serenity is the dominant atmosphere in which Boswell envelops this Flemish picture of his friend.

For the time being, Boswell's mind was relieved of its "wretched changefulness," his inability to sustain a steady view of himself and his society. Though he remarks that meeting a friend cannot provide as much immediate pleasure as meeting a mistress, he goes on to say that the company of Johnson—strongly seconded by the plainness of Taylor's maids—caused him to forget about sex while he was at Ashbourne. Boswell takes this as the triumph of intellectual over emotional pleasure, but Johnson's company may well have satisfied an emotional need even stronger for the

[1] Catharine Macaulay, bluestocking, historian, and "republican," whose principles Johnson had tested by suggesting that her footman sit down to dinner with them.

moment than sexual desire.   It is clear that Boswell takes a much calmer view of his own life: even his unsuccessful attempt to lay a chambermaid at an inn seems a momentary urge, shocking to him only because of the risk of infection rather than the serious lapse into adultery he might have thought it at another time.   And the reader passes over the incident without much attention, another indication of how much our reaction to Boswell's behaviour is directed by his opinion of it.

Wretched changefulness returned to dominate Boswell's life during the autumn and winter of 1777–1778.   He records that on 29 September he ran off from Margaret in a bad humour, on 3 October she was displeased to read in his journal about the chambermaids, on 7 October he was quite well, and on 10 October he got drunk and was horrible to her, being very ill the next day.   The entry of 13 October brings him to the low point of this particular period:

> Exceedingly ill; as dreary and horrible as ever.   Called [on] Grange; groaned and could hardly speak.   Wretched, wretched . . . quite sunk.   Bad cold appeared.

A few days later he set off on a duty visit to Auchinleck, which did not improve his mood.   His father's memory had failed so much that he had forgotten baby David's death.   Boswell's resentment against Lady Auchinleck, who was unpleasantly defensive about her husband, had hardened to the point where he habitually referred to her as the *noverca*.[1]   The Family Melodrama was in full cry:

> Disagreeable mutterings with *noverca* at breakfast, as her pride makes her boast of not complaining.   I unwarily said, "Well, I wish I saw you once seriously ill, that you might be obliged to complain."   SISTER (with peevish grin).   "I believe you do.   To see her in her grave.   To tell her so to her face."   NOVERCA. "Truth will out."   Despised them.   Father bid me tell he would [have] been at Darnlaw's burial if not ill.   *She* would not have it told.   I.   "I'll obey my father's commands."   SHE.   "Yes, that always was the way."   I.   "It was not, but I hope it shall be in time coming."

Margaret's consumptive symptoms again grew worse, and on 28 October 1777 Boswell hurried back to Edinburgh.   She was very ill, and recovered at so slow and irregular a pace that she was unable to leave the house until the latter part of January.   Boswell defended himself against possible loss by fantasies of a second marriage, with Lady Eglinton favoured

---

[1]Virgil's "iniusta noverca" ("harsh stepmother"—*Eclogues*, iii. 33).

as replacement.   (That illusion was sadly punctured when she died in January, aged just over twenty-one.)   In company he "rattled," while at home his mood shifted like a weather-vane.   Time and wine began to tell: one night on the prowl he found himself "*incapax*" (incapable).

It was time for round two of Rule v. Smith.   Gilkie—Maclaurin called him a parody of Boswell—had again popped out irrepressible from gaol, and directly petitioned the Crown to instruct the Lord Advocate to pros-ecute Alexander Rule's murderers.   This manoeuvre predictably having failed, new private criminal letters were prepared, and the relevancy of the indictment argued before the Justiciary Court on 24 November 1777. Again the defendants took refuge in technicalities: Rule, the "prosecutor," was not in court (he seems to have sheltered himself in Berwick beyond the reach of his opponents and the Court itself); the list of witnesses had been signed by Gilkie rather than, as was customary, by the prosecutor; and the indictment left the prosecution free to press charges either for murder or for culpable homicide.   Boswell summarized his performance as "not warm as I have been, but well enough."   Rae answered for the defendants, and the Court argued for two days, finally asking for Infor-mations (statements of the case) from each side.   The eventual ruling came on 26 January 1778, Boswell by now being quite indifferent: Rule's presence could be waived, but Gilkie's signing the list of witnesses was a fatal bar to the present indictment, and expenses were found against Rule.   The pros-ecution was free to draw up criminal letters for a third time; but Gilkie and Boswell desisted, beaten by the law's delay.   Since the trio of defend-ants never came to trial it is impossible to assess their guilt, but they were certainly reluctant to face the charge of murder directly.   At least Gilkie got the last word.   He later published a wheedling letter from Smith asking that bygones be bygones, accompanied by his own noble denunciation of such a dirty evasion of the truth.

In a case of much more general importance, Boswell was one of the counsel for Joseph Knight, a Negro slave imported from Jamaica, who petitioned for freedom on the ground that Scottish law prohibited slavery. Boswell, who like Knight's other counsel served gratis, conscientiously asked Johnson at Ashbourne for an argument in Knight's favour, which was duly supplied and later recorded in the *Life*.   The Court of Session set Knight free on 15 January 1778, but Boswell's heart was on the other side.   Though warmly praising Dundas's speech on behalf of the "sooty stranger" (did periphrasis make Knight less real?) in the *Life*, Boswell chose to argue the case against Knight again there.   He called the abolition movement—and he may well have had a majority of his fellow citizens on his side—a "wild and dangerous attempt . . . to abolish so very important and necessary a branch of commercial interest," continuing:

> To abolish a *status* which in all ages GOD has sanctioned and man has continued would not only be *robbery* to an innumerable class of our fellow subjects, but it would be extreme cruelty to the African savages, a portion of whom it saves from massacre or intolerable bondage in their own country . . . especially now when their passage to the West Indies and their treatment there is humanely regulated.

How sharp the contrast to Johnson's toast: "Here's to the next insurrection of the Negroes in the West Indies!"

The new year began badly. An attempt at conjugal intercourse made Margaret spit blood: "O direful," Boswell says. And there was great family trouble. Several years earlier Margaret's widowed sister, Elizabeth Montgomerie-Cuninghame, had married an Englishman, John Beaumont, in defiance of her family. She was considered a lady of fortune and acted like one; on her death in 1776 she left Beaumont an annuity of £300 and a lease of land worth another £100 a year (as surety for the annuity). Lainshaw was, or had been, worth £40,000 but it was riddled with debt, much of which had been contracted to put money into Beaumont's pocket, and this settlement left her six children by her first marriage almost penniless. The five boys and their sister Annie, who in 1778 ranged in age from about 23 to 16, were high-spirited, reckless, and improvident. The eldest and heir of entail, Sir Walter, a cornet in the Royal North British Regiment of Dragoons, was living on credit like a gentleman. Boswell lectured him severely, suggesting that if he could not live within his meagre means in the army he should return to Lainshaw to try to make the coalworks show a profit. (Sir Walter had the advantage that, until 1799, many colliers technically were still serfs who could not leave a mine without the owner's permission.) The other Cuninghames—only Walter had taken his father's hyphenated surname—were great, hungry nestlings squawking loudly for provision, and it is much to Boswell's credit that he tried very vigorously to help them. He also moved to have the will set aside (Cuninghame v. Beaumont), but on 21 January 1778 the Court of Session decided, 7–3, to let it stand except for the lease in Beaumont's favour, even though, as Kames said, it was a "ruinous deed which indirectly puts an end to the estate." Sir Walter now suggested that he return to Lainshaw and buy out Beaumont's annuity (with what?), but Boswell decided that he had better stay where he was. In late February, Lainshaw was sequestered (put into bankruptcy under trustees).

It had been a bitter year for Margaret: the deaths of her son David and her sister Mary, her own worsening illness, and now the imminent sale of Lainshaw, her family home.   But her health grew better with pregnancy, as is often true for consumptives, and Boswell's mood also improved.   He wandered with a wench to a room in Blackfriars Wynd ("twice"), repeating the prescription the next day, an event unusual only because he felt no self-disapproval; he seems to have convinced himself for the time being that the law of Moses permitted plurality of women.   But whatever the morality of his acts, the physical laws of cause and effect continued to operate, producing the customary *morbus*, and predictably cool relations with his wife.   Buoyed, however, by a month of water-drinking, the rapidly nearing end of the winter session, and the prospect of London, Boswell was even so calm as to think for a moment that the Court of Session might be an important enough sphere for him.   Such spirits could not last; at the rising of the court he felt uneasy for want of "immediate business"— anxiety at the intermittence of a regular occupation—and more fluttered at the thought of his first trip to London in two years, he said, than by the menace of that other great journey, death.   There had been talk of Margaret going south with him for her health; she might join him later.   But Margaret disliked leaving home and children, and on Pringle's advice she stayed in Edinburgh.

This spring's fine London account illustrates how closely Boswell's journal responds to what he is doing, and his skill in evoking scene and mood. It starts not, as usual, with his departure from Edinburgh but two weeks earlier on 1 March, Boswell mistakenly believing that the year had once started in Scotland on that date.   There was fuss, as expected, with his father but not as much as on earlier occasions.   They had reached stalemate: a regrettable lack of close cordiality, but Boswell appreciated his father's stories and steady temper; and he even seemed in better health than he had been for the past two years.   For their parting interview Boswell brought along Veronica, "a little footstool" to raise him so that he would feel less like a boy.   His father raked up some old grievances— Boswell's extravagance, his neglect of the Dundases—but told him since he insisted on going to London, at least to stick close to those who could be of real service to him, a group which certainly excluded Johnson and Paoli. They parted on tolerable terms.

Boswell records the journey and his first few days in London with characteristic sweep.   The journal widens like a river as his life takes on meaning.   He settled with Paoli, where living combined elegant hospitality with home comfort and ease.   He pursued a plan of steady economy, argued cases before Parliament, and tried to sustain London spirits without London giddiness.   Duty calls on Mountstuart and Queensberry produced another £100 loan from Mountstuart, and Queensberry, who would die before the end of the year, promised to ask George Clerk-Maxwell to resign his sinecure, worth £200 a year, as Lord Treasurer's Remembrancer in the Scottish Court of Exchequer, in Boswell's favour.   As before, it remains mysterious why they should discuss so hopeless a solicitation.   What was to be done for Clerk-Maxwell in return?   In a glance over his shoulder Boswell wrote to his father some time in April that he did not wish to depend too much on Mountstuart's help (not forthcoming, of course), and then in summary:

> that I have done well before the House of Commons—and am spending little money—wish that my conduct now may give him satisfaction—that I am grateful for all he has done for me.   Beg to hear from him.

Boswell had brought his *morbus* and water-drinking with him from Edinburgh.   His illness made him uneasy from time to time but hardly altered his habits; he soon renewed his relationship with No. 36, who if she was Mrs. Love must now have been close to sixty.   Whoever she was, the connection (one can hardly call it anything so grand as an affair) continued to afford comfort: "was to try *balsamum femineum*," "vastly snug" at 36's, "refreshed, and 36 said I was *better* than formerly."   The water-drinking was a trial, though Johnson and Paoli gave encouragement.   Boswell constantly found excuses to try something stronger, like mild ale for costiveness; or a sample of tokay, or montepulciano, or rhenish, or anything.   Still abstaining, he argued for drinking and against Johnson; Boswell imagined his behaviour if Reynolds came to visit him in Scotland:

> I take him all in my arms: "My dear Sir Joshua!   I rejoice to see you."   Shall I unsocially let him sit drinking by himself and not take a bottle with him?   No, no.   I *will* take a bottle with you.

Not drinking was "so awkward and particular and insipid."   Johnson warned, "When one doubts as to pleasure, we know what will be the conclusion." But in spite of a few lapses Boswell stuck to water, and as a result thought it the best London visit he had ever made.

Predictable though it is, the instantaneousness of Boswell's response to London never fails to be striking.   Hardly arrived, he was "fully happy in immediate sensation and hope," refuting that melancholy remark of Pope's which continued to haunt him, "Man never is, but always to be, blessed."   Boswell longed to fix his present state of mind, as he had wanted to fix his mood at Auchinleck the previous spring, because happiness for him was so precarious.   Alternatively, he was willing to believe with Johnson that unhappiness was not only his condition but that of all men, designed to encourage us to look to a better world.

The dominant impression Boswell gives is of movement: mass converted into energy.   London was inexhaustible and he was everywhere, a favourite in every social gathering for his adaptability, vivacity, and good humour.   Or almost every company: he intruded when Beauclerk was entertaining some society friends at supper, and got snubbed.   And there were other rifts within the lute.   As even Pringle admitted, he was born for England but it remained impossible to settle there without place or pension.   Further, being an agreeable companion was not enough; to become someone, as Paoli twice more warned him, he must acquire a solid character and a serious position.   To be someone, for Boswell, necessarily included living in London.   This spring he moved one more step towards a fixed resolution: "*must* settle in London," he told himself.

These, however, were long-range considerations, and Boswell was immersed in the present.   For a few days at the end of March he was so busy that the journal shrank to its bones:

Breakfast Burke.   No place of wash.   Dined Sir John Dick's, well.
Supper Lord Mountstuart.

But the record, presumably under the influence of water-drinking, ordinarily is much fuller throughout April.   Sometimes Boswell wrote up memorable days immediately; more often he posted a longer section of journal at a stretch, writing from notes or from "strong, fresh memory."   There was much to report, and Boswell had to remind himself not to indulge in reflection; to gather in significant experience was enough.   (Even entries in somewhat condensed style can be long; that, for example, of 7 April 1778—breakfast at Johnson's, in a coach together, dinner at Streatham—runs to over 2,000 words.)

Naturally Johnson demands to be recorded, but he is far from Boswell's only subject.   He has time for Burke, for Garrick, for anyone like Cleland— "rough cap like Rousseau . . . eyes . . . black and piercing"—who stood out from the crowd.   Nor was he a mere recorder: Burke was informed that he was the only man Boswell could wish to be, and Garrick learned to take Boswell seriously.   Calling on Garrick at breakfast, Boswell was immediately greeted with, "I have not a minute to stop."   Boswell goes on:

I was prompt and flashed upon him, "I am very glad."   Then, strutting up close to the little man and (I think) putting my hands on his shoulders, and looking with his own tragicomic, dubious cast, "Don't give yourself airs." This did with him, and in reply to my "I'm very glad," he smartly took himself: "But I'm vexed."

Then having said he would stay in town an extra day to give Boswell breakfast, Garrick went on,

"Everybody, I find, speaks well of you. But I don't." Said I, "Pray don't talk so." ... We now walked out. I told him, "My good humour is but a sweet sauce to a pretty bitter dish. I have a good deal of *amertume*.[1] I am as proud as Lucifer. I am an old Scot, proud of being descended of ancestors who have had an estate for some hundreds of years."

Having asserted himself, Boswell found it very pleasant to walk arm-in-arm down the Strand with the greatest of actors.

Nor do tête-à-têtes exhaust Boswell's powers of recording; with easy virtuosity he set down a long evening's conversation at The Club, differentiating among Johnson, Burke, R. B. Sheridan, Lord Ossory, George Fordyce, Gibbon, and Reynolds. Dinners were especially worth report: at Paoli's, at Allan Ramsay's, and two at Reynolds's. At Reynolds's on 9 April were Johnson, Langton and his wife Lady Rothes, Richard Owen Cambridge, Ramsay, the Bishop of St. Asaph, and Gibbon; after dinner the company was enlarged by "Hermes" Harris, Percy and his wife, the airy Mrs. Cholmondeley, Hannah More, Dr. Burney, and Garrick. "How rich!" Boswell comments. "This is a great day. Cannot have it anywhere else. This is the place." As he retrieves (to use one of his favourite quotations) "the feast of reason and the flow of soul," time and space fade away; we forget whose table it is, only aware of movement, gesture, and the give-and-take of the conversation, which endures in a continuous present. These are no longer bones but the living creature.

But this wonderful gift to posterity had begun to arouse some hostile comment as his habit of journalizing became widely known. Wilkes, of all people, told him that he was a dangerous man to keep company with, since he restrained others by his habit of recording conversation. Boswell responded accurately, "I don't think it restrains you." Garrick, sneering at his abstemiousness, remarked, "Let it be a law of The Club, either drink or we'll search him, that he mayn't have book. If he won't let wine search him, we will." Boswell's commentary: "Nonsense: as if I had book and wrote in company, and could not carry in my *head*." Later, alone, he would jot down notes in a home-made shorthand, which he also believed rapid

[1]Bitterness.

enough to record speech directly, but it did not stand the trial of Johnson's dictation.

The most valuable kind of conversation, Boswell thought, was that which provided memorabilia, and on occasion this spring Johnson was even willing to help him refresh his memory, though quite capable of saying at the same time, "Don't be scribbling," when Boswell made "little additions" in his presence.   As Boswell later commented in the *Life*:

> He was secretly pleased to find so much of the fruit of his mind preserved; and as he had been used to imagine and say that he always laboured when he said a good thing—it delighted him, on a review, to find that his conversation teemed with point and imagery.

Johnson's character held extremes of affection and antagonism in constant tension.   Competition aroused him; but, beyond this, sometimes he seemed armoured in hostility.   To whom else would it occur to say of a friend:

> Sir Joshua Reynolds, Sir, is the most invulnerable man I know; the man with whom if you should quarrel, you would find the most difficulty how to abuse.

Perhaps as a result of their week of intimacy at Ashbourne and reaction to it, his relationship with Boswell oscillated rapidly between unusual tenderness and real anger.   Johnson's temper, always uncertain, had become as unpredictable as a warm West Indian climate:

> A bright sun, quick vegetation, luxuriant foliage, luscious fruits; but where the same heat sometimes produces thunder, lightning, and earthquakes, in a terrible degree.

The analogy may be too elaborate, but it suggests correctly that Johnson's emotions could resemble forces of nature uncontrollable by society, though in theory he held a very high view of the importance of customs and manners.   He even told Boswell that he regarded himself as a very polite man; "curious this!" Boswell comments in his journal.

Boswell's attitude towards Johnson was itself changing somewhat:

> I had a sort of regret that we were so easy.   I missed that aweful reverence with which I used to contemplate *Mr. Samuel Johnson* in the complex magnitude of his literary, moral, and religious character.

As he knew, such regret was foolish, but the feeling of loss is understandable.   From posterity's point of view it was the reverential regard with which Boswell gazed on his subject, tempered by a detached steadiness of scrutiny, that enabled him to depict Johnson both fully and sympathetically. If Boswell's feeling of inferiority looks like a character weakness in a man who was approaching middle age, it was one he shared with many of Johnson's friends.   And it can be considered in a different way:

> The most sublime act is to set another before you.

Such at least was the attitude that produced the portraits of Johnson in the *Tour to the Hebrides* and the *Life of Johnson*.

Boswell's ease with Johnson, in any case, was intermittent.   He recurred to a more usual attitude when he remarked to Johnson a few days later: "You and I do quite well to travel together.   The composition just fits.   I love to be under some restraint, some awe, and you're as easy with me as with anybody."   Johnson in turn praised Boswell as the best travelling companion in the world.   Then this exchange on Good Friday:

> BOSWELL.   "Sir, there is none of your friends on whom you could depend more than on me."   JOHNSON.   "No, Sir, none who would do more for me of what I'd wish to have done.   Were you to die, it would be a limb lopped off.   And remember, I tell you this that you may not always be wishing for kind words."   BOSWELL.   "Sir, you are very good.   If you were to die, there would be such a blank to me as I cannot express."

Johnson loved to fold his legs and have his talk out and Boswell encouraged him, but that was different from being badgered: "What man of elegant manners teases one with questions so?   I will not be baited with *what*: what is this? what is that? why is a cow's tail long? why is a fox's tail bushy?"   (But, as F. A. Pottle observes, Johnson usually liked being asked why a fox's tail was bushy.)   On Holy Saturday, he gave Boswell a horrible shock by telling him that his company would drive a man out of his own house.   A much more serious break occurred at Reynolds's on 2 May, when fretted by uncongenial company Johnson attacked Boswell with such savagery that Boswell, for the first time in their long friendship, became really angry, purposely avoided Johnson, and might have returned to Scotland without seeing him if Langton had not brought them together at dinner.   When Langton tactfully left the room, they became reconciled, joining, it is to be feared, in a laugh at their host.   The next day, "according to old custom," they dined at the Mitre, where they talked for the only time, as well as Boswell could recall, about sexual pleasure—Johnson thought the difference between duchesses and chambermaids lay in the imagination of the embracer—and then, by some unexplained transition, about the universal mystery of all things.

Near the end of his stay Boswell, all benignant officiousness, secured an interview for Johnson, now writing his *Lives of the Poets*, with Lord Marchmont, who as a young man had been a close friend of Pope's.   When he hastened to Streatham with the good news Johnson, perhaps suspecting some humiliating application on his behalf, became downright crabby:

> JOHNSON.   "I shall not be in town tomorrow.   I don't care to know about Pope."   BOSWELL.   "No, Sir?   There was no means of guessing this beforehand."   MRS. THRALE (surprised).   "I suppose, Sir, he thought that as you are to write Pope's life, you'd wish to know about him."   JOHNSON.   "Why, wish.   If it rained knowledge, I'd hold out my hand.   But I would not trouble myself to go for it." . . .   BOSWELL.   "Lord Marchmont tells me, Sir, Pope left no manuscripts of his own behind him."   JOHNSON.   "He lies, Sir." . . .

In the *Life* Boswell generously ascribes Johnson's response to exquisite irritation, to

> that unhappy temper with which this great and good man had occasionally to struggle, from something morbid in his constitution.   Let the most censorious of my readers suppose himself to have a violent fit of the toothache, or to have received a severe stroke on the shin-bone, and when in such a state to be asked a question. . . .

Another example of Johnsonian, and all too human, behaviour was the Pennantian controversy.   Johnson ran over Percy for some supposed rudeness in an argument about the traveller, Thomas Pennant, in front of a gentleman acquainted with the noble Percys of Northumberland, whom Percy was eager to impress.   Urged by Boswell to make amends, Johnson wrote Percy a handsome recommendation, which Boswell read aloud at a dinner where Earl Percy was present.   But Johnson was offended when he learned Boswell had given Percy a copy of the recommendation, and forced Boswell to retrieve it.   Percy was left badly bruised.

Character, Johnson remarked, is made up of many particulars, and not to be judged by one alone.   Boswell applied this maxim by catching those characteristical instances which make up so much of his portrait of Johnson.   Some are mere gestures, "leaning and swinging upon the low gate into the court, without his hat" as he read Fontenelle's *Mémoires*.   Or he glimpses Johnson ravenously absorbed in a book which he kept "wrapped up in the tablecloth in his lap at dinner, like a dog who folds a bone in his paws while he licks broth."   At other times, Boswell notes the conversation or little story or decisive remark.   To this spring belongs Johnson's ex-

planation of how an acquaintance lived in London on £30 a year: "on
'clean-shirt day' he went abroad and paid visits."   When asked whether
the sermons of the executed clergyman-forger Dr. Dodd were not addressed to the passions, he replied, "They were nothing, Sir, be they addressed to what they may."   He was capable, too, of softer responses, as
in a dispute as to whether the doctrine of Christian charity permitted one
to differentiate among individuals:

> MRS. KNOWLES.   "Doctor, our Saviour had twelve Apostles, yet *one*
> whom he *loved*.   John was called 'the disciple whom JESUS loved. "
> JOHNSON.   (with eyes sparkling benignantly) "Very well indeed,
> Madam.   You have said very well."

Paoli complained that Johnson's conversation was all definitions, but
Boswell greatly admired "his knowing clearly and telling exactly how a
thing is."   Percy offered a fine figure for Johnson's conversation: it was

> strong and clear, and may be compared to an antique statue, where
> every vein and muscle is distinct and bold.   Ordinary conversation
> resembles an inferior cast.

Almost all the preceding remarks appear in Boswell's journal, though
sometimes quoted here in the more polished versions in the *Life*.   Boswell
must have deliberately left out there certain comments that the journal
records, such as Paoli's saying that he was stunned by Johnson's "inarticulate
vociferation"; but much that is brilliantly described in the journal—perhaps
the best bit is the scene with Garrick quoted earlier in this chapter—was
necessarily omitted as irrelevant.   Yet rehearsing these scenes for the *Life*
also prodded Boswell into recalling what the journal had failed to register.
He brings back, for instance, Garrick's precise habits of speech.   The
journal reads: "GARRICK.   'What, is Strahan a good judge of an epigram?
I think as obtuse a man as I have seen.' "   In the *Life* this becomes: "GARRICK.
'What! eh! is Strahan a good judge of an epigram?   Is he not rather an
obtuse man, eh?' "

In one of the most famous scenes he records, Boswell both omits and
recalls.   On Good Friday, as he and Johnson were returning from St.
Clement Danes, Boswell stepped aside for a moment and in the interval
saw that Johnson had been accosted—as the journal but not the *Life* reports—

> by a man whom I did not know.   They stood in the attitude of
> the figures in Newbery's little spelling-book, bowing with curious
> courtesy, Dr. Johnson's hat off awhile:

> > "So, S, T, and U,
> >   Pray, how do ye do?"

> "We thank you—the better
> For seeing of you."

It was Johnson's old college-mate Oliver Edwards, of course, and then follow the details of that memorable meeting.   But the great moment, that "exquisite trait of character" which everyone remembers, Boswell summoned up for the first time in the *Life*:

> EDWARDS.   "You are a philosopher, Dr. Johnson.   I have tried too in my time to be a philosopher; but, I don't know how, cheerfulness was always breaking in."

On 19 May, Boswell paid Johnson a parting visit, and it produced one of his most precise descriptions (given here in the *Life*'s version).   He asked Johnson if he should take a vow not to drink wine.

> JOHNSON (much agitated).   "What! a vow—Oh, no, Sir, a vow is a horrible thing, it is a snare for sin.   The man who cannot go to heaven without a vow—may go—"   Here, standing erect, in the middle of his library, and rolling grand, his pause was truly a curious compound of the solemn and the ludicrous; he half-whistled in his usual way when pleasant, and he paused as if checked by religious awe.   Methought he would have added—to hell—but was restrained.

And then Boswell was away.   On the trip north a clergyman, recalling his *Corsica*, called him an honour to his country.   A stop at Godfrey Bosville's country seat in Yorkshire trapped him in instant ennui, instantly relieved by departure.   On 28 May 1778 he arrived home to a warm welcome.

CHAPTER

8

I

THE OCTOBER 1777 issue of the *London Magazine* carried as its lead article the first of an anonymous series of essays called *The Hypochondriack*. Its seventy numbers, which ran to August 1783, reflect on a wide range of topics, among them fear, hypochondria, love, marriage, parents and children, religion, death, pleasure, prudence (how to get ahead in this world), reserve, penuriousness and wealth, learning, sleep, and suicide. These brief essays—Boswell's, of course—should command attention as his considered opinions about the most vital concerns of living. But contemporaries were unimpressed, and today even assiduous readers of Boswell tend to ignore them.

The Hypochondriack is Boswell's only long work to be a failure; it brought out his weaknesses rather than his strengths. Like the journal, the essay is a highly flexible form, and the eighteenth century responded to all its possibilities from sermon to gossip column. But Boswell had given his attention to two models. *The Spectator* taught manners in the broad sense—modes of social behaviour—as well as new ways of looking at nature, art, and society. *The Rambler* taught morals by probing the complications of the mind and heart. The Spectator, a figure of sophisticated detachment, was the beau ideal of the young Boswell's more dignified hours, but the precepts of the Rambler sank deep within him. Sometimes limiting himself to unarguable common sense, the Rambler was more often impressive through a rigorous but never uncharitable examination of the gaps between what man thinks himself and what he is, between what he is and what he ought to be. These traditional topics of satire took on a graver tone in

Johnson's handling of them. "In no writings whatever," Boswell says in the *Life of Johnson*, "can be found *more bark and steel for the mind.*" Johnson's essays presented a sharply defined, coherent point of view, a most attractive feature to a young man who knew what he felt (but then feelings change so quickly) rather than what he thought (though he knew what he was supposed to think). For Boswell, Johnson's works, like Johnson himself, embodied a moral and psychological integrity as steadying—to return to his metaphor—as the sight of a rock to a man whose head is turning at sea.

Poems and essays were the favoured try-out genres for contemporary aspirants to authorship. Boswell always held a somewhat higher opinion of his poetry than others did, but prose was his natural medium and, when at twenty-one he was a writer in search of a subject, Kames told him that he was "well calculated for writing lively periodical papers." The flexibility of the essay accommodated his pleasure in ranging over opinions and events without much regard to organization. In 1765 he drafted a *Hypochondriack* essay in Milan, which he called No. 10 to suggest that he was already in the middle of a series, and which he was to publish, with literal-minded whimsy, as No. 10 in the *London Magazine*. But, as mentioned earlier, when he actually decided to embark on the series in 1772, Margaret and Temple quickly discouraged him from pursuing it.

Now without preamble he started in again, making no great claim for his efforts. He said in the first *Hypochondriack* that, as well as a preparation for more laborious tasks, essays were pleasant excursions in themselves. In the last *Hypochondriack*, he concluded that his essays had been less lively and more learned than he had anticipated, emphasized their usefulness as mental discipline, and bragged about his talents at the same time as he excused the results by disclosing they were composed while "I had just time enough to do them with rapid agitation." Like Johnson's *Ramblers* is the implied comparison, and he thought some of his sentences as well-written as some of Johnson's.

Boswell's "Rampager" *nom de plume* advertised, at least, the roaring high spirits those letters were supposed to exhibit. The persona of the Hypochondriack points directly to a contrasting and deeper component of his character, one he feared at times was central to it and yet somehow alien, "me" and "not me" at the same time. Further, he believed if he could not free himself from hypochondria he might bring it under control, as he tried to do so much else in his character, by writing about it. In his *Anatomy of Melancholy*, Robert Burton had subjected his ramblings about hypochondria to the precision of scholastic categories; in an equally wandering way though within a much more informal structure, Boswell was also to try to exorcise his feelings.

Hypochondria, as Boswell experienced it, was not a general term for imaginary invalidism or neurosis; it designated a specific illness with a wide range of symptoms—self-contempt, dislike of others, fretfulness and impatience, irresolution, feelings of helplessness, an inability to act or even talk—that collected in crippling depression. Hypochondria was an inexplicable disease, perhaps in part physical, perhaps hereditary, both terrifying and tedious. At worst, it was a total "impotence of mind" that reduced its victim to an agonized or lethargic passivity. And Boswell had suffered from it all his life. He told Wilkes in Italy, "If you would think justly of me, you must ever remember that I have a melancholy mind." Beneath the surface gaiety, the good humour both natural and cultivated, Boswell thought of himself as the Melancholy Man.

Such a character might seem too strong and too special for a long series of essays, but Boswell seldom insists on the full extent of morbidity; hypochondria gives many of the essays little more than a slight colouring. His stylistic model is Addison, not Johnson, the persona taking on a mild and well-bred tone, that of one gentleman speaking to others on subjects of common interest. He throws out what occurs to him as if sitting with a friend; he is the companion rather than the teacher of his public. Such an ingratiating approach, combined with quick intelligence, wide if not deep reading, and easiness of expression—Boswell was almost incapable of writing badly—might appear to guarantee a series of energetic and appealing papers. Careful selection could build up such an impression, but it would be misleading.

Essays investigating broad topics—luxury or subordination or time—demand powerful generalizations. An essayist like Bacon strikes with brilliant sententiousness: "It were better to have no opinion of God at all than such an opinion as is unworthy of Him. . . . Superstition is the reproach of the Deity." Johnson, Boswell's immediate predecessor, builds up steadily to a conclusion through a sequence of insights into ordinary experience:

> Wives and husbands are, indeed, incessantly complaining of each other; and there would be reason for imagining that almost every house was infested with perverseness or oppression beyond human sufferance, did we not know upon how small occasions some minds burst out into lamentations and reproaches, and how naturally every animal revenges his pain upon those who happen to be near,

without any nice examination of its cause. We are always willing
to fancy ourselves within a little of happiness and when, with
repeated efforts we cannot reach it, persuade ourselves that it is
intercepted by an ill-paired mate since, if we could find any other
obstacle, it would be our own fault that it was not removed.

Johnson has thought through his generalizations; when he uses examples, generalizations illuminate rather than derive from them.

Boswell has neither Bacon's command of the aphorism nor Johnson's ability to abstract convincingly from experience. As his other
writings show, to generalize effectively he had to proceed to his conclusions through those minute particulars that are the basis of his biographical method. But in these essays he usually develops his subjects through
a random collection of classical sayings, modern examples, and decorous
personal anecdotes, all leading to an unexceptionable conclusion; and
in the helter-skelter of composition, he was sometimes reduced to using
long quotations as filler. Temple was on the right track when he wrote,
"Your *Hypochondriack* would be more entertaining if you could blend
some story with it." Boswell needed the circumstantial detail that narrative requires; without it he is just another essayist.

The eye on the object is Boswell's source of detail, and even more
important the force of the mind behind the eye. Yet observation rather
than introspection was his strong point: as in his journal he was reluctant
to examine any matter very closely. It was natural enough that he did
not want to recreate depressive moods: "[I am] strangely averse . . . to
present my readers with some of my own particular observations of the
effects of hypochondria." But he also found the minutiae of the physical
world and even the details of daily living wearisome to examine. In
The Hypochondriack, as in his journal, he confessed that "intense inquiry"—even into the nature of words—affected him with giddiness and
a kind of stupor. But then any "abstruse kind of speculation," he thought,
"sickened" his "perceptions of real life": it led directly to religious doubts,
to dreary brooding over Liberty and Necessity, the emptiness of life, the
terror of death, and again—worst of all—the annihilation that might lie
beyond death. Montaigne, the example he is glad to claim elsewhere,
would have given him the best model for these essays, but Boswell could
not let himself wander through his own mind. Modestly, he hopes no
more than to produce "a few cursory observations which will entertain
without fatiguing."

That much may be granted him. He can entertain, and the essays
are too short to have much fatigued their monthly readers. Taken in

batches they become more irritating.   Boswell is at his worst when he
wobbles between what he feels and what he thinks he should advise his
audience.   In his four essays on drinking he cannot reconcile his avidity
for drinking with his fear of being dependent on liquor or with his conviction that a moralist should condemn any but the most moderate indulgence.   So he concludes insipidly that drinking "is a dangerous pleasure."
The essays come alive only when Boswell feels decisively about something
personal:

> I knew a father who was a violent Whig, and used to attack his
> son for being a Tory, upbraiding him with being deficient in "noble
> sentiments of liberty," while at the same time he made this son
> live under his roof in such bondage that he was not only afraid
> to stir from home without leave like a child, but durst scarcely
> open his mouth in his father's presence.   This was sad living.

The most important *Hypochondriack* for Boswell the writer is No. 66,
"On Diaries."   "An hypochondriac," he says, "is particularly prone to think
of himself.   Uneasiness directs his attention inwards.   I have kept a diary
for considerable portions of my life."   Here he brings together some of
his basic ideas:

> It is a work of very great labour and difficulty to keep a journal
> of life, occupied in various pursuits, mingled with concomitant
> speculations and reflections, insomuch that I do not think it pos-
> sible to do it unless one has a peculiar talent for abridging.
> I have tried it in that way, when it has been my good fortune to
> live in a multiplicity of instructive and entertaining scenes, and I
> have thought my notes like portable soup, of which a little bit by
> being dissolved in water will make a good large dish; for their
> substance by being expanded in words would fill a volume.   Some-
> times it has occurred to me that a man should not live more than
> he can record, as a farmer should not have a larger crop than he
> can gather in.   And I have regretted that there is no invention
> for getting an immediate and exact transcript of the mind, like
> that instrument by which a copy of a letter is at once taken off.

In this instance Boswell knows what he wants to say.   But most of the time
he knows only what the world has said, or might say, or should say.

Yet Boswell was pleased with these essays.   "Wrote wonderfully well,"
he congratulates himself repeatedly, the wonder being that he could pull
them together so fast or that in a state of depression he could write at all.
He contemplated a collected edition, and provoked Johnson by asking him
to select the best.   "Nay, Sir," was the response.   "Send me only the good
ones; don't make *me* pick them."   But Johnson, near the end of his life,
was impressed when he heard some read aloud:

> Sir, these are very fine things; the language is excellent, the rea-
> soning good, and there is great application of learning. . . .   I
> would have you publish them in a volume and put your name to
> them.

And Boswell goes on triumphantly to Temple: "He is to revise them, and
then I shall bring them forth in two or perhaps three elegant volumes."

That these volumes first materialized in Margery Bailey's handsome
edition in 1928 has not deprived intervening generations.   A student of
Boswell needs to search them for clues to basic attitudes, but Boswell evaded
the specifics of his own mind: the entertainment they provide is mild, and
Boswell shows no talent for instruction, not because of his moral lapses but
because his mind and opinions, rather than his principles, are interesting.
When Boswell thought abstractly, he thought faintly.

I I

NEAR THE END OF a gloomy summer a break in Boswell's routine came
with a jaunt to the Carlisle Assizes (August 1778).   The ceremonial entrance of the judges—he loved pomp and circumstance—the business of
the court, the lively unfolding of a new society joined to please him.   "I
find myself always easiest among strangers," he remarked, "unless indeed
among my very intimate acquaintance."   And in Carlisle, if he had known,
his future opened for a moment like a chasm.   He got a look at Sir James
Lowther, the great boroughmonger:

> The grand jury were called over.   Sir James Lowther was their
> foreman.   It was agreeable to see a man of his great fortune
> appear doing his duty to his country, both as a Justice[1] and a grand
> juryman.   He had travelled night and day from London to be
> present at the Assizes.   There was a swarthy, Turk-like stateliness
> in his looks and manner.   They speak very differently of him in
> the county.   It seems to be universally agreed that he is a hu-
> mourist.[2]   But some say that he is capricious and proud and dis-
> obliging, and does not choose to have interest by making himself
> agreeable, but by compulsion—by means of his immense wealth.
> Others say that he is very friendly where he takes a regard.

A week of Carlisle was enough; indifferent to the beauties of nature,
Boswell cancelled a trip to the Lake District and returned to Edinburgh.

[1]Justice of the Peace.
[2]An eccentric.

There on 15 September James Boswell, Jr., was born, "a fine, big, stout boy," named according to Scots custom after his paternal great-grand-father. Margaret suffered severely during labour, and for the first time said that she did not want any more children.

Since he had nothing he really wanted to do, Boswell had to look outside himself for stimulus. One animating event occurred late in September when the 78th Regiment of Foot (the Seaforth Highlanders), unpaid and fearful that the regiment had been sold to the East India Company, mutinied and camped out on Arthur's Seat, where well-wishers supplied them with bread, cheese, and beer. After three days they marched down, their demands satisfied. Boswell contributed a lively, sympathetic account of their situation to the *Public Advertiser*, commenting in his journal: "My spirits were now as good as when I am in London, such is the effect of agitation upon me."

Otherwise he was forced to create his own agitation, and it followed the usual routine. In his metaphor, he "strayed into three different strange countries." But he seems to have regularized his habits somewhat. Ports-burgh, an Edinburgh suburb, had become his customary place of recreation, the object of his affection there disguised in his notes under the name of Stevena. Some of his entries are intriguing, but need to be filled out to make sense. 29 January 1779: "Was quite keen, as Peddie[1] would not," so Portsburgh in "vigorous, indelicate frame." 30 January: "Having risked yesterday, out between seven and eight to Portsburgh. Tedious [?delay waiting for door] to open. Man in closet. Wonderful presence of mind; [?bade him be] *to it*. Man off. Going, but allured back: *twice*. Found I was known." That afternoon he had a "solemn conversation" with the Rev. Mr. Falconer, a non-juring bishop, over coffee and old port; "how different from morning!" 19 February: "Portsburgh. Stevena, but took care no multiplication, etc. etc."

Most of his time that autumn and winter Boswell spent in less hazardous ways. In October, after a short, pleasant visit to Valleyfield, he went to Auchinleck, having tried unsuccessfully to secure an invitation for Margaret. His father's indifference to her and the children continued to disturb him, but he thought as usual that the restraint of his father's presence did him good: "Coldness checked fretful fancies as frost kills weeds." He found himself in what he calls "the Auchinleck calm and solemn humour," and once more could almost imagine that he would grow fond of the country.

[1]Margaret.

Legal practice was scanty on his return to Edinburgh, and Boswell took so little interest in it that Lawrie, his clerk, had to warn him to tend to his business.   Only one case was more than routine, that of Campbell's Trustees v. Scotland, a suit stemming from the Stirling burghs election of 1774 in which Boswell had acted as counsel and delegate for Colonel Campbell. Campbell was off fighting in the American War, but his trustees brought suit against his one-time burgh agent, Robert Scotland, who had not only gone over to the enemy during that election but had carried off with him some £3,000 with which he had been entrusted to establish, in Boswell's phrase, "a *beef and claret* interest."   In short, the money was to be used, in illegal though accepted fashion, to bribe the electors.   Scotland made no bones about bribery; in fact, his counsel took the line that any arrangement he had entered into with Campbell could not be enforced because it violated the law.   Ilay Campbell, arguing for his namesake, demanded that Scotland produce his accounts first and then claim an illegal compact.   The Court reluctantly found for Scotland.

Another exciting interruption in Boswell's monotonous existence occurred early in 1779.   The Government had repealed certain penal statutes against Catholics in England, and proposed to extend this reform to Scotland.   But horror of popery was one of the most deeply embedded of Presbyterian fantasies, and conservative ministers in Glasgow and Edinburgh preached bigotry to willing listeners.   Scottish response grew so furious that even the few Catholics asked that the effort at relief be abandoned.   But on 2 February the mob in Edinburgh got out of hand and took deep pleasure in burning and plundering "masshouses" and private dwellings of Catholics, the Lord Provost being afraid to try to protect them. Boswell recounts his own attempt at intervention:

> I went close to the scene of action . . . and having called silence I harangued to them a little very keenly, said I loved a mob [no doubt recalling the one he had led in the Douglas Cause], but was ashamed of them now, for what could the papists do worse than this? . . . A fellow who did not know me said, "You had better not speak so among the mob."   I said, "I'm not afraid of the mob."   One who knew me called out with a significant look and manner, "Mr. Boswell, you know we're in the right," and then was great huzzaing and no more could be said.   It hurt me to see a large book, perhaps some venerable manuscript, come flaming out at one of the windows.   One of the mob cried, "They (i.e. the papists) burnt us.   We'll burn them." Another cried, "Think what they did to our worthy forefathers."

Boswell's feelings were always generous and he loved the limelight. The next day, "inflamed" with port, he again tried to disperse the mob,

and Grange had to pull him away before he got hurt.   Naturally Scotland
was left unreformed.   The class structure of eighteenth-century Britain
rested uneasily on the shifting sands of the multitude, and this episode of
unchecked pillage was a nasty forerunner of next year's Gordon Riots in
London.

A month later Boswell was off to London, where he arrived at Johnson's just in time to sketch him with an aspiring bard, the Rev. William
Tasker:

> Tasker appeared to me to be a foolish, scatter-brained creature.
> He was a lank, bony figure with short black hair.   He had an
> idiotical grin, showing his teeth while he talked, and uttering in a
> squeaking tone while the Doctor read to himself his *Ode to the
> Warlike Genius of Britain,* "Is that poetry, Sir?   Is it Pindar?"   "Why,
> Sir," said the Doctor, "there is here a great deal of what is called
> poetry."   Tasker, while the Doctor read, gave me some abrupt
> exclamations, such as, "My muse has not been long upon the town."
> And (meaning his poem), "it trembles under the hand of the great
> critic."   . . . [JOHNSON.]   "Here is an error, Sir; you have made
> Genius feminine."   "Palpable, Sir," cried Tasker.   "I know it.
> But it was to pay a compliment to the Duchess of Devonshire, with
> which her Grace was pleased.   She is walking across Coxheath,
> in the militia uniform, and I suppose her to be the Genius of
> Britain."   "Sir," [said the Doctor] "You are giving a reason for it,
> but that will not make it right."   . . . I interposed and said, "As
> the Duchess is moving along in her military uniform, with hat and
> feather and everything else, might not the gentleman, instead of
> making Genius feminine, make the Duchess masculine?"

The journal of that visit was to record few such brilliant scenes.   "During my stay in London this spring," Boswell remarks in the *Life,*

> I find I was unaccountably negligent in preserving Johnson's say-
> ings, more so than at any time when I was happy enough to have
> an opportunity of hearing his wisdom and wit.

This decorous statement covered a "multiplicity of engagements."   In better health and spirits than he could remember, Boswell spun like a top
kept steady by its own momentum, his only objection to London that it
involved too much space and too little time.

"Am I not fortunate," he asked Temple, "in having something about
me that interests most people at first sight in my favour?"   Not merely at
first sight; Johnson said Boswell "never left a house without leaving a wish
for his return."   After so many annual visits he had established a large,
dependable network of friends and acquaintances.   In the City, members

of "the Trade" (publishing), like the Dillys, and Boswell's fellow proprietors in the *London Magazine*, now printing *The Hypochondriack*. Wilkes, associated with the Dillys, had been Boswell's friend off and on since their days on the Continent, and Boswell showed surprising affection for him: "I believe I love John Wilkes, the classical individual, better than almost any body," he wrote. (Wilkes was a classicist who published de-luxe editions of Catullus and Theophrastus.)

These solid citizens—Wilkes became a force for law and order during the Gordon Riots—tended to be Dissenters, and liberal in their politics. In contrast stood Boswell's conservative countrymen, some visitors like himself and some settled more or less permanently in London. Among visitors this year he mentions Ayrshire neighbours like the Earls of Cassillis, Eglinton, and Loudoun; and Fullarton of Fullarton. Among the transplanted, Douglas continued to live magnificently in fashionable Pall Mall, though Boswell felt more at ease with his neighbour there, the shrewd, ageing Pringle. And Mountstuart kept up some Scottish connections. Boswell maintained a firm faith in his Maecenas of the puzzling temperament, and while Mountstuart got angry at Boswell's habit of repeating everything, he continued to make gestures about preferment, that never-dying illusion. With the Scots, though very unScottish, can be grouped the Bosvilles, Boswell's wealthy, hospitable Yorkshire "cousins."

Boswell's most important circle of friends derived, of course, from his intimate friendship with Johnson. Johnson himself remained central, the great attraction of London. In one direction he led to the Thrales, in another to various members of The Club. Garrick had died that January— another intimation of mortality—but Boswell cultivated Burke's friendship, and was on easy terms with Reynolds. Closest to him now among Club members was Bennet Langton, tall and thin—he himself said he looked like the stick of an umbrella—a little solemn, a little slow, but learned, friendly, and unaffected. He doted on his numerous children, inflicting them on his visitors, and his mismanagement of his domestic economy was widely deplored. But goodness shone through him, and he at least meant to be tactful. That spring he presented Boswell with a copy of *The Government of the Tongue*, and Boswell was much pleased with what he called this "delicate admonition." He could be himself with Langton, as he never could with Langton's dearest friend, the handsome, acid aristocrat, Topham Beauclerk.

Finally there were the two generals. To James Edward Oglethorpe, senior officer in the British army, Boswell paid the honour he gave to those he admired deeply: he started to make notes for his biography. Next to

Johnson, Pasquale Paoli remained Boswell's most revered friend.   His
house in South Audley Street continued to be Boswell's base of operations,
his chariot always at Boswell's disposal.   Paoli was his conscience and scolded
him when he drank too much; at the same time he was unfailingly patient
and kind.   Most important, he was one of the few of Boswell's friends who
took his career seriously, and his advice over the years was consistent:
Boswell should cultivate people of consequence through his vivacity and
sense of humour, and then by degrees show that he had superior talents
which could be of use to them.   It was not Boswell's way.

The event of the spring was the Hackman affair.   The Rev. James
Hackman fell in love with Martha Ray, mistress of Lord Sandwich and
mother by him of nine children.   She refused Hackman's proposals of
marriage and on 7 April 1779 as she stepped into her carriage after attending a performance at Covent Garden, Hackman shot and killed her.
He then shot and failed to kill himself.   At his trial Hackman asserted that
he had intended only suicide, but had carried two pistols in case one mis-
fired.   The jury followed the lead of one of the judges, the famous Sir
William Blackstone: Hackman intended to kill Miss Ray at least at the
moment he shot her, and his two pistols suggested premeditation.   He was
condemned to death.

As might be expected, Boswell rose to this sensational occasion.   He
struck up an acquaintance with Hackman's brother-in-law, got himself seated
at the defence table at the trial, visited Hackman in gaol, and published in
the *St. James's Chronicle* a sympathetic account of the lesson Hackman's
behaviour offered: "to make us watch the dawnings of violent passion and
pray to God to enable us by His grace to restrain it."   Indeed a newspaper
account, possibly the work of the Shakespearian editor George Steevens,
stated that Mr. Boswell had accompanied Hackman in the coach to Tyburn.
This suggested too close a connection, and Boswell meditated reply.   Pembroke and Burke told him to ignore the newspapers: he was not the only
"Mr. Boswell" and, after all, he had been present at the execution—they
only sent you in Hackman's coach, Burke said—but Boswell issued a wag-
gish denial.   Johnson told him this was the right thing to do, since people
thought that he himself had inserted the paragraph, an indication of the
common and largely correct view of the reason for Boswell's frequent
mention in the newspapers.

The question of whether Hackman's two pistols showed premeditation
set off a violent altercation at The Club between Johnson and Beauclerk,
in which they traded deserved accusations of rudeness.   Johnson resented
Beauclerk's predominance in company, and Beauclerk thought Johnson

should be taught a lesson in politeness; disagreement about Hackman's motives was a spark that set off a latent antagonism.   Burke and Boswell on the sidelines called it a fight between a bear and a polecat.   But as tempers cooled and mutual respect reasserted itself, the quarrel ended in an exchange of compliments.   The miseries of age—and age, as Johnson said, "is a very stubborn disease"—were further cues to Johnson's irritability.   Fortunately, dressed in his Parisian wig and finest suit, he was on his best behaviour for the interview Boswell arranged for him with Lord Marchmont, postponed from the preceding spring.   Marchmont provided some choice anecdotes, and Johnson, delighted, said that he wouldn't have missed this meeting for twenty pounds.

Alarmed at hearing that his father was ill, Boswell left London early this spring, on 4 May, stopping at Southill in Bedfordshire, where he was moved by the affection and edified by the devout fervour of the dying Edward Dilly.   By the time of Boswell's return, Lord Auchinleck was sufficiently improved to travel to Ayrshire but, in a rush of affection or remorse or fear, Boswell voluntarily promised never to go to London again unless his father thought there was good reason for his going.   Lord Auchinleck was now so infirm that he got permission to absent himself from the Bench for most of the summer session.   Not only did Boswell fear the effect of this absence on his practice, but characteristically his view of himself as an advocate was tied to his dependence on his father:

> I resolved to be assiduous this first session of my father's absence as that was to be considered as a trying era for me, because people might imagine that I would not apply to business when he was not present.

Whatever people imagined, his practice was better than it had been the previous summer, though his fees dropped sharply.   Boswell also took to testing Johnson's affection by not writing to him as usual.   Something always survived in Boswell of the child who is naughty because he wants to go through the routine of confession, punishment, and forgiveness; punishment at least indicates concern.   Naturally, the less affection his father gave him, the more he tried to extract from Johnson.   Johnson indeed was concerned, and wrote first to Charles Dilly and then to Boswell directly to find out if he was ill; when he discovered what had happened he felt tricked: "It is as foolish to make experiments upon the constancy of a friend as upon the chastity of a wife."

The summer was insignificant, as insignificant as any Boswell could remember, though there were a couple of breaks in the routine.   In the Pleasance, a straggling street south-east of the city, he made a new ac-

quaintance with whom he engaged in some uncommon act. (At least the
π that indicates sexual relations is upside-down in his journal entry.) And
later that summer he solaced his existence by returning to Portsburgh.
Perhaps he was being philosophical: to a philosopher, Monboddo told him,
women were only an "evacuation." The sale of Lainshaw, though long
anticipated, came as a stunning blow. His spirits dwindled unevenly—he
still had good days—from indifference to boredom to melancholy, which
hard drinking accentuated:

> After having gone to bed with my dear wife, I started up in shock-
> ing gloomy intoxication and raved in solemn rage about my being
> miserable. It was a horrid night.

In this frame of mind, the new coastal batteries at Leith—John Paul Jones
was about—roused all the interest, he said, of potato-beds at Auchinleck.

Salvation materialized, improbably, in the shape of Lt.-Col. James Stuart,
Lord Bute's second son. Boswell's intimacy with Stuart's wife, his "lovely,
enchanting friend," had never led to more than slight acquaintance with
him. Now friendship ripened over the bottle; one night they sat drinking
until seven in the morning. Stuart suggested that Boswell accompany him
on an English expedition, visiting London and his regiment in the North.
For Boswell, mired in a sensual, degrading existence—"nothing gave me
any satisfaction at present but eating and drinking and lying in bed"—the
invitation was irresistible. The mirage of patronage danced before all eyes:
the combined influence of Stuart and his older brother Mountstuart, it was
readily imagined, would carry great weight. Mountstuart, moreover, was
leaving to become Envoy to Turin, and a visit from Boswell would be taken
as a farewell gesture. Even Lord Auchinleck did not oppose this interlude,
which Boswell interpreted as a sign of further decay.

The journal Boswell kept of this jaunt, Leeds to London to Chester
and back to Edinburgh, is the only journal of his later years which has not
been recovered; we would give a good deal to have the Chester section,
which he called "a log-book of felicity." What survives is the account in
the *Life* of two weeks in London (4–18 October), the only "second crop in
one year" of Johnsoniana, and the published version is memorable for what
it leaves out: details of a conversation on marital infidelity in which Boswell
tried to establish the principle that every time a wife refused sexual relations, her husband was entitled to mark it, à la Boswell, in a pocket-book,
and to behave as the fly stung. As Johnson remarked, "Nay, Sir, this is
wild indeed (smiling)." Boswell actually printed the passage but cancelled
it when William Windham remarked on its indelicacy. "It is, however,"

Boswell told Edmond Malone, "mighty good stuff."   He always hated to bowdlerize his material.   This visit also included the occasion on which Lord Newhaven softened Johnson with compliments until Johnson bowed so deeply that, as Paoli observed, he seemed to hold down "his head to have the full pail of flattery poured on."   Boswell bid Mountstuart a cordial adieu, and with him the phantoms of preferment vanished over the horizon.

Boswell had never lost his "wonderful enthusiastic fondness" for the military, and Chester provided all the advantages of garrison life with none of the drawbacks of service in the field.   He admitted it might seem a bit juvenile, but he was "*the great man*" in that scene; the Bishop was cordial, the young ladies most attractive; Chester satisfied, as few places could, his "avidity . . . for delight."   He was as happy there as he had been anywhere, even London, for the same amount of time.   Months after his visit he was still recalling Chester as unique.

Business enforced his return to Edinburgh, but Boswell did not go through the usual post-London letdown, perhaps because association with Stuart and his military friends released some spring of aggressiveness: he himself noted a carry-over of "Stuart's judicious firmness," while Margaret commented that his temper had grown more violent.   If it had, there were abundant compensations:

> I wrote twice the number of pages of law papers that I did in the same space last winter.   I went through business with ability and ease.   I had not the least hypochondria.   I relished life much. I was several times out at dinners and suppers, and had several companies with me; and I was very little intoxicated at any time. . . . I was only once with a coarse Dulcinea, who was perfectly safe.

I   I   I

As Boswell resumes his journal just before Christmas 1779, his concerns are mainly religious and domestic.   His faith constantly threatened, he caught at comfort wherever he could.   When the Rev. Hugh Blair, for instance, suggested that prayer was without efficacy, Boswell reacted by reading a sermon of his old favourite, Ogden, to counteract this dreary and dispiriting view.   Religious doubt had appeared elsewhere in the household.   Every Sunday he heard the children recite sacred lessons, but Veronica, not yet six, announced that after due reflection she did not believe in God: "I have *thinket* it many a time but did not like to speak of it."   Examination disclosed an impeccable line of logic: if God did not exist

she could not die, since there would be no God to take her to him.   Sandy,
a sturdy four-year-old, showed more conviction; told about Adam and Eve,
he said that Adam should have been put in the guardhouse.   But the
senior member of the family refused to discuss his religious beliefs despite
repeated inquiry, and Boswell found his father's lack of manifest faith
disturbing.

There was continuity in training from generation to generation.   Boswell beat Sandy for lying as his father had beaten him; a regard for truth,
he says surprisingly, was the only valuable principle his father had ever
impressed on him.   Certainly his father's influence appears strongly in the
catechism through which Boswell imparted his central loyalties to his heir:

> "What is your first duty?"   "My duty to GOD."   "What is your
> second duty?"   "My duty to the Family of Auchinleck."   "Who
> was the first laird of Auchinleck?"   "Thomas Boswell."   "From
> whom did he get the estate?"   "From his king."   "Who was his
> king?"   "King James the IV of Scotland."   "What became of Thomas
> Boswell?"   "He was killed at Flodden Field fighting with his king
> against the English, for Scotland and England were then two king-
> doms."   "Who was Thomas Boswell's son?"   "David."   "What
> became of him?"   "He fought for his sovereign, Queen Mary, at
> the Battle of Langside, lived a worthy gentleman, and died at
> Auchinleck."   He seems much pleased with this genealogical in-
> struction.   I shall go on with it, and habituate him to think with
> sacred reverence and attachment of his ancestors and to hope to
> aggrandize the Family.

Margaret introduced a discordant note into this litany.   Boswell complained about her attitude:

> I insisted with her that she ought in duty as a wife to be ever
> attentive, ever ready to soothe my temper and be complaisant.
> She said very sensibly that she had been educated without that
> timorous restraint in which I had been kept, and that it was much
> easier for me not to insist on subjection than on her to submit to
> it.

A home thrust, but Boswell continued to insist, at least to his journal, that
Margaret should not contradict "his favourite notions and partialities":

> In particular, she was much to blame in endeavouring to coun-
> teract the principle of *family* which has prevailed in the Family of
> Auchinleck from generation to generation.   She said, and perhaps
> with some truth, that our pride and high estimation of ourselves
> as if German princes (my phrase) was ridiculous in the eyes of
> other people, who looked upon us not only as no better than any

other gentleman's family, but as a stiff and inhospitable family. But as I have great enjoyment in our fancied dignity, and cannot be persuaded but that we do appear of more consequence in the country than others from a certain reserve which has always been maintained, and am also of opinion that this pride makes us act in a nobler manner, I wish to encourage it; and my wife therefore should at least not oppose it.

Part of Boswell's genius is his dispassionateness, here his ability not only to show how large a part fantasy played in his own attitudes, but to set out Margaret's views fairly.   Though he treated her badly at times, he always gave her full credit for admirable spirit and behaviour.   As a Boswell on her mother's side, Margaret from childhood had had firsthand experience of the Auchinleck family's opinion of itself.   And if she failed to share their exalted notions, her feeling for Boswell himself ran deep.   Several times this winter Boswell remarks that she was "very good" or "exceedingly good" to him at night, and whatever conjugal endearment this represents, on one occasion it led Margaret to ask, "Will you ever say again that I don't love you?"

Society had its claims as well as family, and they were all the more binding in an age which valued the group more than the individual.   Dinner and supper were the occasions that brought people together in the winter "dirt and gaiety" of Edinburgh.   Most entertainment took place in the home, but in a more relaxed or celebratory mood the company might gather at Fortune's Tavern or Walker's Hotel or Middlemist's Oyster Cellar, whose speciality the young Robert Fergusson had praised in *Caller*[1] *Oysters*. In theory Boswell fully concurred with the common approval of social occasions.   As he wrote in *The Hypochondriack*:

> I have . . . always thought it the mark of a brutish disposition to feed alone, or even to eat perpetually with one's own family, which is comparatively unsocial and makes one figure a group of beasts in the same den day after day.

In certain moods he thought "good social intercourse" was "the most valuable employment of time."

But practice did not necessarily accord with theory, at least in Edinburgh.   Sometimes Boswell could adapt himself to Scots conviviality, the heavy drinking, the hearty laughter, the frank and often rude banter—"I look upon every jovial company," he could write, "as a forge of friendship"—and a release from the usual rigid rules of decorum.   Yet such

[1]Fresh.

company often left an edge of distaste; drinking, he noticed, never failed to make him ill-bred, and the rough informality of Scottish manners had always grated on him.   Genteel gatherings, on the other hand, were no better; the high flavour of London society made them seem tedious and insipid.   And when overwhelmed with hypochondria he could hardly bear company at all.   Margaret lectured him from time to time on his attitude and behaviour.   The rotation of mutual entertainment was a burden he must endure so that the children would have a place in society.   He must restrain the coarse, abusive style of conversation he affected; he didn't receive a tenth of the invitations he had had before marriage.   Still, by modern standards, the Boswells entertained and were entertained at a lively rate.

Exactly where family turned into society is not easy to mark.   In eighteenth-century usage "family" meant "household," which in Boswell's case included Lawrie, who ate dinner and supper with the Boswells until he acquired a wife and house of his own.   Grange, still living below them in the same building, was also in effect a member of the household, a steady, mild, sometimes melancholy, much-valued companion.   By custom he dined with the Boswells on Christmas Day.   That Boswell felt no need to conceal his hypochondria from either Lawrie or Grange shows they were family.

Boswell's intense regard for Family radiated through his circle of relations.   Of first importance, of course, were his father and stepmother on whom he called, sometimes almost every day, frequently staying for dinner, a grim routine that typically left him "quite sunk."   He remained on his guard with Lady Auchinleck, though once, provoked when she implied that his sympathy for Lieutenant John was hypocritical, he told her she was fit to be captain of a man-of-war.   Lieutenant John himself was a disconcerting nuisance, who intermittently intruded on the Boswells. Boswell versified him in a Ten-Lines-A-Day effort:

> By me sits
> My brother John, disturbed with dreary fits
> Of sullen madness; sometimes on the ground
> His eyes are fixed; sometimes they stare around;
> Sometimes with childish laughter he seems pleased,
> As if his mind were for a moment eased;
> Then on a sudden shakes his hands and head,
> And discontent is o'er his visage spread.

In spite of fears that John would become violent, Boswell treated him affectionately, his only relation who bothered to do so.

Extended family, in its many branches, formed the most important part of Boswell's society in Edinburgh.   This included all the cousins: the Websters (especially Dr. Webster), the Prestons, Commissioner Cochrane and others of the Dundonald family, even distant cousins like Harry Erskine, that favourite among Edinburgh advocates.   Margaret's nephews, the orphaned young Cuninghames, seemed always on hand or under foot on their trips through town.   But Boswell took most pleasure in his Boswell kin.   At one "good clannish dinner," he gathered six Boswells together with his own family: "There is to me a double satisfaction in sociality with near relations," he wrote; "it is like knowing that wine is wholesome while we drink it."

Boswell's closest friends in Edinburgh were Lady Colville at Drumsheugh north-west of the city, and Sir Alexander Dick of Prestonfield southeast of it.   Lady Colville and her Erskine brothers and sister had known Boswell almost too long; they could be narrow, sneering, and censorious, and he and Andrew Erskine had long since drifted apart.   But these drawbacks were balanced by the ease of old friendship: Lady Colville could tell Boswell's mood just by looking at his face.   Sir Alexander, now in his late seventies, was uniformly serene and cheerful, a happy old man who fulfilled the eighteenth-century ideal of living in contented retirement on one's native ground.   Either Drumsheugh or Prestonfield made a fine terminus for an outing with the children.   Drumsheugh now is gone, but the house and garden at Prestonfield retain much of the comfortable look they had in Boswell's time; it is easy there to imagine Boswell sauntering with his companionable host and eating fruit in the orchard, while Sandy rode boldly about on his sheltie.   Grange, likewise welcome at Prestonfield, said it was a "foretaste of future felicity."

Several of the Lords of Session had been kind to Boswell as a young man, but he remained on close terms only with Kames, now very old, for whose biography he was gathering notes.   Monboddo had been a constant adviser during Boswell's quarrel with his father in 1769; their intimacy had faded, but they visited back and forth pleasantly enough.   Hailes continued to restrict their acquaintance to a correspondence mainly on antiquarian matters.   Boswell's one really poor relationship was with the Lord President, to whom he still refused to speak in private, until Dr. Webster offered to act as intermediary between them.   In his best Chester coat and waistcoat, Boswell drove with Webster to Arniston, the President's country place, where all was put right over a hearty dinner.   The great length at which Boswell reports this meeting in his journal underlines its importance; the Lord President's half-brother, Henry Dundas, had become the most powerful political figure in Scotland.

Most of the Lords of Session were a generation or more older than Boswell. Surprisingly, he was not very close to any fellow advocates of his own age. He saw much of them, of course, at dinners, consultations, evening parties, and taverns, but none takes on particular significance. He detested his once good friend and bowling companion, Charles Hay, for "fulsome flattery" and "disgusting meanness." George Wallace, a knowledgeable malcontent, cultivated his friendship but never made much of an impact. Boswell saw more of Maclaurin than any other advocate: they shared a liking for songs, squibs, and pleasantry, but his cool temperament was antithetical to Boswell's, and his religious scepticism persistently disturbing. Nairne, a retiring bachelor, Boswell liked and respected but could hardly have found very congenial. (Sir Walter Scott was to say that Nairne was positively the dullest man he had ever known.) The Hon. Alexander ("Sandy") Gordon and his wife, Lady Dumfries, led Boswell into temptation at the card-table. Boswell got caught up in gambling, had no card sense, couldn't concentrate, and felt irritated and guilty when he lost. Among "writers" and attorneys James Baillie visited the Boswells often; one of his virtues must have been his willingness to lend Boswell money.

Boswell looked to other occupations for many of his friends. The closest of these was that banker and model Christian gentleman, Sir William Forbes, whom he consulted in hours of serious reflection and in his will named with Margaret as guardian for his children. Boswell was on easy terms with various doctors: Thomas Young, who was Margaret's obstetrician; Thomas Gillespie, who took care of Lord Auchinleck's "complaint" at a handsome annual stipend of £200; and Sandy Wood, who tended to Boswell's bouts with gonorrhoea and inflamed toe-nails. His fondness for military company led to invitations to officers of the local garrison. With characteristic attention to old connections, he kept up acquaintance with his Ayrshire neighbours like Lord Eglinton, a passionate Scot and unrepentant hard drinker, and with Eglinton's more congenial heir, Hugh Montgomerie; he took care to call on people like "Old" Lady Wallace, whose niece and step-granddaughter Susan Dunlop was virtually another member of the Boswell family. Margaret took a kind interest in various boarding-school misses, who were about the house a good deal. And visitors provided a variety sometimes not to Boswell's taste: Temple's elegant, lively friend, the Rev. Norton Nicholls displayed a frivolous attitude towards religion that disgusted him. Predictably, Boswell avoided deists and Whigs like Adam Smith.

By now Boswell's swings in mood can cause the reader little surprise. The intermittent though severe hypochondria from which he suffered during the winter of 1780 had one material source in acute financial pressure, which seemed all the more unfair since in 1779 he had spent £100 less of his annual income of £600 than in the previous year.   Besides his old debts he had advanced the young Cuninghames between £700 and £800 on their shaky patrimony to get them started on their careers; now he had to look hard to borrow money himself.   Doggerel condensed the situation:

> Long have I struggled with a load of debt,
> Weak to contract and foolish to forget.

Temple could not, and Eglinton would not, lend him money.   But Charles Dilly came to the rescue with a £200 loan, and Baillie, as mentioned, was willing to help him keep going.   Even so, a couple of months later he asked Godfrey Bosville for a loan of £100 or £200 without success.   In May, Wallace lent him £50.   He was just scrabbling along.

A trip to London that spring was out of the question, and Boswell's hope for a meeting later in the year with Johnson in the North of England proved equally futile.   His spirits grew worse, the lowest point coming in late February: he "could have cried from weak, painful dejection," he wrote; "I exist in misery."   For relief, he tried piety and writing to his friends in England.   On 11 March, when usually he would have been preparing for the trip south, he summarized his outlook:

> Apprehended a failure of my practice now that my father did not attend the Court, and thought I should be unhappy for want of business.   Yet I was sensible that a great deal of the coarse labour of law in Scotland would hurt my mind; and I should have considered that one of my fortune should be satisfied with little practice.   I however dreaded insignificance, while at the same time I had all this year as yet been so averse to the business of the Court of Session that I had no keenness for it, as I once had, and wished always to have anything I had to do decently over.   I saw no opportunity for ambition in this narrow sphere.   What practice I had, I had with the dignity of a gentleman; not having used the artifices which many advocates have done, and not debasing myself by familiarity with vulgar agents. . . .   The Session rose, which was rather dispiriting to me, as I was not to go to London and would mould in inactivity.

A revival of spirits at the beginning of April, and Boswell found a rousing if temporary object to focus his energies.   Decay had forced Lord Auchinleck to resign his Justiciary gown, and he was succeeded by Lord Braxfield (Robert Macqueen).   Braxfield's extraordinary ability accounted for his rise from humble origins, but he was coarse and overbearing—not quite a gentleman. Boswell seized the occasion to write A Letter to Lord Braxfield, a pamphlet inculcating decorum and humanity, deprecating the judges' attempts to overawe juries, and insisting in particular that on their twice-yearly circuits the judges should spend the ample allowances given them as representatives of the Crown to maintain proper state and to provide suitable entertainment for the gentry who paid their respects. (Auchinleck was noted for hospitality and Kames for parsimony on the circuit.)

Begun on 21 April, the pamphlet was published anonymously on 8 May; and Boswell told Nairne, "If I had a pamphlet to write every day, I should be happy." Mystification and puffery accompanied publication: Boswell amused himself by charging others with writing his pamphlet. And with Robert Syme, one of the very few to whom he disclosed authorship, he arranged an exchange of letters in the Caledonian Mercury advocating a meeting of jurymen inspired by his Letter to "assert their rights and privileges." This meeting was never a serious project, and Boswell maintained such discretion that the pamphlet was not certainly attributed to him until this century when his journal revealed the truth. His advice, like most advice, was wasted: Braxfield's savagery in the sedition trials of the 1790s is still well remembered. One exchange, however, did the pamphlet justice. Principal Robertson, known for his florid historical characterizations, remarked, "It is a plain style," to which Boswell replied, "But very well written." Robertson agreed.

War with Spain, declared in 1779, had an important consequence for Boswell: it brought T.D. back from Valencia to begin a new career, and Boswell awaited him eagerly. As a youngster, T.D. had been much under his wing and had sympathized with Boswell in his struggle with their father. Now Boswell badly needed a confidant and an ally in the immediate family, and John, of course, was useless. All that winter Lord Auchinleck had looked "very old and very unkindly," though Boswell cherished every crumb of affection; he even records as unusual his father's saying, "Good-night, my dear Jamie." The old man was weary with failure, his memory going and his emotions exhausted; he seemed indifferent even to the death of his brother Dr. Boswell.

Meanwhile Boswell's spirits remained high. He spoke well in the General Assembly—John Home, the author of Douglas, told him that he had never heard anyone speak better—and, with Margaret in her last month of pregnancy, took to wandering again. Back to Portsburgh or the Pleasance or somewhere during the latter half of May, but family censorship has eliminated the details: journal entries for some five days in May and almost all the period of 6–17 June have been removed.   On 15 June 1780 the Boswells' youngest child, Elizabeth, was born.   We catch glimpses of the eddyings of lust: "Impatient for black [woman]. . . .   Met—more in-different in daylight" (20 June); Portsburgh, "FLASH.   Not pleased after" (27 June); "In a wild desperation, for last time, Pleasance" (14 July).   By then or shortly afterwards, he seems to have been enduring the usual consequences.   But his practice during the summer went well in spite of his fears for it, and his being chosen arbiter in a case with Ilay Campbell, the leading advocate at the bar, shows that he maintained a respectable standing.

T.D. having returned in June, he and Boswell went west in August to spend a month at Auchinleck.   Lord Auchinleck no longer seems to have spent much time on his hobbies: indoors, the collection he had shown Johnson of the classics, with Anacreon as its speciality—a peculiar choice one would think.   Outdoors, his favourite recreation had been pruning trees.   But he filled his day: walked or took airings in the chariot, chewed tobacco, scraped clean the leaves of books and newspapers, and presided almost every night at whist, which he played very well.   Dr. Gillespie was in attendance, since he was in constant need of the catheter.   And Lady Auchinleck protected him with passion, telling Boswell that his father went to Auchinleck

> to be quiet and retired.   That company disturbed him, especially at night; and why have people who wanted to drink and be merry and would go away and say he was useless?   It was hard, when people were willing to give up the world, that they could not be allowed to live in their own way.

Lord Auchinleck may have been willing to give up the world, but he had no intention of relinquishing the management of his estate.   Boswell was positively excluded from any say, dismissed by his father as a "gowk" (fool).   Idle as usual, he spent his time walking and riding about, collecting agates in the Lugar Water and nuts to bring back to Edinburgh for the children, or in mild visiting around the neighbourhood.   There was rou-tine and ceremony.   The miller, George Samson, Lord Auchinleck's foster-brother, died and was buried with due circumstance, Boswell and T.D. being chief mourners.   Sacrament Week began with a sermon on Thursday (Fast Day), continued with sermons for four hours on Saturday, all day until 7 p.m. on Sunday, and another four hours on Monday.   It was a stupefying experience, and Boswell was unable to understand how the people not only endured but enjoyed it. (Burns's *The Holy Fair*, published a few years later, might have enlightened him.)

Still, just as Boswell could mingle in any company, so he could pray with every denomination: Presbyterian, Catholic, Anglican, Methodist, Quaker, different Independent sects, even those whom he called the "descendants of venerable Abraham": all were valuable varieties of religious experience. His sympathies were sensuously Catholic, intellectually Anglican, and socially, when necessary, Presbyterian. Though he never forgot the childhood gloom of a Presbyterian Sunday, he later wrote to Sandy (19 Aug. 1791):

> The difference between the Churches of England and Scotland is not in any essential article of doctrine but only in form, and therefore a sincerely pious man may communicate with both. I therefore seriously recommend to you to receive the Holy Sacrament on Sunday sennight in our parish church. It is obeying the dying command of our Saviour, "Do this in remembrance of me." It is a comfort to our souls, and it is a declaration to the world of our faith. The Family of Auchinleck has long been eminent for giving good example.

Secular amusement was provided by Braxfield and Kames, who stopped by on their way round the Western Circuit of the Justiciary Court: "Lord Kames raved and Lord Braxfield roared—both bawdy." After fourteen years as an advocate, Boswell improved the occasion by asking Braxfield how he had become such an outstanding lawyer, and writing down the answer in detail. He would, we remember, go through almost anything if he was to give a written account of it.

T.D. was a great disappointment. The awkward, enthusiastic cub who had gone off to make his fortune had returned a neat, accurate, unimaginative adult: he had had to look after himself, and he had learned his lesson well. On arrival at Auchinleck Boswell dragged him to the Old Castle to reaffirm that "romantic family solemnity," T.D.'s oath to stand by the Family of Auchinleck "with heart, purse, and sword." But T.D. characteristically pointed out in a codicil that this "custom of the family" had in fact originated with the oath he had taken thirteen years earlier. Boswell respected his decent propriety and attention to business, but found him cold, stiff, and self-centred. (Forty years later, Sandy was to remark on his "provoking formality.") T.D. was only half the confidant and not at all the ally Boswell had hoped for; he was habitually attentive to the *noverca*, if for no other reason than that he needed whatever support his father would give him as he tried to establish himself as a business agent in London.

Disagreement between the brothers came to a climax on their trip back to Edinburgh. Boswell writes:

> David and I had disputed too warmly upon the road in the fore-noon. I said he would be on a larger scale when he had been a winter in London; and I said his behaviour to the *noverca* was *butler-like*. He seemed hurt. I asked his forgiveness for hasty expressions. At night his precision and self-conceit fretted me. He said we should not travel together. I said I would not travel with him for five guineas a day.

This was Boswell's next-to-last stay at Auchinleck as a "young laird," and the last he describes in detail. He continued in old ways, contending with Lady Auchinleck, and begging an affection and approval from his father that were granted only with reluctance. Just before going to Auchinleck, the two had had a little conversation in Lord Auchinleck's room:

> I hoped he was now pleased with me. He said, "*Yes*," but not with warmth. I said if he would tell me anything, it should be done. He said the great point was to be frugal and sober. I spoke of how much he had done. He said he had been lucky in having a good wife—two good wives, he might say. I said he was better now than he had been five years ago. He repeated "three-score and ten years do sum up" down to "remove."[1]

At Auchinleck especially, Boswell remained a boy to his father and, what was far worse, a boy to himself. When he was happy he thought back on his childhood, and when he was unhappy he felt as weak as in those early days and "talked religiously with timid dejection." The conjunction of religion, timidity, and depression suggests Boswell's mother, and the extent to which he identified with her *vis-à-vis* his father. No

---

[1]Lord Auchinleck is repeating the Scottish metrical paraphrase of Psalms 90. 10:

> Threescore and ten years do sum up
> our days and years, we see;
> Or if, by reason of more strength,
> in some fourscore they be:
> Yet doth the strength of such old men
> but grief and labour prove;
> For it is soon cut off, and we
> fly hence, and soon remove.

wonder he hated Lady Auchinleck for having, as he wanted to believe, usurped his father's love. He comforted himself once again by the thought that he was doing his duty in "attending quietly" upon his father.

When Boswell looked into the future he toyed with the improbable idea of living very retired at Auchinleck "in independent tranquillity"—the model his father now offered. At the same time he felt himself "a weak man" and, as before, incapable of taking his father's place. Having failed to achieve emotional independence during his father's lifetime he never would achieve it. But that was the future. Things on balance, he decided, had gone well at Auchinleck; on his return to town he was almost fully recovered from his venereal disease and for the moment "in perfect serenity."

*John Stuart, Viscount Mountstuart (1744–1814). Painted by Reynolds in 1776,
the year he was created Baron Cardiff; he is shown wearing his peer's robes.*

Samuel Johnson, LL.D. (1709–1784). The fifth and last of Reynolds's portraits of Johnson, it was painted between 1782 and 1784 for Dr. John Taylor of Ashbourne.

*Henry Dundas (1742–1811), lawyer and statesman. Reynolds's portrait shows
him in the wig and robes of the Lord Advocate of Scotland.*

Sir William Forbes of Pitsligo, Bt. (1739–1806), banker and one of Boswell's executors. Painted by Reynolds, in 1786, wearing the order of the Nova Scotia baronetcy which his family had held since 1626.

Pasquale Paoli (1725–1807), Corsican general and political leader. Painted by Richard Cosway about 1789.

Edmond Malone (1741–1812), editor of Shakespeare, critic, and book collector.
The portrait was painted by Reynolds in 1778.

Camille Des moulins. *anglice*
Joe Miller Orateur vif & sans Culotte

John Courtenay (1738–1816), M.P., miscellaneous writer, and member of The Club. He was an ardent sympathizer with the French Revolution, as this satirical vignette etching, by James Sayer, proclaims.

James Lowther, first Earl of Lonsdale (1736–1802). Painted by Thomas Hudson, in the 1750s or 1760s, wearing the fancy dress of a member of Dashwood's Hell Fire Club; a mask rests on a pedestal by his side.

"The Pacific Entrance of Earl-Wolf, into Blackhaven," 1792. The engraving, by James Gillray, satirizes a dispute between Lonsdale, depicted here as "Earl Wolf," and the citizens of Whitehaven, over which Lonsdale had virtually full control. The citizens claimed that Lonsdale's coal-mines had caused the collapse of certain houses, and suit was brought against him. Lonsdale threatened to close the mines and thereby ruin the town, and the citizens backed down. All the documents pertaining to the action were printed in Peter Pindar's Commiserating Epistle to Lord Lonsdale, the book being crushed by the wheel of Earl Wolf's carriage.

Sir Alexander Boswell, Bt. (1775–1822), M.P. and tenth Laird of Auchinleck.
The present location of the portrait, by Sir Martin Archer Shee, is unknown.

CHAPTER

9

I

ON 29 OCTOBER 1780, Boswell turned forty and entered middle age. He provides no Inviolable Plan, no helpful review of the past, and none of the resolutions for the future with which he marked important moments in his younger years. His only gesture was a brief comment in his journal: "I hoped to live better from this day." We shall have to draw up his summary for him, and it will involve a good deal of repetition. But life at this point for Boswell was also mainly a matter of repetition.

At the time of his marriage on 25 November 1769, Boswell had been a highly successful young man. He came of good family. He was in excellent practice for an advocate of three years' standing. His *Account of Corsica* had made him internationally known, creating in the process substantial difficulties for the British and French governments. To the author of an early sketch of Johnson, written just a few years afterwards, he was "the celebrated Mr. Boswell." Further, Boswell was heir to the extensive barony of Auchinleck, with a rent-roll of £1,000-£1,200 a year, and proprietor in his own right of the extensive if not very profitable farm of Dalblair. His propaganda had been a powerful factor in the outcome of the Douglas Cause, and he was in high favour with Douglas of Douglas, representative of a most ancient family and one of the richest men in Scotland. His friend Lord Mountstuart, son of the former Prime Minister Lord Bute, seemed likely to become a major political figure. But Boswell had many important friends, in the Scottish legal establishment and the London literary world. He knew almost everyone, and those he didn't know had heard of him. He was in vigorous health and had just married the woman he loved.   One could confidently predict a brilliant future for him.

How had that future slipped away?   This impressive résumé conceals severe problems.   Boswell had become an advocate not by choice but by paternal decree, and his enthusiasm for his profession was intermittent and sometimes wrong-headed. He teased the Bench with jokes like *Dorando*, became too zealous in defence of dubious criminal clients, and wasted his vacations in London when he should have been deepening his knowledge of the law and cultivating his practice.   Clients want, above all else, a solid and reliable lawyer.   Also, he had married his impoverished cousin in direct defiance of his father, who had made his feelings pointedly public by remarrying in Edinburgh on the same day that Boswell was married in Ayrshire.

Many of the sources of trouble lay within.   Boswell was intelligent, flexible, perceptive, and gifted with extraordinary powers of observation and expression.   The one quality everyone remarked about him was his agreeableness—his good humour.   High spirits and an ability to fit himself to any company made him popular everywhere.   But he lacked basic self-confidence: he needed to prove his worth over and over by entertaining his company.   And he was caught between two goals.   Should he try to be like his father, prudent, hard-working, respectable—content to be judge and landowner?   Or should he respond to what he felt were the demands and potentialities of his own nature?

But Boswell found it difficult to distinguish demand from potentiality. He knew what he wanted to be: a great man in London.   But how could he make himself a great man?   He had aimed originally at a commission in the Guards.   He admired the life of courage and honour, the respect the soldier exacts from the civilian.   More important, he loved, and always would, both the discipline and show of military life, the precise routine combined with the heartiness of the officers' mess and the ostentation of a spectacular uniform on parade.   But the Guards had never been within reach, and Boswell was a garrison soldier with no taste for the excitement, danger, boredom, and discomfort of war.

Now at forty he imagined himself in the House of Commons or at the English bar.   To be M.P. for Ayrshire would give consequence if not distinction, and a proper excuse to spend half of the year or more in London.   Or, in spite of the prejudice against Scotsmen, he could fight his way forward at the English bar.   Boswell knew his strengths: he was ambitious, he had great energy, he spoke well, and his ability to make people feel pleased with themselves was an enviable asset.   He had had spectacular success with *Corsica*; could he achieve success in more ordinary ways?

But Boswell's strengths were double-edged.   The stubbornness that led him to Corsica and fame, his persistence and inventiveness in the Douglas Cause, came about because he could give any amount of energy to things he wanted to do.   He had the qualities we attribute to children or adolescents because they show them more clearly than adults: spontaneity, direct responsiveness, self-centredness (but not selfishness), and disregard for others in the pursuit of an immediate goal.   What he could not do was to put himself in harness.   He could not calculate his future, set an aim and drive himself towards it.   He could not play the politician and compromise, work and wait.   Patience and prudence, dignity and restraint, were virtues he commended, but they were virtues beyond his practice. What he wanted—and, as Johnson noticed, he was always wanting something—he wanted now.   Immediate distinction, even in the form of immediate publicity, was everything.   Just as his journal verified his private identity, so his name in print confirmed his public place in society.   And any publicity was better than none: he would criticize himself in print, risk notoriety, come close to reducing himself to a figure of fun, all to get an immediate response.

Still, if Boswell had been less perceptive about himself, blinder and more determined, his career might have corresponded more closely to his desires.   But he knew his weaknesses as well as he knew his strengths, and the knowledge crippled him.   His radical insecurity made him feel weak and incapable of extended effort.   He could not choose to defy his father and move to London, take his chances and find his own way.   At the same time, his resentment of his father was too strong to allow him to take the other path, cooperate with him in Ayrshire politics, cultivate the Dundases, and settle for the gown of a Lord of Session.   Every move was half-hearted, and his failure to choose—the old story—was itself a choice.   His dreams were long-range, and his decisions impulsive or ineffectual.

The rest of the story has been told in the preceding chapters of this volume.   Marriage, which was a step towards independence, stabilized him for a while, and he was inspirited by great events: Paoli's visit, the tour with Johnson to the Hebrides, the John Reid trial.   London became his alternate life, two months of excitement in most springs that made his Edinburgh existence seem all the more dreary.   He tried to vivify this home existence with sensation, too often drinking and whoring.   He fought his father over the entail and lost, the most damaging defeat of his life.

The future turned from a series of hopes and promises—the English

bar, the House of Commons, the estate of Auchinleck—into a blurry, uneasy, indefinitely extended present.   Resigned to servitude, all he could
do was to wait, in horror and expectation, for his father to die.   But the
old man had an iron constitution; he had no intention of dying before he
had to.   And as Lord Auchinleck lived on, Boswell's dependence upon
him deepened.   Partly his outlook was realistic.   Proud though he was of
his growing family, Boswell had given hostages to fortune.   For money in
itself he cared nothing.   He chastised himself for penny-pinching moods,
but he was consistently generous to friends and especially to relations in
need.   He never achieved the success as an advocate which would allow
him to maintain, on his own, the genteel position that his rank as James
Boswell, Esq., required.   He needed the money his father gave him, and
his father kept the screws tight.

Strong feelings reinforced practical considerations.   Recall that at the
beginning of the *Hebrides* Boswell describes himself as "a gentleman of
ancient blood, the pride of which was his predominant passion."   Add, his
pride in the estate of Auchinleck.   Until the signing of the entail, Lord
Auchinleck poised the threat of selling the lands he himself had bought,
the ultimate in rejection; now Boswell felt too close to his moment of
inheritance to jeopardize it in any way.   Also, he retained great respect
for his father's virtues: prudence, good sense, strength of mind, and a
steadiness that marked even his old age.   Much as he needed his father's
money, to the last Boswell hoped even more for his affection and approval.
And he still felt incapable of taking his father's place.

Boswell's basic feeling about himself, though he could only admit it
from time to time, had to be contempt: he could not stand on his own
feet. Fortunately, nature's kindly defences do not allow us to feel unmiti-
gated self-contempt for very long; it would be unendurable.   There are
always others to blame, or various ways in which to rationalize a situation.
By attending assiduously on his father at Auchinleck, Boswell could tell
himself that he was cooperating with the system of things, or at least the
system of the Boswell family.   He could surrender control to his father
and become a child again; he was relieved of responsibility.   And he
could enrich his life with visions of the future, which he communicated to
his public:

> The Hypochondriack . . . has lately returned from having passed
> some time in the country, where in a sound and placid state of
> mind he relished a rural life. . . .   There is a feeling of dignity
> and consequence in being master of land above anything else.

It is the natural dominion of man over the earth, granted him by his Almighty Creator, and no artificial dominion is felt like it. . . . He who is master of land sees all around him obedient to his will. Not only can he totally change the face of inanimate nature, but [he] can command the animals of each species, and even the human race itself, to multiply or to diminish, to continue or to migrate, according to his pleasure.   Limited as he is by our government and our laws, he is very essentially the arbiter of happiness and unhappiness over a district.

Then as session-time and Lord Auchinleck returned to Edinburgh, the clouds darkened again:

FRIDAY 17 NOVEMBER. . . .   How insignificant is my life at present! How little do I read! I am making no considerable figure in any way, and I am now forty years of age.   But let me not despond. I am a man better known in the world than most of my countrymen.   I am very well at the bar for my standing.   I lead a regular, sober life.   I have a variety of knowledge and excellent talents for conversation.   I have a good wife and promising children. . . . TUESDAY 21 NOVEMBER. . . .   I was humbled to think how little I read, and what inconsiderable objects occupied my mind.   I am depressed by the state of dependence in which I am kept by my father, and by being actually in straitened circumstances.   I felt with some warmth Lord Mountstuart's neglect of my interest. SATURDAY 2 DECEMBER. . . .   Groaned from low spirits. . . .

Again Boswell took the public into his confidence:

The Hypochondriack is himself at this moment in a state of very dismal depression. . . .   Let us select some of those thoughts, the multitude of which confounds and overwhelms the mind of a hypochondriack.

His opinion of himself is low and desponding.   His temporary dejection makes his faculties seem quite feeble.   He imagines that everybody thinks meanly of him. . . .   He regrets his having ever attempted distinction and excellence in any way, because the effect of his former exertions now serves only to make his insignificance more vexing to him. . . .   There is a cloud as far as he can perceive, and he supposes it will be charged with thicker vapour the longer it continues.

He is distracted between indolence and shame.   Every kind of labour is irksome to him.   Yet he has not resolution to cease from his accustomed tasks. . . .   He acts therefore like a slave, not animated by inclination but goaded by fear.

Everything appears to him quite indifferent. . . .   He begins actually to believe the strange theory that nothing exists without the mind, because he is sensible, as he imagines, of a total change in all the objects of his contemplation. What formerly had engaging qualities has them no more. The world is one undistinguished wild.

To summarize Boswell's next points: the hypochondriac cannot concentrate; he is perpetually upon the fret; weakly timid or in extremes of rashness or desperation; always anxious, always insecure.

The more he thinks the more miserable he grows; and he may adopt the troubled exclamation in one of Dr. Young's tragedies:

> Auletes, seize me, force me to my chamber,
> There chain me down, and guard me from myself.

> Though his reason be entire enough, and he knows that his mind is sick, his gloomy imagination is so powerful that he cannot disentangle himself from its influence; and he is in effect persuaded that its hideous representations of life are true. . . .
>
> By religion the hypochondriack . . . will have his troubled thoughts calmed by the consideration that he is here in a state of trial, that to contribute his part in carrying on the plan of Providence in this state of being is his duty, and that his sufferings, however severe, will be found beneficial to him in the other world, as having prepared him for the felicity of the saints above, which by some mysterious constitution to be afterwards explained, requires in human beings a course of tribulation. And in the mean time he will have celestial emanations imparted to him.
>
> While writing this paper, I have by some gracious influence been insensibly relieved from the distress under which I laboured when I began it. . . .

Boswell expresses his horrible state of mind with his usual clarity and power, but his remarks about the consolations of religion may strike the modern sceptic as a collection of pious clichés. Not at all. These were deeply felt attitudes expressed in ritualized formulas. But, as already emphasized, beneath them lay those fears of hell or annihilation that Boswell pictured in one of his most powerful analyses of Johnson:

> His mind resembled the vast amphitheatre, the Colosseum at Rome. In the centre stood his judgement which, like a mighty gladiator, combated those apprehensions that, like the wild beasts of the arena, were all around in cells, ready to be let out upon him. After a conflict, he drove them back into their dens; but not killing them, they were still assailing him.

And Boswell himself constantly probed our "unhappy uncertainty as to our salvation."

Boswell could never learn to leave our nature or our fate in mystery. Since Scripture failed to provide sufficient guidance, reason, also God-given, explored the possibilities as far as its feeble powers permitted. And reason ran headlong into a connected and equally agonizing problem, the insoluble paradox of Liberty and Necessity. Johnson could put the problem aside with his celebrated formulation, "All theory is against the freedom of the will; all experience for it," but Boswell was not so fortunate. When he turned in depressive gloom to Providence for consolation, one of his worst tortures was his obsession with free will. It troubled him so much because he knew logically the determinists had the better arguments, but he violently rejected the idea that he could be considered "a *mere machine*, or a *reprobate from all eternity*," even while admitting to himself that "there is not *absolute demonstration* to the contrary." Berkeley and Hume were pernicious because they threatened the substantiality of this world, and on the world's substantiality, as remarked earlier, depended Boswell's own. What in Berkeley's views was to exhilarate Yeats,

> That this pragmatical, preposterous pig of a world, its
> farrow that so solid seem,
> Must vanish on the instant if the mind but change
> its theme,

filled Boswell with dread. But Necessity was worse; it threatened the power of choice, which distinguished human from animal existence.

Religious and metaphysical concerns were deeply if obscurely linked with psychological processes. Locke, the century's psychologist, explained that the mind operated through "association of ideas" (the connecting together of sense perceptions) and "reflection" (the mind's ability to think about its own operations). But lacking the modern theory of the unconscious, Locke was unable to explain how the mind, reflecting upon itself, could become "uneasy" (anxious) without apparent cause. For the philosopher, this psychological question quickly transposed itself into the metaphysical problem of evil, the central question, for example, of Pope's *Essay on Man*. And the existence of evil was inextricably bound up with the question of God's justice. But for the believer, to question God's justice either risked classification as a reprobate and loss of heaven, or led to a complete repudiation of heaven, which equally destroyed any hope of eventual escape from anxiety. "The inscrutable workings of Providence" was a well-known but emotionally unsatisfying answer. The mind went round and round, anxiety leading to religious doubt and religious doubt intensifying the original anxiety. To judge from its writers, insanity in eighteenth-century Britain often took the form of religious obsession, Smart and Blake showing, in some degree at least, signs of a manic state, while in Collins and Cowper it took depressive forms.

For those born under the sign of Freud, these problems assume a more explicable if not more easily soluble form.   Neurotic religious doubt seems a mask for, or displacement of, the anxiety aroused by unconscious conflict or repression.   In this reading, Necessity coalesced with Lord Auchinleck in Boswell's mind: neither allowed him any control over himself.   In turn, Boswell's unconscious aggressive and hostile feelings about his father made him anxious, and he feared losing self-control.   And so, as seen again and again, he felt more secure if his father or Johnson or Temple exerted authority.   But to achieve independence and self-discipline he had to give up his father's authority, which his father prevented him from doing by destroying his self-confidence.   It was a puzzle that Boswell saw different pieces of from time to time, but which he could never put together.

I I

POLITICS WAS ONE of the few areas in which Boswell could allow himself to contend directly with his father.   In September 1780, the General Election brought Sir Adam Fergusson, standing for re-election as M.P. for Ayrshire, to Auchinleck on his canvass.   It was a delicate moment.   Lord Auchinleck supported him keenly, while Boswell again backed the candidate of the "noble association"—the Earls of Cassillis, Eglinton, and Loudoun—who had settled this time on Eglinton's cousin and eventual heir, Hugh Montgomerie.

What complicated the situation was that Boswell was using the election to try to collect an old debt.   In 1768 Fergusson had promised £100 for aid to the Corsican rebels.   On the strength of this promise, their sanguine natures, and the need for haste, Boswell and Andrew Crosbie made large purchases of cannon and shot without the money to pay for them. Fergusson then reneged, arguing that he had never promised the money for cannon (what did he think it was for?), and Boswell and Crosbie found themselves indebted for almost £130 each, beyond their £50 subscriptions. Now before Fergusson's visit, Boswell sent him a "case," temperate and conciliatory but firm in tone, asking for the money.   He thought that on the eve of an election Fergusson would rather pay than be embarrassed. Fergusson's polite answer evaded the issue, and his visit went off without its being mentioned, but Boswell was to discover that Fergusson had no intention of paying a penny unless forced to.

Boswell would later claim that his objection to Fergusson, actually a combination of dislike and contempt, was based on Fergusson's refusal to pay his subscription, but this is hard to credit. As late as 1772 when Johnson denounced Fergusson as "a vile Whig," Boswell had defended him because of his strong regard for religion. It was the election of 1774 that made the difference. Lord Auchinleck's support of the victorious Fergusson not only crushed Boswell's fledgling attempt to make a place for himself in local politics, but it must have strongly suggested that Fergusson was the kind of heir his father would have preferred. Unable to blame his father directly for this attitude, Boswell was reduced to attacking the Dundases, who according to a contemporary jingle, helped "rule aw our lords and lairds like asses," and sneering at Fergusson as a Whig and a parvenu.

These resentments having hardened into convictions, Boswell made the Ayrshire election of 1780 his chief concern for the next six months. He conferred, he worried, he worked hard to round up votes; and when Montgomerie, having adopted Fergusson's own unscrupulous practices at the previous election, "made" enough votes to triumph in October, 65 to 55, Boswell rejoiced exceedingly. But Fergusson did not give up. Appeals first to the Court of Session and then to a Select Committee of the House of Commons—though Boswell did his best as one of Montgomerie's counsel—reversed the result, and Fergusson took his seat on 2 April 1781.

Worse followed. In July, Fergusson was appointed a Commissioner of Trade and Plantations, which necessitated a by-election. To avoid another struggle, Lord North asked Eglinton as a favour to permit Fergusson to be re-elected without a contest; since Fergusson was certain to win in any case, Eglinton agreed. The price was the command of a battalion for Montgomerie. It was the start of an arrangement between the two groups which was to prove disastrous for Boswell's political ambitions.

Keenness about the Ayrshire election kept off melancholy; it also led to a predictable quarrel when President Dundas declared in court that there was not an independent gentleman in Ayrshire. "I fired," Boswell records, "and called out, 'No, my Lord?' 'No,' said he, 'nor yourself neither.' " The President quickly realized he would have to back down— some truths, or half-truths, can be stated only in private—especially when Boswell called on him to press the issue. A little flattery smoothed the process: the President asked Boswell's opinion of the Ayrshire election dispute, and complimented him on his court performance. Then Dundas tried to re-establish their usual relationship by advising Boswell not to get too heated before the Select Committee in London. "My Lord," said

Boswell, "your Lordship certainly does not dislike a man for having a little heat of temper," a sharp reminder of Dundas's impatient bullying of colleagues and advocates.   The President took a convenient opportunity to retract his statement in court the same day.

As Montgomerie's counsel, Boswell had a respectable excuse for going to London, but departure brought on a characteristically unpleasant little scene, also involving the topic of independence, at Lord Auchinleck's (12 March 1781).   Boswell writes:

> Announced to my father (what I believe he knew well enough before) that I was to set out next day, being engaged as counsel. He affected surprise and said *I* was an *independent man* who did not consult him as to my going.   *She*[1] said, "At a certain time of life a son is independent of parental authority."   "No," said he; "I never was independent of *my* father's authority."   She wickedly said, "I am of your opinion.   But that is just as people think." I said, "A man at a certain age is entitled to judge for himself. A man is a fool or a physician at forty."[2]

London provided ample compensation.   Boswell first encountered Johnson in Fleet Street; Johnson, who had been belabouring him by letter for his "hypocrisy of misery," now took him aside, asked kindly about his family, and said, "I love you better than ever I did."   There was a greeting a man could cherish.   A sudden swing to boundless high spirits included a dispensation from worry about conduct; "I *must* allow my temper an easy play," Boswell told himself.   And he did.

An occasion was to grow out of the crucial drama building up at the Thrales', now fashionably installed in Grosvenor Square.   Thrale, supposedly recovered from a stroke of two years earlier, was ominously lethargic; but he refused to admit illness, and the household carried on in its usual fashion.   At dinner on 31 March, Boswell "really fell in love" with the beautiful Sophy Streatfeild, monotonously identified as the learnèd weeper: as a prodigy of female scholarship she knew Greek, and she could produce tears at will.   Thrale's attentions to her made his wife very jealous. There the next day, Boswell caught one of Johnson's most revealing moments: Johnson was criticizing their hostess for her habit of talking thoughtlessly:

> "And yet" (with a pleasing pause and leering smile), "she is the first woman in the world.   Could she but restrain that wicked

[1]Lady Auchinleck.
[2]A Scottish proverb.

tongue of hers, she would be the only woman in the world.   Could she but command that little whirligig—"

An instant illustrates all Johnson's intimacy with the woman he loved.

Then, three days later (4 April), Thrale stubbornly gorged himself into a fatal stroke.   It was a very heavy blow to Johnson; he had lost a friend, he wrote, "whose eye for fifteen years had scarcely been turned upon me but with respect or tenderness."   It was also the final, tragic turning point in Johnson's life, though that was not to become apparent for some while.   Johnson diverted his own sorrow and helped the first woman in the world by bustling about in the management of Thrale's brewery, which was sold shortly afterwards for the immense sum of £135,000.

The play of Boswell's temper at Thrale's death brings his biographer to the most embarrassing action of his career.   Within two weeks he had produced and sung to friends an *Ode by Dr. Samuel Johnson to Mrs. Thrale upon Their Supposed Approaching Nuptials*:

> If e'er my fingers touched the lyre
> In satire fierce or pleasure gay,
> Shall not my Thralia's smiles inspire?
> Shall Sam refuse the sportive lay?
>
> My dearest darling, view your slave,
> Behold him as your very Scrub,[1]
> Ready to write as author grave,
> Or govern well the brewing tub.
>
> To rich felicity thus raised
> My bosom glows with amorous fire;
> Porter no longer shall be praised;
> 'Tis I myself am Thrale's entire.[2] . . .
>
> Ascetic now thy lover lives,
> Nor dares to touch, nor dares to kiss;
> Yet prurient fancy sometimes gives
> A prelibation of our bliss. . . .
>
> Convulsed in love's tumultuous throes,
> We feel the aphrodisian spasm;

[1] Lady Bountiful's man of all work in *The Beaux' Stratagem*.

[2] A commingling of puns.   Tetty was Mrs. Porter when Johnson married her.   "Thrale's entire" was a popular malt produced by the brewery; also, an "entire" (short for "entire horse") is a stallion.

Tired nature must at last repose,
Then wit and wisdom fill the chasm.

Nor only are our limbs entwined,
And lip in rapture glued to lip;
Locked in embraces of the mind
Imagination's sweets we sip. . . .

This is exceptionally clever for Boswell, by far the best poem he ever wrote. The anonymous lampoon was an eighteenth-century custom and pleasure, and clearly Boswell never felt it wrong to publish scurrilous newspaper squibs, though otherwise he directed them at people he disliked. And no one who heard his song seems to have disapproved of it. Still, the *Ode* remains an embarrassment.

The combination of unusual wit and extraordinary tastelessness suggests that Boswell wrote his *Ode* under strong emotional pressure. Wit was serving, as Freud argues it does, to express an otherwise inadmissible hostility. People were beginning to speculate that Mrs. Thrale might marry Johnson, and Boswell, after talking with Johnson's good friend William Scott, reports that "we both wished it much." Immediately Boswell adds: Scott "saw clearly the Doctor's propensity to love *the vain world* in various ways."

Johnson might be impelled by fortune and consequence as this comment suggests, as well as by the lust the *Ode* concentrates on. But what urged Boswell to this performance? Contrary to what he says, he never could have wished for this marriage. He was jealous of Mrs. Thrale and afraid that if Johnson married her their friendship would dwindle to nothing. When his father remarried he could express intense anger openly, because he felt anger had a legitimate basis. Now he could do no more than make savage fun.

It was ludicrously inappropriate, to begin with, to think of Johnson as a lover, just as it had been when Johnson had fantasized at Dunvegan about keeping a seraglio. How could one imagine "that majestic teacher of moral and religious wisdom" (so he calls Johnson to make his own reaction credible) quivering with the everyday compulsions of physical desire?

Elsewhere, though Boswell depicts Johnson's peculiarities vividly, he always makes sure that Johnson's greatness and goodness shine through them. Johnson's sexuality, however, seemed not only grotesque and embarrassing but threatening. Though he often, and sincerely, deplored his own addiction to sensuality, Boswell, at the same time, was proud of his sexual "qualifications" and attractiveness. We remember his boast to Temple that he was "too many" for Margaret, and that other women—"and well-educated women too"—had prized him more as a lover.   A man's estimate of his sexuality is central to his self-respect.   Boswell, whose ultimate ground of assertion was this sexual vitality, willingly admitted that Johnson was far his intellectual superior.   But Johnson should stick to the intellectual.   He had always been too ugly, in Boswell's naïve opinion, to have been attractive to women.   By commenting that he could recall only one conversation with Johnson about sexual intercourse, Boswell tacitly insists on his sexlessness: he had outlived sexual impulse.   Johnson should confine himself to his sphere, and Boswell would remain unchallenged in his own. And yet there was a threat.   Boswell's warm love for Johnson depended in part on his not being sexual; yet the *Ode* shows how strongly Boswell could imagine, in sport at least, Johnson's possible sexual feelings—quite believable feelings at that.

If these speculations about what was going on in some confused though energetic corner of Boswell's mind seem too ingenious, there is a fine modern re-creation of what Boswell consciously must have told himself:

> If Boswell's *Ode* sprang from malice, it was only the sunny malice of a faun which Meredith saw lurking in the smile of the Comic Spirit. . . .   The intention was wit or *double entendre*, what he himself called ludicrous fancy . . . and, without slacking for a moment his sense of love and admiration of the Rambler, could imagine the risibility inherent in the Rambler's idiom if applied to lovemaking.   The externalizing of such fancies, he felt, did no harm if the results did not get reported to the persons concerned; and he really seems to have felt no more sense of treachery in developing them than he would have if Johnson and Mrs. Thrale had been characters of his own invention.   He was by no means the only one among Johnson's close friends who made Johnson matter for comedy in ways which they would have been most unwilling for Johnson to know about.   Garrick convulsed The Club with imitations of Johnson's tumultuous fondness for Tetty.   Reynolds wrote dialogues satirizing Johnson's tendency to choose his side in an argument by sheer whim and to silence his opponent by interruption. . . .

Impulse satisfied, Boswell seems not to have worried at all that Johnson would hear of his new song.   On Good Friday (13 April), a day after its composition, he went "solemn" with Johnson to St. Clement Danes, as usual; and on Easter Sunday he dined with Johnson.   After dinner Boswell started to sneak off to a religious debating society that Johnson disapproved of.

> As I got the door shut, the Doctor, whether lounging in garden or lurking in corner, knew I was gone, opened the door and roared

after me, "Mr. Boswell!   Mr. Boswell!"   I had turned the corner
of Allen's house[1] and was stealing off, pretending not to hear.
But as I took a check of conscience in practising any artifice with
my revered friend I came back.

Conscience, however, permitted Boswell to tell a half-truth and escape
again.

In contrast to his easiness about Johnson, Boswell almost openly expressed his fear (the wish being its father?) that Mrs. Thrale had been told
of his *Ode*.   His note of condolence (26 April), if that is the proper term
for it, runs very oddly: "Mr. Boswell . . . hopes she will believe he feels all
he ought to do, though his gaiety of fancy is not to be subdued."   At least
twice later he grew concerned that Johnson had heard of the *Ode*, but
apparently Johnson never did; it would have taken a bold man to apprise
him of it.   Mrs. Thrale did not learn of its existence until she read stanzas
quoted from it in the *Life of Johnson*, and showed no sign of suspecting that
Boswell was its author.

So much of the time we are confined within Boswell's own view of
himself that a generous glimpse of him in society from the diary of Charlotte
Ann Burney is very welcome.   Charlotte was Fanny's twenty-year-old younger
sister, pretty, impressionable, and a bit of a rattle.   Dinner was at John
Hoole's—the translator of Ariosto and Tasso—on 7 April, with Johnson
present, though still suffering from the shock of Thrale's death.   Charlotte
rated most of the men present as dull to objectionable, but then there was

> the flower of the flock, Mr. Boswell, the famous Mr. Boswell, who
> is a sweet creature.   I admire and like him beyond measure.   He
> is a fine, lively, sensible, unaffected, honest, manly, good-humoured
> character.   I never saw him before.   He idolizes Dr. Johnson,
> and struts about, and puts himself into such ridiculous postures
> that he is as good as a comedy.   He seems between forty and fifty,
> a good-looking man enough.   N.B. He has a wife in Scotland, so
> there is no *scandal* in being in raptures about him.

Charlotte goes on to report the puns and repartee and laughter of the
occasion in detail.   Boswell was in his gayest mood, and they hit it off
marvellously.   "He is a charming creature," Charlotte concludes; "he told
me he would call here, but I am afraid he won't."   Boswell did call on her
father, Dr. Burney, three weeks later, but Burney was not at home, and
that marked the end of the young Charlotte's acquaintance with Mr.
Boswell.

[1]In which Johnson lived.

The high point of Boswell's spring was dinner at Mrs. Garrick's on 20 April; she was entertaining for the first time since her husband's death two years earlier.   The guests included Johnson, Reynolds, Burney, the elegant Mrs. Boscawen,[1] the intellectual Elizabeth Carter, and Hannah More (whom Mrs. Garrick called her chaplain).   The ghost of Garrick, in the form of his portrait, hovered benignly above them.   Boswell remarks, "I had said to Mrs. Boscawen at table, 'I believe this is about as much as can be made of life.'   I was really happy.   My gay ideas of London in youth were realized and consolidated.   I did my part pleasingly."

In the drawing-room after dinner, Johnson put on an exhibition of comedy and authority.   He recalled that John Campbell, a reputable author, had married a printer's devil.   When Reynolds showed surprise, Johnson defended her:

> (looking very serious and very earnest), "And she did not disgrace him;—the woman had a bottom of good sense."   The word *bottom*, thus introduced, was so ludicrous when contrasted with his gravity that most of us could not forbear tittering and laughing; though I recollect that the Bishop of Killaloe kept his countenance with perfect steadiness, while Miss Hannah More slyly hid her face behind a lady's back who sat on the same settee with her.   His pride could not bear that any expression of his should excite ridicule when he did not intend it; he therefore resolved to assume and exercise despotic power, glanced sternly around, and called out in a strong tone, "Where's the merriment?"   Then collecting himself and looking aweful, to make us feel how he could impose restraint and, as it were, searching his mind for a still more ludicrous word, he slowly pronounced, "I say the *woman* was *fundamentally* sensible,"[2] as if he had said, hear this now and laugh if you dare.   We all sat composed as at a funeral.

The day ended on a more feeling note.   As Johnson and Boswell on leaving the Adelphi looked over the Thames, Boswell recalled the recent deaths of two friends who had lived there, Garrick and Beauclerk.   "Ay, Sir," said Johnson tenderly, "and two such friends as cannot be supplied."

Boswell responded fully to every happening, even the most transient. He held a widow in his lap in the stage-coach, "a very desirable armful," and when she left he kissed her "repeatedly and warmly, and wished to be

---

[1] Mrs. Boscawen was to find herself described in the *Life of Johnson* where Boswell says, "Her manners are the most agreeable, and her conversation the best, of any lady with whom I ever had the happiness to be acquainted" (*Life*, iii. 331—29 April 1778).

[2] The American reader may need to be reminded that "fundament" is a British term for "buttocks" or "anus."

better acquainted with her." "I catched fire," he told Mrs. Stuart, "by the incessant rapidity of my whirl through this enchanting metropolis but Passion Week[1] cooled and quieted me." Not for long. He found it hard to keep his equilibrium. He attended mass regularly at the Portuguese Chapel; but he also drank too much, "ranged," and was ill after a riot with Admiral Keppel. Various suspect names make their appearance in the journal: Dinah, No. 35, Madame de Wurtz, Fanny Bates. Lady Elgin (his very early flame, Martha Whyte) left him "quite divinely amorous"; he "procured solace" from a Mrs. Spencer. Paoli spoke frankly:

> For all my regard, if the King would send you as Secretary with me to Corsica to restore our affairs, I would say, "I will not have him. From his fault[2] I cannot trust him." Cure [yourself] of this and you will be asked by men in power; it will be their interest. But you must appear [in your better character] to them. They will not draw you from the waves. The malignity of human nature likes to see you struggle. But get to shore; be firm, be able, and they will have you.—Yesterday morning your wit was fine; it was clear, limpid as water, not muddied by porter or wine. . . .

The same day Johnson also scolded him for drinking too much. Symptoms of gonorrhoea appeared. His *Hypochondriack* for May was on prudence.

One incident illustrates the stresses in Boswell's character. On 22 April he dined too freely at the Duke of Montrose's, and then proceeded to a gathering of notables at Miss Monckton's, a bluestocking and lion-hunter. Boswell tells his own story:

> I certainly was in extraordinary spirits and above all fear or awe. In the midst of a great number of persons of the first rank, amongst whom I recollect with confusion a noble lady of the most stately decorum, I placed myself next to Johnson and, thinking myself now fully his match, talked to him in a loud and boisterous manner, desirous to let the company know how I could contend with *Ajax*.

In particular, Boswell carried on about the pleasures of the imagination, asking whether he should not be happy if he thought the beautiful Duchess of Devonshire were in love with him?

> My friend with much address evaded my interrogatories, and kept me as quiet as possible; but it may easily be conceived how he must have felt. However, when a few days afterwards I waited upon

[1]8–15 April.
[2]Drinking.

him and made an apology, he behaved with the most friendly gentleness.

Boswell not only recounts this story about himself in the *Life*, he drags it out in a footnote with the verses in which he asked Miss Monckton's pardon for his behaviour. He seemed to be what Johnson called one of those "unaccountable volunteers in sincerity." But as a biographer he could not have made a shrewder move; who could doubt the authenticity of the scene, and in consequence the generosity of Johnson's response? The narrative itself makes all its points with succinct poise: Boswell's alcoholic self-deception, Johnson's kindness, even a slight touch at the company itself with its "noble lady of the most stately decorum." The verses could have been omitted, though they have a kind of endearing silliness. He obtained from Miss Monckton, he says, an Act of Oblivion.

But periods of excess were balanced by happier occasions: a three-day visit to Richmond to see Mrs. Stuart; an evening at the Royal Academy with much talk worth abbreviated report; and a second Johnson-Wilkes dinner at Dilly's (8 May). This time Johnson required neither manoeuvering to get him there nor soothing once he had arrived. He and Wilkes joined again in "extravagant sportive raillery upon the supposed poverty of Scotland," and Johnson told the story of Bet Flint who, when acquitted of stealing a counterpane, said, "Now that the counterpane is *my own*, I shall make a petticoat of it." As the closing tableau of the occasion, Boswell presents Johnson and Wilkes

> literally tête-à-tête, for they were reclined upon their chairs with their heads leaning almost close to each other and talking earnestly, in a kind of confidential whisper, of the personal quarrel between George the Second and the King of Prussia.

Boswell also went to Court four times, and had a long conversation with George III about Paoli. As anyone could have predicted, he was entranced with Court life, or its visible manifestations; he declared he would like to know the King better, and admired the Prince of Wales much ("thought I could follow him"). The next summer he would suggest to Paoli that "perhaps some happy opportunity may occur" for Paoli to hint to the King that Boswell wished to be near his person. Boswell would serve, defend, and worship the father of a whole people. It was the Guards all over again on a grander scale, combined with his early dream of becoming one of the brightest wits at the court of George III.

Spring brought one fine success: two interviews in May with Lord Bute,

who lived in splendid isolation.   For years Boswell's desire to meet him had
been frustrated by the unwillingness of either Mountstuart or Col. James
Stuart to provide an introduction.   Now he appealed directly to Bute:

> It is not from affected singularity but from absolute despair that
> I venture this chance.—If your Lordship is gracious enough to
> give me leave to wait on you, your Lordship will do a kindness
> which will be more gratefully felt than any bounty which you
> conferred while Prime Minister.

Boswell gives no reason for writing this particular letter, but some
years earlier in his journal he defended his determination to become acquainted with the great:

> Let me value my forwardness.   It has procured me much hap-
> piness.   I do not think it is impudence.   It is an eagerness to
> share the best society, and a diligence to attain what I desire.   If
> a man is praised for seeking knowledge though mountains and
> seas are in his way, is it not laudable in me to seek it at the risk
> of mortification from repulses?

As usual, Boswell's approach was received graciously.   The Great Man
(Boswell's own term) greeted him with, "Nothing could induce you to see
an old man going out of life but your love for antiquities."   In two long
conversations, Bute found himself talking on all sorts of topics: Pitt, the
negotiations at the end of the Seven Years' War, Corsica, Wilkes, Scotland,
his children; and inevitably James Boswell, who told him that he had been
leading two lives, "living with people who sat up late, and people who rose
early": too much for anyone.   Boswell's talent for establishing an easiness
which approached intimacy, his prized ability to "tune" himself to others,
had proved itself again.   At the end of May, Bute responded so far as to
send for Boswell, but a previous engagement prevented a meeting.   And
Boswell never called on him again, presumably because Bute lived mostly
in rural retirement.

Johnson seems almost to disappear from Boswell's journal in May.   In
the *Life* to explain his lack of material, Boswell says, "I was at this time
engaged in a variety of other matters, which required exertion and assiduity, and necessarily occupied almost all my time."   This explanation is
disingenuous: he saw Johnson on a number of occasions but recorded little
about him after 22 April (Miss Monckton's).   When it came time to write
up Johnson's second meeting with Wilkes for the *Life*, all we know that
Boswell had as guide was the terse note, "Dined Dilly's."   When Boswell
remarked in the middle of May that they had not met for a week, Johnson

replied, "Then, Sir, let us live double."   Mostly Boswell filled his journal
with the King or Bute; or an innkeeper named Rudd, who gave him fine
cold buttock of beef; or Charles Macklin, who had acted with Mrs. Oldfield
and Colley Cibber, now 81 but still on the stage.   Boswell even preserved
their supper bill (ten shillings apiece).

But the last scene of Boswell's London stay brings him back to Johnson.
On 2 June, Boswell called for him at Bolt Court—Johnson was eating
oranges in the sun—and off they went to Squire Dilly's at Southill.   On
the way Boswell contrived a small pilgrimage to the home of Edward Young,
whose poetry had impressed him so much in early life; Young's son supplied
anecdotes, not all of them accurate, and they strolled in the garden.
Southill was placid, and after taking Communion Boswell felt infused with
serenity.   He told Johnson, "I'd fain be good, and I am very good just now.
I fear GOD and honour the King; wish to do no ill, and to do good to all
mankind."

It is a comment worth pausing at.   When Boswell remarked about
himself to Lord Graham a few weeks earlier that he was a *very* good man,
Graham replied, "You only know what a good man is."   Graham was right,
of course, in the obvious sense, but also in another more significant for
Boswell the writer: he did recognize a good man because, as he said about
himself, in his heart he was one; and this goodness was essential to the
vision that made his biographies possible.

The climax of their little excursion came with a visit to Luton Hoo,
Bute's magnificent country seat.   Warming to his prospects, Boswell said
that he expected to be much here when Mountstuart succeeded his father;
Johnson, an accurate prophet, replied, "Don't you be too sure of that."   It
was the King's Birthday, and they drank his health at the local inn.   Johnson, the King, Bute intermingled: it was a great day for Boswell's Tory
soul.   Would it not be rational, he asked Johnson, for him to join "the
great circle of life" in London if he could?   Johnson could only assent to
this abstract proposition and give him his blessing.   Then Boswell was on
the road to Edinburgh.

I I I

THIS SPRING BOSWELL TRIED TO CONVINCE himself that the gulf
between London and Edinburgh was purely a matter of distance, that he
could bring his good spirits back with him.   Instead, he suffered the usual
sickening plunge.   By now his life has become unbearably repetitious, for

him and for us.   He knows he is walking on a treadmill, but each step continues to hurt, and the cries of distress are still painful.   He feels "insignificant and subjected to a wretched destiny," while being aware, occasionally at least, that this is the destiny he has allowed to be inflicted on him.   But he cannot endure this realization.   The mark of the neurotic is not that things are hell, which they are for many people much of the time, but his conviction that there is nothing he can do about them.

The burden of the generations remained central.   Again Boswell complains that he has too little authority over his children, while it is embarrassingly obvious that his father has too much over him, even if he puts a different face on their relationship to the world.   He wrote to Burke, "I am sure you will approve of my anxious, my almost childish care to humour an aged parent."   (It was not an attitude likely to appeal to Burke, who had broken away from his own strong-willed father.)   Two consecutive *Hypochondriacks* (June and July 1781), "On Parents and Children," show his true feelings plainly: a son must acquire "that manly resolution without which we never enjoy liberty," while fathers who injudiciously try to keep an authority over their sons "must either reduce them to unfeeling stupidity, or keep them in perpetual uneasiness and vexation."   But excess of awe is better than their being associates in profligacy.   [What odd alternatives!]   Parents have natural affection for their children, but it takes a Commandment to enforce a child's love for his parents.   A father should not keep his son in such scanty circumstances that the son wishes for his death.

But writing was not enough to give Boswell relief.   He asks himself, "Why keep a journal of so 'weary a life'?"—even the deep impulse to record wavers.   He contemplates suicide.   Not only is the will paralysed but he cannot even think clearly: he is reduced to that state he calls "impotence of mind."   The parallels to Hamlet are unexpected, yet they make sense.

Still, this was real life and Boswell struggled on.   Pringle had retired, weary and fretful, to Edinburgh, and Boswell, who loved him, paid the lonely old man assiduous attention.   (He was so obviously a surrogate for Lord Auchinleck.)   Pringle, in turn, said that Boswell's company did him more good than anything else; with his shrewd understanding of Boswell's temperament, he told him, "I know not if you will be at rest in London. But you will never be at rest out of it."   London certainly gave Boswell high notions of company.   Visiting Pringle one night, he was depressed to discover that the only other caller was one of the greatest men of the age: Adam Smith.   Like Garrick, he found Smith's talk "flabby."

An Auchinleck visit in the autumn provided Boswell with some moments of relief, though his father was cold and his father's women venomous. But Lord Auchinleck finally acknowledged decay by asking Boswell to go round the estate and report on conditions. He returned to Edinburgh to find that Margaret had miscarried, in what was to be her last pregnancy. He grew fat and swinishly sensual.

Depression began to lift in December 1781. Boswell's practice was busy, and it came to him in a dream that he ought to acquire "preciseness and peremptoriness of mind."

> I was in strong spirits all day, and was sensible that a great deal of my unhappiness is mere cloud which any moment may dissipate. I thought that at any period of time a man may disencumber himself of all the *accessories* of his identity, of all his books, all his connections with a particular place, or a particular sphere of life; and retaining only his consciousness and reminiscence start into a state of existing quite new. That therefore I should be more *myself* and have more of the "mihi res, non me rebus, submittere." [1]

Missing journal pages testify that strong spirits found their usual outlet.

The new year began coldly when Lord Auchinleck lectured Boswell about exceeding his income. Margaret was spitting blood, and Johnson enforced the obvious in remarking that if she died he would lose his anchor. But the fall of the North Ministry in March 1782 revived Boswell's political ambitions. His general hopes became focused on Burke's friendship for him, since Burke was certain to come into office; he also shared a prized fantasy with him:

> Would the King . . . but of himself transplant me into a better climate, how pleasant would it be! But I wish not to indulge romantic visions. I am advancing to be called to the English bar, as another string to my bow. In short, I am eagerly looking out.
>
> In the mean time, I have an aged father whom it is my pious wish as well as my interest to please; and as he disapproves of my going to London without a sufficient reason, I beg to hear from you whether my being upon the spot this spring may not be of some advantage to me. The "noctes cenaeque deum" [2] which I enjoy there are a sufficient reason in my own mind. But you can understand at once that something else must weigh with him.

Burke, however, failed to collaborate in this innocent fraud, and without money or excuse Boswell was stuck in Edinburgh.

[1] Loosely, "[a resolution] to make the world submit to me, rather than submitting myself to it" (Horace, *Epistles*, I.i.19—*submittere* for *subiungere*).

[2] "[O] nights and suppers of the gods!" (Horace, *Satires*, II.vi.65).

Suddenly a real opening appeared: the vacant office of Judge Advocate in the military establishment in Scotland, worth £180 a year. He wrote off at once to Burke, now Paymaster-General of the Forces in the new Rockingham-Shelburne Ministry, and Burke did his best. The office was disposed of, at Dundas's wish no doubt, to the heir to the M.P. from Selkirkshire, but Burke's willingness to help raised Boswell's self-esteem greatly. He took Burke's suggestion to turn to Dundas for help, and Dundas, now consolidating his control of Scotland, responded to a letter followed by a "serious conversation" in a vague but friendly way. Boswell went west to Auchinleck in May with spirits "pure as crystal" (a month's regimen of water-drinking had helped). Alone there, he exulted "in the consciousness of a line of ancestors, and in the prospect of being *Laird* myself, and ruling over such a fine Place and such an extent of country."

On returning to Edinburgh, Boswell found Margaret so alarmingly ill that he began a special journal devoted to her health. (As Geoffrey Scott said, "In the elaborate bookkeeping of experience, he was always opening new accounts.") And laid up with influenza himself, he had time to compose his most considered statement of his feelings about her. It is long, but paraphrase will not do it justice:

I made a good many excerpts from *Tom Jones*. My wife disliked Fielding's turn for low life. . . . But it is human nature. She has nothing of that English juiciness of mind of which I have a great deal, which makes me delight in humour. But what hurts me more, she has nothing of that warmth of imagination which produces the pleasures of vanity and many others, and which is even a considerable cause of religious fervour. *Family*, which is a high *principle* in my mind, and genealogy, which is to me an interesting amusement, have no effect upon her. It is impossible not to be both uneasy and a little angry at such defects (or call them differences); and at times they make me think that I have been unlucky in uniting myself with one who, instead of cherishing my genius, is perpetually checking it.

But on the other hand, I consider her excellent sense, her penetration, her knowledge of real life, her activity, her genuine affection, her generous conduct to me during my distracted love for her and when she married me, and her total disinterestedness and freedom from every species of selfishness during all the time she has been my wife. And then I value her and am fond of her, and am pained to the heart for having ever behaved in a manner unworthy of her merit. I also consider that a woman of the same imagination with myself might have encouraged me in whim and adventure, and hurried me to ridicule and perhaps ruin, whereas my excellent spouse's prudence has kept me out of many follies,

and made my life much more decent and creditable than it would
have been without her.   She was very apprehensive today and
sadly dejected. . . .   She has always a dreary terror for death.
Indeed he is the King of Terrors. . . .

Then Boswell's thoughts took a different direction:

My dear wife's illness was more distressing to me that I reflected
she had never had the advantages to which the match she had
made entitled her, my father having kept me upon a small allowance, and he and his women having treated her with shameful
coldness.   When I thought she might perhaps die before my coming to the estate of Auchinleck, which would place her in a situation
which she so well deserves, I was grievously vexed; and as a wife
is to be preferred to a father, especially when he lives only to
continue the harsh and unjust power of a stepmother, I could not
help viewing his death as a desirable event.   I know not what to
think of this.   Certainly the death of a father *may* be a desirable
event.   It is nice to determine in what cases.   A son should be
able to give strong reasons.   I have given mine; and I do not see
as yet that I am in the wrong.   It is not upon my own account
that the wish rises.   It is a wish formed upon the principle of
choosing the least of two evils.

Boswell had so narrowed his view of his situation that no other alternatives could occur to him.   If he did not wish for his father's death on
his own account, it certainly did not run counter to his wishes, or some of
them.   And he was honest enough to admit to himself that he again felt
a pleasurable agitation in "flights of fancy" about being a widower, though
his thoughts shocked him.   "I put down a fair transcript of the phases of
my mind."   It would be a new start all round.

And these phases were highly changeable.   "I was in strong spirits,
which I never recollect to have been at the time of the Races,[1] hypochondria
being by some curious periodical influence always with me at that time."
He attributed well-being to a light diet and avoidance of fermented liquor.
It is very surprising he failed again to realize that his worst attacks of
hypochondria tended to develop after his jaunts to London; this year,
staying at home had eliminated the usual distressing contrast.

On 10 August 1782 the Court of Session rose, and a week later Boswell
and Margaret crossed the Forth to Valleyfield with hopes for a pleasant
vacation.   Here they joined Veronica, who had been spending the summer
with her Preston cousins ("grown a good deal bigger, but had a coarse

[1]Race Week at Leith took place during the latter half of July.

appearance and the Fife accent"). The country agreed with Margaret. On horseback she "looked so genteel," says Boswell, "that I was as much in love with her as a man could be." But a two-hour ride brought on more spitting of blood.

Here we must backtrack a little. Boswell had been very attentive to his father the previous winter, but their relationship was incurable. Lord Auchinleck's health continued to deteriorate: for the past year he had required a catheter three times a day, and when he took exercise his urine was bloody. But he clung grimly to his seat on the Court of Session. The Lord President, his old and close friend, told Boswell that many days his father didn't know what was going on, though he had "flashes of understanding." "I alwise[1] know when he understood. . . . Jamie . . . the best thing that can happen to him is to die quietly." In a final reassertion of will, Lord Auchinleck bought a house in the New Town to assure his widow of a handsome dwelling. Boswell suspected her machinations so much that he asked William Lennox, the coachman at Auchinleck, to spy on her.

In the past, illness had softened Lord Auchinleck, but now he was steadily harsh. "Have you seen your wife the day?" he asked Boswell, as if Boswell rarely saw her. "Ye'll get cold quarters there," Lady Auchinleck promised him, when that May he told them he was going to Auchinleck. A few days later Boswell took up the subject again with spirit, and had the satisfaction of making her blush. As Boswell left, his father showed a last gleam of tenderness:

> He was mild and even kindly, and bid me see how many larches were cut, and seemed willing to purchase Haugh multures.[2] When I went away he took me by the hand, *like* a father, and said, "Fare you well, my dear James." My heart was warmed.

This was a momentary respite. Gillespie told Boswell that his father "showed no more signs of religion than a stock or a stone"—and Boswell continued to be very anxious that his father die a true Christian. At the same time, Gillespie warned him that Lord Auchinleck's temper would not soften as he grew older and his bladder complaint got worse. What comfort there was came from the sympathy of onlookers like Gillespie, Commissioner Cochrane, and even their Ayrshire neighbour and Boswell's old enemy, the Lord Justice Clerk. Most pleasing of all was the deathbed testimony of his affectionate kinsman, James Boswell of Balbarton, that Lord Auchinleck was a good man for himself, but Boswell was the best man of the name.

---

[1]Always.
[2]Rights belonging to the miller at Haugh.

The deep hurt Boswell continued to feel shows itself in a dialogue he recorded that summer between himself and Sandy, now six years old:

I. "Sandy, does my father like me as well as I like you?"
s. "No."
I. "How do you know that?   I am sure he gives me more money than I give you."
s. "But giving money's not liking."
I. "How so?"
s. "You give money to beggars."
I. "What do you see that makes you think my father does not like me so well as I like you?"
s. "Because he never speaks much to you.   If he liked you to come and see him, he would not let you just sit.   You speak a great deal to me."

The situation deteriorated.   One evening at the beginning of August, Lord Auchinleck spoke with "contemptuous disgust" of Lieutenant John. Boswell, shocked, said, " 'He's your son, and GOD made him.' "   Lord Auchinleck "answered very harshly, 'If my sons are idiots, can I help it?' " A few weeks later "a very disagreeable scene of ill humour" after dinner at his father's, just before the Boswells left for Valleyfield:

For all the money that is spent by his women, there is meanness at his table in grudging claret, which very seldom appears.   When Dr. Webster is there, a bottle is set down to him; and as it is a great chance no more will be allowed, I generally never take any of it.   Today I chose a glass of it, and said easily, "Doctor, will you give me a glass of your wine?"   He made me welcome, to be sure.   As I was taking the bottle to me, my father said with a snarl, "That's Dr. Webster's bottle, man."   "I know," said I.   "But the Doctor makes me welcome, and I like to take a glass of claret when I'm with a man who can afford it.   But if it is disagreeable to you, I shall not take any of it."   He was ashamed when I thus spoke out.   But he looked displeased.   I repeated, "If it is disagreeable to you that I should drink claret, I shall let it alone." He wished to have the meanness concealed, and said, "Never fash[1] your head."   So I drank claret.   Lady Auchinleck called for another bottle of claret.   This roused him, and with a vengeance he filled my glass with sherry.   I was stunned, and hesitated for a little what to do.   I once thought of instantly leaving the company. But I luckily restrained myself; said, "It's all one"; and then putting some claret into my glass, said, "I'll make burgundy of it."   After this the other bottle of claret was decanted; I partook of it as if

[1]Bother.

nothing had happened, and he was quiet.   It was really wretched treatment. . . .

My dear wife was hurt by my father's treatment of me and thought I should have instantly resented it, because submitting to it seemed mean.   She said, "If a father slaps his son in the face when he is a man, the son ought not to bear it peaceably."   I was much disturbed reflecting on it.   But her temper is keen, and the Commissioner convinced me next morning that I did well not to take notice of it.

It was the last time Boswell and his father spoke.   On 29 August a messenger came express to Valleyfield with the news that Lord Auchinleck was dying.   Boswell returned at once to Edinburgh:

Was told by Robert Boswell[1] of illness particularly.   Went upstairs. Miss Peggie:[2] "Don't go in hastily; not an agreeable sight."   Went in.   He took no notice as I passed, curtains open.   Went round; she[3] sitting by curtains.   Shook hands.   I asked if in pain.   "Has the pains" (or "struggles" or some such word) "of dissolution on him."   Her hardness was amazing.   I wished to go near.   She said, "It will confuse his head.   Don't torture him in his last moments."   I was benumbed and stood off.   Wept; for alas! there was not affection between us.

Margaret returned from Valleyfield, and they went back and forth between James's Court and Lord Auchinleck's house in the New Town. That night Lady Auchinleck said to Boswell, "There's all that remains of him."

Wished to stay all night.   Miss Peggie like a devil.   Went home to bed.

Raised.   Went back.   Women servants gathered.   Miss Peggie: "Come and see."   [He was] very low.   Stayed in room.   She[4] carried off, Robert Boswell attending.   Miss Peggie's flutter shocking.   Strange thought: "Still alive, still here!   Cannot he be stopped?"   Breathing [grew] high, gradually ceased.   Doctor closed eyes.   Miss Peggie's exclamations.   Up all night. . . .   Breakfasted next morning. . . .   Over to wife: had spit blood. . . .   Writing letters in giddy state.   At night looking at his Skene[5] [from] affection and nervousness cried and sobbed.

[1]Boswell's first cousin, Dr. John Boswell's eldest son.
[2]Margaret Boswell, Lady Auchinleck's sister.
[3]Lady Auchinleck.
[4]Lady Auchinleck.
[5]A law book with MS. notes that Lord Auchinleck had lent Boswell a month earlier, after first refusing to.

The hand of his father lay heavy on Boswell, even in death.   When
he got the news in Paris of his mother's death, he rushed feverishly to a
brothel.   Now when two days later he started to make love to Margaret,
a thought interposed: "What! when he who gave you being is lying a corpse!"
He stopped.

For the honour of the family the funeral at Auchinleck on 4 September
was sumptuous, as Boswell had long planned it to be; in fact, the bills,
which survive neatly bundled, show that it cost nearly £300, almost a fifth
of the estate's annual rents.   It was a beautiful day; Boswell felt manly if
confused, and remained perfectly sober amid the usual hearty excesses of
a Scots funeral.   On 18 September he brought his wife and children to
Auchinleck, she for the first time since 1770, and they for the first time in
their lives.

At last, he was Boswell of Auchinleck.

CHAPTER

10

I

OTHER AMBITIONS WERE imaginative possibilities at best, but Laird of Auchinleck was the substantial place in society which Boswell had always known he would inherit. Now he was master in the home of his ancestors, ruler of a domain rich in romantic beauties of rock, wood, and water that he had long since gilded with classical associations. From his "elegant house," the Laird could ride ten miles forward upon his own territories, his land actually extending half as much again from the rich Trabboch barony west of Auchinleck House to his own desolate Dalblair in the east. At a time when £1,000 a year was a quite comfortable income, the estate's £1,500 rent-roll looked ample. Some 600 people lived, if not at his command, at least under his immediate direction. He was principal heritor of Auchinleck parish, with the right to present the minister, and a heritor in several surrounding ones. Already well known, his new position added solidity. To the polite world he was James Boswell, Esq., of Auchinleck; but to his tenants and neighbours, equated with the estate itself he was simply "Auchinleck." Whatever happened, he could always "just be an old Scottish baron and Tory": the rank and independence he had been born to gave him importance in his own eyes. For the rest of his life his goal was to acquire even greater importance in the eyes of others.

But Boswell reacted to his accession with an uneasiness swelling almost to panic. His father's selfish refusal to teach him how to manage the estate and, worse, his lifelong undermining of Boswell's self-confidence, now precipitated all his fears of being unequal to his father's place. As soon as he had installed the family at Auchinleck he set off for London, but Margaret, still very ill and feeling abandoned, had such a violent spitting of blood that he was recalled before he had gone thirty miles. A firm letter from Johnson, urging frugality and close attention to her, "the prop and stay of your life," confirmed his resolution to weather it out by himself.

Boswell's recourse was to flood Johnson, his other prop and stay, with his problems. He had felt "drawn irresistibly" to consult Johnson:

> I imagined I could neither act nor think in my new situation till I had talked with you. . . . It was my determination that I should maintain the decorum of the Representative of Auchinleck, and I am doing so.

Decorum did not preclude a violent assault on his stepmother, the source of great emotional, and now material, deprivation. He told Johnson that she had totally estranged his father from him and his family, destroyed family letters (a serious crime to Boswell), misused her locality lands[1] for immediate profit, and so forth. His chief grievance was the size of Lord Auchinleck's settlements on her. Even though Henry Dundas, as one of his father's trustees, told him she might have had more, shouldn't he try to have the settlements set aside on the ground of undue influence?

Having relieved his feelings, Boswell let bad enough alone. Anxiety died away, and he quickly experienced the power and comfort of his position. He instituted family devotions, and planned a stately progress to each of the churches of which he was a heritor; he took great satisfaction at Mauchline Church in sitting at the front of the family loft with his tenants ranged behind him. He needed to learn to compute rents and expenses, so he started arithmetic lessons with Alexander Millar, his domestic chaplain and his sons' tutor. Fairlie of Fairlie, a noted agricultural "improver," contributed three days of valuable advice. To stay close to affairs in his absence, he instructed James Bruce, his overseer and lifetime confidant, to send him a weekly journal of weather and work on the estate, and these "returns" from Bruce and his successor, Andrew Gibb, were kept up faithfully until Boswell's death.

Immediately he took his place in Ayrshire society. In twos and threes the county came to pay its respects, and soon he found occasion to express strong views at meetings of the local gentry. On his birthday, 29 October, he had the pleasure of expounding his political sentiments at a meeting of the Ayr Quarter Sessions. The only kind of liberty, he said, that the people (the non-propertied class) of Scotland had ever seemed concerned about was "ecclesiastical liberty, and particularly an opposition to patronage, of

[1]Estate lands which Lady Auchinleck possessed in liferent, the source of her income.

which at present their heads were full." As for political liberty, the representation of the county, violated by the large number of nominal and fictitious votes (which had elected Sir Adam Fergusson), was "a representation of *shadows*." Boswell continued:

> Sometimes in a fit of Roman enthusiasm, I have thought a Member of Parliament should be a man of pure patriotism with enlarged views for the general good of his country, regardless of all inferior motives. But when in a more rational frame I have thought (as I believe most of us think, would we honestly speak out) that a Member of Parliament is just a fowler for the county: and that he who brings down most birds, that is, most places and pensions for his constituents, is the best Member. I have indeed observed that this fowler is chiefly careful of himself in the distribution of the fowls; and he puts me in mind of the honest Irishman who, when three of them sat down to supper with two chickens and a turkey before them, stuck his fork into the turkey and said, "Every man his bird."

Assuming, Boswell went on, that property was the proper basis for the suffrage, he was still in doubt as to two points: whether a gentleman's number of votes should be in proportion to his "stake" in the government, the extent of his property; and whether peers should exert influence in an election to the House of Commons. But he was sure

> that it would be a high gratification of his ambition to represent the real freeholders of a respectable county, gentlemen living upon their estates, with whom he could mutually enjoy good beef and claret as worthy friends and neighbours, to receive their instructions when going up to Parliament, and to the best of his abilities promote the advantage of the county in general and of the freeholders as individuals. But it pained him to the heart that these honest and honourable gentlemen should be deprived of their representation by a parcel of votes invented by the cunning ingenuity of certain lawyers.

These were the arguments Boswell was to repeat throughout his political struggles in Ayrshire. A female, and so presumably a detached, observer wrote that Boswell's speech evoked the loudest applause of any, and "spoke out the concealed sentiments of most of his contemporaries." On his motion, nominal and fictitious votes were denounced by a majority of two to one. Fergusson would no longer be able to brush him aside.

Boswell's accession as Laird marked a new start in life, comparable to his marriage in 1769, and the effect was dramatic. The crisis created by his father's death and his new responsibilities brought out an undeveloped side of his character. He was what he wanted to be, "rational and active." Margaret too, wonderfully recovered, looked like the Miss Peggie Montgomerie he had courted. As he told Dempster:

> I am grown fond of country affairs, which surprises me more than anything I have ever yet met with in the course of my existence. . . .
> I am very well—not by a strong anchor as [you boast] but by riding before a brisk gale.

This new lively interest in rural activities seemed to him like developing a sixth sense.

But the consequence and show of being Boswell of Auchinleck could not long conceal his unpleasant financial situation. Lord Auchinleck had combined the income from his estate with his salary of £700 a year as a Lord of Session and £200 a year as a Lord of Justiciary, the latter continued as a pension after his retirement in 1780. He was "abundantly economical," according to a contemporary, John Ramsay; certainly in his later years he restricted his entertaining to old friends and relations. On the other hand Boswell, though he gives no figures, could hardly have been able to count now on much more than £200 a year from his legal practice to add to his income from the estate.

Then there were the consequences of living for years beyond his means. In a "State of My Affairs" (1 September 1782), drawn up immediately upon becoming Laird, Boswell's comfortable bookkeeping assured him that his debts (£1,456) exceeded his assets (£1,013) by only a few hundred pounds. Neither figure reckoned with reality. Old friends like Douglas of Douglas, Mountstuart, Sir John Dick, and Paoli were creditors for more than half the amount he owed, and they were unlikely to clamour for repayment. But his assets were almost entirely illusory: he valued a sixth share in the foundering *London Magazine* at £250, and the remainder consisted in uncollectible loans to relations and close friends. With great casualness he wrote down, but omitted from these calculations, £3,000 in debts, secured mostly on the estate, which he intended to let run. At 5% or 6%, the interest alone on this amount came to £150 or £200 a year.

On these self-imposed burdens, Lord Auchinleck had piled settlements to the limit allowed by the entail. Even his choice of trustees had added insult. Dundas could be justified as a shrewd nomination to this group of six, since Lord Auchinleck, on his deathbed, had extracted his promise to help T.D. Stobie, Lord Auchinleck's clerk, whom Boswell detested for his impertinence, had his place as Lady Auchinleck's "doer" or agent; every year he would spend several weeks at Auchinleck collecting her rents. But the inclusion of Fergusson was a gratuitous slap in the face. No wonder

Boswell hated him.   After paying Lord Auchinleck's debts, the trustees in 1784 completed their work by handing over what remained of his personal estate, about £43.

The annuities, however, were a permanent charge on the estate: £60 for Lieutenant John (d. c. 1798), £50 (£200 the first year) for Dr. Gillespie (d. 1804), even £10 apiece for Dr. John's daughters, Elizabeth (d. 1806) and Anne (d. 1821), as long as they remained unmarried.   The stunning disclosure was the extent of the settlements made on Lady Auchinleck. Her jointure was a respectable £150 a year but, in time, as Lord Auchinleck quarrelled with Boswell over the entail and grew more and more dependent on his wife, he gradually increased her provision.   Now she had locality lands worth £325 a year (Boswell estimated they could be made to yield £500), a life interest in the new house in St. Andrew Square (£100 a year), and its furnishings outright (£1,000).   For a spinster whose income had once come to a grand total of £40 a year, she had done herself proud.

Boswell was commonly considered as very well-to-do and tried to live as if he were, but he had to confess to Dundas in 1784 that he had only £500 a year at his disposal, when Dundas thought he had twice as much. He himself could never keep track of all his expenses, but we can name a few: improvements on the estate (£100 to £300 a year), rent for the house in James's Court (£90 a year), the governess Miss Young's salary (£40 a year); anyone with a family can specify some of the rest.   Then there were what were called "public burdens": the minister's stipend, local taxes, and so forth.   Like many lairds of the time, Boswell defied augury and spent money without thought as long as he could, gambling on his prospects. It took him time to realize the justice of Johnson's observation that debt was not an inconvenience but a calamity.

For the moment, Boswell understandably ignored the implications of his balance sheet and concentrated on the potentialities of his new state in life.   Back in Edinburgh in November, steady and vigorous, he was eager to return to the Court of Session, where he would never see his father again.   His practice was better than expected; he pleaded, he said, with force, ease, and pleasure; and in a burst of aggressiveness he successfully asserted his position as Lord Eglinton's counsel-in-ordinary when he saw causes being tried by another advocate, something he could not have done, he said, in his dependent days: Eglinton's agents "now saw that I was not so simple or so weakly delicate as to permit it."

What engaged his imagination, however, was the spectacle of Lord Kames, now 86, not so much dying as fading into insubstantiality.   Kames was one of that remarkable group of thinkers which gave Edinburgh its reputation as the Athens of the North.   Sharp-witted and strong-willed, with a coarse outspokenness that could lapse into brutality, he had written energetically, and occasionally with distinction, on whatever came within range: "feudal law, history, trade, philosophy, drains, poetry, and sub-soil." He could arouse dislike—one acquaintance said he united the obstinacy of a mule with the levity of a harlequin—but he could also be very kind, as he had been to the young Boswell.   Boswell had repaid him by having an affair with his newly married daughter, though happily Kames never learned of it.

Some eighty-two pages of notes, chiefly conversation, for Boswell's contemplated biography of Kames survive, far more material than for any of his other unfinished biographical projects.   Disjointed and repetitious, they are also lively and readable, though they do not depict Kames with all the sharpness of profile Boswell could give his major subjects when he had meditated upon them.   But they illustrate clearly his desire to see into the mystery of the eminent and enviably stable.

Especially Boswell hovered about Kames, as he had about Hume, in his dying moments, and for a highly reasonable motive: now, if ever, he would get an honest opinion about that most important of concerns, the hereafter.   (His materializing at the end may seem ghoulish, but he comforted the old man in his loneliness at the same time that he tried to elicit his final responses, and Lady Kames welcomed him: "This is a good man," she told her husband.   "He's very good to us.")   Their conversation, of course, was not confined to the future, and as they ranged over past and present it had its jarring moments.   One day Boswell goaded the dying man into a long argument by talking about his stinginess.   But Kames also knew Boswell's weak points.   When Boswell went on about his new delight in the country, Kames warned that it might pass like a fit of religious enthusiasm.   And that dryasdust annalist, Lord Hailes, was moved to record one exchange, when Boswell affected in public to treat Kames as a revenant:

> [Boswell] addressed him thus, "Lord Kames, you are welcome from the other world, what news?"   "The only news that I have is that your father is coming back to see how you are behaving yourself."

Their private conversation was more serious.   Kames asserted, indisputably, that there was "an impenetrable veil between us and our future state," but when Boswell urged, "We may conjecture about it," Kames replied, "with that spring of thought, that kind of sally for which he was ever remarkable, 'You'll not go to Hell for conjecturing.'"   The field was wide open.   Some time earlier Kames had intimated that there had not been just one revelation to Christians but several, to Muhammadans and others, a notion to which Boswell himself inclined.   Now they began to speculate specifically about the nature of Heaven.   Could they not anticipate refined versions of earthly pleasures, eating and music?   Kames agreed:

> "Why not have the pleasure of women?"   "Why not," cried I with animation.   "There is nothing in reason or revelation against our having all enjoyments, sensual and intellectual."

And Kames was clear that man's creation in God's image meant that God had a physical form, though he could not tell "in what manner and with what rapidity He darts from one part of the universe to another."   Boswell found this a new idea.

Still, Kames all in all was a disappointment.   He did not shock Boswell as Hume had with his unruffled infidelity, but there was "nothing venerable, nothing edifying, nothing solemnly pious at the close of life."   On 21 December 1782, he made his last appearance in public.   Boswell

> just saw him in the Court of Session like a ghost, shaking hands with Lord Kennet in the chair, and Lords Alva and Eskgrove patting him kindly on the back as if for the last time.

But, according to folklore, Kames turned in the door as he was leaving and cried, "in his usual familiar tone, 'Fare ye a'weel, ye bitches!' "   He died less than a week later (27 December).

I I

ON THE SAME DAY, Boswell set out for Auchinleck to spend the Christmas recess in estate business and visits to neighbours.   He was as happy at Auchinleck as he had been when a boy, and added to happiness the loftiness of being Laird.   He told himself:

> I was just as I wished to be.   I was quite satisfied with my character and conduct at present.   It was what would have pleased my father and my grandfather.   May I ever behave in like manner at the seat of my ancestors!

He had drunk little since his attack of influenza the previous summer, but took no credit: for the first time in his life he was experiencing what he called constitutional sobriety and was freed from the rage of drinking.

And in almost every journal entry he reports himself "in sound, cheerful spirits."

It may seem odd that Boswell could not take his sound spirits for granted. He recorded them because his emotional weather was as unpredictable to him as the weather outside: he went through each day never knowing how his mood would change. Of course he could make general predictions: he would feel exuberant in London and dismal in Edinburgh—no one, he said, ever had a more "local" mind—just as he could expect that it would grow hot in summer and cold in winter.

He was not in touch with himself. As remarked earlier, his incessant self-commentary observes rather than analyses his emotions. Yet his assertion that to examine oneself or others at close range leads to the same disgust that Gulliver felt when he looked at the ladies in Brobdingnag is strikingly inaccurate in one respect. Gulliver's disgust is physical and sexual, while Boswell never shows any revulsion from the body. But there is something ugly inside him that threatens to overwhelm him if it ever surfaces, feelings of worthlessness (nothingness) that he can suppress only if he is active, involved in something, and important to others.

The crash came shortly after his return to Edinburgh:

> 15 JANUARY 1783. . . . I began to have a little return of bad spirits.
> 16 JANUARY. . . . My spirits were pretty good. But the enamel of my sound mind was a little broken. . . .
> 17 JANUARY. . . . The Court of Session was irksome to me. . . .
> 18 JANUARY. To what purpose waste time in writing a journal of so insipid a life? . . .

He had a cold and sore throat. Does the body affect the mind and vice versa, or are they just synchronized? Boswell had often wondered himself. The Laird was all-important at Auchinleck, but in Edinburgh he was just another advocate, and not a remarkably successful one at that. He remained definitely dissatisfied with the Scots bar.

> 20 JANUARY. Was sadly impressed with a conviction of the transient nature of human life with all its concerns and occupations.

[Translation: *I* can accomplish nothing.]

> 28 JANUARY. I looked back with wonder and wishfulness on my healthful state of mind last autumn and this winter till after my return from Ayrshire which I had flattered myself was to be permanent. . . . [Company at supper.] I was in such want of spirits that I not only had difficulty to speak a little and affect attention, but was obliged to go for a little and lie down on my bed, just for a kind of relief from teasing pain.

Talking was as fundamental an expression as writing of Boswell's selfhood.
When depressed he could hardly talk at all, while he says that he could
talk twice as much as usual in London.

The shadow of his father hung over him. As he told Kames, he
frequently imagined he could still consult his father, that in making improvements at Auchinleck he thought he was doing what his father would
approve, and that he wanted to preserve the notion his father would always
see what he was about. Only God always sees what we are about. When
his father was alive, Boswell could realize at times that his father was another
ordinary mortal. Now Lord Auchinleck had turned into a fixed image.
Dining at Lady Auchinleck's, he felt a "tremulous awe" when he passed
the room where his father had died. He began to drink again sporadically.
Then Johnson came down on him with a letter so rigorously opposed to
Boswell's settling in London or his drinking at all that he felt "a good deal
hurt." Practice dwindled away, but he told himself that "a gentleman of
good fortune never gets much practice at our bar" and he had more than
anyone else in his situation had ever had; besides, he wasn't fit to undertake
a great load of business. A transient flow of good spirits led to bewilder-
ment: "I *must* believe that man is in many respects subject to influence quite
unknown to him."

Fortunately, when it came to his writing Boswell could estimate its
value without regard for the views of others. His series of *Hypochondriack*
essays was coming to a close because his partners in the *London Magazine*
didn't care for them: "I was not in the least affected by this, because I had
no opinion of their taste in writing, for they wished rather for a *merry essay*."

He turned to London like a magnetic needle. As the time for his
spring jaunt approached, his immediate source of discontent breaks into
his journal and his depression begins to lift:

> 18 FEBRUARY. Was rather better, but quite dissatisfied with the
> narrow sphere here, and perpetually languishing for London em-
> inence.
> 19 FEBRUARY. Felt all at once in the Court of Session a happy
> state of mind which made me view it with complacency instead of
> disgust. I wondered, while I experienced how little reality there
> is in external things.

He realized it was all in his head, but what was in his head he didn't know.

On 14 March 1783 Boswell set off for London by public stage-coach
rather than the usual private post-chaise, a concession to economy, with
stops at Moffat to visit Lieutenant John, difficult as always and drinking
hard, and at Carlisle to keep up his acquaintance with Percy, newly made

Bishop of Dromore.   The stage-coach was a punishment he resolved never to inflict on himself again.   Though he still distances "all human concerns as scenes in a drama" with no effect on him, the journal has begun to take on its old expansiveness, a sure sign of better spirits.   As soon as he had landed at Dilly's he started on the rounds of that "very extensive acquaintance" of which he had reason to be proud: Oglethorpe, Dempster, Godfrey Bosville, his brother T.D., Reynolds, his cousin Captain Preston, Langton, on and on.   He had forgotten the "hard exercise" that London required.

This spring Boswell, a middle-aged Rasselas, intended to make his "choice of life."   (He himself echoes the phrase twice.)   As he saw it, there were three possibilities:

1.   He could stay at the Scottish bar with a good chance of becoming a Lord of Session like his father.   This was not merely his own estimate; his friend, Sir William Forbes, a singularly clear-headed man, wrote to Langton shortly after Lord Auchinleck's death that Boswell had a "very fair prospect of arriving at a seat on the Bench in due time."   This alternative would allow him to maintain a highly respectable position in Scotland, pay off his debts, and continue to visit London for two or three months every year.

2.   He could live in London much of the year by being chosen M.P. for Ayrshire or by securing preferment through his friends.   The political scene provided some substance for what otherwise would have to seem regression into fantasy.   Fox and North had joined in their notorious Coalition, and Burke was coming back into office as Paymaster of the Forces at £4,000 a year.   And perhaps some other friend would help.   Paoli and Pembroke disclaimed any influence, but there was always Mountstuart.

3.   He could transfer to the English bar.   To the old models, Mansfield and Wedderburn (now Lord Loughborough), was added the example of Thomas Erskine, the impoverished youngest son of the Earl of Buchan, who, after unproductive stints in the navy and army, had achieved dazzling success immediately upon being called to the bar in 1778.   It was true that Erskine was a brilliant speaker with a formidable talent for making his weight felt in the courtroom, but Boswell had enough trial experience to have confidence in his own declamatory powers.   And Paoli, telling him that Erskine was taking giant strides towards honours and riches, as early as 1780 had encouraged him with explicit comparison:

You should expect at least equal success were you willing to emulate him in assiduity and diligence, which are his to the highest degree.

Transfer to the English bar was the riskiest and most appealing alternative.

Other people built castles in the air, Boswell said, but he tried to live in his. To attempt his third alternative now would have far-reaching consequences not only for himself but for his family. "The great difficulty," he told himself before leaving Edinburgh, "is to settle between foolish fancy and spirited ambition; and probably I shall dream and balance till it is too late to exert." A complicating factor was that his first and third choices were entirely in his power, the second very little so.

As always when he had difficulty in making up his mind, Boswell sought advice compulsively. He blamed the timid restraint in which he had been kept as a child for depriving him of the power of decision. In this instance, however, he was not looking for advice but approval. He wanted to be told to throw caution to the winds and transfer to the English bar. Consulting friends had the supplemental advantage of reminding them of his desire for a place, but primarily he wanted them to quiet an uneasy conscience. He knew that the English bar was a gamble against odds, and he knew that he would be exposing Margaret's impaired lungs to the smoke of London. To stay in Scotland was the prudent choice, the only drawback being that he hated Scotland. And somewhere in the depths, perhaps never articulated, was the guilt and joy of defying his father.

Burke was the friend he counted on most. Boswell had taken him as a model in active affairs and in the affections of domestic life. Burke, he imagined, had full satisfaction in existence. When he needed an example of the greatest of minds, he thought of Burke. When he wanted to praise his performance in court, he told himself his talents were "Burkeish." In turn, hadn't Reynolds written that Burke declared Boswell was "the pleasantest man he ever saw, and sincerely wishes you would come to live amongst us," a compliment all the more exquisite because it had to be sincere? And hadn't Dundas told him he *knew* Burke wanted to help him? Boswell stayed close to Burke this spring, pressed his needs, exerted his affability, and was rewarded by an invitation to Gregories, Burke's country estate. This stay in Eden, and Boswell hardly thought it less, was even shorter than Adam's; the day after his arrival he was called back to London by the news that Lt. David Cuninghame, one of Margaret's nephews, had killed his antagonist in a duel and was himself dangerously wounded.

Mountstuart, too, had been activated on the short list of patrons. Having returned from his post at Turin the previous autumn after offending the King of Sardinia, he was now to display his diplomatic talents as Ambassador to Madrid. Paoli had assured him that Mountstuart's liking for him was genuine, but Boswell, as always, found his friend an enigma, and asked Johnson for explanation:

> He is, I really believe, noble-minded, generous, and princely.   But his most intimate friends may be separated from him for years, without his ever asking a question concerning them.   He will meet them with a formality, a coldness, a stately indifference; but when they come close to him and fairly engage him in conversation, they find him as easy, pleasant, and kind as they could wish.   One then supposes that what is so agreeable will soon be renewed; but stay away from him for half a year, and he will neither call on you nor send to inquire about you.

Though he was beyond Johnson's powers of analysis, Mountstuart himself made one point clear about the political facts of life:

> There are but three ways in which a man can have weight with a Minister: talents, Parliamentary interest, or a great deal of money to buy Parliamentary interest.

This comment was made apropos of the Duke of Gordon, but if the Duke, as Mountstuart thought, lacked such resources, what could Boswell offer?

Since Mountstuart is soon to disappear from this story, it is enough to add that in his self-conception as a princely nobleman Mountstuart never entertained any sordid notion of exerting himself strongly on his own behalf or on anyone else's.   In 1792 he succeeded as Earl of Bute; a few years later, George III raised him a step in the peerage.   Otherwise he lived on in easy self-satisfaction, leaving no mark behind.

Then there was Dundas.   Boswell had written to him the previous spring magnanimously forgiving the political injuries Dundas had inflicted on him in Ayrshire, and inviting Dundas in reparation to help him gain preferment.   Dundas replied good-humouredly but made no promises. The previous July Boswell had caught him in the Parliament House for one of those "confidential conversations" he thought so significant: was it irrational to wish for something in London?   No, but Dundas stalled; he would have to consider Boswell's situation and talk to him again in a few months.   In London Boswell now found him "open, frank, and hearty" and was highly gratified when Dundas read aloud important letters to and from Lord Shelburne and William Pitt in their attempt to stave off the Fox-North Coalition.   Dundas had just lost his post as Treasurer of the Navy but was unconcerned: his hold on Scotland made it dangerous for any Ministry to turn him into an enemy.   He advised Boswell to stay at home.

The current market price of a seat in Parliament was £3,000 and tenure in the existing political confusion was precarious.   The first thing for a man was to be "round" in himself: a free and independent agent.   If Boswell worked assiduously at his profession, that and his family status would give him a good claim to a judge's seat, a claim which Boswell understood him to say he would support.   Or perhaps Boswell could dash into Parliament if opportunity offered.

Boswell's constantly shifting attitude towards Dundas mixed admiration, liking, envy, and contempt: Dundas had risen quickly to high office and great influence; he was friendly but he had been Boswell's junior at school, and Boswell found his manner somewhat too bluff.   He was not *sympathique*.   Possibly it was his close association in Boswell's mind with Lord Auchinleck.   Something, at least, always interfered with Boswell's approaches to him.   This was regrettable; Burke or Mountstuart might become helpful, but Dundas already had power.   Yet Boswell seemed to go out of his way to snipe at him.   He accused Dundas of being a salesman for Scotland, a topsman (chief drover) for a herd of cattle.   Dundas replied calmly that as an agent for Government he held a trust, and "maintained ably that the forty-five Scots Members[1] were as independent in proportion to numbers as the English."

Boswell, of course, looked first and last to Johnson to make up his mind for him.   Johnson, however, was increasingly ill and difficult.   More and more he had come to depend on Mrs. Thrale's providing a home where, as he said, he could "use all the freedom that sickness requires." But freedom for him meant agonizing restraint for her, and she began to loosen their ties.   Distraught from having had to give up Gabriel Piozzi, the Italian music-master she loved, because her children and society at large disapproved of the match, she was now impatient to get away to Bath. Boswell's arrival represented the changing of the guard.   Johnson, vulnerable and uncomprehending, felt abandoned and wanted Boswell to play his customary role of sympathetic listener and affectionate helper; he had no intention of pandering to foolish ambitions.   At the end of their first meeting Johnson recited his newly written stanzas on the death of Robert Levett, that "obscure practiser in physic" (Boswell's phrase) who had been one of Johnson's household for many years.   It is one of the most moving elegies in the English language:

> Condemned to Hope's delusive mine,
>   As on we toil from day to day,

[1] Of the House of Commons.

By sudden blasts or slow decline,
  Our social comforts drop away.

Well tried through many a varying year,
  See Levett to the grave descend;
Officious,[1] innocent, sincere,
  Of every friendless name the friend. . . .

In Misery's darkest caverns known,
  His useful care was ever nigh,
Where hopeless Anguish poured his groans,
  And lonely Want retired to die.

No summons mocked by chill delay,
  No petty gain disdained by pride,
The modest wants of every day
  The toil of every day supplied.

His virtues walked their narrow round,
  Nor made a pause nor left a void;
And sure th'Eternal Master found
  The single talent well employed. . . .

Johnson then turned and said, "You must be as much with me as you can.
You have done me good. You cannot think how much better I am since
you came in." (Writing to Robert Chambers in Calcutta a few weeks later
about the painful loss of common friends, Johnson excepted Boswell: "He
is all that he was, and more.")

Two days after this first encounter, they got to Boswell's problem:

JOHNSON. "It is too late to indulge fancy. It may do in a young
man but not at your age, not in a man with wife and five children."
He even checked every ambitious wish which started from me,
and wanted to beat me down to dull content with my present state.
He said, "Talk no more in this way. People will only laugh at
you, or be vexed as I am."

But Boswell thought to himself:

In my coolest moments, and after employing the powers of judgement and reflection which GOD has given me, with a fair wish to
be well-informed, I am clearly persuaded that a man of my family,
talents, and connections may reasonably endeavour to be employed in a more elevated sphere than in Scotland, now that is in
reality only a province. But if I find after some time that there

[1]Quick to be helpful.

is little hope of being so employed, I shall set my mind to be satisfied with a judge's place in Scotland.

And he remembered then that Johnson had told him to empty his head of Corsica.

Such opposite views on so vital a topic promised a rocky spring, but soon Johnson and Boswell settled into their old relationship and routine. Boswell was assiduous in gathering Johnson's conversation; he got advice to explore Wapping, and got told—it was quintessentially Johnsonian—to clear his *mind* of cant.   Good Friday they spent as usual together; having returned from St. Clement Danes, they sat on stone seats by Johnson's garden door and let their thoughts drift: country hospitality, the uses of orange peel, the expense of garden walls, oratory (Walker the elocutionist had joined them, and they were now in Johnson's study), the origin of language, Dr. Dodd.   Mrs. Burney came in, and the conversation shifted to the costliness of Garrick's funeral and the wisdom of erecting residential buildings near madhouses.   On every subject Johnson showed his usual strong, decisive sense occasionally marked by stubborn prejudice.

The most revealing conversation that spring took place on Easter Sunday in Johnson's house, with the host absent.   Contemporary notions of propriety prohibited its inclusion in the *Life*; Boswell labelled it "Extraordinary Johnsoniana—*Tacenda*" (to be suppressed), and put it away.   Boswell and the untalented painter, Mauritius Lowe, are sitting with one of the household ménage, Mrs. Desmoulins, who had known Johnson all her life.

> Said Lowe: "Now, Ma'am, let us be free.   We are all married people.   Pray tell us, do you really think Dr. Johnson ever offended in point of chastity?   For my own part I do not believe he ever did.   I believe he was chaste even with his wife, and that it was quite a Platonic connection" (grinning a smile with his *one* eye to me).   MRS. DESMOULINS.   "Ah, Sir, you are much mistaken. There never was a man who had stronger amorous inclinations than Dr. Johnson.   But he conquered them." . . .   LOWE.   "I do still think the Doctor never has had any inclination for women." MRS. DESMOULINS.   "But he has."   LOWE.   "I do not believe his marriage was consummated."

Mrs. Desmoulins then repeated Garrick's story about peeping through the keyhole of the Johnsons' bedroom, and said that she thought Mrs. Johnson had never loved him.

> MRS. DESMOULINS.   "They did not sleep together for many years. But that was her fault.   She drank shockingly and said she was

not well and could not bear a bedfellow." . . .   LOWE.   "He has
had no passion."   MRS. DESMOULINS.   "Nay, Sir, I tell you no man
had stronger, and nobody had an opportunity to know more about
that than I had."   LOWE.   "I am sure, Madam, were I to indulge
that passion, I should think you a very agreeable object."   BOSWELL.
"You'll forgive me, Madam.   But from what you have said, I beg
leave to ask you if the Doctor ever made any attempt upon you?"
MRS. DESMOULINS (Lowe and I closing in upon her to listen).
"No, Sir, I have told you he commanded his passion.   But when
I was a young woman and lived with Mrs. Johnson at Hampstead,
he used to come out two or three days in a week, and when Dr.
Bathurst lived there, he'd go and stay with him till two or three
in the morning.   The maid went to bed, as she could not be kept
up, and I used to sit up for him; and I have warmed his bed with
a pan of coals and sat with him in his room many an hour in the
night and had my head upon his pillow."   BOSWELL.   "What, when
he was in bed, Madam?"   MRS. DESMOULINS.   "Yes, Sir.   He'd
desire me to go out of the room, and he'd go to bed; but to come
back in a little while and talk to him—and I have come and sat on
his bedside and laid my head on his pillow."   BOSWELL.   "And
he showed strong signs of that passion?"   MRS. DESMOULINS.   "Yes,
Sir.   But I have always respected him as a father."   BOSWELL.
"What would he do?   Come now" (Lowe like to jump out of his
skin), "would he fondle you?   Would he kiss you?"   MRS. DES-
MOULINS.   "Yes, Sir."   BOSWELL.   "And it was something different
from a father's kiss?"   MRS. DESMOULINS.   "Yes, indeed."   LOWE.
(approaching his hand to her bosom), "But would he? eh?"   MRS.
DESMOULINS.   "Sir, he never did anything that was beyond the
limits of decency."   LOWE.   "And could you say, Madam, upon
your oath, that you were certain he was capable?"   MRS. DESMOU-
LINS.   "Y-Yes, Sir."   BOSWELL.   "But he conquered his violent
inclination?"   MRS. DESMOULINS.   "Yes, Sir.   He'd push me from
him and cry, 'Get you gone.'   Oh, one can see."   BOSWELL.   "So
you saw the struggle and the conquest."   MRS. DESMOULINS.   "I
did."

The conversation continued.   Mrs. Desmoulins admitted that she had
often wondered what she would do if Johnson proceeded to extremities.
She had no "inclination" for Johnson, but her awe of him would have
prevented resistance.   BOSWELL.   "I cannot imagine it[1] of any woman.
There is something in his figure so terribly disgusting."   But Mrs. Desmoulins had the last word: "Yet, Sir, one cannot tell.   His mind is such."

This was one of Boswell's best springs in London.   As before, his
liveliness, good humour, and "insinuating urbanity of manners," made him

[1]Inclination.

popular everywhere.   He paid several visits to the Stuarts at Richmond Lodge.   He made an excursion to Woodford with his rich cousin, Capt. Bob Preston, to visit some of Preston's old cronies: a convivial day, and he hitched a ride back in a cart, singing "Gee-ho, Dobbin" to the imperturbable Londoners.   He recorded in detail Captain Inglefield's story of the sinking of the *Centaur* off Newfoundland, and his nightmare voyage in the ship's boat to the Azores.   (Byron drew vivid details from Inglefield's own *Narrative* for the shipwreck passage in the second canto of *Don Juan*.) Boswell wheeled round with the world but felt remarkably steady, master of his bottle, he claimed, though his journal records that insensibly he drank more and more as time went on.   On Sunday 18 May he went to high mass in the Portuguese Chapel: "Was devout as I could wish; heavenly and happy.   Vowed before the altar no more *filles* while in London.   A memorable moment."

Still, he had Temple on his hands.   Temple had business near Berwick and Boswell urged that they meet in London and travel north together, arguing that they had not met since 1775 and their friendship would wither. Temple's enthusiasm waned as the time for departure to London approached.   Home life was boring, his wife ill-tempered, his children expensive at school or a nuisance at home.   Babies continued to appear and, like the Sorcerer's Apprentice, Temple could seem to do nothing about it. Faced with another infant—Octavius, the eleventh and last—he wrote, "Oh, Boswell!   How oppressive it is to have so large a family!"

And yet . . .   He made the point in his sparse journal, a querulous counterpoint to Boswell's exuberant one: "Notwithstanding the uniformity of *home*, still preferable to anywhere else: more satisfaction, more enjoyment."   There were the compensations of blessed routine: a good book, the morning ride, the evening walk, even the comforts of family.   He tried to beg off in what Boswell characterized as a "languid, uxorious letter," and his "unkind" answer bullied Temple into making the trip.   But Boswell, too, was having doubts.   He wrote to Grange a few days before Temple's arrival that Temple's "feeble spirits and contracted sphere of acquaintance" might produce "some suspicion of my neglecting him while I am hurried round a large circle of company and amusement.   I must frankly caution him."

Everyone's expectations were fulfilled.   Temple visited his few friends, and Boswell did his share: he introduced Temple to Burke, took him to dine with Dilly, Wilkes, and Paoli; they called on Oglethorpe and Johnson, and took a jaunt to Richmond Lodge.   Little pleased.   The confusion of London was distracting and the distances tiring; dinner in a coffee-house was disagreeable, the conversation was too often insipid.   (Temple did admire Paoli and the Pantheon.)   Then one night while he was writing peacefully to his wife, Boswell broke in drunk from the Duke of Montrose's, having had his pocket picked of his gold watch.   There is some discrepancy in dates and events, but the loss of the watch appears in Boswell's journal at the end of a most lively day: he had spoken well on an appeal before the House of Lords, his one piece of business in London, and won his case with increased costs; an excellent dinner followed at Le Telier's tavern with Lord Pembroke as host, "good port, sherry, and claret and iced water.   A magnificent upper room.   All quite in high tavern style."   Unslaked, Boswell had summoned the landlord and they drank four more bottles of claret. Then

> sallied forth shockingly drunk, and picked up a girl in St. James's Street.   Went into park; sat on bench and toyed, but happily had sense enough left not to run risk.   However, when we rose and walked along, missed watch.   She denied.   Grew sober; said she should go to watch-house.   She broke off in St. James's Street. Watchman, two chairmen, and a soldier catched her, and we marched to St. James's watch-house.

The journal account ends here at the bottom of a page with a blank reverse, so Boswell probably never finished it.   Nor, it appears, did he get his watch back, since he seems to have been advertising for it a month later.

That Sunday, Temple exploded in his journal:

> Gave an account of everything so far to my wife.   No pleasure here.   Nothing but noise and madness.   O for my wife and quiet parsonage! . . .   Called on Boswell.   Went to church.   Bl. irregular in his conduct and manners, selfish, indelicate, thoughtless, no sensibility or feeling for others who have not his coarse and rustic strength and spirits.   Sorry I came to town to meet him. Detaining me here to no purpose.   Seems often absurd and almost mad, I think.   No composure or rational view of things.   Years do not improve him.   Why should I mortify myself to stay for him? . . .   Boswell came to us[1] in the evening in his usual ranting way and stayed till 12, drinking wine and water, glass after glass.

It certainly was hard to detach Boswell from London.   Where else was existence so exciting, where else was he so happy?   Johnson, in a mild moment, even encouraged his hopes of preferment.   Boswell admitted that he had no claim on Burke beyond friendship.   "However," he said, "some people will go a great way from that motive."   Johnson replied,

---

[1]Temple was lodged with a friend, Christopher Hawkins.

"Sir, they will go all the way from that motive." When Boswell, still considering alternatives, spoke of retiring to a desert (a metaphor for Scotland?), Johnson told him that it would be civil suicide.

Their last conversation that spring was intimate and tender. Boswell was in a confessional mood, and complained,

> It is incredible how absurd and weak I am, with talents—I mean in conduct and in speculative opinions; for I do very well when I come to an argument in law. I have not force of mind.

In response, Johnson spread out into general maxims of prudence:

> Endeavour to get as much force of mind as you can. Live within your income. Always have something saved at the end of the year. Let your imports be more than your exports, and you'll never go far wrong.

Boswell invited him to Auchinleck, and Johnson said he would gladly come if he grew better:

> Were I in distress, there is no man to whom I should sooner come than to you. I should like to come and have a cottage in your park, toddle about, live mostly on milk, and be taken care of by Mrs. Boswell. She and I are good friends now, are we not?

He told Boswell to stick to his practice and aim at a judge's place. He was "quick and lively, and critical as usual." Boswell, who still believed that his character could be deliberately formed, couldn't decide whether he should be a grave, reserved solid man or "a fine, gay, flashy fellow." Johnson's answer, as preserved, is succinct but sufficient: "This is mighty foolish." His "manly conversation" animated Boswell; he again felt a transfusion of mind. Johnson took him in his arms and uttered the usual parting formula, "GOD bless you for Jesus Christ's sake," followed by a reminder to say good-bye to Mrs. Williams as he left.

After attending the anniversary dinner at Chelsea College, the old soldiers' home, with Burke, an occasion which had delayed his departure from London for several days, Boswell picked up Temple at Dilly's and they set off. The next day, at Southill, he put down his resolution, fixed by Johnson and Burke, to stay in Scotland:

> I am then to be steady to the great point of being of consequence in my own country and having my wife and children comfortable and creditable—with the addition of London, The Hague, Paris, to enlarge and enliven. And keep up the piety of your family.

The trip north did a good deal to mend matters between Boswell and Temple, though after communicating at Berwick on Sunday Boswell got drunk and was seen staggering on the ramparts, which Temple thought "both wrong and indiscreet."   Still, he stuck up for his friend: when, later, the vicar was so ill-bred as to mention the incident, Temple wanted to slap his face.   But despite repeated invitations, Temple was not to be lured to Edinburgh: "Cannot go to Boswell; for what purpose?"   As late as the next spring he was still scolding Boswell: if you do move to London,

> I shall be better pleased with you than last summer.   You will be more settled and tranquil and not imagine your importance depends on a multiplicity of unnecessary and uninteresting engagements, you will have leisure to attend to my feelings as well as your own, and not oppress me by that boisterousness and indelicacy contracted among your friends at the Scotch bar.

For all that, they found their way back to their old affection, and Temple writes:

> How pleasing it is to look back to our early intimacy! how consoling to have a friend with whom we are under no reserve!   It atones for many disagreeable things and is one of the chief satisfactions in life.   May this mutual satisfaction be long, very long, preserved to us!

I I I

AGAIN THE DROP into the void.   When the journal resumes on 1 August Boswell is in Edinburgh, his mood black.   He had made his decision, it was the approved one, and he was as miserable as ever.   "Wasting my days in provincial obscurity"—that is what he felt.   In this state of mind, the news of Dundas's dismissal as Lord Advocate a few days later did not much agitate him, though he wrote immediately to Burke, asking to be made Advocate or Solicitor-General or joint Solicitor-General or just given something.   In return, he would help to establish the Coalition's popularity in Scotland.   It was a feeble letter, and Burke's reply, though friendly, was discouraging.   Harry Erskine, a Coalition partisan, was appointed Advocate; Sandy Wight, an authority on Scots election law, became Solicitor. (According to the often-repeated anecdote, Dundas offered to lend Erskine his Advocate's gown since Erskine, he thought, would need it for so short a time.   Erskine replied that he realized Dundas's gown was made "to *fit any party*," but he would not "put on the *abandoned habits* of his predecessor.")

Now at Auchinleck, Boswell's "uneasiness of low spirits" gave way to "dull indifference, a sort of callous stupor."   Entertaining company was an anxious and laborious task, badly relieved by drinking. Johnson had suffered a stroke in June, and though he recovered rapidly Boswell's anticipation of his death oppressed him with dreadful gloom. He neglected estate affairs, and reverted to his old habit of passing the time at Auchinleck in pottering about: "collecting ferns and rushes for dung, and such things." An unpleasant sign of returning energy appeared when some careless expression of Margaret's aroused "a paroxysm of horrible passion" that left him shaken by his own behaviour. "It is amazing," he thought, "how much everything depends on the state of our minds at the time, and how little the state of anyone's mind is known to others." Still he was elected preses (chairman) first of the Quarter Sessions and then of a general meeting of Ayrshire landowners, which approved a petition again condemning nominal and fictitious votes; it was his pleasure as well as duty to forward it to Fergusson. At least his neighbours respected him. "I *must* submit to life losing its vividness," he told himself.

Then frustration and anger found a focus. He wrote a furious letter to Burke (20 November):

> The choice of a Solicitor-General in Scotland has not only vexed me as a gentleman of such connections in every view as give me good reason to think myself ill-used, but I can assure you discredits the present Ministry more than they are aware. You flattered me with hopes that they were to have no understrapping manager of affairs on this side of the Tweed. But this appointment is a wretched proof to the contrary.

Sir Thomas Dundas, Henry Dundas's distant relation and enemy, and most notable as "a fine fellow at Newmarket," was pulling the strings in London for the Coalition Ministry; Boswell thought him responsible for Erskine's and Wight's appointments. He continued:

> You think it is not easy to sour my temper. But I should think meanly of myself did I entertain no resentment of the total neglect which I have had the mortification to experience, at a time when I had reason to think and when it was generally thought that I could not fail to receive some mark of attention from Administration.

Without waiting for Burke to reply—he never did—the next day Boswell asked Erskine directly why he hadn't been appointed Solicitor; the response was awkward excuses and professions of willingness to be of service.

This delayed reaction—Erskine had been appointed Lord Advocate three months earlier—had no rational basis. Boswell had never approved of the Coalition, and he had nothing to offer it except his hunger for preferment.   Now the Ministry faced far more serious problems.   Fox's unpopular East India Bill had given the King the opening needed to dismiss him, and in mid-December the 24-year-old William Pitt became Prime Minister, though the Coalition still commanded a substantial majority in the House of Commons.   Pitt had Henry Dundas's strong, essential support.   Ilay Campbell became Lord Advocate; Dundas had been right about the gown.   Boswell's Tory soul fired with enthusiasm and a clear conscience; on 20 December he proposed an Address from the Faculty of Advocates congratulating the King, but his colleagues were too prudent to commit themselves during such unprecedented political turbulence and unanimously rejected it.   Three days later he wrote to Pembroke and Mountstuart for their help towards the Solicitorship (it went to the Lord President's son, young Robert Dundas), and between 26 and 29 December 1783 Boswell wrote a short pamphlet called *A Letter to the People of Scotland*. "At a crisis of doubtful event," he would "stand forth with honest zeal as an ancient and faithful Baron."

The 1783 *Letter* is a firm, clear, lively attack on Fox's East India Bill, which makes two central points: (1) the Bill violates the property rights of the East India Co.; (2) the Bill violates the Constitution by setting up a commission with immense power appointed by Parliament, which diminishes the royal prerogative.   The effect of the pamphlet did not depend on the originality of these arguments—they were commonplaces—but on the telling manner in which Boswell phrased them.   The letter format was a means for adopting an easy tone of voice; the pamphlet is a speech, and Dempster told him that if it had been delivered in the House of Commons it would have been the best speech on the subject.   As long as he could keep his exhibitionism under control, Boswell was a first-rate journalist with a shrewd sense of his audience; here, for example, the informal asides on Oglethorpe, the disastrous American War, and heritable jurisdictions serve as slight digressions to relieve the line of argument.   In the House of Commons, Dundas even alluded to a clever remark in the *Letter* about Jack Lee, the Coalition's Attorney-General.   Lee had asked what value had the East India Co.'s charter, "a skin of parchment with a waxed seal at the corner," compared to the happiness of thirty million subjects and the preservation of the empire?   Taken out of context the quoted phrase became notorious, and Boswell wrote, "If an Attorney-General were hanged it might be said with vulgar triumph, 'What is an Attorney-General but a carcass dangling at the end of a rope?' "

This joke seems slight, but the pamphlet was effective.   The reviews struck just the right notes: the *European Magazine* called it "judicious and masterly," the *English Review* praised its "pleasantry and good humour," and the *Critical Review* commented that "Mr. Boswell has always distinguished himself by an attachment to public liberty." Only the *Monthly Review* dissented, remarking sourly on Boswell's overdeveloped sense of self.

Private reactions were equally flattering and more significant. Congratulatory letters came from two Ministerial figures, Dundas and Lord Graham, but the prize was a short letter from Pitt himself praising Boswell's "zealous and able support" of the public cause. Only Mountstuart, who had taken a "warm part" with the Coalition, maintained a disquieting silence that, despite repeated appeals, announced the end of their connection. It was the price Boswell had to pay. Paoli, warning him that his convivial nature would be little help in politics, went on: "You have entered the lists; you must now fight, for your new friends feel obliged to you for what you have done on their behalf in equal measure, perhaps, as your old friends have cause to be disgusted and offended." Even Johnson rallied round. The previous December he had written: "Of the exaltations and depressions of your mind you delight to talk, and I hate to hear. Drive all such fancies from you." Now he wrote, "Your paper contains very considerable knowledge of history and of the Constitution, very properly produced and applied. It will certainly raise your character, though perhaps it may not make you a Minister of State."

Boswell had already entered the lists before hearing from Paoli and Johnson. In the *Letter* he had stated that its purpose was to arouse Addresses from Scotland to the King denouncing the East India Bill, and he pushed the good work himself. He persuaded his cousin, Sir Charles Preston, to sponsor one from the burgh of Culross, and wrote it himself to make sure of its effectiveness. In Midlothian, where the Dundases were reluctant to back an Address openly, Boswell initiated one through Sir Alexander Dick, which was carried by a large majority. The undertaking closest to his heart was an Address from Ayrshire where, in spite of opposition, he pushed one through on 17 March 1784, along with a vote of thanks to Pitt and an implied rebuke to Fergusson for his past support of North and the American War. (He might have remembered that Dundas had backed both North and the War; perhaps he did remember, and wanted to emphasize to Dundas that times and opinions had changed.) On the way to London for this spring's stay, he stopped at York, a very important political centre, for a meeting of the county freeholders to consider an Address; when the chairman was uncertain who had carried the day Boswell persuaded him that the pro-Pitt faction was in the majority, and the Address was adopted.   Hearing at York on 26 March that Parliament, as expected, had been dissolved, he turned back to Edinburgh.

All during the first three months of 1784, Boswell's spirits rose.   He was confined to the house in January by another bout of gonorrhoea but abstemiousness calmed his spirits and he grew thin.   He revised the *Hypochondriack* and his legal practice at least made a "decent show."   He claimed to be enjoying domestic life more than usual, though that may have led to what he called an unfortunate "domestic disturbance," carefully left unspecified, which recurred from time to time.   Possibly Margaret caught him in pursuit of the governess Miss Young.

But the *Letter*'s reception was gratifying; it gave him the short-term success needed to revive confidence.   It ought to do him good with a Tory administration, and surely with the King himself.   He pleased himself with fancying that some great man, "to whom my congenial sentiments and good talents might recommend me, would call me into a respectable employment, and not improbably bring me into Parliament."   This wish had a terrible irony to it if it was the *Letter* that brought Boswell to the attention of Lord Lonsdale.

CHAPTER

11

I

IN THE LATER eighteenth century, Scottish county elections focused on one easily grasped issue: the outs vs. the ins. Of course, in 1784 the King's stubborn backing of the Pitt Ministry against the Coalition majority in the House of Commons had precipitated a constitutional crisis, which stirred excited discussion. But the success of Boswell's Ayrshire Address demonstrated the attraction of Government, the cornucopia of places and preferment; and when Eglinton went over to the party in power—a Scottish characteristic—his candidate, Montgomerie, and the sitting Member, Fergusson, were left with nothing to disagree about. Family alliances and friendships, interested and disinterested, would determine the election. True, there were other candidates: John ("Fish") Craufurd, the Glencairn-Dumfries nominee, supported the Coalition, but he had too few friends to carry the election. Sir John Whitefoord, with only 11 out of the 230-odd freeholders' votes at his disposal, was busy campaigning: he hoped to squeeze in, if not at the present election then at the next one; and, while pledged to mutual consultation with Fergusson, he was soliciting Montgomerie's help.

Boswell, meanwhile, had manoeuvred himself into an unhappy position. As early as January 1783, in a burst of unnecessary enthusiasm he had renewed allegiance to Eglinton as his "chief" in the county, and to Montgomerie as candidate. In fact he told Eglinton he would support Montgomerie even if Eglinton did not, an impossible situation since Montgomerie could not stand without Eglinton's support; then Boswell added that he would offer himself as a candidate if Montgomerie were to withdraw. Slowly he came to believe that this tangled statement committed him to Eglinton under any circumstances, which aroused his misgivings. And doubts recurred. Was it proper, he asked Johnson in November 1783, for peers to manipulate elections? His mentor replied that their interference constituted usurpation. Boswell then spread the word that if Montgomerie did not stand, he would oppose Fergusson himself.

This news having reached Eglinton, he despatched Hamilton of Bargany, an "old, sly politician," to confer with Boswell (17 January 1784). Boswell blurted out that he must support any candidate, even the devil, of Eglinton's choice this time, but he would take care in the future not to commit himself. Bargany offered excellent advice: insist to Eglinton that whatever Administration he supported—at this point Eglinton was still watching developments—should give Boswell some legal office. Was Boswell interested in becoming Sheriff-Depute of Ayrshire? This could be a crucial question if Boswell meant to advance his career in Scotland since, as mentioned earlier, this county office was a well-recognized training ground for the Court of Session. Boswell was lukewarm: he didn't much want the job, but he wouldn't refuse it. He was then left to consult his conscience. Did not the interests of the State override private considerations? Yet if he had made Eglinton a positive promise it must be kept: otherwise "any scoundrel might plead *principle* for breaking his word." "It is exceedingly difficult," he told himself, "to have it believed that a man is honest in altering a political opinion."

But, in any case, the situation seemed to have possibilities. The faint indication of a split between Eglinton and Montgomerie over the Ayrshire Address, which Eglinton opposed, led Boswell to announce in a newspaper letter "To the Real Freeholders of the County of Ayr" (19 March 1784) that he intended to stand if Montgomerie did not. And somehow he had acquired the idea that Montgomerie, if elected, would pass the seat along to him in case he obtained an office incompatible with it. When Montgomerie did announce his candidacy, Boswell threw himself into the campaign, recruiting votes and holding busy conferences with Dundas. He also did his part in Edinburgh by singing his *Midlothian Address* in praise of Dundas and the local candidate, James Hunter Blair, at an election dinner, the first of many such compositions and performances. (Singing at public or private dinners was a widespread entertainment; Boswell had a fine voice, and composed lively doggerel.)

But Dundas found the situation unnecessarily complicated. Why should Fergusson and Montgomerie contest the seat, when either would back Pitt? He would fight on the "common public bottom" if he must, but he preferred a comfortable give-and-take among gentlemen. Besides, Craufurd was threatening to support Montgomerie, which would ensure his victory.   So Dundas reached an agreement with Eglinton: Montgomerie would come in this time, and Fergusson at the next election.   (Nor would Fergusson be forced to sit out this session of Parliament.   Edinburgh, now in Dundas's pocket, had been allowed to re-elect Hunter Blair.   After a discreet interval of a few months, he retired on some pretext in Fergusson's favour, became Lord Provost of Edinburgh, and was rewarded with a baronetcy two years later.)   Neither side in Ayrshire, naturally enough, was anxious to publicize their arrangement, since Fergusson had originally campaigned under the standard of independence, and Eglinton—or so Boswell later claimed— degraded himself by this compromise.

Like the fruit of many illicit conjunctions, however, the agreement could not be concealed for long and the news of it burst, according to Boswell's later report, like a bomb.   No public announcement was needed: when Montgomerie was returned on 20 April 1784, everyone could see that Fergusson was supporting him, and it was unlikely that he had experienced a sudden conviction of unworthiness.   Boswell comforted himself with the reflection that to have promoted the Ayrshire Address was enough for one laird to have done.   But he had done more; in the fluster of the campaign he had written a complacently unpleasant letter to Fergusson (5 April), saying that he intended to stand at the next election on the interest of the real freeholders:

> If I am honoured with your support in that character, I presume you will throw into the same scale your share of those unconstitutional votes which, until we obtain relief from the present miserable election law, must it seems be employed by the real interest in self-defence.

Since Fergusson hardly wished to admit to the arrangement he had entered into, his reply was noncommittal.

The day of the Ayrshire Address had been the high point of the campaign for Boswell.   It united his ideas about the importance of county meetings, the status of the Family of Auchinleck, and the monarchical principles he had acquired from Johnson.   "I felt myself just what I could wish to be, except that I had not actual employment from the King."

Another reassuring development had been a meeting with Burke. Boswell had sent him a copy of his East India *Letter* and receiving no acknowledgement feared that Burke, deeply involved with Fox's East India Bill, was seriously offended.   Now hearing that Burke was to be installed as Lord Rector of the University of Glasgow, Boswell hurried to meet him— and narrowly escaped death on the way when his horse threw him and a

cart-wheel passed within an inch of his head.   When he arrived at the
Saracen's Head Inn where Burke was staying, Boswell sent in a careful
letter (the much corrected draft survives) to test the temperature, but Burke
came out to meet him right away, as friendly as ever.   Boswell admired
him in his Lord Rector's gown: "So great a literary honour sat very becomingly on one who had no solemn appearance, but a pleasant air of genius."

The election had delayed Boswell's migration south long past his usual
time, and he was anxious to get to London.   Johnson's health was clearly
breaking up.   He was suffering from asthma, dropsy, and chest constric-
tion; he slept a great deal.   And he was gripped by fear.   "O! my friend,"
he wrote to Taylor, "the approach of death is very dreadful."   Catching
at every possibility, Johnson asked Boswell to present his case to the medical
eminences of Edinburgh, and they were prompt to say what they could.
Dr. Gillespie offered solid advice, and Sir Alexander Dick, who had long
since given up practice, sent gentle, garrulous letters, extolling the virtues
of currants, mushrooms, rhubarb, and especially garlic.   Dr. Hope corresponded with Brocklesby, one of the doctors attending Johnson; and
Boswell carried with him what was encouraging in the opinions of Drs.
Cullen and Monro.   Naturally, he did not pass on their diagnosis of what
today is called congestive heart failure, for which they could suggest little
but laudanum to keep the patient comfortable.

Boswell set off for London at the end of April, but in spite of his hurry
he dallied two or three days *en route* to kindle a new romance.   His object
was the poet Anna Seward, remembered faintly by posterity as "The Swan
of Lichfield."   She was in her early forties, earnest, strong-minded, and
fluent in the stilted conventional verse of the period.   Also, she was definitely attractive.   Continuing his pursuit after arrival in London,
Boswell wrote to ask for a lock of "that charming auburn hair I admired
so much that delicious morning I was last with you.   It will be a *talisman*
against all temptation till I return to you."   She replied quickly and warmly,
but she had spotted the cloven hoof in the "voluptuous inclination" Boswell
had displayed at their last meeting; after he left, she had wept from vexation.   Theirs could only be a mingling of true souls.

Like Congreve's Mirabell, Boswell then "proceeded to the very last act
of flattery," and wrote an extravagant review of her throbbing verse-epistle
novel, *Louisa*.   Crowning her with Johnson and Garrick among the geniuses of Lichfield, he asserted that

> every part of this story is exquisitely told, with the genuine sen-
> timents of a tender and generous heart, and the elegant language
> of a rich imagination.

Having picked up a reference to Pope's Eloisa in the prefatory remarks to *Louisa*, he wrote to her again with a line from *Eloisa to Abelard*:

Give all thou canst—and let me dream the rest!

His strategy appears in a note on the draft of the letter: "I studied to restrain myself from exuberant rhapsody, and not dress too rich a fly.   We shall wait as 'the patient angler.' "   Miss Seward (even today it seems presumptuous to call her Anna) was touched, especially since she attributed the call for a second edition of *Louisa* to Boswell's review, and the lock was forthcoming.   (It survives, auburn still.)   All gratitude, Boswell promised another call on his return journey.

London was irresistible to the point that even journalizing was forgotten; much of the surviving record dwindles into a list of engagements. After having been confined to his house for four months, Johnson was wonderfully recovered, "copious and animated in conversation, and appearing to relish society as much as the youngest man."   He recounted a curious story about himself and Langton, to whom he was deeply attached and whose piety he found exemplary.   During his illness Johnson had asked Langton to tell him in what ways his life had been faulty.   In response, Langton had given him a list with several Scriptural texts recommending charity.   As Johnson told it,

> "When I questioned him what occasion I had given for such an animadversion, all that he could say amounted to this—that I sometimes contradicted people in conversation.   Now what harm does it do to any man to be contradicted?"   BOSWELL.   "I suppose he meant the *manner* of doing it: roughly—and harshly."   JOHNSON.   "And who is the worse for that?"   BOSWELL.   "It hurts people of weak nerves."   JOHNSON.   "I know no such weak-nerved people."

Boswell adds:

> Johnson, at the time when the paper was presented to him, though at first pleased with the attention of his friend, whom he thanked in an earnest manner, soon exclaimed, in a loud and angry tone, "What is your drift, Sir?"   Sir Joshua Reynolds pleasantly observed that it was a scene for a comedy, to see a penitent get into a violent passion and belabour his confessor.

The last comment on the incident belongs to Burke:

> It is well if, when a man comes to die, he has nothing heavier upon his conscience than having been a little rough in conversation.

At the beginning of June, Boswell escorted Johnson to Oxford on his first jaunt since his illness, and then hurried back for a gala performance of the *Messiah* in Westminster Abbey.   Mary Hamilton, who moved among the bluestockings, describes him at this occasion:

> At a quarter before nine Dr. Burney and Miss Palmer[1] came for me in Dr. Burney's coach.   Sir Joshua Reynolds and Mr. Boswell followed in Sir Joshua's chariot. . . .   We got in without any difficulty.   The lower part was already filled with people, but Dr. Burney got us the proper seats for hearing the music.   Sir Joshua introduced me to Mr. Boswell (the Mr. Boswell who wrote the history of Corsica).   From nine to twelve passed away very agreeably in conversation with Miss Palmer and these three sensible men and in remarking the countenances of the company. . . .   Mr. Boswell is one of those people with whom one instantly feels acquainted.   We conversed together with as much ease and pleasantry as if we had been intimate a long time. . . .   I was so delighted that I thought myself in the heavenly regions, 513 performers, the harmony so unbroken that it was like the fall of waters from one source, imperceptibly blended.   The spectacle too was sublime.   So universal a silence.   So great a number of people. . . . It was over at four o'clock.

Boswell returned to a hearty welcome in Oxford, where he and Johnson stayed with Johnson's old friend, William Adams, Master of Pembroke. There is a glow over their last excursion together.   Johnson mellowed in the relaxed atmosphere.   They spent a happy day with the well-known Tory, Dr. Thomas Nowell, at his beautiful villa outside Oxford on the Isis; Boswell says, when "I thought of Dr. Nowell, Dr. Johnson, and myself sitting together, it seemed the very perfection of Toryism.   I relished the old port and hugged myself."   Another little tour took them to Wheatley, "a very pretty country place," for a pleasant dinner with Boswell's sometime protégé, the touchy poet William Julius Mickle.

But Johnson's deep conviction of human suffering seldom left him; he argued vigorously that life offered more misery than happiness, agreeing with Boswell that "no man would choose to lead over again the life which he had experienced."   Death seemed very near.   When urged by a group at Adams's to compose some family prayers, Johnson in great agitation called out,

> "Do not talk thus of what is so aweful.   I know not what time GOD will allow me in this world.   There are many things which I wish

[1]Reynolds's niece, who lived with him.

to do." Some of us persisted, and Dr. Adams said, "I never was more serious about anything in my life." JOHNSON. "Let me alone, let me alone; I am overpowered." And then he put his hands before his face, and reclined for some time upon the table.

But there was a terror beyond death. When Adams "suggested that GOD was infinitely good," Johnson refused to take comfort:

> "I am afraid I may be one of those who shall be damned" (looking dismally). DR. ADAMS. "What do you mean by damned?" JOHNSON. (passionately and loudly) "Sent to hell, Sir, and punished everlastingly."

He did not despair, but could face the future no longer: "I'll have no more on't."

Still, the expedition was a success. Years earlier on Johnson's going to the Hebrides, Mrs. Thrale had encouraged him: "Dissipation is to you a glorious medicine, and I believe Mr. Boswell will be at last your best physician." Now Johnson remarked to Taylor that he loved to travel with Boswell, and to Mrs. Thrale that Adams had treated him

> as well as I could expect or wish; and he that contents a sick man, a man whom it is impossible to please, has surely done his part well.

The great question of Boswell's removal to the English bar was still very much in agitation, but now he was telling others what he intended to do rather than asking their opinions. He informed Bishop Barnard, "I have reasonable hopes to distinguish myself in Westminster Hall, and I have not a faint prospect of getting into Parliament." Neither hopes nor prospect are specified nor could have been. The real reason for his move, as he admitted in the same letter, was that after years of suspense he *must* make it. Dundas said the experiment would not prevent him from retreating to a judge's place in Scotland. And he extracted Johnson's approval, conditioned by several warnings:

> You must take care to attend constantly in Westminster Hall. . . . You must not be too often seen at public places, that competitors may not have it to say, "He is always at the playhouse or at Ranelagh, and never to be found at his chambers." And, Sir, there must be a kind of solemnity in the manner of a professional man.

Boswell must never let his annual expenses exceed his income. Yet Johnson thought that he could hardly lose by the move, and friends would do all they could for him:

If after a few years you should return to Scotland, you will return with a mind supplied by various conversation, and many opportunities of inquiry, with much knowledge, and materials for reflection and instruction.

Paoli also contributed his usual clear-sighted advice:

Mankind as individuals are cunning; as a multitude they are drunkards. Take care of them. If you are a pleasant bottle companion, they will not employ you as a lawyer; they will not trust you with their property. But they will give their voice to make you a Minister of State.

As we have often seen, Boswell wrote down much good advice, both his own and that of others. But he so seldom acted on it that, evidently, the recording of advice was enough in itself to ease his conscience. He could never be wise or prudent for long, because the urge to be himself, whatever that was at the moment, was far too strong for him to resist. He had learned early that following inclination was the main road to happiness, and recognized at least from time to time that "immediate enjoyment," whether of sensation or reflection or hope, was the great object for him to pursue. With more self-control he might have prospered and been forgotten, for his gift depended on his carrying out inner promptings.

Margaret acquiesced in his decision after first expressing her disgust with an immediate problem at Auchinleck. Lieutenant John, now on a visit, was the most disagreeable companion she had ever lived with. He refused to come to meals at the appointed times, and then

his sullen pride is shocked that he is not waited for as if he was something above the common. . . . I trust in God you will give him no encouragement to pitch his tent here; otherwise adieu to every comfort. . . . Your brother rides your horse, I may say, all day, and mounts or dismounts perhaps ten times in a mile. I see him now moving in a slow, solemn manner up the avenue. . . .

In your letter on a certain subject you desire me not to oppose you. I never had any desire to do it. I only wish you to be perfectly settled in your own mind and convinced of the propriety of quitting your country and profession, for in that case England or anywhere is equally the same to me, so put me quite out of the question; and if *you* resolve, I am already prepared in my heart to follow you or accompany you, where I have not to sail. But my weak lungs and seasickness forbid that method of transporting myself.

The pathetic saving clause testifies to the inroads of age and illness, but Margaret's heart was still as staunch as when she had accepted Boswell's proposal fifteen years earlier, promising to live with him if necessary in retirement on £100 a year.   Besides, she hadn't promised not to encourage others to offer objections to Boswell's plans, and she asked both Robert Boswell, Boswell's man of business in Edinburgh during his absences, and Mrs. Stuart, her old intimate, to try to persuade him to change his mind.

But why had Johnson given his approval?   Though admitting he had never known anyone like Boswell with such a *gust* for London, Johnson had never thought much of his ambitious schemes.   When the previous March Boswell announced that he had hopes of standing for Parliament, Johnson wrote to Langton, "Whether to wish him success, his best friends hesitate."   Now Johnson wrote to Mrs. Thrale at Bath (31 May 1784): "Bozzy . . . is for his part resolved to remove his family to London, and try his fortune at the English bar.   Let us all wish him success."

Johnson's change of mind remained mysterious until 1974, when a letter from him to Sir William Forbes (7 August 1784) was first printed:

> When Mr. Boswell first communicated to me his design of re-moving his family to London, I thought of it like all the rest of his friends; for a while it seemed possible that his desire might evaporate in talk, or that the trouble and difficulty of such a migration might overpower his inclination.   I was therefore con-tent to say little, but what I said, he will tell you, was all discour-agement.   By degrees, however, I found his ardour for English honour and English pleasure so strong that he would have con-sidered all open and declared opposition as envy, or malignity, or distrust of his abilities.

So Johnson withdrew his prohibition on the following terms: (1) that Bos-well not make the move until he had saved enough money to bring his family; (2) that while he resided in London, he should live on his income without incurring debt.

Johnson continued:

> To these conditions he will own that he has agreed. . . .   The danger is, and that danger is very great, lest he should be driven by his passions beyond the bounds which he has consented to fix.   The mischief then may be such as both you and I sincerely wish him to escape.   I have told him with as much energy as I could call to my assistance that he is too rich for an adventurer, and by a game so hazardous and daring he stakes more than he can win.
>
> Since I began this letter I have received from him a gloomy account of his perplexity and irresolution; and his present intention is to delay his removal.   To gain time is a great

advantage.   Reason and the advice of his friends will probably prevail.   Every reason against his removal will be stronger another year.

Despite the temporary improvement in Johnson's health, he remained a very sick man.   He ate so much at Paoli's one day that Boswell whispered to their host not to press further food on him.   "Alas!" said the General, "See how very ill he looks; he can live but a very short time.   Would you refuse any slight gratifications to a man under sentence of death?"   On 22 June Johnson dined at The Club for the last time, where his appearance, Boswell says, evoked

> evident marks of kind concern about him with which he was much pleased, and he exerted himself to be as entertaining as his indisposition allowed him breath to be.

To prolong life, Johnson spoke of wintering in the milder climate of Italy, and several of his friends, with Boswell and Reynolds taking the lead, started to make arrangements.   Francesco Sastres, an Italian teacher and translator, agreed to accompany him, but Johnson would need more money, so Boswell approached Thurlow, the Lord Chancellor, to ask the King to augment Johnson's pension.   This "pious negotiation" (Boswell's term) was kept from Johnson, until a sympathetic letter from Thurlow encouraged Boswell to break the news.   Johnson was very moved:

> He listened with much attention; then warmly said, "This is taking prodigious pains about a man."—"Oh, Sir" (said I, with most sincere affection), "your friends would do everything for you."   He paused—grew more and more agitated—till tears started into his eyes, and he exclaimed with fervent emotion, "GOD bless you all." I was so affected that I also shed tears.—After a short silence, he renewed and extended his grateful benediction, "GOD bless you all, for JESUS CHRIST's sake."   We both remained for some time unable to speak. He rose suddenly and quitted the room, quite melted with tenderness.

Boswell stayed an extra day in London for a "choice dinner" with Reynolds and Johnson, just the three of them, to speculate about the increased pension, Johnson hoping that it would be doubled rather than take the form of a grant of a thousand pounds; £600 a year would give him the prospect of passing "the remainder of his life in splendour, how long soever it might be."   Then it came time to part.   Boswell says,

> I accompanied him in Sir Joshua Reynolds's coach to the entry of Bolt Court.   He asked me whether I would not go with him to

his house; I declined it from an apprehension that my spirits would sink. We bade adieu to each other affectionately in the carriage. When he had got down upon the foot-pavement, he called out, "Fare you well"; and, without looking back, sprung away with a kind of pathetic briskness, if I may use that expression, which seemed to indicate a struggle to conceal uneasiness, and impressed me with a foreboding of our long, long separation.

Boswell left London on 1 July, and on the same day Johnson received word that Mrs. Thrale had married, or was going to marry, Piozzi. For several years Johnson had perceived that her affection for him was waning, but this was a mortal wound. Their exchange of letters is famous: Johnson's violent recrimination, her spirited defence, and his last letter to her:

> I therefore breathe out one sigh more of tenderness, perhaps useless but at least sincere. . . . Whatever I can contribute to your happiness I am very ready to repay, for that kindness which soothed twenty years of a life radically wretched. . . . The tears stand in my eyes. . . .

Mrs. Thrale wrote to him only once more, arranging though she was in London that her letter should be sent from Bath, in order to avoid an interview that could only be agonizing and futile.

Mrs. Thrale had the tenacity of her feelings. She had made a *mésalliance* both in rank and religion. Her three eldest daughters, who disliked her anyway, refused to have anything to do with Piozzi, whose connection to the family blemished their marital prospects. The equally repellent pity or scorn of her friends—though Mrs. Montagu and Mrs. Chapone were charitably inclined to think her mad—and the newspaper jokes about the wealthy widow who had sacrificed all for lust, left her unshaken. But to let the storm blow over, she and Piozzi departed for the Continent in September.

Johnson now had nothing to keep him alive except an indomitable will and a horror of death. It was hardly surprising that he should wish Boswell near: "They that have your kindness may want your ardour," he wrote. That summer, he wandered out of habit to Lichfield and Ashbourne and then back to Lichfield. After all their expectations, Thurlow was embarrassed to report that no increase would be made in Johnson's pension, offering at the same time to provide £500 or £600 out of his own pocket as a "mortgage" on Johnson's pension, a gift disguised as a loan. Johnson declined with gratitude and dignity. It was "a gloomy, frigid, ungenial summer"; hope dimmed, but he struggled on. "I will be conquered," he said; "I will not capitulate."   He got back to London on 16 November.

<h1 style="text-align:center">I I</h1>

TO RETURN TO Boswell.   At Doncaster *en route* to Edinburgh, he wrote a remarkable letter to Temple, recapitulating experiences, thoughts, and hopes.   First, Anna Seward in Lichfield:

> Though not now a *girl*, she is still beautiful.   Her eyes are ex-quisite—her *embonpoint* delightful, her sensibility melting.   Think of your friend—you know him well—reclined upon a sofa with her, while she read to him some of the finest passages of her *Louisa*.   How enchanting!   Many moments of felicity have I en-joyed.   Let me be thankful.

This, however, was the only kind of felicity Boswell was to enjoy with Miss Seward.   Whatever her feelings towards Boswell, she had given her heart, and certainly nothing more, to John Saville, vicar choral of Lichfield Ca-thedral, who was separated from his wife; and despite gossip they remained the closest of friends until he died in 1803.

Boswell then turns to spiritual considerations:

> Were there not hope of a more perfect world, would it not be an advantage to be less feeling in every respect than either you or I am in this?   But there *is* hope of a world where we shall be happy in proportion to our refined faculties.   My dear friend! from the first dawn of our intimacy, from our worshipping in Porter's Chapel on Christmas day, all through life, religion has been our chief object, however smaller objects coming close to us may have at times obscured our view of it.
>
> Allow me to say that I think both you and myself exceedingly selfish.   We are perpetually thinking of our own enjoyments, our own cares; and perpetually writing to one another of them.   Nor can either of us allow that the other has much reason to complain.   Yet I am conscious at present that my uneasiness at not being able to get your son out to India is truly sincere. . . .

Then came talk of the law:

> I breakfasted and dined with Jack Lee[1] the day but one before I set out.   Found him hearty and friendly in advising me as to what

[1]In spite of Boswell's joke about dangling his carcass at the end of a rope, the former Attorney-General had become a good friend.

I am to read to have as much English law as will be necessary for
me to begin with.   I am not to go to a special pleader.[1]   It would
cost me a considerable sum of money and be a servitude ill-suited
to my time of life.   I am to acquire *elements* and *forms* by private
study.   It is amazing with what avidity I read to fit me for trying
what I wish for so much.   But when a man acts from himself he
proceeds with all his might.   Let us see if my *resolution* (which
after years of wavering came at once upon me with wonderful
power) will make me an eminent barrister.   I am *sure* with what
I have already done upon many public occasions that in all jury
trials where popular declamation is of consequence I shall be distinguished.   General Paoli, who is truly a wise as well as a good
man, counsels me to depend upon myself and not to court others.
"Be always armed," said he.   "Show that you have abilities.   They
will apply to you." . . .   When you have read Lord Melcombe's
Diary you will see that I do right to make him a beacon, for he
was continually courting statesmen.   In a life of him in the *European Magazine* it is justly remarked that his great fault was not
having a proper respect for himself, which made his talents and
fortune and rank in life of less consequence than they might have
been.   "*Memento,*" said I to myself.

Boswell resumed his letter two days later in Carlisle.   It had been a
hard journey: the coach was full, and he had had to travel as an outside
passenger for more than a hundred miles.   But delay would have alarmed
Margaret painfully.

And certainly I should be most unwilling that she should suffer
any uneasiness, for her constant and generous affection is highly
to be valued.   I have found at the post-office here a charming
letter from her. . . .   Now that I am *resolved* to try my fortune at
the English bar, you and all my friends must encourage me, as
Dr. Johnson, *mirabile dictu,* does in his powerful manner. . . .   You
cannot imagine with what firmness I am prepared to live in London upon a small scale for some time, and after having entertained
(I may splendidly) the first company at my table to entertain none
at all.   Burke says this is very manly.

There would be difficulties: to maintain Auchinleck in repair, to pay
travel expenses, to keep his debts quiet and gradually clear them off.

To restrain my eagerness for variety of scenes—to conduct myself
with prudence.   But strict economy will, I trust, do a great deal—
and a determined attendance on Westminster Hall, and a course
of study and practice of the English law will give me a desirable

---

[1] A specialist in the technicalities of pleading (see below, p. 320).

steadiness.   Your visits to *town* will be cordials to me.   But remember you must make full allowance for the difference between
your feeble and my robust constitution.   I must, however, have
a philosophical resolution not to be cast down though I should
have no practice.   Of this I am aware as a thing possible.   My
retreat to the Bench in Scotland will, I trust, be secured.   Did I
mention to you that I talked over my scheme fairly to the King,
and that His Majesty was graciously pleased to listen to me, and
talked of it afterwards to the Lord-in-Waiting?   I think my pretensions to employment as a lawyer of fifteen years' good practice
in Scotland in all questions of the law of that country should be
strong.

(It must be recalled that transferring from the Scots to the English bar
was not like moving from practice in one county or state in the United
States to another.   Scots law was completely different from English law
not merely in its forms but in its foundation since it was based on civil, and
so ultimately on Roman, law, while English law was based on common law.
Boswell, for example, would have had no occasion in Scotland to consult
Blackstone's *Commentaries*, now coming to be regarded as a fundamental
legal text.)

Boswell continued:

Would you were here with me today.   I could talk to you and
listen to you alternately from morning to night.   It is unpleasant
for me to go to Edinburgh for the remainder of the summer
session, and to be stared at and talked to with Scottish familiarity
concerning my change of situation.   *Nunc animis opus Aenea, nunc
pectore firmo*.[1]   I shall say little.   The great consolation is my permanent consequence as Baron of Auchinleck, which is believed to
be of much more value than I know it to be.   What pleasure shall
I feel when I am free from debt!   May I not indulge the ambitious
hope of being a *baron* indeed—of being created by my Sovereign
Baron Boswell of Auchinleck in the County of Ayr.[2]   I *have* indulged
that hope ever since I saw Sir James Lowther introduced into the
House of Lords. . . .[3]

No one can summarize Boswell's recollections of happiness and visions
of glory better than he.   And they were visions he thought he could realize.
Boswell could be high-spirited about his fantasies: regretting once that the
King had not yet given him office, he said to an acquaintance, "Monsieur,

[1]"Now, Aeneas, thou needest thy courage, now thy stout heart!" (Virgil, *Aeneid*, vi. 261,
trans. H. R. Fairclough, Loeb ed.).
[2]The style of the Lord Chancellor.
[3]As Earl of Lonsdale on 2 June.

il ne me manque que la base. Je suis déjà la statue." But at a deeper
level he continued to transform hope into belief.

Then, in only two weeks, the wind had shifted into the east, as he
reports in his next letter to Temple (20 July 1784):

> All is sadly changed. I was three nights completely well with my
> family at Auchinleck. Then my wife accompanied me to Edin-
> burgh, where I was no sooner arrived than at once, as if plunged
> into a dreary vapour, my fine spirits were extinguished, and I
> became as low and as miserable as ever. There certainly never
> was a mind so *local* as mine. How strange, how weak, how un-
> fortunate is it that this my *native city* and my *countrymen* should
> affect me with such wretchedness. I have been harassed by the
> arguments of relations and friends against my animated scheme
> of going to the English bar. I have lost all heart for it. My
> happiness when last in London seems a delirium. I cannot ac-
> count for it. I have at that time thought of English law as of an
> *end* without perceiving the *means*; for, upon endeavouring to ac-
> quire it, I perceive myself incapable of the task; at least I imagine
> so. Then upon making out a "State of My Affairs" I find my
> debts amount to so large a sum that the interest of them and a
> moderate annual appropriation of rents for a sinking fund[1] will
> leave me no more than what will maintain my family in Scotland,
> but would by no means support it in London, unless I could submit
> to live in penurious privacy, which my wife with her admirable
> good sense observes would deprive me of all the felicity which
> London now yields me. That, when I go thither at present as a
> gentleman of fortune, I am on a footing with the first people,
> easy, independent, gay. But were I settled as a man of business,
> labouring uphill and anxious for practice, my situation would be
> quite different. Add to all this the weakness of her lungs renders
> her very unfit to live in the smoke of London. Last night she
> had a return of spitting of blood. In short, my friend, I tell you
> *in confidence* that I am *satisfied* that my airy scheme will not do;
> and, moreover, that if I cannot obtain an office from His Majesty,
> I must drag on a life of difficulties.
>
> I entreat of you to comfort me. Say nothing to any human
> being of my having altered my resolution. But let it remain as a
> matter in *agitation* against which they who wish me well in this
> country are endeavouring to persuade me.
>
> But alas! what is to become of my ambition? What of my
> love of England where I am *absolutely certain* that I *enjoy life*, whereas
> *here* it is *insipid*, nay *disgusting*. O could I but have the *perfugium*[2]
> in study which you have. The coarse vulgarity all around me is

[1]Money set aside to reduce the principal of a debt.
[2]Refuge.

as shocking to me as it used to be to Sir John Pringle.   Dr. Blair
accosted me with a vile tone, "Hoo did you leave Sawmuel?"   What
right have I to be so nicely delicate? . . .

May I not get into Parliament for a few sessions?   Colonel
Hugh Montgomerie would gladly give me his seat for Ayrshire
could he get a place. . . .

22 July.   I am rather better and my scheme revives.   O would
but *Rex meus* patronize me!

It is puzzling how Boswell could have got so much further into debt
in two years, but clearly he had.   He had bought a small farm, Foardmouth,
for under £100, and otherwise made no capital expenditures.   But he had
lived like the gentleman of fortune he was reputed to be.   And the poor
harvest of 1782 must have put the tenants behind in their rents.   At the
end of 1782, he had owed the Edinburgh banking-house of Forbes, Hunter,
and Co. about £275, and they were liberal in advancing money; by the end
of 1784, he owed them £1,375, which alarmed them into the unusual step
of securing their loan on Boswell's house in St. Andrew Square, occupied
for life by his stepmother.   As one of the guardians of his young nephew,
George Campbell of Treesbank, he borrowed £300 from Treesbank's estate
at the beginning of 1784, and at the end of the year would be forced to
borrow another £100 so that Sir Walter Montgomerie-Cuninghame and
his two brothers, David and Henry, could post bond for having deforced
the King's messenger.[1]   And Boswell had paid off virtually none of his
debts.

Boswell's misery in Edinburgh resulted from the incompatibility between environment and temperament.   Or temperaments.   Like most of
us he suffered from the discrepancy between what he was and what he
wanted to be.   More troublesome, he wanted intensely to be the two different people whose characters he had ingenuously presented to Johnson
as alternatives: the grave, retired Tory baron, and the gay, flashy blade.
The solid, consequential James Boswell, Esq., of Auchinleck was Boswell
the member of society, while the volatile, good-natured Boswell, the life of
every gathering, was Boswell the individual.   Naturally, he wanted it both
ways, wanted others to respect his dignity while they allowed him room to
play the fool or, in his language, give vent to his irrepressible fancy.

Edinburgh was provincial grey, the colour of its winter skies.   Its
worthy, respectable, hard-working citizens poked, Boswell thought, into
his affairs and jeered at his stateliness.   But they equally disapproved of

---

[1]Prevented a King's messenger from doing his duty, which may well have been to arrest
one of them for debt.

the whimsical, spontaneous Boswell, whose indiscreet openness was construed as malice.   The good people of Edinburgh wanted him to conform,
to exist at their level, to be like them.   When he didn't, their satire was
like grappling, he said:

> They tear your hair, scratch your face, get you down in the mire,
> and not only hurt but disfigure and debase you.

Boswell could have shielded his individuality by turning eccentric, like
Monboddo or Kames, but he was never self-sufficient enough to ignore
the sentiment of the community.   "Black, law black," was the dress of choice
in Edinburgh; he wore it, but it didn't suit him.

Above all, Boswell associated Edinburgh with his father, while even
his language showed how closely he identified himself with London.   "If
I am not so solid a man as my father," he wrote, "I am much livelier and
of more extensive and varied views."   London he praised similarly "as
comprehending the whole of human life in all its variety, the contemplation
of which is inexhaustible."   It offered a sophisticated, highly intelligent
society, a rapidly shifting scene, a mingling of wealth, elegance, memorable
conversation, and freedom.   It was at the centre of things, and Boswell
belonged to its most respected intellectual group.   His highly developed
social talents were in demand; his unusualness was appreciated.   Here a
man was free "from remark and petty censure"; here and here alone

> a man's own house is truly his *castle*, in which he can be in perfect
> safety from intrusion whenever he pleases.

Boswell then quotes an acquaintance:

> The chief advantage of London . . . is that a man is always *so near
> his burrow.*

Though his temperament was entirely different, Boswell belonged in London as much as Johnson did.

From July 1784 to the following November, Boswell's life was a depressive blank.   At some point he wrote to Johnson full of "dejection and
fretfulness," and Johnson, near despair himself, reproached him for "affecting discontent and indulging the vanity of complaint."   Johnson continued:

> Write to me often, and write like a man.   I consider your fidelity
> and tenderness as a great part of the comforts which are yet left
> me, and sincerely wish we could be nearer to each other. . . .   My
> dear friend, life is very short and very uncertain; let us spend it

as well as we can.—My worthy neighbour, Allen, is dead.   Love
me as well as you can.

Feeling that he might have been too harsh, Johnson wrote again a week
or so later, with an account of his own mortal sufferings and a bit of an
apology:

> Before this letter, you will have had one which I hope you will
> not take amiss; for it contains only truth, and that truth kindly
> intended. . . .   This may seem but an ill return for your tender-
> ness; but I mean it well, for I love you with great ardour and
> sincerity.   Pay my respects to dear Mrs. Boswell, and teach the
> young ones to love me.

Boswell, now at Auchinleck, preserved a hurt silence.   Johnson
wrote for the last time, mingling censure and affection; he also reported
that dropsy was gaining on him.   Boswell felt "callous by reiteration of
misery." Even years later he could not understand why Johnson, whose
life was permeated with melancholy, could think his depression affected.
Johnson indeed complained quite as much as Boswell, but he managed a
stoic tone while Boswell sounded like a child in pain.   Johnson fought his
melancholy, and Boswell's submission to it as an inexplicable infliction
must have seemed both contemptible and alarming: what happened to
Boswell could happen to him.   At the end of his life, the contrast between
his deadly illnesses and Boswell's never-ending complaints must have struck
Johnson as insulting.   Nor does it seem to have occurred to Boswell that
though Johnson had heard often enough of Boswell's hypochondria he
had never seen Boswell in a fit of depression.   His Boswell was always in
high spirits.

On his return to Edinburgh in November 1784, Boswell's dark mood
started to break up.   Still, feeling neglected by Dundas, he wrote in his
journal:

> I was discouraged to think that my merits were so coldly consid-
> ered; and I indulged a kind of satisfaction in discontent, and
> earnestly wished for an opportunity to treat the world with
> disdain.

When Margaret urged, as she had in the past, that they entertain more
for the sake of the children, and added if he mixed in company he would
find people were better than he now thought them, Boswell replied in his
journal:

> All this was very proper.   But my indolence, joined with the sad-
> ness of disappointed eagerness for distinction, made me live almost
> entirely without society at Edinburgh.

And then his father's death was still "a gloomy, dejecting thought. How vain is human life!"

But ambition was reviving, encouraged by the intervention of his friend Sandy Gordon (now elevated to the Bench as Lord Rockville) with Dundas. As Boswell summarizes Rockville's report:

> Mr. Dundas said my pamphlet on Fox's East India Bill was excellent, that the Ministry felt it. And that if anything of two or three hundred a year had fallen then, he believed I would have got it. Lord Rockville kindly said, "Has he not the same merit yet?" Lord Rockville told my wife privately that my jocularity was against me in my claim for a judge's place, as also my openly declaring my antipathies to many people. He was very desirous I should have a more sedate behaviour. This was very friendly.

Margaret had taken it upon herself to write to Dundas urging him to dissuade Boswell from settling in London, but Dundas had avoided a reply, according to Rockville, because the matter was so delicate.

Boswell himself, a few days later, went directly to Dundas for an hour-long confidential conversation. Dundas was cordial and talked of consulting Pitt or the Attorney-General (Richard Pepper Arden) or Thurlow about possibilities. But with no more than £500 a year to spend, Boswell should only think of settling in London if he was given an office of some hundreds a year or could be assured of immediate practice. To plead poverty never helped anyone to preferment. Nor should Boswell go to the Bench in Scotland without carrying something with him; once a judge, he could make no further claim. Dundas admitted that he himself wouldn't settle in Scotland if a place of £10,000 a year were created for him. He repeated his praise of Boswell's *Letter* and his comment that Boswell might have been given some office at the time if one had fallen vacant. He would help Grange to some little appointment if opportunity offered, and said he had already tried to place T.D.

This interview invigorated Boswell with prospects all the more exciting for their vagueness. Margaret remained somewhat sceptical: perhaps Dundas was artfully trying to eliminate Boswell from his long list of candidates for the Bench. In view of what was shortly to occur, it is natural to wonder which of them was right, and one answer is neither. Dundas was cheerful, sanguine, and a thorough politician. He would help Boswell if he could; why not? But there were many others closer to him or with better claims to office. And he had more significant and immediate concerns.

I I I

So, UNHAPPILY, did Boswell.   On 17 December 1784 came the news he most dreaded: Johnson had died four days earlier.   Boswell at least had the consolation that he had recently written him two kind letters, and that he had read one of them before his death.   "I was stunned and in a kind of amaze," Boswell wrote, his immediate feeling being "just one large expanse of stupor.   I knew that I should afterwards have sorer sensations." His mind's "great SUN," as he had once described Johnson, had set.   He made love to Margaret that night.   Reaction to Johnson's death took its first clear form in his journal for the next day:

> My resolution was to honour his memory by doing as much as I could to fulfil his noble precepts of religion and morality.   I prayed to GOD that now my much respected friend was gone, I might be a follower of him who I trusted was now by faith and patience inheriting the promises.

As numbness wore off, he wrote to Reynolds:

> How dismal a blank does his departure make!   I stretch after him with enthusiastic eagerness.   I cannot doubt he is exalted to immortal felicity.

Immediately following Johnson's death, Dilly had written to Boswell

> in the true spirit of *the trade* wanting to know if I could have an octavo volume of 400 pages of his conversations ready by February. . . .   I answered him that I had a large collection of materials for his life, but would write it deliberately.   I was now uneasy to think that there would be considerable expectations from me of memoirs of my illustrious friend, but that habits of indolence and dejection of spirit would probably hinder me from laudable exertion.   I wished I could write now as when I wrote my *Account of Corsica*.   But I hoped I should do better than I at first apprehended.

He was also uneasy that Johnson had not remembered him in his will with a book, as he had others—Johnson had made his will in a great flurry just before his death—but comforted himself with the tokens of affection Johnson had given him during his life, and resolved to make the most of their connection "in an honourable way."   And, as always when it came to writing, he was quick to decide how to proceed.   Less than a week after hearing from Dilly, he replied that in the spring he would publish the account of his tour to the Hebrides as a prelude to the larger work, the life of Johnson, and asked whether Dilly would go halves in an edition. Dilly answered that he could have all the profits from the *Hebrides*.

His father's death had not only made Boswell Laird of Auchinleck, it had given him the liberty to choose what future he could. Now Johnson's death freed him to produce the works that would give him lasting fame. As in the earlier situation, Boswell had to reconcile the claims of mourning and release. He justified his great opportunity as a writer quite sincerely by construing his Johnsonian narratives as monuments of piety, as well as works composed for reputation and profit. But a dream on the night of 5 February 1785 gives some clues to his mind's attempt to resolve the background turmoil:

> I was with my much respected friend, Dr. Johnson. I saw him distinctly, sitting in a chair opposite to me in his usual dress. He talked something which I do not perfectly recollect about his library not being in such order as he could have wished, and gave as a reason his being hurried as death approached. He then said in a solemn tone, "It is an aweful thing to die." I was fully sensible that he had died some time before, yet had not the sensation of horror as if in the presence of a ghost. I said to him, "There, Sir, is the difference between us. You have got that happily over." I then felt myself tenderly affected and tears came into my eyes, and clasping my hands together I addressed him earnestly: "My dear Sir! pray for me." This dream made a deep and pleasing impression on my mind. I this morning invoked him to pray for me if he heard me and could be of influence. He did not absolutely disapprove of invoking departed spirits. GOD grant us a happy meeting!

Six weeks later, at Carlisle, Boswell dreamt again about Johnson:

> Did not recollect he was dead but thought he had been very ill, and wondered to see him looking very well. I said to him, "You are very well, Sir." He called out in a forcible, pathetic tone, "O no!" He said, "I have written the letter to Paoli which you desired." He then expressed himself towards me in the most obliging manner, saying he would do all in his power (or words to that purpose) to show his affection and respect, and seemed to search his mind for variety of good words.   ——

These reassurances from the beyond and from within were complemented by good packets of Johnsonian recollections for the projected *Life of Johnson* from Adams, Miss Seward, and Johnson's old school-friend, Edmund Hector. The process of compilation was under way.

Boswell passed the winter in surprisingly good spirits. As a stout Ayrshire laird, he admitted to "a rage for buying land," and in spite of his debts he borrowed £470 to buy a farm called Willockshill that protruded uncomfortably into his estate. Also he tidied up his affairs by making a settlement on Margaret and the children in case of his death, Margaret to receive a quarter of the Auchinleck rents, just as his stepmother had. He read part of the manuscript of his Hebridean journal to Cosmo Gordon and Hugh Blair, and was pleased to find they agreed with him that it might be published much as written. He would sit down quietly in the retirement of London and execute it easily, he promised Dilly and himself.

The political front, however, was discouraging. When Boswell began to press Montgomerie on his assumption that he was the heir apparent to Montgomerie's seat in Parliament, Montgomerie proved regrettably evasive. "I perceived," said Boswell,

> that I had indulged a fallacious notion of his having a reciprocal wish for my obtaining what I was so happy he had at last obtained. It hurt me a good deal. I resolved to stand upon my own legs and exert myself to secure if possible a respectable share of the independent interest of the county, by which in the midst of contending parties I might perhaps be successful.

Further disappointment followed. James Erskine, Knight Marshal of Scotland, died on 27 February 1785. His sinecure, worth £400 a year, was very desirable, and Boswell wrote to Dundas immediately for it. Dundas replied that he and Pitt between them had received 37 applications for the post and, since it was compatible with a seat in Parliament, M.P.'s had first option. "You must be aware," Dundas wrote, "how impossible it is to resist the claims of persons so stated and brought forward in competition with others who, however respectable, have certainly not the same pretensions to bring forward." To him who hath shall be given in abundance. Dundas ended by saying that he had not forgotten his most recent conversation with Boswell but that it would be disingenuous to encourage him to settle in London. These remarks Boswell found honest and friendly, but in his reply he lamented his situation:

> As to fortune I have indeed a competency though not enough to purchase a ticket in the great lottery of Parliament. But I do believe the cravings of ambition are as painful as those of hunger. I will not despair. I may perhaps never be able to soar. But I shall have a good deal of flutter yet before I lay my head under my wing.

The cravings of ambition.   For almost twenty-five years Boswell had hoped—and what he hoped he assumed—that he would some day sit in the House of Commons or fill some lucrative office, in a favourite phrase, enjoying *otium cum dignitate*[1] and the pleasures of London; for the same amount of time he had been badgering his friends for help.   Now he was tired of courting the powerful, tired of working hard in elections and being ignored in the division of the spoils.   Now every prospect from that approach had vanished.   He was at a dead end.   As he had resolved that winter, he would have to help himself, stand on his own principles and his own legs.   If he could not advance by serving the Ministry, he might succeed by becoming such an annoyance that the Ministry would be forced to buy him off, or by putting himself in the forefront of independent opposition.

The honest pretext Boswell needed to channel his sense of grievance and to start him on the path of independence emerged on 27 April 1785, when the Lord Advocate, Ilay Campbell, introduced a bill in the Commons to reduce the number of Lords of Session from fifteen to ten in order to augment the salaries of the remainder.   Three days later Boswell, once more in London, noted in his journal: "Resolved now, pamphlet against diminishing Lords of Session."

Boswell had made his decision: he would stand as the guardian of Scotland's constitutional rights and political liberty against the encroachments of Parliament and the sovereignty of Dundas.   Sincere patriotism would launch a remarkable exercise in propaganda.   As a preliminary puff, Boswell gave warning in a letter in the *St. James's Chronicle* (12 May 1785):

> Having called to you with so much success last year to oppose Mr. Fox's East India Bill, I resolved to call to you again on this momentous occasion.   My friends and countrymen, be not afraid. I am *upon the spot*.   I am *upon the watch*.   The Bill *shall not pass* without a spirited appeal to the justice and honour of the Commons of Great Britain.   Collect your minds.   Be calm, but be firm.   You shall hear from me at large a few days hence.

This pamphlet too he called, *A Letter to the People of Scotland* (distinguished here from the East India *Letter* as the Diminishing Bill *Letter*).

Tactics were more perplexing than strategy.   Of course Boswell could, and did, advance the basic conservative objection to the "rage for *innovation*" (eighteenth-century language for total change amounting to revolution).

---

[1]"Dignified ease" (Cicero, *For Sestius*, xlv. 98).

Specifically, the Bill infringed on the Articles of Union between England and Scotland, always a sore point to the Scots.   Alter the Court of Session and all the Articles of Union are in danger: the land-tax might be increased and the Presbyterian Church of Scotland disestablished.   In a country lacking juries in civil trials, to lessen the number of judges narrows further the restricted appeal a Scot has to his fellow citizens.   Moreover the whole political interest of Scotland rests in the hands of these judges, who pass on nominal and fictitious votes; a decemvirate may emerge.   And half-seriously Boswell maintains that a reduction in the number of judges would be unfair to that deserving group, the Faculty of Advocates: "It is *unjust*," he argues, "to lessen the number of prizes after the lottery has begun drawing, after we, by an expensive education and much time and labour, have purchased our tickets."   He freely admits, however, that at this time the "serious and important office of a Lord of Session" was too confined to satisfy himself.

But the Bill merely serves as a starting point from which to survey the ignoble extent of Scottish politics:

> The Stuarts, the Hamiltons, the Erskines, the Craufurds, the Montgomeries, the Douglases, the Grahams, the Somervilles, the Cathcarts, the Kennedies, in short all the men of blood and of property, who ought to be men of consequence

have allowed the Ministry to appoint a *locum tenens*[1]—Dundas, "sometimes called *Harry the Ninth*"—to drive

> the people of Scotland to St. James's and the Treasury as a sales-man drives black cattle to Smithfield.

Dundas, Boswell concedes, has acted badly in only two specific instances: he attacked Sir Lawrence Dundas in his Orkney home base, and he persuaded Boswell's father to make votes, despite his horror of the nominal and fictitious.   If Scotland must have a Protector—the allusion is to Cromwell—then Boswell has no objection to Dundas.   On the contrary:

> I trust to the generosity of his feelings that, as he *knows* he once did me a severe injury which I have from my heart forgiven, he will be anxious to make me full amends if ever it shall be in his power.   The desire of elevation is as keen in me as in himself, though I am not so well fitted for party exploits.

("Party" was close to a dirty word to begin with, and Dundas had already acquired a reputation for shifting parties at convenience.)   As an example

[1]Deputy.

of shady happenings, Boswell goes into detail about the 1774 Ayrshire election and the recent rumoured bargain between Eglinton and Fergusson, a bargain, he says, that some of Eglinton's friends will repudiate as degrading to him and obnoxious to themselves.

The controlling factor in the Diminishing Bill *Letter* is Boswell's reversion to the role of the *naïf*: not here the simple admirer of the hero, as in *Corsica*, but the honest soul who blurts out what everyone else whispers, and in the process reveals himself completely.   Twice he alludes to a favourite couplet:

> I love to pour out all myself, as plain
> As downright Shippen or as old Montaigne.

(Shippen was a sturdy Jacobite of Pope's time, as noted for his integrity as Montaigne was for his open revelation of himself.)   And so Boswell presses on the public his love for Margaret and his relationships with many well-known figures: Dempster, Lord Ossory, Burke, Wilkes ("excuse my keeping company" with him), Thurlow, Mountstuart, Jack Lee among them.   The list leads up to the two major political rivals of the day, Fox and Pitt, and finally alludes to a conversation between a "Great Personage" and "one of the most zealous royalists of the age."   No contemporary needed a key to recognize these figures as George III and the author.   Despite this wealth of connections, Boswell testifies to his own independence, integrity, and sense of honour.

A summary suggests little of the rich flavour of this intensely personal and highly entertaining pamphlet, characterized by a modern commentator as "racy, full of good stories, and animated by zest, intelligence, and good humour."   We can afford a detached view and, in any case, eighteenth-century politics were more personal than they are today; pamphlets were speeches, and newspapers trafficked freely in innuendo and low abuse. Still, the Diminishing Bill *Letter* must have given a shock to some of Boswell's friends: Lord Rockville campaigned for a seat on the Bench unavailingly until a political wave threw him in; Maclaurin, Nairne, and Wallace are all eager for the same promotion.   Monboddo is gratuitously described as a "grotesque philosopher, whom ludicrous *fable* represents as going about avowing his hunger and wagging his tail, fain to become cannibal and eat his deceased brethren."   Boswell even makes one confession about himself that contained the potential for disaster:

> Though not blessed with high heroic blood, but rather, I think,
> troubled with a natural timidity of personal danger which it costs
> me some philosophy to overcome, I am persuaded I have so much

real patriotism in my breast that I should not hesitate to draw my
sword in your[1] defence.   It is the ROYAL CAUSE.

Surely Lord Macdonald recalled this intimation of cowardice six months
later.

Some time afterwards Boswell claimed that

the *mode* in which [the *Letter*] was written was intended with a full
consciousness of what the event justified, that a mixture of argument with a variety of topics would most effectively excite general attention to a subject not very promising.

It was another ticket in the lottery, a conscious gamble that this *Letter*,
"hastily written upon the spur of the occasion," would come across as the
spontaneous revelation of an odd but lovable and entirely trustworthy
character, motivated fundamentally by the public good.   Sincerity, self-
interest, and ostensible purpose all work together, just as ten years in the
future Burke would be able in his *Letter to a Noble Lord* to convert his deep
self-pity into the basis for a resonant attack on his political enemies in
Britain and the Revolutionists in France.   But Boswell had some idea of
how risky his approach was.   At one point during the month it took to
compose and print the *Letter*, which as Boswell pointed out was fed to the
press as he wrote it, he cancelled some comments in "unpleasing uncertainty" only to reinstate them in later pages.   And near the end of the
Letter he lost control.   In his last *Hypochondriack* essay and in the East India
Letter of 1783, Boswell had apologized for any egotistical intrusions.   Here
he took the opposite approach:

Allow me, my friends and countrymen, while I with honest zeal
maintain *your* cause—allow me to indulge a little more my *own*
egotism and *vanity*.   They are the indigenous plants of my mind:
they distinguish it.   I may prune their luxuriancy, but I must not
entirely clear it of them; for then I should be no longer "as I am"
and perhaps there might be something not so good.

With this prologue, he inflicts on the reader a long genealogical note and,
anticipating objection, responds, "I wish all this to be known; and you who
censure it have read it, and *must* therefore know it."   He was suffering
from a desperate case of exhibitionism.

The apologia is a hard literary form to carry off; even Swift's *Verses*
on the Death of Dr. Swift and Pope's *Epistle to Arbuthnot*, which also introduces
a long genealogical note near the end, puzzle and irritate some readers.

[1]Pitt's.

Boswell's rhetorical model in his *Letter* is not Cicero, whose vanity is of a more pompous sort, but Sterne.   Like *Tristram Shandy*, the Diminishing Bill *Letter* records the supposedly immediate reflections and concerns of the author rather than a carefully thought-through argument; it is what modern theorists call a work of process rather than product.   But where Sterne teases the reader, Boswell is all friendly openness.

To succeed, Boswell had to dare all, and one advertisement promised the following topics:

> The security of the Union destroyed; the Presbyterian Kirk in danger. . . .   Mr. Dundas's prodigious power. . . .   Sketches of the Lord High Chancellor Thurlow, Earl of Lonsdale, Earl of Upper Ossory, Lord Palmerston, Lord Advocate of Scotland, Hon. Col. James Stuart. . . .

All the way up to "a Great Personage."

This approach worked for the press.   According to the *Critical Review*, the Diminishing Bill *Letter*

> contains many sensible observations and, to use the author's own words, is richly sprinkled with "egotism and vanity"; but these qualities, from the lively and eccentric manner in which they operate, serve only to render it more entertaining.

The *English Review* was more reserved: though praising the work as Boswell's best performance, it concluded that

> if the abilities of the writer had been greater than they are, we should have excused more readily his eternal vanity and egotism.

The *Monthly Review*, kinder than it had been to the East India *Letter*, found that

> a peculiar vein of humour runs through the whole of this performance, which must please and cannot offend; and the *Letter* is such, that if it does not universally produce conviction, it will afford instruction and amusement.

Differences in opinion about the Diminishing Bill *Letter* depended precisely on those qualities that Boswell's advertisement for himself flaunted: some found them entertaining but others were repelled.   Finally, at home, the *Scots Magazine* took a determined stand:

> Mr. Boswell, with a patriotic zeal that claims applause, warns his countrymen of the dangerous innovation that is meditated in the Court of Session. . . .

The Diminishing Bill itself was tangled in a net of ironies. Dundas seems to have had the simplest of motives: higher pay and greater efficiency. Apparently he and Campbell believed that the Bill was too routine to bother the other Scottish Members about, and this was a bad miscalculation. No sooner had Campbell brought the Bill forward than Fergusson, of all people, pointed out that though he approved of it, by the Articles of Union the Bill needed the Royal Assent before it was introduced. When it reappeared in watered-down form on 3 June, it still met strong Scottish resistance and was postponed until the autumn session.

Boswell's pamphlet was by no means all sunny geniality, and its sting aroused "An Ayrshireman" to attack it in a long letter in the *Public Advertiser* (14 July 1785) as an incoherent rhapsody which calumniated Fergusson, who

> from his earliest days displayed uncommon talents, and has all his life been as remarkable for a steady, uniform discretion as you have been for a want of it, which is saying a great deal, James, and is perhaps one cause of your vexation.

(It is true that Sir Adam Fergusson—Burns's "aith-detestin,[1] chaste Kilkerran"—could not have been more respectable.) "An Ayrshireman" disputes Boswell's version of the 1774 election and brings up the quarrels over the entail. "From the regard I had for your worthy father," he remarks, "I wish that your petulant vanity and violent versatility did not mark you out so conspicuously an object of contempt and ridicule." Most tellingly, "An Ayrshireman" compares Boswell to Lord George Gordon, the half-mad leader of the anti-Catholic mob that had terrorized London in the Gordon Riots of 1780. Gordon was notorious for instigating Addresses, and Boswell had just presented an Address in protest against the Diminishing Bill from his tenants, "two-hundred and eighty-nine men all fit to bear arms in defence of their King and country," to the King on 24 June.

Boswell's answer (*Public Advertiser*, 27 July), was firm, manly, and effective. Ordinarily, he said, he disdained anonymous attacks and would have ignored "An Ayrshireman's" personal scurrility, but he was moved by the advice of an unnamed "honourable friend" (Colonel Stuart) "to descend from recording the wisdom and wit of DR. JOHNSON to a contest about *Sir Adam Fergusson*." "An Ayrshireman" had led with his chin when he gave Boswell the chance to rehearse the deadly particulars of the various Ayrshire election arrangements, which Fergusson undoubtedly would have

[1]Oath-detesting.

preferred to leave in decent obscurity.   As for Boswell's unhappy differences with his father they were none of "An Ayrshireman's" business; in any case, his father would never have tried to upset the entail, as "An Ayrshireman" had asserted he might.

The Diminishing Bill might have died anyway without Boswell's intervention, but he certainly catalysed the opposition to it.   Nine Scottish counties petitioned against it, with Boswell leading the successful fight at the October 1785 meeting of the Ayrshire freeholders to declare that the attempt to hurry the Bill through Parliament was "most improper and disrespectful."   Ilay Campbell's anonymous answer to Boswell's pamphlet, *An Explanation of the Bill Respecting the Judges in Scotland* aroused no attention at all, and in December Dundas was forced to drop the Bill.   Another restricted to increasing the judges' salaries, of which Boswell approved, was adopted in June 1786.   Dundas learned a lesson: under no circumstances in the future would he ever propose or support the reform of anything.

Boswell had achieved his stated purpose, and one Ayrshire enthusiast said if he could also bring about the introduction of juries in civil trials he would deserve a statue of gold.   And he was celebrated in an anonymous broadside, *Auld Reekie—1785: In Imitation of Fergusson*:

> But loes me o' you, JAMIE BOSWELL,   [But you please me]
> For you're a *cock*, I'm sure, that crows well,
> Our Scottish lairdies' spirit grows well
>   To like your logic;
> Had on, my lad! gif your bowl rows well   [Hold]
>   Ye'll crack their project.

The general reaction of his own class was quite different.   He had feared challenges, first from Dundas and then Fergusson, but the worst happened: they ostentatiously paid no attention to him at all.   Harry Erskine, no friend to Dundas, did remark that the Diminishing Bill *Letter* was properly priced at half a crown, since no one with a whole one would write or read it.   But Boswell was stubborn; when Colonel Stuart also compared him to Lord George Gordon for presenting his tenants' Address, Boswell wrote in his journal, "I, however, think well of it."   It took his new friend, Edmond Malone, whose opinion he trusted and valued, to shake his self-satisfaction.   Malone wrote bluntly in the autumn of 1785:

> You cannot imagine how much mischief your own pamphlet has done you and how slow people are to allow the praise of good thinking and good writing to one whom they think guilty of such indiscretion in that pamphlet as a man of sound sense (they allege) would not be guilty of.

Boswell replied quickly that he would "henceforth *to a certain degree* be more cautious," and he thought it expedient to insert a letter in the newspapers apologizing for any intemperate expressions he might have used. But to what extent could he muffle his vanity and egotism? They were, as he said, cherished integral parts of his character.

Boswell's presentation of himself might have won him a following among the voters of Westminster or Middlesex but, once the excitement waned, the respectable landed gentry of Ayrshire cast a cold eye. In winning his battle, Boswell had alienated every politician with whom he had dealings: Pitt, Dundas, Eglinton, Fergusson. Worse, he had established a reputation for foolishness that, highly exaggerated by Macaulay, lingers today.

CHAPTER

——————

12

I

ON 30 MARCH 1785 BOSWELL arrived in London to prepare his *Journal of a Tour to the Hebrides with Samuel Johnson, LL.D.* for the press. But he had never had a London spring without Johnson since his elopement from Glasgow in 1760, and conscience took a holiday. Settling at Paoli's, he was almost immediately swept round in a wild swirl of dinners, executions, and girls. One "great day" started with brandy, breakfast, more breakfast, "quite intoxicated," "Westminster double," more brandy, "wild glow," Burke, Wilkes, Mrs. Cosway,[1] supper at Eglinton's, two bottles of claret, and ended most unexpectedly "quite sober." The complete entry for the next day reads, "General [Paoli] ill from disturbance. Resolved no more. Lay all forenoon." On such occasions Boswell enjoyed sin and enjoyed repentance.

In the midst of life there was the reminder of death. On 28 April Boswell watched nineteen criminals—thieves, a forger, a stamp counterfeiter, three men who had returned from transportation before the expiration of their terms—depart from Newgate to the other world. Then there were the girls, who figure in his expense account as "sundries," usually ranging from one to three shillings and sixpence, with eightpence prudently laid out in "armour." It was London in all its giddy variety, with the customary excursions to the Stuarts at Richmond, and with Preston to Woodford—always a hearty occasion. There he acquired a long-promised Chinese gong with which he alarmed Dilly's street, the Poultry, on his

———

[1]The beautiful young painter of miniatures to whom Paoli was strongly attached. The next year in Paris Thomas Jefferson fell deeply in love with her.

return.   Later its "noble sound, louder than that of the great bell of St. Paul's but more melodious," rejoiced a musical gathering at the Lord Mayor's.   And he was in great social reputation.   Lady Ossory said her daughter had begged off dinner with her grandmother to have dinner with him, the grandmother returning word that if she had known Mr. Boswell was to be among the company she would never have issued the invitation. Boswell's comment on the occasion is succinct: "Was brilliant."

So passed Boswell's first month in London.   But at its very end came the most significant event of his later literary career: a "most agreeable day" with Edmond Malone, beginning with a company at dinner and ending with a tête-à-tête until 2 a.m.: "full of bar scheme and encouraged." Malone must also have encouraged him to embark on his appointed task, since Boswell mentions working on the *Hebrides* the next day for the first time since his arrival in London.   Dilly (publisher) and Henry Baldwin (printer) began to push him by setting up a printing schedule.   "You must *feed* the press," they told him, and he answered, "Alas, dinners, etc.   I *feed myself*."   (Because of the limited supply of type, the *Hebrides* was printed as Boswell furnished Baldwin with copy, the type being distributed as each sheet or so was run off.)   On 2 May Boswell did provide some copy, perhaps a specimen for Baldwin to work out the format with.   But he had already found another distraction in putting together his Diminishing Bill *Letter*. "Sundries" took on a name, Polly Wilson (perhaps the "Westminster double" mentioned earlier).   And then a location and a personality: wandering down Ludgate Hill past the Old Bailey near Dean's Court, Boswell encountered a "pleasing and honest" girl, who is cleverly concealed in the journal as "ysteB htimS" ("ys" for short).

The vigour and rapidity of Boswell's traversal through the wide range of London life is preserved in F. A. Pottle's summary:

> Those who relish Boswell in elliptical effervescence will treasure the record . . . of Friday 13 May 1785, where he begins his day with Betsy Smith ("twice"), breakfasts with Mrs. Mary Knowles, the Quakeress, attends a Quaker meeting, sees Lunardi ascend in a balloon, tours the wards of Bedlam, dines with Dr. Scott, the admiralty and ecclesiastical lawyer, and ends the day ("intoxicated much") in St. Paul's Churchyard, singing ballads with two women in red cloaks.

To add a few details from the journal which round off this admirable abridgement:

> Had pocket picked.   Fell in street.   Got home by help of two different worthy men, ——— and ———.

Memory could not retrieve their names.

Boswell had taken a liking to ys, and the inns being full the next night they walked briskly to her friend's place in Whitechapel: "*Three* then. Insisted she should repeat LORD's Prayer. Strange mixture. Wondrous fondness." Two days later, "something not right" appeared; a consequence of relations with ys or Polly or some other Miss Sundry, perhaps the first, since a couple of weeks later Boswell conveyed a very reluctant Betsy (the journal has thrown off disguise) to St. Thomas's Hospital, where he paid her half-guinea entrance fee. No matter; at Court on 20 May he had a refreshing conversation with his Sovereign about balloons (the leading topic of conversation that spring), the forthcoming *Hebrides*, and the eventual *Life of Johnson*. The King encouraged him: "There will be many foolish lives first. Do you make the best."

Long afterwards in his "Memoir" of Malone, James Boswell, Jr., recounted how Malone and his father met. At Baldwin's one day, Malone accidentally picked up the sheet at the beginning of the *Hebrides* which includes Boswell's character sketch of Johnson, and was so impressed by its spirit and fidelity to the original that he asked to be introduced to its author. The story is inaccurate in at least one respect: Boswell and Malone had met in 1781, and had been in company together several times since. But it is likely to be true in substance. After Boswell's death Malone virtually adopted young James, who must have cherished the story of Malone's association with his father. We can guess that Malone picked up the sheet at Baldwin's with considerable curiosity, told Boswell how striking he found the portrait of Johnson, and Boswell responded by indicating that he needed help.

At least Boswell took the initiative in establishing their collaboration. The Diminishing Bill *Letter* was published on 26 May 1785, clearing the decks. In a memorandum for Sunday 29 May Boswell told himself, ". . . Home and dress calm after seeing Malone, and have him to breakfast Monday. Go on strictly now with *Hebrides*." The next day he did breakfast with Malone: they discussed the challenge Boswell feared from Dundas as a result of the *Letter*; and Boswell lodged his will with him, which suggests how fast intimacy developed. On 3 June, Boswell spent "almost all the forenoon with Malone revising *Hebrides*." They had entered on a close friendship and one of the most productive collaborations in literary history.

Edmund Malone was forty-three years old. Member of a distinguished and prosperous Irish legal dynasty, he had practised dutifully at the Irish bar for ten years and stood without success for the Irish Parliament, but his father's death provided him with a competency of £800 a year, and in 1777 he escaped to London to take up a scholar's career. When he started to help Boswell with the *Hebrides*, Malone was in the middle of producing his monumental ten-volume edition of Shakespeare, published in 1790. He was slight, fastidious, reserved rather than shining in company, and rightfully confident of his literary judgement. He was also a loyal, warm, and most helpful friend. His abiding disappointment was his failure to find a wife. An early and enduring attachment to Susanna Spencer led to painful frustration when she went mad, and various later advances towards matrimony were also unsuccessful. According to Boswell (*crede experto*), Malone was "too soft in his manners" to please the ladies. The consolation, to call it such, of bachelorhood was that he could give himself to his literary interests with passionate perseverance. He became the greatest Shakespearian scholar of the century.

Malone's willingness to help with the *Hebrides* was characteristically generous—he was always giving literary friends a hand—but Boswell's reasons for seeking assistance seem more diffuse. The *Account of Corsica* had established his reputation as an author, but he had written nothing of any length since. Pamphlets he knew he could manage. But his reluctance to begin preparation of the *Hebrides* for the press suggests that he was uneasy about undertaking a sustained piece of work. Did he dread solitude, those long hours of working alone? Could he keep himself at it? In the event, Malone became far more than a taskmaster and companion; he provided a stylistic standard and a model audience.

Like most great writers, Boswell had a good deal of confidence in his talent, but his Hebridean journal was an impromptu private performance that would need extensive revision before it was turned outwards to appear as a public memoir of Johnson. In particular, he worried about his phrasing: was it slovenly? did he use Scotticisms? On their tour, Boswell had said he wished Johnson would turn the journal into good English, and Johnson told him, "Sir, it is very good English." But Malone was confident he could improve it. If he knew anything, he knew how to put together a literary work, in English acceptable to a cultivated audience.

Their first decision concerned linked questions of format and copy. Boswell had started to sink his material under topographical heads (St. Andrews, Laurencekirk) as Johnson had done in the *Journey to the Western Islands*, but after preparing a specimen along these lines, Reynolds, Sir Joseph Banks, and others unnamed (certainly including Malone), persuaded him to revert to his original day-by-day notation. This was a vital decision for it committed Boswell to the immediacy of journal presentation. And Malone must have initiated him into the labyrinthine method of preparing copy which Boswell used here and in the *Life of Johnson*. The prime rule was never to transcribe one word more than was necessary. When revisions, additions, deletions, and transpositions made the original journal pages impossible to follow, they were supplemented by loose leaves, called "papers apart," which were cued to the main body of the manuscript by a series of signposts. A modern printer would reject this wondrous tangle at sight, but Baldwin's compositors deciphered it with remarkable accuracy.

Malone's guidance and hand appear everywhere in the manuscript, revising this phrase, clarifying that reference or sequence of ideas, smoothing out Boswell's simple paratactic sentence structure. Typically, "agreeable schemes of curiosity" turns into "occasional excursions," and "might push the bottle about" is dignified as "urged drinking." In the journal, Johnson's sermon, "in a boat upon the sea" between Raasay and Skye, takes place "upon a fine, calm Sunday morning"; Malone elevates this to "in a boat upon the sea, which was perfectly calm, on a day appropriated to religious worship." The text gains in precision and "elegance," while it loses in directness and force. Boswell, however, must have been responsible for recasting indirect speech ("he said that") in dramatic form ("JOHNSON").

More important than verbal alterations were the heavy substantive changes Boswell and Malone made as they focused the *Hebrides* on Johnson—actions, reactions, pronouncements on men and manners, effect on the natives. Many of Boswell's own hopes, fears, and acts of piety became irrelevant, as did a good deal of patient description and measurement. This last was no loss; as Boswell himself admitted, "I find I can do nothing in the way of description of any visible object whatever." A mechanical factor came into play: Boswell had chosen an octavo format with a large type-face and wide margins so that, midway, he realized he must throw out material by the handful if the book was not to become unpleasantly thick and expensive.

The need to cut detail and maintain decorum accounted for other large chunks of discarded journal. Boswell's ample reports of meals disappeared—"Shall the dinner *stet*?" is his wistful marginal query at one point. When Boswell complained, amidst the hospitality of Raasay, about the lack of privies in Scotland, "Mr. Johnson laughed heartily and said, 'You take very good care of one end of a man, but not of the other.' " This remark went. Even plain field-notes could be too outspoken for the contemporary audience. Boswell says,

> I observed tonight a remarkable instance of the simplicity of manners or want of delicacy among the people in Skye. After I was

in bed, the minister came up to go to his. The maid stood by and took his clothes and laid them carefully on a chair, piece by piece, not excepting his breeches,[1] before throwing off which he made water, while she was just at his back.

Johnson's dignity also had to be preserved. Even in the heat of argument, he could not be permitted to recall the Rev. Kenneth Macaulay as "the most ignorant booby and the grossest bastard." It might have damaged his reputation to include his remark that for five years of his life he made a bowl of punch for himself every night. But perhaps lack of space rather than a suspicion of triviality deleted mention of his fishing for cuddies at Ullinish. Boswell, elsewhere, hangs on to that kind of detail.

The nature of the collaboration between Boswell and Malone appears most clearly in their give-and-take about changes in the second edition. As soon as the first edition was published at the end of September 1785, Boswell left for Auchinleck; when a second edition was immediately called for, Malone was put in charge of the proofs, and discussed alterations with Boswell in voluminous correspondence. Both discovered obvious ways to improve the book, but some basic stylistic disagreements emerged. The charge that he had committed a Scotticism always brought Boswell to his knees; otherwise he could be highly resistant to suggestion. When Malone wanted to substitute "It gave me pleasure to behold" for "I loved," in "I loved to behold Dr. Samuel Johnson rolling about in this old magazine of antiquities," Boswell responded "I think 'I loved' a good warm expression." (Though Malone seldom made a change without Boswell's approval, he felt strongly enough about this phrase to substitute "I was pleased to behold.") His preference for conventional diction shows itself when he says of one phrase, "It is too colloquial, not book language, and nothing got by it." A related objection arose to another passage in which Johnson was discussing free will:

> But stay! (said he, with one of his satiric laughs). Ha! ha! ha! I shall suppose Scotchmen made necessarily, and Englishmen by choice.

"I wish the 'ha! ha! ha!' were omitted," Malone wrote. "It is only fit for the drama. What can a reader do with it? It adds nothing." Boswell replied, "I resign the 'ha! ha! ha!' to your deleting pen." But when Malone wanted to cut out the emphatic "myself" in the phrase, "I myself," Boswell argued, "I like the passage as it stands. I like *myself.—Moi.* It is more *avowed.* So let it remain."

[1]He would have worn nothing underneath.

Moi. Malone realized that everything in the journal came through Boswell's perceptions, that his attitudes and responses were central; but occasionally they could seem ridiculous or irrelevant, and he wanted to spare Boswell public derision. The debate over Veronica exemplified a major issue:

> Mr. Johnson was pleased with my daughter Veronica, then a child of about four months old. She had the appearance of listening to him. His motions seemed to her to be intended for her amusement; and when he stopped, she fluttered and made a little infantine noise, and a kind of signal for him to begin again. She would be held close to him, which was a proof from simple nature that his figure was not horrid. Her fondness for him endeared her still more to me, and I declared she should have five hundred pounds of additional fortune.

Malone invoked the reinforcement of their friend, John Courtenay, a spirited, witty, warm-hearted Irishman, M.P. for Tamworth: Courtenay, he wrote,

> wishes with me that Veronica had been left quietly in her nursery. He agrees entirely also with me in thinking that is no defence to say, "That is my mode or turn"; and that any part or passage of a book that is vulnerable does not barely operate by itself against the writer, but also casts a shade over other parts that are excellent and invulnerable.

Boswell was troubled:

> Perhaps you and Mr. Courtenay are right as to Veronica. I am convinced you are right as to the effect in *general* of weak parts in a book, and that "my way" is no excuse. But to omit Veronica *now* would do no good. . . . So I insist on retaining it. . . . Let me add however that had Veronica not been printed I should *perhaps* have left it out. To omit it *now* would be to invite attacks, by flying.

Besides, Boswell added, in his next letter, "Veronica is herself so fond of her appearance that she would be much mortified if I should delete her." Malone gave way but, as he feared, Veronica invited ridicule and duly made her appearance, in one of the Collings-Rowlandson caricatures of the *Hebrides*, knocking Johnson's wig over his forehead while Boswell looks on enraptured. Yet Boswell was right in the long run: the description is another fine example of his ability to evoke a scene with a range of implications.

Malone pressed on in the pursuit of correctness until Boswell, his spirits drooping at Auchinleck, rebelled: "Are you not too desirous of perfection? We must make *some* allowance for the book being a *journal*." Still, he was properly appreciative: "Your kind attention to my book is wonderful." And again, "You have certainly the art of book-making and book-dressing in the utmost perfection."

Boswell's own revisions tended to be brief, though occasionally he recalls a detail omitted at the time or adds a comment about later events. One revision, however, gives a striking example of his need to bring a scene into line with his mental image of it. Johnson had burst into one of his mysterious paroxysms of laughter at The Club, and only Garrick reacted, saying, according to the journal, "Mighty pleasant, Sir; mighty pleasant, Sir!" But this didn't come close enough to suit Boswell and, after experimenting further in the manuscript, he came up with a new version in the first edition of the *Hebrides*: "Only Garrick in his significant smart manner, darting his eyes around, exclaimed, '*Very* jocose, to be sure!'" What is remarkable is that Boswell had not even witnessed the scene himself; Langton had told him about it. But he could see that the repetition of the original phrase was clumsy, and he *knew* Garrick's characteristic speech and manner.

Such changes, both wholesale and minute, demonstrate how professionally self-critical a writer Boswell was, but they may also seem to cast doubt on Boswell's repeated assertions of authenticity in the *Hebrides*. To the entry for 18 August, very near to the work's beginning, he appended a footnote: "My journal, from this day inclusive, was read by Dr. Johnson." A few days later, in recounting the conversation between Johnson and Monboddo, Boswell advances his most extreme claim:

> My note of this is much too short. "Brevis esse laboro, obscurus fio."[1] Yet as I have resolved that *the very journal which Dr. Johnson read* shall be presented to the public, I will not expand the text in any considerable degree, though I may occasionally supply a word to complete the sense, as I fill up the blanks of abbreviation in the writing; neither of which can be said to change the genuine journal.

Not only does Boswell continue to remind the reader several times that Johnson had read the journal, he includes Johnson's comment that it "might be printed, were the subject fit for printing." Finally, in a footnote to 26 October, Boswell writes:

[1]"In trying to be concise, I become obscure" (Horace, *Art of Poetry*, ll. 25–26).

Having mentioned more than once that my journal was perused
by Dr. Johnson, I think it proper to inform my readers that this
is the last paragraph which he read.

Also Johnson had authenticated the journal as a whole by calling it "a very
exact picture of a portion of his life," and showed his satisfaction with
Boswell's report by approving Boswell's intention to write his biography.

But Boswell didn't direct his claims only to the public; he told Malone,
who knew the truth, "*authenticity* is my chief boast." To make sense of his
assertion it has to be taken in its contemporary context. No one in the
eighteenth century hesitated to revise letters, memoirs, or journals for
publication, and justifiably if the point of publication was to edify: effect
was more important than authenticity.

> Lives of great men all remind us
> We can make our lives sublime.

Longfellow reduces the point to doggerel, but it still holds: who is going
to be inspired by learning that his hero was vain or stingy or cowardly or
mean to his children? Yet all such contemporary publications claimed, at
least implicitly, to be authentic.

Boswell's assertion of authenticity might seem to us more warranted
if he had restricted it to Johnson's own words. No one could think, then
or now, that every word of Johnson's Boswell reported was exact. But
Boswell did write down, as nearly as possible, Johnson's key words, and he
was very reluctant to alter them, though occasionally he softened some of
Johnson's harsher comments or provided him with rather more elevated
language than he had used. (After 22 October when his journal fails,
Boswell attributes far less direct discourse to Johnson.) And once printed,
Johnson's language acquired the status of Sacred Writ. "I am determined,"
Boswell told Malone in revising for the second edition, "not to alter *now*
in *any* degree *any* saying of Dr. Johnson's." Boswell shows no qualms
otherwise about rewriting his journal; he had provided its material himself,
and that he can recast either for stylistic reasons or to bring it closer to
memory. Deletions hardly counted. What is authentic is Boswell's memory as proved genuine by the record of the journal, and that is what he is
proud of.

In his Dedication of the *Hebrides* to Malone, Boswell writes:

In every narrative, whether historical or biographical, authenticity
is of the utmost consequence.... The friends of Dr. Johnson
can best judge, from internal evidence, whether the numerous
conversations which form the most valuable part of the ensuing

pages are correctly related. To them therefore I wish to appeal for the accuracy of the portrait here exhibited to the world.

As one of those who were intimately acquainted with him, you have a title to this address. You have obligingly taken the trouble to peruse the original manuscript of this tour, and can vouch for the strict fidelity of the present publication.

The confidence with which Boswell makes these statements shows that neither he nor Malone felt any compunction about their revisions of the original, nor did they perceive any disingenuousness in concealing Malone's role in revision. *Essentially* this is the very journal Johnson read, though not the very words.

Malone was not Boswell's only collaborator. Another had been pressed into the service to settle a delicate question about the story within a story: the account of Prince Charles Edward's wanderings after the Battle of Culloden. What was Boswell to call "that person who in 1745–1746 attempted to recover the throne upon which his ancestors sat"? It would be insulting to call him "the Pretender," but "Prince Charles" might suggest that he had a right to the crown. The authority on this question—could there be a higher one?—was the King himself. Off went a letter to the King, with protestations of the most fervent loyalty, saying that if Boswell received no reply he would assume that His Majesty disapproved of "Prince Charles." The lack of a response did not at all discourage Boswell; this letter, like his letter introducing himself to Rousseau, was only the first move in the game.

On 15 June at Court, the King, no doubt being made aware of Boswell's impatience, drew him aside. Boswell pressed his question and the King turned it away; Boswell persisted and again the King hedged. All this hesitation, Boswell knew, was meant to test him:

> The trial was now over. The King found I was a man. He stepped a little forward, and inclining towards me with a benignant smile equal to that of any of Correggio's angels, he said, "I think and I feel as you do." My heart glowed with emotion, and I felt an admiration and affection for my King such as a warm royalist alone can imagine.

Yet somehow the question still seemed unanswered:

> KING. "But what designation do you mean to give?" BOSWELL. "Why, Sir, 'Prince Charles' I think is the common expression." His Majesty appearing to hesitate or demur, I proceeded. "Or shall it be 'the grandson of King James the Second?'" KING. "Yes."

Then the King pointed out that the nomenclature didn't matter in any case, since the matter of right was unquestionable.

According to another account, written down long afterwards, the King tried to escape at one point, but Boswell

> with his left hand took the King by the right elbow and fairly brought him round, saying at the same time, "Suppose, Sir, we call him the grandson of the unfortunate James the Second?" to which the King replied, "Very good, very good indeed, Mr. Boswell," and immediately proceeded to speak to other persons in the circle.

This is at least *ben trovato*, and may have some truth to it. Boswell, retiring bedazzled, wrote in a footnote to the *Hebrides*:

> I *know*, and I exult in having it in my power to tell, that THE ONLY PERSON in the world who is entitled to be offended at this delicacy[1] "thinks and feels as I do"; and has liberality of mind and generosity of sentiment enough to approve of my tenderness for what even *has been* Blood Royal.

But another consideration had later occurred to Boswell, and the note goes on:

> That he is *a prince* by *courtesy* cannot be denied, because his mother was the daughter of Sobieski, King of Poland. I shall, therefore, *on that account alone*, distinguish him by the name of *Prince Charles Edward*.

Which, after one mention of "the grandson of the unfortunate King James the Second," Boswell proceeds to do.

Of course the deeper purpose of Boswell's manoeuvre was to call the King's attention to himself, but he strangely failed to realize what a sensitive issue he had chosen to badger the King about. One does not speak of the rope in the house of the hanged man. A week later he plucked at the King's attention again by presenting the Address from his Auchinleck tenants against the Diminishing Bill. This time the King's conversation was restricted to asking when Boswell expected to return to Scotland. "A hint this," Boswell recognized. In fact, the earlier interview had boomeranged. He learned from Langton that in a bad humour one day the King said of Boswell, "He asked me how he should name the Pretender. I did not care how."

With his important book under way, Boswell decided it was time to

---

[1]Not calling Charles "the Pretender."

compose his features for posterity, and Reynolds agreed to paint his portrait: fifty guineas, to be paid out of Boswell's first earnings at the English bar, or at any rate in five years.   (In the end Reynolds made him a present of the portrait, well repaid by the Dedication to him of the *Life of Johnson*.) The Willison portrait, painted in 1765 at Rome, shows a silken Boswell in furred scarlet and green, with graceful hands, a soft, alert face, and some determination about him.   In maturity, Boswell appears in blue coat, white stock, and powdered wig, steady and dignified.   The face has taken on assured and self-conscious importance.   Still, some hint of cheerfulness lingers about the mouth, and the eyes remain always alert.

From an agreeable companion Reynolds had become a close friend, in spite of the difference between what Boswell spoke of as his equal and placid temper and Boswell's own ups-and-downs.   And as the summer wore on, the outlines of what was to be known as "the Gang" began to form: Reynolds, Boswell, Malone, and Courtenay—Reynolds and Malone the bachelors, Boswell virtually one in London, and Courtenay not a man to let himself be much tied down by a wife and seven children.   Others were loosely linked to the group, like William Windham, a charming, gifted, self-doubting M.P. of an old Norfolk family, much admired as the perfect gentleman, with special interests at the time in balloons, mathematics, and prize-fighting.   The Gang, Reynolds remarked, had many pleasant days together that summer; it was to be the great comfort of Boswell's life that they were to have many more.   Malone and he worked constantly on the *Hebrides*, but there was time for an occasional rural outing with "the ladies" (Malone's sisters, Henrietta and Catharine, and his sister-in-law, Lady Sunderlin).   There was the usual round of relaxed dinners and suppers with old friends—among them Wilkes, Dempster, Dilly, and Langton—as well as the Paoli and Cosway group.   Boswell became a great favourite of William Ward, M.P., the late Godfrey Bosville's son-in-law, and he "*felt* that with such connections all things, even quarrels, appear not distressing." Richard Akerman, Keeper of Newgate, introduced him to a club called "Friends round the Globe," which met every evening at the Globe Tavern (admission and one evening's bill, 5*s*.7*d*.).   Boswell called existence a delicious life in a delightful metropolis, a "paradise" even in the dead summer season.

One dinner at Courtenay's can stand for others.   Its "choice company"—Boswell gave the list to the press—included Windham, Dempster, Malone, and Burke.   When Boswell expatiated on his important interview with the King, Dempster asked "with sly pleasantry, 'Why don't you write oftener to him, Boswell?' "   Burke, Boswell reports, gave us an admirable dissertation on a good conjugal life, which made an impression on me. He showed that it was a great bond of society, and that we must not expect a continuation of the fervour of love, but be satisfied with a calm friendship. He said a husband would come to be as little disgusted with little indelicacies about his wife as with his own. . . .

The conjugal life otherwise did not occupy a great deal of Boswell's thought; he almost never mentions Margaret this summer. Betsy Smith, however, had not been forgotten. She had been discharged (or had decamped) from St. Thomas's:

I . . . met her in the Old Bailey, looking wonderfully well. But she frankly told me she would not take a place; she would rather resume her former life. I said, "You are a pleasing, honest creature, but the most profligate being I ever knew." . . . All my arguments were in vain. She said she'd be her own mistress. Said I: "At the mercy of every brutal ruffian." She said masters and mistresses had bad tempers. Said I: "What have many of the men that you must submit to?" I told her I was ashamed, but I loved her. I was vexed at such an instance of depravity. But it was curious. It verified Reynolds's maxim that human nature loves *gaming*: agitation, uncertainty.

When Boswell next mentions looking for Betsy, she had changed her lodgings, leaving no address; and unless she is hidden once more in the journal, this time as "Chelmsford," she disappeared from Boswell's knowledge.

But Boswell did not lack for agitation. On 9 August he received a card from a Mrs. Stewart asking him to call and, as he anticipated, it was Margaret Caroline Rudd, the celebrated adventuress, whom Boswell had interviewed shortly after her acquittal on charges of forgery in 1776. As will be remembered, he had found her sufficiently alluring to write a poem called *The Snake* about her, but nothing ensued except a few feverish kisses. Now she claimed she wanted a recommendation to the Lord Chancellor so that she might get justice from a man who had abandoned her after six years. She begged Boswell not to forget her; "it was a romantic scene," he thought. When he called again a few days later, Mrs. Rudd claimed to have an independency "and would not form another connection unless it were very agreeable." They got closer to the point on 10 September:

Told her honestly not in circumstances. " 'Tis tantalizing." "Come and see me sometimes and you shall not be tantalized."

Then one or the other remarked:

Should like to have a child between you and me; curious being. It would find its way in the world.

Mrs. Rudd's child certainly would have.   The meeting attests to Boswell's continuing attractiveness, vitality perhaps masking the double chin and other signs of wear and tear that show about the face in Reynolds's portrait.

The actual "connection" apparently did not take place until late November, when Boswell says in his journal: "Had cravings.   Visited Mrs. R. Indifferent.   Then gross folly."   But long before, his talk of seeing her helped to bring on a lecture from Reynolds, usually the most permissive of friends.   The immediate awful example was Boswell's model of urbanity, Lord Pembroke:

> ". . . a good, pleasant boy.   Never having been accustomed to refuse himself anything, he has gone on on all occasions, 'I will have this woman'; but by taking such gratifications he loses what is more valuable: the consequence which he should have in his country from his rank, fortune, and talents.   He is conscious he is not the great Earl of Pembroke."   This was a very instructive lecture to me.   Sir Joshua also talked of Mrs. Rudd, and said that if a man were known to have a connection with her, it would sink him.   "You," said he, "are known not to be formally accurate" (or some such phrase) "in your conduct.   But it would ruin you should you be known to have such a connection."   I did not see why this should appear so peculiarly bad.

Characteristically, Boswell's mind went off in another direction:

> I am very lucky in my intimacy with this eminent man.   It is truly enviable.

Boswell listens to the emotional tone: that Reynolds is his intimate friend, not what Reynolds says, is what sinks in.

Boswell never could see why some escapade should hurt him.   If he had been a Byron or Shelley who could scorn the public, his attitude would have made more sense.   But he was dependent precisely on that world whose opinion he flouted.   He shared its values; it was only that he felt its standards of conduct did not apply to him.   Prim Fanny Burney did not represent the more tolerant segment of contemporary opinion, but when the news reached her long after the affair was over, she was properly appalled: Boswell

> is now an actual admirer and follower of Mrs. Rudd!—and avows it, and praises her extraordinary attractions aloud!

Perhaps an incident earlier in the summer had made Reynolds more sensitive than usual to the public voice.   Boswell, who persuaded him to come along to the execution of five convicts at Newgate, had provided a fine, extended account of their last moments for the *Public Advertiser* (7 July 1785), which appeared under the heading of "Execution Intelligence." What must have disconcerted them both was the first paragraph of this "Intelligence":

> While a great concourse of spectators were assembled, the first person who appeared upon the scaffold yesterday morning was Mr. Boswell. *That* was nothing extraordinary, but it was surprising when he was followed by Sir Joshua Reynolds.—"Evil communications corrupt good manners."—It is strange how that hard Scot should have prevailed on the amiable painter to attend so shocking a spectacle.

Apparently the printer had grouped a number of paragraphs about the event without regard to source or congruence. Reynolds stoutly assured Boswell that he was glad to have been present, and defended the value of public executions, but he could hardly have been pleased by such notice. In any case, there were plenty of others in at the death. Whether such occasions deterred the potential criminal may be doubted, but they certainly provided the Londoner's equivalent of a blood sport. And Boswell, after the Diminishing Bill *Letter* and the forthcoming *Hebrides*, could expect constant petty attack in the newspapers.

Boswell and Malone made great headway on the *Hebrides* because they were able to take so much of it from the journal. On 21 September 1785 Boswell returned to Court where the King, who now kept to a safe line with Mr. Boswell, asked again when he planned to go north. Boswell replied that his book had detained him longer than expected, but His Majesty should have a copy the next evening. Indeed, next day, Boswell sat at Malone's with a "jury" (Reynolds, Brocklesby, Dempster, Langton) on the finished work, and they "applauded it much." Two days later he left London and, after a short stop at Jack Lee's place in County Durham, arrived at Auchinleck on 3 October.

I I

THE *HEBRIDES* WAS an instant success, widely reviewed and excerpted. The first edition of 1,500 copies sold out almost at once, and two more editions were called for during the next year. But it was a work that fitted customary genres and expectations awkwardly, and the critics, conscious they upheld standards of taste and judgement in an ever-collapsing world, were more hesitant than the public. Everyone, of course, had to admit that the book was continuously entertaining, but was it also instructive? Indeed, was the entertainment itself seemly?   Even John Nichols, who wrote a very favourable review of it for the *Gentleman's Magazine*, failed to see or at least to remark that it had taken unusual skill to put together what he called a "plain and simple narrative of the ordinary business and manner" of Johnson's life.   And most critics had strong reservations—of one or more of three kinds.

First, what should biography include?   A few years later, Vicesimus Knox, who could be relied on to impart sonority to any cliché, declared apropos of Boswell:

> Biography is every day descending from its dignity.   Instead of an instructive recital it is becoming an instrument to the mere gratification of an impertinent, not to say a malignant, curiosity.

Biography should conceal blemishes; it needs a vein of panegyric to arouse "ardour of imitation."   Johnson himself, in the *Lives of the Poets*, had been unusually blunt about the failings of his subjects, but that did not disarm Boswell's critics.   The *English Review* put the point:

> But allowing to Dr. Johnson all the merit which his warmest ad-mirers ascribe to him, was it meritorious, was it right or justifiable in Mr. Boswell to record and to publish his prejudices, his follies and whims, his weaknesses, his vices? . . .   It was counteracting, we should imagine, his design, which, if we mistake not, was to hold up Dr. Johnson in the most respectable light.

Second, and a closely connected point, was Boswell's inclusion of so much minutiae.   Detail was associated with low forms like the novel or comedy or satire; it had no place in an elevated or instructive work.   In the *Account of Corsica* Boswell adhered to conventional practice: his Plu-tarchian depiction of Paoli could not accommodate unedifying detail.

In the *Hebrides* Boswell's approach was guided by intuition rather than theory: what he chose to do, without wholly grasping his own method or its implications, was to present Johnson through a mosaic of widely varied and apparently unselected detail, from which his unique character would enable him to stand forth triumphantly.   But, of course, Boswell's mind composed each scene.   In his journal, for example, he wrote at Loch Ness:

> To see Mr. Johnson in any new situation is an object of attention to me.   As I saw him now for the first time ride along just like Lord Alemoor, I thought of *London, a Poem*, of *The Rambler*, of *The False Alarm*; and I cannot express the ideas which went across my imagination.

Then, in revision, his mind winnowed and sharpened the scene's implications:

> To see Dr. Johnson in any new situation is always an interesting object to me; and as I saw him now for the first time on horseback, jaunting about at his ease in quest of pleasure and novelty, the very different occupations of his former laborious life, his admirable productions, his *London*, his *Rambler*, etc. etc. immediately presented themselves to my mind, and the contrast made a strong impression on my imagination.

Boswell focuses his imagination clearly: Alemoor and *The False Alarm* disappear, and the titles of Johnson's works, *London* and *The Rambler*, bring out the striking contrast between Johnson at home and Johnson on his travels.

Still Boswell, in the *Hebrides*, was more defensive on the issue of minutiae than on any other. He excuses his description of Johnson's clothes with, "Let me not be censured for mentioning such minute particulars. Everything relative to so great a man is worth observing." Yet later he concedes, "I must again and again apologize to fastidious readers for recording such minute particulars. They prove the scrupulous fidelity of my journal." And, at the very end of the work, he justifies printing Johnson's conversation by appealing to examples, from Xenophon to Joseph Spence, of earlier collections of apophthegms, memorabilia, ana (sayings), table-talk, conversations, and anecdotes.

Time has dispatched these first two objections to the book, but the third, expressed by many contemporary critics, may always persist: it involves Boswell's depiction of himself again as the *naïf*. Not just the *naïf* simple, the landlubber who clings to his useless rope as the ship drives on Coll; but the *naïf* complex, who reveals his own tricks—how he soothed or deceived Johnson or led him to talk, how he danced to keep the Hebrideans happy. Others have exploited the role of the *naïf*: Chaucer the pilgrim; a wide-eyed Pope; Burns the farmer turning naïveté into manly simplicity; Frost hiding within New England pastoral. But Boswell is the greatest writer in English to play the *naïf* consistently. While it fitted his personality, or one aspect of it, he was reaching far beyond personality for a role that his friend Courtenay caught in one couplet about him:

> With fond delight we praise his happy vein,
> Graced with the naïveté of the sage Montaigne.

"I cannot give it up," Boswell told Malone, when there was talk of revising these lines; "the similarity to Montaigne is quite characteristical." Montaigne wrote in his prefatory "Author to the Reader": "If I had lived among those nations, which (they say) yet dwell under the sweet liberty of nature's primitive laws, I assure thee I would most willingly have painted myself quite fully and quite naked."   His *Essays* show a mind moving through a naïve openness to a wisdom beyond that of the respectable, clever, or good, and Boswell, who shared the same goal of naked depiction, hoped to achieve the same effect.   Everywhere he reveals those trivial thoughts and feelings that many people are too embarrassed even to admit having, let alone expose for the entertainment of the public; they induce shame rather than guilt, and so are more closely concealed.   Crimes may arouse sympathy; gaffes elicit only amusement.

But reviewers could not easily penetrate beyond performer to author, and it must be admitted that Boswell did not *always* anticipate how he would appear to those in front of the footlights.   At best, commentators, like "Johnsonophilus" in the *Gentleman's Magazine*, said that Boswell's "artless manner of relating the common incidents of their journey evinces his veracity."   The *English Review* dismissed him as an "agreeable trifler," and the *Critical Review*, in its impenetrable complacency, seems typical enough to quote at length:

> We cannot easily leave Johnson, but his companion will not forgive us if we pass him without notice; and why should we omit to mention him, whose vivacity has confessedly enlivened the didactic gravity of the literary Colossus—whose good-humoured vanity generally pleases?   Excuse us, Mr. Boswell; though we sometimes smile *at* your volubility, yet we go with you cheerfully along.   Life has too many grave paths; let us catch the fluttering butterfly occasionally in the flowery meadows; he will not detain us long, and may deceive the length, sometimes the tediousness of the way.

Boswell lacked high seriousness.   The reviewers might have recalled Sterne: gravity is "a mysterious carriage of the body to cover the defects of the mind."

With a critical vocabulary restricted to "instruction," "entertainment," and "decorum," the reviewers were too limited in technique to be able to explain, or even to suspect the need of explaining, why the *Hebrides* was so wonderfully readable.   Without trying to make that appeal fully explicit, some reasons for it can be suggested.   It is unified by a constant cross-play among topics: some immediate (Ossian, emigration), some personal or contemporary (Burke, subordination), some perennial (evil, the variety of human nature)—as they recur in varying contexts and are perceived from varying viewpoints.   But the *Hebrides* also has an inherent structure:

it moves from the civilized (Edinburgh and the Lowlands) through the primitive (the Highlands and Hebrides) back to the civilized (the Lowlands and Edinburgh), with all the shadings and ironies that the travellers' experiences of "civilization" and "nature" provide. The savage-shopkeeper debate, which opens the work's central issue, is settled when near the end of their tour Johnson and Boswell laugh heartily "at the ravings of those absurd visionaries who have attempted to persuade us of the superior advantages of a *state of nature.*" (This is one literary work where art is accounted superior to nature.)

Further, the sustained tension in the Johnson-Boswell-Scots triangle supplies each new situation with the potential for almost any reaction—comic, explosive, or harmonious—while the inner play between Johnson and Boswell strengthens the narrative line. Tension is heightened by contrast between Johnson and whomever or whatever—a Highland guide, an old Presbyterian minister, a small pony. Boswell builds on a fundamental incongruity; as he wrote to Garrick from Inverness:

> Indeed, as I have always been accustomed to view [Johnson] as a permanent London object, it would not be much more wonderful to me to see St. Paul's Church moving along where we now are.

The underlying suspense of the *Hebrides*—how will the situation work out?—is resolved by Johnson's reaction to Iona, the grail of their pilgrimage. And this reaction has been foreshadowed by reversal when Johnson assumed the accoutrements of an ancient Caledonian bard.

All these factors are equally characteristic of well-made novels; one important factor that differentiates the *Hebrides* from them is Boswell's carefully cultivated sense of authenticity, the sense that the scene we are reading about actually occurred. The ordered selectivity of the imagination seems to give way to the rich randomness of experience. The sense of familiarity reinforces the effect, taken to the point today where the devotee authenticates the narrative by travelling over the same route. Authenticity in itself is never enough, of course; there are plenty of dull authentic narratives. Rather, authenticity provides the foundation for Boswell's vision of existence.

First he had to get down his sense of Johnson. The opening static character sketch dissolves into activity: the face, figure, gestures, voice (the "bow-wow" utterance, "the *Messiah* played upon the Canterbury organ"), the convulsive movements, the manner in company, the moments in retirement with Boswell. Johnson invigorates as well as dominates the scene, but its unfailing interest comes from Boswell's choice of what to record, and this does not depend on Johnson: Boswell shows the same power to capture attention in the London Journal of 1762–1763.

Take, for instance, a scene where Johnson's part is less prominent than usual:

> There was a comfortable parlour with a good fire, and a dram went round.   By and by supper was served, at which there appeared the lady of the house, the celebrated Miss Flora Macdonald. She is a little woman of a genteel appearance, and uncommonly mild and well bred.   To see Dr. Samuel Johnson, the great champion of the English Tories, salute[1] Miss Flora Macdonald in the Isle of Skye was a striking sight; for though somewhat congenial in their notions, it was very improbable they should meet here.

As elsewhere, Boswell calls attention to the scene, then stands back and leaves the reader to fill it in.   He goes on:

> Miss Flora Macdonald . . . told me she heard upon the mainland, as she was returning to Skye about a fortnight before, that Mr. Boswell was coming to Skye, and one Mr. Johnson, a young English buck, with him.   He was highly entertained with this fancy. . . . He was rather quiescent tonight, and went early to bed.   I was in a cordial humour, and promoted a cheerful glass. The punch was super-excellent.   Honest Mr. Macqueen observed that I was in high glee, "my *governor* being gone to bed."   Yet in reality my heart was grieved when I recollected that Kingsburgh was embarrassed in his affairs, and intended to go to America.   However, nothing but what was good was present, and I pleased myself in thinking that so spirited a man would be well everywhere.   I slept in the same room with Dr. Johnson.   Each had a neat bed with tartan curtains, in an upper chamber.

Boswell takes his usual roles of participant and reporter.   The scene is concrete in its thick specificity but contains little detailed description. The narrative moves, as the mind ordinarily moves, by association, shifting rapidly and sometimes unexpectedly in topic and mood, yet it is held together by a consistent tone, genial and urbane, that invites the reader to share Boswell's feelings of enjoyment and wonder.

One of the strongest attractions of the *Hebrides* for eighteenth-century readers must have been its high-level gossip, especially Johnson's pronouncements on contemporaries.   Immediate curiosity will no longer propel the reader forward, though Johnson's acute and energetic opinions sustain interest.   But whatever Boswell's openness about other living men

[1]Kiss.

and women, it does not compare with his honesty about himself and John-son.   His willingness, even desire, to expose himself is persistent, in spite of self-remonstrance:

> It is the same to many men with regard to the mind as to the body. I would not strip myself naked before everyone, and would be shocked to occasion another being so exposed.

This reservation came to nothing.   In the *Hebrides* Boswell exploits his honesty again and again.   He is willing to gamble that frank self-revelation and faithful report about others will interest his readers as much as it does himself.   And honesty is essential to that attempt at an exact transcript of life, which he knows is impossible to achieve but which remains his goal. Others go higher or deeper, depict a broader or more intense range of experience, but no one suggests more convincingly that, day by day, this is what life is like.   And in giving his life permanence in the *Hebrides* Boswell converts it into art.   Nor should the reviewers have been expected to realize that Boswell was pioneering a new mode that has produced the modern biography.

It is more surprising that they did not focus sharply on the revelation of the frankness with which Johnson and Boswell discussed their contem-poraries.   Boswell got plenty of warnings from friends, especially after the publication of the *Hebrides*, that his kind of reporting was unacceptable, and immediately, as we shall see, he got himself into serious trouble.   But such frankness was a matter on which Boswell, for artistic or whatever reasons, was at least half-blind.   "I think it proper to say," he wrote in the penultimate paragraph of the *Hebrides*,

> that I have suppressed everything that I thought could really hurt anyone now living.   With respect to what *is* related, I thought it my duty to "extenuate nothing, nor set down aught in malice"; and with those lighter strokes of Dr. Johnson's satire, proceeding from a warmth and quickness of imagination, not from any malev-olence of heart, and which, on account of their excellence, could not be omitted, I trust that they who are the object of them have good sense and good temper enough not to be displeased.

It all depends on whose ox is being gored.   The Scots in general were not delighted by the revival of Johnson's well-known, disparaging opinions reinforced with the new, so-called lighter strokes of satire, though Boswell tried to disarm reaction by suffixing commendatory letters about his journal from Hailes, Dempster, and Forbes.   Surely Johnson was carried away by controversial zeal when he insisted that before the Union the wine available to the Scots was too weak for them to get drunk on.   The conversation degenerated into an exchange of insults.   BOSWELL.   "I assure you, Sir, there was a great deal of drunkenness."   JOHNSON.   "No, Sir, there were people who died of dropsies, which they contracted in trying to get drunk." But at Auchinleck, it will be recalled, when someone innocently asked Johnson how he liked the Highlands, the answer expressed a considered, though irritable, opinion:

> "How, Sir, can you ask me what obliges me to speak unfavourably
> of a country where I have been hospitably entertained?   Who *can*
> like the Highlands?   I like the inhabitants very well."   The gentle-
> man asked no more questions.

General reflections, however, do not carry the sting of individual animadversion.   A few complained aloud that their names were scattered along the entertaining trail of Boswell's indiscretions, and the mention ratified by Johnson's concurrence or silence: the blind poet, Thomas Black-lock, declared that he had never been troubled by religious doubts; and the Auchinleck minister, John Dun, denied that Johnson had said he knew no more about the Church of England than a Hottentot.   Others kept public silence, though Lord Gardenstone could read that he had made as much fuss about establishing the village of Laurencekirk as if he had founded Thebes; Lord Erroll's family (he was dead) that sleeping at Slains Castle had frightened Boswell with memories of Erroll's father, the traitorous Lord Kilmarnock; and Sir John Dalrymple that Johnson had mercilessly parodied his prose.   Lord Monboddo could discover that he provides the running joke for the first half of the *Hebrides*, as Sir Alexander Macdonald does for the second.   But Boswell had little to fear from old or reverend gentlemen, and he despised Dalrymple for having refused a challenge.

One bit of exquisite badinage cost Boswell an important friend.   Re-marking that Holyrood Chapel had been left unrepaired, Boswell went on:

> [I] particularly complained that my friend Douglas, the repre-
> sentative of a great house and proprietor of a vast estate, should
> suffer the sacred spot where his mother lies interred to be un-
> roofed, and exposed to all the inclemencies of the weather.   Dr.
> Johnson, who, I know not how, had formed an opinion on the
> Hamilton side in the Douglas Cause, slyly answered, "Sir, Sir, don't
> be too severe upon the gentleman; don't accuse him of want of
> filial piety!   Lady Jane Douglas was not *his* mother."—He roused
> my zeal so much that I took the liberty to tell him he knew nothing
> of the Cause, which I do most seriously believe was the case.

Elementary tact should have suppressed that exchange.   Despite a "hand-some letter" of apology, Douglas treated Boswell with great coldness thereafter.

Then there was the mighty quarrel with Mrs. Thrale (now Piozzi) generated by one incidental mention of her.   Boswell and Johnson were discussing Johnson's unwillingness to praise Garrick in the Preface to his edition of Shakespeare.   Boswell writes:

> I spoke of Mrs. Montagu's very high praises of Garrick.   JOHNSON. "Sir, it is fit she should say so much, and I should say nothing. Reynolds is fond of her book[1] and I wonder at it, for neither I nor Beauclerk nor Mrs. Thrale could get through it.

What made the remark so damaging was that if Mrs. Piozzi ever attempted to regain the social position her second marriage had cost her, she would need all the help she could get; Mrs. Montagu was the acknowledged leader of the British female intelligentsia, and to the usual sensitivity of authors united great wealth, strong opinions, and a formidable presence.   (The Boswell-Piozzi story will be continued.)

Even praise could be deadly.   Johnson admired Burke for his "great variety of knowledge, store of imagery, copiousness of language," but when Principal Robertson added that Burke had wit, Johnson replied, "No, Sir, he never succeeds there.   'Tis low; 'tis conceit.   I used to say, Burke never once made a good joke."   At this point in the first edition Boswell saw fit to insert a footnote more than a page long in small print, trying to refute Johnson by citing a few examples of Burke's wit and the favourable opinions of Wilkes and Reynolds.   Unfortunately, these samples seemed trifling or overingenious, so for the second edition Malone, whose sense of tact occasionally deserted him, concocted an addition, almost as long as the original note, that talked of Burke's "lively and brilliant fancy" as only one "of the many talents he possesses, which are so various and extraordinary that it is very difficult to ascertain the rank and value of each."   Boswell thought the "rich plumage" of this rider so splendid that he wanted to put Malone's name to it, but Malone refused to allow public acknowledgement.   Still, to give proper credit, Boswell explained the whole affair in a letter to Burke (20 December 1785).

Anyone not lost in self-admiration would have found this note fulsome. The matter was worse for Burke.   He was fully aware of his great powers, and liked compliments as well as the next man.   But he was constantly vilified in the press, and had become sensitive to the point of paranoia

[1]*An Essay on the Writings and Genius of Shakespeare*, 1769.

about such public discussion. To find his attributes debated in print aroused a complicated embarrassment, for which he could not even blame his torturers because they meant well. In his intricately ironic answer to Boswell's letter, Burke says,

> I am extremely obliged to you and to Mr. Malone (to whom I beg my best compliments) for your friendly solicitude with regard to a point relating to me about which I am myself not very anxious; the reputation for wit . . . is what I certainly am not entitled to; and, I think, I never aimed at. If I had been even so ambitious, I must show myself as deficient in judgement as I am in wit. . . .
>
> I shall be well content to pass down to a long posterity in Doctor Johnson's authentic judgement, and in your permanent record, as a dull fellow and a tiresome companion, when it shall be known through the same long period that I have had such men as Mr. Boswell and Mr. Malone as my friendly counsel in the cause which I have lost. . . .
>
> I ought not to take this public reprimand amiss. My companions have a right to expect that when my conversation is so little seasoned as it is with wit, it should not, out of respect both to them and to myself, be so light and careless as it undoubtedly always has been and is. . . . I ought therefore to thank you for informing the world of this censure of our deceased friend that I may regulate myself accordingly. . . .
>
> I am sure there are very few who (let them be qualified as they will) shall be indiscreet enough to interrupt, by the intrusion of their ideas, the strong flow of your real wit and true humour, who will not be great enemies to their own entertainment, as well as to the satisfaction of the rest of the company. . . .

Burke never trusted Boswell again.

Worse came from elsewhere. Alexander Tytler, an advocate with literary pretensions, had told Johnson that he knew *Fingal* was genuine because he had heard a great part of it repeated in the original. Johnson soon discovered that Tytler knew no Erse, and later remarked to Boswell, "Did you observe the wonderful confidence with which young Tytler advanced, with his front ready *brazed?*" Tytler took exception to this anecdote in a violent letter. Boswell replied that he had understood Tytler to say he had no objection to the story being printed; he was willing to change it, but he wanted an apology for "hasty expressions" in Tytler's letter. Tytler was willing to forgive the offence, but felt too affronted to apologize. The matter hung fire until Boswell returned to London (17 November 1785), where Malone and Courtenay convinced him that he must have an apology, and a firm letter implying a challenge if one was not forthcoming brought Tytler around.

The quarrel with Tytler was just a curtain-raiser, and even before it was concluded the main drama had begun.   To appreciate it one must recall that in the eighteenth century a gentleman's honour was his most sacred possession; if he lost it, both self-esteem and social position vanished. The duel was the final test of that honour.   The state prohibited duelling, religion denounced it, and a moment's thought showed its stupidity and unfairness; but custom overruled them all.   Even the Duke of York fought a duel in 1789.

The person most abused in the *Hebrides* was Sir Alexander (by 1785 Lord) Macdonald.   His portrayal, both under his own name and anonymously, was essential to the book's structure, but Boswell felt some compunction at having hit him so hard and so often, and cancelled one leaf in the first edition which gave his name, though for the sake of completeness he reinserted the material later as the character of "a rapacious Highland Chief."

In revising for the second edition, Boswell felt further qualms; apparently someone in Edinburgh suggested that Macdonald might take offence.   Boswell wrote from Auchinleck to Malone about this matter just before setting out for London:

> When you and I look back upon the accumulation of just censure concerning L—d M—d and think how little appears with his *name* (and nobody has a right to apply anything said without it), we must wonder that the little we suffered to escape displeases.   Yet I declare I am sorry that *any* part of it appears (with his *name* I mean).   My wife thinks that attacking his *cheer* is adopting Dr. Johnson's *low-bred* notion of the importance of a *good table*, and she thinks I had no right to *report* Dr. Johnson's saying that Sir A. was "utterly unfit for his situation," which she thinks a severe reflection which will stick both to himself and his family.   She has been in sad anxiety lest he should call me out, and was going to write to you entreating you would prevent it.   I have no great fear of *that*.   But why be in any degree a public executioner?   I therefore enclose for your consideration what I would propose to introduce instead of: "Instead of finding the Chief of the Macdonalds" etc., and, if you approve, that leaf shall be cancelled a second time.   I have the milk of human kindness in abundance.
>
> I have been much disconcerted by my wife's affectionate fears. If the *Remarks* come from him, he has retaliated and we have no more to do.[1]   Yet I still doubt if it would not be better on my own account to make the proposed change.   So it must be well weighed when our heads are laid together.

[1] Macdonald had nothing to do with this attack on the *Hebrides*.

If you could have an opportunity to know for *certain* that Lord M—d does not take it *hot*, a few lines to Mrs. Boswell, James's Court, Edinburgh, would relieve an excellent woman. To say that a man does not *entertain* liberally—and that a gentleman educated in England is totally unfit for the Hebridean situation are surely no *severe* reflections, and what is *anonymously* said ought not to be taken as "levelled at me."

It is sad that there should be such mixtures of alloy in human happiness. The fame of my *Tour* is darkened somewhat by censures as if I were ill-natured. But I am now amidst narrow-minded, prejudiced mortals.

The changes Boswell made in the second edition of the *Hebrides* reduce the comments on Macdonald by name to something like decency. But Boswell's attention was elsewhere: the time had come for him to make up his mind at last about his move to the English bar, and the decision was agonizing. Then, first he heard rumours from Mrs. Bosville, Macdonald's mother-in-law, and her son William that Macdonald intended to abuse him in the newspapers. Next William told him that Macdonald intended to do no more than break off acquaintance with him. The blow fell in London on 27 November:

On my return home, found a most shocking, abusive letter from Lord M. which I thought made it indispensable for me to fight him. Was quite dismal. Such a dreary force upon me in my gloomy state was terrible. I thought of my dear wife and children with anxious affection. Could not rest. Had a thousand thoughts.

Macdonald's letter, though turgid from rage and habitual affectation, would have disturbed anyone:

Your violation of the acknowledged laws of hospitality by the wanton affront put upon me in [the *Hebrides*] after such a lapse of time is without a parallel in the annals of civilized nations, and could only have proceeded from a mind tainted with prejudices of the most dark and malignant kind, unsusceptible of the least spark of generosity and refinement, and accustomed to arrogate to itself a licence to treat mankind in general with indignity and insolence. . . .

You think proper, without any ceremony or regard to Doctor Johnson's memory, to father a few rude sayings to me upon him whose good sense shielded me from any such offence, while its influence ingratiated him with everybody who came within the peal of his enlightened conversation. . . .

To your outrageous and fanciful aspersions you have united the grossest dissimulation, and prostituted your very encomiums to the cause of malignity.

This last charge referred to the Latin alcaics Macdonald had composed in honour of Johnson's visit. Because they

> contained a compliment due to Mr. Macpherson,[1] they have not been deemed worthy of any notice in your memorabilia or *ana*, which, as to their offensiveness to many respectable families and societies, may with greater force of truth be written in the masculine gender and in the dative case.

Then to show he had kept his hand in, Macdonald added some Latin verses, which read in part: "Damn me if with a heavier weapon [than the pen] I do not tickle your ass's head, till the blood flows down and the bare skull reeks horridly where I have ripped off the hide."

"It is not my intention," Macdonald continued,

> to comment upon your mass of fabricated apophthegms, which bubble upon the surface of an heated imagination, and, like the workings of a vat, throw up the briny foam of your equinoctial reveries to the gaping world. But . . . I think it is time to justify myself, as one of many individuals, from the obloquy with which it abounds to swell your volume, and gratify your avarice.

Macdonald's syntax had slipped out of control, but he recovered to defend himself at length from charges of miserliness and a determination to drive his tenants to emigrate. He concluded,

> Every true Englishman will abhor the man . . . who makes a rude effort to mingle his gall with the essence of private friendship. . . . This may suffice for the present; and I shall think my time which I have dedicated to a restoration of your judgement well bestowed if it shall be the means of rescuing one man from detraction.

The letter was unsigned.

Boswell had to respond in some way, but his conscience was uneasy. Implicitly Macdonald himself had admitted that, as everyone knew, he was the "rapacious Highland Chief" and "penurious gentleman" censured, which demolished Boswell's excuse that many of his references to Macdonald were anonymous. Paoli, who had no need to prove his courage, told Boswell not to resent Macdonald's letter, and Bosville said Macdonald merely wanted to frighten him and publish their correspondence in the newspapers if he could make Boswell retract any of the remarks he had made in the book. Malone and Courtenay concurred that Boswell should take no notice of the letter: it was unsigned and, while saying that no apology would

---

[1]The "translator" of Ossian.

be accepted, did not in itself constitute a challenge.   But Boswell wanted Macdonald to know that his deletions in the second edition were unforced, so he sent a letter via Bosville telling him so, which also apologized for certain exceptionable passages.

The quarrel might have rested there if Courtenay, who had a little of Sheridan's Sir Lucius O'Trigger in him, had not worried Boswell with the possibility that Macdonald might show his abusive letter around or even publish it; the situation must be clarified before Boswell returned to Edinburgh.   Complicated negotiations followed between Boswell and Macdonald, with Courtenay as intermediary, which are preserved in a series of formal "papers" (letters and notes).   In brief, Boswell pressed for assurance that Macdonald would make no use, public or private, of the offending letter, with the threat of a challenge if Macdonald refused.

Macdonald's aims were to make Boswell sweat and to convince the world that Boswell had made changes in the second edition under pressure. To fight a duel would spoil both aims, and besides it was dangerous.   So he stalled as long as he could, and he knew his man. Boswell tried to convince himself that it was all an accident: "What mischief may imprudent publications bring upon even a good man!"   But this excuse didn't make him feel any better, as successive entries in his journal show:

> My anxiety was most distressing. . . .   I was in sad agitation. . . . Awaked very ill both in body and mind.   I thought of my wife and children with tender pain, and had death before my eyes. . . . I wrote to my wife before dinner, under an apprehension it might be the last letter.   Courtenay, on my asking him, directed me how to stand and fire a pistol.   My heart failed me, but I found myself under an absolute necessity to go on.   Courtenay said he thought Lord M. a mean poltroon, who, conscious that he was not to proceed to the last extremity, as he could at any time put an end to the matter, wished to appear bold and work my feelings; for it seems he had proposed to refer the affair to a committee of the gentlemen who attend the Mount Coffee-house. . . .   What misery, real and imaginary, do I endure.
>   Had not slept five minutes all night.   The alternative of killing or being killed distracted me. . . .

All this time the dance of punctilio went on.   First Macdonald pretended he had to consult his friends.   Then he wrote a letter that said nothing to the purpose.   Boswell, Malone, and Courtenay were now sure that Macdonald just meant to play on Boswell's fears, "conscious that he could at any time get off."   Yet Boswell continued to suffer:

The night was passed somewhat more easily, but I was still in feverish agitation. . . . It was terrible to think that *death* is *certain* at *some* period.   But a *violent* death, especially when a man by his fault occasions it, is shocking.   I endeavoured to cherish pious hope.

(As Tytler remarked in his Commonplace Book about *his* quarrel with Boswell, "It is amazing how a man that can so ill extricate himself from scrapes should not be more careful how he falls into them.")

Macdonald got in a last hit: he agreed to revise his letter and retract certain accusations, such as that Boswell had invented Johnson's remarks— a charge which upset Boswell seriously—but this "second edition,"as Macdonald called it, left the original statements perfectly legible, just as the second edition of the *Hebrides* could not obliterate the first.   On 13 December Macdonald declared the matter at an end, the papers were enclosed in a wrapper for posterity, and honour was declared satisfied.

But Macdonald, whether he showed his letter about or not, let it be known in some way that he had attacked Boswell, so when the second edition of the *Hebrides* appeared at the end of December 1785 it was assumed that Boswell's statement, in a note at the end, that he had omitted "a few observations . . . which might perhaps be considered as passing the bounds of a strict decorum" had been extorted from him.   The aftermath can be quoted directly from F. A. Pottle's detailed account, from which this description of the Macdonald affair has been abridged:

> Macdonald was in a position to deny this, but it would have been asking too much of human nature to expect him to rescue Boswell from such a predicament.   The satirists at once pounced on the situation.   Peter Pindar's *Congratulatory Epistle to James Boswell, Esq.*, which appeared in February 1786, contained the following pungent couplets:
>
>> Let Lord Macdonald threat thy breech to kick,
>> And o'er thy shrinking shoulders shake his stick;
>> Treat with contempt the menace of this Lord,
>> 'Tis History's province, Bozzy, to *record*.
>
> In a footnote to this passage, Wolcot[1] says expressly that Lord Macdonald sent Boswell "a letter of severe remonstrance," in consequence of which Boswell omitted "the scandalous passages relative to this nobleman."   Boswell replied in the newspapers early in March, and in the *Gentleman's Magazine* for April 1786.   He denied that the passages in question were scandalous, and he fur-

[1]"Peter Pindar's" real name was John Wolcot.

ther denied that they had been omitted because of any protest
from Macdonald.   It suited the purpose of Wolcot and others not
to believe him.   In *Bozzy and Piozzi* he is reminded that "from
Macdonald's rage to save his snout" he "cut twenty lines of defamation out"; and when the famous Collings-Rowlandson caricatures appeared in June 1786, one of them was entitled, "Revising
for the Second Edition."   Macdonald holds Boswell by the throat
and points sternly with his stick at an open copy of the *Tour*.[1]
Two leaves, on which the page numbers 165 and 167 appear, have
been torn out and lie on the ground, and Boswell, in an agony of
terror, is begging for mercy.   It must have been maddening to
realize that he had in his possession documents which would amply
vindicate his honour, but that this same honour forbade his making them public or even hinting at their contents.   All that he
could do was to file them away in his archives, to show at least to
his descendants that he had acted with dignity and resolution.

[1]Cited as *Hebrides* in the present volume.

CHAPTER

————

13

I

WITH THE RESOLUTION of the Macdonald crisis, Boswell could let his attention revert to his long-standing dilemma, now in its most acute stage. London, for many years, had represented to him emergence into full consciousness. There in 1760, he said, the late Lord Eglinton had first opened his eyes to the *savoir vivre*: "I lived under his roof in London and was first introduced by him into what alone deserves the name of life."

Ever since, Boswell's most cherished goal had been to fix himself in London, and his far-fetched schemes—a commission in the Guards, a seat in Parliament—even the fantasy that the King, with bounteous gesture, would bestow a place at Court on him, showed how desperate this desire was. The only remotely feasible way to achieve this aim would have been to become an English barrister at once, or to transfer to the English bar after practising as a Scots advocate for a few years. The first possibility his father simply prohibited, and the second, as remarked, Boswell never dared to try while his father lived, for fear of forfeiting his father's approval and financial support, and quite possibly losing his inheritance. Death three years earlier had removed that barrier, but still he wavered. Now he had to decide.

Boswell had summoned up the arguments against and for this move again and again. Here they will be summarized for the last time. The arguments *con* were many and solid. He was forty-five years old; English law had an entirely different basis from that of Scots law, and was mined with technicalities about which he knew nothing; he was heavily in debt, London was expensive, and his family would have to live in straitened circumstances that would affect their social position; his wife was seriously ill with consumption, and without doubt would suffer, mentally and physically, from being transplanted; finally—a powerful consideration—the move would inevitably estrange the family to some degree from Auchinleck, their ancestral home.   The last had been one of his father's chief arguments against his scheme, and now as a command from the beyond it was difficult to ignore.

The arguments *pro* dwindled to two, one almost delusional and the other almost irresistible.   First, he hoped he would become, overnight, a brilliant success, rise rapidly in wealth and reputation, and achieve the high office that alone would satiate his ambition.   The example of Thomas Erskine lured him on like a will-o'-the-wisp.   But if Erskine had been favoured by fortune, he had put himself in a position to take advantage of it.   He had kept terms simultaneously at Trinity College, Cambridge, and at Lincoln's Inn; had continued to study with a special pleader even after he had been called to the bar at the age of twenty-nine; and combined verbal fluency with iron self-confidence.   Vain as a peacock and notorious for the enthusiasm with which he talked for hours about himself, Erskine also worked hard and he knew how to make the most of his abilities in the courtroom.   According to Sir William Holdsworth, the foremost of English legal historians, he was "the greatest advocate who has ever practised at the English bar."   Boswell admired the results of Erskine's efforts, and ignored their causes.

Second, of course, was his need for London.   Boswell was not undergoing some sudden change in objective brought on by midlife crisis, nor was his wish to live in London whimsical and easily dismissed.   In Scotland, he was more than dull and discontented: he was often so depressed that he could barely exert himself at all.   In London he breathed abundantly: the hurry, the crowds, the range of his experience and the variety of his acquaintance—brilliant, or at least of high rank or well mannered or genial—fulfilled him.   Boswell needed city air.   Like his friend Sir Michael Le Fleming he preferred the smell of a flambeau in the playhouse to the country fragrance of a May evening.   For him life at its fullest had always been found at Charing Cross.

He was never in doubt as to the right choice, but both choices were right.   If he stayed in Scotland the income from his estate and even moderate practice would enable him to live comfortably and gradually pay off his troublesome debts; he had some claim to a place on the Court of Session, with its snug salary; his respectable social position was assured; and pride of family, his "predominant passion," would be satisfied by the traditional ways of living at Edinburgh and Auchinleck. But could he condemn himself untried? Scotland operated on him, he said, like the *grotta del cane* near Naples; he would choke to death. It is impossible to imagine Boswell as a lifelong bachelor but, whatever his misgivings about deserting Auchinleck, had he remained one he would unquestionably have settled in London, just as Malone had done. Instead, Boswell had given hostages to fortune, and to make his move he had to claim that his family would benefit too. The boys would go to English public schools, the girls acquire English manners, and Margaret—well, Margaret would stand by him as he boldly attempted to aggrandize the name and fortune of Boswell of Auchinleck.

All along, Boswell had oscillated between optimism and prudence about his removal to London, but now that decision was upon him the pendulum swung wildly. Every day, sometimes every hour, he changed his mind. On his return to London (21 November 1785), "all seemed confused." As usual in moments of crisis, he consulted everyone: Paoli against, Mrs. Stuart for, Colonel Stuart against, Langton for. Dempster, who had had longer experience with Boswell and his anxieties than anyone else in London, treated the question lightly; he told Boswell not to worry about appearances, but just to follow his inclination.

After his distracted two weeks with Macdonald, Boswell immediately faced a short-term problem: dare he return to Scotland even for a visit? He needed to go home; indecision had not only depressed him, it had made him physically sick. He wrote in his journal (16 December):

> Awaked gloomily ill. Sallied forth in a kind of despair. Breakfasted with Seward,[1] and was a little relieved by talking of melancholy and hearing how he often was afflicted with it. I was sensible it was wrong to speak of it. But the torment was such that I could not conceal it.

He felt "all restlessness and vexation." Two days later he wrote that T.D., the most resolute opponent of his move,

> complained of my never almost seeing him, and pressed upon me my duty as the head of our Family, entreating me to reside at Auchinleck. I was moved, and regretted much my feverish fancy for London.... In the evening I went early to bed. A poor existence.

Boswell tried to avoid inner conflict by relying on others' advice, but when he renounced responsibility for his choice he merely substituted the anxiety of helplessness.

---

[1] William Seward, a man about town and agreeable friend.

On the same day that T.D. told him to go home and stay there, Boswell decided to submit his "case" to Thurlow.   He had come to know Thurlow slightly when applying for an augmentation of Johnson's pension the previous year, and had announced to the world in his Diminishing Bill *Letter* that now Johnson was gone, "I bow the intellectual knee to Lord Thurlow." Perhaps this posture caught Thurlow's attention; he recognized Boswell so markedly in the House of Lords in June 1785 that Boswell sent him a grateful note.   This he followed by presenting a copy of the *Hebrides* to Thurlow, who acknowledged it politely.   Now, writing in the impersonality of the third person, he was ready to make his pitch.   It was breathtaking. Filled with "ambitious restlessness," Mr. Boswell wanted to transfer to the English bar but was afraid he could not learn enough about English law to practise successfully.   If he could be appointed King's Counsel and a Bencher of the Inner Temple, he would then be willing to retire to a judgeship on the Court of Session in Scotland.   Actually it might be embarrassing to return to Scotland just now:

> His having thwarted Mr. Dundas in his job[1] of diminishing the number of the Lords of Session has drawn upon him the displeasure of that provincial despot, and his having had candour enough to speak without prejudice of Scotland in his tour with Dr. Johnson has given very general offence to an irritable people.

If Lord Thurlow would honour him with his attention and advice, "it would animate him to pursue with resolution whatever plan his Lordship may be pleased to point out.   He is miserable without stated occupation."   Or perhaps he *should* make a trial of the English bar?   He would be leaving for Edinburgh in four days to pass the holidays with his family—implying the favour of an early answer.

Boswell had used this approach with great success in the past.   Again and again, older men of unusual ability, even genius, had responded to ingenuous appeal.   Rousseau had been willing to advise the youthful traveller, and Johnson to exert continuing authority.   But circumstances now were entirely different.   Of some 350 English barristers in 1783 only 17 held the valued honorary rank of King's Counsel; while a Bencher of the Inner Temple, usually a lawyer of many years' standing, was a member of its governing body.   And Boswell was no longer a charming youth but a man of forty-five.   Surely his argument that he deserved high promotion because he was *un*qualified must be unique.

---

[1]"Transaction in which private advantage prevails over duty or public interest" (*Concise Oxford Dictionary*, 6th ed.).

Boswell had, however, come to two decisions.   As he told Thurlow, he had made up his mind to return for a visit to Edinburgh, and that resolve immediately improved morale.   And as for the English bar, he wrote in his journal, *"My wife's inclination shall determine.   Let me remember this."*   Since Boswell shared the ordinary attitude of the time that the head of the family always made any important decision, this looks like complete abdication.   But Margaret had already decided, as he pretty well realized. She knew he would always be tormented until he tried it; she had written agreeing to live in London, and telling him not to worry if later they had to retreat to Scotland, for as "a true Montgomerie" (his description of her in the Diminishing Bill *Letter*) she could find many excuses.

Scotland turned out to be easy.   Nor did it seem such a long way from London; he would not be cutting himself off from his roots.   He enjoyed being with his wife and children again very much, though Veronica spit blood, a bad sign in a family riddled with consumption.   The Lord President praised an able Petition from the bench and invited him to dinner: "a very hearty day."   Yet, on the whole, it would not do:

> I felt with disgust the vulgar familiarity of some of my brethren, and contrasted it with the manners of my London friends.   It provoked me a little that my literary superiority seemed to have no effect here.

Still, he had to take into account Thurlow's reply, which was long, tactful, and firm:

> Your succedaneum is to be called to the bar and to the place of King's Counsel and to the Bench of the Inner Temple at once. This idea shows how much you are a stranger to the situation you think of.   The thing is impossible, morally speaking, and if done by an act of power it would . . . place you at a still greater distance from the common chance of success.
>
> If you think the parade of such a circumstance would forward your approach to the Scottish bench or grace it, I am too much afraid it would be differently received by the world, and produce a different effect.   But as I shall not be consulted on that subject, my thoughts upon the means of obtaining a judge's robe will be of little use.[1]   The road of merit you are familiar with.   If the rectitude of your sentiments and the sufficiency of your talents require any further advantage-ground, that will be gained by taking that situation at the bar and in practice which your talents entitle you to expect.

[1]Thurlow means that Dundas controlled appointments to the Court of Session.

This letter, Boswell says, "sunk me a good deal.   But my excellent wife suggested that I could not take it as a *decision*, but only as an able evasion of taking any charge of me."   Margaret seems to have missed the point, as Boswell certainly had.   Temple rubbed in doubt with the dexterity of an old friend: "It is pity you have said so much on the subject of your removal and so unguardedly."   But even he felt that Boswell would never enjoy tranquillity without making the experiment.

The decision, in fact, had been taken.   On the subject of his transfer to the English bar, Boswell was like a pillow: any argument made an immediate impact, but somehow he always resumed his original purpose.   He told Malone, "You speak philosophically when you say that I consider my movement to London much too deeply.   It *must* be now, after going so far."   At Newcastle on his return trip to London (28 January 1786), he summoned resolution in a special memorandum.   Spirit admonished Will in Boswell's early manner:

> You felt *serenely* that there is nothing wild or even difficult in making a trial of your abilities as an English barrister, and that the transition from London to Auchinleck, and connection between them, may appear quite easy and plain.   All depends upon the state of the mind, and *that* probably on the state of the blood and other corporeal circumstances.   Many Scotch people are not strange in London. . . .   Are not numberless, worthy, quiet families there?   The very *hopes* there are better than *realities* in a narrow sphere to a man of *fancy* who is not without a *moderate fortune*. Occasional clouds pass away as if they never had been, and then all the train of events and variety of ideas are valuable and pleasing.

Only the last sentence makes much concession to actuality: it is the process of living rather than attainment of the goal that matters.

Boswell's decision, confirmed by another round of friendly consultations in Scotland, seemed the most prudent possible.   He would try the English bar for an indefinite period, and if unsuccessful would retire with dignity to the judge's seat in Scotland he took virtually for granted.   Actually, it was a dishonest decision, made in bad faith, fundamentally unrealistic—Boswell tended to save his sense of reality for his biographies—but necessary and inescapable.   No matter that all his reasons were flimsy; he had reasons that reason knew nothing of: immediate enjoyment remained the driving impulse of his life no matter what he destroyed in reaching for it.   Worst of all, the move was half-hearted.   Every time he could permit himself to look clearly at the future he realized he would fail, and that awareness crippled him.   All he committed himself to was endless shilly-shallying.   The practical way to succeed in London was to make withdrawal impossible, so that he would have to exert every effort not to fail.　But Boswell didn't cast the die and pass the Tweed with unyielding resolution; he straggled across.　His father might summon him to return at any moment.

Boswell often thought of his love for London in terms of fancy vs. judgement; now that he was converting fancy into fact, he wanted to rationalize the change:

> The truth is that *imaginary* London, gilded with all the brilliancy of warm fancy as I have viewed it, and London as a scene of real business, are quite different; and as the *changes* of fanciful sensation are very painful, it is more comfortable to have the duller sensation of reality.

In other words, permanent residence in London would even out the sharp changes of mood which shifting between London and Scotland had always occasioned.　But the fancy-judgement polarity was superficial and misleading.　For Boswell, proper judgement consisted in following his fancy (as Dempster told him), because he could only do very well what he very much wanted to do.

He was called to the bar at the Inner Temple on 9 February 1786, and on the thirteenth took the necessary oaths in the Court of King's Bench. With two other new barristers, he gave an inaugural dinner that afternoon in the Inner Temple Hall.　His fellow hosts had one or two friends apiece (including Spencer Perceval, later Prime Minister), while Boswell, who had taken charge of the affair, invited ten guests: Daines Barrington (Bencher and antiquarian), Reynolds, Wilkes, Malone, Courtenay, young Strange (son of the noted Scots engraver), Brocklesby, Dilly, Baldwin, and T.D. It was splendid:

> a course of fish; a course of ham, fowls, and greens; a course of roast beef and apple pies; a dessert of cheese and fruit; madeira, port, and as good claret as ever was drank.

The Hall lustre was lighted for the first time in thirty years.　All told, the affair cost £18.

Unfortunately his move to London was immediately dampened by a run-in with Burke.　Boswell had touched on some "calumny" against Burke in order (he later said) to be enabled to refute it.　Burke, still sore from the Boswell-Malone anatomy of his wit in the *Hebrides*, suspected that Boswell intended to rush into print about it, and blew up.　"We parted on sad terms," Boswell wrote.　"I was very uneasy. . . .　Wrote to Burke.　This affair was happily settled in letters between us.　I need not give the detail."

He never does specify the calumny, and since Burke was libelled in the press as everything from a Jesuit to a sodomite, the range of possibility is too wide to permit a plausible guess.   Burke admitted that he had reacted too warmly, but advised Boswell not to give slander publicity by refuting it.   "Depend upon it," Boswell replied.   "I shall profit by your counsel."

And leopards change their spots.   Boswell's stock-in-trade was to repeat, if not calumny, at least what people said about each other.   This side of his character deserves further discussion.   Though he announced he was exceedingly unwilling to be provoked to anger, Boswell had discovered other modes of aggressiveness.   He admitted early to "a most particular art of nettling people without seeming to intend it," though he claimed he seldom made use of it.   When irritable the hypochondriac, he wrote, is "rather pleased with seeing the slighter sort of uneasiness which is produced by raillery."   But tale-bearing was his "usual fault," his major "bad habit." It was the indirect counterpart of that direct confrontation he delighted in.   As C. B. Tinker said, Boswell loved friction.

Another lure had fetched Boswell southwards, one that he had not discussed with Margaret.   He makes no mention of having seen Mrs. Rudd during the period of crisis before Christmas, but now he hastened to her, drawn by her "talents, address, and irresistible power of fascination."   She was pleased to see him so well, and appointed a meeting the next day. Boswell summarized that occasion in one word, "Wonderful."   He called on her the following day "gratefully," and thereafter was as assiduous in visiting her as he was in his attendance at the law courts.

He also made two efforts to catch what he felt about her:

Tasting wondrous tree of old made us know the difference between good and evil.   Tasting thee, my Margaret,[1] the reverse, for it confounds it, and all thy arts and all thy evil is lost in the blaze of thy charms.   Thus I at first exclaimed—till through time and on a calm and steady view I found that it was true.   My eyes were opened and that all the bad imputed to thee was false, and I now saw thee good, generous, etc. etc.

If the Roman Emperor who had exhausted delight offered a reward for the inventor of a new pleasure, how much do I owe to thee, who hast made the greatest pleasure of human life new to me.   I used to look on love with feverish joy or childish fondness. All madness or folly, though delight.   Thou hast shown me it rational, pure from evil.   How keen the fire that thus clears the dross from the most precious ore.

[1]Margaret Caroline Rudd.

Boswell never complains that his wife is sexually cold—for that matter he never makes such a complaint about any woman—and though she was less interested in sex than he was, he always reports enjoyment or pleasure. But Mrs. Rudd was an accomplished courtesan who knew all the sources of excitement, and Boswell, with his unconstrained interest in sex, could fully appreciate her.   She was the sensual high point of his life.

Still, Mrs. Rudd did not deflect him from his new career.   Boswell had started to promote his transfer to the English bar with a small publicity campaign the previous autumn: newspaper items linking him with Jack Lee, whom he regarded as his principal supporter in his new situation. But Dilly, his conduit to the newspapers, had advised him sharply to desist; he was only opening himself to ridicule.   As well as encouragement—"your parts and learning are at least equal to many that have in any time been very successful in our profession"—Lee offered urgent advice: prudence, labour, diligence, avoidance of attempts to figure in the higher ranks of life.   More concretely, he wondered at Boswell's eagerness to affront the Scots in general and Dundas in particular in his Diminishing Bill *Letter*, and after a quick look at the *Hebrides* he wrote,

> I can hardly conceive of anything more injurious to a man's success
> as a lawyer than that it should be thought that he has such a
> copiousness of communication that he must reveal everything he
> knows.

Boswell could have replied honestly that he drew a careful line between professional confidences and matters he communicated to friends and the public, but this distinction was likely to be lost on prospective clients.

And so on to the bar in a shower of newspaper squibs.   Boswell's preparation consisted in a glance or two at Blackstone, and the purchase of a notebook in which to record cases in the law courts, which were held mainly in Westminster Hall, Guildhall, and on circuit.   Once, making notes on cases had been standard procedure for the aspirant but the technicalities of pleading had become so intricate and were so rigorously adhered to— the most trivial mistake was enough to nonsuit—that most new lawyers now put in several years' work in the office of a special pleader before even bothering to appear in the courts, where nothing useful could be learned, according to a contemporary writer on legal education, "until some knowl- edge of the *general principles* of law, as well as of the *practice*, be first ac- quired."   Still, this writer (Thomas Ruggles) continued,

> Many young men may be daily seen in the jury and crier's boxes
> in the King's Bench, armed at all points for note-taking, working

hour after hour in vain; many of the notes there taken being inanity itself; a kind of *crambe recocta*,[1] which no art can make palatable or skill methodize into law or common sense.

The notebook Boswell kept for the next year and a half might have been lying open before Ruggles as he wrote these words.   But Boswell started on his new career—in his words—with a firm and serene mind and a bright imagination.

His journal tells the story better than any paraphrase:

14 FEBRUARY.   Attended Lord Mansfield's sittings at *nisi prius* in Westminster Hall, and was both entertained and instructed.
16 FEBRUARY.   Attended Lord Mansfield's sittings with great relish.
17 FEBRUARY.   Attended the sittings with great relish.
18 FEBRUARY.   Attended the sittings with relish.
20 FEBRUARY.   Attended the sittings.
21 FEBRUARY.   Attended the sittings.
22 FEBRUARY.   Attended sittings.
23 FEBRUARY.   Attended the sittings.
3 MARCH.   I did not attend the sittings at Guildhall after this Hilary term.[2]   I am sorry I did not, as I should have learnt a good deal, and as I should have had at least one brief, as Mr. McDougal, clerk to Mr. Irving, informed me; for an acquaintance of his wanted to employ me and did not know where I was to be found.   The truth is there is very little room for counsel at Guildhall, and besides I was as yet at a very great distance while in Portman Square.[3]   But I might have taken my quarters at Dilly's.   I shall henceforth attend at Guildhall.

Boswell had already been handed his first brief (fee, two guineas), a case of perjury for which he had been suggested by the plaintiff, an Edinburgh "writer," who had employed him there.   "I was very happy," he wrote, "to get business the second week I was at the bar, when many able men stand for years unemployed.   I had a boyish fondness for my first brief and fee, and put up the guineas as *medals*."   He was junior counsel to Erskine, and led off with a little natural trepidation but did well.   The case was lost instantly because the attorney who instructed them had neglected to have the previous trial record properly authenticated.   Erskine was friendly and tactful, saying that he had taken the liberty to direct Boswell so "that no puppy might have it to say you did not do it as it ought

[1]Hashed-up repetition.
[2]Hilary was one of the year's four very brief terms, but further sessions were held after the terms were concluded.
[3]Where Boswell was still living with Paoli.

to be done." And he underlined what Boswell had just witnessed: "To know the forms is the difficulty of our profession."

Boswell also took the precaution of calling on Thurlow to explain why, despite the clear implication of Thurlow's letter, he was now to be found at Westminster Hall. It was a matter of "strong impulse," Boswell said, and Thurlow blandly agreed that this was an irresistible plea. He was more interested in discussing the *Hebrides*; he had read every word of it, he said,

> and yet one cannot tell how. Why should one wish to go on and read how Dr. Johnson went from one place to another? Can you give a rule for writing in that manner? Longinus could not.

Nor could Aristotle. Thurlow raised a central question about Boswell's narrative powers. Boswell was so elevated by this gracious reception that he called on Margaret Caroline, who was already in bed and furious at the lateness of the hour. They had their first quarrel.

Private reactions to the *Hebrides* were accumulating. Two points predictably bothered the book's readers. The first was Boswell's "foible," as Wilkes called it, about pride of family. Even Temple, who praised the book handsomely, could not resist one thrust: "I never knew before that you were allied to the Royal Family. No wonder you write to your cousin George." The second, already discussed, was Boswell's freedom in his treatment of the living. Sir William Forbes tempered his compliments with bankerly caution: "I trust with some confidence that you will pay a particular attention in your life of Dr. Johnson to insert nothing that can give either pain or offence to any mortal." Forbes's confidence was misplaced. Boswell firmly repelled any concessions not only to concealment, but to revision:

> People must be satisfied to appear as they really did. Should they be allowed to improve and enlarge their conversations upon afterthought, the labour would be endless and the book not authentic.

Those most alarmed, naturally, were the relations of Boswell's prospective biographical subjects. George Drummond, Lord Kames's son, for one, tempered his praise for the *Hebrides* with his fear that his father would suffer from Boswell's frankness. "A thousand pages of encomium," he wrote, "would not compensate for a single line that had a tendency to *derogate from the dignity* of [my] father's character," and he demanded a power of veto over any biography Boswell produced. Since a dignified

Kames was beyond biographical imagination, Boswell dropped the project as hopeless.

Otherwise, Joseph Cooper Walker's reaction was typical, if extreme: the *Hebrides* is "exquisitely entertaining.   I have hardly ate, drank, or slept since I got it."   Reynolds liked it so much that he quickly read it twice and, in offering to send his copy to the Duke of Rutland, Lord Lieutenant of Ireland, wrote:

> Boswell has drawn [Johnson's] character in a very masterly man-
> ner.   The Bishop of Killaloe, who knew Johnson very well, I think
> will subscribe to the justness and truth of the drawing.

Sir Egerton Brydges recalled late in life, "I never took up many books with more intense curiosity than Boswell's *Journal* . . . on the day of its publication."   Admiration could become excessive; Boswell dismissed one letter as "a rhapsody from some anonymous fool on my *Journal*."   Best of all, Boswell heard that the King and Queen liked his book.   Actually, as Fanny Burney reports her, the Queen sounded bemused by the prospect of the *Life of Johnson*.   Boswell, she said, "is so extraordinary a man that perhaps he will devise something extraordinary."

In view of her later passage at arms with Boswell about Johnson, Anna Seward's responses to the *Hebrides* deserve a paragraph to themselves.   She was reading it aloud to three friends: "Good God! how does your book grapple our attention as we eagerly travel through its pages!"   But Miss Seward was perhaps unique in admiring Boswell far more than her towns-man, about whom she had deeply mixed feelings.   When several months later she reported again, she made her attitude emphatic: Johnson

> was the most extraordinary composition of great and absurd, of
> philanthropy and malignance, of luminous intellectual light and
> palpable darkness that were ever blended in the human breast.

She had written about the *Hebrides* to her friends

> in the warmest spirit of encomium upon the characteristic strength,
> gay benevolence, scenic graces, and biographic fidelity, which adorn
> its pages; observing how valuable a counterpart they form to Doc-
> tor Johnson's own *Tour*.   In one we discern through a medium
> of solemn and sublime eloquence in what light the august wan-
> derer beheld Scotland, her nobles and her professors, her isles
> and her chieftains.
>
>   In the other we perceive in what light the growling philoso-
> pher must have appeared to the inhabitants of those northern
> regions.

Boswell was highly flattered.

Public controversy over the work, from serious argument to light epi-gram, was everywhere.   Boswell had always wanted to be a public figure, and now he had achieved at least notoriety.   In the *Hebrides*, he had pro-vided Johnson's text on literary attack with a commentary: "Fame," Johnson said,

> "is a shuttlecock.   If it be struck only at one end of the room, it will soon fall to the ground.   To keep it up, it must be struck at both ends."   Often have I reflected on this since; and instead of being angry at many of those who have written against me, have smiled to think that they were unintentionally subservient to my fame by using a battledore to make me *virum volitare per ora*.[1]

The paper wars were on, and now he was continually aloft.

Pindar, the most energetic English satirist between Churchill and By-ron, was the first opponent to wound, though his *Congratulatory Epistle*, which appeared in February 1786, now seems tame enough in its abuse: Boswell is a "charming haberdasher of small ware," who caught up scraps from Johnson's mouth and should search his privy for further remains. But in a note Wolcot asserted that Boswell was turned away from society's doors because "our Great People want the *taste* to relish Mr. Boswell's vehicles to immortality.   Though in London, poor Bozzy is in a desert." Some people, of course, were afraid that Boswell would hand them down to posterity, but his journal shows fully that he was never a social outcast. Still, this was the kind of comment that began to haunt his reputation.

Boswell was more irritated by the prose Postscript, a dialogue between Johnson and Pindar, in which Johnson is made to say, "Were I sure that James Boswell would write *my* life, I do not know whether I would not anticipate the measure by taking *his*."   A lawsuit charging libel seemed to offer possibilities.   Boswell wrote about the dialogue to Malone:

> Absurdly malignant as this really is, it *may* be believed by many people, and therefore *may* injure the success of my *Great Work*. I own I am not much afraid of this.   But if I thought that a verdict would be obtained merely to proclaim the falsehood of the fellow and punish him in the most *tender* part, his *purse*, I certainly should prosecute.   And you will consider if this would not give an op-portunity to announce the Work in the most splendid manner. Erskine would expatiate upon it as not only to be the life and conversation of the first genius, etc. etc. etc., but the history of

[1]Virgil, *Georgics*, iii. 9: "Fly victorious through the mouths of men" (trans. H. R. Fair-clough, Loeb ed.).

literature and literary men during a considerable period. . . .   Do consult with Mr. Courtenay as to this, for it appears to me a very good use might be made of such an action.

Nothing further is heard of this idea.

I I

PINDAR AND THE NEWSPAPERS were sidelights to Boswell's occupation. Virtually all barristers went on one of the six circuits held twice a year, to build up a practice that often brought cases to London.   Boswell had chosen the Northern Circuit (Yorkshire, Durham, Northumberland, Westmorland, Cumberland, and Lancashire), no doubt because of its proximity to Auchinleck.   On the day of his departure, Boswell called on Lee, who, though too old and infirm to follow the circuit himself any longer, gave advice "like a Nestor": "Attend regularly the courts, take notes, think nothing beneath you, and have as much conference with your brethren upon law as you can."   M.C.'s farewell was more touching:

> Never shall I forget the scene.   So good, so generous, was she. Elegantly dressed: satin *couleur de rose*; her hair in perfect taste— not to be discomposed.   A kind wish to give me felicity before a separation.

She inspired him to write a love lyric, *Larghan Clanbrassil*, the first since his youth.   Sandy later printed it in all innocence as *Song to an Irish Air* "by the Late James Boswell, Esq."   The first two of its four stanzas will suggest the flavour:

> O Larghan Clanbrassil, how sweet is thy sound!
> To my tender remembrance as Love's sacred ground!
> For there Marg'ret Caroline first charmed my sight,
> And filled my young heart with a flutt'ring delight.
>
> When I thought her my own, ah! too short seemed the day
> For a jaunt to Downpatrick, or a trip on the sea;[1]
> To express what I felt then, all language were vain,
> 'Twas in truth what the poets have *studied* to feign.

However, Margaret Caroline deceives, and her lover flees his dear native shore, though continuing to remember her in enchanted moments: an ending which points up the disparity between literature and life.

Lawyers on the circuit travelled as a pack, with the junior counsel,

[1]Pronounced in eighteenth-century fashion, as "say."

Boswell on this occasion, deputed to arrange for their mess, keep track of bills and records, etc.   He took to his duties with too much convivial enthusiasm, and picked up a case of his old complaint.   For a while it worried him seriously and Malone, his confidant, urged him to return to London without delay.   But he was taking notes assiduously and enjoying himself too much to cut the circuit short, and it turned out that his illness, as he told Malone, was by "no means such as I had just reason to apprehend . . . in this *last* excursion into the *wilds* of Venus."   The best excuse he could think of was, "I am no hypocrite though sadly inconsistent."   ("Inconsistency" was a Boswellian code word for deviation from precept.)   He made his last extended entry for the circuit in his journal for 5 April 1786 at Lancaster:

> Dined at the mess moderately.   Evening went to the assembly, but wisely did not dance.   Played at whist and drank tea with the ladies, and was quite gay.   Here now did I *perfectly* and *clearly* realize my *ideas* of being a counsel on the Northern Circuit, and being an easy gentleman with Lancashire ladies, with no gloom, no embarrassment.   *How* I was so well I know not.   A constancy of this *may* be the existence of some.

The next day's entry consists of one sentence: "Last night a feigned brief had been left at my lodgings."   And he makes no further comment. But the story is famous from another source.   The Northern Circuit entertained itself with primitive jokes—it even held a Grand Court of High Jinks in various towns—and a feigned brief was irresistible, Jack Lee having been handed one at York some years earlier.   The ringleader in the present proceedings was John Scott, K.C., a very able lawyer, in his later incarnation as Lord Eldon well remembered as the most reactionary of Lord Chancellors:

> Next came Fraud, and he had on
> Like Eldon, an ermined gown.
> His big tears, for he wept well,
> Turned to millstones as they fell.

In old age, Eldon buffed up some anecdotes for his grandson, and his story ran that Boswell having been found one evening dead drunk on the street, his colleagues clubbed together a guinea for him and half a crown for his clerk, and sent him a brief the next morning with instructions to move for a writ of *Quare adhaesit pavimento*: "Wherefore it (or he) adhered to the pavement."   Eldon goes on:

> Boswell sent all round the town to attorneys for books that might enable him to distinguish himself, but in vain.   He moved, how-

ever, for the writ, making the best use he could of the observations in the brief.   The judge was perfectly astonished and the audience amazed.   The judge said, "I never heard of such a writ; what can it be that adheres *pavimento*?   Are any of you gentlemen at the bar able to explain this?"   The bar laughed.   At last one of them said, "My Lord, Mr. Boswell last night *adhaesit pavimento*.   There was no moving him for some time.   At last he was carried to bed, and he has been dreaming about himself and the pavement."

Like many of Eldon's anecdotes, this one amused more than it convinced when it got abroad in Twiss's *Life of Eldon* (1844).   Still, it was one more mark against Boswell.   The real story did not emerge until 1953 when Lt.-Col. Ralph H. Isham gave the missing brief to the Yale Boswell collection.   The brief states that a "poor, industrious" defendant named John Timperley, who informed on smugglers, was being sued by a "noted smuggler," David Duffus:

> Upon the 14th of April last as the defendant was attending the Custom House upon the quay at Liverpool, the prosecutor called him a "ragged-arse dog" and told him he would give him a douse on the chops, upon which the defendant, irritated by this foul language, threw a dead cat in prosecutor's face, which is the whole foundation of the present malicious prosecution.

Boswell was instructed to get the case dismissed, "and do not forget to plead hard for costs."   Nothing is said of anyone adhering to a pavement, but Boswell endorsed the brief, "a circuit joke by which I was for some time deceived."   With his high notions of dignity, Boswell would not have enjoyed being made a fool of, but apparently he held no ill will; he later called Scott "as shrewd and candid a counsel as [there is] in Westminster Hall."   The feigned brief did, however, add insult to injury, since Boswell had received only two briefs during this excursion.   This was not at all surprising; well-known or local attorneys got almost all of the business, and barristers of several years' standing could go briefless round the circuit.

Boswell's spirits on the Northern Circuit were sustained by novelty and the publication of Mrs. Piozzi's *Anecdotes of the Late Samuel Johnson*.   Though she was still happily honeymooning in Italy, Mrs. Piozzi was eager to get her view of Johnson before the public.   She had been the most important person in his life during his last twenty years; inevitably she would be writ large in the forthcoming biographies, and her enemies would not be kind. Many of her papers were still in England but she had her commonplace-book, "Thraliana," with her in which she had recorded many Johnsonian sayings and stories.   These she rewrote to better effect to supply somewhat more than half of the *Anecdotes*; the rest came from a memory not re-markable for precision and shaped by self-interest.   ("Memory," as André Maurois said, "is a great artist.")   Some London friends—notably Sir Lucas Pepys, Samuel Lysons, and Michael Lort—were instructed to see the book through the press.

Mrs. Piozzi wrote easily and evocatively, and her book provides some sharp vignettes of Johnson, though a collection of anecdotes is necessarily disconnected and full of exaggerated point.   Still, the public was avid for the new-fashioned biography that Boswell had popularized in the *Hebrides*, and the first edition of the *Anecdotes* sold out on the day of publication, to be rapidly followed by several more.   Apart from those who condemned it, as they had Boswell's book, for revealing the blemishes as well as the virtues of its subject, the major reason for the uneasy impression the book still leaves was defined by Horace Walpole: "Her panegyric is loud in praise of her hero—and almost every fact she relates disgraces him."   Mrs. Piozzi's two aims were, in fact, cross purposes: to exhibit Johnson as a great figure, with whom she had long lived in intimacy; and to demonstrate that she was perfectly justified, in spite of this long intimacy, in deserting a lonely, sick old man in order, as everyone knew, to contract a mismatch with Piozzi: a foreigner, a fiddler, and a Catholic.   (Mrs. Vesey, a chief of the blue-stocking coterie, described him as "very black, low, and mean.")

Mrs. Piozzi was by no means insincere in her contradictions.   Her letters to and comments about Johnson during their long, close relationship show an easy familiarity deepening over the years to great affection and respect.   Even after Thrale's death—in her account the watershed in the friendship—she wrote to Johnson (21 October 1781): "Love nobody better than your truly faithful and obliged servant."   Johnson had never loved anyone as he loved her.   But as his health worsened he made more and more demands on her attention, just when her feelings had turned towards Piozzi.   Her responsibility for Johnson was as much an impediment to a second marriage as her daughters' disdain for her suitor.   If Johnson had supported her once she made her decision to marry Piozzi, the world could have done little but murmur.   But he had rejected her implicit appeal; and now, having made the break with society, as she thought back over the past she realized that Johnson had often been harsh, difficult, and selfish.   Guilt overlaid with resentment saturated the *Anecdotes*.

But Boswell had specific grounds for complaint.   In January 1785 the *St. James's Chronicle* had published two letters harshly criticizing Mrs. Piozzi and both her husbands, while touting Boswell as the ideal person to write Johnson's life.   Much pleased, Boswell inquired a couple of weeks later about the identity of his admirer, in a letter to the same newspaper. Already upset by the remark in the *Hebrides* that she could not get through Mrs. Montagu's *Essay on Shakespeare*, Mrs. Piozzi immediately intuited that Boswell's inquiry was a subterfuge to cover his authorship of the anonymous letters. So she included in her *Anecdotes* a vigorous paragraph condemning his breach of her frequent hospitality, which ended by comparing him to Aaron the Moor, the Iago-like villain of Shakespeare's *Titus Andronicus*. Fortunately, Lysons began to worry about the authorship of the anonymous letters, and investigation having revealed that in fact their author was George Steevens, known as "the asp" for his delight in slandering his literary friends in print, Lysons excised the offending paragraph in proof.

Otherwise, Mrs. Piozzi's text noticed Boswell just once by name, though he figures transparently, unflatteringly (and inaccurately) as the Mr. B— who defended the adage *in vino veritas*. Also there was mention of an anonymous someone who practised

> a trick . . . of sitting steadily down at the other end of the room to write at the moment what should be said in company, either *by* Dr. Johnson or *to* him.

Mrs. Piozzi then comments:

> There is something so ill-bred and so inclining to treachery in this conduct, that were it commonly adopted all confidence would soon be exiled from society, and a conversation assembly-room would become tremendous as a court of justice.

This rebuke loses some of its force when Mrs. Piozzi, a few lines later, naïvely reveals the existence of her commonplace-book, with its happy store of Johnsoniana. She was as guilty as Boswell of recording and publishing private conversation, though not of having taken it down at the moment or in public. Had she recorded conversations "recently," Boswell was to retort in the *Life of Johnson*, "they probably would have been less erroneous; and we should have been relieved from those disagreeable doubts of their authenticity with which we must now peruse them."

One other intervention by Mrs. Piozzi's friends had a most unhappy consequence. Hearing that Mrs. Montagu had been mortified by her reputed reaction to the *Essay on Shakespeare*, Mrs. Piozzi protested to all and sundry, including the author herself, that her position had been entirely misrepresented, though she could never bring herself to state explicitly that she had read the book through. Instead of leaving well enough alone, Pepys and the others decided to concoct a Postscript to the *Anecdotes* from phrases in one of her letters to him, which, after quoting Boswell, states,

> I do not delay a moment to declare that ... I have always com-
> mended [the *Essay*] myself, and heard it commended by everyone
> else; and few things would give me more concern than to be
> thought incapable of tasting, or unwilling to testify my opinion of
> its excellence.

Boswell and Mrs. Piozzi were becoming embroiled in an unnecessary battle.

Apart from his tactless statement about the Montagu *Essay*, Boswell
had made few references to Mrs. Thrale in the *Hebrides*, but they were all
pleasant ones which made it clear how significant a part she played in
Johnson's life. As late as 1782 he told her, "I have invariably thought of
you with admiration and gratitude." Now Boswell was angry. He wrote
to Malone that the passage about the anonymous someone who took notes
in company

> is *undoubtedly* levelled at me; for it describes what the jade has
> often seen me do—but with Dr. Johnson's *approbation*; for he at
> all times was flattered by my preserving what fell from his mind
> when shaken by conversation, so there was nothing *like* treachery.
> I must have the patience of *Job* to bear the book of *Esther*. But
> I shall trim her *recitativo* and all her *airs*.

Since Boswell here seems to be admitting that he took down conversation in company, which the knowledgeable have long denied, narrative
must yield briefly to explanation. Boswell further replied to Mrs. Piozzi
in the *Life* by defending

> that anxious desire of authenticity which prompts a person who
> is to record conversations to write them down *at the moment*. Un-
> questionably, if they are to be recorded at all, the sooner it is done
> the better.

What Boswell actually did was to scribble condensed notes—a few
words—his "portable soup" (or contemporary equivalent of our beef-broth
cube): "a hint, such as this," he says, "brings to my mind all that passed,
though it would be barren to anybody but myself." "I find," he remarks
elsewhere, "that if I neglect to make memorandums at the time, I cannot
bring up my journal with any accuracy." In writing up the end of the
Hebridean journal, where he had only the briefest notes to go on, he
admitted to himself:

> My journal cannot have the same freshness and fullness when
> written now as when written recently after the scenes recorded.
> But I hope I shall preserve some valuable remains or fragments.

But Boswell refers to jotting down a few words and in many, if not most,
situations even this would have been impossible to do. As Geoffrey Scott

pointed out, Boswell would hardly have interrupted himself to take notes, but he seldom records conversations where he is not a participant.

That Boswell recorded conversation was well known, but most people regarded this habit as a fairly common and harmless eccentricity, at least until the publication of the *Hebrides*. It never occurred to Boswell to deny that he recorded conversations *in company*, because the charge was so preposterous. To recall some earlier points: when he boasted to Johnson (10 April 1778) about a method of abridging words which enabled him later to set down conversations completely, Johnson immediately challenged him by reading "slowly and distinctly a part of Robertson's *History of America*," which Boswell could record only "very imperfectly." It is obvious (to cite Geoffrey Scott) that if Johnson knew Boswell had recorded his conversation on the spot—and after fifteen years' acquaintance he could hardly have been unaware of it—he would have had no reason to challenge Boswell to this test. Then further, when Garrick protested that Boswell either should drink or submit to being searched for his "book," Boswell commented irritably in his journal, "nonsense, as if I had book and wrote in company, and could not carry in my *head*."

Yet Boswell was anxious to give himself a clue as quickly as possible. On one occasion, Johnson discussed the topic of conversation itself so brilliantly that, Boswell says in the *Life*,

> I was fixed in admiration, and said to Mrs. Thrale, "O for short-hand to take this down!" "You'll carry it all in your head," said she; "a long head is as good as shorthand."

At this point Boswell continues in his journal, though not in the *Life*:

> I have the substance, but the felicity of expression, the flavour, is not fully preserved unless taken instantly.

"Instantly" does not mean on the spot, but before his vivid sense of the scene had time to fade. (Perhaps, however, this is one of the occasions on which Mrs. Thrale observed him making a note.)

It was exactness of phrasing, "felicity of expression," that Boswell was most anxious to preserve or recover, and which sometimes eluded him. But an example from the *Life* shows how close he could come in his mind to re-creating it. Boswell had quoted Johnson as saying that Burke's "vigour of mind is incessant," but when he found his original note he corrected the phrase to "stream of mind is perpetual."

Still, if Boswell's recording of Robertson's *History* was very imperfect, how can we believe in the authenticity of his Johnsonian conversations?

Again it is helpful to recall that, as Johnson's test makes clear, Boswell was not a stenographer. He could *not* take down conversation, sentence after sentence, verbatim. What he could do was to remember and record the highlights of a conversation. Many people can bring back in great detail a crucial scene, an unusual event, a trip to a strange place; and occasionally someone displays a memory for daily occurrences over a long period. Boswell, as he himself said, "had naturally an excellent memory, and that memory became still better through cultivation." He had trained himself thoroughly in his journal, from at least the age of twenty-one, to preserve long stretches of conversation, ordinarily—to repeat—by remembering key phrases, sometimes with the help of a cursory note. He combined this general power of recollection with intelligence and the ability to select matter of general interest. As Brydges, his contemporary, remarked, Boswell was notable not only for an extraordinary memory but for "quickness of apprehension, for no one can remember what he does not understand."

Given a clue, Boswell seems to have been able to summon up a scene in sharp detail long after it had occurred. Others have the same power of memory for other kinds of material; Sir Walter Scott absorbed certain works into his memory as he read them. Perhaps in Boswell's case the process resembled the way in which some people recall a much-loved poem: lines come back one after another, and the phrasing sorts itself out.

Once in a while the accuracy of Boswell's memory can still be demonstrated from external sources, but there are two convincing pieces of contemporary evidence for its correctness. One has already been mentioned, the report of Johnson himself, who read Boswell's journal throughout the Hebridean tour and called it "a very exact picture of a portion of his life." The second is that none of their contemporaries, except those with an axe to grind, ever disputed the authenticity of the conversations Boswell reports. Even Percy, who was furious with Boswell for recording the Pennantian controversy and other humiliating stories in the *Life*, never disputed the correctness of Boswell's account. On the contrary, the repeated general complaint was that he had stuck embarrassingly close to the truth.

A detached acquaintance of Johnson's, William Weller Pepys, is an excellent witness to the impression Boswell's account made on those who knew both men. Pepys wrote to Hannah More (24 October 1785) that the *Hebrides* is

> a most faithful picture of [Johnson], so faithful that I think anybody who has got a clear idea of his person and manner may know

as much of him from that book as by having been acquainted with him (in the usual way) for three years.

Boswell could not take issue with Mrs. Piozzi on his having made notes in company, no matter how unfair her account of his practice. But her *Anecdotes* showed, in his opinion, that she was "a little, artful, impudent, malignant devil," a venomous insect that meant to bite him "as much as she can that she may curry favour with Mrs. Montagu." The Postscript had left her hopelessly vulnerable, especially when he remembered as he told Malone—"O brave we!"—that she had read much of his Hebridean journal shortly after it had been written, and never claimed that her opinion of Mrs. Montagu's *Essay* was misrepresented. What would have added zest to his rebuttal was the report that Mrs. Piozzi and Mrs. Montagu had gone through a warm epistolary reconciliation. If he had known the details he would have been even more pleased. Mrs. Montagu generously acquitted him of

> any wilful falsehood, yet poor man! he is so often in that condition in which men are said to see double, the hearing in the same circumstances may probably be no less disordered.

Boswell's response, printed in several newspapers and magazines in April 1786, was deadly: Johnson, not he, had said Mrs. Thrale couldn't get through the *Essay*; Mrs. Piozzi's Postscript did not deny that fact; Johnson on several occasions had made it clear he thought little of the *Essay* and did not correct Boswell's journal on this point when he read it; and, finally, Mrs. Thrale had read the journal herself without objection. Originally Boswell had omitted her name out of delicacy, but a friend persuaded him that he had

> no right to deprive Mrs. Thrale of the high honour which Dr. Johnson had done her, by stating her opinion along with that of Mr. Beauclerk, as coinciding with and, as it were, sanctioning his own.

Convinced, Boswell had restored her name.

Nothing remained to be said, but Boswell couldn't let the subject go. He submitted some *Piozzian Rhymes*, under the signature, "Old Salusbury Briar," to the *Public Advertiser*, in which he ridiculed the *Anecdotes*, Mrs. Piozzi's flattery of Mrs. Montagu, and her selfish marketing of Johnson for profit—a charge to which he was equally open. The next day he treated the same readers to a prose item:

Mr. Boswell's retort courteous to the *stiletto* postscript has played the very devil in the assembly of *stockings*, whose *colour* shall be nameless. It has run among the learned legs flaming and *hissing* like a well-charged *cracker*. But, as is foretold in the celebrated motto, "Altius ibunt,"[1] the sparks have flown up and singed *hairs less in sight* of several *grey* cats. Goody Galimatias[2] herself may well say, "I wish that designing woman had let me alone."

But perhaps Mrs. Montagu should have been pleased by the uproar; by public demand her *Essay* went into another edition.

This was no private quarrel. The merits of the rival biographers so enlivened London that, according to Hannah More, who disliked them both, the topic spoiled conversation. Soame Jenyns, whose *Origin of Evil* Johnson had trampled on years before in one of his most celebrated reviews, retaliated with an *Epitaph* on him, which ended:

> Boswell and Thrale, retailers of his wit,
> Will tell you how he wrote, and talked, and coughed, and spit.

Boswell's enthusiasm for publicity may have diminished when he read Pindar's next effort, *Bozzy and Piozzi* (published 24 April 1786), which takes the form of a mock-pastoral contest in which Boswell and Mrs. Piozzi appeal to Sir John Hawkins, whose "official" biography of Johnson was in process, to decide "which bore the palm of anecdote away" by citing stories from their works. Pindar realized that he had only to vulgarize their minutiae very slightly to get an amusing effect. So an early exploit of Boswell's turns into:

> When young ('twas rather silly, I allow),
> Much was I pleased to imitate a cow.
> One time, at Drury Lane with Doctor Blair,
> My imitations made the playhouse stare.
> So very charming was I in my *roar*,
> That both the galleries clapped and cried, "*Encore.*"
> Blessed by the general plaudit and the laugh,
> I tried to be a jackass and a calf;
> But who, alas, in *all things* can be *great*?
> In short, I met a terrible defeat:
> So vile I brayed and bellowed, I was hissed;
> Yet all who *knew* me *wondered* that I *missed*.
> Blair whispered me, "You've lost your credit now:
> Stick, Boswell, for the future to the cow."

[1] "They will attain a higher point [who strive at things the most exalted]."
[2] Mrs. Montagu, who had used this uncommon word for "meaningless talk" in her *Essay*.

Near the end of the poem, the two biographers turn on each other:

MADAME PIOZZI
Who told of Mistress Montagu the lie,
So palpable a falsehood?—Bozzy, fie.

BOZZY
Who, maddening with an anecdotic itch
Declared that Johnson called his mother *bitch*?

MADAME PIOZZI
Who, from Macdonald's rage to save his snout,
Cut twenty lines of defamation out?

Predictably Hawkins, who is also banged around a bit, orders them both to desist. Writing about the earlier Pindar poem, Temple made a comment applicable to both: Pindar is "a lying, scurrilous fellow, yet you must own he has sometimes a fair hit at you." And Temple was Boswell's intimate friend.

What has fixed Boswell's image almost ineradicably, however, is the twenty Collings-Rowlandson caricatures, which were published on 9 and 15 June 1786. They have become so conflated with the *Hebrides* in the minds of many readers that it is difficult to avoid thinking they were commissioned for it, like Tenniel's illustrations for *Alice in Wonderland*. Pindar's satires are both lively and easily forgotten, but these engravings are witty, and certain of them portray scenes in the *Hebrides* indelibly: Walking up the High Street ("I smell you in the dark"); The Dance on Dun-Caan; Sailing among the Hebrides; the Contest at Auchinleck. Still, they are caricatures; they distort; in order to be amusing they naturally emphasize the moments when Johnson and, much more often, Boswell can be made to look absurd. They catch the vivacity of Boswell's book and his own bounce and swagger, but necessarily ignore his great talents for discriminating individuals through characteristic speech and for presenting them as fully human. And, as already discussed, Revising for the Second Edition, which shows Macdonald pointing with his stick at the manuscript while Boswell begs for mercy, is libellous. But the Collings-Rowlandson caricatures will always shadow Boswell, just as Pope will never entirely escape his reputation as the wicked wasp of Twickenham.

I I I

WHILE STILL ON the Circuit, Boswell had confessed his venereal dereliction to Margaret Caroline, and received a "spirited, romantic, and kind"

response.   Back in London he resisted seeing her until he thought himself
free from infection: it was Easter and she was most amiable.   The next
Sunday they dined at her lodgings, where Boswell "felt strangely"; with
some friends they went after dinner to visit the Magdalen Hospital for
penitent prostitutes (Courtenay having asked "pleasantly" whether Boswell
intended to leave her there).   She referred with tenderness to her sometime
lover, Daniel Perreau, whom she had helped to the gallows for forgery,
and Boswell told her she was an "affectionate creature."   "We walked to
her lodgings.   I disliked this *low* association.   Home."   Boswell saw her
no more, but he did not forget her.   Temple scolded him that summer:
"How can you think of Caroline Rudd?"   The next year, having dreamt
that she and his wife were contending for him, Boswell called on Mrs.
Rudd, but she had been put in the Fleet Prison for debt and he did not
pursue her there.

Home at this point meant, as it had for years, General Paoli's.   With
his family soon to join him, Boswell rented a dark, old-fashioned, and, as
it turned out, rat-infested house on Great Queen Street, near to the Inns
of Court, and he moved into it on 16 May 1786.   Simultaneously, Margaret
shipped some furniture to London by sea, and auctioned off the rest of
their Edinburgh belongings.   She and the children moved for good from
the flat in James's Court to Auchinleck, where they waited for word on the
move to London.   But Boswell was uncertain.   The mental excitement
that made him happy slowed until he came to rest.   In his new solitude,
his situation lay plain before him.   He wrote to Margaret (18 May 1786):

> I see numbers of barristers, who I really believe are much better
> qualified for the profession than I am, languishing from want of
> employment.   How then can I reasonably hope to be more suc-
> cessful than they?   The encouraging speeches made me by many
> people, I suspect, were made merely to please me, or without any
> serious consideration.   I indeed see the necessary application to
> be much more difficult than I imagined, yet on the other hand
> my long-indulged notion that I might rise to wealth and honour
> at the *English bar* is not yet quite subdued; and it may be advisable
> to make a farther trial to get myself thoroughly satisfied so as
> never again to be disturbed by it, should I not succeed. . . .
>   At this moment it seems to me a curse that I ever saw London,
> since it has occasioned so much vexation to my family, and may
> estrange us from our own fine Place. . . .   Oh, my dearest, most
> valuable friend, counsel me!

His depression grew worse.   Serjeant Bolton, a distinguished lawyer,
advised him to attend a special pleader as a sign that he was in earnest

about business, but Boswell couldn't face the drudgery.   All May he hung about, doing nothing.   Margaret was ill again, and he was on the rack with guilt until she grew better.   In June he was supposedly attending the King's Bench, but he took any excuse to absent himself.   Malone and Courtenay tried to keep up his spirits, and Paoli was as hospitable as ever; they were his steady comforts.   Sir William and Lady Forbes came on a visit, and Lady Forbes accused him of his connection with Mrs. Rudd, which he assured her "did not exist," i.e., no longer existed; he persuaded Forbes "to contradict the ill-natured report."   (It is hard to find what was ill-natured about it, since he had publicized the liaison so widely himself.) Margaret got Mrs. Stuart to call on him; if she reported him "dreary in solitude," Margaret intended to come to London immediately at all risks. Boswell and Mrs. Stuart agreed that they would leave it to Margaret to do whatever was most agreeable to her.

And he wavered and wavered.   He would return to Auchinleck since "all my English bar scheme," he wrote, "was chiefly with a view to how it would *tell* in my 'Life' in the *Biographia*." [1]   Malone told him not to be uneasy; no one cared whether he was at the English bar or Scotch bar or any bar at all, and his encouragement triggered one of those memorandums in which Boswell tried to fix his momentary resolutions:

> Remember how well Mr. Malone made you.   You saw that London and Auchinleck may be *united*.   If you go there every year, the distance will be nothing.   Your *records* and *memorandums* of the Inner Temple will be in the Family archives, and you *may* have a fortunate display and get a brilliant fortune.   Be firm, then, and see what time will produce.   If you sink, you will be in worse misery.   But be habitually sober and *retenu*.

He was still giving himself the same admonitions he had given himself at twenty-one.

Then a letter from Margaret, who zigged when he zagged.   Evidently, when faced with the actual prospect of removal, her courage faltered.   She told him he was very selfish to ignore her uneasiness about transplanting the family and deserting Auchinleck, and he agreed with his "Dearest Life" (as he always begins his letters of his later years to her) that he should abandon the English bar.   But how to do it?   A winter of London would not hurt her, and he would have made a fair trial of his chances at Westminster Hall.   Besides, there was the *Life of Johnson*, which Malone told him he could write only in London.   Yet he felt he couldn't settle to it in

[1]The *Biographia Britannica*, the chief biographical dictionary of the time.

London, where he was used to "agitation." And he loved and missed his wife.

On the same day (3 July 1786) that he wrote this letter, he gave a bachelor's dinner-party in his half-furnished house: Courtenay, Malone, Ward, Reynolds, Wilkes, and Forbes:

> A good plain dinner: a turbot, roast beef, beans and bacon and other vegetables, and a cherry and currant tart; claret, port, sherry, cider, porter, small beer. I worked myself into tolerable spirits. But there was an inward gloom from the thought that I was to give up London. But, alas! is not my *station* at Auchinleck? We had an excellent day. Courtenay, Malone, and Sir W. Forbes stayed till past twelve.

He hit bottom the next day. The forces on him were exerting equal pressure, and he was unconscious of his own will. So restless that he could not remain in the King's Bench, he walked beyond Cornhill, where he had tea and buttered toast in a coffee-house.

> When I got into the streets again I was so depressed that the tears run down my cheeks. I thought of my dear wife and children with tender affection. I upbraided myself for being so long absent from them. I upbraided myself for neglecting Auchinleck.

He stopped to see a Scottish client (he had no English ones), and couldn't help talking to *him* about abandoning the English bar. He then called on William Scott (like his brother John, a distinguished lawyer):

> We talked seriously of my attempt in Westminster Hall. He thought I might now judge, for if I was to succeed at all it must be by a *coup de main*; and he was for my quietly returning to the Scotch bar. . . . I came to my solitary house, drearily, as to a prison. What a poor, wretched day!

Boswell was casting about everywhere. He had left his card twice at Douglas's, and had written to Mountstuart asking for a reconciliation. Neither responded. His most serious venture was to submit a long "case" to Dundas, an extraordinary document in which he goes into the most personal details of his hopes, financial situation, his "credulity" about the English bar and failure there, for the benefit of a man whom he had successfully attacked in public just a year earlier. Having injured him (the old cry, but it was from the heart), Dundas should now provide "kind assistance," "able advice," and a seat on the Court of Session. Apart from the unfortunate Diminishing Bill *Letter*, his exertions on behalf of Pitt and Dundas had been spirited and useful. It would not be judicious for Pitt (*read* or Dundas) to disregard him "and perhaps produce that sourness which is incident to human nature from the feeling of being ill used, and which therefore may be justified." Since a judge's place was not immediately available, would Dundas please find him something worth £200 or £300 a year to take to the Bench with him, and which meanwhile would help to support him in London. Would it not, in any case, be improper for him to quit Westminster Hall until he had tried his chances for a year?

Boswell was counting on the same approach he had used towards Thurlow: the warm, impulsive opening of himself to advice and assistance. In effect: this is what I am; take care of me. The *Probationary Odes for the Laureateship*, a collection of clever satiric parodies of contemporary figures, caught his general approach exactly in an "appendix" to the Diminishing Bill *Letter*, where "Boswell" says of one of the "candidates," Lord Mulgrave:

> But though *I* laugh at *him*, how handsome will it be if *he* votes against Dundas to oblige *me*. My disliking him and his family is no reason for his disliking me.

To Boswell's eloquent plea for help, Dundas made no reply.

It would be intolerably tedious to record Boswell's wretched and endless fits of irresolution if he did not draw us into his alternations of pleasure and misery until they acquire some of the familiarity and obsessiveness of our own; and if we were not aware that, unknown to his conscious self, he had already made his decision. He would never go back to the Scots bar even as a Lord of Session. If Dundas had offered him a seat—an impossibility—he would have found an excuse to decline it. In fact, his letter to Dundas, however eloquent, was not at all calculated for that purpose. Rather, it was Boswell's bill of complaint against Dundas, Pitt, himself, and Fate. Nor would he ever return permanently to Auchinleck, though Paoli told him he was past the age of ambition, and should rest happy with his wife and children. London would always be his home.

Finally he started to work on the *Life of Johnson*. For years, of course, during Johnson's lifetime Boswell had solicited information about his early years and his writings from him or their friends, and begged anecdotes and reminiscences. Soon after Johnson died, as already noted, he began to write to people like Anna Seward, Adams, and Hector for information, and he continued to make inquiries throughout 1785, though his attention naturally was concentrated on the *Hebrides* as the prelude to the much more comprehensive work. Then came the Macdonald débâcle and the transfer to the English bar. After his return from the Northern Circuit, Boswell had stayed in London for a Scottish appeal in the House of Lords on 24

April, and then went to Oxford with Malone in search of Johnsonian materials.   May, as stated, he spent wavering and worrying.   Once again Malone lifted his spirits and stiffened his resolution to stick at the English bar, in a session that ran until three in the morning.   On 5 June 1786, the journal records the first decisive step: "At home all forenoon sorting materials for Dr. Johnson's *Life*."

Boswell had started collecting his stores with no very apparent notion of what spirit would animate them.   At the beginning it was enough to gather in all the facts he could: anecdotes, sayings, letters, juvenilia, accounts of Johnson's writings, poems, and so forth.   He could decide what to make of this heap of material later.   Many of his early references to the *Life* stress that it was to be a memorial to Johnson, like that collection, *Ménagiana*, the friends of the French philologist, Gilles Ménage, had erected to give him "immortal glory."   It would be a "great literary monument," an "Egyptian pyramid," a "mausoleum" for all of Johnson's remains.   And it would be a collective work, a cairn to which each could contribute his stone.   It is from this point of view that he told Blair, with exact truth:

> I will venture to promise that my life of my revered friend will be the richest piece of biography that has ever appeared.   The bullion will be immense, whatever defects there may be in the workmanship.

Massiveness is one of the *Life*'s attributes, but Boswell, long before, had made an important decision that would also give it vitality: he would write the *Life* in "scenes," i.e., he would dramatize Johnson's career rather than present it in elevated summary.   And in his description of his emerging work to Barnard as "a valuable treasure of literary anecdotes," he added a different, powerful element: "and of the genuine emanations of his energy of mind."   The *Life* would display reason irradiated by energy.

Sorting was a major task in itself.   The composition of the *Hebrides* had been fairly easy; he and Malone stuck mainly to the journal, making room here and there for some supplementary letters.   Now he had to wrestle with all sorts of material, beginning with his massive journal with its clutter of auxiliary notes, and all those other documents he was accumulating.   Momentarily he was so overwhelmed that Malone had to supply an organizing principle: "Make a skeleton with references to the materials, in order of time."

So he began.   One day he worked so hard he skipped dinner and tea, which left him faint and uneasy.   Of another, he wrote: "Sorted till I was stupefied." After his low point early in July he turned ascetic, and for three days took only tea and dry toast for breakfast, and boiled milk and dry toast for dinner: this period gave him a real start. There were also other tasks: questionnaires to be submitted to Hector and to Frank Barber, Johnson's black servant; and negotiations upon "a delicate question" with Hawkins, Langton acting as intermediary. The "question" must have concerned the handling of Johnson's irregular sexual conduct after he first moved to London, information both Boswell and Hawkins had acquired surreptitiously from Johnson's diaries. Malone kept him to his task, and he worked himself into good spirits. An invitation from Lord Lonsdale, soon to be discussed, cheered him. For diversion there were little jaunts into the country with Malone and Courtenay, including one picnic that anticipates Mrs. Elton at Donwell Abbey:

> It was a delightful day. We did not find the gipsies; indeed we did not look much for them, but dined under a tree. I wished for a room and table and chairs. We were troubled by ants. However it was very well.

Boswell had transferred from the Northern to the Home Circuit, which was less expensive, less rowdy, and of course conveniently close to London. He could spend two or three days in Chelmsford or Maidstone and return for the dinners, conversation, and company that kept him content. One dinner at Wilkes's in Kensington, still a semi-rural suburb, seems memorably liquid: "turtle, venison, ices, fruit, burgundy, champagne, cyprus, claret, etc., coffee, tea, and liqueur." Malone and he ate lobster and drank wine and water at Courtenay's when they returned to town. As he said, "This was a day."

The breakup of the Edinburgh household had already claimed one casualty: Grange. With his "placid smile," he is so mild that he fades into the background of Boswell's life, but he was the steadiest of friends to the whole family. In deteriorating health and with little to look forward to in his later years, he relied heavily on Boswell's comfort and support. When Boswell decided to transfer to the English bar, he had tried to console Grange with assurances that they would meet every year and that he would make every effort to obtain some place or sinecure for him. He wrote from London to cheer Grange and applied to Dundas and Pitt on his behalf in vain. Temple asserted that Grange was a martyr to sloth, but whatever the truth of that remark Boswell's desertion of Edinburgh, sealed by the family's removal from their common quarters in James's Court, was an irremediable stroke. They were his family too. Boswell got the news of his death on 3 August; now there was no longer anyone in Edinburgh he had to see; he would return to his birthplace only once more, and then for a very brief visit.

Two weeks later Boswell set off for Auchinleck.   He wrote gratefully to Malone from Carlisle to say how much he owed to him, now that he was thoroughly involved with the Home Circuit and on the track "of I know not what success."   He arrived home on 21 August 1786.   Of the last seventeen months he had spent less than three with his family.   He would never be separated so long from them again.

CHAPTER

14

I

THE DECISIVE FAMILY move from Auchinleck to London came at the end of September 1786. The family's presence was a solace to Boswell, but also very much a responsibility. It fixed the difference between being a London visitor and a settled man of business. Temporarily Sandy and Jamie were sent to an academy in Soho Square, while Veronica and Euphemia attended a day-school in nearby Lincoln's Inn Fields. Margaret weathered the transition surprisingly well, and soon made herself at home in the London markets and shops.

But Boswell had no practice, and it was not a lively period. They had few callers; depression reduced Boswell to a regimen of playing draughts for a hundred apples a game with young Treesbank, who was hanging about waiting to join his regiment. Boswell fretted when he lost, Treesbank "having somehow got the knack of it." He attended the courts without much hope, suffered from nervous headaches, and dined so often with Malone, his great resource, that Boswell commented that he had better board with him. With Malone, he said, "I am always happy." When Boswell's doubts about himself spread even to the *Life*, Malone came to the rescue:

> One morning we revised a part of it, which he thought well of, and dispelled my vaporish diffidence; and he surprised me another day with a page of it on two different types that we might settle how it was to be printed.

In his despondency, Boswell prodded Dundas about his "case," and Dundas was human enough to take his small revenge. He replied in the third person that he had not realized Boswell's communication needed a written answer. While he had "not the least disposition to depreciate" Boswell's political services, he could not admit—turning Boswell's argument in the Diminishing Bill *Letter* against him—"that political merit of any kind is the proper road to judicial preferment." And he added that though he did not regret that *Letter* on his own account, he certainly did on Boswell's.

Then lightning struck. Boswell, as will be explained, had made the acquaintance of Lord Lonsdale and, apparently relieved from doubts as to the interference of peers in elections, asked Lonsdale to make him Recorder (chief legal officer) of Carlisle. Lonsdale countered by inviting Boswell to be Counsel to the Mayor at the forthcoming Carlisle by-election, an offer which Boswell was happy to accept.

Whatever attitude contemporaries took towards Sir James Lowther, since 1784 first Earl of Lonsdale, they all agreed he belonged to a species of one. Actually he was an extreme illustration in real life of a common eighteenth-century fictional type, the rich squire who must have his own way in everything. Given the hold of the more powerful gentry over neighbour as well as tenant, the type owed more to reality than to imagination. Lonsdale came from an old, well-established Cumbrian family, and his father had been Governor of Barbados; but he owed his rise to prominence to the deaths of three kinsmen, which brought him a baronetcy and a fortune, estimated at £2,000,000, that made him the richest commoner in England. In 1761, at the age of twenty-five, he married Lord Bute's eldest daughter, but the marriage was a failure; apart from a sister, the only person he ever seems to have cared about was the daughter of one of his tenant farmers, whose body after death he kept in a glass-lidded coffin so that he could continue to admire her beauty.

Lonsdale wanted power, absolute power, but on a local scale; he had no Ministerial ambitions or many ideas of doing good. With the concentration that others give to acquiring paintings or manuscripts, he collected seats in the House of Commons to dominate the counties and boroughs of northwestern England and to make himself a force to be courted at Whitehall. By 1784 he controlled nine seats, two each for Westmorland, Cockermouth, and Haslemere (a rotten borough in Surrey whose seats he had bought), and one each for Cumberland, Appleby, and Carlisle. His Members were known as "Lowther's ninepins." He knew only his own will, and his control over that was intermittent. The intensity of his ambition generated an equally intense opposition.

In general, Lonsdale had earned a bad reputation. As Sir Nathaniel Wraxall said, his fiery and overbearing temper combining with a fearless disposition, scarcely under the dominion of reason at all times, led him into perpetual quarrels, terminating frequently in duels; for he never declined giving satisfaction, and frequently demanded it of others.

More succinctly, Junius called him "the little, contemptible tyrant of the North." Tyrant yes, but far from contemptible; like Macbeth, he inspired "curses not loud but deep," and the reason they were not loud was his ruthlessness with opposition. One offensive shopkeeper he had pressed into the navy and kept at sea for ten years. His assertion that he owned not only the port and mines of Whitehaven but everything in it, including earth, fire, and water, led the authors of *The Rolliad* to write:

> Even by the elements his power confessed,
> Of mines and boroughs *Lonsdale* stands possessed:
> And one sad servitude alike denotes
> The slave that labours and the slave that votes.

Though not many adopted it, there was another way of looking at Lonsdale, most favourably presented by Dempster, a man of unquestioned integrity: "I most sincerely congratulate you," he wrote to Boswell some time later,

> on your being known to and well with Lord Lonsdale, who has always been a favourite of mine. We sate long beside each other in the House of Commons and I could never discover a spark of sordidness about him—a *homo sui juris*[1]—with such a mass of eccentric force—and rare peculiarities so directly the reverse of a Roman senator after the fall of the Republic.

A mass with force exerts attraction, and Boswell had felt it from his first momentary but impressive glimpse, quoted earlier, of Lonsdale in 1778 as foreman of a Carlisle grand jury. He acquired a more decided aura when Boswell witnessed his induction into the House of Lords. Wealth and Power put on the robes of Rank. When Boswell described to Johnson how the metamorphosis from commoner to peer of the realm had (he said) made his mouth water, Johnson, though a firm friend to social gradation, advised him to consider the transient nature of all human honours. What Boswell considered, of course, included both the transformation he wanted to emulate and the patron he had hoped his East India *Letter* would bring him. He tried to approach Lonsdale through Eglinton, but Eglinton had

---

[1] A law unto himself.

no wish to oblige—in fact, liked frustrating him, so Boswell thought—which reduced him to expressing his enthusiasm in print.   In his Diminishing Bill *Letter* he implored Lonsdale to come to the aid of the Scots:

> We are his neighbours.   *Paries proximus ardet.*[1]   We all know what
> HE can do . . . HE whose soul is all great—whose resentment is
> terrible, but whose liberality is boundless.   I know that he is dig-
> nified by having hosts of enemies.   But I have fixed his character
> in my mind upon no slight inquiry. . . .   LOWTHER! be kindly en-
> treated!—*"Come over to Macedonia and help us!"*[2]

Though his countrymen might have had trouble grasping why they should exchange their native "Harry-the-Ninth" Dundas for a despot from among their old Border enemies, Boswell was quite clear about the dif-ference between them.   Dundas was just another schoolmate, who had somehow bellowed and shoved his way to power; Lonsdale was not only a striking figure in himself but he displayed all the attributes of authority, and Boswell loved authority.   In the *Hebrides* his tone lowered to a rev-erential mutter about

> the ancient family of Lowther, a family before the Conquest. . . .
> A due mixture of severity and kindness, economy and munifi-
> cence, characterizes its present Representative.

And Boswell became a volunteer partisan for Lonsdale, as he had earlier for Corsica and for Douglas, collecting votes for the Lonsdale candidate in the Lancaster by-election of March 1786, and in May cheering on the side at the Select Committee hearings on the Carlisle by-election, which nonetheless unseated Lonsdale's choice, John Lowther.

By this time Boswell had met several members of Lonsdale's entourage, and public flattery must have been taking hold, since suddenly on 21 July 1786 he received an invitation from Lonsdale to dine on that great delicacy, a turtle, three days later.   Boswell confided to his journal:

> This was truly a stirring of my blood.   I strutted and said to myself,
> "Well, it is right to be in this metropolis.   Things at last come
> forward unexpectedly.   The great LOWTHER himself has now taken
> me up.   I may be raised to eminence in the State."   Yet as I was
> not at all acquainted with him, had never called on him, and he
> had not left a card for me, I suspected that this invitation might
> be a trick attempted upon me.

---

[1] "['Tis your own safety that's at stake when] your neighbour's wall is in flames" (Horace, *Epistles,* I. xviii. 84—trans. H. R. Fairclough, Loeb ed.).
[2] Acts 16:9.

Malone's servant, sent to reconnoitre, found the invitation was genuine, but Boswell hung back.   The summons was abrupt and he was already engaged for dinner that day; he decided to stand on his dignity as "an ancient Baron," decline politely, and call on Lonsdale instead.   So they became acquainted, and so Boswell became Mayor's Counsel.

The extent of the franchise was the key question in the new by-election.   In 1780, Lonsdale had had to share the two Carlisle seats with the Earl of Surrey, the city returning Surrey himself and William Lowther, Lonsdale's cousin and heir.   Determined to correct this situation, Lonsdale had forced the City Corporation to admit almost 1,450 non-resident farmers and coal-miners as honorary freemen in October 1784 and January 1785.   The slave that laboured and the slave that voted often were one and the same.   They were known as "toadstools" or "mushrooms," as upstarts of a sudden political growth, and gave Lonsdale his pamphlet title of "James, Earl of Toadstool, commonly called Jimmy Gripeall."   But their right to vote was in hot dispute.   At the April by-election, John Lowther, the Yellow (Lonsdale) candidate, had easily outpolled John Christian, the Blue candidate, with their help; in reversing the result, the Select Committee had thrown out the mushroom vote in practice but had not ruled on it in theory.

Surrey having succeeded as Duke of Norfolk, another by-election became necessary in autumn 1786 and Lonsdale chose to try the same manoeuvre again; he did not have time to win over enough of the old voters, and in any case this tactic had proved successful elsewhere: the mushroom vote was the means by which the Duke of Devonshire exerted influence in Derby, and it was crucial in the borough of Bedford and city of Durham.   Edward Knubley was the Yellow candidate, while Norfolk, who was himself reaching out for five seats, backed Rowland Stephenson, a rich London banker who had bought a nearby estate.

The polling, which began on 30 November and continued for fifteen days, was a contentious business in which Boswell found himself in the crucial position of passing on the validity of the mushroom vote.   This grand question arose on 7 December, and Boswell delivered an extended ruling "with animation and force" confirming its admissibility.   The squibs and broadsides which enlightened the voters included a dialogue called *Bozzi and Sir Jozzi* (the Mayor, Sir Joseph Senhouse), and an advertisement for a magician's performance, which promised that Senhouse would swallow "*Bozzonian Pills*, each the full size of an HEN'S EGG, enough to choke any other man."   "A Westmorland Freeholder" scored a point by asking how the defender of the rights of mankind in *Corsica* could turn into the public adulator of Lonsdale.   But the legal situation was at least technically opaque enough to justify Boswell's decision.   Knubley was duly elected, and duly unseated on petition to the House of Commons.

Carlisle held special significance for Boswell.   It gave him great pleasure to remember that Carlisle had provided his first sight of England as a young man, when he admired everything English; it brought back thoughts of how his honoured father had kept him from settling in England, and the desperate melancholy he had endured at twenty.   Now the Laird of Auchinleck was directing English proceedings, and he felt "a real rise in dignity . . . as the ally of the great Lowther of Westmorland."

Ally, however, was not the *mot juste*.   For the first time, Boswell had an opportunity to observe Lonsdale at close range and for an extended period.   He was unquestionably impressive; as Boswell put it in the pidgin Italian which he was using here and there in his journal as a flimsy concealment, Lonsdale was

> un esempio di un aggregato di grandezza—antichitá di famiglia— territorie immense—nobilta di creazione—forza d'intelletto—violenza—interesso di Parliamenta.

His force of personality was sufficient in itself to revive Boswell's spirits, and led him to recall Johnson's remark that a madman loves to be with someone he fears.   And like Lord Auchinleck, Lonsdale evoked in Boswell a feeling of the "solidity of life."   His handsome features, his pronunciation, his memory, were striking: he amazed with the amount of poetry, both Latin and English, he could repeat.

Boswell, who liked to study great characters, had ample opportunity to ponder these traits.   Lonsdale did not pretend to conversation; he harangued every night, while M.P. s and other dependants sat "quietissimi." Nor did he tolerate competition; if any of his auditors dared whisper to each other, they were immediately recalled to attention.   Even a servant's heavy tread roused him to call out, "Don't make such a noise.   It makes me strain my voice."   No one, of course, tested his patience by arguing with him.

Lonsdale's matter consisted in circumstantial accounts of acquaintances and election contests, but at times he grew personal.   He was but a steward, he said, for his possessions: from him whom much has been given, much is required.   He confided, "I may have children yet.   I shall certainly do my endeavour."   So, Boswell thought to himself, Lady Lonsdale must go. Most revealing was a story of school-days, when as a fag Lonsdale had had to pump water at half-past five in the morning until his hands were numb. There was a fire at one end of the room, which the big boys would not let the little boys near.   The pissing place was at the other end of the room "and the big boys would not take the trouble to go to it, but would piss by the little boys' beds."   Boswell drew the moral:

> What shocking tyranny! I could not help thinking it curious that he had once been thus kept in subjection. . . .   It makes a very pernicious succession of slavery and tyranny.   The big boys recollecting what they have suffered are barbarously severe upon the little boys, and perhaps his own *domination* has been inflamed by that education.

Lonsdale's hangers-on protected themselves as best they could.   They fell asleep during his monologues, complained about but drank his bitter port—claret was too expensive—and huddled together in the conspiracy of the miserable.   They told tales out of school: how he was anxious to save sixpence but would throw away thousands at one time on an election. Col. James Lowther, M.P. for Westmorland, disconcerted him by taking half a sheet of his stationery; he would not let J. C. Satterthwaite, M.P. for Cockermouth, read one of his newspapers.   When Lonsdale admitted that if he could follow his own inclinations, he would become an old don in a Cambridge college, who spent two months a year in London to be near the British Museum, Colonel Lowther remarked afterwards that this was just a way of talking to make people wonder: "He had no pleasure in anything in this life, so that he might as well be in one place as another." Nor were Boswell's prospects promising: Lonsdale would ask nothing for his friends, Satterthwaite said, because he wanted only dependants.   And they despised themselves: "You see," said another, "who we are that he has about him."

After a week of close quarters, Boswell commented:

> I now began to feel a load of weariness and to be surfeited of that greatness which was much enforced by my own imagining.   But it was necessary to persevere.

Two days later,

> I could hardly stand the repetition of strong dissertation.

The next day:

> I saw him a *forcible* Lord Macdonald.   He eat (all but four that Dr. Dun inadvertently took) a whole plate of fresh oysters without offering anybody one.   Colonel Lowther and Saul had stolen away and dined at another public house comfortably and had some good wine.   They were frightened to have it discovered, but it came

out.　Lonsdale *gronda*[1] the Colonel: "I should not have gone somewhere else and paid for my dinner when I could have dined here."
This was a striking refutation of "Whose soul is all great."[2] Yet
perhaps his exorbitant tyranny and extreme narrowness may be
reckoned great in a bad sense.　He was much in his usual style
tonight.　I was much fatigued and got early to bed.　All these
traits I mark as *disjecta membra*[3] out of which I may afterwards
complete the *real* character of one of whom I *imagined* so highly.
I was kept in a kind of fever of agitation, and also in that kind of
awe which I had not experienced but in my father's company—
seeing all round *kept down*.　My absence from home was very hard
upon me.

To divert himself, Boswell started to publish a pro-Lonsdale ballad
until it occurred to him that this might not seem impartial in the Mayor's
Counsel; nor would it help his professional reputation to become known
as a ballad-maker for a faction.　Then one night Lonsdale unexpectedly
relaxed, and shared some white wine—hitherto denied—with him.　Boswell says,

> He was now for the first time that I have seen him *really* pleasant,
> with an agreeable smile upon his black countenance, and all of us
> talking a little in our turns.

There the record stops.　But after the polls closed, Boswell was carried
off to Lowther Castle in Westmorland, escaped with difficulty, returned
to London in high spirits just in time for Christmas, and wrote Lonsdale
what Boswell called "a letter of sincere compliment," and others might read
as an exercise in obsequious gratitude.　He had something to be grateful
for: a fee of 150 guineas, 50 more than promised.　And naturally he looked
ahead to even more substantial rewards.

Among the most vigorous congratulations on his new friendship were
those from the Bishops of Killaloe and Dromore, perhaps reflecting their
acquaintance with the exigencies of ecclesiastical preferment.　Barnard
(Killaloe) wrote:

> If you had been permitted to choose out of the British dominions
> a patron the most capable of conducting you to honour and profit
> you could not have pitched upon one more fit your purpose than
> Lord Lonsdale: he has wealth, he has interest, he has business
> enough to keep you employed, and he has other boroughs left

---

[1]Scolded.
[2]Boswell's characterization of Lonsdale in his Diminishing Bill *Letter*.　See p. 346.
[3]Unconnected parts.

though he loses Carlisle.   So *coraggio*, my friend; something will turn up trumps yet at Westminster Hall, and a *fico* for sweet Edinburgh.

Percy (Dromore) was equally sanguine:

... a lasting connection with a nobleman distinguished for the zeal and spirit with which he serves his friends, and I already anticipate the happiest consequences to you from that connection; especially his bringing you into Parliament for one of his numerous boroughs, an event which I consider as no less certain than splendid to your fortunes and establishment in England.

It could be assumed that Percy knew the local situation at first hand; he had been Dean of Carlisle for four years.   To the confident, rolling tones of these two Anglican (Irish Establishment) deep divines, the Rev. Dr. Hugh Blair joined the simpler and more hesitant accents of the Church of Scotland: "Lord Lonsdale certainly is one very good and useful patron."   But was one patron enough, Blair wondered: the bar was always uncertain.

While waiting for manna, Boswell returned patiently and fruitlessly to Westminster Hall.   His main concern, however, was the *Life*, still far from completion, though he told Barnard and the newspapers that he was holding up his work until Hawkins's *Life of Johnson* appeared, and that his own book was "in great forwardness."

Hawkins was an even more serious threat than Mrs. Piozzi.   He was publishing a full-scale biography rather than a collection of random anecdotes, and he had known Johnson for forty years, ever since the days Johnson had worked as a hack writer for Cave on the *Gentleman's Magazine*. Johnson's own enthusiasm about Hawkins had been tempered: he conceded that Hawkins was penurious and mean, with "a degree of brutality and a tendency to savageness," but he was an honest man at bottom if thoroughly unclubbable; and Johnson let no one else attack him.   As a trustworthy man of business, Hawkins was a natural choice as one of Johnson's executors, and when he pinched two volumes of Johnson's diary a few days before his death, Johnson forgave him because of the high-minded motive he professed: to keep them out of the hands of an unnamed someone (Steevens) who might misuse them.   For all Boswell knew, Hawkins had wonderful material about Johnson's early career; and prefixed to the standard edition of Johnson's works his *Life* could easily be taken as official.   At the least, Boswell faced the biographer's nightmare: someone will publish an extended treatment of his subject just before he does.

The son of a carpenter, Hawkins had been articled to an attorney, and was building a career in that unrespected vocation when he made a fortunate marriage. According to Horace Walpole, his wife eventually brought him £30,000; whatever the amount, it was enough for Hawkins to abandon the law for gentility. He became Chairman of the Quarter Sessions for Middlesex and, Boswell sneered, "upon occasion of presenting an Address to the King, accepted the usual offer of knighthood." Actually, Hawkins's knighthood had nothing to do with presenting an Address; he had straight-forwardly solicited it for having administered the King's justice to the best of his respectable lights, so that his rival Sir John Fielding, Chairman of the Quarter Sessions for Westminster, would no longer out-title him. He was also known for having published an industrious *History of Music* (1776).

Hawkins was intent on using Johnson's biography to impart the lessons a long life had taught him, and these included the necessity of hard work, attention to duty, loyalty to whatever Ministry was in power, and the bad effects of a playhouse: "No sooner is a playhouse opened in any part of the Kingdom than it becomes surrounded by an halo of brothels." (Presumably Hawkins had also reflected on the advantages of marrying well, but these he does not mention.)

Johnson himself pointed many a moral. "Truth obliges me to say"—and Hawkins does not flinch—that Johnson's "outward deportment was in many instances a just object of censure." "His garb and the whole of his external appearance was not to say negligent, but slovenly and even squalid." "The source of Johnson's misery throughout his life" was an "inertness and laxity of mind," which resulted from "the neglect of order and regularity in living and the observance of stated hours." And "he indulged himself in the dangerous practice of reading in bed." Not only did Hawkins criticize Johnson's *London* for uttering "vulgar complaints," and assert that except for the Preface Johnson had produced a poor edition of Shakespeare, he repeatedly expresses his contempt in general for a professional author—and what else was Johnson? He was particularly offended that Johnson made his faithful black servant Frank Barber his residuary legatee, instead of two relations, one a lunatic and the other a connection by marriage. Having labelled Barber a cuckold, Hawkins concludes his biography by saying that Johnson's will "may serve as a *caveat* against ostentatious bounty, favour to negroes, and testamentary dispositions *in extremis*."

In disposing of Johnson, Hawkins digresses to other horrid examples, like Samuel Dyer, who, after the most praiseworthy Dissenting education, with "a sober and temperate deliberation resolved on a participation of [the world's] pleasures and enjoyments," grew so indifferent to religion that he fell into an "easy compliance with invitations to Sunday evening parties," and ended possibly as a suicide after losing his fortune and honour by speculating in stocks.   Even Goldsmith, though "a man of genius and of very fine parts," is called an idiot: in response to an offer of assistance from the incoming Lord Lieutenant of Ireland, Goldsmith had suggested that he help Goldsmith's brother instead, which showed that Goldsmith had "no sense of the shame, nor dread of the evils, of poverty."   More dangerous are sentimental immoralists like Fielding, Sterne, and Rousseau, "men of loose principles, bad economists, living without foresight," who think they make up for their failings by "more tender affections and finer feelings than they will allow men of more regular lives, whom they deem formalists."   As will now be quite clear, Hawkins's main concerns were to award marks of praise and mostly blame like a schoolteacher, and to justify his own way of life to his unsympathetic contemporaries.

It is too bad that Hawkins didn't concentrate on reminiscences of Johnson.   He does provide a splendid description of an all-night party at the Ivy Lane Club: "about five Johnson's face shone with meridian splendour though his drink had been only lemonade."   Occasionally he catches Johnson's genuine tone; when his surgeon refused, despite his urging, to pierce deeper into Johnson's leg to relieve his dropsy, the dying man said, "You all pretend to love me, but you do not love me so well as I myself do."   And precisely because of his lack of temperamental affinity, Hawkins makes some shrewd though limited comments on Johnson's character: Johnson had "no genuine impulse to action, either corporal or mental"; his indolence and melancholy were mental diseases which caused him to see "human life through a false medium."

But Hawkins's self-absorption, his pompously turgid style entangled in legal jargon—"whereof, whereon, wherein, hereby, thereby, and wherein before," was one reviewer's impression—his enormous and tedious digressions, above all his general malevolence towards Johnson and the world, made him an irresistible target.   The most merciless commentator was the great classical scholar, Richard Porson, who wrote a "Panegyrical Epistle on Hawkins v. Johnson," under the name of "Sundry Whereof."   He points out, for instance, that Hawkins "never misses an opportunity of using the pronoun of the first person": *my* own coach, *my* servants, *my* servant, *my* lands, *my* country house, *my* gate in the country, *my* gardener, etc., not to mention the "I's" and "me's."   It will be sufficient to quote Sundry Whereof's admiring summary:

> The compass of learning, the extent and accuracy of information, the judicious criticisms, the moral reflections, the various opinions,

legal and political, to say nothing of that excess of candour and charity that breathe throughout the work, make together such a collection of sweets that the sense aches at them.

Under such attack, Hawkins's book sank rapidly.

With great relief, Boswell announced in the *Public Advertiser* (21 May 1787):

> He does not regret the deliberation with which he has proceeded, as very few circumstances relative to the history of Dr. Johnson's private life, writings, or conversation have been told with that authentic precision which alone can render biography valuable. To correct these erroneous accounts will be one of his principal objects; and, on reviewing his materials, he is happy to find that he has documents in his possession which will enable him to do justice to the character of his illustrious friend. He trusts that in the mean time the public will not permit unfavourable impressions to be made on their minds, whether by the light effusions of carelessness and pique, or the ponderous labours of solemn inaccuracy and dark, uncharitable conjecture.

Boswell's last sentence referred, of course, to Mrs. Piozzi's *Anecdotes* and Hawkins's *Johnson*. In particular, Hawkins intimated that Johnson's friendship with Savage in London, while Tetty remained in Lichfield, had led him into sexual irregularities that troubled his last moments. Boswell himself later touched on the same point, with much greater finesse: in spite of Hawkins's "strange, dark manner" of hinting around the subject, Johnson (Boswell says) had nothing "of more than ordinary criminality weighing upon his conscience." One might add, that if judged by Boswell's conduct rather than his beliefs, there was nothing criminal about it at all.

I I

SPRING 1787 WAS difficult. Boswell was working hard on the *Life*, mostly by himself though with Malone keeping him to it. But the family situation had become strained. Margaret was ill and fearful, and thought only of returning to Auchinleck. When Boswell stayed away from The Club, he got angry because she failed to praise his sacrifice: "She with a high spirit said she wished me to do what was most agreeable to me." Fortunately Malone, whom he had chosen even before the move to London to "command" him as "guide, philosopher, and friend," gave the command he wanted to hear: "He said if I should quit London and return to Scotland, I would hang myself in five weeks. I begged he would prevent me."

Margaret got worse and Boswell cried bitterly.   Sandy, now a boy of eleven, comforted him, Boswell wrote in his journal, "like a man older than myself, saying, 'O Papa, this is not like yourself.' "   Grievances piled up: Lee, the great encourager of his move to the English bar, was quite indifferent to his lack of success, and Burke was cold.   Boswell went on a water regimen, as he often did now when depressed.

As the season went on, Boswell's spirits fluctuated according to the state of Margaret's health.   When the King, "with a pleasing look," asked him at the levee (11 May) how the biography was progressing, Boswell, disloyal to his fellow author, replied, "It will be some time yet.   I have a good deal to do to correct Sir John Hawkins."   His situation, as he summarized it to Forbes (8 May 1787), was volatile:

I have upon the whole had a very good life since we parted.[1]   Sir Joshua, Malone, Courtenay, and I have been so much together and so "loath to part" that we have got the name of the *Gang*. Then there has been the extensive variety which it would require a volume to relate, but which you can very well imagine.

As to the law, I cannot say that the prospect is as yet brilliant; but I have no reason to complain of this my first year as an English barrister, when I consider that I was employed as Counsel for the Mayor in the election at Carlisle, and received a fee of one hundred and fifty guineas.   Such chances keep one's hopes alive and I cannot help thinking that it would be wrong were I to abandon Westminster Hall without a longer trial.   I may venture to say to *you* that the thought of shrinking into the narrow sphere which I quitted after many a weary, languishing day distresses me.   I am more and more confirmed in my love of London.   In short, you see plainly how it is with me.

But on the other hand, the alarming return which my wife has had of her dangerous illness and the apprehension that the air of London is hurtful to her presses me in a most interesting manner. I thank GOD she is at present better, but she has so many turns that appearances are sadly precarious.   The expense of living too is greater than I flattered myself it might be, and this independently of giving my children such advantages in point of education as I am very desirous they should have.   Thus am I painfully distracted by different considerations. . . .   A little time may clear the prospect.   My wife's constitution may be reconciled to London, and my rent roll is every year increasing. . . .   My life of Dr. Johnson is in great forwardness; but on account of many avocations, and of additional materials which come to me from different quarters, I shall not be able to have it in the press till July or

[1] The previous July.

August, so that it cannot be published till the end of this year or the beginning of the next.

The more he worked on the *Life*, the clearer the idea Boswell got of the kind of material he was looking for. After thanking the Rev. William Maxwell for some "genuine, high-flavoured Johnsoniana," he wrote:

> I ought to apologize for having given you so much trouble; but I had *understood* that you had *minutes* of his conversation, and I was anxious to have had transcripts of them because, however strong the faculty of memory may sometimes be, I am persuaded that no recollection can be so authentic as a relation committed to writing *at the time*. We are apt to imagine that we have *heard* what has been conveyed to us through some other medium. I am sure you will forgive my frankness when I give you as an instance of this what you communicate in the belief of its being a saying of his as to Scottish education, which is indeed a sentence in his *Journey to the Western Islands*.

For some time Boswell had been content to let himself be driven along the stream of life because that was what best suited him; now he started to make some casual attempts at navigation. In June he called on Dundas for a "friendly conversation" about his "case," but nothing came of it. And he wrote to Lonsdale reminding him of his application for the Recordership of Carlisle. Lonsdale's reply was flattering: "I don't believe we shall either of us regret the time we spend together." In July and August, Boswell dutifully went round Essex, Hertford, and Surrey on the Home Circuit; no business, but he enjoyed himself. Now he thought of making a quick trip north alone to tend to estate matters but conscience awakened. He wrote in his journal (13 August 1787):

> RESOLVED I would take my wife with me to Auchinleck. She might die, and I should upbraid myself for not having given her the benefit of travelling, change of air, and rural amusement. Besides, her good sense and activity would be of essential service to me. I also resolved to take Sandy, as his heart was quite set on it. . . . My wife was much pleased.

In the end Veronica also went along, and they arrived at Auchinleck on 20 August, just in time to enjoy the pleasures of Sacrament Week.

Boswell simply notes, "Mr. Russel preached in tent," but the name alone can evoke that wonderful counterpart of this scene, in Mauchline two years earlier:

> But now the L—'s ain trumpet touts,
>   Till a' the hills are rairan,

An' echos back return the shouts,
  Black [Russel] is na spairan:
His piercin words, like Highlan swords,
  Divide the joints an' marrow;
His talk o' H-ll, whare devils dwell,
  Our vera "sauls does harrow"
    Wi' fright that day.

A vast, unbottom'd, boundless *Pit*,
  Fill'd fou o' *lowan brunstane*,   [full of flaming brimstone]
Whase raging flame, an' scorching heat,
  Wad melt the hardest whunstane! . . .

Burns had also memorialized Boswell's own chaplain, the short and
exceedingly stout Alexander Millar, in the same poem:

Wee [Millar] niest the Guard relieves,   [next]
  An' Orthodoxy raibles;   [babbles]
Tho' in his heart he weel believes,
  An' thinks it auld wives' fables:
But faith! the birkie wants a *manse*,   [fellow]
  So, cannilie he hums them;   [humbugs]
Altho' his *carnal* Wit an' Sense
  Like hafflins-wise o'ercomes him   [half]
    At times that day.

It *was* true that Millar desperately wanted a parish, and the Boswells
had persuaded Lord Eglinton to present him to the living of Kilmaurs.
But the parishioners, furious at being denied their own choice, nailed the
church shut; and "the most cutthroatlike fellows" met the new incumbent
with such menaces of sticks and stones that he found it prudent to slip out
of the back of the manse.   Millar was very angry at Burns.   He wrote to
Boswell:

> I doubt not but the liberty which Burns hath taken with me in his
> poems has prejudiced some, but it can only be with those who
> know me not.   I never was in company with the *fellow*, nor would
> I know him if I now saw him.   He is publishing again, in which
> edition, I have reason to believe, that poem is to be left out.

Yet there was also dissension among the godly, as Millar had informed
Boswell a few days earlier:

> Mr. Russel, I am certain, is the person who acts for [the insubor-
> dinate parishioners] behind the curtain. . . .   He makes it his busi-
> ness to create and foment disturbances in every parish within his
> reach where the presentee happens not to be one of his sycophants.

Happily, after a few months the parishioners became reconciled to their new minister.

The several days of high-powered preaching that distinguished Sacrament Week no doubt slowed everyone's sense of time; otherwise the month at Auchinleck passed quickly. Margaret revived in her native Ayrshire. Boswell looked after the estate and made progress, he thought, in canvassing the county against the next election. Thurlow, as Lord Chancellor, had pronounced against nominal and fictitious votes the previous April, and though his decision had not yet taken effect at the local level the elimination of these votes would slightly improve Boswell's slim chances of representing Ayrshire. Earlier, Fairlie had pointed out the contradiction between legalizing mushroom votes in Carlisle while opposing nominal and fictitious votes at home but, besides the technical difference between the two cases, that was the way the world wagged. (He had also urged Boswell to apply for the vacant Sheriff-Deputeship of Ayrshire, i.e., to *work* towards Parliament or the Bench, an old possibility that now seemed hopelessly provincial.)

Boswell marked the happiness he felt in a memorandum dated "Dumfries, 24 September 1787":

> Recollecting my worthy friend Grange and many former ideas connected with this place, how wonderfully well am I tonight. The very wish of my heart in early years, when I used to read *The Spectator* with Temple, is realized. I am now a barrister-at-law of the Inner Temple, have a house in London, am one of the distinguished literary men of my age. And, at the same time, have an extensive estate, a number of tenants all depending upon me; in short, have, when I please, the *potentiality* of a prince. Yet persevere in attending the Essex Sessions.

The family left Auchinleck on 24 September, with the tenants lined up to bid the Laird farewell. Malone had kept him in touch with London:

> We had yesterday a very good quiet day at Sir J. Reynolds's: Edmund Burke, Mr. Laurence, Sir J., and myself. The true cause, I perceive, of B.'s coldness is that he thinks your habit of recording throws a restraint on convivial ease and negligence. I think after once your great work is done, which you seem to refer *ad Graecas Kalendas*,[1] it will be of consequence to declare that you have no thoughts of that kind more. . . . No packet or box from Bowles.— What an insufferable procrastinator, almost as great a one as another person of my acquaintance.

[1] "To the Greek Kalends," a non-existent date.

But Boswell preferred to believe that it was his zeal against Fox's East India Bill that accounted for Burke's "shyness."

He returned to embarrassments on all sides in London. Money was an immediate difficulty. Captain Preston wanted repayment of £500 that Boswell had borrowed in more exuberant days, and Boswell had no idea of where to raise the money; Dilly and Baldwin came to his rescue. What would happen if the loan of £500 he had procured for his cousin, Bruce Boswell, were called in? (Bruce had used the money to captain an East Indiaman on a disastrous voyage, had been cashiered by the East India Co., and was seeking reinstatement.) Boswell found money where he could, but was so ashamed of borrowing £200 from William Gibb, an excise officer at Ayr, that he appears only as "Mr.———" in Boswell's list of debts.

The family also presented worrying problems. Margaret, Boswell wrote,

> complained of the expense of London, of the injury it did her health and that of both my sons, and of the obscurity in which my daughters must be. I was sensible of all this. But my aversion to the narrow, ill-bred sphere was very strong.

Jamie was an engaging child, full of "vivacity and love of learning," but Sandy, who suffered from an undescended testicle and a hernia, was becoming unruly at home, and his mother could not be persuaded to trust him to a boarding-school. And Boswell felt he could not afford to send Veronica and Euphemia to a school where they would acquire "elegance of manner."

Nor had his prospects improved in any discernible way. He anxiously insisted that Dundas, who had taken a friendly part in Bruce Boswell's affair, come to dinner; he was thinking again of a judge's place in Scotland. Dundas was frank, good-humoured, and offered nothing in the way of help. The law was equally barren, and he was glad to take Malone's advice "to attend laxly" at Westminster Hall and "get on diligently" with the *Life*. This Boswell could and did do. For two months that autumn, through persistent gloom that modulated into frequent restlessness, he kept writing: "at *Life*," "*Life* all day," "some *Life*." Malone's continuing support was essential, as Boswell's record shows:

> Went to Malone's and read him a year's journal of Johnson's conversation for *Life*, which I feared was of little value. He cheered me by praising it.

> Awaked very uneasy. Lay in bed till noon and drank coffee. Then rose very low-spirited. Westminster Hall. Malone's, and

told him how ill, and how I apprehended at such times my friends were tired of me. . . . Courtenay was engaged to dine with him, and he *insisted* that I should stay. I was prevailed on; and by a pleasant, social, convivial interview, I was restored to serene cheerfulness.

Boswell complained that his social circle in London had contracted with permanent settlement, but it is hard to feel sorry for anyone who could gather Malone, Reynolds, the actor John Kemble, the dramatist Arthur Murphy, Brocklesby, and Langton for dinner; or who dined out constantly that autumn: with Paoli (several times), Mrs. Bosville, Dilly (twice), Kemble, Brocklesby, Lonsdale (twice), Metcalfe, Langton (twice), at The Club, a half-dozen times with Reynolds, and too often to count accurately with Malone.

On one particularly entertaining occasion, after attending Robert Jephson's *Julia* at Drury Lane, the group (Malone, Kemble, young Jephson, Courtenay, and Boswell) assembled at Malone's to partake of "a noble haunch of venison, a brace of grouse from Auchinleck, and a barrel of oysters; port, sherry, claret, hock, and burgundy." "We had a most jovial meeting," Boswell reports, "and sat till between four and five. I walked home, but was much intoxicated." The next morning he was shocked that his family had seen him in such a state, and vowed to avoid indulgence for three months. It could hardly have been a novel sight. A year later, Jamie wrote to his mother about another outing:

> Mrs. Buchanan invited one Dr. Burn to keep papa company and drink a bottle or two with him, he is an odd sort of a fellow for he refuses every thing and then take evry thing, they drank about two bottles together but neither of them was the worse of it which you know was a lucky thing indeed.

These dinners were no casual recreations: starting in late afternoon and often going on into the morning, they were the centre of Boswell's intellectual and social life. With such friends, it is not surprising he resisted retreat to the dull, coarse society of provincial Edinburgh, or to the company of bucolic dependants, occasional visitors, and chance passers-by at Auchinleck, where custom insisted that every caller be entertained.

Dinner with Lonsdale, however, was part of his necessary attendance. Writing in the third person, Boswell once more pressed him for employment:

> The office of Recorder of Carlisle which he has presumed to solicit would put him in a situation for which he most earnestly wishes. . . . He begs leave to suggest that the appointment of a gentleman of

family and fortune would be creditable for that ancient Corporation, and that he would feel it in such a manner as to make him do his duty not only with fidelity but with a warmth of zeal. The appointment would be of considerable consequence to him in his profession, and would afford him at once an ostensible reason for returning to the Northern Circuit, which he is now convinced would be most advantageous to him.

It was not the position itself, which involved few duties and paid only £20 a year, that Boswell cared about. But it was an honour and a precedent: Lonsdale had made the previous Recorder, Edward Norton, an M.P.

Was Boswell surprised at Lonsdale's response? Was he almost resigned to failure, acting on desperate impulse or going through the motions as he seems to do with Dundas? It is hard to guess, but when Lonsdale said in effect, "Yes, I will make you Recorder; we go north tomorrow," Boswell unexpectedly hesitated. As he explained to himself: "I was agitated at finding now that LOWTHER really had resolved publicly to befriend me, but I was somewhat embarrassed." He had several engagements, he explained, and the *Life* to finish. But Margaret was in favour of his going, and T.D. "thought *it could do no harm*." He accepted.

I I I

BOSWELL'S ACCOUNT OF this northern trip (21 December 1787–7 January 1788) is the most brilliant of his later journals, but only its climactic scene can be quoted at length. The start was peculiar though customary: Lonsdale dawdled for hours, leaving his companions to hang about; then he sent the coach in one direction while he walked in another to meet it, since he never got into his coach at his own door. The daily routine of his three companions varied entirely at his whim. At best he and Boswell sang songs from *The Beggar's Opera* to help pass the time. But for the most part it was a hard trip, with Lonsdale irritable at every delay and stingy with the postilions:

> His way was to call, "Boys, I'm in a great hurry; make haste or I'll give you nothing. I am not to waste my lungs calling to you. I have looked my watch. If I have to call to you again, you shall have nothing. If I must waste my lungs, I must save my cash."

Even before they started, there had been talk of Parliament. Colonel Lowther said the way to get anything from the Great Man was to find someone to oppose it: "What! would you bring Boswell into Parliament?"

He thought Boswell might be chosen for Cockermouth in place of Hum-
phrey Senhouse, who hated Parliament, and soothed Boswell's fears of
being without a voice of his own by saying that Lonsdale acted honourably
towards his Members.   But Satterthwaite reminded him it was understood
that no Member opposed his patron.   Perhaps Boswell had begun to remember what he had written many years earlier in *The Hypochondriack*:

> Independency is a truly dignified state, and in proportion as a
> man recedes from it, he sinks into meanness.   He who subjects
> himself to a servile compliance with the will of another from in-
> terested views of obtaining the greatest advantages is justly de-
> spised by men of spirit as an abject being.

Lowther Castle, their first destination, had burned in 1726 and only
the two large wings remained.   There was little food and it was very cold,
since Lonsdale refused to keep the fires going.   The servants ignored the
guests, rightly considering them merely another class of dependants.   Satterthwaite, assuming that Boswell had sunk into being just another retainer
like himself, again talked freely of Lonsdale's refusal to procure good
situations for his followers, to prevent them from standing on their own.

> He . . . told how a gentleman observed how great a man [Lonsdale]
> might be if he were but commonly civil.   "Nay," said another, "if
> he were but commonly *un*civil."   He said no man of parts had
> ever submitted to go along with him.

This, Boswell wrote,

> struck a damp upon me, and I saw how fallaciously I had imagined
> that I might be raised by his interest, for I never would submit to
> be dependent. . . .   I now foresaw many difficulties in being Re-
> corder, as he could not bear even decent attention to be paid to
> his opponents in the Corporation.

The first night at Lowther after dinner, Lonsdale entertained the company
by reading aloud three acts—"I think," says Boswell, whose attention may
have wandered—of John Home's historical tragedy, *Alonzo*.

The following day, Christmas, it snowed.   They were to set off for
Whitehaven Castle, which Lonsdale had refurbished grandly, but he decided to wait until the weather improved.   On the 26th, Lonsdale talked
for three hours without intermission.   "His camp *butcher*" (Boswell's italics)
cooked oxcheek broth, tripe, and a bit of venison for dinner, and all sat
"in vile, timid restraint."   Boswell was shocked to discover that Lonsdale
still owed £2,000 from last year's Lancaster election.   (In fact, Lonsdale
was notorious for not paying his bills, and is best remembered for his shabby

financial treatment of the Wordsworth family.) He asked himself how the Laird of Auchinleck could hang on a savage, and wrote, "I thought I heard my worthy father say, 'James, I left you independent.' "

Two more days of isolation at Lowther undid Boswell:

> I viewed with wonder and regret my folly in putting myself at such an age as my 46th year into a new state of life by becoming an English barrister. I saw that it was not a life of spirited exertion as I had supposed, but of much labour for which I had ever been unfit, and of much petulant contest which in some states of my changeful mind I could not bear. Being made Recorder of Carlisle *to bring me back to the Northern Circuit*, as I had put it in my application to L., I considered as again involving me in a tiresome, expensive, ineffectual struggle to get business which I had no probability of obtaining.

All the arguments for returning to Scotland recurred.

> I meditated calmly on the infatuation of a gentleman of a large estate, fine Place, and excellent house dooming himself to trouble and servile vexation.

At 1 p.m. that day (the 28th), there were still no signs of Lonsdale or breakfast, so Boswell packed his travelling-bag, hitched a ride in a cart, and thought longingly of Margaret. But then he began to fear she might despise him for running away, and that Lonsdale might resent his departure in more drastic fashion. When the cart left the main road, he walked the rest of the way to Penrith. Here he met George Saul, a local subordinate, who told him that Lonsdale would indeed object to his taking French leave. Restored by coffee, muffin, and toast, Boswell picked up his bag and trudged back, almost five miles through the snow, cold, and dark weather, to face Lonsdale directly.

Boswell reviewed his folly in coming to the English bar, and urged his unfitness to be Recorder.

> "Sir," said he, "You applied to me for this several times, and at last mentioned your returning to the Northern Circuit as a reason for your having it. I thought of it deliberately for some time. I never consult—neither the Officer[1] nor Garforth nor one of them. . . . It is said it is easier to get into a situation than to get well out. If a man does not get out well, it is a reflection on the person who put him in. . . . What I should say to the Corporation: 'Here is a man of great sense, of talents, who when a thing is

[1]Col. James Lowther.

properly prepared can judge of it with ability.'　And the business
is all prepared by the Town Clerk." ...

"Your Lordship is very kind.　You put it in the most favourable light.　I am now ambitious to have it. ...　Your Lordship has not only the power to give me the place, but you have
given me fortitude to take it.　I am of an anxious temper."

"You can think of it for four or five days or a week, and it
shall be as you please.　If you had had as much to do in life as I
have had, you would not have that anxious temper."　This conversation gave quite a new turn to my spirits.

The next day they got away in a coach and six through the high-piled
snow.　The hangers-on repeated that no one submitted to Lonsdale except
from self-interest: two had sons whose Eton education he paid for; a third
had his eye on a post as Collector of Customs at Lancaster.　Boswell wearily
summarized his situation:

I felt myself very awkward amidst such people.　But I thought
what does the world *imagine* as to the *consequence* of living intimately
with the great Lowther, the powerful proprietor of £50,000 a year?
And in the world's estimation, one wishes to exist high.

Lonsdale continued to be unpredictable.　Boswell had brought his *Life*
notes for 1778 with him, and Lonsdale came into his room one day when
he was working on them.

"Here," said he, "is a room which may be celebrated.　It may be
said such and such things were written here."　When he chooses
to pay a compliment, nobody can do it more graciously.

Then again the atmosphere grew stifling.　No one even dared ask for
wine; Lonsdale measured it out himself.　A letter from Margaret showed
she was very ill, and when Boswell pressed for a date for his election,
Lonsdale replied, "I am *thinking* of it."　Boswell trembled with agitation,
while Lonsdale as its Colonel paraded the Westmorland militia about, or
taking him under the arm showed him complacently over his vast Whitehaven properties.　Finally, on 10 January 1788, Boswell was allowed to
proceed to Carlisle, where he was elected Recorder the next day; he was
back in London on the 14th.　From his wife's appearance he saw "that she
had been at the gates of death."

I V

THE NEXT FEW PAGES of Boswell's journal, summarizing the rest of
January and February, are a babble of relief.　The Warton brothers, Joseph

and Thomas, were in town, which always stimulated literary dinners; and Warren Hastings's trial for plundering India—Boswell, as always, the fervent admirer of a powerful figure—was a spectacle of far greater fascination than any play at Drury Lane.   But money was short again, scarcity aggravated by a gathering at Dilly's when Boswell played whist until 4 a.m. and lost almost £20, while Margaret waited up for him.   Though he assured Lord Rockville, "I would give up very favourite objects for her health and happiness," the most he did for Margaret was to comment that when Malone and young Jephson came to supper,

> It was wonderful what a change to the better their agreeable society made on my wife and daughters, who had been long shut up in almost constant dull solitude.

Boswell later accused Mrs. Stuart of neglecting her once closest friend.

Margaret now exerted full pressure.   She brought out all the old arguments about Scotland, bearing down heavily on his father's wish that Boswell live at Auchinleck, and she found new points to make:

> That if my living in London had any probability of advantage, I might be justified; but that I must now be satisfied that I could not give the application necessary for the practice of the English law, and that indeed I led a life of dissipation and intemperance so that I did not go on even with my *Life of Dr. Johnson*, from which I expected both fame and profit; in short, that I did nothing; and that I found myself neglected by those who used to invite me when I came to London only for a month or two; that my circle was now confined to a very few, for that people shunned a man who was known to be dependent and in labouring circumstances.

Her arguments carried great weight, Boswell admitted, but he could not bring himself to return to the stifling country he had finally escaped.

The one result of Margaret's lecture was to start Boswell working again on the *Life*.   Though he feared that interest in Johnson was fading, at least he had become increasingly confident about his method.   He wrote to Percy (9 February 1788):

> It appears to me that mine is the best plan of biography that can be conceived, for my readers will as near as may be accompany Johnson in his progress and, as it were, see each scene as it happened.

He could be much more open with Temple, who had asked whether he had the vanity to think his biography would be better than Mason's *Gray*:

> Mason's *Life of Gray* is excellent, because it is interspersed with letters which show us the *man*. . . .   I am absolutely certain that

> *my* mode of biography, which gives not only a *history* of Johnson's
> *visible* progress through the world and of his publications but a
> *view* of his mind in his letters and conversations, is the most perfect
> that can be conceived, and will be *more* of a *life* than any work that
> has ever yet appeared.   I have been wretchedly dissipated so that
> I have not written a line for a forthnight.   But today I resume
> my pen and shall labour vigorously.

And so he did, finishing fifty-two pages in a week.   He still had six years
of Johnson's life to write, and now spoke of publication in September or
thereabouts.

Then the competition produced its most unsettling effort, Mrs. Piozzi's
Letters to and from the Late Samuel Johnson.   Boswell confidently expected
"much entertainment"; instead, he was deeply hurt.   He told himself in
his journal (7 March 1788):

> I was disappointed a good deal, both in finding less able and
> brilliant writing than I expected, and in having a proof of his
> fawning on a woman whom he did not esteem, because he had
> luxurious living in her husband's house; and in order that this
> fawning might not be counteracted, treating me and other friends
> much more lightly than we had reason to expect.   This publication
> *cooled* my warmth of enthusiasm for "my illustrious friend" a good
> deal.   I felt myself degraded from the consequence of an ancient
> Baron to the state of an humble attendant on an author; and,
> what vexed me, thought that my collecting so much of his con-
> versation had made the world shun me as a dangerous companion.

Boswell could rationalize anything Mrs. Piozzi wrote, but he could not
evade Johnson's own words.   His basic feeling was jealousy.   Johnson was
not that much taken with luxurious living, but he did want a home where
he was welcomed and indulged.   Thrale always looked upon him "with
respect and benignity"; his letters to Mrs. Thrale showed how much more
he loved and depended on her than on anyone else.   Boswell—or "Boz"
or "Bozzy" half the time—often appears in the *Letters*, usually as gay, good-
humoured, and full of energy; but now and then Johnson speaks of him
disparagingly, the more to emphasize his intimacy with the mistress of his
heart.

More disquieting—to the point that Boswell cannot bring himself to
articulate it precisely—was the attitude he calls "fawning."   Johnson often
asks Mrs. Thrale to "manage" him, tells her to "keep strictly to your character of governess," speaks of the Thrale children as his brothers and sisters,
says, "I wish to live awhile under your care and protection": in brief, as he

admits to her late in life, "I am miserably under petticoat government and yet am not very weary nor much ashamed."

If Johnson's other friends characteristically saw him as potent and authoritative, sometimes displaying an angry irritability that could suggest a cruel streak, with Mrs. Thrale his intellectual superiority became mixed with something approaching an unpleasant subservience. Johnson wanted it both ways: to be respected for his abilities and so dominate the situation; and to be pitied and taken care of as a helpless being. There is an infantile component in any deep feeling of love, but in this case the child pleads constantly out of its most desperate fear, "Don't abandon me," and inevitably is abandoned for someone not only more physically exciting, but more emotionally satisfying because he stands on his own feet. And while Mrs. Piozzi primped up her letters extensively for publication, she never pretended to equal Johnson in affection.

Though much discouraged, Boswell was determined to proceed: "I am going on with the *Life*—anything to the contrary notwithstanding. It *will* be a valuable collection," he insisted to Malone immediately after reading Mrs. Piozzi's *Letters*. Luckily, about a month later he ran into Lysons, who had helped Mrs. Piozzi with her *Letters* as he had earlier with her *Anecdotes*, and Lysons obligingly filled in some of the blanks Mrs. Piozzi had created for publication. It seems fair to guess that Lysons also confirmed Boswell's suspicion that Mrs. Piozzi had omitted certain of Johnson's complimentary remarks about him.

But we now know that Mrs. Piozzi had omitted only two significant references. The first has been previously quoted. On 19 June 1775, Johnson had written to her:

> Do you read Boswell's journals? He moralized and found my faults, and laid them up to reproach me. Boswell's narrative is very natural and therefore very entertaining; he never made any scruple of showing it to me. He is a very fine fellow.

This was too much praise on the still sensitive point of her having read the journal, though with some hesitation she elsewhere let allusions to reading it stand. In the second omission, Mrs. Piozzi actually spared Boswell. As she printed it, Johnson's letter of 18 May 1776 reads:

> B— went away on Thursday night with no great inclination to travel northward, but who can contend with destiny? . . . He paid another visit, I think, to ✳ ✳ ✳ ✳ ✳ before he went home. He carries with him two or three good resolutions; I hope they will not mould upon the road.

The tone of this comment was dubious, but then Johnson's second sentence had originally read:

> He paid another visit, I think, to Mrs. Rudd before he went home to his own dearie.

Whether Mrs. Piozzi spared Boswell out of magnanimity, or because she knew he had a possibly damaging letter of hers in his hands, is anyone's guess.

By and large, Mrs. Piozzi's *Letters* raised her reputation, and even Malone, who disliked her, thought better of Johnson's letters than Boswell did.   Taylor represented a minority opinion when he had urged Mrs. Piozzi not to publish them:

> I shall be greatly grieved to see the ridiculous vanities and fulsome weaknesses which [Johnson] always betrayed in his conversation and address with his amiable female friends exposed.

Equally stirred by women and convinced of his own unattractiveness, Johnson tended to be pathetically grateful for any interest they took in him.

Taylor's comment shows the detachment of an old friend, but Boswell was far more disturbed by Johnson's letters, and not merely because they ran counter to the character of Johnson he was constructing in the *Life*. Earlier his only conscious fear had been that marriage to Mrs. Thrale would lessen Johnson's love for him, certainly remembering how Lady Auchinleck had come (so he thought) between him and his father.   But Boswell's jealousy was not merely of the usual sibling variety; it was quasi-sexual. Physically he had found Johnson repulsive, and nothing suggests he was repressing any contrary feeling.   But emotionally *one* component of Boswell's reaction to Johnson was a responsive passivity; in that respect he and Mrs. Thrale had been rivals, but her gender made a reciprocal relationship more comfortable.   To realize just how dependent Johnson had been on her was very upsetting.

Hurt found its release in anger.   He would punish them both. Boswell wanted to make a sexual relationship between Johnson and Mrs. Thrale seem ridiculous by insisting upon it, a tactic that had the further advantage of recalling her reputation for lubricity.   So he now published the *Ode by Dr. Samuel Johnson to Mrs. Thrale upon Their Supposed Approaching Nuptials*, which he had written in 1781 when that possibility had alarmed him; he gave it the fake publication date of 1784, the year of her marriage to Piozzi to emphasize the irony of the situation, and added an Argument:

> ... Touches on his jealousy of Signor Piozzi—exults in his supposed victory over his rival—describes the congratulations on the

nuptials between him and his dearest dear lady, but characteristically hints at the malignity of human nature—represents the envy with which their happiness is beheld—weary of continence, solaces himself with the prospect of future enjoyment—paints it with vigorous strokes and glowing colours—takes care to give it the delicate sanction of sentiment. . . .

Boswell also published *A Thralian Epigram* in the *Public Advertiser* (13 May 1788), picking up the phrase, "battering ram," which Mrs. Piozzi had used in her recent Epilogue to Bertie Greatheed's tragedy, *The Regent*:

If Hesther had chosen to wed mighty SAM,
Who, it seems, drove full at her his BATTERING RAM,
A wonder indeed then the world would have found:
A woman who truly preferred SENSE to SOUND.

But his wit was wasted on the public.

Meanwhile the crisis at home was approaching. Margaret's health had grown worse. On 9 March she had "a severe fit: cough, spitting blood, high fever." Her doctor, Sir George Baker, told Boswell what he had long dreaded, that her disease was incurable. Margaret knew it. "Oh, Mr. Boswell," she said one afternoon, "I fear I'm dying." Boswell was miserable, but at the end of March he noted in his journal:

My being so much abroad appeared very unkind to her, though I was *conscious* of sincere regard. At the same time, let me fairly mark the modifications of feeling by time and circumstances. I certainly had not that tenderness and anxiety which I once had, and could look with my mind's eye upon the event of her being removed by death with much more composure than formerly. This I considered as humanely ordered by Providence; yet I was not without some upbraidings as if I were too selfish, from leading what may be called a life of pleasure. My enthusiasm for my *Family*—for *Auchinleck*—has abated since I plunged into the wide speculative scene of English ambition.

The old ties were loosening. He summarized a letter to Lady Crawford: "Of my uneasiness between wishing to do what is for [my wife's] comfort and my love of London." Adjustment to Margaret's mortality was too difficult a process for him to cope with. He had never been very good at doing what he didn't want to do, and now he was worse than ever. In robust health himself he tried religious consolation, but Margaret was too rational to be soothed: "Oh! I am terrified for the dark passage," she told him. Though he knew he shouldn't, he so enjoyed one night at Malone's that at 5 a.m. he and Courtenay and young Jephson walked to

Hampstead, had a hearty breakfast at Highgate, and then walked back for another breakfast at Malone's, a round trip of eight or nine miles. Boswell didn't get home until noon, when he found Margaret "so agitated with anxiety that she was more feverish and spit more blood." On 29 April:

> At night was much distressed by seeing my wife in one of the feverish fits which come upon her at that time. She wandered and roved[1] strangely. Her relief from them is by laudanum. Then follows a profuse sweat, which weakens her much. She has been also for some time, with a few intervals, troubled with a looseness. She was so emaciated that it was a pain to her to sit up in bed. I was in dismal apprehension.

Apprehension sent him out the next night to get so drunk that he lost his ring (luckily recovered from a pawnbroker), sprained his ankle, and couldn't remember how he got home.

Boswell had begun looking elsewhere for support. He had written to Temple at the end of February, urging him to visit London: "*Come, come, come. . . .* O my friend, let us have some more comfortable hours *in our own old way.*" This appeal roused Temple, who replied, "I long much, very much to see you." But, as usual, he was hard to move. A month later, Boswell entreated Temple not to fail him and, as he summarizes his letter, "relieve me from the dismal apprehension that 'my friendship with Temple has perished.' " It hadn't, though Temple postponed his trip until the next year.

Except for occasional stints on the *Life*, he did nothing. He kept away from Westminster Hall, though John Scott encouraged him by saying that two years at the bar were not a sufficient trial, that he should ride the Northern Circuit both spring and summer, and that he could float back and forth between the English and Scottish bars. He persuaded Burke to come to dinner for the first time; Burke was quite easy and polite (Boswell's terms), and complimented him on his fine family. He went to Court where the King stuck to Scotland and the weather, called on his friends, and sometimes even on those who weren't, like Horace Walpole, whom he thought the same as ever: "genteel, fastidious, priggish."

Others saw Boswell too. The journalist John Taylor, writing long afterwards, describes him in his energetically social later years:

> It is no wonder that Mr. Boswell was universally well received. He was full of anecdote, well-acquainted with the most distinguished characters, good-humoured, and ready at repartee. There

---

[1]"Was delirious"—a Scotticism.

was a kind of jovial bluntness in his manner, which threw off all restraint even with strangers and immediately kindled a social familiarity.

One night that spring Taylor saw him at the theatre with Jamie, there to watch Macklin play Shylock, followed by Sir Archy MacSarcasm in his own farce, *Love-à-la-Mode*.   Young James

> was then quite a boy, and stood on the bench while his father held him round the waist. . . .   Jack Johnstone sung a song in character, each verse ending with the word, "*whack*," which he gave with great power of lungs.   Little Boswell was so delighted with this song that his father roared for a repetition with a stentorian voice to please the child, and Johnstone readily sang it again.

This was the Boswell so often seen abroad; Margaret had become a figure of reproach, and he could not keep himself at home.   Out to dinner again, he wrote:

> I was inwardly shocked at my rage for pleasure, which made me leave a distressed wife, who would never have left me even in the slightest illness.   But I braved all tender checks, and truly I came to be satisfied that I had done right; for I added to my stock of pleasing subjects for recollection, and had I stayed at home, should have fretted and done my wife more harm than[1] good. . . .   It was a very pleasant day.   I really felt how uneasiness may be perfectly removed for a time by variety of ideas.

He reverted to another pleasing idea, that continuous intoxication made him happy, and Malone had to lecture him on his drinking and lack of progress on the *Life*.   He became sexually restless, but restrained himself.

Though Margaret knew her husband far too well to expect better behaviour, she still resented his desertion of her bitterly.   He puts down one exchange which illustrates how the situation was deteriorating:

> Home; was asked unpleasingly, had I been drinking?   Glad of an excuse to go out.   Went to Piazza:[2] beefsteak and brandy punch. Quite English.

Sandy Wood, their old Edinburgh surgeon, wrote to urge his getting Margaret back to Auchinleck as soon as possible, but Boswell was enjoying London and lingered.   Finally, in a rush, he persuaded Margaret to leave

---

[1] Boswell wrote "and"—a Freudian slip?
[2] A coffee-house.

Veronica at Mrs. Stevenson's fashionable, expensive boarding-school in Queen Square, and on 15 May 1788 the rest of the family started for Auchinleck. The next day they reached Stamford, where Margaret became delirious and said she would go no further. What choice did she have but to go on to the end?

CHAPTER

15

I

EXCEPT FOR THE special instance of the Northern Circuit (July 1788), Boswell's journal now fails for a year, the longest break in the record since his marriage in 1769. Then the journal had lapsed because it had become superfluous: the excitement and happiness of marriage, the gradual settling into the regularity of legal practice and comfortable domestic habit, did not demand notation. Also, not only do all happy families resemble each other but their members begin to blur together, while, as mentioned earlier, no form of writing emphasizes individual distinctness so much as a journal. To abandon his recording practices was a sign that Boswell, so to speak, had turned over a new leaf. It took a sharp break in routine, Paoli's visit in the autumn of 1771, to make him revert to his old compulsion, in the form of brief notes; he resumed the fully written journal in the spring of 1772 when he anticipated his London jaunt and first prolonged separation from Margaret. Once more he would have things he wanted to say only to himself.

Boswell's reasons for abandoning his journal in 1788 were entirely different. Whether he was in good spirits or bad, Auchinleck did not offer much to arrest attention: if your thought and conversation are of bullocks, what is the use of writing them down? Ever since he had become Laird, Boswell had bothered less and less with journalizing at Auchinleck, and after 1789 he gave up entirely. His correspondence with his overseers, first James Bruce and later Andrew Gibb, together with various estate records, gave a sufficient account of business and daily life; while his Book of Company provided an exiguous but adequate list of visitors, local jaunts, and liquor consumed.

Margaret's illness slowed the journey to Auchinleck to six and a half days instead of the usual four or five, and even at that they travelled too quickly because of her impatience to be in her own room again. Once home she ran a constant fever and was "sadly distressed and dismally apprehensive." Boswell shared his standing attitude with Forbes: "No man ever loved a woman more than I have loved her from our early years, and no husband was ever under greater obligations to a wife." He had grown anxious enough about Margaret to detach himself from London; for once he wanted to be at Auchinleck. Now that he had temporarily subdued his own inclinations in order to comfort her, he was in sound spirits, led a busy, active life, and enjoyed the unusual peace of a quiet conscience.

If Boswell had had the sensibility we associate with Gray or Dorothy Wordsworth, if he had shared their ardour for the sublime or picturesque, no doubt he would have formulated a dozen accounts of the beauties of Auchinleck. Even better, he might have described it with the easy, unself-conscious observation he brought to his depiction of people. He might have written like Burns, not as a tourist but from within his surroundings:

Upon a simmer *Sunday morn*,   [summer]
  When Nature's face is fair,
I walkèd forth to view the corn,
  An' snuff the callor air;   [fresh]
The rising sun owre Galston muirs
  Wi' glorious light was glintan;
The hares were hirplan down the furrs,   [hopping . . . furrows]
  The lav'rocks they were chantan   [larks]
      Fu' sweet that day.

But Boswell's perception of Auchinleck had early frozen into a cliché: "the romantic rocks and woods of my ancestors." "Romantic" here means "attractively wild"; he was thinking first of the ruined Old Castle, situated high above a rocky, well-wooded glen at the intersection of the Lugar Water and the Dippol Burn. But it was no deep romantic chasm to evoke further fantasies. Nor did history touch his imagination. The celebrated skirmish of Airdsmoss had taken place at Dalblair, where that precious vessel, Richard Cameron, and eight of his little band of Covenanters, who had sworn to exterminate Charles Stuart and all the sons of Belial, were themselves slain by government troopers in 1680. There the fallen were later commemorated:

In a dream of the night I was wafted away,
To the moorland of mist where the martyrs lay;
Where Cameron's sword and his Bible are seen
Engraved on the stone where the heather grows green.

But the Killing Time had not yet been enveloped in the vitality and glamour of Scott's reconstruction, and Boswell never mentions Cameron, whose austere and exultant fanaticism he would have dreaded.   Sometimes he walked out on the roof of the House after tea and enjoyed the prospect, but at its most inspired his fancy stretches only to say of a snowfall: "I like that appearance.   Nature is like a man with fine linen well washed and his wig well powdered."   As he always was quick to admit, Boswell hardly saw the landscape at all.   It was a tract of space to be crossed between human habitations.

What Auchinleck did make substantial for its owner was the mystique of Family.   "Ancestors" is the evocative word in his cliché.   The land had come to him through a long line of males descended from Thomas Boswell, who had fought and died with his king, James IV, at Flodden Field in 1513.   Boswell's principal ambition, as he told the late Lord Eglinton in 1763, was to improve and beautify his paternal estate.   Nor, apparently, did he then foresee any conflict between that and his other early hopes centred in London.

Today Auchinleck House stands stripped to its bones, facing an untidy hayfield and backed by oak trees and what were once kitchen gardens.   It looks a bit disconsolate, abandoned—as indeed it is until funds permit further repairs.   Most of the *via sacra*, the three-mile "holy way," gravelled and tree-lined, that Lord Auchinleck had been so proud of constructing between the House and village church, is now a well-maintained public road; the visitor turns from it onto the short unkempt section remaining within the property.   The rectangular grey stone block of the House, slightly relieved by flanking pavilions, with its fine plain front in the Adam style, makes no attempt to blend with the countryside; this is a gentleman's seat—"very stately and durable" as Johnson said—which dominates the area and still gives pleasure in its directness and simple proportions.   The conspicuous motto on the front reads:

> Quod petis hic est,
> Est Ulubris, animus si te non deficit aequus—

which may be translated freely as, "What you seek is here at Auchinleck, if you have a good firm mind."   The sentiment was characteristic of Lord Auchinleck, Boswell said, "but the *animus aequus*" (the good firm mind) "is, alas! not inheritable, nor the subject of devise."

With the draining of the reedy semi-marshlands the modern landscape is now much greener, the fields richer, but the estate has shrunk to nothing. In Boswell's time it was a barony which spread over five parishes.   "Barony" is no Boswellian embellishment, but a precise legal term: land held directly of the Crown, which gave its owner, even in the late eighteenth century, jurisdiction in his baron court over petty civil and criminal cases.   As the "young laird" (heir), Boswell had often exulted in his eventual power, but possession, he found, brought responsibility as well as consequence.   T.D. and Sandy could stand in for him, and Fairlie rode over now and again to give advice on new farming methods, which the tenants might stubbornly resist: they were interested in short-term profit and the owner in long-term improvement.   Boswell's cousin, Bruce Campbell, "a gentleman of great skill and long experience," helped with the management; and the overseers took charge of day-to-day business.   But Boswell still had to make or approve all the necessary, tedious decisions about farm rentals, cottage repairs, crop rotation, timber sale, estate improvements, and, most difficult, the human variables: which tenants to encourage or reward, and which, after due warning, to threaten with the law or evict.   And his attention had to descend to the price of a grass crop or the sale of a cow.   He even felt it necessary to instruct James Bruce that when the man came to make the experiment in draining, he must have his victuals with small beer in the House.   Equally Boswell was responsible for the selection and salary (perhaps £5-£10 a year) of the schoolmaster and, as patron of Auchinleck parish, for the far more solemn duty of presenting the minister and paying most of his £50-a-year stipend.

Nellie P. Hankins, whose study of the estate has been drawn on heavily here, has sketched a composite day at Auchinleck:

> Hugh Hair was clipping the hedges; James Bruce, the overseer, was instructing his son Sandy, the gardener, in the skills of the kail yard and in planting the grounds in a style befitting "plans of noblemen's seats"; Quentin Dun was spreading burnt limestone on Tenshillingside Park; old John Wyllie was busy washing bottles in the brew-house; William Lennox, the coachman, whose allowance for boots and breeches was one pound from Martinmas to Whitsunday, was readying the chaise and comparing the merits of Dash, Old Browning, and Sharper as coach horses.   On the washing green, John Wilson's wife was bleaching the holland (linen) which she herself had woven; Grissie Wilson was gathering eggs; and Jenny Watt, the milkmaid, was caring for a cow "of an excellent kind" (probably an early Ayrshire).   Inside the house Bell Bruce, the housekeeper, was supervising the bottoming of a press bed; James Morton was sweeping the chimneys, and Alexander Pedin was repairing the spit in the kitchen; Agnes Wardin, a housemaid, was leaving her tasks for a moment to enjoy the tea

which was supplied her in addition to her annual £4 of wages; and in the sun-filled window the pet finch was singing.

Like Johnson, Boswell believed that a man born to an estate had a moral obligation to take care of it and its people.   No tenant, he told Gibb, "upon my estate has reason to fear that I will be a hard master."   Within the limits of the inevitable proprietor-tenant struggle, he made this assertion good: the orphan got new clothes, the old man a rebuilt cottage or a bottle of wine or a crown "as a kindly remembrance."   He liked collecting his rents in Auchinleck Kirk next to an open fire and with the ancient bellman in attendance.   He enjoyed inspecting the fields with James Bruce, talking to the tenants, and receiving the deference that was his due.   And he had a special regard for the tenants of long standing, like the Murdochs, Pedins, Caldows, Templetons, and Samsons (appropriately the millers), some of whom had been at Auchinleck before records were kept.   Still, Boswell had summarized his basic feelings about farming and country life in a *Hypochondriack* years earlier:

> A man of vivacity, unless his views are kept steady by a constant golden prospect of gain, cannot long be pleased in looking at the operations of ploughing, dunging, harrowing, reaping, or threshing.

> A hypochondriac proprietor is sick and sick again and again with ennui, and is tempted with wild wishes to hang himself on one of his own trees long before they are able to bear his weight.

As Johnson remarked, "They who are content to live in the country, are *fit* for the country."

Once more, and this time it was almost miraculous, Margaret started to recover.   Boswell told Malone that she had

> a very favourable remission of her severe and alarming complaints. The country air, asses' milk, the little amusements of ordering about her family, gentle exercise, and the comfort of being at home and amongst old and valuable friends had a very benignant effect upon her; and I would fain flatter myself that she may recover though not full health, yet such a degree of it as that she may enjoy life moderately well.   Her preservation is of great importance to me and my children, so that there is no wonder that I suffer frequently from anxious apprehensions which make me shrink.   I sometimes upbraid myself for leaving her, but tenderness should yield to the active engagements of ambitious enterprise.

Enterprise meant the Northern Circuit, the prominent reason Boswell had given Lonsdale for wishing to be made Recorder of Carlisle.   T.D., who had all of the family pride with none of Boswell's genius, volatility, or flights of optimism, encouraged him with "a dreary remonstrance" that he was lessening himself by the futile pursuit of practice, but Boswell endeavoured to keep resolution firm: "I attend diligently," he assured Malone; "I take good notes, I feel a gradual accession of knowledge, and I look forward with hope." This statement suggests someone of twenty-seven rather than forty-seven, and in fact Boswell's combination of age and inexperience was awkward. Some of his forty or fifty fellow counsel "in their half-impertinent, half-ludicrous way" tried to make him Junior again, but he resisted firmly and successfully. However he had to pay a two and a half guinea fine and submit to the reinstatement ritual of "Grand Night," when the Circuit held mock-court; Boswell rode about backwards on the back of another barrister (who stood in for a ram), repeating:

> Here I am,
> Riding on a black ram,
> Like a deserter as I am.
> My contrition sincere, O Grand Court, don't disdain,
> But, good Mr. Junior, let me have my place again.

Apparently Boswell had invented this ceremony himself two years earlier, but that did not reconcile him to the fun: "The din and foolishness did not please me like the first time, when there was novelty and hopes of success as an English counsellor."

Boswell's ample Northern Circuit journal (1–29 July 1788) had little more to record than the strenuous social life of the legal round: dinners with the Archbishop of York—where Boswell was distinguished by being asked to stay the night—and the Bishop of Durham, balls, tourist visits to castles, calls on local ladies, whist at the Circuit mess. It was "a very good way of getting over life" Boswell thought,

> to a man who has often struggled in "the miry clay"[1] of a melancholy existence. There was a manly steadiness about me which I enjoyed much, and I was animated with thinking that I was in a *great* lottery.

In the *Life of Johnson* Boswell was to comment that some prominent contemporary lawyers had "by no means thought it absolutely necessary to submit" to a "long and painful course of study." To think of the law as a lottery—Boswell tried the lottery itself too—conveniently transferred responsibility for success from Boswell's shoulders to the broader ones of Fortune. Did he recall that most lottery tickets turn up blank?

[1]Psalms 40:2.

At Durham, Boswell met the first known Johnson-Boswell enthusiast, William Ambler, a fellow Recorder. Ambler overdid the compliments. One evening at a dance, Boswell wrote,

> Ambler was somewhat troublesome by pressing me; and by way of being on [terms of] Johnsonian familiarity, he called me (in northern broad dialect) *Bozzy*, which I did not like; so I would not sup after the dance.

This was the initial sign that literature was shaping life, that Boswell would fade into the legend of himself which he had largely helped to create.

As the weeks went on, Boswell's patience with his colleagues wore thin. He began to complain daily of "coarse jocularity," "rough vulgarity," "vulgar jocularity." A good deal of the blame he could take to himself. On his first Northern Circuit he had played the ingratiating hail-fellow-well-met, and even now he enjoyed being the promoter of festivity; but his simple-minded brethren found it hard to grasp that fundamentally he was a proud country gentleman of good family. They snickered when he got a brief. T.D.'s criticism stuck in him: he was lessening himself, if in a good cause.

One night (25 July) at Naworth Castle Boswell absurdly offered (his phrase) to fulfil local custom by emptying a glass which held a full quart of ale. Imagining himself protected by "a breastplate of ale," he began to drink port with impunity, and chased the port with brandy. Some of his companions had kept up with him; they got on their horses and rode wildly into Carlisle, Boswell at one point tumbling off when he tried to dismount. A kind friend supported him to his lodgings.

The next day, he decided that this was no way to enter the city of which he had the honour to be Recorder. The Circuit began to seem an ambitious but ill-judged experiment; then, after a long, losing evening at whist, he decided it was an expensive dissipation that deprived his wife and family of the legitimate comfort of his presence. But he also felt the claim of persistence and made it out as far as Lancaster, virtually the Circuit's end, before returning home in the middle of August.

Boswell now turned his full attention to politics. An accidental encounter with Pitt and Dundas the previous March had momentarily extinguished any illusions of Ministerial aid. Pitt, who refused to recognize his existence, had "looked cold and stiff and proud," which was the way he always looked, though Dundas took pleasant notice of him. Boswell reminded himself that he "had done the King's cause essential service" and deserved reward; Dundas had promised in writing, so Boswell believed, to help him obtain promotion, and had said "upon his honour" in the summer

of 1787 that he had not resented the Diminishing Bill pamphlet.   Boswell
told himself:

> I trusted that he would keep his word, or rather I was *determined*
> that by and by he *should*; otherwise he should answer to me.

This was a fierce-sounding threat.

But until Dundas kept his word Boswell's remaining hope, apart from
Lonsdale, lay in Ayrshire.   He had vacillated about further involvement
there, announcing to the world through the *Public Advertiser* at one point
that now he was Recorder of Carlisle he was withdrawing as a Parliamentary
candidate.   Then the rumour that Montgomerie was to be given a lucrative
appointment and vacate his seat stirred ambition once more.

National politics provided an unusual complication to the Ayrshire
scene.   Despite being snubbed, Boswell felt he had to support Pitt against
Fox, which severely limited his options.   He explained his position in a
letter to Malone (12 July 1788):

> Having been a declared candidate for the county ever since the
> last election[1] I found such an appearance of stirring that it was
> proper for me to begin my canvass directly, in which I tell *you*,
> not ostentatiously, that I have met with more success than I
> expected.

If nominal and fictitious votes were eliminated, the Ayrshire roll would
drop from over 200 to some 85 voters, which would give Boswell what
chance he had.

> I stand between two parties—the State Coalition interest[2] which is
> to support one candidate, and a strange coalition between Lord
> Eglinton and Sir Adam Fergusson, who are both with the present
> Administration, but which has given great offence to many of their
> friends, who will therefore prefer me who am of the same political
> way of thinking without having the exceptionable circumstance of
> being in a confederacy to enthral the county.

On his way to the Northern Circuit, Boswell published an "Address
to the Real Freeholders," and in September rode the county for two weeks.
He was joined as a candidate by that other perennial independent, Sir John
Whitefoord; the Eglinton-Fergusson group chose William McDowall of
Garthland (Renfrewshire) as a stopgap until Fergusson could come into his

---

[1] Of 1784.
[2] The local adherents of the Fox-North Coalition.

own again, while the great lords of the State Coalition (Cassillis, Dumfries, and Glencairn) fixed on Cassillis's nephew, Sir Andrew Cathcart.

Boswell erected his banner at a meeting of the "real freeholders" in Kilmarnock on 25 September 1788, which unanimously resolved to support him against the outlander McDowall.   The brave newspaper account, however, mentions only two other freeholders by name, so it is likely very few attended.   But Boswell would have been willing to stand alone, as long as his stance was prominent.   Young James Cuninghame, his wife's nephew, declared that he wanted more than "merely to pass through life unnoticed like a mushroom," and Boswell was of the same mind.   If he couldn't be important, he wanted to look important.

A few days later, Boswell in his capacity of Recorder addressed the grand jury at Carlisle.   It was his most significant public speech and he was proud of it.   After briefly reviewing the historical development of our excellent government, in which he touched on the shock of the Glorious Revolution and the monarchy's recovery of strength under the present benignant sovereign, Boswell presented his credo:

> "Fear GOD and honour the King" is a text which cannot be too frequently recalled to our minds.   The union of religion with government—"submission for the Lord's sake"—produces that reverence for our rulers which, if men have [it] not, they may be restrained but are not gently governed. . . .   The better Christians we are, the happier shall we be in our civil connections with each other and in our allegiance to the sovereign.   Our duty will be easy, and we shall realize that beautiful expression in the liturgy that "service is perfect freedom."

The champion of Corsican liberty had come to rest in the most irreproachable Tory view of the intertwined supremacy of Church and State.   In France different theories were about to make themselves felt.

I I

THOUGH HE HAD EXPECTED to finish the draft of the *Life* at Auchinleck, for months Boswell had not written a word.   He would have to devote himself to it in London and, worried about his lack of progress, even threatened to drink no more wine until he finished.   Of course this was not meant to be taken literally.   He and Malone missed each other.   Malone and his relations had taken a house, Cobham Park, in Surrey, and he urged Boswell to visit: "Make what haste you can here that you may not lose some pleasant hours, which, as life passes away, become more and more valuable." Auchinleck had started to depress him again, but it was not easy to leave. He had decided to take the two boys, and Veronica was still at Mrs. Stevenson's in London; Margaret, to be left behind, was anxious about the children's health and miserably fearful she would never see the absent ones again. On 20 October 1788 they set off, and after a quick detour to call on Anna Seward in Lichfield—that flame remained alight— they arrived in London on the 26th.

Still Boswell did not resume his journal, the first time he had not done so on arrival in London. He felt too guilty: his place was at Auchinleck with Margaret, if not at Edinburgh in the Court of Session. London was a selfish indulgence, too plain to rationalize and too painful to confront. He suffered severely: conscience could not keep him at home, but it would not let him rest abroad. Much of what is known about his life for the next few months comes from a series of letters to Margaret, which reveals his uneasiness, her hurt, and the deep intimacy between them. He had made the bad mistake of telling her about Margaret Caroline Rudd (after all, he had told everyone else), and she realized, of course, that Mrs. Rudd was her first serious rival. Painfully conscious of the effect of consumption on her attractiveness, and of Boswell's susceptibility to temptation, Margaret was convinced that the affair was still going on; and her suspicion, groundless for once, further embittered their separation.

Nor could Malone help this time. After a day and a half at Cobham Park, Boswell fled to London, unfit for company. From there he wrote to Margaret (9 November 1788):

> Yesterday morning I was alarmed in a terrible manner. The postman's loud rap shook my nerves, which for a week and more had been very bad—and a letter with the mark Mauchline, sealed with black and directed by Phemie, was delivered. The circumstance of its being sent directly and not under Mr. Garforth's cover seemed to imply unusual haste and added to my fears. I was almost afraid to open it, which I did in great agitation—and when I saw your handwriting I fervently thanked GOD. The poor boys were in the room, and you may imagine how they were affected. . . .
>
> I was so much relieved by finding you had written me any letter at all, that I bore with much tranquillity certain passages which otherwise would have pained me a good deal. Sensible as I am of conduct which I so sincerely blame that I can scarcely believe it to be true, and of which I have repented most seriously and with vexation of mind, I cannot but think it hard that the regard which I express should be doubted or rather not credited,

when I am sure that notwithstanding many culpable deviations there never was a more lasting attachment, more true esteem, or more tender love.   During this last separation I have felt it deeper than ever, and when I have been depressed by a return of melancholy joined with contrition, how distressing must such reflections as are in your letter be to me.   The creature to whom you allude I told you was totally dismissed from my attention, and I solemnly protest that I have not corresponded.   How shameful would it have been if I had after what I assured you, or indeed in any view.   If you can, for this one time more, generously and wisely forget and forgive, I think my feelings have been such there shall never again be any occasion for just complaint.

Would it have raised Boswell's spirits at this point to have read the following letter to Bruce Campbell?

Mauchline, 13 November 1788

I enclose you for Mr. Boswell the ballad you mentioned; and as I hate sending waste paper or mutilating a sheet, I have filled it up with one or two of my fugitive pieces that occurred.   Should they procure me the honour of being introduced to Mr. Boswell, I shall think they have great merit.   There are few pleasures my late will-o'-wisp character has given me equal to that of having seen many of the extraordinary men, the heroes of wit and literature, in my country; and as I had the honour of drawing my first breath almost in the same parish with Mr. Boswell, my pride plumes itself on the connection.   To crouch in the train of mere stupid wealth and greatness, except where the commercial interests of worldly prudence find their account in it, I hold to be prostitution in anyone that is not born a slave; but to have been acquainted with such a man as Mr. Boswell I would hand down to my posterity as one of the honours of their ancestor.
        I am, Sir, your most obedient and very humble servant,

ROBT. BURNS

Burns tended to adopt an air of honest manliness when approaching possible patrons—he protests rather much—but these compliments have a more convincing sound than usual.   He and Boswell never met.

Public attention for the next few months was focused on the sudden prostration of the King.   At the beginning of November he fell ill: his eyesight, hearing, and memory were impaired; unable to sleep, he was violently agitated and talked incessantly—once for nineteen hours at a stretch.   Delirium and fever developed, and the doctors thought he was near death.   The fever subsided, but the delirium did not.   Oaths and indecencies poured out, he turned away from the Queen to whom he had always been devoted, and made too plain his violent desire for fifty-year-old Lady Pembroke. He thought London was under water, and wanted to send his yacht from Windsor to rescue some manuscripts. He conferred the highest dignities on pages, attendants, and all who approached him. In a lucid interval, he confided that he had thought he was inspired, and also that he could see Hanover through Herschel's telescope. In desperation, the Court called in a clergyman turned madhouse-keeper, who put the King into a strait-waistcoat at the first sign of stubbornness. Modern authorities think he suffered from a rare hereditary physical disease called porphyria. But to his bewildered physicians and Ministers, he was simply as mad as the vexèd sea. And no prognosis of recovery commanded general confidence.

A regency was imperative but the Prince of Wales, like all Hanoverian heirs, was hostile to the King's Ministers, and Pitt proceeded with all possible deliberation. The Opposition's greedy haste to grasp power only made his reluctance to abandon office seem the more sensible. Moved by the Prince's claim to an unrestricted regency, Boswell started to put together one of his "very warm popular pamphlets." But ambition did not halt there; if the King could not help him, perhaps the Prince would. He was seized by a vision of moving among the Prince's friends, the Carlton House set, and started to write a "Song for Carlton House" in which various dignitaries are addressed familiarly, and for which he prepared a newspaper puff describing it as "*studiously* composed for a worthy gentleman when half-seas-over, when at the enchanting point of incipient intoxication." But prudently he waited to see which way Lonsdale, who was ill and ardently courted by both sides, would swing. Lonsdale went over to the Prince, but by that time Boswell's zeal for the Prince's cause had momentarily cooled.

Still the political uproar had its small pleasures. He wrote to Margaret (23 January 1789):

> Sir Adam Fergusson's having gone against Pitt is *capital*, as the phrase is. He means to prevent the Regency Ministry from being against him in Ayrshire. But he will find himself mistaken. I shall consider calmly whether to avow myself against *both* the Coalition candidates, as they both now are.

Whatever political misstep Fergusson made, he quickly regained his footing.

For some time Boswell had thought the more strings that attached him to Lonsdale the better. Where else could he turn? And Lonsdale graciously entrusted some delicate negotiation to him, which Boswell took as a "very honourable distinction." In response he declared (23 November 1788):

> I am a zealous friend to our limited monarchy and wish to support the Crown against faction, but I am attached to no party but to your Lordship. In the present or any other opening for me, I shall most gratefully be, my Lord, your Lordship's very faithful, humble servant.

"The business alluded to," he told Margaret, "is highly flattering to me, but is a *secret* which I might communicate to *you* were we together, but would not put in writing." (Its nature remains unknown.) Lonsdale even condescended to call one day when Boswell was out:

> Sandy did not hear his name and talked to him, he says, quite easily, but takes credit to himself for perceiving something grand in his countenance. Jamie had heard who it was, and stood in a corner frightened. . . . What you write to me as to my being ill-suited to *dependence* is excellent. But where I have a high respect and look up to superior strength of mind, I am greatly assisted.

Lonsdale's favour revived Boswell's spirits, as he reassured Margaret:

> I am wonderfully well, so be no longer uneasy about me. Poor Jamie said to me just now, "Papa, you say that I'm a great charge trusted by Mama to Sandy and you. But you are the charge trusted to us, for she writes to both of us to take care of you."

Alternating between despair at getting practice and "visionary hopes that it may come all at once," Boswell had determined on a year's further trial. Margaret sensibly suggested that his ignorance of English legal forms would expose him, but he replied that "the *rank* of *barrister* is, however, something and might be turned to account." (Malone once said in exasperation, "You will never cease to delude yourself with *sound*.") Since Margaret's illness made it most unlikely she could ever return to London, they gave up the house in Great Queen Street. Boswell considered chambers in the Temple, but their dreariness and promise of solitude made him shudder. After much searching he found "a neat, pretty, small house in Queen Anne Street West, quite a genteel neighbourhood"; though it could not accommodate the whole family it would serve as a kind of camp lodging until better could be had. And Malone lived on Queen Anne Street East, very convenient for dinners, visits, and literary consultations.

Since his return to London, Boswell had made real progress on the *Life*. By the middle of November he was half done with 1783; a month

later he had reached June 1784; and on 10 January 1789 he wrote to
Temple:

> On Saturday[1] I finished the Introduction and Dedication to Sir
> Joshua, both of which had appeared very difficult to be accom-
> plished.   I am confident they are well done.   Whenever I have
> completed the rough draft, by which I mean the work without
> nice correction, Malone and I are to prepare one half perfectly,
> and then it goes to press, where I hope to have it early in February
> so as to be out by the end of May.

Boswell was trying to defend himself against Temple who, having
abandoned effort himself, was quick to assault his illusions.   On the verge
of fifty, Temple declared, it was too late to trifle; one ought to have more
than a reputation for wit and pleasantry; "one ought to be something."
Then he modulated into the pathetic: what had happened to the "pleasing
ideas of eminence and distinction" of their youth?   Still, Temple conceded
the attraction of London since "agitation and an object are necessary to
your well-being."   Boswell responded in unison: "In the country I should
sink into wretched gloom, or at best into listless dullness and sordid ab-
straction."

And he worked and worked and worked, with great speed and care.
Boswell has never been given sufficient credit for the hard labour the *Life*
cost him.   Though he complains or boasts to his friends of his exertions,
he says little to himself in the journal about the pleasures and pains of
composition; they were too much a part of the accepted routine to need
comment.   Yet he went to bed every night knowing that much remained
to be done, and waited for the access of energy that morning would bring.
This extended stretch of heavy work on his great biography has been
ironically overshadowed by a "keenness of temper and a vanity to be distinguished *for the day*," which, he said, "make me too often *splash* in life."
Just as Johnson, the most indolent of men, had produced that most laborious of works, the *Dictionary*, so Boswell, with his constant eye to immediate prominence, yet wrote by far the longest biography composed in
English up to that time.

And the thought of Margaret was always with him.   "The *separation*,"
Boswell wrote to her in December 1788,

> distresses me more than I can tell, and I often say to myself, "Is
> there anything in this world equally valuable to *me* as being with
> my dear M.M.?"   It is truly unfortunate that I have such a restless

[1]3 January.

ambition and so little tranquillity.   But if Lord Lonsdale should prove a real friend to me, I may yet have it to say that I did well to try my fortune here. . . .   I hope in GOD that a winter in the country and a particular time of life being fairly over may make you healthy so as to be able to come to London if necessary.

When Margaret complained, he answered:

How *can* you say I am better off without you?   Be assured that I feel our separation more than you can imagine.   At this very time I am much in the frame that I was in the summer that we returned from Ireland, and you recollect what *that* was.[1]   I get into fits of extreme impatience to be with you, and sometimes into fits of sad fear.

But Boswell—it exasperates and charms—could seldom resist honesty:

Yet I am upon the whole wonderfully well, owing, I do believe (though perhaps I should be sorry for it), to my living very *heartily* and being in much variety.

As his contribution to variety, Boswell gave a dinner (26 January 1789) in Queen Anne Street West for Barnard, Windham, Tom Warton, Reynolds, Seward, the Earl of Moray, ever-cheerful Jack Devaynes (the King's Apothecary), and Mr. O'Reilly, "an Irish gentleman of ancient blood."   He described the occasion to Forbes:

I can have such a thing as this rarely, but it is wonderfully agreeable.   However, I have it often, or rather am had at it often, in other houses.   We were—I am sure I myself was—very, very happy. It may be perhaps more rational for me not to be in London; but also, my dear friend, as Johnson said, "sensation is sensation," and what can compensate to a man for the want of high intellectual enjoyment? . . .   I am very impatient that I am not in Parliament. My *fermentation* is not over yet.

Prominent among his entertainers was Reynolds, who "was never more happy," according to the painter Joseph Farington, "than when . . . Mr. Boswell was seated within his hearing" (an odd expression, since Reynolds was so deaf he had to use an ear-trumpet).   Reynolds gave the most celebrated dinners in London, his table reputedly costing him £2,000 a year. The money was not spent on grandeur.   But his "enlarged hospitality," Boswell was to say in dedicating the *Life* to him, made his house in Leicester Fields (now Square) "a common centre of union for the great, the accomplished, the learned, and the ingenious."   According to Courtenay, liter-

---

[1]Boswell refers to the summer they became engaged.

ature was the chief topic and politics was forbidden; wit and humour were encouraged, except for story-telling and premeditated *bons mots*.

Courtenay continues:

There was something singular in the style and economy of his table that contributed to pleasantry and good humour: a coarse, inelegant plenty without any regard to order and arrangement. A table, prepared for seven or eight, was often compelled to contain fifteen or sixteen. When this pressing difficulty was got over, a deficiency of knives and forks, plates and glasses, succeeded. The attendance was in the same style; and it was absolutely necessary to call instantly for beer, bread, or wine, that you might be supplied before the first course was over. . . .

The wine, cookery, and dishes were but little attended to; nor was the fish or venison ever talked of or recommended. Amidst this convivial, animated bustle amongst his guests, our host sat perfectly composed, always attentive to what was said, never minding what was eat or drank, but left everyone at perfect liberty to scramble for himself. Temporal and spiritual peers, physicians, lawyers, actors, and musicians composed the motley group, and played their parts without dissonance or discord.

Boswell summarized dinner at Reynolds's in a phrase: "quite a hurly-burly, but very pleasant."

Given such attractions and the need to complete the *Life*, Boswell finessed the Northern Circuit, with its expense and rough, unpleasant company. His prospects centred in London. He continued to berate Pitt, though Temple advised a calmer approach: "A person of your family, fortune, and situation appearing so solicitous for office and preferment cannot raise you in the idea[1] of a Minister"; Boswell's last letter to Pitt "had a tendency to give offence" rather than obtain its object. (Pitt was notorious for not answering his mail, so it is quite possible that he never even bothered to open Boswell's letters.) But when Temple ventured doubts as to his dependence on Lonsdale, Boswell insisted that Lonsdale showed him more and more regard, and hoped that Lonsdale would do even more for him than he already had. In any case, he declared once more, he was in the great lottery of life, and even if he did not win a considerable prize the agitation involved provided present enjoyment.

Then Boswell's attention was drawn homewards. At the end of February Margaret began to grow worse again. She had been too active, though perhaps it made no difference. The only medical man she trusted was Sandy Wood in Edinburgh, but under the pretext of a social call a

[1]Mental image.

neighbouring doctor, John Campbell, looked in on her: in common chance, he reported, she might live only a month; but Boswell might just as well wait to see if she didn't improve after all before he started for Auchinleck. Boswell himself remembered clearly that she had made surprising recoveries in the past.

In her panic, Margaret recurred to Mrs. Rudd. (Did she wonder what else could detain Boswell in London when he must know how ill she was?) Boswell was patient:

> It pained me to think that after your humane and generous conduct you should be agitated with any suspicions that what I am truly sensible was very bad indeed is not totally at an end. Be perfectly assured that it is, and that you shall have every proof that can possibly be given of sincere regret. You really do not know me well enough; otherwise you would give more credit to me. I entreat then that all remembrance of this unfeeling and criminal conduct, for such I from my heart allow it to be, may be banished from *your* breast. As for me, I consider it to be my serious duty to be forever sorry for it, and to be more and more upon my guard.

Margaret's response was "truly kind."

Boswell had not planned to go back to Auchinleck until Veronica's school term ended in May, and even now he vacillated. There were all the cherished distractions of London that made it, as he said, the best place for the unhappy as well as the happy: illuminations in honour of the King's recovery; the dinner of the Humane Society (350 in attendance) for reviving the apparently dead; the Queen's splendid drawing-room (levee), where, Boswell told Temple,

> I was the *great man* (as we used to say) . . . in a suit of imperial blue, lined with rose-coloured silk, and ornamented with rich gold-wrought buttons. What a motley scene is life.

In spite of his continual protestations of affection, Boswell was reluctant to leave London; but Margaret could also say one thing and suggest another. Now she wrote: "My fever still continues, and I waste away daily," though, aware of his extreme fondness for London, she urged him "with admirable generosity" not to hasten away from it. There is no more reason to suspect her sincerity than to doubt Boswell's. "I should have a heart as hard as a stone were I to remain here," Boswell told Temple. Leaving the boys behind, he gathered Veronica from school and arrived at Auchinleck on 6 April 1789.

It was a terrible time. Boswell could neither face Margaret's condition nor escape it. She was miserably weak and emaciated, hardly able to eat or drink, and Boswell himself said that he had never seen anyone in such distress except old Treesbank, when his face had been eaten away by cancer. Nor could the pious commonplaces of religion comfort her. But she was more firm than Boswell. Though he had come home "on purpose to soothe and console her," politics gave him an excuse to junket about the countryside and drink too much.

Since Boswell wanted to make himself, as he said, conspicuous, he put together an Address to the Prince of Wales, complimenting him on his "admirable moderation and truly patriotic conduct" during the King's illness, which he persuaded six other J.P. s to approve at the Quarter Sessions (5 May); he then circulated it for other signatures, but in spite of its apparently innocuous nature fewer than 40 of the 140 Ayrshire J.P.'s would put their names to it. Their reluctance was understandable. A number of pro-Prince Addresses had been submitted from Scotland during the King's illness, and their sponsors had been marked for political oblivion by the triumphant Pitt and Dundas. It was a wrong-headed move even from Boswell's point of view, since it could only irritate, without damaging, the Ministry, and play into the hands of the detestable Foxite Opposition. Also, as Temple was quick to remind him, the conduct of the Prince's party during the crisis was "generally thought to have been equally unfeeling and injudicious." "You show everyone," continued Temple, "how eager you are for office and preferment, and yet by your own rashness throw obstacles in your way." The best one can say for Boswell's initiative is that he thought it would procure him an introduction to the Prince of Wales, and that Lonsdale would approve of it. He lacked a political gyroscope.

All this time Boswell was conscious that at some point he would be summoned to Lowther Castle to accompany Lonsdale to London where the Corporation of Carlisle faced a crucial lawsuit about the honorary freemen, and the dreaded call came in the middle of May. Visiting a neighbour a few days earlier, Boswell had got drunk and fallen from his horse on the way home, badly bruising his shoulder. He felt unfit for travel, and was afraid that if he left Auchinleck he might never see Margaret alive again. But she urged him to go; neither would admit that she was in immediate danger; and on 18 May he set off. He was too late for the coach, and returned for one more day. In a fragment of surviving journal (the first since the previous July) he wrote, "I shall never forget her saying, 'Good journey!'" Others were more hard-headed: Bruce Campbell asked whether they should delay the funeral until his return, if she died while he was gone.

The party was to start immediately for London as soon as Boswell arrived at Lowther, but as usual Lonsdale took his time. Boswell's shoulder ached badly, and he had an interval for overwhelming remorse. He much preferred Malone's company, but it was to his old and most intimate friend Temple that he could confess freely:

> No man ever had a higher esteem or a warmer love of a wife than I of her. You will recollect, my Temple, how our marriage was the result of an attachment truly romantic. But how painful is it to me to recollect a thousand instances of *inconsistent* conduct. I can justify my removing to the great sphere of England upon a principle of laudable ambition. But the frequent scenes of what I must call *dissolute* conduct are inexcusable. Often and often when she was very ill in London, have I been indulging in festivity with Sir Joshua Reynolds, Courtenay, Malone, etc. etc. etc., and have come home late and disturbed her repose. . . .

Endless self-indulgence, endless remorse. What could better illustrate our compulsion to repeat our worst mistakes? Boswell continued:

> But I *will* go forward. To be *zealous* is with justice a strong recommendation, and such is [Lonsdale's] great Parliamentary influence that, be Minister who will be, [he] may when he pleases get almost anything for a friend. I have no right to expect that he will give me a seat in Parliament, but I shall not be surprised if he does.

Boswell then rehearsed his small chance to represent Ayrshire and his Prince of Wales Address, as well as his intention to "work" the insolent but able Pitt:

> Can [Pitt] wonder at my wishing for preferment when men of the first family and fortune in Great Britain struggle for it. We shall see. Meantime the *attempt* rouses my spirits. What a state is my present—full of ambition and projects to attain wealth and eminence, yet embarrassed in my circumstances, and depressed with family distress, which at times makes everything in life seem indifferent. I often repeat Johnson's lines in his *Vanity of Human Wishes*:
>
>> Shall helpless man, in ignorance sedate,
>> Roll darkling down the torrent of his fate? . . .
>
> How dismal, how affecting is it to see my cousin, my friend, my wife, wasting away before my eyes, and the more distressing it is that she is as sensible as ever, so that one cannot see *why* this is. I entreat all the comfort you can give. Write to me in London directly.

Two years earlier Temple had lost his eldest son, a promising young man, and, though usually all resignation to the Divine Will, he had been impelled to complain to Boswell just that March: "Nor can I explain how the sickness or loss of those I hold most dear should be requisite to improve my nature." Now in response to Boswell's appeal, the immediate demands of the situation had the most impact. "How could you desert her at so critical a time!" he replied.

Boswell had been in London only a week and the Carlisle case had not yet come on, when he heard both from Euphemia and Dr. Campbell that Margaret was sinking. With the two boys he set out on the evening of 4 June 1789 and posted night and day, reaching Auchinleck in just over 64 hours. It was too late. Euphemia came running out of the house in tears. Margaret had died the morning of the day he left London.

Again he turned to Temple:

I cried bitterly and upbraided myself for leaving her, for she would not have left me. This reflection, my dear friend, will, I fear, pursue me to my grave. She had suffered a great deal from her disease for some weeks before her death. But the actual scene of dying itself was not dreadful. She continued quite sensible till a few minutes before, when she began to doze calmly and expired without any struggle. When I saw her four days after, her coun-tenance was not at all disfigured. But alas! to see my excellent wife and the mother of my children, and that most sensible, lively woman, lying cold and pale and insensible was very shocking to me. I could not help doubting[1] that it was a deception. I could hardly bring myself to agree that the body should be removed, for it was still a consolation to me to go and kneel by it and talk to my dear, dear Peggie.

   She was much respected by all who knew her, so that her funeral was remarkably well attended. There were nineteen car-riages followed the hearse, and a large body of horsemen, and the tenants of all my lands. It is not customary in Scotland for a husband to attend his wife's funeral. But I resolved, if I possibly could, to do her the last honours myself, and I *was* able to go through with it very decently. I privately read the funeral service over her coffin in presence of my sons, and was relieved by that ceremony a good deal. . . . I imagined that I should not be able to stay here after the sad misfortune. But I find that I cling to it with a melancholy pleasure.

[1]Suspecting.

CHAPTER

16

I

MARGARET'S DEATH LEFT Boswell numb. Then sensation returned, feelings of grief exacerbated by guilt, just as painful as if his reaction were unique instead of commonplace. Never before had he experienced overwhelming deprivation. He had loved his mother, but she had not dominated his being as his father had; and Boswell's feelings about his father's death were deeply mixed, as well as at once overshadowed by the need to assume his duties as Laird.

Temple was his great source of consolation. "Pour your griefs into my bosom," he wrote, and Boswell complied:

> What distress, what tender, painful regrets, what unavailing earnest wishes to have but one week, one day, in which I might again hear her admirable conversation and assure her of my fervent attachment, notwithstanding all my irregularities.

And nearly two months later:

> My grief preys upon me night and day. I am amazed when I look back. Though I often and often dreaded this loss, I had no conception how distressing it would be. May GOD have mercy upon me. I am quite restless and feeble and desponding. . . . I have an *avidity* for death. I *eagerly* wish to be laid by my dear, dear wife. Years of life seem insupportable. . . . *Why* should I struggle? I certainly am constitutionally unfit for any employment.

Piety comforted him.

Boswell could not yet join Margaret in the grave, and death had enlarged his immediate responsibilities. She had always attended to the

393

children, and he felt unfit, as well as reluctant, to take charge of them. Still, over the next several months, he made the necessary decisions. Veronica and Euphemia, now sixteen and fifteen, were squabbling and needed to be separated. And frankly, Boswell admitted to Temple, the company of Edinburgh-mannered girls could give him no satisfaction. Veronica boarded in London with a Mrs. Buchanan, whose daughter was her closest friend. Euphemia was sent to be polished a bit at an Edinburgh boarding-school. Fortunately, Lady Auchinleck had come to take a grandmotherly interest in the children, and Boswell, whose resentment of her had long since faded, was grateful that she was willing to keep a strict but concerned eye on the headstrong Euphemia. Sandy, almost fourteen and "a very determined Scotch laird," was sent to Eton. Jamie, at eleven, affectionate, precocious, and delicate, continued for the time being as a day-boy at Soho Academy. Betsy, pretty, clever, and young enough at eight to be saved from the contamination of her native manners and accent, was to be isolated from the family at a Chelsea boarding-school, to escape the overindulgence as well as Scottishness that afflicted her brothers and sisters. As Boswell later said to Veronica, with a casual lack of tact, he wanted one daughter who was a true English miss. The family was dispersed.

Boswell also had to dispose of himself, and his first need was to regain some spirit by lessening his sense of guilt. He offered Margaret's close friend, Lady Crawford, a characteristic excuse for his recent behaviour:

> It is not often that all the imperfections of a character are shown with an honest though perhaps imprudent openness. Fairly balance the good with the evil.

A harsh critic might recall Pope:

> Or her that owns her faults but never mends,
> Because she's honest and the best of friends.

Further, Boswell wanted to share the blame with his patron. "Alas! my Lord," he wrote to Lonsdale,

> I fear I gave too strong a proof of my zeal for anything in which your Lordship is concerned.... I thus endeavour to free my mind from a charge of barbarous neglect, which now upbraids me and may attend me to my grave.

This was not a productive line to take, and when Lonsdale failed to respond he inquired anxiously of Richard Penn, another Lonsdale M.P., whether his letter had been received. Penn replied that Lonsdale wished to give Boswell time to recover his reason before writing, but added kindly that

Boswell stood extremely high with their patron.   In time, Lonsdale did manage a decent letter of sympathy, combined with an invitation (or command) to visit Lowther Castle where, he said, "it may be some satisfaction to open your mind upon family affairs to your friend, Lonsdale."

Meanwhile, mourning had to give way to political exigency.   Montgomerie finally received his appointment as Baggage Master and Inspector of the Roads in North Britain (£500 a year), vacating his seat, and the by-election was fixed for 3 August 1789.   Boswell and Whitefoord had joined Cathcart to try to stop McDowall, and Boswell assured Temple that though they would lose they would make an admirable figure.   Even that hope was chimerical.   According to the Opposition count, Whitefoord controlled the swing vote, and with his support Cathcart would win.   Boswell's four sure votes (his own and three nominal votes made by his father) were confidently assigned to Cathcart months before the election.   Boswell was of no importance.   But Opposition efforts were unavailing, since the Eglinton-Fergusson voters felt no uneasiness about taking the trust oath, and McDowall carried the election (3 August 1789) by a large majority of 21.

"To own the truth," Boswell confessed to Temple, "I have very little chance for success at the General Election," which would be held during the next three years.   "But I may negotiate for a *part* of the Parliament." Competing candidates sometimes did arrange to sit sequentially during the same session; and it needs to be stressed that the seat in the House of Commons Boswell hoped for was a conventional goal attained by other members of the landed gentry no better qualified by property or position than he.   What was unrealistic was Boswell's estimate of the concrete political situation and the self-contradictory ways in which he tried to attain office or preferment.

It was time for Boswell to resume his usual routine, which meant rejoining the Northern Circuit.   He got as far as Lowther and funked it. As he told Temple, "My mind was so sore from my late severe loss that I shrunk from the *rough* scene of the roaring, bantering society of lawyers." And Lonsdale told him he could stay away.   But Lowther itself was unpleasant because of his still intense grief and what seems to have been a mean-spirited joke, more cruel in his situation than a direct affront.   One morning Boswell's only wig could not be found.   He suspected a trick, but Lonsdale and Colonel Lowther swore they knew nothing of its whereabouts, and he was forced to show himself in a nightcap, missing the day's excursion and the dance that night.   In his state of distress he did not regret these amusements; but he could not continue an object of laughter, so the next day he rode twenty-five miles into Carlisle, where luckily he was able to get a new wig fitted in a few hours. On his return visit to Lowther several weeks later, the wig materialized. "The way in which it was lost," Boswell told Temple, "will remain as secret as the author of Junius." [1]

In the wreckage, Boswell clung to London and the *Life*. He returned to town in October to summon up the future: finish the *Life*, take chambers in the Temple so that he could at least appear to be seeking practice, and live on in grief-stricken retirement. As late as Christmas, he was confiding to Lady Auchinleck that "what remains of my life will be passed in a pretty obstinate state of indifference." As usual, his financial situation seemed desperate: though his rent-roll now came to £1,600 a year, he had only £850 left after his fixed expenses were deducted, and his five children, he calculated, each cost him £100 a year. Still, when Bruce Campbell suggested that he let Auchinleck House, Boswell replied that he would rather set fire to it.

The future, however, has an obstinate way of not conforming to our expectations. When the journal resumes again in November 1789, Boswell has fallen in with someone identified only as "C.," possibly a well-kept courtesan; Kemble said she was as fine a woman as he had ever seen. Boswell spent a "delicious night" with her, but on a later evening found her occupied with a friend:

> Walked about awhile. Returned; C. not so inviting, and I "with wine and love oppressed." [2] Weakly deficient. Only once; ineffectual wishes. Wakeful night in feverish vexation. To crown all, the FRIEND was to come in the morning, so off early.

Next he feared "mischief" from C., and this little flurry led to a quarrel and another venereal bout. He was drinking excessively, and one night when he staggered out to meet C., Jamie decided to follow and bring him back. "Wretched scene," Boswell notes.

At least the *Life* made progress. By the middle of October, Boswell and Malone had prepared the first thirty pages for the printer; at the beginning of November, he was estimating May 1790 as the date of publication; and by the end of the month he thought a third of the work "settled," so that printing could begin soon. "You cannot imagine," Boswell wrote to Temple (30 November 1789),

> what labour, what perplexity, what vexation I have endured in arranging a prodigious multiplicity of materials, in supplying omis-

[1] Junius was the signature given to a series of able, furious attacks on prominent public figures in the *Public Advertiser* (1769–72). He is commonly thought to have been Sir Philip Francis.

[2] "With love and wine at once oppressed" (Dryden, *Alexander's Feast*, l. 114).

sions, in searching for papers buried in different masses—and all
this besides the exertion of composing and polishing.   Many a
time have I thought of giving it up.   However, though I shall be
uneasily sensible of its many deficiencies, it will certainly be to the
world a very valuable and peculiar[1] volume of biography, full of
literary and characteristical anecdotes . . . told with authenticity
and in a lively manner.   Would that it were in the booksellers'
shops.

Then Boswell broadened his survey:

Methinks if I had this *magnum opus* launched, the public has no
farther claim upon me; for I have promised no more, and I may
die in peace or retire into dull obscurity—*reddarque tenebris*.[2]   Such
is the gloomy *ground* of my mind, but any agreeable perceptions
have an uncommon though but a momentary brightness.   But
alas, my friend, be the *accidents* as they may, how is the *substance*?
How am *I*?   With a pious submission to GOD, but at the same time
a kind of obstinate feeling towards men, I walk about upon the
earth with inward discontent, though I may appear the most cheerful man you meet.   I may have many *gratifications* but the *comfort*
of life is at an end.

"Many gratifications but no comfort" became a formula to which Boswell
would now often recur in times of depression.

   It is understandable that the children were showing many signs of
distress.   Euphemia was unhappy at boarding-school, and Veronica denounced Mrs. Buchanan to Sandy with adolescent intensity as "squealing
like a pig.   She is the most deceitful, artful, cunning, greedy creature you
ever saw."   Sandy was absolutely miserable at Eton and wanted to return
home.   His father told him sharply to "think and act like a gentleman and
not like a spoiled child," but sympathy soon overcame him and he confessed
that he well remembered writing from Utrecht as from the galleys.

   Boswell could not maintain distance between himself and his children:
he confided his griefs and joys; complained of sleeping badly and missing
their mother.   He had lost almost all authority over his two eldest daughters, he confessed to Temple; his only hold was their affection for him.
Even little Betsy scolded him for not allowing her to stay at home over the
Christmas holidays.   Jamie was his great comfort: "an extraordinary boy,"
he told Temple, "he is much of his father (vanity of vanities!)."   Destined
for the bar, he had already taken up the Templar's traditional interest in

[1]Unusual.
[2]"And I shall return to the shades" (Virgil, *Aeneid*, vi. 545).

the theatre and was scribbling plays, including " 'The Siege of Carthage'—
a comic opera in five acts."

There were crumbs of pleasure, like one dinner described to Sandy,
a pie made from three Auchinleck moorfowl and three Auchinleck par-
tridges, given to "such a group of eminent men!": Wilkes, Courtenay,
Malone, Penn, Reynolds, Henry Flood (the great Irish orator), and T.D.
"Wilkes chiefly talked."

Penn, grandson of the famous Quaker and sometime deputy-governor
of Pennsylvania, was Boswell's chief confidant and adviser among Lonsdale's retainers.   He warned Boswell, from long experience, never to break
an engagement with Lonsdale; equally, he encouraged Boswell by saying
that Lonsdale had taken notice of his wish to be in Parliament.   This
disclosure could hardly have been unexpected; it would have taken a thoroughly stupid man to miss Boswell's hint in a congratulatory letter: "May
your steady friends be made to shine around you in their several orbits."
And no doubt Boswell made other leading remarks.

The life of a courtier involves constant attendance and sometimes long
hours.   Lonsdale gave a grand dinner at the London Tavern to celebrate
momentary victory in the cause of the Carlisle honorary freemen—the
cause that had dragged Boswell away from his dying wife—and that night
he did not get home until after 3 a.m.   The courtier lives as well with his
ruler's ups and downs.   Lonsdale could be "absolutely easy and agreeable";
also he could be loud and contradictory, or force too much wine on his guests.
Even the long-suffering Penn was violent one morning against his "shocking
ferocity and undignified manner of living."   But Penn too fed on hope,
specifically that Lonsdale would arrange his appointment as Ambassador
to America; he promised to take Boswell along as Secretary of Legation.

As autumn slipped into winter and winter drifted into spring, Boswell
came fully to life again.   Though Margaret's death had permanently damaged his sense of stability, it had equally lightened his ballast, so to speak;
he floated more freely.   His mood was complex:

> I cannot distinctly describe my present state of mind.   There was
> a ground of sad indifference from the consciousness of the loss
> of my excellent wife, which prevented all anxiety or uneasy re-
> flections with regard to my situation in life, whether a good account
> could be given of my method of living, or whether I should ever
> succeed in any scheme of future advancement.   I felt as if I were
> done with life, that is to say, with any care about it, so that all the
> considerations and fretfulness which I used to have were no more,
> and I experienced quite a new state of existence.   For aught I
> could see then, I might at an after period experience another state

as new, having still the consciousness of identity, which was continually stirring in my mind.   I at the same time had a keen relish
of every pleasure, whether sensual or intellectual.

Boswell's activities are easier to follow.   He had settled into a constant
round of dinners, especially with the Gang, often followed by whist and
supper; there was no Margaret at home to reproach him for wasted time
and late hours.   By the end of January 1790 he was "vastly well," and
"FELT how SUPERIOR being in London" was.   He had a "SOLID discussive
flow of gaiety."   One festive night he was carried to the Marylebone watch-
house for calling the hours in the streets, his defence being that the watch-
men never emphasized the *hour* as they should, but *past* and *o'clock* instead.
Becoming accustomed to a hearty masculine society, he felt bored and
strange in the company of ladies, unless one of them aroused particular
interest.   After one mixed gathering, Malone and Reynolds had to instruct
him that the essence of politeness was "to do what we do not like, that we
may please others."

A sure sign of recovery was that he was contemplating remarriage.
No one, he knew, would accommodate his wayward fancies as Margaret
had, but he could imagine a marriage of convenience with a sensible, good-
tempered woman of fortune.   A series of candidates presented themselves
in the next few years.   There was Lady Crawford's daughter, Lady Mary
Lindsay, a handsome woman of thirty, to whom he appointed himself
knight-errant, and supplier of lavender-water and York gloves.   She preserved her composure.   There was Isabella Wilson, an attractive heiress
whom he had met on the Northern Circuit; a polite exchange of letters
led nowhere.   For years, before and after Margaret's death, he kept a
record of a flirtation with Wilhelmina Alexander, sister of a neighbouring
laird and Burns's "bonnie lass of Ballochmyle."   Their mutual feeling
warmed a bit and then cooled.   He had frank conversations with Miss
Lister, showing her his "singular character."   He admired Jane Upton at
church; Le Fleming was able to introduce him to her mother, but he never
succeeded in meeting the daughter.   William Scott (now Sir William) invited him to dinner with his sister-in-law, Frances Bagnall: fine enough
and an heiress, but not his type.

Not that Boswell had resigned himself to abstinence.   He had almost
fainted when sounded for an urethral stricture that January but, undis-
couraged, by March had found an "enchantress," alternately "disreputable"
and "seducing," whom he describes as

> Lovely Susanna!—not too chaste—
> Wert thou a prude I could not taste

> Thy store of kind, delightful charms
> With bliss ecstatic in thy arms.

She may be the "Angel" to whom he applied a pair of lines dated 28 March 1790:

> I hate hearts.   I hate to be plagued with hearts.
> I once lost my own heart and I felt very strange.

If Boswell is referring to this incident, he soon got his heart back again. Taking Lady Crawford as his confidante as he had once taken Margaret, he summarizes a letter to her as containing an account

> of my having been in a dangerous fever of love.   Entreating allowance for my *égarements*.   One maxim I am *sure* is solid: let no man try *absolutely* to *change* his character.   It is *impossible*.   Let him make the *best* of it, and *lessen* its evil as much as he can.   This is a strange state of being.   My hope of a better is, I thank GOD, constant. . . .   Lady Mary will not deign to write to her *perfumer*. But like the royalist, I am "true as the dial."

Lady Crawford, displeased by the tone of his letters, broke off correspondence for a while.   Temple, however, was fascinated by his "Rousseaulike confession"—"in love at fifty!"—and wanted every detail.   "The more you talk of yourself, your children, your views, your feelings," Temple wrote, "the more you please me."   Details, no doubt, were forthcoming, but they have disappeared.

Boswell's surge of vitality carried him into politics again.   He had won a small victory in the Court of Session: Sir Adam Fergusson was ordered to repay Boswell for his involuntary share of the £100 Corsican subscription Fergusson had reneged on so many years earlier: the amount was only £50 with interest since 1774, and costs, but when Fergusson dragged his heels about payment Boswell determined to extract every last farthing of it.   He began to look towards the next General Election, asserting that with the abolition of nominal and fictitious votes, again under attack, he would have more backing in Ayrshire than Eglinton—a preposterous claim.   In any case, he assured Robert Boswell, "I shall make a handsome appearance, and shall certainly at least *begin* a family interest which *shall* be cherished."

To put himself forward, Boswell planned a pamphlet to be called "The Loyalty of Ayrshire," which would reprint his Diminishing Bill pamphlet and his Address to the Prince of Wales, while it added an attack on Pitt's Regency Bill and an attempt to "silence . . . obloquy" against the Duke of Queensberry ("Old Q"), accurately described by a female contemporary as "a nasty old son of sin" and remembered as the most assiduous of aristocratic lechers.   During the Regency crisis, Queensberry had deserted to the Prince's side and been stranded there on the King's recovery: deprived of his place as Lord of the Bedchamber, he had acquired a widespread reputation as a renegade.   Still, he had two or three seats in the House of Commons at his disposal.   Though Queensberry showed some interest in the project, it never materialized; perhaps it seemed better to leave his conduct unreviewed.

The two great national questions of the day were the impeachment of Warren Hastings and the French Revolution.   Boswell, making his usual claim to disinterestedness, wrote to Hastings that his only motive for cultivating an acquaintance was that of "enjoying the conversation of a man of distinguished abilities, which has all my life been my chief luxury." When Hastings called, he was greeted in a set speech:

> I view you, Sir, with the eye of Lord Thurlow as an Alexander; and though I am not surly and proud, I flatter myself I am in some degree a philosopher.   Your visit, therefore, to me may be compared to that of Alexander to Diogenes; for indeed my small hut is not much bigger than a tub.   Let me add, Sir, that you have saved me the trouble of going into the street with a torch at noonday to look for a man.

Boswell thought this mode of address quite happy, and Hastings, whose own style was orotund, was sufficiently gratified to keep up a friendship.

But admiration for Hastings necessarily increased the distance between Boswell and Burke, the principal manager of Hastings's trial, just when the detestation both felt for the French Revolution should have brought them together.   As early as autumn 1789, Boswell thought the state of France

> an intellectual earthquake, a whirlwind, a mad insurrection without any immediate cause, and therefore we see to what a horrible anarchy it tends.   I do not mean that the French ought not to have a Habeas Corpus Act.   But I know nothing more they wanted.

When Boswell called the Revolution "a diablacy" Burke warmly agreed, but Hastings obsessed him and on that subject Boswell reports him on one occasion "Irishly savage a little, but full and flowing," and on another "really unpleasant."

Boswell intended to combat the Revolution in his own fashion with a tragedy called "The Death of Favras," whose hero in real life was an executed royalist.   In the play, Dumont, "who has his head full of the fiery modern writings about the rights of men, raves like Rousseau" to Favras, who "shows that subordination and right of any sort are coeval and coexistent." Characteristically, Boswell started to publicize the play even before he had worked it out, and he soon lost interest in it.

Paoli, however, took a more optimistic, or at least more pragmatic, view of the Revolutionaries, hoping that they would restore Corsican rights if not sovereignty, and agreed to return to Corsica. Boswell gave a formal dinner in farewell (22 March 1790); they were never to meet again. The help he provided in the Corsican struggle for independence had been invaluable, and Paoli had repaid it as generously as possible: Boswell had a room in his house, an open dinner invitation, and the use of his carriage. There was always a bit of distance between them, partly a matter of temperament, partly because of Paoli's superiority in character. But "uniformly and invariably good and friendly," he gave Boswell disinterested advice and unfailing affection. His departure was an irremediable loss.

Where Boswell's access of self-confidence helped him most was in writing the *Life*. Though the date of publication like the horizon receded steadily before him and he worried about length and format, he pressed on vigorously. By the end of February 1790 he and Malone had reviewed almost half of it, and he could start feeding it to the printer. Hailes warned him to omit minute or trifling detail; Boswell ignored his advice. Bishop Percy, alarmed that episcopal dignity might suffer if his name was attached to petty anecdotes, offered to pay for cancelled leaves, and dangled the hope of further choice contributions if Boswell would accommodate his desire to remain anonymous. Boswell refused in the name of authenticity, even though Percy threatened to take serious offence. The publisher George Robinson reportedly was willing to offer "a cool thousand" for the copyright. But art is long. By the end of March Boswell was forced to admit that he could not be out before the end of October.

In his heightened state of well-being, new schemes began to intrigue him. He would write a history of Carlisle; he would pursue his fortune in the East or West Indies as soon as the *Life* was published. Temple, who was to visit London for their first meeting since 1783, wondered as he chided: "What spirits, what vivacity do you enjoy! What a relish for society and conversation!" Such a course of life would kill Temple in a few months. Write a history of Carlisle: what could Boswell be thinking of? Go to the East or West Indies: "Oh, my friend, how long do you mean to continue on this scene?" Rest your anchor at Auchinleck, Temple advised, and assert your independence.

Courtenay gave Boswell a more immediate warning: "For God's sake, keep yourself a little quiet, for drinking too much every day will harden your blood." Some friends commented on his "false spirits," but his mood did not seem false to him. He felt able to advise Euphemia, who was developing a temper, to imitate his example: "I was once peevish and discontented; and now I do not believe there is a better-humoured man upon earth than myself." Every day he was gaining more and more friends and upon his honour, he said, he would not return to Scotland if he were offered the presidency of the Court of Session.

At one of their recent meetings Burke had sneered that Boswell had the art of reconciling contradictions beyond any man he knew. Boswell conceded that he had been both a Tory and an American sympathizer.

> BURKE. You were not always an American. (This was an unjust suspicion of time-serving.) And then asking Sir James Lowther to come into Scotland to defend liberty! You are the greatest *encyclopédiste* in politics.

Tu quoque would have been an appropriate rejoinder since Burke's political views had been no model of seamless consistency, but the reference to Lonsdale stung. Still, Boswell continued in attendance, though he took a disparaging view of some of his fellow dependents:

> Dined at Lord Lonsdale's: Penn and the two dogs.
> Lord Lonsdale; two dogs.
> Dined at Lord Lonsdale's. . . .   Two dogs dined.

How did he differentiate himself from these members of the animal kingdom?

When Boswell that spring boasted of having the full entrée at Lonsdale's, Temple remarked, "I do not like your making yourself dependent on anybody, and cannot reconcile it with your *pride of family*." This difference in opinion was to be unexpectedly tested when on 14 May 1790 Temple appeared for a happy reunion, bringing with him his eldest daughter Nancy, who, though lame, was a pretty, elegant, accomplished girl of nearly eighteen. Almost simultaneously, Lonsdale ordered Boswell to accompany him to his country lodge near London for the weekend. Boswell tried to beg off, giving Temple's arrival as his excuse, but Lonsdale cared nothing for that. Even this feeble show of resistance irritated him: he took the opportunity of accusing Boswell of keeping "strange company," like Sir Joshua Reynolds! Boswell replied indignantly that he was honoured by being admitted to Reynolds's society. Sadly ruffled by Lonsdale's image of him, he began again to think of severing their connection.

Temple's visit repeated the pattern of his last one in 1783 with variations. He was a difficult guest, fussy and feeble. To give him credit, he had wanted to take separate lodgings, having foreseen the strain on both families; but Boswell had insisted on their staying in his small house. Very much the country cousin, Temple ran through his few friends quickly, and it was a chore to keep him entertained.

The situation was reversed for Nancy and Veronica, her junior by less than a year. Veronica, as Nancy told her mother,

> is really vulgar, speaks broad Scotch, but appears very good hu-
> moured. I am really surprised at Mr. Boswell's keeping her so
> secluded; he never scarce permits her to go out. She seems now
> like a bird got out of her cage, for he must let her accompany me
> while I stay. . . . It is very disagreeable not to be able to stir
> without Miss B.

Add to this, adolescent dread of public embarrassment. After visits to the various sights—Ranelagh, the opera, the ballet, Vauxhall, Westminster Abbey, several plays, the Royal Academy exhibition, and Strawberry Hill—Nancy wrote:

> You cannot conceive how disagreeable Miss Boswell is at these
> places. She is so vulgar and uncouth and such a strange figure
> that she keeps one in continued dread of what she will say or do.
> Away she flies into the thickest of the crowd without any regard
> to herself or us. And then she is so fearful of getting into a
> carriage and makes such a puzzle that I am often tempted to be
> quite out of humour.

These feelings were invisible to their elders. Boswell considered Veronica sensible and cheerful, and thought she behaved quite well in company, while Temple, who called her "very good and attentive," invited her to Cornwall for a long visit. Nancy was in agony: "I am vexed beyond expression about it. I absolutely dislike her and I cannot help it." Fortunately Veronica declined, but Temple, in his later letters, continued to convey Nancy's love to Miss Boswell.

Then, at the end of May, Boswell's spirits collapsed. One morning, he noted in his journal:

> I awaked sadly dejected and under such a fit of hypochondria as
> I had not experienced for a considerable time. I despaired of
> doing any good myself, and timidly shrunk from the thought of
> little James being at Westminster School.

(Boswell may well have chosen Westminster for Jamie, as Eton for Sandy, because they were the only two large public schools to draw their pupils from all parts of the kingdom.)

Circumstances, like his trips north with Lonsdale, often account for Boswell's periods of depression, but at first glance they sometimes can appear inexplicable. He undoubtedly experienced sharper mood-swings than are usual: he said himself that most of the time he was in too high spirits or too low. It seems clear, however, that he does not fit a classic manic-depressive pattern of motiveless change. Rather, his mind registered immediate situation and sensation very sensitively; as remarked earlier, he lacked the customary adult ability to muffle the moment. When mood-swings came rapidly, as on his Italian travels, they reflected the extent to which he felt in harmony with his surroundings; any tourist is liable to experience the same reaction, if to a more limited degree. Where Boswell differed from many others is that prolonged routine of any kind tended to depress him. But send him on a jaunt, give him a scheme, an adventure to seize his fluttering fancy (as he puts it), and he will revive immediately. Agitation and conspicuousness always make him happy. Nor are his shifts in mood so abrupt as he can make them sound; moments of dulness or gloom anticipate the plunge. While there may be shifts that defy interpreting, it is usually helpful to cast about for an explanation.

Though there were difficulties in the present instance that might deepen depression—another financial crisis, uncertainty about the future with Lonsdale, the burden of Temple's visit—the trigger seems suggested in the last sentence of Boswell's journal entry just quoted. Of his children, Jamie most resembled him in temperament and interests and, after Margaret's death, he had come to take something of her place in Boswell's life. Though Boswell feared correctly that Jamie would be very unhappy at Westminster, and thought the school dangerous to his morals—on his arrival the bigger boys forced burgundy on him until they got him drunk—the real threat was emotional. Now, once again, Boswell would be abandoned and lonely.

By the middle of June, with Boswell so depressed that he could "scarcely articulate," Temple was going through his own usual acute nervous crisis in London. Though he admits to occasional moments of enjoyment, the shock of novelty, the loss of sheltering routine, and his acute sense of being out of place distressed him constantly. He wrote only two days after arrival, "Cannot bear London," and time only made his mood worse. He released his feelings in his journal: unmeaning visits, drowsiness from late hours, increased nervousness, "nothing but bustle and hurry," "do not even breathe freely in this thick air," "the noise and roaring of the coaches dreadful both by night and by day." Even his favourite Nancy irritated him: "Taking young people from home occasions anxiety and apprehension"; they have no idea of money and want to buy everything; "girls are very troublesome, fond of finery and wishing to have it all with them, almost to fill the carriage."

Chiefly Temple's resentment fell on Boswell. The Scotch are indelicate and familiar, unlike the neat and orderly English, who are becomingly reserved and fearful of offending. Staying in someone else's house involves disagreeable restraints and obligations; besides, it gives other friends an excuse for neglect. Though the journals of both Temple and Boswell record a continuous effort to amuse him, Boswell's hospitality did not live up to expectations. Further,

> [Boswell] has a strange way of saying everything he knows of people that he thinks will undervalue them. What he says of one to others seldom turns out to one's praise or credit. No recommendation to be thought to be intimate with him. His life known to be very free, and he cannot conceal his love of wine.

The last two sentences, at least, suggest that Temple had been listening to his fastidious friends, like that clerical *petit-maître*, Norton Nicholls.

One savage outburst marks the climax of Temple's rage:

> Never thinks of anyone but himself; indifferent to other people's feelings or whether they are amused. Envious; solicitous to make known what others wish to conceal; no command of his tongue; restless, no composure. Can never be happy, uniform, or to be depended on. Disobliged most of his friends. One while paying court, another wishing to be independent. Not able to bear home or the company of his children. Losing all respect in their eyes by saying the wildest and most imprudent things before them; yet good humoured, lively, and benevolent.

Only disappointed love could be so bitter.

At least Temple kept his feelings to himself. Boswell sought his advice, found him friendly and soothing, and wrote:

> My dear friend Temple was quite uneasy to see the state in which I was. It hurt me particularly that my dismal hypochondria had returned at the time when he had kindly come to see me after a seven years' separation.

I I

BUT TEMPLE WAS FAR from Boswell's main worry. Parliament had been dissolved on 11 June 1790 for the General Election, and three days later Lonsdale summoned Boswell to attend him to Carlisle. Already his

Parliamentary hopes had been virtually crushed: according to Colonel Lowther, when he suggested to Lonsdale that he make Boswell an M.P., Lonsdale replied, "He would get drunk and make a foolish speech."   Again Boswell tried to beg off because of Temple's visit, but Lonsdale remained determined, saying meanly that to conduct the election was all Boswell had to do for his salary.   Penn and Colonel Lowther half-hinted that he must not hang back now.   "Heated" with wine, Boswell "rashly went three times in the course of this day to a stranger."   Temple and T.D. thought he should resign his Recordership immediately; Malone advised him to go to Carlisle, do his duty, see whether Lonsdale would bring him into Parliament and, if not, resign at some later date.

Boswell had excellent precedent for having tried so hard to attract Lonsdale's favour, since he had initiated, even if in each case inadvertently, the Parliamentary careers of a number of well-known politicians: John Robinson, Fletcher Norton (later first Baron Grantley), George Johnstone, Charles Jenkinson (later first Earl of Liverpool), Sir George Macartney (later first Earl Macartney), and, above all, the younger William Pitt himself. But now all Boswell's plans were being resolved into their basic insubstantiality.   The next day Lonsdale's associate, Sir Michael Le Fleming told him that two "blackguards" were to stand for Carlisle, though Lonsdale enjoyed his company and might want to use Boswell as a stopgap if it suited his whim.

Boswell was offended:

> I told Sir Michael warmly that this was quite unsuitable to me; that I was as proud as Lucifer, and that I would have no connection with Lord Lonsdale farther than paying my respects to him as an independent gentleman.

But when he talked of throwing up his Recordership, Lonsdale said that he himself would be criticized for securing the appointment for Boswell; and Boswell agreed to go to Carlisle, do the business, and then resign.

Even before they got underway, Boswell began to complain again that it was hard on him to make the trip, and Lonsdale grew furious:

> "You have some sinister motive."   "How can your Lordship say so?"   "Because I know the man to whom I speak.   I suppose you want to have a large fee."   "Did your Lordship ever see anything in my conduct to make you think so?"   "You asked the Recordership of me.   I did not wish you should be Recorder.   But you were so earnest, I granted it.   And now when duty is required, you would give it up.   What have you done for your salary?   I will advise the Corporation not to accept your resignation till you have attended the Midsummer Sessions as well as the election.   I

suppose you think we are fond of your company.   You are mistaken.
We don't care for it.   *I* should have heard of no difficulties.   I
suppose you thought I was to bring you into Parliament.   I
never had any such intention.   It would do you harm to be in
Parliament."

This was a full discovery.   I had leave of absence for an hour,
went to Malone and told him.   He advised me to go in apparent
good humour and get away as soon as I could.   It vexed me that
I was dragged away from the printing of my *Life of Johnson*, and
that perhaps Malone might be gone to Ireland before I could get
back to London.   At L.'s again.   Time was trifled away till the
afternoon, I am not sure what hour.   L. took me under the arm,
and we walked by Grosvenor Square to Oxford Street, near Hanover Square, to get into his coach.

As we walked, the bringing into Parliament was resumed, and
he showed his poor opinion of me, saying I would get drunk and
make a foolish speech.   I talked too freely of my liberal and
independent views, and of their inconsistency with being brought
in by him unless special terms were granted.   He was provoked.
In the coach the same subject was unfortunately resumed, and I
expressed myself, I do not recollect exactly how, but so as to raise
his passion almost to madness, so that he used shocking words to
me, saying, "Take it as you will.   I am ready to give you satisfaction."   "My Lord," said I, "you have said enough."

I was in a stunned state of mind, but calm and determined.
He went on with insult: "You have kept low company all your life.
What are *you*, Sir?"   "A gentleman, my Lord, a man of honour;
and I hope to show myself such."   He brutally said, "You will be
settled when you have a bullet in your belly."   Jackson[1] sat silent.
When we came to Barnet and entered the inn, I told him he had
treated me very ill and very unjustly.   He said, "I will give you
satisfaction *now*.   I have pistols here."   "If you please, my Lord;
and I will be obliged to you for pistols."   "What, Sir, against myself?
Certainly not."

I went out and inquired if there was any regiment quartered
there, thinking that I might get one of the officers to lend me
pistols and be my second.   There was none.   I returned to him
and said I would go back to London and find a friend, and let his
Lordship know when we could meet.   We had a cold dinner,
during which he said it would seem strange to me when the friend
I should bring would say that his words to me were warranted;
that I was the aggressor and ought to ask pardon; that I had
attacked his honour.   Looking on him really as a madman, and
wishing upon principle never to have a duel if I could avoid it
with credit, I protested that I had no such intention as he sup-

---

[1]One of Lonsdale's retainers, a Carlisle alderman.

posed; and then in order to give him an opportunity to have the matter adjusted, I asked his pardon for using expressions which his Lordship had imagined attacked his honour, but which I solemnly declared were not so meant by me.   He then said he would not have used words to me if he had not thought that my expressions were meant as he had supposed.   Then we drank a glass of wine.

Captain Payne joined us and sat some time.   After he was gone and I was walking before the door of the inn, L. sent for me and, when I came, held out his hand and gave it me, saying, "Boswell, forget all that is past."   Jackson said to me that the affair had been very well settled, and not a syllable about it should ever transpire. He said L. was interested in not mentioning it.   After this we travelled on socially enough, but I was inwardly mortified to think that I had deceived myself so woefully as to my hopes from the GREAT LOWTHER, and that I was now obliged to submit to what was very disagreeable to me without any reward or hope of any good, but merely to get out of the scrape into which I had brought myself.

All Boswell's other projects were shadows and at heart he knew it. He could make a figure in Ayrshire; he could put on his gown and parade in Westminster Hall; but his only solid hope of success had narrowed to Lonsdale's patronage.   He could count himself a man for having stood up to Lonsdale with firm courage at the crucial moment. But, as he wrote soon afterwards to Penn, "An ambitious hope which I had cherished of being connected with and patronized by one of the greatest men in this country is utterly blasted."   He had to recognize that he had truckled to Lonsdale for years; as Johnson remarks, no remorse is more bitter than that following an unworthy action which is also unsuccessful.

Separating from Lonsdale at Lancaster, where Penn was to fight a losing contest, Boswell went on to Carlisle to serve an indeterminate sentence; his irksome captivity would endure until Lonsdale was pleased to release him some time in the next month.   He took a room with the mayor and postmaster, Jeremiah Wherlings (familiar to some as Red-nosed Jerry), who, with a daughter "such as might make a man forget the difference of sex," were his only companions for several days; at least they were good-humoured and obliging, if dull.   "Think what I suffer," he lamented to Veronica, "after the variety of London, where I could hardly bear any company long."   Devoured by hypochondria, he sat listless for hours in front of the fire, rehearsing his situation: the memory of his worthy, rational, steady father reproached him; he felt "eager, vain stretchings of mind" towards Margaret, once his cheerful comforter in all difficulties; he brooded over his inadequacies as a parent.

Hardly had Boswell arrived in Carlisle when he received a discouraging letter from Temple, announcing his intention of returning to Cornwall:

> I have nothing to do, and hardly know how to amuse myself. My few friends are gone, and you have made no provision for my entertainment by means of yours.

Sadly, Boswell replied, "As to making provisions for your amusement from my friends, alas! the selfishness of London is too great." His real consolation now, Boswell wrote, is "that we have met after a long absence the same friends as when we parted."

Boswell needed all the consolation available; what he called "the journal of a diseased mind" was also the record of a diseased body. He confessed to Malone,

> I am again unfortunate enough to have *one* sore of a certain nature . . . which *alone* gives me more pain and alarm than several which I had lately. Whether it be that it is enhanced by apprehension in my feeble state of mind and body from living very low,[1] or that it is of a worse nature than common I cannot say.

He could walk only with difficulty. After two weeks of worry and indecision he got up his nerve, went to the barber-surgeon's and operated himself on his sore, which then started to heal. But his mind remained so feeble that he could hardly transact business; he quoted Ecclesiastes: "The grasshopper is a burthen." He had no ambitious hope left and no defences:

> What sunk me very low was the sensation that I was precisely as when in wretched low spirits thirty years ago, without any addition to my character from my having had the friendship of Dr. Johnson and many eminent men, made the tour of Europe and Corsica in particular, and written two very successful books. I was as a board on which fine figures had been painted, but which some corrosive application had reduced to its original nakedness.

A piteous plea through Penn for release left Lonsdale unmoved; he was, Boswell thought, "certainly the most *cruel* man upon earth."

On 2 July Lonsdale and his entourage finally arrived from Lancaster, and the long process of polling could begin. Lonsdale's only comment on Boswell's distress was to tell him that his looks had improved, and that he

---

[1]That is, drinking very little, during this period of depression.

was all the better for having been quiet in Carlisle.   One day he made a
show of cordiality and the next worked himself into a fury, his only unchanging characteristic being a total lack of consideration for others.   Satterthwaite, one of the blackguards he had set up for Carlisle, suggested
that Boswell record Lonsdale's strange conduct for just one day.

> I said it would not be believed.   "Oh," said he, "I and others will
> underwrite it."   It amused me to think how much I *had* written
> down.

With the end somewhere in sight, Boswell stuck to his job and delivered
his opinion clearly and forcibly in favour of the honorary freemen's right
to vote, wondering all the while at his ability to speak well when his mind
was so weak.   The freemen's vote assured Lonsdale's candidates of election
(to be overturned, as before, on appeal to the House of Commons).   Political passion ran high and Boswell was forced to cope with rioters who
attacked Lonsdale's headquarters, "Mushroom Hall," and seriously injured
some of the people there.   But he survived, and even roused himself to
reassure Veronica:

> It gives me real concern to find that you have entertained any
> doubt of my loving you as much as your brothers.   What, my own
> Ve, could you seriously entertain such a notion?

His own lax talk was to blame.   *"On my assurance,* have no jealousy."   But
he felt far from capable of attending the General Election in Ayrshire.

Boswell's resignation took effect on 12 July 1790, the day of the Mid-
summer Sessions, but Lonsdale kept him hanging on until the election was
formally concluded.   Lonsdale felt used; still, it should have come as no
surprise to him, since his world was made up of users, used, and enemies.
Boswell felt beaten and tender everywhere.   They were like a couple who
have long circled a delicate topic, which once broached becomes obsessive.
For the final day of the polling (14 July), Boswell writes:

> L. again attacked me passionately; said . . . that he had been told
> by a person whom he believed that before I was acquainted with
> him, I had said that I should have one of his seats in Parliament;
> and that when I got the Recordership, I had said I had now got
> one step.   I in vain assured him that I never had talked in that
> manner, and I appealed to Penn that I had uniformly declared,
> whenever the subject of L.'s bringing me into Parliament was men-
> tioned, that I had no claim on him and did not expect it.   Penn
> confirmed this.

Lonsdale recurred to the Recordership, remarking

that when it should be observed that I was not at his house as usual, he would say that I had earnestly asked the Recordership, and thrown it up in the most unhandsome manner. It was difficult to be patient under such savage injustice. But I was quiet, and Penn afterwards told me that he was glad I was.

After all this, Lonsdale insisted that Boswell dine with him, and then

asked me to go to his private dining-room and eat fruit.[1] I played the game all through and went, hugging myself in the thought of being free from him and setting out early next morning. . . . I said not a word when we separated, for fear that some other crotchet for delay would come into his head. I had drunk so much wine as to have a headache. It was near two in the morning when I got to my lodgings.

But he was free. "I parted from the Northern Tyrant in a strange, equivocal state, for he was half-irritated, half-reconciled," he told Temple. "But I promise you I shall keep myself quite independent of him."

On a previous occasion, Boswell wrote:

I thought of his great interest. Insensibly I tried to please him and was afraid of offending him. He soon noticed it and could not keep from profiting a little from it. I realized it too. I was highly shocked by it. . . . Is Boswell so far overcome by vile interest as to depend on the moods of a young lord? I recollected myself. I made my Lord realize I was as proud as ever. I did it too emphatically. We began to dispute about our characters, and each stated bluntly all the other's defects and all his own merits.

Here Boswell is discussing his relationship not with Lonsdale, but with Mountstuart twenty-five years earlier. All his life, Boswell had alternately flattered his patrons and asserted his independence. Either attitude consistently maintained might have earned him the advancement he wanted, but their unpredictable mingling would strain any relationship. Could he not grasp that the more he fawned, the more Lonsdale would despise him? And then to whine about hardship and to prate about independence: Lonsdale must have found it intolerable.

Boswell tried to live up to the realities of his situation. "I deserve all that I suffer," he wrote to Temple. But his head was still muddled about what had happened and he could rapidly contradict himself, as he did in a letter to Forbes:

[1]Fruit was very expensive.

I always said Lord Lonsdale would not bring me into Parliament. *In confidence*, my dear Sir, it is obvious why. . . . I did flatter myself his Lordship's opinion of me was such that he would have thought it right to give me one of his seats upon liberal principles such as would have suited my character, and that he would have been induced to use his great power in advancing me, which I believe would have been to his credit.

One would like to ask, why would Lonsdale, of all boroughmongers, have given Boswell the special terms he had not granted even to the younger Pitt when he had introduced him into Parliament? Why would he have thought it to his credit to advance Boswell? Surely, we think, Boswell must have known somewhere in his mind that he was deceiving himself. His attitude seems as irrational as that of an adolescent lost in the heady fantasies of first love. Earlier he had written to Margaret, "Fortune, I trust, will at last favour me, for I am sure I deserve it." Why did he deserve it? What could he have answered except that he had the same prepossession in his own favour that we all share? Each of us deserves an exemption from the general laws that govern humanity, but most come sadly to realize that the world does not share this opinion.

Even at this point Boswell could not sustain belief in his own full responsibility. His letter to Forbes continues:

I cannot blame myself; for I acted upon a probability of good to my family, in which I was encouraged by many people to whose opinion I thought I could trust.

After Boswell's return to London, Malone explained the cross-purposes involved. Boswell provides a summary:

Both L. and I had been deceived: he had concluded that a man who had praised him so highly when all the world abused him was willing to be his dependant, and would think it an honour; and therefore he had sent me a card of invitation to dine with him without being acquainted with me or having called on me, thus treating me as an inferior character; and I had flattered myself that this powerful lord would exert his influence particularly to promote me.

I I I

THE IMMEDIATE TASK was to get on with the *Life*, and Boswell laboured hard if intermittently at it. It demanded continual legwork, running out to Cornhill, for instance, to authenticate just one small piece of information; and he had to make this kind of effort, he said, hundreds of times. Then the shaping of the whole: "You cannot imagine," Boswell told Forbes, "how tedious it is to revise and correct a work with the nicety which Mr. Malone has taught me to do it." But equally, "You cannot imagine what a rich and various treasure it will contain." Malone was invaluable: he had put five sheets (twenty pages) through the press during Boswell's absence, and he was consistently kind and active. Still, by September, it became apparent that the work would run to two quarto volumes instead of one as planned. Temple quoted the proverb, "A long book is a great evil"; there was no help for it. Boswell reproached himself for not working harder. Malone, having delayed his departure for Ireland in order to help him as well as to read the last proofs on his own edition of Shakespeare, left in mid-November; Boswell was on his own.

Even in the depths of depression at Carlisle, Boswell insisted, "I *must* endeavour to raise myself in one way or other, and either succeed or persevere till a comfortable stupor comes upon me." Like Micawber, he told himself that "something fortunate would start up." But now he was consciously content to drift; if he lacked direction, at least he felt no positive pain. What a delight it was to sit at dinner, high above Piccadilly, looking across London to the Surrey hills, to see the country and not be in it. He told Robert Boswell that T.D. was tending to affairs at Auchinleck

> while I in this immense metropolis—this intellectual world—this—
> I cannot say enough of it—am endeavouring to obtain as much
> felicity, or rather as much forgetfulness of the reverse, as I can.

Either felicity or forgetfulness or just sexual need entailed familiar indulgences. Boswell made the most of opportunity: one evening he cut out of a rubber of whist at Reynolds's for a half-hour visit in Old Burlington Street, enough time for his purpose. He drank and "wandered." On another evening,

> the heat of the weather and various draughts of wine and water
> had thrown me into a fermentation, so that in walking home I did
> not shun a very fine object and——.

Apart from satisfying natural curiosity about how others cope with their lives, there would be little need to recur to Boswell's ways of passing the time if, as we have seen, he did not make so much of them himself. In his later years he could never keep himself away from wine and women for long, nor could he accept his own behaviour, which he regularly characterizes as foolish and absurd. He lacked even the excuse of displeasing his father or his wife; now no one cared what he did. Nor did he feel the exuberance of youth, when he had "sallied forth like a roaring lion after girls." It was just the repetition of quick release, indifference interspersed with guilt. The serious problem Boswell's conduct created for him was that it tended to set up a vicious circle: loose living eroded his self-esteem, always a quality in short supply, and the lower his self-esteem sank, the more recourse he had to drinking and whoring.

Though Boswell had avoided Auchinleck that summer, sending T.D., as remarked, as his deputy, he had not lost any of his intense pride in the home of his ancestors. He emphasized to his heir, Sandy: "Remember always our ancient Family, for *that* is the capital object." (Sandy needed no reminder; he loved Auchinleck, and acquired grand views of the family importance.) That autumn Knockroon, a pretty little property contiguous to Auchinleck which belonged to a distant cousin, John Boswell, came on the market. It had descended to him through a younger son of the fourth laird of Auchinleck, and our Boswell regarded it with a feudal eye as "an ancient apanage, a piece of, as it were, the flesh and blood of the Family." He told Sandy that he would rather live on bread and water than let it be sold to strangers. And it would do very nicely for another younger son, Jamie.

But where would he find the money to buy it? "Were I to have the promotion which I am sure I deserve," he wrote to Robert Boswell, "the whole price would soon be paid and forgotten." It was dangerously easy for him to take just one step more and assume he would be favoured by Fortune, as he liked to reassure himself he would; in any event he could not resist the temptation to buy the property and worry later about paying for it. Outbid the highest fair offer for Knockroon, he instructed Bruce Campbell, and it cost £2,500, which he later admitted was exorbitant. Fairlie lent him £1,500 on the security of the land, but raising the other £1,000 became an anxious embarrassment the next winter (1791), especially since he was having to repay the £500 he had borrowed for Bruce Boswell. He seriously considered selling the copyright of the *Life*, if Robinson were still interested. But the matter never came to negotiations; Dilly and Baldwin loaned him the money in anticipation of royalties.

The acquisition of Knockroon did not imply that Boswell contemplated returning to Auchinleck. London remained the place where "continual openings for advantage" appeared, and there Boswell could at least make use of his social talents. He was "the harbinger of festivity," Farington recalled, with "a happy faculty of dissipating that reserve which too often

damps the pleasure of English society." Or, as his Club-mate Dr. Richard
Warren put it, he was one of those persons who instantly inspire cheerfulness. Reynolds, now blind in one eye, had stopped painting and was
also at loose ends; they teamed up to dine together two or three times a
week, often at City banquets, long, elaborate anniversary entertainments
for a hundred or more, and Boswell advertised himself and Reynolds as
those "two inseparable companions of the illustrious Order of the Knife
and Fork." His knack for effective topical verse and readiness to perform
made him much in demand as an after-dinner singer.

One such performance took place at a grand dinner of the Humane
Society the previous March, marked by "an affecting procession of a considerable number of fine children and several grown persons who had been
restored by the exertions of this benevolent society." Boswell's second
stanza is the funniest:

> Lo! a troop of grateful creatures,
>   Which our institution boasts;
> Dim, nay, dead were once their features—
>   But for us they had been ghosts.

But the most memorable occasion of this kind occurred at the Lord
Mayor's Day feast (9 November 1790). Knowing that Pitt himself was to
be present, Boswell on the very day rapidly put together a ballad called
William Pitt, the Grocer of London, Pitt being an honorary member of the
Worshipful Company of Grocers. The song celebrated a notable recent
success, Pitt's conclusion of a favourable trade convention with Spain.
Though Pitt had left by the time Boswell got up to sing, the ballad was
enthusiastically received and repeatedly encored. The second (and last)
stanza will give its flavour:

> Though fleets in vain-boasting hostility ride,
>   Still BRITAIN is queen of the main;
> The secret well kept now comes forth with due pride;
>   And lo! a convention with Spain.
> Too noble to brag, as we're never afraid,
>   'Tis enough that we've had a good pull;
> There's a GROCER of LONDON who watches our trade;
>   And takes care of th'estate of JOHN BULL.

A rousing chorus follows. Boswell was so proud of the piece that not only
was it spread all over the newspapers, but he had it reprinted as a broadside.
Still, however much he hoped for political recognition, he valued his reputation for independence more. When a newspaper letter charged servility, he answered that he wished to let "the wasps of Opposition" know

that I am vain of a hasty composition, which has procured me large draughts of that popular applause in which I delight. Let me add that there was certainly no *servility* on my part, for I publicly declared in Guildhall between the encores "that this same Grocer had treated *me* arrogantly and ungratefully; but that from his great merit as a Minister I was compelled to support him!"

Boswell was following his established back-and-forth pattern but it made no difference, since Pitt was coldly indifferent to any overtures of this kind.

Then, once more, Ayrshire seemed to offer an opening, though others might have thought it a mirage or even an hallucination. Fergusson had been unanimously returned as M.P. in July 1790, but hearing a rumour that he was to get a place and vacate his seat, Boswell made a strong appeal to Dundas (16 November 1790):

I assure you *solemnly upon my honour* that in the year 1784 when I was of no inconsiderable service to the present Administration, you gave me your *word* and *hand* after dinner at Hillhead[1] that you would give me your interest to be Member for my own county, which has ever been and ever will be the fond object of my ambition. I have never claimed that *promise*, because it was made after we had participated largely of your generous wines, and *I wish to do as I would be done by*. . . . Mr. Pitt (I am utterly at a loss to know for what) has treated me arrogantly and ungratefully

—that is, because you have prejudiced him against me, though Dundas may not have caught the implication—

as I can state to you at our leisure. Meantime I nevertheless am compelled for my own interest as Laird of Auchinleck and as a sincere lover of my country to support him. Colonel Fullarton is a candidate for Ayrshire. *That great county must not go into Opposition.*

Not only had Boswell never claimed this promise, he had never mentioned it specifically enough anywhere for the present-day reader to spot a reference to it. In reply, Dundas reminded Boswell that he was engaged by his agreement with Eglinton for two Parliaments, and either insinuated or stated directly—his letter is lost—that the whole incident was a product of Boswell's fancy. This roused Boswell. He realized, he answered, that his appointment was to depend on Montgomerie's vacating his seat during his term in office, and the approval of Eglinton—with whom, incidentally, Boswell was now on very bad terms—but said he had never been aware

[1]Dundas's country place in Midlothian.

that the agreement covered more than one Parliament. (This, it must be said, contradicts Boswell's own assertion in his Diminishing Bill pamphlet, though perhaps he might have entered the technical disclaimer that he had never heard this arrangement specifically acknowledged.)

Boswell continues:

> As to your compliment on my lively fancy, it has never yet exerted itself in inventing facts; nor am I one of those who are blessed with an accommodating memory that can recollect or invent facts as it may suit self-interest for the time.

This was a hit at Dundas, who was widely regarded as having most accommodating principles. Then Boswell asked:

> As my services to the present Administration are admitted, and my attachment to it, upon independent principles, still continues . . . will you or will you not give me what interest you may have in Ayrshire, that I may represent it?

The question was now rhetorical and, in any case, Fergusson did not vacate his seat. What had happened, clearly, was that Boswell had spun his cobweb—what if Montgomerie resigned, and what if Eglinton agreed to support him—and Dundas had made agreeable noises. With a face "tinged with convivial purple," Dundas was known to be as great a lover of generous wines as Boswell, but even in his most festive moments he was far too shrewd to make such a fantastic commitment.

I V

WHATEVER ELSE FAILED, Boswell still had the *Life*, fast nearing completion. In that arch, self-conscious, but alive style which makes her Boswell's only rival among contemporary British diarists, Fanny Burney preserves a moment of him at Windsor (October or November 1790), where she was an enfeebled drudge-in-waiting to the Queen. She encountered him at the gate of St. George's Chapel, and he asked for her help:

> "My help?"
> "Yes, Madam; you must give me some of your choice little notes of the Doctor's; we have seen him long enough upon stilts; I want to show him in a new light. Grave Sam, and great Sam, and solemn Sam, and learned Sam—all these he has appeared over and over. Now I want to entwine a wreath of the Graces across his brow; I want to show him as gay Sam, agreeable Sam,

pleasant Sam; so you must help me with some of his beautiful billets to yourself."

I evaded this by declaring I had not any stores at hand. He proposed a thousand curious expedients to get at them, but I was invincible. . . .

He then told me his *Life of Dr. Johnson* was nearly printed, and took a proof-sheet out of his pocket to show me; with crowds passing and repassing, knowing me well, and staring well at him; for we were now at the iron rails of the Queen's Lodge.

I stopped; I could not ask him in: I saw he expected it, and was reduced to apologize, and tell him I must attend the Queen immediately. . . . Finding he had no chance for entering, he stopped me again at the gate, and said he would read me a part of his work.

There was no refusing this; and he began with a letter of Dr. Johnson's to himself. He read it in strong imitation of the Doctor's manner, very well and not caricature. But Mrs. Schwellenberg was at her window, a crowd was gathering to stand round the rails, and the King and Queen and Royal Family now approached from the Terrace. I made a rather quick apology and, with a step as quick as my now weakened limbs have left in my power, I hurried to my apartment.

You[1] may suppose I had inquiries enough, from all around, of "who was the gentleman I was talking to at the rails?" And an injunction rather frank not to admit him beyond those limits.

Boswell tried again the next day to get Miss Burney's letters, but she remained invincible.

Not only was Malone a constant help with the *Life*, he was also the one person who could make Boswell feel better when he got depressed. And some time about the beginning of 1791, Boswell became badly depressed again, "worse than I almost ever was," he told Sandy; "perpetually gnawed by a kind of mental fever," he told Temple. Malone, still in Ireland, got full reports of his state of mind: he was continually uneasy, everything was gloomy and hopeless, his financial situation (as discussed earlier) was desperate. He was overcome by timidity; would Malone decide whether he should take Robinson's offer for the *Life* if it was still open? Would Malone lend him some money? (The answer to that was "no.") He still had 80 pages of copy before him, and the *death*, to be "concise though solemn," to compose. At the end of January he had written, "Indeed I go sluggishly and comfortlessly about my work. As I pass your door I cast many a longing look." Two weeks later he added, "I am strangely ill, and doubt if even you could dispel the demonic influence."

[1]Her sister Susan.

And to whom could he turn, Boswell asked Malone, "in this great metropolis, where hardly any man cares for another?"   For 25 February 1791, he wrote in his journal: "It was not pleasing to find that Sir Joshua had all this time known that I was in sad spirits, and never once called or sent to inquire about me.   We must take our friends as they are."   But Courtenay was a true friend, who made repeated efforts to comfort him, though it was a difficult task even for this genial soul, who firmly ignored his own appalling financial circumstances.

Courtenay wrote to Malone (22 February 1791):

> Poor Boswell is very low and dispirited and almost melancholy mad—feels no spring, no pleasure in existence—and is so perceptibly altered for the worse that it is remarked everywhere.   I try all I can to rouse him but he recurs so tiresomely and tediously to the same cursed, trite, commonplace topics about death, etc.— that we grow old, and when we are old we are not young—that I despair of effecting a cure.   Dr. Warren and Devaynes very kindly interest themselves about him, but you would be of more service to him than anybody is. . . .   Seward gave B. a supper t'other night (a French pie)—the company an opera singer and a young French architect—yet it did not do.   He complains like Solomon that "all is vanity."

To Boswell's pitiful appeals, Malone responded, as he always did, with a detached, clear-headed analysis of the situation:

> Without being a very strict moralist, one may say that it is surely *unwise* to indulge in such excesses *habitually*, and that the sure consequence of wild and intemperate riot for one half the year must be the lowest depression during the other.

And what about Boswell's professions of piety? Why did he not try to live up to his religious principles?

Temple, on the other hand, could be relied on to pour out full, consoling sympathy:

> It makes my heart bleed to find you complaining again. . . .   Friend of my youth, whom I have loved with uninterrupted affection, do not give yourself up to dejection and despair but cherish pleasing expectation, and let us flatter ourselves that much good is yet in reserve. . . .   Let me know whatever you are doing, and you shall hear from me every day if it will be any relief to you.

By the time these letters arrived, Boswell had already experienced a sharp moment of relief.   On 1 March 1791, after dreaming that Margaret had "distinctly pointed out in her own handwriting the propitiation of our

Saviour," he awoke suddenly recovered.   And though salvation proved temporary, at least his mood was not so dark as before.   He had promised Courtenay the previous November that until 1 March 1791 he would not drink more than four good glasses of wine at dinner and a pint after it, so perhaps the thought of release from this promise helped to improve his spirits.   Warren actually advised him to drink more since he was dependent on wine, and to cut down when he felt better.   A week after his promise expired, at a dinner of the Stewards of the Humane Society, an occasion known for its relaxed atmosphere, the drinking went on until Boswell lost all knowledge of time.

Boswell always paid attention to Malone's admonitions; he gave himself the same advice.   Indeed Malone's analysis of Boswell's behaviour is so sensible that it takes a while to realize it is mistaken.   Drinking did not depress Boswell nor did sobriety maintain his moods of well-being; that he should have realized from his youthful period of sober abstinence in Holland, which he passed in gloomy despair.   Activity, purpose, public recognition, and sensual gratification were his openings to happiness: an existence of what he once called *"vives secousses"* (lively shocks).

The previous December Boswell had planned to publish the *Life* on Shrove Tuesday (8 March 1791); by the end of February, the publication date had been put off until the end of March; and by 6 April to Easter Monday (25 April).   Before the great day, he had decided to indulge himself in a poem.   He had always had a genius for poetry, he believed, a genius which he defined as ascribing many fanciful properties to everything; and he gave it full utterance in *No Abolition of Slavery, or, The Universal Empire of Love*, which appeared anonymously on 16 April.   It is surely the strangest piece he ever wrote.   Three hundred octosyllabics combine his last year's romance with an attack on abolitionists and a review of major political figures.   To attack slavery was to attack property, and eighteenth-century orthodox opinion always ranked property rights above mere personal rights.   The Rights of Man, now being disseminated by the French Revolutionists, caused all sound-thinking people to shudder: they led to democracy, then anarchy, and finally to the destruction of civil society. Subordination, Boswell argued, was the key to private as well as public relationships:

> From wise subordination's plan
> Springs the chief happiness of man.

By being subordinate to their owners, Negroes not only come to share the benefits of civilization, they are better off materially than they were in a state of liberty.   (How far from Rousseau and Corsica!)   In fact, Boswell claims they are much better off than the London poor, and his description of laughing, happy Negroes, singing as they toil, anticipates the best ante-bellum Southern fantasies on the subject:

> Of food, clothes, cleanly lodging sure,
> *Each has his property secure.*

The twist comes when Boswell relates this argument to the convention that the lover is the slave of the beloved.   Overextending analogy, Boswell compares gaining the favour of his "beauteous tyrant" to making the dreaded slave passage from Africa to the Americas, "between the decks of hope and fear."   His mistress must have thought him one of the blacks of Angola, who were supposed to be the most ferocious.   (Boswell, all his life, was intrigued by the darkness of his complexion.)   Now he enjoys his "bless-ings" all the more.   The draft of his poem, which survives, extends this position to cover thousands of "fine folks," who would be better off "in good subjection" than "lounging in idle misery."   Perhaps this line of reasoning was omitted in deference to his audience.

Most of *No Abolition of Slavery*, however, is taken up with attacks on Wilberforce, Windham, Burke, Courtenay (who obligingly supplied some lines himself), and other supporters of abolition.   Fox is condemned for undermining established institutions, and Pitt comes in for both praise and blame.   Even Thurlow is criticized for wobbling during the Regency crisis. In contrast, "an ancient Baron of the land" will stand by his King and, when "the Royal image" is "in a cloud," by the Prince of Wales.

No Abolition of Slavery does have a peculiar logic, and could be defended as ingenious or even clever.   Its argument derives from Pope's in the *Essay on Man* that the Great Chain of Being is identical with the chain of love which unites all nature.   But this abstract notion of the theme contradicts the concrete impression the poem makes of a mind moving in an unmapped orbit.   For Boswell it was a *jeu d'esprit* that gave him a chance to express some strong opinions to the world without being held accountable for them. The world did not care.

Boswell's final judgement on the *Life* before giving it to the public comes in a letter to Dempster (30 April), and it repeated what he had been saying all along: "I really think it will be the most entertaining collection that has appeared in this age."   On 13 May, forty-one London booksellers purchased upwards of 400 sets (two volumes at two guineas).   On 16 May 1791, the twenty-eighth anniversary of his first meeting with Johnson in Davies's back parlour, Boswell's *Life of Johnson* was published.

I

BOSWELL'S *Life of Johnson*, "the delight and boast of the English-speaking world," is by common consent the greatest biography ever written. Beyond that judgement, disagreement about its nature and characteristics is so various and deep that this chapter must restrict itself to five issues: (1) biographical theory and practice as they are related to the *Life*; (2) the making of the *Life*; (3) its presentation of Johnson; (4) Boswell as author and character; (5) eighteenth-century and modern critical opinion of the *Life*.

A satisfactory theory of biography depends on the assumption that a biography is a work of fact and not fiction. Fact and fiction evoke fundamentally different mental sets, and faced with a written work a reader is profoundly uneasy until he knows which set is appropriate. Tell a six-year-old a story, and the first question he will ask is whether it is real or pretend. For adults, the question of whether the Bible is a work of fact or of fiction, even if fiction of the greatest significance, arouses argument so passionate that until a few centuries ago it could cost a man his life, and can still cost him his job. Authenticity, Boswell's proudest claim for the *Life* as for his other biographical works, meant above all to him truth to fact.

The differences in response to fiction and fact are far easier to suggest than to define. Fiction widens into potentiality, while fact offers the pleasing resistance of the actual. Fiction may move us more deeply, but we trust fact. Fictional characters can be developed to any degree of complexity, but who can say where the resonance of real persons like Garrick and Burke dies out? Fictional narrative can please with wonderful invention, but factual narrative invites increased alertness: if this happened to someone else, it could happen to me.

The mental set of fiction derives from imagination, and of fact from memory. Of course the two must overlap: imagination becomes unintelligible if it loses touch with what we already know, while memory involves imaginative reconstruction. But there are essential distinctions between "imaginative" modes, like drama or the novel, and "memorial" modes, like biography and history.

Imaginative works are closed forms, while memorial works are open ones. *Don Quixote* is a self-limiting novel; nothing more can be learned about its hero because he was not a real person. But the *Life of Johnson* is permeable, so to speak; the adequacy of its Johnson can be checked by information from other sources, just as we impart to Boswell's depiction certain characteristics drawn from other works about him. A character in a novel has only to be plausible, but the subject of a biography must be credible. At most, novels can be compared; biographies can be corrected. Usually a biography is too full of the unresolved dissonances typical of our own lives to attain the satisfying conclusion of a novel.

The eighteenth century thought much more highly of factual literature than of fiction; today the opposite is true. This shift in prestige to the imagined or imaginatively reconstituted is partly responsible for obscuring the biographical traditions on which Boswell drew. Virtually all serious biography before Boswell's time was ethical; its model in purpose was Plutarch's *Lives*, and its aim to instruct and to judge. This noble tradition now seems pompous because of our distaste for the explicitly didactic, but Johnson justifies it when he asserts, "We are perpetually moralists, but we are geometricians only by chance." Johnson is not suggesting that we adopt a high moral tone or spy on our neighbours. He is merely emphasizing that the most important decisions we make every day are ethical decisions. Basically, we are ethical beings; our intellectual knowledge of the world is, by comparison, unimportant. And biography has the advantage over history, its rival among memorial genres, of offering individual rather than general models of thought and behaviour. "I esteem biography," Johnson told Lord Monboddo, "as giving us what comes near to ourselves, what we can turn to use."

But the kernel and origin of biography is the anecdote, nothing more than the story one person tells to a second about a third; and the tradition of anecdotal biography is also long, going back at least to Xenophon's *Memorabilia* of Socrates. One basic distinction between the two types is that in ethical biography incident serves the humble function of illustrating moral points, while in anecdotal biography incident comes to the fore and the ethical is apt to be left to fend for itself.   In the eighteenth century, though anecdotal biography had strong admirers, including Johnson himself, it was open to the charge that it pandered to idle curiosity—a frequent criticism, as mentioned, of the *Hebrides*—and lacked redeeming moral value.

Johnson's two important pre-Boswellian biographers neatly illustrate the extremes of ethical and anecdotal types.   Hawkins's *Life of Johnson* plucks out the moral *exempla* to be derived from Johnson's career, but Johnson himself peers through only at intervals.   In contrast, his character—often in its most unpleasant moods—emerges vividly in the brief, disjointed stories that make up Mrs. Piozzi's *Anecdotes*, which is a classic of moral confusion.

Boswell made the necessary connection: his *Life of Johnson* embodies a crucial moment in the history of biography because in it he unifies the ethical and anecdotal traditions.   (In the same period, Gibbon similarly unified the traditions of philosophical and antiquarian history.)   And Boswell extended a third biographical element, the role of psychological analysis.   For this he had Johnson's example in the *Lives of the Poets* to go on.   But he also had his own journal-practice as background, as well as models of introspection ranging from confessions and autobiographies by splendid saints and sinners, like Augustine and Rousseau, to those of spiritual and temporal journalists whom a contemporary unkindly referred to as "a thousand . . . old women and fanatic writers."

General tradition and concrete example operate in any particular biography through its major determinants: materials, methods of presentation, and, most important, purpose.   And purpose in the biography of a writer also has shifted over the years.   In the recent past, the usefulness of a "critical biography," one that purports to connect life and work, was thought to consist mainly in giving the work a limiting context.   Although biography, in this approach, cannot fix intention in the old-fashioned sense of "Milton wanted to show in *Lycidas* that . . ." it can establish, while making more precise, a possible range of meanings.   A knowledge of Boswell's life and character, for example, rules out the notion, which has actually been advanced, that the *Life of Johnson* is basically a covert attack on its subject.

But this is a minimal view of the function of critical biography, and reflects the clichés of formal criticism, the most anti-biographical of theories, rather than even its usual practice.   Intent on preserving the isolated purity of the literary work, its good-for-nothingness except as a locus of aesthetic and moral values, the formal critic ostensibly restricted his analysis to the thing-in-itself, while constantly drawing—though without notice—on what in rigorous theory was inadmissible evidence, starting with his knowledge of the writer's career and era.

Today, when the range of critical approaches has widened beyond the narrow verities of formal criticism, we are permitted an ampler view of critical biography. To understand any literary work requires, to begin with, a grasp of its genre and of its historical context. Equally essential is a personal context—of which Boswell's is a model at its fullest—that biography provides to put the subject's work in adequate perspective. The work never provides sufficient information in itself for proper interpretation. To fully grasp Johnson's *Lives of the Poets*, for instance, it helps to know something about the circumstances in which Johnson wrote it, his own feelings about his subjects, and his personality and prejudices.

A modern biographer might focus on his subject's writings, but in Boswell's approach Johnson's writings took their place in a more inclusive vision of Johnson as a struggling moral hero of everyday life—a hero and a life to be presented on an epic scale. In the Advertisement to the second edition, Boswell points to his epic model when he compares the *Life* to the *Odyssey*, in that

> amidst a thousand entertaining and instructive episodes the HERO is never long out of sight, for they are all in some degree connected with him; and HE in the whole course of the history is exhibited by the author for the best advantage of his readers.

Boswell then quotes two lines from Horace (given here in Francis's translation):

> To show what wisdom and what sense can do
> The poet sets Ulysses in our view.

Nor is it surprising that Boswell thought of a moral struggle in epic terms: what else is *Paradise Lost*, which has hung over all later English epics? The *Life of Johnson* takes its place among the many eighteenth-century versions of epic: Pope's translation of the *Iliad*, *Rape of the Lock*, and *Dunciad*; *Tom Jones*; *The Decline and Fall of the Roman Empire*; and those strangest of mutations, Blake's major prophecies. When the epic returns in changed but recognizable form, its hero, the narrator of Wordsworth's *Prelude*, is like Johnson an ordinary man who has taken on some of the aura of the sublime.

Within the epic framework, Boswell wanted to present his hero both fully and exactly.   Fullness, given his materials, was a comparatively easy achievement.   "I will venture to say," he writes at the beginning of the *Life*, that Johnson "will be seen in this work more completely than any man who has ever yet lived."   Full presentation of a hero aligns Boswell with the ethical tradition.

Exactness, on the other hand, might seem an impossible ideal.   As Geoffrey Scott says:

> Boswell has an image which describes his aim: a "life" should be like a flawless print struck off from the engraved plate which is bitten in our memory. . . .   Biography should be nothing less than this duplication of an image in the mind.

Or, to cite Boswell directly, "I must be exact as to every line in his countenance, every hair, every mole."   If this was beyond anyone's power he could at least create, in his celebrated phrase, a "Flemish picture" of Johnson that expanded anecdotal biography beyond any earlier conception.

The sheer quantity of Boswell's material, beginning with his massive journal, put fullness and exactness within reach.   But quantity also helped to force a new biographical approach on him.   In his "Memoirs of Pascal Paoli," where his notes were somewhat sparse and he wanted to disguise the fact that his visit to Paoli had lasted only a week, Boswell suppressed dates and filled out his account by interspersing what Paoli said and did with general comment on the Corsicans.   A contrasting problem emerged in the *Hebrides*, where he worried that his narrative would be choked with detail; there he experimented by abridging it under topographical headings (St. Andrews, Laurencekirk), until he reverted with great success to the day-by-day entries of his original journal.

But the method that served for a three-month narrative like the *Hebrides* would not do for a far more comprehensive portrait and, as early as 1780, Boswell had determined to write the *Life of Johnson* "in scenes," that is, to centre his presentation on conversations which would approximate scenes in a play.   This was a key decision and it meant that Johnson, whom Boswell praises in the opening sentence of the *Life* as the greatest of biographers, could not provide an appropriate model.   Though Johnson included dialogue and anecdote, the principal interest of his *Lives of the Poets* lay in his unrelenting judgemental commentary.   This suited neither Boswell's aim nor his material.

Instead, early in the *Life* Boswell announces, "I have resolved to adopt and enlarge upon the excellent plan of Mr. Mason, in his *Memoirs of [Thomas] Gray*."   Well known at the time, William Mason's *Gray* was unusual in being made up of a long series of the subject's letters—which Mason, we now know, rephrased, bowdlerized, truncated, spliced together, and misdated—linked by a trickle of mealy-mouthed explanation.   But even in these butchered versions Gray's letters, as Boswell remarked to Temple, "show us the *man*."   They present Gray so directly, they reveal so much about him, that Mason the memoirist is forgotten and Gray stands before us plain.   Self-presentation and self-revelation by his subject to the greatest extent possible: this too was part of Boswell's plan.   Of course he had been born knowing how to set figures directly before an audience, as he had shown in his earlier studies of Paoli and Johnson.   But Mason's example may have crystallized his decision about how to present Johnson in the *Life*, and at the least it offered a convenient precedent.

To the union of the ethical and anecdotal on an epic scale, Boswell joined, then, one more innovation of the greatest significance to biography: mimesis, the setting of a subject immediately before the reader.   "Presentness" was the decisive effect Boswell wanted to achieve: to get Johnson to present himself, to reveal himself, first in conversation, but also in all those documents Boswell quotes or summarizes: letters, prayers and meditations, essays and biographies with working notes and discarded readings, political pamphlets, definitions, parodies, fables and allegories, decisions on literary disputes, an appeal for votes, poems, legal opinions, a novel, and even the minor forms of eulogy—dedication, obituary, and epitaph. Johnson appears further in what was said about him in various forms, from diplomas to memorable opinions: Garrick's "Johnson gives you a forcible hug and shakes laughter out of you, whether you will or no"; Goldsmith's "he has nothing of the bear but his skin"; Dr. John Boswell's "a robust genius born to grapple with whole libraries."   Presentness is the brightest of Boswell's talents.   He became the first mimetic biographer and he remains without equal.

I I

IF THE GLORY of art is to conceal art, then the *Life of Johnson* belongs in the first rank.   Finally the naïve notion has passed that Boswell practised a primitive stenography, so that he had no more to do than to copy out his tablets, but its long persistence testifies to Boswell's success: it was the effect on which all other effects depended.   The making of the *Life* had to be a much more complicated task.

Boswell's rawest material was the condensed notes which he made as soon as possible after the event recorded, sometimes on the same day.

When he had expanded these, presumably they were to be disposed of, though a good many survive besides those which he never wrote up. Sometimes as late as the *Life* itself he would expand a brief jotting into a whole speech or scene. So the note, "Johns[on] great on Lit[erary] Prop[er]ty. Creation for autho[r]. But consent of nations ag[ainst]," became a Johnsonian utterance 170 words long.

But the journal was the prime source for most of the scenes displayed in the *Life*, with torn-out leaves used directly as copy. As in revising for the *Hebrides*, Boswell dramatized as much as possible; indirect discourse was recast as dialogue and, in playing back scenes in his mind, vivifying detail, sometimes in the form of stage directions, might materialize in so advanced a stage as proofs. These directions could be as brief as "smiling," or expand to "standing upon the hearth rolling about, with a serious, solemn, and somewhat gloomy air." But in every case they fix an expression or gesture or tone of voice.

We know that Boswell's reports of conversations could not be verbatim. But as early as 1762, Boswell wrote of an hour-and-a-half session with David Hume, which he preserved in a 900-word précis: "I have remembered the heads and the very words of a great part of Mr. Hume's conversation"; and this much he could claim. What the *Life* provides is a selection or epitome of Johnson's talk. Once well acquainted with his phrasing and syntax—*"strongly impregnated with the Johnsonian ether"*—Boswell could surround pivotal words with characteristic diction. (In a contest of Johnsonian mimicry, the umpire Hannah More adjudged superiority to Garrick in reading poetry and to Boswell in familiar conversation, a convincing testimonial to his ability to catch Johnson's voice, phrasing, and manner.) If Johnson didn't say precisely what Boswell records him as saying, he said something very much like it.

But how accurate is this presentation? In the Advertisement to the first edition, an essay in self-praise, Boswell called attention to the work the *Life* had necessitated:

> The labour and anxious attention with which I have collected and arranged the materials of which these volumes are composed will hardly be conceived by those who read them with careless facility. The stretch of mind and prompt assiduity by which so many conversations were preserved, I myself, at some distance of time, contemplate with wonder; and I must be allowed to suggest that the nature of the work in other respects, as it consists of innumerable detached particulars, all which, even the most minute, I have spared no pains to ascertain with a scrupulous authenticity, has occasioned a degree of trouble far beyond that of any other species of composition.

Boswell's final claim is excessive, but his feeling is understandable.   He had first to deal with that "great sand-drift of 'particulars' he had accumulated since 1763," while he collected and sifted the contributions of others.   Since authenticity is the scaffolding of the *Life*, he was careful, for the most part, to cite his authorities wherever it counted, constantly reassuring his reader that the narrative is solidly based, yet at the same time leaving to him some of the responsibility for assessing the evidence.

Attention to truth was a distinguishing feature of the Johnsonian school, but even before Boswell met Johnson his father had beaten the same principle into him.   He was continually on guard.   "Carelessness as to the exactness of circumstances is very dangerous," he said, "for one may gradually recede from the fact till all is fiction."   In writing, "one must clear head (lave it [1] as a boat of water) of imagination to give authentic narration." When Boswell came to a disputed point, such as who was responsible for Johnson's pension, he cross-examined every witness, a procedure Johnson had taught him to extend from the courtroom into daily life:

> *Lord Bute told me* that Mr. Wedderburn, now Lord Loughborough, was the person who first mentioned this subject to him.   *Lord Loughborough told me* that the pension was granted to Johnson solely as the reward of his literary merit. . . .   *Mr. Thomas Sheridan and Mr. Murphy*, who then lived a good deal both with him and Mr. Wedderburn, *told me* that they previously talked with Johnson upon this matter. . . .   *Sir Joshua Reynolds told me* that Johnson called on him. . . .

In preparing the *Life* for publication, the only sustained help Boswell received was from Malone, and the precise extent of that help will not be clear until the manuscript is fully deciphered and edited.   But already it is evident that Malone's share, though substantial, was less than it had been in the case of the *Hebrides*.   Malone got Boswell started on the *Life* and kept him at it.   When Boswell had completed most of the draft he read it aloud to Malone, who made suggestions; then they worked together through about half the proofs—this book, like the *Hebrides*, was being printed off as they concluded revision—before Malone's departure for Ireland.   Malone had taught Boswell how to go over a manuscript with diligence, and continued to offer advice from across the Irish Sea:

> Pray take care of colloquialisms and vulgarisms of all sorts.   Condense as much as possible, always preserving perspicuity, and do not imagine the *only* defect of style is repetition of words.

[1]Ladle it out.

Boswell replied sadly that the difference between what they had revised together and what he had done by himself was only too visible, but it has never been apparent to readers.

Pursuit of accuracy entailed no unthinking reverence for documents, and the process of reworking that Boswell applied to his own Johnsoniana he applied even more vigorously to the accounts contributed by others, subjecting them "to every conceivable mode of revision: summary, paraphrase, expansion, conflation, interpolation, and so forth." A modern editor of the "His Very Self and Voice" persuasion would have left them as they were, but such compilations are material for a biography, not its substitute. Biography cannot consist of bits and pieces, the unmediated clamour of conflicting views. Documents must be fused within a smooth, coherent narrative. Authenticity depends on accuracy as the basis for the biographer's image of his subject. Still, "*perfect* authenticity," as Marshall Waingrow remarks, "is to be found not in the discrete historical fact, but in its representation—in the control of implications."

Method of presentation, however, does depend in the *Life of Johnson* on the discrete fact, and Boswell was much more confident than he had been in writing the *Hebrides* that particulars were vital, with the selection and arrangement of these particulars regulated by

> a massively detailed conception of Johnson's character, operating
> to shape into unity all the multifarious and potentially discordant
> elements of a very long book.

Boswell necessarily builds his world out of facts, but facts as construed by a powerful and wide-ranging sense of actuality, comparable to what we call imagination in a novelist.

Does this mean, as G. B. Shaw asserted, that Boswell was the dramatist who invented Johnson? Shaw is right to the extent that all biographers invent their subjects; just as we speak of Lockhart's Scott and Strachey's Victoria, so this is Boswell's Johnson. Boswell's aim was authenticity, not "objectivity." There never was nor ever can be an "objective" Johnson; even Johnson's own view of himself, though privileged, is only one view among others.

I I I

IN HIS PRESENTATION of Johnson, Boswell was able to fit material to purpose smoothly. The first fifth of the *Life*, which describes Johnson's career until their meeting in 1763, serves to introduce the detailed portrait of the mature man.   The structure of the main section, a potentially difficult problem, was handled very simply.   Johnson's life in his middle and late years lacked eventfulness or even much incident: except for excursions to Scotland, Wales, and France in successive years, each year saw him follow a familiar round.   So Boswell emphasized continuity by dividing his material chronologically, year by year, without chapter breaks.   This mechanical organization provides just enough dividing lines to give the material a shape without impeding its flow: the movement through scene, summary, commentary, and quotation that builds up the *Life*'s alternation between drama and documentary.   At the same time, chronological organization satisfied Boswell's desire that the reader " 'live o'er each scene,' " with Johnson, "as he actually advanced through the several stages of his life."

Lacking narrative urgency, the *Life* at its basic level of appeal is picked up with anticipation, put down with equanimity, and returned to with pleasure.   "The book of Boswell is ever, as the year comes round, my winter's-evening's entertainment," wrote Richard Cumberland.   Sir Walter Scott thought it "the best parlour-window book that ever was written." George Mallory caught some sense of the *Life*'s engagingness in a simple impressionistic comment:

> The plain fact is that it is impossible to read Boswell without feeling better. . . .   With Boswell we never want to leave the world for something better, but we want to live in it and enjoy life to the full; and we want especially to love other men.

The *Life* does keep calling the reader back.   Boswell compensates for the lack of sustained development or intriguing suspense with local effects: the constant shift from conversation to reflection to letter; and the use of multiple perspectives: Johnson as he sees himself, past and present, in reminiscence and diary entry; Johnson as Boswell sees him; and, in unusual diversity, Johnson as other contemporaries see him.   We keep coming back to Johnson from different angles.   Individual scenes, the most famous being the Johnson-Wilkes meeting at the Dillys' dinner in 1776, combine surprise, recognition, reversal—all the techniques dramatists use; but these effects always return us to the centre of interest, the life and opinions, the progressions and digressions, of Johnson himself.   His "exuberant variety of . . . wisdom and wit," operating within a framework of predictable attitudes but always forceful and unexpected in expression, focuses and holds the reader's attention.

At the same time, Boswell stresses the stability of repetition.   The unity of the *Life* is largely thematic: the same topics, though raised from shifting points of view, appear again and again.   Also, the cast of characters changes with reluctance; even the same actions recur:

> BOSWELL.   "Let us dine by ourselves at the Mitre, to keep up the old custom, 'the custom of the manor,' the custom of the Mitre." JOHNSON.   "Sir, so it shall be."

Time, too, repeats itself.   After 1763, except for two autumnal interludes, it is always spring in the *Life*.   The years themselves pass in the steady march of days.   How familiar and comforting to the habitual reader of the *Life* are its temporal cadences: "on Monday, April 6," "on Thursday, April 9," "on Friday, April 10," "on Saturday, April 11."   These markers lack any individual distinctiveness or importance; it is only the sequence that counts, as it insists on dailiness, on the way we all experience life, just day by day.

Setting is equally generalized and unemphatic.   Sometimes a few props; but usually Boswell does no more than indicate place, and continues:

> There was a pretty large circle this evening.   Dr. Johnson was in very good humour, lively, and ready to talk upon all subjects.

The details are precisely sufficient to let us know where we are; they provide solidity without specification.

The character of Johnson, at the centre of the *Life*, also is static.   The modern biographer tends to conceive of his subject in terms of development; but Boswell, like his contemporaries, believed that the boy is the man in miniature, and thought instead of persistent, lifelong traits. Johnson of course had a career: he attended Oxford, progressed from failed schoolmaster to London author by profession, became the dominant literary figure of his time: in turn poet, biographer, lexicographer, essayist, novelist, editor, and critic.   But from the beginning his innate intellectual superiority, his "astonishing force and vivacity of mind," his "supereminent powers" displayed themselves.   And other characteristics were equally prominent: "jealous independence of spirit and impetuosity of temper," "dismal inertness of disposition," and "morbid melancholy."   Activated by his conviction of free will and deep Christian belief, Johnson struggled to reform, and was caught, according to one Boswellian formulation, in the "vibration between pious resolutions and indolence."   Boswell insists sympathetically on this striving, on both accomplishment and failure.   But the bases of character do not change.

Though character was static, the eighteenth century gave it range by insisting that it was composed of contradictions, and Johnson's contradictions were emphatic; he was all the more difficult to portray, as Steevens pointed out, because "his particularities and frailties" were more strongly marked than his virtues.   Boswell was intent on depicting him as "blinking Sam" and all, but his faults had to be put in perspective; this meant that Boswell had to counteract the common misconception that Johnson was a gloomy, brutal pedant, while avoiding the opposite extreme of the hero as grand old character.

A contemporary biographer might have taken refuge in a "ruling passion," just as a modern biographer might reduce Johnson to fit the pattern of what very loosely may be called "the authoritarian personality": guilty, domineering, perfectionistic, rigid in religion and politics, self-disapproving and harsh towards others—a giant in chains.   Insecurities within emerged as hard-edged formulations: "The woman's a whore, and there's an end on't."   But equally Johnson was honest, warm-hearted, helpful, and hugely affectionate.   A biographer could impale himself on these contradictions, as Mrs. Piozzi had; her Johnson was not only repulsive, he was unbelievable to those who had known him.

Boswell solved this problem of presentation brilliantly.   In the *Hebrides*, he had begun with a block sketch of Johnson.   Now far more confident of his method and material, Boswell could rely on an accumulation of minute particulars to build up "a full, fair, and distinct view" of Johnson's character: it is an *emergent* picture that makes the reader acquainted with Johnson in the same way he comes, little by little, to know a friend.

In amassing particulars, Boswell takes full advantage of his claim to "authentic precision."   Since it predisposes the reader to believe in his truthfulness, Boswell does not need to worry about plausibility.   A fictional character is judged on the basis of congruence: does the reader, relying on experience, find his traits coherent?   But a real person puts the burden of explanation on the observer: what patterns make sense of his actions? And Boswell had piled up, from his own records and those of others, a collection of examples that showed an unusually complex range of acts and characteristics.   He exhibited not only the well-known Johnson, decisive in opinion and abrupt in response, but a Johnson who was tender and warm in feeling; who had a sense of humour—grave, robust, or sly—"which gives an oiliness and a gloss to every other quality"; who even exhibited a "politeness and urbanity" for which he did not often get credit.   At the same time, Boswell can put unpleasant incidents into perspective with explanation—"the fretfulness of his disease unexpectedly showed itself"—or examples of Johnson's deep sympathy and ready practical assistance.   As

Waingrow says, Boswell presents Johnson's weaknesses under aspects of his strengths.

We learn so much about this Johnson because there is so much to learn. Sometimes Boswell points up opposites: the slovenly body contrasted with the acute mind; the contractions, tics, and mutters with the strength, precision, and aptness of expression. Taken as a whole, Johnson gradually grows in impressiveness: he demonstrates "wit" (defined by James Thomson as "vivid energy of sense") and "wisdom" (the same common sense concentrated to high generality). Wit and wisdom combine in his power to penetrate to the core of ordinary experience. In Percy's phrase, he "at once probed the human heart, where the sore was."

And so, gradually, Boswell not merely asserts but establishes a dominant image of this "great and good man," of Johnson's generous humanity, which then allows him to concede almost any number of limitations and failings without essentially depreciating Johnson's character. Though the *Life* was written in "admiration and reverence" (its last words), for Boswell warm partisanship was compatible with shrewd observation and, at moments, detached amusement. Boswell sees all round Johnson. He is not only a hero but an extraordinary specimen of human character. The great philosopher can scold the waiter about roast mutton: "It is as bad as bad can be. It is ill-fed, ill-killed, ill-kept, and ill-dressed." He can be shown as overbearing, narrow-minded, susceptible to flattery, greedy for victory, superstitious, and self-deceived. Most dangerous, Boswell can make him look comic:

> If we may believe Mr. Garrick, his old master's taste in theatrical merit was by no means refined; he was not an *elegans formarum spectator*.[1] Garrick used to tell that Johnson said of an actor who played Sir Harry Wildair at Lichfield: "There is a courtly vivacity about the fellow"; when in fact, according to Garrick's account, "He was the most vulgar ruffian that ever went upon *boards*."

But Johnson's shortcomings humanize him, and even his small acts become attractive. Boswell writes:

> He sent for me to his bedside and expressed his satisfaction at this incidental meeting with as much vivacity as if he had been in the gaiety of youth. He called briskly, "Frank, go and get coffee, and let us breakfast *in splendour*."

Boswell's insistence on full credibility allows him to move from detail to generalization and back again with ease. We believe that Johnson showed

---

[1] "A nice observer of the female form" (Terence, *Eunuch*, iii.5).

an "eager and unceasing curiosity to know human life in all its variety," in part because of the scenes already exhibited, and in part simply because Boswell says so.   Johnson's character takes on a density that makes other fine biographical portraits, such as the acute and elegant profiles of Strachey, seem as impoverished as the ordinary fictional figure.   No one ever travelled all over this man's mind.   In Boswell's depiction, Johnson attains a "critical mass," like Don Quixote or Hamlet; he becomes capable, within the broad limits of his beliefs and prejudices, of saying or doing anything and, indeed, his unpredictability becomes a compelling attribute.   Readers agree with John Nichols that "every fragment of so great a man is worthy of being preserved"; even the most trivial detail—that he tried to pole a large dead cat along a stream—makes him that much more visible.   And when these details are amassed, Johnson's significance overflows any single interpretation, and causes each age to construe him differently.   His contemporaries, to simplify, beheld the great lexicographer, moralist, and critic; for the nineteenth century he became the epitome of strong uncommon sense; and some modern commentators suggest an anguished figure sustained by force of will from moment to moment over the void.

Boswell's portrayal, however, does not focus on an isolated Johnson; like most eighteenth-century writers, he thinks of the individual first as a social being.   Johnson must have a human context.   And so the importance of Boswell's large treasure of Johnsonian conversation.   It was the "peculiar value" of the *Life*, whose main business, Boswell said, was to record it.   But it was also the central activity of the *Life* in all its settings: tête-à-têtes, small casual gatherings, formal dinners, meetings of The Club.   Here are the great scenes that make Johnson's a *dramatic* portrait, the single most distinctive and most often discussed aspect of the *Life*.

Though from time to time Boswell collects what he calls "gold dust" (detached remarks), Johnson's sayings carry more weight when they emerge in such social contexts, often under the pressure of informal argument. Johnson believed conversation was a high art where a man's intellectual ability truly proved itself, while public speaking was merely a knack.   Conversation for him naturally turned into contest, and Johnson was formidable: he could speak on any subject with fluency and impact; his adroitness of response was notorious; his talk "teemed with point and imagery"; and if all else failed he knocked down his opponent with sophistry or sarcasm. Again and again Boswell illustrates its "unexampled richness and brilliancy," which only Burke among contemporaries could rival.   In talking, Johnson is brought close up: we are in the same room with him; he sits directly in front of us and we see the expression on his face; he speaks to us; we hear him laugh and growl; we could almost reach out and touch him.

The great web of conversation that helps to bind the *Life* together establishes the public Johnson, the "literary Colossus." The shadow behind it is the private Johnson, the figure of uneasy solitude, the business of whose life was to escape from his own thoughts—from the mind, as many agreed, that preyed on itself. Johnson had an unusual gift for spontaneous enjoyment—"What, is it you, you dogs! I'll have a frisk with you"—but recurrent melancholy, ranging from depression to despair, darkens his portrait throughout. Boswell has been criticized, perhaps rightly, for not sufficiently stressing Johnson's fear of madness; though as Mrs. Thrale admitted—and she had seen Johnson convulsed with anxiety—he could persuade no one to believe in his fear. But the *Life* is full of black expressions: "Je ne cherche rien, je n'espère rien"; "a kind of solitary wanderer in the wild of life . . . a gloomy gazer on a world to which I have little relation"; "I would consent to have a limb amputated to recover my spirits"; "terror and anxiety beset me." Most frightful of all was the approach of death. Yet just as Johnson fought to demonstrate superiority over his companions, so he struggled to keep mastery over himself. After citing one particularly troubled passage from Johnson's "private register," Boswell comments:

> What philosophic heroism was it in him to appear with such manly fortitude to the world, while he was inwardly so distressed.

Courage, Johnson once remarked, is considered the greatest of the natural virtues.

While it is the most banal of truisms that Boswell thought of Johnson as a father, in the *Life* he recurs to the formula he had used in the *Hebrides* and presents Johnson principally as "a majestic teacher of moral and religious wisdom." Johnson considered himself "as entrusted with a certain portion of truth" and he was willing to impart it. To begin with, he taught his fellow man "the boundless importance of the next life," with all the implications of that fundamental belief. Next, the most orthodox of eighteenth-century secular maxims: our first duty is to society, which is founded on respect for rank and property. Subordination (Johnson's favourite topic) is essential "to the fair and comfortable order of improved life."

When Johnson moves from these generalizations to specific issues of, say, politics, his views, so responsive to the times, now seem inert. It is clear that Johnson's reputation as a thinker cannot depend on particular opinions.   One could fill an anthology with his "wrong" ideas on many subjects: Wilkes's expulsion from the House of Commons, the American Revolution, religious toleration, the prose of Swift and the poetry of Gray—on and on.   But, as often noted, even when his views are outrageous Johnson makes them worth refuting.

It is Johnson the moralist, rather, whose stoic vision continues to command attention.   His own achievements demonstrated some of the possibilities of life, while at the same time he continually insisted on its limitations. Life is "supported with impatience and quitted with reluctance"; it "is a progress from want to want, not from enjoyment to enjoyment"; even at best, "every man is to take existence on the terms on which it is given to him" and these terms may be highly restrictive.   We are always hemmed in.   As he warned Boswell, "Do not expect more from life than life will afford."

Conversation, as remarked earlier, often starting from a commonplace, elicits many of those observations "deep and sure in human nature," which show, as Boswell said, that Johnson's moral precepts were practical, appropriate to the recurring concerns of daily existence.   His *dicta philosophi* (philosophical sayings) carry conviction because they are based on "a very attentive and minute survey of real life."   They carry that weight of rightness, or at least of finality, which led Boswell to declare Johnson's "conversation was perhaps more admirable than even his writings, however excellent."

It is almost exhilarating when Johnson concludes, near the end of the *Life*, that existence is far more miserable than happy: this judgement offers the solidity of facing the worst.   And in any case benevolence, which Johnson once defined as the chief duty of social beings, is a constant in this world, as is our hope of immortality in the next.   Boswell lightens this austere outlook by stressing Johnson's fierce Anglican commitment—he is a militant and triumphant defender of the faith—and his constant practical exertions on behalf of deserving and undeserving alike.   And Boswell repeatedly shows the gloomy moralist seizing with avidity the pleasures of the day.

Other heroes face the unusual; Johnson confronts the ordinary.   His finest bit of advice came late in his intimacy with Boswell: whatever good breeding requires you to say, "My dear friend, clear your *mind* of cant." Johnson is a hero of awareness, of the examined life.   And together with awareness, integrity; Johnson is never just the same, yet he is always of a piece, and always himself.

The most significant lesson Johnson offers is the example of his own

life, and nowhere more so than in its close.   A stroke was followed by the
intermeshing pains of insomnia, asthma, and dropsy; he was deprived not
only of the Thrales but of his familiar household companions, Levett and
Mrs. Williams; others might consider him "the venerable sage" serenely
abstracted from the world, but he faced the realities of sickness and solitude.
His irritability was more apparent, his fear of death more immediate when,
as he said, mortality presented its formidable frown, but he continued to
cling tightly to life.   Reynolds's last portrait of Johnson, "with its fallen lip
and suffering indomitable eyes," catches the essence of this final struggle.

Death is the culmination of the old man's story as marriage is of the
young man's, and Boswell leaves Johnson to recount his own last summer
and autumn, through a series of letters that go over and over the same
pathetic ground of declining health and lessening hope.   But he remained
intellectually alert and emotionally responsive: "Sir," he said to one friend,
"I look upon every day to be lost in which I do not make a new acquaintance."   To the last he maintained his "animated and lofty spirit."
When hope ceased, he refused further medicines, even opiates, so that he
could render up his soul to God unclouded.

Johnson finally is a hero as he emerges in his strengths and weaknesses—in the light and shade of Boswell's biography—because he grappled
in extreme form with the beasts that can menace anyone: poverty, disease,
loneliness, melancholy, sexual frustration, religious doubt, fear of insanity,
dread of the inevitability of death.   But his determination to survive and
his willingness to assume responsibility for himself, to manage his mind
and to keep control of his life, persisted to the end.   This is a picture of
Johnson that can be put to use.

I V

BOSWELL SAYS, "I love to exhibit sketches of my illustrious friend by
various eminent hands," and these reminiscences, especially of the not-so-
eminent William Maxwell and Bennet Langton, are valuable additions to
his account.   But Johnson is more directly defined in the context of conversation: in sharp, varied interchanges with Garrick and Goldsmith, in
reconciliation with Wilkes, in his many moods—angry, critical, loving—
with Langton.   He appears least clearly *vis-à-vis* Burke, whose fuzzy presentation is one of the *Life*'s major disappointments.

Johnson's principal interlocutor, of course, is Boswell himself, and
though in the Dedication he emphatically warns against identifying Boswell

the author with Boswell the character, that confusion has always been the easiest way of misreading the *Life*.   Certainly Boswell the author demonstrates a remarkable intelligence.   As F. A. Pottle says:

> The easy and delighted comprehension which [Boswell's] dramatic record shows at every point can be explained only by assuming that he had a mind that stretched parallel to Johnson's throughout the whole range of topics discussed.

Intelligence was matched to an equally remarkable ability to get what he perceived down on paper.   "With how small a speck does a painter give life to an eye," Boswell had observed long before he came to write the *Life*, and this touch he imitated in the precision of his own detail.   Yet he is careful not to let his phrasing call attention to itself.   If, as Ruskin said, the symmetry of Johnson's style is "as of thunder answering from two horizons," then Boswell's style is as limitlessly transparent as the sky.   The effect, often remarked, is to convince the reader that no medium intervenes between him and the scene being described, though Boswell has shaped it with care.

Here is the opening of one scene:

> Garrick played round [Johnson] with a fond vivacity, taking hold of the breasts of his coat and, looking up in his face with a lively archness, complimented him on the good health which he seemed then to enjoy; while the sage, shaking his head, beheld him with a gentle complacency.

The physical movement makes its own point, the playing round Johnson, taking hold of the breasts of his coat, as the small Garrick (he seems to have been no more than 5′4″) looks up at the 6′ Johnson.   These details recalling their long intimacy—who else would have dared take Johnson by the lapels?—are shaded by phrases, "fond vivacity" and "lively archness," that suggest Garrick's mixture of attitudes: polite congratulation, fondness, play-acting—Garrick notoriously play-acted all the time—and the overtones of other responses: detachment, self-consciousness, even a touch of irony. In contrast Johnson, abstracted as "the sage," stands almost immobile—the fox plays round the hedgehog—but his reaction is ambiguous: is the shaking of the head a disclaimer of health or an intimation that he sees through Garrick's posing?   "Gentle complacency" (French, *complaisance*, the manners of the well-bred) at least implies a benevolent if wary attitude. This tiny sketch, which occupies only a sentence, vibrates with the depth of a celebrated, complex friendship, while adding one more element to it.

To examine even so short a passage minutely is like concentrating on the brushwork of a Cézanne, or freezing a film to examine individual frames.   But the ease and naturalness of Boswell's style carries us along quickly; we are not meant to stop to analyse the ebb and flow of suggestion underneath the clear verbal surface, to become explicitly aware of all the possibilities one sentence contains.   The casual tone, the fluid movement, hide the subtle complications that give the scene its fullness, just as the elegant straightforwardness of Pope's couplets conceals some of the most difficult of English poetry.

The re-creation of even so brief an interchange requires a mind alert to the nuances of social behaviour, attuned to the intricate play of relationships.   Yet if Boswell displays this kind of insight, what of the Boswell who could write himself down an ass?   As in the *Hebrides*, Boswell's success has been, in part at least, his undoing: since Boswell the character is so clearly and fully developed it becomes difficult to keep in mind that Boswell the author observes him with some of the detachment with which he observes his other characters.   And certain of Boswell's personal qualities, observable in the character portrayed, were very helpful to the author: vividness of sensation, openness of perception, immediacy and concreteness of response.   Because he is unusually honest with himself, he can see others better for what they are.   His plasticity, his ability to take on the tone of his company, even the childlikeness that can disregard received notions of decorum: all these contribute to the writing.

Boswell the questioner, manipulator, and stage manager, also has evident links to Boswell the author, but in revealing these roles to the audience, Boswell reinforces the persona of the "artless I," which he was willing to adopt once more because here, as in the *Hebrides*, it brought out Johnson so well.   In remarking this persona for the final time, it should be stressed that this was an accepted technique, a possibility inherent in the "plain" or "simple" style that Hugh Blair, whose lectures on rhetoric Boswell had attended at the University of Edinburgh, called "naïveté":

> That sort of amiable ingenuity[1] or undisguised openness, which seems to give us some degree of superiority over the person who shows it; a certain infantine simplicity which we love in our heart, but which displays some features of the character that we think we could have art enough to hide; and which, therefore, always leads us to smile at the person who discovers[2] this character.

Only once, at the end of the *Life*, does Boswell mention the "peculiar plan of his biographical undertaking," at the point where he offers his

[1]Ingenuousness.
[2]Reveals.

apologies "if he should be thought to have obtruded himself too much" on the reader's attention.   But clearly from the beginning he had been aware of his special place in the story, and willing to take the risks of misapprehension that prominence entailed.   Like Johnson, his failings are more strongly marked than his virtues.   He reveals that at times he was vain, snobbish, insecure, insatiably curious (a more admirable trait in a biographer than in a friend), and intrusive; he tells how he drank and misbehaved. The *Life* also provides full evidence that most people found him intelligent, attractive, good humoured, perceptive, and excellent company: as Johnson said, Boswell was welcome wherever he went.

What has really damaged Boswell's reputation is the direction in which he extends self-revelation.   Like most of us Boswell sometimes acted very foolishly, but while other writers would bury such moments as deeply as possible, he is willing to exploit them if they can be turned to use—and, occasionally, it must be admitted, when they cannot.   Boswell's eagerness to thrust his faults forward can become disturbing.   He quotes Johnson as saying, "There is something noble in publishing truth, though it condemns one's self"; there can also be something exhibitionistic about it. While it is inaccurate to infer that Boswell had no sense of shame, he had less than most people.

Yet it is also easy to exaggerate the extent to which Boswell depreciates himself, as his detractors, who perhaps like him are insecure and self-conscious, are liable to do.   Gray's remark that the title of the "Memoirs of Pascal Paoli" should have been "A Dialogue between a Green Goose and a Hero" evolved into the paradox that Macaulay made explicit: Boswell wrote a great book *because* he was a fool, a paradox that a moment's thought shows is a contradiction.   Great books are written by great authors.   That's how we recognize a great author: he has written a great book.

"I surely have the art of writing agreeably," Boswell told Temple, with very considerable understatement.   Boswell had a much more remarkable gift, an almost mysterious power, what G. O. Trevelyan spoke of as

> that rare faculty (whose component elements the most distinguished critics have confessed themselves unable to analyse), which makes every composition of Boswell's readable, from what he intended to be a grave argument on a point of law, down to his most slipshod verses and his silliest letters.

Boswell does show a rare faculty, both in general outlook and the ability to express it.   Trevelyan's comment leads towards Proust's insight: style is not a question of technique but of vision.   The interrelationship of vision and technique is ultimately impenetrable; it is impossible to say *where* or *how* Boswell came by his power to look at the world as he did, but, in his case, technique is so much an externalization of vision that one is tempted to agree with Croce that the two are identical.

What can be grasped is the world Boswell created in the *Life*, which opens out in time and scope as the title promises:

> The whole exhibiting a view of literature and literary men in Great
> Britain, for near half a century during which [Johnson] flourished.

Unlike the *Hebrides*, where movement and change of setting are indispensable, the scene here hardly varies: the dining-room, the drawing-room, and the tavern; seldom out-of-doors and rarely a glimpse of the bedchamber. Yet the *Life* never seems limited; it pours forth a variety of character and daily incident that no novel of the time can match.

If interest in certain contemporary topics (luxury, subordination, emigration, slavery) is now extinct, the *Life*'s figures have something still memorable to say about enduring ones: politics, religion, marriage, friendship, melancholy, death, and relations between the sexes. If the *Life* gives ample credit to misery, Boswell also fills it with enjoyment, as in the gathering at Mrs. Garrick's when he "whispered to Mrs. Boscawen, 'I believe this is as much as can be made of life' "; and at the level of social happiness it is. The *Life* is lively with the ordinary round of eating, talking, and visiting; it is a study in vitality: a crowded canvas of animated figures, against the background of London, representing the full tide of human existence.

The world of the *Life* is unified by Boswell's sensibility, and when seen as the transformation of life into art it becomes all the more impressive: from an existence marked by distress, long delays, half-willed actions, bad faith and broken promises, hastily snatched pleasures, wild illusions, the daily impediments of vanity, intemperance, lust, and despair, he has constructed with confident firmness a serene, generous world in which character and incident appear in undistorted perspective. The poet, as Sidney says, turns Nature's brazen world into a golden one. Yet rather than an invented world Boswell's is a fully realized one, which resists reduction to the much more selective constructs of fiction. And the *Life*, like the *Hebrides*, is very much literature of the world we know: Boswell took great pleasure in its daily operations and he left its rough edges. He was a connoisseur of the quotidian.

Carlyle, the most acute as well as the most absurd of Boswell's critics, attributed his greatness as a writer to his "open loving heart." The phrase is romantically indefinite but also highly suggestive, especially if expanded

into terms we feel more at ease with.   The delight Montaigne had taken
in exploring his own mind, Boswell took in exploring the world of society.
They had much in common, as Boswell insisted: urgent curiosity—about
the familiar as well as the strange—combined with detachment; shrewdness,
tolerance, and geniality.   Very little human was alien to them.   Boswell
also could assimilate others, let them "sink in" on him, and represent them
with a full sense of their humanity.   When he presents his characters, he
does not interpose his personality between us and them: they stand life-
size.   Most of the time he saves his moralizing for the footnotes.

A friend of mine remarks that if God wrote a novel it would be *Anna
Karenina*.   Certain writers—Chaucer, Shakespeare, George Eliot, Tolstoi—
have the ability to suggest that they depict, in heightened consciousness,
the world of normal vision, the world we share because it is created by the
overlapping of our separate ways of perceiving existence.   Boswell also
projects normal vision, and though he does not compare with these wonderful writers in strength of invention or depth of imagination, he approaches them in power of realization.   As W. K. Wimsatt says, he is "a
visionary of the real."

Boswell's vision of his world is so convincing that it has overflowed to
help colour an epoch.   Just as we tend to see the Scottish world through
Burns or Scott, and the Victorians through Dickens, so the atmosphere of
the *Life* suffuses our sense of later eighteenth-century England.   Boswell
says himself that he Johnsonized the land, and it is because of him we
identify this period as the Age of Johnson.   At the same time Boswell is
unique.   In snatches later writers can reword him amusingly, as when
Lamb says that "the author of *The Rambler* used to make inarticulate animal
noises over a favourite food."   But attempts to reproduce Boswell's tone
and viewpoint in an extended work fail; even Thackeray, in *The Virginians*
and *Henry Esmond*, produced only pastiche, in which the picturesque distances and the quaint diminishes the eighteenth-century world.

If you have a mean, pedantic spirit you will write a mean, pedantic
biography, no matter who your subject is.   And the reader will infer your
character from your work.   By the same reasoning, if a writer realizes a
world notable for its sense of spaciousness, its fullness of presentation, its
rightness of proportion, then these qualities dominate his deepest vision
of life.   Carlyle argued that Boswell's *Life of Johnson* was "the best possible
resemblance of a Reality; like the very image thereof in a clear mirror."
Several of Johnson's friends were talented writers; several sensed or knew
that he was an heroic figure.   But only Boswell, with his acute intelligence,

his brilliant technique, and his open loving heart, could fully realize that greatness.

V

IN HIS "MEMOIRS," published immediately after the *Life of Johnson*, Boswell stated with understandable complacency that the *Life* had been "received by the world with extraordinary approbation." It was a best seller: of the 1,750 copies printed, 888 had been sold in the first month after publication. And it was soon trailing a string of parodies, a good omen of success.

Not everyone liked it, of course. The Critical Reviewer complained of dull anecdotes and the impropriety of reporting private conversations. Both subject and biographer displeased him: Johnson for "brutal severity," and Boswell for "affected self-importance" and "passive fawning insensibility." Some of Johnson's friends objected once more to the revelation of his weaknesses and eccentricities. The eighteenth century liked to stick its heroes, whatever their private failings, into marble togas, literally in the case of Bacon's sculpture of Johnson in St. Paul's. But, from the start, Boswell had been determined to write a life not a panegyric: when Hannah More—to repeat a well-known story—"begged he would mitigate some of [Johnson's] asperities," Boswell told her "roughly" that "he would not cut off his claws, not make a tiger a cat to please anybody." As Dr. Burney later remarked in his usual mild way, Boswell had numerous good qualities but delicacy was not among them: "He was equally careless what was said of himself or what he said of others."

Percy would have sworn to the last statement. Not only did he stand displayed as a thin-skinned sycophant in the wonderfully funny and humiliating account of the Pennantian controversy, but he seemed a special target elsewhere. In particular, when Boswell told Johnson that Percy was writing a history of the wolf in Great Britain, Johnson asked why he didn't write a history of the grey or Hanover rat, so called because it had made its appearance in the country at the same time as the House of Hanover. JOHNSON. " 'I should like to see *The History of the Grey Rat* by Thomas Percy, D.D., Chaplain in Ordinary to His Majesty' (laughing immoderately)." Nor was Percy pacified by Boswell's comment: "Thus could he indulge a luxuriant sportive imagination when talking of a friend whom he loved and esteemed." After the publication of the *Life*, Percy could hardly be per-

suaded to speak to Boswell or to attend meetings of The Club when Boswell
was to be present.

And one can hardly blame others for taking offence.   Richard Hurd,
Bishop of Worcester, for example, spoke fiercely to his commonplace book
about

> a striking likeness of a confident, overweening, dictatorial pedant,
> though of parts and learning; and of a weak, shallow, submissive
> admirer of such a character, deriving a vanity from that very
> admiration.

But then Hurd had learned from Boswell's work that he had been Warburton's toady, and when "well-advanced in life" had engaged in "unjust
and acrimonious abuse of two men of eminent merit."

Even Wilkes, who might have been expected to relish the *Life*'s high
spirits, had mixed feelings about it.   He told Boswell it was "a wonderful
book," but wrote more openly to his daughter (during a dry spell):

> The earth is as thirsty as Boswell, and as cracked in many places
> as he certainly is in one.   His book, however, is that of an enter-
> taining madman.

Wilkes may not have cared for the remark that his reconciliation with
Johnson reminded the Bishop of Killaloe of the lion lying down with the
goat.   But, to do him justice, he had objected to the *Hebrides* also.   Perhaps
his literary tastes, unlike some of his writings, had always been conventional.

There were others who damned Johnson himself, literary tyrant and
Hottentot, "puffy pensioner" with his "insolent bigotry," along with Boswell.
Horace Walpole spoke for some when he wrote:

> With a lumber of learning and some strong parts, Johnson was
> an odious and mean character. . . .   His manners were sordid,
> supercilious, and brutal; his style ridiculously bombastic and vi-
> cious; and, in one word, with all the pedantry he had all the
> gigantic littleness of a country schoolmaster.

And others grew angry on behalf of their friends.   Norton Nicholls, who
had been one of Gray's intimates, wrote to Temple (21 July 1791):

> I have run through Boswell's *Life of Johnson* and can never forgive
> the disrespect shown to Mr. Gray. . . .   Indeed, I never before
> met with (to use a gentle term) so unguarded a publication.

Boswell's own friends joined in the criticism of one aspect of the *Life*,
its depiction of Goldsmith as a highly talented writer who often made a
fool of himself.   But Boswell did not make a comic butt of Goldsmith;

Goldsmith had made one of himself.   As Reynolds, his best friend, admitted, Goldsmith would "sing, stand upon his head [or] dance about the room" to attract attention.   Nor did anyone question that Goldsmith spoke and acted precisely as Boswell said he did; one can object at most that Boswell is just to him rather than generous.   On the other hand, Boswell could have been faulted more than he was for his tiresome sniping at Hawkins and Mrs. Piozzi, and for using the few opportunities available to make personal attacks on Gibbon, whose contempt for religion pressed on an exposed nerve.

But the common reader found the *Life* irresistible, and so did a majority of the reviewers.   Reporting that it had been "received by the public with extraordinary avidity," John Nichols, in the *Gentleman's Magazine*, struck the general note: "a literary portrait is here delineated which all who knew the original will allow to be THE MAN HIMSELF."   Ralph Griffiths, in the *Monthly Review*, was "astonished at Mr. B.'s industry and perseverance!—to say nothing of the multiplicity and variety of his own occasional [1] and pertinent observations."   Johnson appeared "in his mind's undress. . . . All is natural, spontaneous, and unreserved."   Griffiths urged that any reader would say to "the reporter":

> Give us *all*, suppress nothing; lest in rejecting that which in your estimation may seem to be of inferior value, you unwarily throw away gold with the dross.

The *Life* was so entertaining, so delightful, so quick to capture and hold attention that no one realized immediately that it was a major addition to English literature.   The *English Review* considered it a great gift to the lovers of light amusement: "The airy garrulity of the narrative will effectually recommend these volumes to volatile and desultory readers."   The serious presumably turned to such works published that year as Beloe's translation of Herodotus and Cowper's of Homer, both given longer reviews in the *Gentleman's Magazine* than the *Life*.   Like the *Hebrides*, the *Life* was not received at its true value because it lacked literary dignity.

But as early as 1795, the year of Boswell's death, Robert Anderson, with strong assistance from a letter by Malone in the *Gentleman's Magazine*, had arrived at a reasonably accurate estimate:

> With some venial exceptions on the score of egotism and indiscriminate admiration, his work exhibits the most copious, interesting, and finished picture of the life and opinions of an eminent

---

[1]Directed to specific occasions.

man that was ever executed, and is justly esteemed one of the most instructive and entertaining books in the English language.

The eccentricities of Mr. Boswell, it is useless to detail. They have already been the subject of ridicule in various different forms and publications by men of superficial understanding and ludicrous fancy. [What follows is Malone.] Many have supposed him to be a mere relater of the sayings of others; but he possessed considerable intellectual powers for which he has not had sufficient credit. It is manifest to every reader of any discernment that he could never have collected such a mass of information and just observations on human life as his very valuable work contains, without great strength of mind and much various knowledge; as he never could have displayed his collections in so lively a manner had he not possessed a very picturesque imagination or, in other words, had he not had a very happy turn for poetry, as well as for humour and wit.

Just a few years later James Northcote recognized that "very few books in the English language bid fairer for immortality than [Boswell's] *Life of Johnson.*" Macaulay's pronouncement in 1831, issued with his usual flat self-sufficiency, fixed its reputation: "Eclipse is first, and the rest nowhere." At the time of publication Boswell himself must have cherished the Latin verses contributed by Sandy from Eton, and Jamie from Westminster, welcoming the long-awaited emergence of the *Life.* Jamie's verses have not survived, but Sandy's begin bravely if unsyntactically:

> Adveniit tempus jamjam, quae musa tacebit,
> Quae non cantabit gloria magna modis?[1]

But no sign of public approval could match George III's remark: "Mr. Burke told me it was the most entertaining book he had ever read."

Contemporary objections to the *Life* have, or should have, faded with the years. But modern critics have found new charges to make. One, that Boswell suppressed some materials and bowdlerized others, is of course the exact opposite of contemporary complaint, and shows profound ignorance of eighteenth-century standards of decorum. In general, the question, "How much should a biographer tell?" is a non-issue: any biographer like Boswell who wants to present his subject whole tells all he can find out, thinks pertinent, and hopes he can get away with. A second charge, that Boswell was inaccurate, is almost ludicrous when his performance is compared with those of his rivals. For his time Boswell made an

[1]Now the time approaches, what muse will be silent,
What muse will not sing your great glory in its measures?

extraordinary effort to collect the facts, and the more facts the more chance for error. No biographer gets every fact right, nor do any of Boswell's few, easily corrected errors substantively affect his portrait of Johnson. A third charge, that Boswell slighted Mrs. Thrale's significance, has more merit. But circumstances—closeness to the events related, their rivalry, and the general conviction of Johnson's friends that she had deserted him in the shabbiest manner—made a just appraisal out of the question. Boswell assumes rather than brings out properly her central role in the last twenty years of Johnson's life.

A serious problem for some modern Johnsonians is that Johnson the conversationalist obscures Johnson the writer. It may be true that Burke declared Boswell's *Life* would be a greater monument to Johnson than all his writings; it is certain that both Macaulay and Carlyle, in the nineteenth-century vein of thinking the poet more significant than the poem, emphatically agreed. But even though Boswell himself found Johnson's conversation more impressive than his writings, he also praised Johnson's works highly—he said in his journal that they were the food of his soul—and surely he is not responsible if others have either agreed or disagreed with him.

In contrast to the old misconception that Boswell was no more than a reporter, an occasional modern will say that while Boswell's material is worthwhile, he had the temerity to provide a commentary; he interprets what he records. Here is a well-known example from 1784:

> [Johnson] bore the journey very well, and seemed to feel himself
> elevated as he approached Oxford, that magnificent and venerable
> seat of learning, orthodoxy, and Toryism.

Isn't this sheer Boswell? How dare he pretend to know what was going on in Johnson's mind? But Boswell's statement is modest; he says merely that Johnson "seemed to feel himself elevated." Thousands of biographers have looked far more confidently into their subjects' heads without incurring reproach. And Boswell was there as his censurers were not; he could see Johnson's expression and sense his mood. Boswell had a right, perhaps a duty, to interpret Johnson's reaction.

It may seem curious that Boswell, almost two hundred years after his death, is sometimes attacked as if the critic held a personal grudge. But Johnson still exerts such a powerful attraction that sibling rivalry continues to burn, with Boswell as the envied and hated eldest brother. In more than one instance, Boswell has been vigorously abused at the very same time that his material was being copiously appropriated.

The adequacy of any depiction of Johnson will always remain a matter of individual judgement. Yet assessment of Boswell's portrayal involves more than subjective reactions. It has to take into account such factors as contemporary testimony to the power and fidelity of his image of Johnson, the testimony not merely of reviewers but of men who knew Johnson very well, like Adams, Malone, or Reynolds, who said that "every word in it might be depended upon as if given upon oath." In addition, though Boswell shapes his particulars he never invents them, while his closest rivals among English biographers, Lockhart and Strachey, were notoriously indifferent to mere fact. As soon as credibility is damaged, to some indefinable extent our trust is reduced and so our pleasure in the work.

Finally, it has been objected that Boswell spent no more than 425 days with Johnson, so he could not have known him as well as Hawkins or Mrs. Thrale. Certainly Hawkins knew him much longer, and Mrs. Thrale more intimately, but like most of us they were too engrossed in their own dear selves to give the equally clear-sighted and obsessive attention to another that Boswell paid to Johnson. The *Life* in itself sufficiently refutes such criticism, but this line of argument can be profitably pursued. Boswell recorded Johnson directly and extensively over a period of 21 years. For much of that time he knew he was going to write Johnson's biography. For over three months during their Hebridean tour, they lived together in very close quarters. And though Boswell failed to make notes about many of the days they spent with each other, those days helped to impart a rich familiarity to the ones he does record. Imagine how valuable it would be to a modern biographer to spend even one day with Johnson! Imagine having watched him, listened to him, been grumbled at and blessed and hugged to him like a sack!

CHAPTER

18

I

GOSSIP COHERES INTO LEGEND, and legend hardens into history.   In a letter to an aspiring editor of private correspondence in 1798, Percy spread what was to become the received version of Boswell's last years:

> You were so kind as to furnish me with the octavo edition[1] of Boswell's *Life of Johnson*.   You may not perhaps have heard what occasioned his death, which soon followed that publication.   In consequence of his violating the primary law of civil society in publishing in that work men's unreserved correspondence and unguarded conversation, he became so shunned and scouted that with very agreeable talents for lively converse, a fund of anecdotes, and a considerable elevation in society, he was so studiously excluded from all decent and good company as drove him into deplorable habits of drinking, which speedily terminated a life that seemed radically formed for long duration.

"It is to be feared," as a modern scholar says, "that Percy had allowed himself to state as fact what he thought ought to have happened."

The "Memoirs of James Boswell," which appeared in the *European Magazine* for May and June 1791, put about a different version of Boswell's history.   Boswell had persuaded Reynolds to paint him on the publication of the *Hebrides*; now, safely anonymous, he himself presented his best, though quite recognizable, face to his public.   His readers were told that there was little need to make private inquiries about his life, "as from a certain peculiarity, frank, open, and ostentatious, which he avows, his history, like that of the old Seigneur Michael de Montaigne, is to be traced

[1]Of 1793.

451

in his writings." The "Memoirs" themselves trace the familiar story: illustrious ancestry, an early "almost enthusiastic notion of the felicity of
London," the Grand Tour, and participation in the Douglas Cause. Especially Boswell looked back to his marriage to his cousin-german, with
whom he had

> from their earliest years lived in the most intimate and unreserved
> friendship. His love of the fair sex has been already mentioned,
> and she was the constant yet prudent and delicate confidante of
> all his *égarements du cœur et de l'esprit*.

He praised Margaret, accurately and poignantly, for "excellent judgement
and more sedate manners" than his own, for "admirable sense, affection,
and generosity of heart," for "no common share of wit and pleasantry."

Necessarily Boswell summarized his literary career: *Corsica*, which made
him famous; his two letters *To the People of Scotland*; the *Hebrides* "so well
known and so successful that it is unnecessary to say anything of it"; and,
of course, the just-published *Life*. Less expectedly he quotes or alludes to
a good many of his poems, under the mistaken impression that his talent
for easy, unpremeditated verse had been underestimated.

Boswell defended his move to London by including part of Johnson's
letter of 11 July 1784, in which he had given the most guarded consent to
the shift to the English bar. Politics were even more lightly glossed over.
Boswell had resigned as Recorder of Carlisle because of the town's incon-
venient distance from London, but admittedly no good reason could be
given for his political obscurity:

> It was generally supposed that Mr. Boswell would have had a seat
> in Parliament; and indeed his not being among the Representa-
> tives of the Commons is one of those strange things which occa-
> sionally happen in the complex operations of our mixed government.

On the writer's taking thought, though, reasons did suggest themselves.
Boswell is too independent, too much the "downright Shippen," for great
patrons. In Ayrshire, the power of the Minister for Scotland (Dundas)
had been exerted against him at the last General Election, but he "has
declared his resolution to persevere on the next vacancy." He is a steady
Royalist and Tory, but able to mingle in perfect good humour with Whigs,
Republicans, Dissenters, Independents, Quakers, Moravians, and Jews. As
for self-presentation, it comes as no surprise to learn that he displays "egotism and self-applause . . . yet it would seem with a conscious smile."

Boswell must be allowed to speak without interruption on the subject
of Margaret's death:

This melancholy event affected him very much, for it deprived him of the woman he loved and the friend he could trust.   He had recourse to piety for relief; but his expression of what he felt was, "There is a wound which never can be entirely healed.   I may have many *gratifications*, but I fear the *comfort* of life is over."

He however did not resign himself to unavailing grief, but endeavoured to dissipate his melancholy by occupation and amusement in the metropolis, in which he enjoys perhaps as extensive and varied an acquaintance as any man of his time.   We find him at least extremely gay, and occasionally exercising his poetical talents.

Boswell's *Grocer of London*, it appears, was greeted with great applause, and he is generally considered to be the author of a poem of some length, entitled *No Abolition of Slavery, or, The Universal Empire of Love*.

This was the version of his life Boswell had been telling himself and all who would believe him, and much of it was true.   The "Memoirs" is also an extended dust-jacket blurb, the most elaborate puff in Boswell's publicity campaign for his great biography.   The *Life*'s runaway success made puffing unnecessary, but Boswell, an old hand at arousing public interest, enjoyed it as a game demanding an agile, resourceful mind, and took to the newspapers.   He announced that Mrs. Piozzi's attempt to defend herself against his charges of inaccuracy—this "attempt" was Boswell's invention—would be an excellent advertisement for the *Life*; that allowing for the difference in price, the *Life* had sold far more copies than Burke's *Reflections on the Revolution in France*, its rival for prominence among current publications; that the *Life* is a union of matter and spirit; that it is like portable soup: "the LION's *marrow* of a JOHNSON"; that it would be a more durable monument to Johnson than the one to be erected in St. Paul's; that Langton is "the character perhaps most highly held forth" in it; and that it is a pity Reynolds's portrait of Boswell could not have been reproduced in it along with Johnson's, since the *Life* is "a work in which *both* their minds are depicted in a vivid style."   Finally, though Boswell himself calls the *Life* his *magnum opus*, it is more properly an *opera*,

for it is truly a composition founded on a true story, in which there is a *hero* with a number of *subordinate characters*, and an alternate succession of *recitative* and *airs* of various tone and effect, all however in delightful animation.

In these fragmentary comments, Boswell is a brilliant reviewer of himself.

Boswell also informed the public that the *Life* had brought him so many invitations he could "be *literally* said to *live* upon his deceased friend." But Percy was right in one respect: some among Boswell's extensive acquaintance did fear his recording conversation. The one known example involves his long-time friend, Sir William Scott. Boswell had invited himself to dinner at Scott's—forced a passage, as he himself put it—and Scott replied that he sometimes invited their friends without Boswell because they feared that relaxed moments would eventually be placed in "the glare of public light." Do come, Scott said, "but no *letterpress* upon the occasion." Boswell was sensitive and defensive:

> I should be curious to know *who* they are that are conceited and absurd enough to imagine that I could take the trouble to publish *their* conversation because I have recorded the wisdom and wit of Johnson. But I own I wonder, my dear friend, at *your* saying, *"No letterpress upon the occasion."* It is too ridiculous.

Scott's cautiousness was understandable, and his reply to this protest, though conciliatory, was firm. Boswell was willing to smooth over the dispute, while asking

> that you and my other friends will inculcate upon persons of timidity and reserve that my recording the conversations of so extraordinary a man as Johnson with its concomitant circumstances was a *peculiar* undertaking, attended with much anxiety and labour, and that the conversations of people in general are by no means of that nature as to bear being registered, and that the task of doing it would be exceedingly irksome to me. Ask me then, my dear Sir, with none but who are clear of a prejudice which you see may easily be cured. I trust there are enough who have it not.

Yet, virtually at the same moment, Boswell wrote to Burke:

> It is long since I relieved myself from the anxious and laborious task of making minutes of conversations of value, which however I wish to resume in some degree, and am pressed to it by Malone because there is much wisdom and wit fresh from the source in casual talk which should not be lost. You gave me a delicious repast[1] when you communicated to me what the Sovereign and yourself said of my labours, and particularly when you repeated your very friendly defence of my writing down the conversations of Johnson. If you will, in the leisure of Margate, take the trouble to let me have for my archives at Auchinleck a written state of an interview so precious to me I shall be exceedingly obliged to you.

Not only did Boswell want to preserve every detail of this flattering interview, he was also testing Malone's assertion that Burke's coldness re-

[1]MS."repose."

sulted precisely from this habit of recording. Burke wrapped his response, as he often did when irritated, in an elaborate simulation of politeness:

> We shall, I trust, find ourselves hereafter as much obliged to your invention as hitherto we have been to your recollection. I am sure that something original from you will be well received. Whether, in the present possession of the favourable opinion of the world as you are, it will be prudent for you to risk the further publication of anecdotes, you are infinitely more competent to judge than I am.

As for his conversation with the King,

> Since then other things, not of much moment I admit, have made my recollection of the conversation far worse than then it was. . . . The King, by his manner of questioning me, seemed to be affected properly with the merit of your performance; and I said, what I thought, that I had not read anything more entertaining; though I did not say to His Majesty, what nothing but the freedom of friendship could justify in my saying to yourself, that many particulars there related might as well have been omitted. However, in the multitude of readers perhaps some would have found a loss in their omission.

Boswell seldom again bothered to report conversation fully, and even complained he had lost the faculty of recording. Rather, he had lost interest. The ongoingness of life no longer seemed purposeful or exciting; its point was gone, and with it Boswell's great gift—that private vice he had developed into a public benefit—and fundamental vocation.

Still, his reputation lingered. In 1794 he warned Sandy, who had been providing him with amusing sketches of old friends in Edinburgh:

> You must be very cautious of letting other people know that you are such an *observer* and such a *censor morum*,[1] as they may be apt to misunderstand and form a wrong notion of you. I speak from experience, because I am certain that there is not in reality a more benevolent man than myself in the world; and yet from my having indulged myself without reserve in discriminative delineations of a variety of people, I know I am thought by many to be ill natured; nay, from the specimens which I have given the world of my uncommon recollection of conversations many foolish persons have been afraid to meet me, vainly apprehending that *their* conversation would be *recorded*.

But the point should not be overstressed: if some people avoided Boswell, many others were happy to receive him, including a number who

[1]Critic of behaviour.

made his acquaintance through the *Life of Johnson*.   As a modern commentator points out, Boswell

> continued to the end to move in very decent society.   During
> March 1794 (the last full calendar month recorded in his journal)
> he dined at home eight times (one of those times with invited
> guests) and twenty-three times abroad, never alone and generally
> by invitation.   His hosts included a former governor-general of
> India, an earl, a marquess, and two bishops—really *three* bishops,
> for on one occasion he was invited by special request of a bishop,
> his fellow guest.   It is really too bad that one cannot say that one
> of these bishops was his old friend, the Bishop of Dromore.

To the successful belong the fair, in this instance Mlle A. Divry, a "gay little *Parisienne*," one of whose talents was to provide supper, "un morçeau de poulet avec une bonne salade."   In their mostly undated correspondence, Boswell signs himself her "mauvais sujet"—misunderstanding, she applied the term, quite appropriately, to herself—while she talks of knitting him garters.   But Mademoiselle was hard-headed as well as delicious.   In what must be one of her first letters (23 June 1791), she spells out the terms of their relationship: since he can't afford to keep her she has to maintain other acquaintance, and he has no right to get angry because she isn't at his disposal at all times.   Take care, she ends tartly, especially of your faults.

This little tiff passed, and later notes in Mademoiselle's phonetic French show that she at least got what she could from him: the loan of an unspecified "bagatelle"; a bottle of wine to entertain milord—but Boswell should drop in for a moment at dessert; renewal of some pawn-tickets; help with her lawyer's expenses (forget the past, she says, and think only of my misfortunes).   From Newgate (15 August 1791), an appeal during her period for a bottle of white wine.   Finally, the break.   She wrote:

> How can you count on me after the way you've acted?   Here's
> your *congé*, and don't bother me any more.   I'm happy; that's all
> you need to know.

Seeing her a year later at a theatre in Cornwall, Boswell felt her attractiveness again for a moment.   But they ignored each other, and he told himself she was "a mercenary and base creature."

This *divertissement* did not interfere with Boswell's matrimonial schemes, whose newest object was Miss Harriet Milles, "daughter of the late Dean of Exeter, a most agreeable woman *d'une certain age*, and with a fortune of

£10,000." Boswell conducted this courtship in his characteristic fashion: he told Miss Milles that he had kissed her name and then, just as he had done with Zélide twenty-five years earlier, he asked her to admit her partiality for him without committing himself at all—saying, in fact, that he might not even be interested in her. She promptly refused encouragement.

No longer distracted by Lonsdale, Boswell also rejoined the Home Circuit, where he was received (he said) like the Prodigal Son. He travelled to Hertford, Chelmsford, Kingston, Guildford, and Maidstone, without a single brief; but he enjoyed himself greatly, especially on a side trip to review the Grand Fleet at Portsmouth under the auspices of his Irish cousin, Captain Macbride. The *Life* had now sold 1,200 copies. Then, by travelling night and day, he reached Auchinleck on 28 August 1791, just in time to attend services on Sacrament Sunday.

It was Boswell's first return home since Margaret's death. Sandy—sensible, well-disposed, and passionately attached to Auchinleck—spent a month with him there, but Boswell immediately sank into languor and gloom. The house seemed melancholy and deserted, full of memories of Margaret. He felt unequal to dealing with his tenants or anyone else, and took refuge in restless movement about the county: to Fairlie at Fairlie, and Lady Crawford at Rozelle; to Ayr for the Justiciary Court circuit, where he found his old colleague Lord Eskgrove; to neighbours, relations, and friends at Garallan, Netherplace, Sundrum, Gadgirth, Ballamyle (formerly Ballochmyle), Kilmarnock, Adamton, Ayr (election of magistrates, Michaelmas Head Court), Coilsfield, back to many of the same places, to Caprington and Robertland. One small, precious moment of triumph came at the Head Court where, after a debate with the old enemy Sir Adam Fergusson on the old subject of nominal and fictitious votes, the freeholders expunged them from the roll. On 18 October Boswell fled from Glasgow to London on the fast mail-coach, again travelling night and day. "I visited a good deal," he told Temple, "but, alas, I could not escape from myself."

Even London could not relieve his depression. The world and his prospects were dark. He had held Auchinleck for nine years, he complained, but burdened with debts, unavoidable estate improvements, and the children's education, he had gained "only a scanty and difficult subsistence." When he wrote to Miss Milles to retract his "unreasonable request," she replied with cold candour: "I must again declare my full and fixed determination not to receive your visits or to continue any correspondence with you."

Then, also, Reynolds, once the most genial of friends and a constant recourse, was moping silently because he feared total blindness. Boswell found Reynolds's gradual decline very painful, but he forced himself to visit often. Near the end Reynolds withdrew into himself: Boswell informed Barnard, "He does not wish to see his friends, takes laudanum, and dozes in 'tranquil despondency,' as Burke expressed it." His death (23 February 1792) made a blank; "no man," Boswell wrote a year later, "feels it more than I do." It was also a heavy blow to the Gang and to the larger circles in which Reynolds had occupied a prominent place. As Malone observed, Reynolds had served as "a point of concentration, as it were, to those who had the happiness to enjoy his society, which it is scarcely to be expected any other can supply."

In writing to Paoli, who was exhausted by age and his own problems in Corsica, Boswell tried to present a balanced report of his situation: the *Life* continued to sell wonderfully (1,400 copies disposed of), he had a genteel house in Great Portland Street, and his two eldest daughters conducted themselves rationally. But he was miserably unoccupied, and hampered by that "alternate agitation and depression of spirits to which I am unhappily subject." He thought of applying directly to the King for preferment—no doubt hoping that Paoli would recommend him.

To a similar indictment of the world, Temple responded:

Ever dissatisfied, ever repining. People think you too independent, too volatile for business. Wedderburn and Dundas had no manor, no old castle, were not ambitious of the reputation of wit and authorship. I am at a loss what to say, what to advise. . . . You want high place and office. But can you be useful, can you go to all lengths with your party? . . . You must afford [patrons] inducement to seek you, and I fear they will not think your virtues and talents fit for their use. They are too refined, too conscientious. Disdain them all then; be the baron, the wit, the philosopher; do not appear to court them, and it may be they will court you.

Despite complaints of frustrated ambition, Boswell's attitude towards existence had changed fundamentally since Margaret's death. Where earlier his anxiety to sustain the happiness of the moment led him to recur uneasily to Pope's "Man never is, but always to be, blessed," now he had grown fond of quoting a different verse from the *Essay on Man*: "Hope travels through, nor quits us when we die." He was trying to rest in the imperfect present, and keep up his hopes in the future. And his final hope was that we may be—must be—blessed in the hereafter.

For when Boswell turned towards the years ahead, the outlook fright-

ened him so much that he blocked his reaction: his distress at this time
seemed, as usual, inexplicable to him.   The invigorating bustle roused by
publication of the *Life* had died away, and what was there for him to do?
He could glimpse but not sustain a realistic estimate of his prospects as a
lawyer and political aspirant: such an estimate would have crushed him.
Had he been able to find a steady occupation that he thought compatible
with his talents and social position, he would have been much happier in
his last years.   But none materialized, and in periods of high spirits when
energy abounded he snatched at every chance to entertain and distract
himself.   "I am conscious," he was to write to T.D.,

> that I can expect only temporary alleviation of misery, and some
> gleams of enjoyment.   But these it is my *right*, nay I think my
> *duty*, to have.

Pleasure had become a necessity.

And family life hung over him.   As Boswell confessed to his stepmother, his habits of life were not at all domestic.   Sandy had left Eton to
study law at the University of Edinburgh; Jamie was still at Westminster
and Betsy at Blacklands.   But Veronica and Euphemia were an embarrassment.   Though fond of them, Boswell could not afford to provide
them with a proper social life; nor did he intend to waste his own time
with unidea'd girls.   His dislike of dining *en famille* was so emphatic that
one obituarist could assert that Boswell's "companionable qualities led him
to be more absent from home than any man of his time."

Essentially he was idle, and for an idle man in London club life was a
very pleasant way of organizing existence, especially if like Boswell he was
a clubbable man.   Reynolds had done him a final, important favour by
arranging for his election in July 1791 as Secretary for Foreign Correspondence in the Royal Academy.   This honorary post led to his joining
the Royal Academy Club, a group drawn from the full membership who
dined together once a fortnight during the winter, and which included the
painters Copley, Farington, Hoppner, Humphry, Smirke, Stothard, West,
and Zoffany; the sculptor Nollekens; and the architects Bonomi, Chambers,
Dance, and Wyatt.   Among these artists Boswell found fellow spirits whose
meetings were more enjoyable than those of The Club itself.

Boswell also belonged to the Essex Head Club, that group Johnson
had founded in his last desolate days to secure himself company three
evenings a week; it had easy attendance rules and Boswell enjoyed its
conversation and air of decorum.   The occasional lonely evening could be
filled in at several other clubs: the Free and Easy (whist); the Eumelian,

which had a distinguished membership; and the lively Friends round the Globe.

Yet always restless, unable to settle for a life of small enterprises and mild rewards, Boswell looked everywhere for social excitement.   Not merely the recurrent satisfactions of eating and drinking though, as he said, no man appreciated these pleasures more.   But he clung to London because there he continued to find the spectrum of company and the constant intellectual round, the interplay of thought and pleasantry—wisdom and wit—that he found essential to happiness, and for which he was particularly fitted.

Perhaps no man, he said of himself, was "so universally easy and of more address in social life," and on this point the world largely agreed with him.   Everyone granted his gaiety of disposition and, to return to what Burke had said of him, so much innate good humour that "a man might as well assume to himself merit in possessing an excellent constitution." Yet, if so, Boswell's face was becoming one with his mask.   He had always, of course, been highly self-conscious.   Now, to an extent hard to gauge, his youthful spontaneity—that wholehearted responsiveness to the moment—had given way to a more studied attitude.   His character thickened with age.   He no longer complained of having to entertain his company; he wanted to entertain it, looked for the instantaneous appreciation that could momentarily compensate for his deep dissatisfaction with himself.

Two witnesses from his earlier years even preferred his talk to his writing.   Henry Mackenzie, the sentimental novelist whom Sir Walter Scott was to call "our Scottish Addison," said Boswell set the table in a roar but that his "wit always evaporated when he wished to write it."   And Boswell's Ayrshire neighbour, the commonsense philosopher Dugald Stewart, recalled listening with delight to his stories:

> They were much more amusing than even his printed anecdotes;
> not only from the picturesque style of his conversational, or rather
> his convivial, diction but perhaps still more from the humorous
> and somewhat whimsical seriousness of his face and manner.

Yet this underlying dissatisfaction drove Boswell to distract himself by shifting his company often, and his power to entertain could degenerate into a routine performance.   One hostess, while admitting his occasional usefulness "in removing reserve" and "causing mirth in company," complained that "he was only induced to exert himself when he had a desire to shine before somebody."   Her feeling that Boswell cared for no one must have owed something to his absorption and refuge in his public role. Malone, far better acquainted with him, objected violently to this view when it appeared in an obituary.   To assert, Malone said, that Boswell "was convivial without being *social* or *friendly*" was

> a falsehood which all who knew him intimately can peremptorily contradict.   He had not only an inexhaustible fund of good humour and good nature, but was extremely warm in his attachments, and as ready to exert himself for his friends as any man.

Still, Boswell could go over the edge of excitement.   According to her daughter, Lady Lucan hated him because he never left her house until he was perfectly drunk.   A reading of the *Hebrides* led Lord Fife to seek out his company shortly before Boswell's death:

> But the voice was so loud and he drank so much and talked so much that I decided it was more comfortable to me to *read* him than to *hear* him.

Fife was himself in his long-winded sixties, a master proser, but this must be an accurate description of Boswell on a bad day.

Cumberland gives a sense of the more frequent good days, when he wrote about Boswell long after his death:

> I loved the man; he had great convivial powers and an inexhaustible fund of good humour in society; nobody could detail the spirit of a conversation in the true style and character of the parties more happily . . . especially when his vivacity was excited and his heart exhilarated by the circulation of the glass and the grateful odour of a well-broiled lobster.

And Boswell's charm stuck with him to the last.   Even Fanny Burney had to concede its formidable power, though she was furious at his recording of Johnson in the *Life*.   After one meeting, she wrote:

> How many starts of passion and prejudice has he blackened into record that else might have sunk, for ever forgotten, under the preponderance of weightier virtues and excellences!
>
> Angry, however, as I have long been with him, he soon insensibly conquered, though he did not soften me: there is so little of ill-design or ill-nature in him, he is so open and forgiving for all that is said in return, that he soon forced me to consider him in a less serious light, and change my resentment against his treachery into something like commiseration of his levity; and before we parted we became good friends.   There is no resisting great good humour, be what will in the opposite scale.
>
> He entertained us all as if hired for that purpose, telling stories of Dr. Johnson, and acting them with incessant buffoonery.   I told him frankly that if he turned him into ridicule by caricature,

I should fly the premises; he assured me he would not, and indeed his imitations, though comic to excess, were so far from caricature that he omitted a thousand gesticulations which I distinctly remember.

One of the basic sources for the *Life*'s impact was that Johnson, physically and mentally, was so deeply imprinted on Boswell's imagination that he could reproduce Johnson at will.

During these final years, Boswell's circle of friends expanded in several directions.   Windham took Reynolds's place in part in the Gang; and Seward, who came to live a few doors away, became a frequent companion. The Earl of Inchiquin, an elderly Irishman who had carried off Reynolds's heiress, the fair Palmeria (Mary Palmer), called Boswell's presence at dinner a "certain pleasure."   He ventured into the immediate countryside: Sir William Chambers, the architect, entertained him at Whitton; John Cator, a wealthy banker who had been Thrale's executor, invited him to spend the Christmas holidays at Beckenham; Dr. John Coakley Lettsom, a noted Quaker physician, often asked him to bowls and dinner at his house-library-museum in Camberwell Grove.   Lettsom gave Boswell good advice about drinking, and Boswell published an ode celebrating him.

Boswell also spent more time with his friends in the City, counting on a welcome and a dinner at Dilly's or Baldwin's or the apothecary John Hingeston's.   Perhaps he thought his connections there would be useful to his law practice: "I must keep in with those men," he told John Taylor. But his main interest had to lie in joyous occasions, the company roused by drink and song.   Nichols warmly recalled Boswell deputizing at Dilly's table when their host was called away on business: in that capacity Boswell sometimes "tried the strength of *the oldest bin*."

The larger the company, the more elaborate the entertainment, the greater opportunity to put himself forward, the more Boswell liked it.   One such opportunity involved him in his last significant battle with the newspapers.   In June 1791, Boswell had entertained the gathering with his own ballad at an anniversary election dinner for Alderman William Curtis, chosen as M.P. for London the previous year.   Curtis's family had for several generations manufactured sea-biscuits in Wapping and, as a later mock-epitaph suggests, he was something of a rough diamond:

> Here lies William Curtis, late London's Lord Mayor:
> He has left this here world, and has gone to that there.

No matter.   Boswell's song was "loudly applauded" and widely publicized. But the London newspapers now took to referring to him as the City

Laureate, not a complimentary allusion since the last holder of that title
had been Elkanah Settle, the mighty rival of Dryden, who had sunk to
playing the dragon in his own farce at Bartholomew Fair.

Boswell was undeterred.   At the second anniversary dinner (June
1792), with more than 250 in attendance, he sang his ballad again with
further topical stanzas.   The *Public Advertiser*, his favourite newspaper,
loyally reported that his performance had met with universal approbation,
but other newspapers were caustic.   The *Morning Chronicle* said that Boswell "chaunted some miserable doggerel of his own composition," which
"the company bore with exemplary patience," while the *Diary*, which printed
the whole song, commented that Boswell

> in his ardour to show his wish to leave his loyalty beyond all ques-
> tion made a speech in which he was running amok at men who,
> equally violent with himself, thought and acted on different po-
> litical principles, when he was very properly checked and called
> to order by the President.

Boswell defended himself in the *Public Advertiser* under the pseudonym of
"Old Stingo" against what he called party attempts to depreciate his ballad,
which he also brought forward as a broadside; but a paragraph in the *St.
James's Chronicle* may have given him pause:

> *Notoriety.*—Nothing, says a literary friend, can be a stronger evi-
> dence of the force of this passion than that a man of real wit,
> learning, and genius, endowed with qualities to ensure him the
> respect of the wise and the worthy, should court popularity by
> what might be almost called gross buffoonery at a City feast.—
> What would Dr. Johnson have said to see his friend and *biogra-
> pher* . . . mounted on a stool for the entertainment of an election-
> eering meeting?

For whatever reason Boswell never exposed himself again to such ridicule.

Happily, Boswell's energy found paths besides political self-advertise-
ment.   One of his finest traits was his willingness to help others, beginning
with his multitudinous relations.   For years he had done, with patience
and affection, what was possible for his brother John.   The Cuninghames
were now on their own, but other connections were scrambling up the great
ladder of preferment.   Young Treesbank had needed help with a cornetcy
in the army; George Webster looked for promotion in the East India Co.;
John Boswell at Ayr—"Young Knockroon" until Boswell bought the estate—was trying to secure a promised office as Clerk to the Ayrshire Justices
of the Peace.   And the line of the deserving extended even to Montgomery
Boswell, who, though blighted as the son of the Leith dancing-master, had

been shrewdly named after Margaret's family: he wanted to be made a surgeon's mate.

Sometimes results were quite satisfactory, as when Bruce Boswell found his proper niche as naval storekeeper in Calcutta. A great triumph was to nag Dundas until he fulfilled his promise to do something for T.D. In early 1791 Dundas made him a clerk in the Naval Pay Office at the modest salary of £150 a year, but a toehold was all this worthy, industrious, punctilious, and stingy man needed; he worked his way up until he was affluent enough to buy Crawley Grange, an extensive estate in Buckinghamshire, which was eventually inherited by Betsy's son, Col. Bruce Boswell.

Outside the family, Boswell helped Temple mount a major campaign to get the crucial promotion from midshipman to lieutenant for Temple's son Frank. Dundas was their main target but no possible source of aid was neglected. Still, Boswell was willing to come to anyone's assistance. He procured a humble position as a tide-waiter (a customs-house post) for Alexander Dawson, an old college-mate; he wanted to send a boy who had picked his pocket to a better life at sea; he rescued from a harsh master an apprentice encountered in the street. In the absence of family, he arranged the burial of his old friend Royal Ross. If he couldn't provide money or concrete assistance, he gave practical advice. When Janet Little, the Scotch Milkmaid, in expectation of the usual handsome present asked permission to dedicate her *Poetical Works* to him, he suggested she try one of the Ayrshire ladies instead; Flora, *suo jure* Countess of Loudoun and all of eleven years old, duly accepted the honour and subscribed to a dozen copies. This is only a selective list of charitable undertakings; Boswell's generous temperament must have engendered, over the years, many little nameless, unremembered acts of kindness and of love.

The poor, unfortunate criminal especially touched his heart, and the most spectacular case he ever engaged himself in was that of Mary Broad, the Girl from Botany Bay. A Cornish girl, Mary had been transported for stealing a cloak to that newly established penal colony, where she married William Bryant, smuggler. Made reckless by the threat of starvation, on 28 March 1791 they and their two very small children escaped with seven other convicts in the Governor's six-oared open boat, and headed for Dutch Timor three thousand miles away. It was an appalling journey: soaked through for the first five weeks from the perpetual rain; in constant danger of shipwreck from a leaky boat and mountainous seas; suffering first from hunger and then thirst; always in fear of being killed and eaten by natives whenever they landed or came near shore. But they arrived safely after a voyage of ten weeks, and were soon on their way to England, prisoners once more.   Bryant, the two children, and three of their fellow convicts died on the voyage home.   The Government was not inclined to press for death, the penalty for escape from transportation, but neither did it want to encourage more such attempts, so in July 1792 the convicts were committed to Newgate.   According to the *London Chronicle*, they found the prison "a paradise, compared with the dreadful sufferings they endured on their voyage."

Boswell, whose spirits had picked up at the end of the preceding winter, immediately took over.   He appealed repeatedly to Dundas and Evan Nepean, Under-Secretary of State, for a pardon; collected seventeen guineas as a subscription for Mary; and inquired about her family's reputation from Temple, who reported they were eminent for sheep-stealing.   In May 1793 Dundas issued Mary an unconditional pardon, and a story that her father had inherited thousands of pounds persuaded Boswell to encourage her to return to her relations; he settled an annuity of £10 a year on her in case, as it turned out, that the inheritance was a delusion.   Nor did he forget her fellow convicts, who were freed in November 1793.

It is no depreciation of Boswell's vigorous and unselfish efforts on behalf of Mary Broad and the other convicts that Boswell's friend, William Parsons, a minor poet, chose this incident as the basis for an amatory epistle in which Mary is made to lament her separation from her benefactor:

> Though every night the Strand's soft virgins prove
> On bulks and thresholds thy Herculean love,

Mary remains Boswell's true mistress.   Exiled in Cornwall she complains,

> Was it for this I braved the ocean's roar,
> And plied those thousand leagues the lab'ring oar;
> Oh, rather had I stayed, the willing prey
> Of grief and famine in the direful bay!
> Or perished, whelmed in the Atlantic tide!
> Or, home returned, in air suspended died!

No, Mary will go back to London, where she and Boswell will perish together:

> For thou, relenting, shalt consent at last
> To feel more perfect joy than all the past;
> Great in our lives, and in our deaths as great,
> Embracing and embraced, we'll meet our fate:
> A happy pair, whom in supreme delight
> One love, one cord, one joy, one death unite!
> Let crowds behold with tender sympathy
> Love's true sublime in our last agony!

> First let our weight the trembling scaffold bear,
> Till we consummate the last bliss in air. . . .

Near-tragedy returns as farce.   Boswell's relationship with Mary had been completely innocent, but Parsons could take advantage of his reputation.

I I

OTHERWISE, 1792 WAS AN uneventful year.   Boswell asked to join Lord Macartney, departing as the first British ambassador to China, and was relieved to be turned down.   Veronica played the harpsichord and Euphemia sang; they had gathered a circle of musical friends, and one day Haydn, the impresario Salomon, and the well-known singer Mme Mara came to dinner.   Boswell travelled to Margate as one of the committee to lay the corner-stone of the Sea-Bathing Infirmary, "a rock of benevolence." As Temple noticed, he was "in a perpetual hurry and bustle, not owing to serious business but the want of it."   "I *cannot* forget my irreparable loss," Boswell told his cousin Robert; "yet I *enjoy* a good deal in somewhat a feverish manner."

His behaviour during a visit to Hatfield House, while on the Home Circuit that summer, illustrates the last statement.   As he explained to his host, Lord Salisbury, he had dined three days running with the officers of the Guards, and passed the next in a jovial bout with fellow barristers at Hertford.   Of the following day at Hatfield, it was necessary to write:

> My Lord, I am exceedingly hurt to hear from different quarters that my conduct on a day very memorable to me was by no means decorous. . . .   I can only say that the magnificence and genuine cordiality of the scene intoxicated me.   What followed I wish may be buried in oblivion.

His apology was accepted.

By August upwards of 1,660 copies of the *Life* had been sold, and the second edition, octavo in three volumes, had been in the press for some time.   (When he came to settle accounts on the first edition that November with Dilly and Baldwin, his profit was over £1,550 on a sale of 1,689 sets.) There was talk he would write a biography of Reynolds but, as he told Barnard, he was dubious about undertaking it: Reynolds "had not those prominent features which can be seized, like Johnson's."

Boswell could not bear returning to Auchinleck that August, so Sandy served as his deputy.   Instead, with Veronica and Euphemia in tow, he accepted Temple's standing invitation to Cornwall, a jaunt that gave existence a momentary focus and revived his journal, which had lapsed on 10 April 1791. The first event he had to record was embarrassing enough: on the way he stopped to see Betsy, who was staying with the family of a fourteen-year-old school chum, named Williams. Boswell felt "awkward and uneasy" because Miss Williams had complained to Betsy and the mistress of their boarding-school about his behaviour on a recent occasion in London:

> It seems after dinner, when I had taken too much wine, I had been too fond. Betsy told me the particulars, of which I had no distinct recollection, but I was vexed that such a thing should have happened, which might easily be exaggerated into very bad usage of the child of those to whom my little daughter is under great obligations.... I wondered at Betsy's judgement and prudence, who, when I talked of what Miss Williams had complained of, said she would do what she could to make her forget it, and desired I would not speak of it to her, for she would be very angry if she knew it had been repeated to me. Surely girls are more forward in understanding than boys in general.

Boswell had always had a weakness for adolescent girls; he once told Burke he would like a seraglio of them.

After spending two days with the hospitable but perpetually fretful Bishop of Salisbury (an old friend, John Douglas), Boswell and his daughters went on to a lively welcome from another old friend, Lord Pembroke at Wilton, where he marvelled at the sight of the unsophisticated Veronica and Euphemia sitting with their host under the magnificent Van Dycks in the double-cube room. Then they hastened west and the journey turned into a public event. He was the celebrated Mr. Boswell, and all of Cornwall turned out in hospitality: Sir William Lemon, M.P. for the duchy, whose daughter Maria he found particularly alluring; Sir Christopher Hawkins, M.P.; Robert Lovell Gwatkin, who was married to one of Reynolds's nieces; Sir Francis Basset, M.P. and boroughmonger; Francis Gregor, the other M.P. for the duchy; Lord Falmouth; Lord Camelford, the stately head of the Pitt family; Lord Eliot, his old London friend; and on their return through Devon, Lord Lisburne, Temple's sometime patron.

He'd had a wonderful tour in Cornwall, Boswell reported near its end to Malone, but that was not to boast of happiness. "Would to GOD," he continued, "I were safe in London." Travel and visiting were a constant constraint, and rural views tedious. "My mind *rusts* very soon in the country, especially in damp weather," he wrote in his journal; and he complained to his hosts that he was never asked to drink his fill. The best part of his

stay in grey and showery Cornwall was his sessions with Temple, in particular the day they sorted Boswell's letters to him since 1757. Among all
his changes, Boswell could trace continuity: "warmth of heart and imagination, vanity, and piety." His puritanism and timidity had disappeared,
he thought; to the modern observer, they may seem to contribute to his
self-reproach about drinking and sex, and need to entertain others. One
Sunday, he says in his journal:

> As my friend and I rode calmly between his churches, I observed
> that he held a creditable, actual station in society, whereas I held
> none. Yet we both agreed that I was better as the distinguished
> biographer than as a Lord of Session. We recollected Dundas
> when our companion at college, when we thought him much our
> inferior, and wondered at his great preferment. When I talked
> of *insisting* on having some promotion through Dundas, Temple
> advised me never to ask any little place, but to assume it as my
> right to have a considerable one.

That evening Miss Susan (Sukey) Frood, a dressmaker, sang sacred music
to them. She will reappear.

Boswell would have liked to station Veronica (19) and Euphemia (18)
in Temple's care till the next spring, but he feared they would fret; they
didn't seem to be enjoying the trip very much. Nancy Temple, who had
a mean tongue, described them to her dearest friend, Padgy Peters, as
"boisterous and unpleasant," though with pretensions to refined sensibil-
ities. On one short sea passage, Euphemia

> all the way over . . . blubbered and sobbed like a child. Can you
> conceive anything more ridiculous and absurd than a woman al-
> most six foot high behaving in this manner?

When they reached the other side, Veronica

> must likewise show her timidity and delicacy. . . . Imagine Miss
> Boswell, all terrified and alarmed, dart through a gate into a field,
> tearing her gown to tatters every step she took—

all because she was afraid that Temple on horseback would ride over them.
At tea the mention of ghosts made Euphemia throw herself down on the
floor and sob. "Next Sunday," Nancy continued,

> I trust they will turn their backs to St. Gluvias, and may their faces
> nevermore appear in it is my sincerest prayer. Mr. Boswell is a
> curious genius too; he is perpetually falling in love, as he calls it;
> and then he can do nothing but talk of the angelic creature. In
> a man more than fifty, such behaviour is folly. In short, I am

truly weary of them all and, if the truth were known, I believe they are full as weary of this (to them) stupid place.

And, in truth, the visit at the parsonage had its difficulties: Mrs. Temple showed her dislike of Boswell openly, and he declared (to his journal) his disgust with her mean dress and peevish manner. But the two fathers remained oblivious to the strains among the girls, and each admired the other's offspring greatly.

Boswell, as he told Blair, languished out of London; it was necessary to the "fitful fever" of his life. Yet shortly after his return from Cornwall, depression struck again. Everything troubled him. "I had no hope of happiness in this world," he wrote, "yet shrunk from the thought of death." Without practice, he was indignant at seeing others with briefs in Westminster Hall. Seeking sympathy and willing to share the responsibility for his failure, he turned to Malone:

> As he had been one of my encouragers to try my fortune at the English bar, I lamented to him my want of success. He said if I had confined myself to it, I possibly might have had practice. But I had chosen a wide and varied course of life. I had no reason to *complain*. That was *just* enough, but I could not help being *vexed*.

Summarizing his state of mind just before Christmas, Boswell wrote in his journal:

> I had been during all this fit of hypochondria miserably restless. I had some gratification, but a poor one and that mixed with upbraidings, by lying long in the mornings in a kind of half-sleepy stupefaction. When I came downstairs I was listless and fretful. I breakfasted without appetite having, as it were, a bitter taste which communicated itself to everything. . . . I often called on Malone, and found him fully occupied in historical and biographical researches, on which he was intent while I had absolutely no pursuit whatever. The delusive hope of *perhaps* getting into some practice at the bar was *now* dead or at least torpid. The printing of my second edition of Dr. Johnson's *Life* was the only thing I had to do. That was little, and was now nearly ended. I hurried into the streets and walked rapidly, shunning to meet people as much as I could, my perceptions being liable to such soreness from even looks and manner that I suffered acute pain on being accosted, and this was augmented by an unhappy imagination that it must appear how inefficient and troubled I was. . . . I had scorbutic eruptions on different parts of my body, which fretted in the night, and I supposed that the *humour* which they indicated to be in my blood was one cause of my present indisposition. I

called on an old acquaintance near Maiden Lane and had a momentary change of ideas, but no vivid sensation of existence.

Boswell inked over this last sentence, though in general his interest in,
and guilt about, casual sexual encounters had diminished. He does mention certain unspecified "experiments": "on three—one new," and "on one
new, but with no good influence on my spirits." Also, he "most improperly
domesticated but not all night. It was, however, a temporary feverish relief
from gloom." Sex could not release the libidinal energy which had been
drawn back into him by depression; it could not bridge the gap that opened
at such times between him and other people. And though the self-
reproaches persisted, after Margaret's death Boswell had abandoned any
serious belief in reformation. He alternated between drinking heavily and
not drinking at all, but none of the senses could give relief to the spirit.
Even the brilliance with which he records his moods, as in the long passage
just quoted, failed to restore his confidence and self-respect.

CHAPTER

19

I

DEATH CAME to the rescue.   The Rev. John Dun, Boswell's first tutor
and for fifty years minister of Auchinleck parish, died on 10 October 1792.
Boswell, as patron of the parish, was responsible for choosing his successor.
Recommending a candidate, Colonel Fullarton wrote with the jocosity of
the enlightened:

> Many trumpeters of the Gospel will be anxious to labour in that
> vineyard, and of course you will be assailed with solicitations as
> various as the forms and colours of the caxons[1] which adorn the
> pastors of our church, from the ample, bushy cauliflower or dal-
> mahoy to the smug, meagre curl closely adhering to the lank
> withers of the more rigid votaries of John Knox, predestination,
> and original sin.

This attitude did not recommend itself to Boswell, who took his duty
with great seriousness.   The parish minister held an important and sensitive post.   Spiritually he guided, or tried to guide, a congregation which
found hair-splitting theological argument both intensely significant and
delightful; temporally he might have to mediate between tenants and landlords.   (Though the ministry was also the high road of social mobility, few
attained the status of Mrs. Elspeth Buchan of Irvine, Ayrshire, who, after
being informed in 1783 that she was the third person of the Godhead,
soon collected a band of Buchanites.)   Many more candidates than parishes
were available, and Auchinleck was a very desirable post.

Since the responsibilities of landowner and minister often intersected,

[1]Wigs.

471

the patron naturally looked for someone congenial, but Boswell demanded further qualifications.   He wanted an old-fashioned minister, who preached revelation as well as providing the "cauld harangues" of morality.   And his choice had to be acceptable to the parishioners; "their edification," he wrote to Blair, "shall be my primary object."   To make a conscientious selection he was even willing to abandon London in mid-winter liveliness for a quick trip to Auchinleck (February 1793) to take soundings on the spot.   By this time he had collected many recommendations from clergy and gentry, respectful but urgent advice from the parish elders, and Andrew Gibb's confidential reports on candidates and local feeling.   It is unnecessary to detail the conferences and correspondence involved—Boswell docketed forty-three letters on the subject—before he and the parish settled on the Rev. John Lindsay to their common satisfaction.

Concentration on a specific project brought a welcome lift in mood. Boswell wrote to Malone from Auchinleck (20 March 1793): "I have been wonderfully active, and in health and spirits almost incredible; and never once drunk."   He felt so well, in fact, that he ventured to Edinburgh for ten days, his first visit since his departure in 1786; here, he told Forbes, "my wonder and cordial gladness were at once excited in an extraordinary degree."   Evidently Edinburgh was willing to forgive, or at least to overlook, the failings of its errant son.

But even before Boswell's departure from London, public events had begun to shock him out of depression.   The news of Louis XVI's execution had arrived on 24 January 1793, and immediately Boswell started to collect subscriptions for a monument to his memory in Westminster Abbey.   Pitt and Dundas stepped on that plan, but it illustrates the special horror with which the French Revolution filled Boswell and almost all of his friends. It was not inspired by the French declaration of war on 1 February; war with France was an old extramural sport.   What made this war different was that native radicals and reformers, encouraged by French doctrine and military success, threatened to demolish the political and social structure of Britain.   Or so the ruling class believed, and it reacted accordingly. When the mob burned down Joseph Priestley's meeting-house in Birmingham because he sympathized with the French Revolutionaries, Bishop Barnard, a good hater, sent Boswell "a real and genuine brick" from it. And Boswell gave his own vehement voice to the Government's cruel repression of political dissidence.

He had not abandoned the law entirely, and in April 1793 a "very good speech" in an appeals case in the House of Lords brought a courteous word from Thurlow, no longer Chancellor but still a man of great influence.

Given this opening, Boswell called and came to a long-desired point: would Thurlow be his patron?   A hard-headed bulldog of a man, Thurlow suggested a *quid pro quo*: Miss Boswell should call on Miss Kitty, his illegitimate daughter.   A great lady, Boswell reflected, could get away with contracting such an acquaintance, but the social cost was too high for his daughters. He would never abandon the idea that he could get something for nothing.

Meanwhile interest in the *Life* remained wonderfully high, showing itself in letters of praise, suggestion, and correction.   Boswell was especially pleased when his old friend Andrew Erskine, having read the *Life* "with infinite avidity," reported that he found it "an inexhaustible mine of wit and good sense."   For the second edition Boswell had collected extensive material: anecdotes from Nichols, Reynolds, Maxwell, and in particular Langton, as well as many of Johnson's letters to Langton.   And he brought back details about Johnson from his own memory:

> Such was the heat and irritability of his blood that not only did
> he pare his nails to the quick, but scraped the joints of his fingers
> with a penknife till they seemed quite red and raw.

Boswell also took the opportunity to include some of the compliments paid to the *Life*; for example, Vicesimus Knox, who had deplored the *Hebrides*, now stumbled on this insight: the *Life* "is a most valuable work. Yours is a new species of biography."   And, characteristically, Boswell provided further personal details: the attentive reader could learn that the author himself was "a lover of wine"; that he had conducted a correspondence with the late Elizabeth, Duchess of Northumberland; and, in a transparent reference, that in Westminster Hall merit did not always assure success.

One kind of addition, however, was unfortunate: feeling that the world did not take his ideas with adequate seriousness, Boswell decided to impart them in some lengthy footnotes.   "I am sure," he told Blair, that "the opinions [the *Life*] enforces, whether political or religious, should be diffused amongst all the subjects of the King of Great Britain and Ireland." He had never been an impressive thinker on general topics; now he prided himself on high and inflexible attitudes, and a distressing number of his notes seem less intent on affirming his own orthodoxy than on insulting those who differed from him.

Boswell could have used the second edition to soothe some ruffled feelings, especially those of Percy and James Beattie, who resented Johnson's remark that Beattie, while in London, had concealed his wife's existence.   But Boswell was unyielding in matters of fact, and his allusion in the second edition to Beattie's "extreme sensibility" on the subject was worse than saying nothing at all.   Another critic, Anna Seward, took to the *Gentleman's Magazine,* and the literary world was edified by a dispute over two early poems, one about a duck and the other about a sprig of myrtle, attributed to Johnson.   Though describing herself as "a defenceless female," the Swan of Lichfield hissed a good deal, and others joined in, prolonging the controversy for several months.   Boswell triumphed easily, but victory over a lady in a public squabble was inglorious.

It is hard to understand why contemporaries did not praise Boswell's genius as a writer more often.   But certainly one reason was that Boswell would not play the part of the serious author.   In the second edition of the *Life* he reproduced a significant passage from the Preface to his *Account of Corsica*:

> I have an ardent ambition for literary fame, for, of all possessions, I should imagine literary fame to be the most valuable.   A man who has been able to furnish a book which has been approved by the world has established himself as a respectable character in distant society, without any danger of having that character lessened by the observation of his weaknesses.   To preserve an uniform dignity among those who see us every day is hardly possible, and to aim at it must put us under the fetters of perpetual restraint. The author of an approved book may allow his natural disposition an easy play, and yet indulge the pride of superior genius when he considers that by those who know him only as an author he never ceases to be respected.

Boswell returned to the soul-animating strain of authorial fame in the Advertisement to the second edition, and it involved him in the only quarrel he ever had with Malone.   According to the account Malone gave years later, he persuaded Boswell to tone down the Advertisement but then he saw "by accident" at the printer's (was he suspicious?) the addition of a "wild rhodomontade" to it.   This led him to "entreat" Boswell

> not as a favour but as a *right* that you would cancel whatever relates to me in the former Advertisement; for *noscitur a socio*[1] is a very true adage, and you cannot degrade yourself without injuring at the same time the characters of those whom you mention as your friends.   Poor Sir Joshua is in his grave, and "nothing can touch him further"; otherwise he could not but blush that his name should appear at the head of a Dedication followed by such an Advertisement as the compositor has now in his hands.   Yours

[1]A man is known by his companions.

always very sincerely in *private*, but by no means wishing to be *pilloried* with you in *public*.

The offending paragraph, which survives in a proof, reads:

It is impossible for me, as an enthusiastic *Tory*, not to tell the world what I feel, and shall express with that reverential fondness which characterizes a true royalist.   Soon after the death of my illustrious friend, HIS MAJESTY one day at the levee, after observing that he believed Dr. Johnson was as good a man as ever lived, was graciously pleased to say to me, "There will be many lives of Dr. Johnson; do you give the best."—I flatter myself that I have obeyed my SOVEREIGN's commands.

Not only was Boswell shamelessly praising himself, he was violating the rule that the King's private observations were never to be made public. But he reacted calmly, endorsing Malone's complaint "a strange letter," and attributing his "*hyper*critical" reaction to irritation about the "stabs" at him in Steevens's recently published fourth edition of Shakespeare.   He had talked to Courtenay, Boswell replied, and

I assured him, as I do yourself, that I was fully satisfied you acted with real friendship towards me; but I could not help thinking very erroneously; for surely every man is at liberty to put himself forward in the style he likes best, and the praise of his friends in a very different style must not be confounded with his own personal rhodomontade.

But since Malone was so outraged, he would submit their difference to the Bishop of Salisbury.   This paragraph was dropped but "having afterwards got into a higher flight of spirits," Malone recalled, Boswell added four more paragraphs of (justified) puffing and self-complacency, which even much later struck Malone as perhaps the most exceptionable passage in the whole *Life*.   Sandy, with his very firm notions of the family dignity, thought his father should have taken a stronger line, but Boswell told him he had given as good as he got.   He needed Malone.   Yet he had always wondered why he shouldn't say just what he felt.

Boswell never lacked for literary projects, taken up with varying degrees of seriousness: a life of the poet Robert Blair; an account of Walton to prefix to his *Lives*; memoirs of the Family, or of his uncle Alexander Webster; a quarto edition of *The Beggar's Opera* with fine plates; a life and edition of Steele.   Nor did he ever lose his ability to discriminate and express character, as this late bit from the journal illustrates:

Dined at Mr. Cator's with Mr. Jeffreys, town clerk of Bath, a great crony of Lord Camden's, a sly, talking old fellow with an affectation of heartiness, and withal such a knowledge of legal forms and their history as made me ashamed of my ignorance.

At least once in Cornwall, his hosts had shown an understandable apprehension that he might make a book out of them, but his jaunt there had been too short and uninteresting. He did have one feasible project, his long-considered account of his Continental travels, feasible because he could only do sustained work on a topic of which he himself made a part. He outlined his plan to Forbes, who was travelling in Italy (11 May 1793):

> Your *travels* afford you an ample and various field for the exercise of your observation, reflection, and let me add description; for I trust you have kept a copious journal, and will bring us home a great deal peculiarly agreeable. I am preparing *my* Travels (notwithstanding Johnson's discouraging me) and believe they may be ready for publication next winter. They will not have much of inanimate subject matter, though I flatter myself there will be some good touches too on several topics of that nature. But for conversations, with Voltaire, Rousseau, Tissot, John Wilkes, Gaubius of Leiden, Abbé Jerusalem of Brunswick, Morgagni of Padua, and a wonderful number of other persons, with letters, anecdotes, etc., etc., etc., they will be, I *say it*, delightful. I cannot yet say how many volumes they will make. That will depend on the size, as to which pray advise me. Methinks duodecimo volumes or small octavo will be best, as they will go round the world in carriages.

Even in their surviving fragmentary state, Boswell's materials provide some of our finest glimpses of such men; given fullness and continuity, his "Travels" would have been a worthy companion piece to the *Hebrides*.

A writer of course has to disregard his friends' well-meant advice. When Forbes urged, as he always did, that Boswell excise any remark which could possibly offend anyone in any manner, Boswell replied:

> Although I should be very sorry to hurt any worthy person, I can by no means think it a duty to abstain from censuring the unworthy or laughing at the ridiculous, though they should be vexed.

And Temple deprecated the whole scheme: "I don't think you have anything interesting or novel to say, but your NAME may make it sell." But then Temple could comment ingenuously about the *Life*, "Strange that you should be able to compose a book so much liked!" Perhaps he was suffering from author's pique. Years previously Temple had sent a sketch of Gray to Boswell, who inserted it as an anonymous piece in the *London Magazine*; Mason discovered it there and used it as his summarizing "char-

acter" in his *Memoirs of Gray*.   Temple ever after fancied that characters
were his forte, but Boswell had refused or ignored his generous offer to
provide a similar one of Johnson.

Still, Boswell would never have let himself be discouraged about a
writing project by anything Temple said; it was just that he could not bring
himself to undergo the labour entailed; and he left the materials for his
travels among the other papers entrusted to his literary executors, in the
hope that a book could be quarried from them for the benefit of his younger
children.

Now he planned to embark on his travels once more, this time to view
the Combined Allied Armies besieging Valenciennes.   But the jaunt had
to be postponed: coming home drunk on the night of 5 June 1793 he was
knocked down, robbed, and left lying stunned in the street.   A young
Templar named Pughe, passing by, got him home with the help of the
watchman and patrol.   He had suffered a bad cut on the head, and was
confined for several days with pain and fever.   Temple admonished him
in Shakespearian terms: what if he were to be cut off in the blossom of his
sins, unhouseled, disappointed, unaneled?   Boswell replied in the fervour
of reform:

> This . . . shall be a *crisis* in my life.   I trust I shall henceforth be
> a sober, regular man. . . .   Your suggestion as to my being carried
> off in a state of intoxication is aweful.   I thank you for it, my dear
> friend.   It impressed me much, I assure you.

The incident's more lasting effect was on Boswell's morale.   To prepare for Valenciennes, he visited Warley Camp where Langton was serving
as a major in the Lincolnshire militia.   But he quickly deserted, with
apologies:

> I was sorry to leave you sooner than you kindly wished.   But it
> was really necessary for me to be in town; and, as I candidly owned
> to you, I had enough of a camp.   In my convalescent state another
> disturbed night would have hurt me much.
>   O London! London! there let me be; there let me see my
> friends; there a fair chance is given for pleasing and being pleased.

But again even London could not keep depression from deepening,
nor the news that the second edition of the *Life*, published on 17 July 1793,
was off to a wonderful start: 400 copies sold in a week.   Boswell's heart
hadn't been in its preparation; the first edition had established his reputation, and the second involved work without hope of comparable return
in fame, though with some anticipation of profit.   Textually it was chaotic:

material received late was inserted out of chronological order; the second
of its three volumes was burdened with a supplement of 21 pages; and the
first volume had at its beginning not only the index (as in the first edition),
but "additions . . . recollected and received after the second edition was
printed," a "chronological catalogue" of Johnson's prose works, "corrections," and "additional corrections"—37 pages of Johnsoniana thrown in
at random.

Following the publication of the second edition, the only occupation
Boswell could find was to bring out the *Principal Additions and Corrections*
to the *Life*, a 44-page pamphlet distributed free to owners of the first
edition.   The Critical Reviewer carried on about it as before: would Johnson have been so much at ease with Boswell "if he had seen the ready tablet
and the ambushed pen prepared to stab the soul of confidence and mutual
fellowship?"   This was virtually Boswell's last attention to Johnson; nothing
indicates he did more towards preparing the third edition, brought out by
Malone in 1799, than to make a few corrections in a copy of the second.

News of the death of Col. Thomas Bosville, Godfrey's second son, at
the battle of Lincelles, extinguished military ardour completely, and Boswell gave up his Continental expedition.   With nothing to do—James at
Auchinleck with Sandy, and Malone in Stratford looking through Eliza-
bethan records for traces of Shakespeare—Boswell pined in London, thinking of all the friends who were dead or gone: Reynolds, Pringle, Godfrey
Bosville, Oglethorpe, Paoli, and of course Johnson.   One day in early
September he ran into Lord and Lady Inchiquin and they asked him to
dinner.   Afterwards, his hosts went to the theatre, and Boswell says:

> When I found myself in the street, just warmed with wine and
> having nobody on whom I could call, I thought the best thing I
> could do was to steal into bed, which I did a quarter before seven.
> Strange kind of life.

He lay in bed as usual till past nine the next morning.

Then London began to fill again.   James and Malone returned, and
Temple hurried up to town to press Dundas in person for Frank's appointment as lieutenant.   Temple had a tale to unfold, in fact two.   The
first concerned Nancy.   On their return trip from London in 1790, they
had met a Rev. Charles Powlett, smooth, personable, and articulate.   He
and Nancy were soon engaged, but they faced the old problem of money.
Powlett's late father was the illegitimate son of the Duke of Bolton and the
celebrated actress Lavinia Fenton (the original Polly Peachum in *The Beggar's Opera*), whom he married after the death of his first wife.   Our Powlett
moved in a fast set, which included the Prince of Wales; he lived on air,

credit, and expectations, the last in particular from his uncle, another Rev. Charles Powlett.   Temple liked the young man very much, but he was firm that he and Nancy could not get married without a proper income, say £300 a year.   In the mean time Powlett and his mother, laden with impedimenta, had moved in with the Temples and were starting to get on Temple's feeble nerves.

At this point the Nancy-Powlett story crossed Temple's own.   Mrs. Temple had died the previous March.   Throughout their married life Temple had constantly complained about her peevish disposition, sexual coldness, and indifference to her children; shortly before her death he told Boswell, "She hardly knows what an agreeable sensation is of any kind." But Temple's love for her had always increased in direct proportion to the geographical distance between them; their final separation made him realize she had been an angel, and he could hardly bear to live without her. Or without someone.   To help with the children the twenty-eight-year-old Sukey Frood had moved in as housekeeper, and soon Temple fell deeply in love with her.   It was a delusion, an infatuation, delirium, he told Boswell and himself, but love persisted.   Boswell advised diversion or, as a last resort, escape from St. Gluvias.   Nancy and Powlett were horrified.

Temple's mission in London was successful, but as soon as he returned to Cornwall he got into a most violent dispute with Powlett: for some failure in respect Powlett had deprived Octavius, Temple's nine-year-old favourite, of food for 24 hours.   The Powletts were soon on their way.   But Nancy and Powlett hit on a venomous means to keep Temple from marrying Sukey: they got Frank, also no doubt shocked by paternal lust, to assert that he had had sexual relations with Sukey.   Though she denied it, Powlett spread the story all over the duchy.   In his reeling world, Temple clung to the image of his closest friendship.   He wrote to Boswell:

> Six-and-thirty years!   How thankful ought we to be that in an entire intimacy of so long standing, no difference, not the slightest coolness, has ever damped the satisfaction and joy with which we saw or heard from each other.

Now Temple spoke very differently of Powlett: "a diabolical, mean, dirty creature it is."   This opinion was reinforced by letters from the elder Charles Powlett, whose relations with his nephew had become very strained after he had married *his* housekeeper *en secondes noces*.   (Utterly selfish, Nancy thought it.)   Temple had already learned that Powlett had left debts "of mere extravagance and dissipation" amounting to £600 behind him in Hampshire when he moved in with the Temples; Powlett Sr. now imparted the tale of his nephew's debaucheries as a Cambridge undergraduate.   Un-

der stress Nancy had become "indelicate, disrespectful, violent, undutiful."
Of course Temple had forbidden the marriage, pointing out accurately
among other causes for dissatisfaction that neither Nancy nor Powlett had
any notion of economy.   Boswell sympathized with his anger at filial disregard.

Boswell's amorous adventures were both more casual and more mysterious: "an old acquaintance in Queen St." sometimes entertained him;
"excellent," he notes of one visit.   But the next day, "*domesticated*; almost
discovered.   Never again."   His escape occurred on 20 August, and he
didn't return until 13 October.   Two new enigmatic signs appear in the
journal: "C"; and then "somewhat heated with wine, ⁓⁓⁓," followed the
next day by, "⁓⁓⁓ ⁓⁓⁓."   A guarded entry the following winter suggests that he thought he had impregnated someone, and others that he
was infected once more: both fears seem to have been false alarms.

All this time Boswell had been indulging fantasies of marrying Maria
Lemon, and Temple responded enthusiastically, "the lovely Maria! the idea
is transporting!   Such a connection would be like beginning life anew."
But in his sober hours Boswell reminded himself that his uncertain temperament, the memory of Margaret, and a "tender regard" for his children
put a second marriage out of the question.   He would not inflict on them
the pain his father had on him.   In fact, no one he could love would have
put up with him as Margaret had, and the constraints of marriage were
now too irksome for him to endure.

I I

ONE BY ONE, Boswell's illusions were deserting him.   For two years he
kept chambers in the Inner Temple before giving them up as a totally
useless expense.   He still made an occasional appearance in his barrister's
dress in Westminster Hall, but that pretence deceived no one, not even
himself.   He also travelled the Home Circuit twice a year, picking up a
few petty cases; it gave his life variety.   But he had so little business—not
one brief during Epiphany Sessions in January 1794—that he resolved to
go round only from time to time, if at all.

Also his health may have begun to deteriorate.   Temple nagged him
to have some "bumps" (cysts?) on his head removed.   He had put on weight,
Sandy joking that they would have to find a strong young horse for him
at Auchinleck "that can stand the labour which you will give him, which is
none of the least."   George Dance's sketch of Boswell, done in April 1793,

shows a well-set, double-chinned gentleman; and the undated Lawrence semi-caricature of roughly the same period is lively and appealing.   But Farington, the following October, thought him "much altered for the worse in appearance."

And there was his state of mind: "I was incessantly thinking on myself." To escape, he continued to dine out as much as possible, the length and elaborateness of dinner often enabling him to evade the tyranny—and futility—of reflection.   A series of selected entries (partly summarized earlier) for February–April 1794 shows his routine: dined Farington, "a truly joyous, social day"; dined Wilkes, "a cheerful day"; dined Lord In-chiquin, "a hearty day"; dined Penn, "a capital dinner and good wine; enough, yet not to excess"; dined Bishop of Salisbury, "a good rational day, yet wine enough"; dined Ross Mackye (almost his father's last surviving friend), "quiet and agreeable"; dined Dilly, "an extraordinarily good din-ner, even for Dilly."   Boswell's City friends knew how to entertain; Wind-ham had to ask whether Curtis and Dilly would yield him to other company "for one day."

Not that such entertainment was invariably pleasurable: a grand set dinner with John Bleaden, "mine host" of the London Tavern, resulted in total oblivion; and a dinner at Lord Townshend's Boswell summarized as "a weary day and little wine.   Early to tea. . . .   I had got into bad hu-mour . . . and stole home soon.   I am become too fastidious."   A visit from Robert Boswell and a friend, exuding Edinburgh, also dampened his spirits.

But to say that Boswell cheated the hours in sociability catches only part of the truth.   He moved constantly among friends—Malone, Courte-nay, Langton, Windham, Wilkes, to name the most prominent—that would have given social and intellectual pleasure to anyone at any time.   And of this group he was the most gifted as well as the most entertaining member.

Lack of money continued to restrict Boswell's own hospitality, but he mentions one dinner for Lords Eliot and Sunderlin, Malone, Wilkes, Windham, Courtenay, and T.D.: "a rich day" even though Wilkes did all the talking, which Malone did not appreciate.   Between war and a bad harvest in 1792 his tenants were suffering, and their rents were in arrears. He was living in the narrowest manner, he told Sandy; improvements at Auchinleck in 1793 had cost him almost £300; the children's education continued to be a large, fixed expense; annuities and the interest on his debts were crippling.   Asked to go over the London household food bills, T.D. reported excessive expenditures on bread, butter, and eggs, though, as Boswell explained, "the two young ladies eat very little."   Twice he stayed away from The Club to save money.

Then, once more, he imagined the possibility of official employment. In July 1793 the National Convention in Paris had voted Paoli a traitor, and he responded by proclaiming Corsica an independent nation. Since the country was too weak to stand on its own, Paoli wanted Britain to take it under her protection as ally or subject state, and a British commission, under Sir Gilbert Elliot, landed in Corsica in January 1794 to carry on negotiations. By March it was common knowledge that Britain and Corsica were near some sort of arrangement.

Boswell was by far the Briton most closely identified in the public mind with Corsica. He wrote urgently to Dundas, reminding him that by letter eleven years earlier Dundas had engaged to help him, and that for four years Boswell had not pressed his claim; now he wished to be made Minister to Corsica. A "cold, ministerial" response informed him that his services in Corsica were unwanted. "Courtenay was clear from it," he wrote in his journal,

> that Dundas had no inclination to do anything for me, but the contrary. I was not very sorry that this particular application had failed, for I had begun to shrink from the thoughts of quitting London and going among foreigners, etc. etc. But it hurt me to think that Dundas, after his apparently cordial professions, was minded to neglect me totally. However, I thought of pressing him resolutely.

Corsica was annexed, and Elliot, the Ministerial choice as Viceroy, had great claims: he was among the earliest of the Portland Whigs who had gone over to Pitt, and had been Commissioner of Toulon during the British occupation of 1793. But he made a poor Viceroy: his importance went to his head; he quarrelled with Paoli and drove him back into exile in London, alienating the Corsicans from Britain; and the French forced the British abandonment of Corsica in autumn 1796. Still the post, or even a subordinate one, would have been far too strenuous for Boswell, who was no longer capable of sustained exertion.

Temple and Boswell kept in close touch with each other's situation. "I tenderly sympathize with you in your disappointments and the uneasy state of your mind," Temple wrote; "I fear D. is no longer to be relied on. His insolence is provoking." But Boswell's own conduct was censurable:

> Unless you correct this propensity to *joviality* you will injure your health, your faculties, your *glory*, perhaps shorten your life; and be guilty of a species of suicide.

Boswell must do penance for some unspecified lapse by not dining out for a week.

Temple himself, however, was in such a state of upheaval that he needed all the advice and support Boswell could provide.   Shortly after his wife's death, Temple wrote:

> I . . . am even healthier and stronger than in my brightest years. You must be so too, or you could not feel as you did for the young and luscious Maria.

Emotional pressure squeezed confidences out of him:

> It is very odd, Boswell, but the very last time I found the parts so cold and so little sympathy that I said to myself I never would again; and indeed it proved to be the very last time.   It is unaccountable but, notwithstanding so many proofs, no sensation was ever experienced in one party but two or three times; yet dissatisfaction was expressed if an attempt was made to draw back.

Temple accounted for the "unaccountable," by saying that women didn't have sexual desires.   As for himself, he had been more addicted to "certain gratifications" for the past three or four years than ever before. Cut off from Sukey, Temple had found a new object for his affections in a scornful young lady visiting Bath, whom he was courting by letter; he wrote insipid poems, which he asked Boswell to get inserted in the *European Magazine* to impress her.   (They were not.)   He had spoiled Nancy, he realized, and wanted to get out of reach of her "whining folly."   "It never seems to enter her thoughts," he wrote, "that it is her duty to endeavour to please and entertain me."   Best of all would be to have his wife again. Occasionally he drew back to look at himself: "Alas! are all my ambitious views to conclude in St. Gluvias Vicarage and in being *infatuated*?"   Later, "I believe you will think I am a little deranged; I fear I am."   And, as he grew older, he had taken to falling off his horse.   Yet the turbulent course of events had shaken him out of his habitual depressive state, and he showed surprising resilience: "Let us be gay while we may," he wrote in one of his last letters to Boswell.   In the summer of 1794, Norton Nicholls persuaded him to let Nancy marry Powlett, once he acquired an income of £400 a year.   Sukey's fate is unknown.

In spite of his own ferment, Temple saw clearly what was happening to Boswell:

> Your drinking is owing to want of employment and pursuit and the native activity of your mind.   [Then, two days later.]   While out of employment, *office* I should say, why not attempt something? It would quiet your restlessness, occupy your thoughts, and your *magnum opus* would give it currency.   Let me then retract what I

said about your Travels, and set about them.   You possibly may
make something entertaining out of your journal and our correspondence. . . .   Engage in something, and get out of the feverish existence that at present irritates and distracts you.

One piece of literary good news was that 800 sets of the second edition of
the *Life* had been sold by the middle of March 1794, and Boswell expected
the whole edition to be exhausted within another year.

As he told Sandy, Boswell was "spoiled by the luxurious variety of
conversation which the metropolis affords," but it was time to go down to
Auchinleck.   He was driven by guilt about being an absentee landlord,
and by the hope of saving money.   To take Veronica and Euphemia was
expensive but it would look odd to leave them behind in London, and he
owed them the chance to find suitable husbands.   Boswell's life as a man-
about-town precluded introducing even Sandy to many of his friends; and
the girls, abandoned to their own innocent devices, had drifted into the
undesirable society of musicians and French emigrés.

Fulfilling his obligations lightened Boswell's mood; when he arrived
at Auchinleck on 1 July 1794, he wrote to James that he was "in wonderfully
good spirits and looking forward with glee" to his stay.   James and Betsy
remained at school, but Sandy came from Edinburgh to join them.   Veronica and Euphemia, who had not returned to Auchinleck since their
mother's death in 1789, put on London airs and complained about dulness
and vulgarity; but when they got into company late that summer they took
enthusiastically to country doings.

For a few weeks Boswell contentedly applied himself to estate affairs.
London echoed far off.   When James wrote to congratulate him on being
appointed Lord High Chancellor of Corsica, a title bestowed by the newspapers, Boswell replied that they were welcome to their fun.   Even Windham's appointment as Secretary at War stirred only dim hopes of preferment.

Then his spirits drooped, and all the grievances that had soured his
existence recurred.   He wrote to James, now sixteen:

The country does not at all suit me.   I have no relish of its amusements or occupations.   My temper is gloomy and irritable, and I
am continually fretted by hearing of trespasses upon my woods
and lands, and tenants falling behind in their rents.   Add to this,
that my circumstances are so straitened that I am in a wretched
state of uneasiness how to get my family supported, and at the
same time pay the annuities and interest of debts which must be
annually cleared.   The expense of living here is much greater to
me than in London. . . .   I do not think I have had two comfort-

able days, putting together all the hours which should be reckoned
so, since the first of July when I arrived here.

And to Malone:

> I have been uncommonly moderate in wine, so cannot blame my-
> self.   I have done some good to my estate, my tenants, and the
> neighbourhood.   But my existence has been not only negatively
> dull, but it is positively uneasy.   I must do my daughters the justice
> to say that they have conducted themselves very well.   So it is
> *myself alone* that must answer. . . .   I can see no prospect in life,
> but a thick fog.

Boswell tried to guard against pity or contempt for his folly by acknowledging it himself: "I still indulge a visionary, pleasing hope that I
may obtain some preferment of consequence."   James replied with the
cruel clearsightedness of youth, "Read and write, for your preferment must
be on Parnassus."   And he offered suggestions: "Write any little pamphlet
or anything to keep you going—write a play."   Now that Corsica was in
the news, why not an abridgement of his *Account of Corsica*?   T.D. dutifully
called for a new edition of the same work.   But Boswell, in return, insisted
on sticking to his delusions:

> I will try to avoid repining.   Yet at the same time, I cannot be
> contented merely with literary fame and social enjoyments.   I
> must still hope for some creditable employment, and perhaps I
> may yet attain to it.

Once more it was Temple who most fully grasped Boswell's situation
and needs:

> You complain of your ill success in life and so do all who do not
> succeed, but perhaps our disappointments are owing to ourselves.
> You affected a character incompatible with assiduity and busi-
> ness. . . .   I am almost afraid that the variety and dissipation of
> London are absolutely necessary for you.   Your mind to preserve
> its proper tone must be agitated.

Boswell always had a straightforward, urgent sense of his desires but, apart
from his writing, little comprehension of what he could accomplish.   In
February 1794 he wrote in his journal:

> My constant cause of repining is having indulged hopes of attain-
> ing both to consequence and wealth, so as to raise my family to
> higher consideration; and finding no prospect of attaining my
> ambitious objects, I tried to soothe myself with the consideration

of my fame as a writer, and that by the good management of my estate and saving, I might in time pay my debts.

Trying to *soothe* his mind with his fame as a writer! Boswell has been more widely read in the second half of the present century than any other writer of his time. But nothing could satisfy that ambition which, he once said, "has ever raged in my veins like a fever."

"Thus it is that characters are written," says Johnson; "we know somewhat and we imagine the rest." Even when the modern biographer, more informed than Johnson, finds his documents piled like Pelion upon Ossa, how difficult it is for him to set aside his own perceptions so that he can attend to those of his subject. The only character he is certain to illuminate is his own. As best he can, the biographer tries to enter into Boswell's visionary schemes of ambition or intense pleasure in social life—"I just sat and hugged myself in my own mind"—or his grief for Margaret's death, which, he wrote to Forbes as late as 1794, "is still at my heart in painful tenderness. Indeed I feel the want in so many respects that there is no forgetting the misfortune." Or his talent for adventure, or the terrible, restless gloom that sometimes poisoned him day after day, month after month. "One great advantage in my distress," he says in this same letter to Forbes, "is an habitual piety." He was made up of contrarieties in uneasy coexistence.

Auchinleck was painful, but Boswell hung on. Temple had praised his conscientiousness about his children: "How eccentric soever, you always do your duty by them." Boswell certainly spent a disproportionate amount of his income on educating the two boys and Betsy; he had neglected Veronica and Euphemia, but now he was trying to make it up to them. He was deeply attached to all his children, even when he was feeling some of the usual parental irritation with the developments of adolescence. Sandy had acquired a Scots accent and "loud familiarity of manner" by living so much among his inferiors. He domineered over the country people, who talked of Boswell as "the old man." But he wrote to Sandy as he wrote to all his children, combining tactful, encouraging advice with an easy warmth: just as Lord Auchinleck had rewarded him for memorizing Horace's odes, so he advised Sandy that "veins of classical quotation running, let me say, shining" through a gentleman's conversation gave it a peculiar advantage. He had hopes, he told James, that Sandy would make a good lawyer and be a credit to the family; in fact, he thought Sandy studied too hard at the law. Boswell also quarrelled much less with the older girls than he had in London, where they tormented him, as mentioned, by running into company with fiddlers and singers and leechlike emigrés.

Their manners continued to displease him—he had apologized to Lord Pembroke for their being Scotch misses and not fine ladies—but they had good hearts.

In turn, Boswell's children loved him. Two years later, during a tour of Germany, Sandy wrote when he came to Dessau:

> I was now at the court where my father was betwixt thirty and forty years ago, and of which I had heard so much when sitting on his knee and listening to the stories which he told of the old princes and their hospitable splendour. The impressions in early days are always most strongly marked, and are the visionary solace of many an hour.

Betsy, who was a favourite, jumped for joy when she heard that a letter had come from her father. And several years after his death, Euphemia spoke about him "with much feeling."

But it was James who was closest to his father's heart. They were companions and missed each other constantly. James was high-spirited, clever, sensitive, sensible, and everyone loved him. Even Lady Auchinleck said, he is "really a fine boy . . . so steady and companionable that you feel immediately attached to him." Though Courtenay kindly took an interest in him, and T.D. occasionally issued an invitation to a dull Sunday dinner, Boswell's stay at Auchinleck was a long, dreary separation for the young man who once ended a letter with, "I remain again and again, and will ever be, your affectionate son."

Boswell let the girls have their head and their giggle. They entertained and junketed around the neighbourhood. Chaperoned by Sandy, they spent a week at the Ayr races; they met some officers of the 4th Dragoons at Kilmarnock, who involved Boswell in a drinking bout that left him "quite overcome." The same officers were part of a crowd that descended on Auchinleck, and Boswell complained of "a day of excessive vitality." He told Sandy, "I can *fight a battle* of entertaining company occasionally. But never was any man more unfit for much of it." He started a "Pathetic Song" about "gay hopes indulged in youth, and the apathy which years and disappointment produce." But left to himself and his library he passed some comfortable hours.

Christmas came and went. "I weather it out here wonderfully," Boswell wrote to James, "but I must really get to town when it grows full and animated." He told Forbes mysteriously, "I have good reasons for continuing my attendance in Westminster Hall." In the new year his spirits fully revived with the prospect of escape, and James was welcoming: "Oh, Sir, it is perfectly impossible to tell you how glad I am that you are returning so soon." The girls went to Edinburgh for a visit, and Boswell met them

at Moffat for the return trip. He was back in London by the middle of
January 1795.

I I I

THERE WAS SO MUCH to do. He canvassed London for Alderman
Eamer; went down on his knees to kiss the manuscript of *Vortigern*, a
recently discovered play by Shakespeare; flirted with Mary, *suo jure* Countess of Orkney; and complained vigorously to Paoli in Corsica "that the
Ministry of this country has shown both gross neglect and ingratitude in
not naming me to one of the appointments there under the new government." Ever eager for news of the next world, he gave a dinner for an
interested circle to consider a strongly supported ghost story: Lieutenant
Wynyard and a fellow officer on Cape Breton Island had seen an apparition
of Wynyard's brother in England just at the moment, as they later learned,
of his death.

Also he took up the cause of one last criminal, the celebrated swindler
Major James George Semple (or, among many aliases, Semple-Lisle), imprisoned for shirt-stealing. Semple's shady dealings were so extensive that
at a previous arraignment in 1786, 120 people had come forward to accuse
him of fraud or theft. Now he was busy offering his services on desperate
military ventures to the Government, or talking about the "charming woman"
who was to abandon her husband, he said, and go off with him to America
where her family would support them. But first he had to get out of
Newgate, and he prodded Boswell so hard for help that Boswell bridled:
"I have been doing all for him I decently could," he wrote to John Kirby,
the Keeper of Newgate (11 April 1795), "and perhaps a little too much,"
in urging Semple's case to John King, Under-Secretary of the Home Department. Nothing came of Boswell's efforts, but Semple, despite being
transported, carried on a colourful career for a number of years before
vanishing from sight as a common thief.

One significant act of these last months long remained undiscovered.
Boswell's promise to reward Veronica's infant fondness for Johnson seemed
a whim whose lack of fulfilment was all the more disappointing to his
admirers because of its symbolic value. To borrow from the greatest of
Boswellians, F. A. Pottle, for the last time:

> The two great affections of Boswell's life were Johnson and the
> Family of Auchinleck, and it caused him real grief that the objects
> of his love were not themselves in harmony. His wife disliked

Johnson, his father despised him.   But Veronica, a babe in arms, had ranged herself on his side.   She was Family, she liked Johnson.   He *ought* to have shown her some extraordinary mark of gratitude.

And he had.   On 3 March 1795, he produced a deed at The Club giving Veronica her additional £500, and had it witnessed by the Duke of Leeds, Lords Macartney and Palmerston, and Sir William Scott.   The document was found at Malahide Castle in 1937.

Once again existence exhilarated Boswell.   The journal gives a glimpse of him begging a biscuit from a fine miss in a coach, as alive as ever.   He wrote to Sandy (18 March 1795):

> As to wine, I for some time indulged largely. . . .   But for some days I have been *moderate*, and feel myself happier.   In truth I am wonderfully happy at present.   What a varied life do I lead! Yesterday dined with Lord Delaval at his princely house in Portman Square, where I am this winter for the first time *at home*; today at Newgate; tomorrow with the officers of the Guards at the Tower; Friday with a great clothier in Aldermanbury, married to a niece of my rich friend Cator—the 30,000 at least man.   The Earl of Inchiquin has given me dinner after dinner with admirable parties at his house.   In short I am invited *here* as you at *Edinburgh*. But *memento* you are a *young laird* in a *plotting town*.   (But I am not afraid of you.)   I am caressed without any interested view in this *liberal metropolis*.   I have had one or two capital dinners at my house.   I shall have some when you come.

Something even suggested that Dundas was more favourably disposed than previously, and Boswell planned one further approach.   He did not intend to return to Auchinleck until August.

On 14 April, Boswell was taken violently ill at a meeting of The Club, and had to be carried home.   He was suffering from fever, chills, violent headache, and nausea.   He improved enough to dictate a letter (24 April) in the third person congratulating Hastings on his acquittal and declaring that as soon as Mr. Boswell recovered, "he will fly to Mr. Hastings and expand his soul in the purest satisfaction."

But his illness persisted, and on 4 May T.D. informed Temple that a swelling in Boswell's bladder had mortified.   (As Farington observed, Boswell's disorder "fell upon *those parts* which happened to be the weakest.") Four days later Boswell himself started a letter to Temple, but got only as far as, "I would fain write to you with my own hand but really cannot." He went on:

> My son James is to write for me what remains of this letter, and I am to dictate.   The pain which continued for so many weeks

was very severe indeed, and when it went off I thought myself quite well; but I soon felt a conviction that I was by no means as I should be, being so excessively weak, as my miserable attempt to write to you afforded you a full proof.   All, then, that can be said is that I must wait with patience. . . .   I feel myself a good deal stronger today, notwithstanding the scrawl.

James continued in a postscript:

You will find by the foregoing . . . that he is ignorant of the dangerous situation in which he was and, I am sorry to say, still continues to be.

Malone was later to blame Boswell's drinking and himself for what happened.   He wrote to Forbes that after Boswell's return from Scotland,

He seemed to think himself entitled to more than usual indulgence, in which he went on so rapidly that I had no longer, as formerly, any kind of influence over him.   But could I have foreseen the sad consequences, I would have exerted myself more strenuously, and I am confident that by the exertions of Mr. Windham, Mr. Courtenay, and myself, his life might have been saved, for he was ductility itself and had a high opinion of us all, and would, I am sure, have entered into any engagement with respect to temperance that we should have proposed to him.

Briefly it seemed as if he might pull through.   On 13 May T.D. wrote to Temple that "good hopes are entertained of his recovery," but was forced to add in a postscript, "My brother has not been so well this last night; I hope by my next to give you better accounts."   James sent another bulletin to Temple on 16 May, reporting that Boswell's condition was much the same, but he had to admit on the 18th,

Since I wrote last, my father is considerably worse; he is weaker, and almost all the nourishment he takes comes off his stomach again.   He had expressed a very earnest desire to be lifted out of bed, and Mr. Earle, the surgeon, thought it might be done with safety.   But his strength was not equal to it, and he fainted away. Since that he has been in a very bad way indeed, and there are, I fear, little or no hopes of his recovery.

Death came at 2 a.m. on 19 May—according to a modern diagnosis from uraemia: "the result of acute and chronic urinary tract infection, secondary to postgonorrheal urethral stricture."   Two days later, Malone wrote to Windham:

I suppose you know poor Boswell died on Tuesday morning without any pain.   I don't think he at any time of his illness knew his danger. I shall miss him more and more every day. He was in the constant habit of calling upon me almost daily, and I used to grumble sometimes at his turbulence; but now miss and regret his noise and his hilarity and his perpetual good humour, which had no bounds. Poor fellow, he has somehow stolen away from us without any notice, and without my being at all prepared for it.

His record has lived on, in part in a correspondence that Forbes said, after examining it, contained

the most striking memorials of the high degree of estimation in which he was held by as numerous and respectable a circle of acquaintance as almost any private gentleman, I believe, could boast of.

Then in *Corsica*, the *Hebrides*, and the *Life of Johnson*. Finally in that journal which has made him famous a second time in this century.

Boswell was buried in the Family vault at Auchinleck on 8 June 1795.

TEXTUAL NOTE

CAPITALIZATION, punctuation, and spelling are my own, and not those of the text cited. Unless otherwise indicated, translations are also mine. Manuscripts cited without a source are in the Yale Boswell Collection, whose forthcoming Catalogue will identify documents in detail. Since Boswell's journal (including memoranda and notes) and correspondence, whether or not at Yale, will be published in full in the research series of the Yale Boswell Editions, they are identified here only by date. Much of this material, especially the journal, is already in print in the reading or research series of the Yale Editions, but published sources usually are cited only in cases where I was unable to consult the originals. Other documents (miscellaneous papers, printed papers, legal papers, accounts) in the Yale Collection are identified by the numbers assigned to them in the forthcoming Catalogue. In a number of instances where full annotation would have overwhelmed the text, I have provided only illustrative references; a detailed listing of sources will appear in appropriate volumes of the research series. Page numbers in the reading series of the Yale Boswell Editions refer to the McGraw-Hill rather than the Heinemann edition, where the two differ. References are omitted in the notes where the text provides adequate identification.

Subjects which run over a page, whether consisting of single or grouped items, are located by the page on which the subject begins, not, as is usual with footnotes, by the page on which it ends. When annotation for a given item appears to be lacking, glance back over the notes for a page or two preceding.

The following abbreviations and short titles are used:

A: Accounts (in the Yale Boswell Collection).

Ayrshire . . . Burns: Ayrshire at the Time of Burns (vol. 5 of the *Collections* of the Ayrshire Archaeological and Natural History Society) [ed. John Strawhorn] 1959.

Bailey: James Boswell, *The Hypochondriack*, ed. Margery Bailey, 2 vols. 1928.

Beinecke: Beinecke Rare Book and Manuscript Library, Yale University.

Berg: Henry W. and Albert A. Berg Manuscript Collection, New York Public Library, Astor, Lenox and Tilden Foundations.

Bettany: *Diaries of William Johnston Temple, 1780–1796*, ed. Lewis Bettany, 1929. References are given either by date or page number.

Blunt: *Mrs. Montagu, "Queen of the Blues,"* ed. Reginald Blunt, 2 vols. 1923.

Book of Company: Book of Company at Auchinleck since the Succession of James Boswell, Esq. in 1782 (Hyde).

Boswelliana: *Boswelliana, the Commonplace Book of James Boswell, with a Memoir and Annotations* by the Rev. Charles Rogers, 1874.

Boswelliana MS.: Manuscript from which the preceding was extracted (Hyde). References are by page numbers given to the photostat in the Yale Boswell Office. *To be distinguished from* Boswelliana *followed by a number—e.g.* Boswelliana (M25)—*which refers to documents in the Yale Boswell Collection.*

BP: *Private Papers of James Boswell from Malahide Castle, in the Collection of Lt.-Colonel Ralph Heyward Isham*, ed. Geoffrey Scott and Frederick A. Pottle, 18 vols. 1928–34.

Buchanan: David Buchanan, *The Treasure of Auchinleck: The Story of the Boswell Papers*, 1974.

C: Letters to Boswell and correspondence of others (in the Yale Boswell Collection).

Cal. Mer.: *Caledonian Mercury* (Edinburgh).

Chambers: Robert Chambers, *Traditions of Edinburgh*, 2 vols. 1825. References to the 1912 edition specify that date.

Clifford: James L. Clifford, *Hester Lynch Piozzi (Mrs. Thrale)* 2nd ed. 1952.

Collins: P. A. W. Collins, *James Boswell* (vol. 77 of "Writers and Their Work") 1956.

Consultation Book: Manuscript consultation (fee) book of James Boswell, 1766–1772 (NLS, Adv. MS. 3.1.10).

Corsica: James Boswell, *An Account of Corsica, The Journal of a Tour to that Island, and Memoirs of Pascal Paoli*, 3rd ed. 1769.

Cumberland: Richard Cumberland, *Memoirs*, 2 vols. 1807.

Defence: *Boswell for the Defence, 1769–1774*, ed. William K. Wimsatt and Frederick A. Pottle, 1959.

DNB: *Dictionary of National Biography from the Earliest Times to 1900*, ed. Sir Leslie Stephen and Sir Sidney Lee, 22 vols. various printings.

Earlier Years: Frederick A. Pottle, *James Boswell: The Earlier Years, 1740–1769*, 1966.

Edin. Adv.: *Edinburgh Advertiser*.

Edin. Eve. Cour.: *Edinburgh Evening Courant*.

ELH: *ELH: A Journal of English Literary History*.

Extremes: *Boswell in Extremes, 1776–1778*, ed. Charles McC. Weis and Frederick A. Pottle, 1970.

Farington: Joseph Farington, *The Farington Diary*, ed. James Greig, 8 vols. [1922–28].

Farington, "Memoirs of Reynolds": Joseph Farington, "Memoirs of the Life of Sir Joshua Reynolds," in *Literary Works of Sir Joshua Reynolds*, ed. Edmond Malone, 5th ed. 1819.

Fasti Scot.: Hew Scott, *Fasti Ecclesiae Scoticanae*, 7 vols. 1915–28.

Ferguson: Richard S. Ferguson, *Cumberland and Westmorland M.P.'s, 1660–1867*, 1871.

Fifer: *The Correspondence of James Boswell with Certain Members of The Club*, ed. Charles N. Fifer, 1976.

Fletcher: James Boswell, *Life of Johnson*, ed. Edward G. Fletcher, 3 vols. 1938.

Foladare: Joseph Foladare, *Boswell's Paoli* (vol. 48 of *Transactions* of the Connecticut Academy of Arts and Sciences) 1979.

Fullarton: Colonel [William] Fullarton of Fullarton, *General View of the Agriculture of the County of Ayr*, 1793.

Gent. Mag.: *Gentleman's Magazine*.

Ginter: *Whig Organization in the General Election of 1790*, ed. D. E. Ginter, 1967.

Grand Tour I: *Boswell on the Grand Tour: Germany and Switzerland, 1764*, ed. Frederick A. Pottle, 1953.

Grand Tour II: *Boswell on the Grand Tour: Italy, Corsica, and France, 1765–1766*, ed. Frank Brady and Frederick A. Pottle, 1955.

Hebrides: James Boswell, *Journal of a Tour to the Hebrides with Samuel Johnson, LL.D.* 1785. This is the first edition, to be distinguished from *Life*, vol. v, which reprints the third edition. (Cf. *Tour*.)

Houghton: Houghton Library for Rare Books and Manuscripts, Harvard University.

Huntington: Henry E. Huntington Library, San Marino, California.

Hyde: The Hyde Collection, Somerville, New Jersey.

Hyde, *Friendship*: Mary Hyde, *The Impossible Friendship: Boswell and Mrs. Thrale*, 1972.

Hyp.: Boswell's *Hypochondriack* papers (see Bailey above).

J: Journal (in the Yale Boswell Collection).

John. Misc.: *Johnsonian Miscellanies*, ed. G. B. Hill, 2 vols. 1897.

Johnson, *Lives*: Samuel Johnson, *Lives of the English Poets*, ed. G. B. Hill, 3 vols. 1905.

Journ.: Boswell's Journal. References to both published and unpublished journal are by date.

Journey: Samuel Johnson, *A Journey to the Western Islands of Scotland*, ed. Mary Lascelles, (vol. 9 of the Yale Edition of the Works of Samuel Johnson) 1971.

Jury: *Boswell: The Applause of the Jury, 1782–1785*, ed. Irma S. Lustig and Frederick A. Pottle, 1981.

Kay: John Kay, *A Series of Original Portraits*, 1877 (paginated as 2 vols. but often bound as 4).

L: Letters from Boswell (in the Yale Boswell Collection).

Laird: *Boswell, Laird of Auchinleck, 1778–1782*, ed. Joseph W. Reed and Frederick A. Pottle, 1977.

Legal Calendar: Index file in the Yale Boswell Office to Boswell's printed legal papers.

Letters HW: *The Yale Edition of Horace Walpole's Correspondence*, ed. Wilmarth S. Lewis et al. 48 vols. 1937–83.

Letters JB: *Letters of James Boswell*, ed. C. B. Tinker, 2 vols. 1924.

Letters SJ: *Letters of Samuel Johnson*, ed. R. W. Chapman, 3 vols. 1952.

Lewis Walpole: Lewis Walpole Library, Yale University.

Lg: Legal Papers (in the Yale Boswell Collection).

Life: James Boswell, *The Life of Samuel Johnson, LL.D.* ed. G. B. Hill, rev. L. F. Powell, 6 vols. 1934–64. References are given by date as well as page number, so that any edition can be used.

Life MS.: Manuscript of the preceding (mainly in the Yale Boswell Collection).

Lit. Car.: Frederick A. Pottle, *The Literary Career of James Boswell, Esq.* 1929.

Lond. Chron.: *London Chronicle*.

Lond. Mag.: *London Magazine*.

LPS 83: James Boswell, *A Letter to the People of Scotland on the Present State of the Nation*, 1783.

LPS 85: James Boswell, *A Letter to the People of Scotland on . . . Diminishing the Number of the Lords of Session*, 1785.

M: Manuscripts by James Boswell (in the Yale Boswell Collection).

Mem.: Memoranda.

More: Hannah More, *Memoirs*, ed. William Roberts, 4 vols. 1834.

Morgan: Pierpont Morgan Library, New York, New York.

Morison: *The Decisions of the Court of Session [1540–1808] . . . in the Form of a Dictionary*, ed. William M. Morison, 21 vols. 1801–05 [i.e. 1810]. Reference is by volume and page number.

Murray: John Murray, "James Boswell in Edinburgh [1772–74]" Diss. Yale, 3 vols. 1939.

Namier and Brooke: Sir Lewis Namier and John Brooke, *The House of Commons, 1754–1790*, 3 vols. 1964.

New CBEL: *The New Cambridge Bibliography of English Literature*, ed. George Watson et al. 5 vols. 1974–77.

Newhailes MSS.: Manuscripts in the Possession of the Late Sir Mark Dalrymple of Newhailes, Bt., now in NLS.

Nichols, *Anec.*: John Nichols, *Literary Anecdotes of the Eighteenth Century*, 9 vols. 1812–15.

Nichols, *Illus.*: John Nichols and John Bowyer Nichols, *Illustrations of the Literary History of the Eighteenth Century*, 8 vols. 1817–58.

NLS: National Library of Scotland, Edinburgh.

Notes: Boswell's journal notes.

OED: *Oxford English Dictionary*, ed. James A. H. Murray et al. 24 vols. 1888–1933.

Ominous Years: *Boswell: The Ominous Years, 1774–1776*, ed. Charles Ryskamp and Frederick A. Pottle, 1963.

Osborn: James Marshall and Marie-Louise Osborn Collection, Beinecke.

P: Printed Matter (in the Yale Boswell Collection).

Piozzi, *Anecdotes*: H. L. Piozzi, *Anecdotes of the Late Samuel Johnson, LL.D.* (in vol. 1 of *John. Misc.*).

Pol. Car.: Frank Brady, *Boswell's Political Career*, 1965.

Pottle, "Art and Authenticity": Frederick A. Pottle, "The *Life of Johnson*: Art and Authenticity," in *Twentieth Century Interpretations of Boswell's "Life of Johnson,"* ed. James L. Clifford, 1970.

Powlett: Collection of Rear-Admiral P. F. Powlett, Norwich, Norfolk.

Pride and Negligence: Frederick A. Pottle, *Pride and Negligence: The History of the Boswell Papers*, 1982.

Pub. Adv.: *Public Advertiser*.

Ramsay: John Ramsay of Ochtertyre, *Scotland and Scotsmen in the Eighteenth Century*, ed. Alexander Allardyce, 2 vols. 1888.

Reg. Let.: Boswell's Register of Letters.   In Reg. Let. entries, "R." stands for "received" and "S." for "sent."

Rosenbach: Rosenbach Museum & Library, Philadelphia.

Scots Mag.: *Scots Magazine.*

Sheffield: Sheffield City Libraries, Wentworth Woodhouse Muniments.

SHR: *Scottish Historical Review.*

Smith, "Mushroom Elections": Martin J. Smith, "The Mushroom Elections in Carlisle, 1784–1803," in *Transactions* of the Cumberland and Westmorland Antiquarian and Archaeological Society, 81 (1981).

Somervell: Fettercain Papers deposited by Mrs. Peter Somervell in NLS (Acc. 4796).

SRO: Scottish Record Office, H. M. General Register House, Edinburgh.

Stat. Acct.: *The Statistical Account of Scotland,* ed. Sir John Sinclair, Bt. 21 vols. 1791–99.

St. James's Chron.: *St. James's Chronicle.*

Taylor: John Taylor, *Records of My Life,* 2 vols. 1832.

Ten Lines: Boswell's dated exercises of heroic verse.

Thraliana: *Thraliana: The Diary of Mrs. Hester Lynch Thrale (Later Mrs. Piozzi)* ed. K. C. Balderston, 2 vols. 1942.

Topham: [Edward Topham] *Letters from Edinburgh Written in the Years 1774 and 1775,* 1776.

Tour: *Boswell's Journal of a Tour to the Hebrides with Samuel Johnson, 1773,* ed. Frederick A. Pottle and Charles H. Bennett, new ed. 1961.   This text provides the journal Boswell kept at the time of the tour, from which he later extracted his published account (*Hebrides*).

Tour MS.: Manuscript of the preceding (in the Yale Boswell Collection).

Waingrow: *The Correspondence and Other Papers of James Boswell Relating to the Making of the "Life of Johnson,"* ed. Marshall Waingrow, 1969.

Walker: *The Correspondence of James Boswell and John Johnston of Grange,* ed. Ralph S. Walker, 1966.

Werkmeister: Lucyle Werkmeister, "Jemmie Boswell and the London Daily Press, 1785–95," in *Bulletin* of the New York Public Library, 67 (1963).

Whitley: W. T. Whitley, *Artists and Their Friends in England, 1700–99*, 2 vols. 1928.

NOTES

PROLOGUE
  p. 2
  "Natural power"] *Earlier Years*, p. 35.

  "Melting and transporting rites"] Journ. 13 Mar. 1763.

  "The great, the gay, and the ingenious"] "Memoirs" in *Lit. Car.* p. xxxi.

  p. 3
  "A winter's safe copulation"] Journ. 20 Jan. 1763.

  p. 5
  Johnson's judgement of *Corsica*] From Johnson, 9 Sept. 1769 (*Life*, ii. 70).

  "I had got upon a rock"] *Boswelliana*, p. 328 (dated 27 May 1783).

  p. 7
  Lord Auchinleck pruning] Ramsay, i. 166 n. 1.

CHAPTER 1
  p. 9
  Wilkes] Journ. 20 Apr. 1772.   A hero of the mob, Wilkes had been imprisoned for
seditious and obscene libel, 1768–70.   He was elected Sheriff of London and Middlesex in
1771.

  p. 10
  Hume's opinion] Hume to the Comtesse de Boufflers, [?Feb.] 1766 (*Letters of David Hume*,
ed. J. Y. T. Greig, 1932, ii. 11).

  Agitation of mind] "If the Abbé du Bos's system be true, that the happiness of man
consists in having his mind agitated . . ." (Boswell, "On the Profession of a Player," *Lond.
Mag.* 39, 1770, 516).   Many later references show that Boswell fully agreed with du Bos.

  p. 11
  Relationship with Lord and Lady Auchinleck] To W. J. Temple, 19 June 1770 (Morgan—
circumspect behaviour); From Erskine, 12 Dec. 1769.   Visiting terms: Lt. John Boswell's
"Diary," many references from 1 Dec. 1769 to 14 June 1770 (MS. formerly in the possession
of Dr. Alexander Boswell).   From Temple, [?25] May 1770 ("women at forty"); To Temple,
19 June 1770 (Morgan—"honest man").

  Capt. Alexander Montgomerie-Cuninghame] From Margaret, 7 Feb. 1770; *Earlier Years*,
pp. 260–61 (Lord Auchinleck's complaint); To Margaret, 7 Feb. 1770.

  p. 12
  Moving] To Margaret, 7 Feb. 1770; To Grange, 31 May 1770 ("admirable").

  Lamb] "A Bachelor's Complaint of the Behaviour of Married People," *Essays of Elia*.

Grange and Margaret] Journ. 7 Oct. 1774 ("real, comfortable friend"). For their relationship, see Walker, pp. xxx–xxxii.

Temple and Boswell] "Old and most intimate friend" is Boswell's constant formula for
Temple (e.g. *Life*, ii. 316—before 24 Mar. 1775). Temple to Margaret, 15 Dec. 1769 ("easiness
of temper"); From Temple, 20 Feb. 1770 ("I am uneasy").

Temple's difficulties] General situation (Bettany, pp. xii–xiii, xxii–xxiii). From Temple,
26 Apr. 1770 (heartily sick). Study of medicine: e.g. From Temple, 15 Dec. 1769. Literary
projects: e.g. From Temple, 18 Jan. 1771.

Temple and Hume] Temple had met Hume very early, Boswell speaking in 1758 of
having been "introduced to your friend Mr. Hume" (To Temple, 29 July 1758—Morgan).
Much later Temple wrote that Hume's "futile metaphysics sowed the first seeds of poison in
my infant mind" (From Temple, 27 Nov. 1788). Asking Hume's advice: e.g. From Temple,
26 Apr. 1770. Hume thought well of Temple (From Temple, 26 Mar. 1772).

p. 13
Temple teases Boswell] To Temple, 7 May 1770 (Morgan—not wholly satisfactory letter);
From Temple, [?25] May 1770.

Legal practice] Number of cases: Consultation Book, 1769–70, which omits a few cases
mentioned elsewhere. A sampling of seven of Boswell's cases from 1769 to 1771 in which
printed records list counsel gives him as sole counsel in one, as "J. Boswell *et alii*" in a second,
and he is not named at all in four in which he is known to have participated. In the seventh,
the important case of Hamilton v. Rutherford *et al.*, counsel for Hamilton are listed as Alexander Lockhart, Henry Dundas, and James Boswell; and counsel for Rutherford as Robert
Macqueen, Ilay Campbell, Andrew Crosbie, and Claud Boswell (Morison, xvi. 13,933).

Lord Auchinleck's allowance] Journ. 2 Jan. 1775.

Harris's background] *Earlier Years*, pp. 329, 392–93. Apparently Harris sold cloth goods
and miscellaneous items like straw hats (Papers in the Case of William Harris, Lg19:1, pp.
35, 44).

Harris's further career] Details from *Scots Mag.* 31 (1769). 669, 32 (1770). 337; Papers
in the Case of William Harris (Lg17:5, p. 4; Lg18:2, pp. 6–7; Lg19:1, pp. 51–52). Ramsay,
i. 133 (Lockhart); From Neill, 30 Aug. 1768; To Grange, 31 May 1770 (knowing "from him,"
execution).

p. 14
Assembly as debating school] John Cunningham, *Church History of Scotland*, 2nd ed. 1882,
ii. 367–68; Henry Mackenzie, *Account of John Home*, 1822, pp. 61–62.

Practice in the Assembly] Boswell usually received two or three guineas as fee for each
cause in the General Assembly, instead of his customary one or two guineas (Consultation
Book). *Moderator's Advice* (From Maclaurin, 25 May 1770—poem enclosed). An altered and
expanded version is printed in Frank Miller, *The Mansfield Manuscript*, 1935, pp. 37–39.

Popular and Moderate parties] Cunningham, ii. 366–80; W. L. Mathieson, *The Awakening
of Scotland, 1747 to 1797*, 1910, ch. 4. Andrew Crosbie, *Thoughts of a Layman Concerning
Patronage and Presentations*, 1769, ably presents the Popular case.

The ministry] Carlyle suggests the religious attitudes of the poor brilliantly in his memoir
of his father, "James Carlyle of Ecclefechan," *Reminiscences*, ed. J. A. Froude, 1881.

p. 15
St. Ninians] Consultation Book, 25 and 27 May 1770. The case is summarized in Cunningham, ii. 378–79, and in Murray, ii. 201–06; the proceedings are reported in some detail
in *Scots Mag.* 1767–75: 31 (1769). 226 (extensive and populous), 32 (1770). 285 ("weak voice").
For Boswell's appearances in the case, see *Mansfield Manuscript*, p. 38 n. 53. On Thomson's

death in 1787, the parish paid over £600 for the right of presentation (*Fasti Scot.* iv. 314–15; *Ordnance Gazetteer of Scotland*, ed. F. H. Groome, 1901, p. 1443).

Court of Session Garland] Quoted here from MS. version in the National Library of Scotland. It is endorsed, "1770, by James Boswell, advocate, son to Lord Auchinleck." For the revised and enlarged version Maclaurin sang and in which he may have had a share, see Chambers, ii. 158–67, and *The Rothschild Library*, 1954, i. 95–96.

p. 16
London Chronicle] *Lit. Car.* pp. 245–47 (contributions).

"Rampager"] Boswell marked 16 of these "lively essays" (Journ. 24 Aug. 1774), dating from 1770 to 1782, as his (P152). *Pub. Adv.* 12 May 1770 ("to rampage"), 27 Aug. 1777 (book titles), 7 July 1770 (Smelling Medicine).

"On the Profession of a Player"] *Lond. Mag.* 39 (1770). 397–98, 468–71, 513–17. Boswell owned a one-sixth share in the *London Magazine* (*Earlier Years*, p. 436).

p. 17
Boswell on himself] To Temple, 9 Sept. 1767 (Morgan—"I will be myself"), 7 May 1770 ("well do I know"). Marriage and practice: e.g. *Life*, ii. 140 (after 18 Apr. 1771).

p. 18
Baby dies] To Temple, 1 Sept. 1770 (Morgan—Margaret in labour, "you may imagine"); To Grange, 29 Aug. 1770; From Temple, 4 Sept. 1770; To Temple, 6 Sept. 1770 (Morgan—"Nature has given").

Temple's visit] From Temple, 30 Sept. 1770 ("how can I"); To Temple, 6 Oct. 1770 (Morgan—"I am fully").

p. 19
Ayrshire visit] Margaret's widowed sister, Elizabeth Montgomerie-Cuninghame, had inherited Lainshaw; their sister Mary was the wife of James Campbell of Treesbank. To Temple, 6 Oct. 1770 (Morgan—trip); From Temple, 27 Dec. 1771 ("learn a little dissimulation"). Not asked: e.g. To Johnson, 14 Feb. 1777 (not in *Life*); Reg. Let. R. Lord Auchinleck, 8 Oct. 1778.

Winter session] From Lumisden, 15 Dec. 1770; Consultation Book, 1770–71.

Miller v. Angelo] Details in James Boswell, Petition for Miller, 14 Feb. 1771 (Houghton); Morison, xv. 12,395–96; Kay, i. 69; W. F. Gray, "An Eighteenth-Century Riding School," *Book of the Old Edinburgh Club*, 20 (1935). Boswell's Petition calls the defendant Francis Angelo Tremamondo; Gray gives the name used in the text.

p. 20
Correspondence with English friends] From Bosville, 10 Jan. 1771: Wilkes was alderman for the ward of Farringdon Without. From Temple, 18 Jan. 1771; To Johnson, 18 Apr. 1771 (*Life*, ii. 139–40); To Garrick, 30 Mar. 1771 (invitation); From Johnson, 20 June 1771 (*Life*, ii. 140).

Assembly] To Grange, 22 May 1771 (immersed in business). "Memorandum Book of John Grant, 1771," ed. G. D. Henderson, *Miscellany* of the Third Spalding Club, i (1935). 125 ("Boswell, the advocate"). Consultation Book (fees). *Scots Mag.* wrote up all six cases: 33 (1771). 271–80, 328–30; 34 (1772). 191–95, 225–32; Boswell himself inserted the speeches in the St. Ninians cause (*Lit. Car.* pp. 219, 223). Walker gives further details about these causes (p. 266 n. 11). *Life*, ii. 246 (7 May 1773—doubts about patronage); *Scots Mag.* 34 (1772). 192 ("I did not expect").

p. 21
McMaster] *Fasti Scot.* ii. 351; *Scots Mag.* 33 (1771). 277, 34 (1772). 275; *Life*, ii. 171–72 (5 Apr. 1772).

James's Court] Robert Chambers, *Traditions of Edinburgh*, 1912, pp. 55–61 (many details); Journ. 17 Feb. ("parliament"), 7 Feb. 1776 (dislike of exclusiveness); To Grange, 22 May 1771 ("large enough," Margaret fond of flat); Temple to Margaret, 19 Apr. 1771 (cheaper).   The Boswells' flat was in the west entry, the left-hand one on the third storey facing south, or sixth facing north (John H. Burton, *Life of David Hume*, 1846, ii. 136–37; E. C. Mossner, "Dr. Johnson *in Partibus Infidelium?*" *Modern Language Notes*, 63, 1948, 516–19).   Presumably the Boswells "flitted" (moved) at Whitsunday, in Scotland a quarter-day (15 May), traditional for entering on leases.   Walker, p. xxix (Grange moves in).

Literary projects] *Guy Mannering*, ch. 37: Pleydell is said to have been modelled in part on Andrew Crosbie.   From Hailes, 29 Aug. 1766 and 3 Mar. 1770; From Temple, 26 Apr. 1771 ("I long to see").   Sweden: From Temple, 26 Apr. 1771; *Life*, ii. 156 (23 Mar. 1772).

p. 22
North of England tour] To Grange, 27 Aug. 1771.

Paoli's tour] *Lond. Mag.* 40 (1771). 433–34; *Life*, v. 382 n. 2 (Lord Auchinleck's description of Paoli); Journ. 24 Mar. 1772 (convoy to Haddington).

Paoli's entertainment in Edinburgh] Notes of Paoli's Tour (J22).   Dr. Gregory Grant: Kay, ii. 110–11 (musical suppers); Chambers, i. 219–20 (the same entry).   Perhaps the Miss Ords were invited because they spoke Italian (*Anecdotes and Egotisms of Henry Mackenzie*, ed. H. W. Thompson, 1927, p. 77).

p. 23
"Tall, *buirdly*"] Chambers, i. 221 n.

Paoli's remarks] Notes of Paoli's Tour.   Boswell recorded the conversation in a mixture of English and French, the latter translated here without specification.   The reconstruction is occasionally conjectural.

p. 24
Boswell and Corsica] *Lond. Mag.* 40 (1771). 433 (his part in making Corsica famous). "I said to General Paoli, it was wonderful how much Corsica had done for me, how far I had got in the world by having been there.   I had got upon a rock in Corsica and jumped into the middle of life" (*Boswelliana*, p. 328—dated 27 May 1783).

CHAPTER 2
p. 25
Auchinleck] Journ. 30 Mar. 1772 (his great object); To Grange, 20 Oct. 1771 (activities at Auchinleck, misses Margaret); "Rampager," *Pub. Adv.* 25 Nov. 1771 ("digging deep").

Dalrymple] *Lond. Chron.* 24 Oct. and 28 Nov. 1771; From Hailes, early Dec. 1771 (Newhailes MSS. 7,228—"he visited me"); To Langton, 4 Nov. 1773 (Johnson's visit restores contact).

Return to London] First mentioned in To Garrick, 18 Sept. 1771 (Houghton), written immediately after Paoli's departure.

p. 26
Burnett v. Clark] Morison, x. 8,491–92 (cause); Chambers, ii. 175–76 (general account); *Scots Mag.* 61 (1799). 730–31 (seat for eminent guests): such is the story, but Kay suggests plausibly that Monboddo may have sat below the Bench because of his deafness (i. 20 n. 2).

Legal practice] Quotations in order: Notes 8, 20 Jan., 1, 5, 7 Feb. 1772.   *Life*, ii. 196–200 (after 9 May 1772—vicious intromission).

McDonald] Papers in the Case of George McDonald (Lg20:5—charge, "young, hardy Highlanders"); Notes, 15, 17 Feb. 1772 (manly and calm).   Murray summarizes the case from contemporary periodicals (ii. 215–16).

Scots lawyers in London] See index to *Defence*.

Hastie] To Johnson, 3 Mar. 1772 (*Life*, ii. 144–45—stipend); *Life*, ii. 183–86 (11 and 14 Apr. 1772).   The fullest account of the case appears in John Craigie, J. S. Stewart, and T. S. Paton, *Reports of Cases Decided in the House of Lords upon Appeal from Scotland*, 1849–56, ii. 277–83, where Hastie's stipend is said to be £30 a year.

Reasons for trip to London] Journ. 20 Mar. 1772.

p. 27
Quarrel with Margaret] Notes, 13 Mar. 1772 ("romping"); From Temple, 26 Mar. 1772 (miscarriage).

London journey and arrival] Journ. 14–20 Mar. 1772: 17 (comely figures), 19 (cold fowl, ideas run "into their old channels"), 20 Mar. ("do you want").

p. 28
Firmness of mind] E.g. Journ. 21 Mar. 1772.

English projects] David: e.g. Journ. 9 Apr. 1772; *Life*, ii. 195 (before 9 May 1772). To Garrick, 18 Sept. 1771 (English bar); Journ. 20 (calls on Queensberry), 25 Mar. 1772 ("amiable young nobleman").

p. 29
Douglas] Namier and Brooke, ii. 330–31 (career).   Boswell later wrote that Douglas flattered himself with the idea of being created Earl of Douglas (Journ. 17 Mar. 1776); he was made a baron in 1790.   Journ. 24 ("made way," Douglas should spend more time in Scotland), 29 Mar. 1772 (should look back on Cause).

House of Lords] Journ. 10 (hearing Mansfield a feast), 14 ("I amused my mind"), 15 Apr. 1772 (Garrick's comments).   Boswell had asked Smith's opinion on the case (Journ. 14 Apr. 1772).

p. 30
Boswell's impressions of London] Journ. 22 (larger), 25 Mar. 1772 ("like one at a great table").

Breakfast] Arnold Palmer, *Movable Feasts*, 1952, pp. 10–11; Journ. 7 Apr. 1772 (Eglinton's).

Supper] 11 p.m. was a very late hour for supper (Journ. 12 Apr. 1772).   Journ. 24 Mar. (Pringle), 6 Apr. (Macdonald), 29 Mar. 1772 (Mansfield).   At least Pringle said that Lord Auchinleck was *his* best friend (From Pringle, 4 Mar. 1773).   Johnson: Journ. 28 Mar., 11, 15 Apr. 1772.   *Life*, iii. 149 (15 Sept. 1777—Johnson's definition of friendship).

Dinner] Palmer, pp. 12–14.   Chop-houses and coffee-houses are grouped here with taverns. The only dinners Boswell did not specify are two which he almost certainly ate at the Thrales' (Notes, 22, 28 Apr. 1772; *Life* MS. p. 363—before 9 May 1772), and one which he seems to have eaten with Johnson at the Crown and Anchor Tavern (*Life* MS. p. 362—before 9 May 1772).   All other dinners are recorded in the journal and notes (20 Mar.–11 May 1772). Journ. 26 Nov. 1762 (dinner at landlord's in 1762); *Life*, iii. 258 (9 Apr. 1778—Elphinston's Martial).

p. 31
Dinner with Ross] Journ. 15 Apr. 1772.   The *Essay on Woman* parodies Pope's *Essay on Man*, which begins:
      Awake, my St. John! leave all meaner things
      To low ambition, and the pride of kings.

Dinner at Mrs. Montagu's] Journ. 14 Apr. 1772.

"Honest Whigs"] Journ. 9 Apr. 1772 (Priestley reads *Corsica*); *Earlier Years*, p. 563 (explanation of "Honest Whigs").

Other dinners] Journ. 20 Apr. 1772 (Lord Mayor).   Foote: Journ. 2 Apr. 1772; William Cooke, *Memoirs of Samuel Foote*, 1805, i. 124–25 (set of plate).

p. 32
Correspondence with Johnson] To Johnson, 3 Mar. 1772 (Hyde—not in *Life*); From Johnson, 15 Mar. 1772 (*Life*, ii. 145).   In her copy of the eighth edition of the *Life*, Mrs. Thrale wrote in the margin opposite her name, "Not I, I never loved him" (Fletcher, i. 465).

p. 33
First meeting with Johnson] Journ. 21 Mar. 1772 (meeting), 6 Aug. 1776 ("Gothic, Salic").

Dinners with Johnson] Journ. 23 (Mitre), 31 Mar. 1772 ("state of marriage," "vile Whig"); *Life*, ii. 128 (middle of 1770—"ill-assorted marriages"); Journ. 6 Apr. 1772 (Macdonald). "Pretty" means "fine" or "attractive."   Missing dinner: *Life*, ii. 178 (9 Apr. 1772—"a man is always pleased"); Journ. 9 Apr. 1772.   Journ. 15 Apr. 1772 ("as usual risked"), 5 June 1784 ("Johnson's harsh attacks"), 10 (Oglethorpe), 11 Apr. 1772 (Goldsmith talking carelessly); *Life*, i. 27 (introductory remarks—"companionable ease"); Journ. 17 (Good Friday), 19 Apr. 1772 (Easter).   Thrales: Notes, 22, 28 Apr. 1772; *Life* MS. p. 363 (before 9 May 1772).

p. 35
Boswell's plan to write Johnson's life] Journ. 31 Mar. 1772 ("nobody could furnish"). Melanchthon: To Johnson, 30 Sept. 1764 (*Life*, iii. 122 and n. 2—28 June 1777); *Earlier Years*, p. 157.   *Life*, ii. 60 (after 26 Apr. 1768—on publishing Johnson's letters); Journ. 13 Apr. 1772 ("really a genius").

p. 36
Last days in London] Reg. Let. S. and R. Mar.–May 1772 (correspondence with Margaret); To Grange, 9–11 May 1772 (anxiety); Notes, 29 Apr.–9 May 1772: 30 Apr. ("hipped black"), 3 ("bad women"), 6 ("Liberty and Necessity"), 9 May ("Father's joke").   *LPS 85*, p. 99 ("a jewel").

p. 37
Garrick] Notes, 9 May 1772 (Dempster's opinion); Journ. 31 Mar. 1772 ("fine, sly malcontent"); Notes, 8 May 1772 (Rantum-Scantum); *Life*, ii. 326 (27 Mar. 1775—"Davy has some"); Notes, 9 May 1772 ("all elegance").   Connubial ardour: *Life*, i. 98–99 (1736); Extraordinary Johnsoniana—*Tacenda* (Journ. 20 Apr. 1783); *Jury*, pp. xix–xx.

Departure] Notes, 11–15 May 1772; To Grange, 9–11 May 1772 ("admirable health," felicity); Notes, 11 May 1772 (Johnson's parting comment).

CHAPTER 3
p. 39
Return to Edinburgh] Notes, 16 May–7 June 1772: 30 May ("close evening").   Reid's *Inquiry*: Journ. 19 July 1764, 16 Sept. 1769.

General Assembly] Notes, 18 May–2 June 1772.   (Boswell's diary entries from Apr. 1772 to Mar. 1773 are mainly notes, but occasionally expand into journal.   They are all called Notes here.)   Consultation Book (fees); To Grange, 3 June 1772 (rent).

Marykirk] *Scots Mag*. 34 (1772). 271; *Lond. Mag*. 42 (1773). 188–91, 227–29, 296–99, 340–44; Murray, ii. 183–85.

p. 40
Trouble with Lord Auchinleck] Notes, 9 Aug. 1772 (dispute over "renunciation"); *Earlier Years*, pp. 80–81 (history of "renunciation"); From Temple, 5 Oct. 1772 (Margaret's lack of

settlement, entail).   Knowledge of law deficient: From Pringle, 19 Sept. 1772; From Johnson, 24 Feb. 1773 (*Life*, ii. 206).

Tacit bargain] *Earlier Years*, pp. 56–57, 414–17, 441–42, 470–71; Journ. 15 Oct. 1773 (tenderness of a child).

Worsening relationships] To Temple, 21–24 Sept. 1772 (Morgan—Lieutenant John); From Temple, 5 Oct. 1772 (Lady Auchinleck ill disposed towards Boswell, he scolds Boswell); *Roxana*, para. 14; From Temple, 16 July 1775 (Margaret's distaste for her mother-in-law); To Temple, 19 June 1775 (Morgan—Lord Auchinleck ignores Margaret); Notes, 11 Aug. 1772 ("parted"); From Temple, 5 Oct. 1772; From Pringle, 19 Sept. 1772 (cheerful, attentive).

p. 41
Boswell's autumn] Notes, 1 Sept. 1772 ("Cytherean").   Fits of temper: e.g. Notes, 15, 27, 28 Sept. 1772.   Genital problem: Notes, 17 Oct. ("you drank"), 7 ("still very uneasy"), 10 Nov. 1772 ("declared safe").

Lamplighter] A guess, based on Boswell's apparently having consulted Wood earlier (Notes, 27 Oct. 1772), and the fact that he was known as "lang Sandy Wood" (Kay, i. 163), suggesting that he could light a street-lamp without step or stick.

Privy Council records] Notes, 24 Aug., Sept.–Oct. 1772; From Johnson, 31 Aug. 1772 (*Life*, ii. 202); Journ. 24 Nov. 1775.   This was one activity Lord Auchinleck approved of (From Johnson, 27 Oct. 1779—*Life*, iii. 414).

Hypochondriack] Notes, 29 Sept., 11 Oct., 5, 8 Nov. 1772; From Edward Dilly, 10 Sept., 5 Oct. 1772; From Temple, 5 Oct. 1772 (Margaret's disapproval, "hucksters and pedlars!").

Visitors] Notes, 25 Sept. (Pennant), 5 Oct.–17 Dec. (Langton), 12–18 Nov. 1772 (Banks and Solander); Johnson to Mrs. Thrale, 25 Aug. 1773 (*Letters SJ*, i. 344—Monboddo's displeasure); "Some Anecdotes of the Late Voyage of Mr. Banks and Dr. Solander," *Lond. Mag.* 41 (1772). 508–09.

The Ayr Bank] The full history of the Ayr Bank remains to be written, but the basic facts appear in *The Precipitation and Fall of Mess. Douglas, Heron, and Co. by a Committee of Inquiry*, 1778.   Its theoretical defects are explained in Adam Smith, *The Wealth of Nations*, 1776, bk. ii, ch. 2; and its economic context illuminated in Henry Hamilton, "The Failure of the Ayr Bank, 1772," *Economic History Review*, 2nd ser. viii (1956). 405–17, which is summarized in Henry Hamilton, *Economic History of Scotland in the Eighteenth Century*, 1963, pp. 317–23. Other accounts appear in Andrew W. Kerr, *History of Banking in Scotland*, 4th ed. 1926, ch. 9; and S. G. Checkland, *Scottish Banking: A History, 1695–1973*, 1975, pp. 124–34.   Figures here are taken from Robert Somers, *The Scotch Banks*, 1873, p. 103.   See also Frank Brady, "So Fast to Ruin: The Personal Element in the Collapse of Douglas, Heron and Company," *Collections* of the Ayrshire Archaeological and Natural History Society, 11 (1973).

Smith's analogy] *The Wealth of Nations*, bk. ii, ch. 2, para. 76.

Ayr Bank's failure] According to Checkland, demands on the shareholders and their families continued well into the nineteenth century (pp. 132–33).   For the aftermath, see also Sir William Forbes, *Memoirs of a Banking-House*, 1860, p. 42 n.

p. 42
Industrialization of Ayrshire] J. H. G. Lebon, "The Beginnings of the Agrarian and Industrial Revolutions in Ayrshire," *Ayrshire . . . Burns*, pp. 150–72.   In 1787 the owners of the Muirkirk works approached Boswell for permission to build a blast-furnace, and also prospected for minerals.   A contract was prepared, but the project was abandoned (Henry Hamilton, *The Industrial Revolution in Scotland*, 1932, p. 184 n. 5; see also *Stat. Acct.* vii. 606–07).   Boswell gave his consent to the building of the Catrine mill (From and To Claud Alexander, 5 and 14 Mar. 1787).   A coal mine and some quarries were worked on the

Auchinleck estate in Boswell's time (To Bruce Campbell, 1 Mar. 1786—NLS; Reg. Let. R. Bruce Campbell, 10 Apr. 1787, S. Bruce Campbell, 10 and 12 Apr. 1787; *Stat. Acct.* xi. 431). N. P. Hankins, who kindly answered questions on this matter, will provide further details in her forthcoming research edition of Boswell's Estate Correspondence.

Reflections] *Lit. Car.* pp. 89–92 (description); Inscription to Lord Kames (M249); *Edin. Adv.* 20 Nov. 1772 (review attributed to Boswell on internal evidence).

p. 43
Boswell as advocate] Notes, 12 Dec. (fees), 20 and 27 Nov. 1772 (examiner).

Fullarton v. Dalrymple] Summarized partly from Fifer, p. 21 n. 11, some phrases verbatim. *Records of the Burgh of Prestwick* [ed. John Fullarton] 1834, p. 102 (Fullarton the successful candidate); Court of Session Cases (Lg21, p. 19—"casual commotion"); Notes, 9–10 Dec. 1772 (Walker's tavern and after). For advocates' meetings with their clients, see *Earlier Years*, pp. 294–95.

p. 44
Whist] Notes, 12, 19, 21, 29 Dec. 1772, 6 Jan. 1773.

Masquerade] Notes, 15 Jan. 1773; *Lit. Car.* pp. 252–53; Topham, p. 246 ("encourager of intrigue"); widely reported in periodicals. The account in the *Edinburgh Advertiser*, evidently supplied by Boswell, regretted "that this facetious gentleman's talents were locked up in dumb show" (19 Jan. 1773).

Family gathering] Notes, 8 Jan. 1773. Lord Dundonald, a hearty gentleman of over 80, was Boswell's mother's uncle. Boswell admired his vitality but thought his stories improper for one of his age (Journ. 22 July 1774). Lady Preston, Sir George's wife, was Dundonald's sister. Alexander Webster, whose late wife had been Boswell's maternal aunt, was known as Dr. Bonum Magnum from his fondness for claret. Dr. John Boswell, Lord Auchinleck's brother, had a character sympathetic to Boswell's.

Remarks in Court of Session] Court of Session Cases (Lg21, p. 54). Boswell records the Lord President (Robert Dundas) as complimenting him in another case: "I like to see a paper drawn in this way. The Answers are very well drawn, and without any reflections" (ibid. p. 76).

p. 45
Meal-mobs] The basic study is S. G. E. Lythe, "The Tayside Meal Mobs, 1772–3," *SHR*, 46 (1967). 26–36, which can be supplemented in certain details. Unemployment and decline in wages: Hamilton, *Economic History*, pp. 153, 364, 366. Local bad harvests: *Scots Mag.* 35 (1773). 18. Rise in prices: *Scots Mag.* 34 (1772). 118 ("the poor cannot long").

Riots] Fullarton, p. 75 ("objects of public execration"). Details: *Scots Mag.* 34 (1772). 692 ("total want of meal"), 35 (1773). 14–20, 164. The Cupar mob supposedly numbered 900 or 1,000 people (*Scots Mag.* 35, 1773, 16) out of a total population of some 3,000 (extrapolation from the figures in *Stat. Acct.* xx. 603).

Trials] *Scots Mag.* 35 (1773). 329–31 ("painted in very lively colours"); Lythe, pp. 33–35. The prosecution admitted that the evidence against Cameron and Tosh was insufficient, and they were acquitted. Boswell may have furnished material for the published account of the trial, but the only evidence is the circumstantial reporting of the arguments. He had previously defended meal-rioters in 1767 (*Earlier Years*, pp. 328, 538–39).

p. 46
Birth of Veronica] Notes, 14, 15 Mar. 1773. Her name had come into the family through her great-great-grandmother, Veronica van Aerssen van Sommelsdyck, Countess of Kincardine, after whom the baby's maternal grandmother had been named.

Aftermath of the meal-riots] Lythe, p. 36 (granaries); Sir Henry Craik, *A Century of Scottish*

History, 1901, ii. 54–55 (Honest and Industrious Poor, police).   For the general impact of such riots, see R. B. Rose, "Eighteenth Century Price Riots and Public Policy in England," *International Review of Social History*, vi (1961). 277–92.

On returning to London] From Temple, 2–3 May 1772 (to return every spring); Journ. 13 Apr. 1772 (to bring Margaret); To Johnson, 26 Feb. 1778 (*Life*, iii. 219—Margaret's dislike of travel).

p. 47
Move downstairs] See note to p. 21 above, and add Notes, 15, 17 May 1773.   Robert Chambers, in saying that Boswell entailed this flat but that an Act of Parliament enabled his son Alexander to sell it (*Minor Antiquities of Edinburgh*, 1833, p. 97), may have confused it with the house Lord Auchinleck later bought in the New Town.   Boswell never owned the flat in James's Court and moved out in 1786 (From John Buchan, 9 Nov. 1786; To Robert Boswell, 20 Nov. 1786).

Letters before departure to London] Reg. Let. 29 Mar. 1773; To and From Goldsmith, 29 Mar. (Hyde) and 4 Apr. 1773.   Goldsmith's reply is notable to Boswellians as the first item that Colonel Isham purchased (1926) from Boswell's descendant, the fifth Lord Talbot de Malahide, in acquiring the Boswell Papers now at Yale.

Goldsmith and Kenrick] *Life*, v. 97 n. 3 (24 Aug. 1773—"irascible as a hornet," which is Johnson's phrase); Oliver Goldsmith, *Miscellaneous Works*, 1801, i. 103–08 (quarrel); *Life*, ii. 210 (3 Apr. 1773—"I fancy, Sir").

p. 48
Boswell on Goldsmith] Journ. 25 Dec. 1762 ("curious, odd, pedantic"); *Life*, i. 421 (1 July 1763—envy), ii. 217–19 (13 Apr. 1773—luxury), 223 (15 Apr. 1773—the King's projected visit), 233 (29 Apr. 1773—"I know of no comedy"); Goldsmith, *Life of Nash*, para. 2 (affections and follies); Journ. 7 Apr. 1773 ("most generous-hearted"); *Life*, i. 412 (after 25 June 1763—"his mind resembled").

p. 49
Mansfield] Journ. 6 ("kind of enthusiast," specimens, "choice expression"), 11 Apr. 1773 ("cold instrument").   Boswell feared, correctly, that he had offended Mansfield by speaking well of Wilkes: *Earlier Years*, p. 386; Journ. 29 Mar. 1772; To Mansfield, 14 Feb. 1783.

Boswell's reporting] Journ. 8 (dinner at Paoli's), 5 (Burke), 6 (*Lond. Mag.* meeting), 11 Apr. 1773 (Christ's Hospital); *Life*, ii. 231 (27 Apr. 1773—"little fishes").

p. 50
Johnson on keeping a journal] Journ. 11 Apr. 1773.   A modern critic: W. K. Wimsatt, "The Fact Imagined: James Boswell," *Hateful Contraries*, 1965, p. 175.

Recording of Johnson] Journ. 11 Apr. 1773 (all for twopence); *Life*, ii. 232 (29 Apr. 1773—Hebrides); Journ. 7 Apr. 1773 (comments on Garrick, Burke, Percy); Notes, 19 Apr. 1773 (Boswell just hatched); Journ. 7 (Garrick, Beauclerk, and Goldsmith on Johnson; Chesterfield), 9 (Good Friday), 11 Apr. 1773 (Easter).

p. 51
Election to The Club] *Life*, v. 76 and n. 2 (21 Aug. 1773—"got into our club," Boswell's gloss, Burke's opinion, "Sir, they knew").   In asking for Percy's support, Boswell said that Reynolds, Johnson, and Goldsmith favoured his election (To Percy, 16 Apr. 1773—Fifer, p. 27), and Johnson told him that Beauclerk was "very earnest" for him (*Life*, v. 76—21 Aug. 1773).   *Life* MS. p. 398 (30 Apr. 1773—Beauclerk's coach); Notes, 30 Apr. 1773 ("in flutter"); *Life*, ii. 240 (30 Apr. 1773—Johnson charges him).   Boswell says in the *Life* that he met Burke for the first time on the night he was chosen for The Club (*Life*, ii. 240—30 Apr. 1773) but, as just indicated, he had already reported in the *Hebrides* that Burke had objected to his election.   In fact, they had met the year before (above, p. 36).   But Boswell seems to have

mislaid his notes for 1772 when he came to write up that portion of the *Life* (*Defence*, p. 133), which may account for his forgetting when he had met Burke. Equally it seems possible that his relationship with Burke had become so sensitive that he unconsciously suppressed Burke's earliest criticism of him.

The Club's significance for Boswell] *Life* MS. p. 398 (30 Apr. 1773—"I question"); *Life*, i. 477 (Feb. 1764—Literary Club), v. 108–09 (25 Aug. 1773—faculty), ii. 242 ("the most *unscottified*"). The other Scots elected to The Club before Boswell's death were Smith, the physician and chemist George Fordyce, the diplomat and antiquarian Sir William Hamilton, and John Douglas, Bishop of Salisbury.

p. 52
London journal of 1773] Notes, 30 Apr. 1773 ("not able"). Presumably Boswell had condensed notes for much or all of this period; those for 11 Apr.–15 May have been recovered. Also, more fully written notes survive for 15, 21, and 30 April, preserving in each case a long Johnsonian conversation.

Dinner at the Dillys'] *Life*, ii. 247–56 (7 May 1773); Notes, 7 May 1773 (long legs in air).

p. 53
Langton's will] *Life* MS. pp. 418–20 (10 May 1773). W. J. Bate comments perceptively on this incident in *Samuel Johnson*, 1977, pp. 486–87.

CHAPTER 4
p. 54
Sensation] *Life*, v. 23 (14 Aug. 1773—"I smell you"). G. B. Hill vividly summarizes Edinburgh sanitary conditions in *Footsteps of Dr. Johnson*, 1890, pp. 46–47. *Life*, v. 95 (23 Aug. 1773—"sensation is sensation"), 140 (1 Sept. 1773—Culloden); *Tour*, p. 416 (*savoir vivre*).

Boswell and travel] To Johnson, 28 July 1777 (*Life*, iii. 129–30—"incidents upon a journey"). Remarkably good traveller: this description is adapted from F. A. Pottle, *Tour*, p. x. Heightened consciousness: "My mind had been kept upon its utmost stretch in [Johnson's] company" (Journ. Review before 14 June 1774).

p. 55
Johnson and travel] *Journey*, p. 32 ("our business"); *Life*, v. 264–65 (28 Sept. 1773—mind a great mill); *Journey*, pp. 22 ("diminutive observations," inconveniences, pleasures), 148 ("whatever withdraws").

p. 56
Life of Savage] Johnson mentions himself some twenty-four times in *Savage*, but the reader is seldom made aware of him as a person.

Account of Corsica] *Grand Tour II*, p. 189 ("never was I"). General discussions: *Earlier Years*, pp. 258, 362–67; Frank Brady, "The Strategies of Biography and Some Eighteenth-Century Examples," *Literary Theory and Structure*, ed. Frank Brady, John Palmer, and Martin Price, 1973, pp. 257–62. The Benbridge portrait is reproduced in *Earlier Years*, following p. 102.

Ready-made scenario] *Life*, v. 20 (14 Aug. 1773—John Bull, citizen of the world). Wilkes had called Boswell a citizen of the world as early as 1765 (*Earlier Years*, p. 209). For a sense of what the phrase meant to Boswell, see A. D. McKillop, "Local Attachment and Cosmopolitanism—the Eighteenth-Century Pattern," in *From Sensibility to Romanticism*, ed. F. W. Hilles and Harold Bloom, 1965.

Characters of Johnson and Boswell] *Life*, v. 17–19 (introductory remarks—Johnson), 51–52 (18 Aug. 1773—Boswell). Rochester: *An Allusion to Horace*, l. 60.

p. 58
Mary, Queen of Scots] *Life*, v. 40–41 (16 Aug. 1773). In this passage Boswell's "would have been glad" must mean "were glad," since Highland regiments had served in the Seven Years' War.

Flannan Islands] *Description*, ed. Donald J. Macleod, 1934, pp. 97–98. Johnson criticizes Martin for not delighting his readers with "uncouth customs" and "wild opinions" (*Journey*, p. 65), which shows he had not looked at the book for a long time.

p. 59
"A system of life"] *Life*, v. 13 (opening paragraph).

Conditions in Highlands] Summarized in Gordon Donaldson, *The Scots Overseas*, 1966, ch. 4; and T. C. Smout, *A History of the Scottish People, 1560–1830*, 1969, ch. 14. Ramsay, i. 168–69 (Lord Auchinleck's broad Scots); *Journey*, p. 88 ("to the southern inhabitants"). Highlanders praised for not stealing: John Mason, "Conditions in the Highlands after the 'Forty-five," *SHR*, 26 (1947). 138. *Rob Roy*, ch. 10 (Bailie Jarvie).

p. 60
Edinburgh] *Life*, v. 371 (29 Oct. 1773—Robertson). Hume: at least he had been in St. David Street in July (Notes, 9 July 1773). *Life*, v. 29–30 (15 Aug. 1773); *Tour*, p. 17, n. 10 (blockhead and rogue); Johnson to Mrs. Thrale, 17 Aug. 1773 (*Letters SJ*, i. 341—Boswell's rooms, Old Town). Where sources for details of the tour are not specified, it means that the material can be easily located chronologically in *Journey*, *Life*, v., or *Tour*. When possible, *Life*, v. is cited rather than *Tour*.

Monboddo] *Life*, v. 77 (21 Aug. 1773—"a wretched place"), 111 (26 Aug. 1773—"other people").

p. 61
Erroll] *Life*, v. 103 (24 Aug. 1773—"exceedingly pleased"): the *Tour* reads "excessively pleased" (p. 74). *Complete Peerage*, ed. G. E. C[okayne] and Vicary Gibbs, 1910–59, v. 100 (Erroll's appearance).

p. 62
Slains to Inverness] *Life*, v. 132 (30 Aug. 1773—on Druid temples), 115 (26 Aug. 1773—"grand and affecting"), 511 (kangaroo); *Tour*, p. 331 ("the great thing"); *Life*, v. 53 (18 Aug. 1773—pistols), 72–73 (20 Aug. 1773—lemons). They carried lemons at least as far as Glenelg (*Tour*, p. 111).

Johnson on the Highlands] *Journey*, p. 30 (Loch Ness). The reader may wish to compare this description with Boswell's: "It was a delightful day. Loch Ness, and the road upon the side of it shaded with birch trees, and the hills above it, pleased us much. The scene was as sequestered and agreeably wild as could be desired, and for a time engrossed all our attention" (*Life*, v. 132—30 Aug. 1773). *Journey*, pp. 33 ("gloom and grandeur"), 39 ("hopeless sterility"); *Tour*, p. 263 (sand-dunes). Fear of vacuity of mind: W. J. Bate, *The Achievement of Samuel Johnson*, 1955, ch. 2. *Life*, v. 112 (26 Aug. 1773—"wild objects").

p. 63
Old woman] *Journey*, pp. 32–33; *Tour*, p. 100. Boswell added sixpence more after a taste of whisky. The old woman's fears had some oblique basis in precedent: "In this same hut in 1746 an officer of the Duke of Cumberland's army is said to have caused the death of an elderly woman who had resisted his attempt to rape her granddaughter" (*Tour*, p. 418).

p. 64
Boswell's journal] *Life*, v. 312 (14 Oct. 1773—preparation for biography), 279 (3 Oct. 1773—"very exact picture"), 307 (12 Oct. 1773—twice as long), 262 (27 Sept. 1773—raises

opinion), 128 and n. 2 (29 Aug. 1773—criticism), 253 (23 Sept. 1773—argument), 307 and n. 2 (12 Oct. 1773—"ejaculations"), 227 (19 Sept. 1773—see little of each other), 159 (7 Sept. 1773—"I did not exert"); *Tour*, pp. 328–29 ("roving among the Hebrides").

p. 65

Johnson journalizing] *Tour*, p. 38 n. 1 ("wonderfully minute"); *Journey*, p. 40 ("I sat down"); Johnson to Mrs. Thrale, 15–21 Sept. 1773 (*Letters SJ*, i. 359—"the use of travelling").

The Highlands and Corsica] *Tour*, pp. 196–97; *Life*, v. 236–37 (22 Sept. 1773).

Chivalric romance] *Journey*, pp. 77 ("the adventurer"), 155 ("the fictions").

Homer] *Journey*, pp. 39, 66, 71.

p. 66

To Glenelg] *Journey*, pp. 40–41 ("the imaginations"), 48 ("Cyclops"), 49 ("lay in linen").

Sir Alexander and Lady Macdonald] From Macdonald, 26 Apr. 1773 (welcome), 26 Nov. 1785 (expected the travellers earlier); BP, xvi. 222 (Macdonald sends boat); *Tour*, p. 113 ("jumping"); Johnson to Mrs. Thrale, 6 Sept. 1773 (*Letters SJ*, i. 348—"verge of European life"); *Tour*, p. 115 (like someone in lodging-house). A modern scholar: Mary Lascelles, "Notions and Facts: Johnson and Boswell on Their Travels," in *Johnson, Boswell, and Their Circle*, 1965, p. 216. Johnson to Mrs. Thrale, 15–21 Sept. 1773 (*Letters SJ*, i. 358—on Macdonald leaving Monkstadt early).

p. 67

Macdonald and his people] From Macdonald, 12 Sept. 1769 (good relations). For the importance of the chief's education, see Smout, p. 344. *Life*, v. 378 (3 Nov. 1773—soul of an attorney).

p. 68

Emigration] *Life*, v. 180 (12 Sept. 1773—a short settlement). Macdonald later disputed both the extent and ill effects of emigration from his lands (From Macdonald, 26 Nov. 1785), but 2,000 of his tenants were said to be preparing to emigrate in 1771 (*The Lyon in Mourning*, ed. Henry Paton, 1895–96, iii. 259).

Sir Alexander and Lady Macdonald further] *Tour*, p. 242 (Johnson mimics Lady Macdonald). *Thralia dulcis*: *Life*, v. 158 (6 Sept. 1773—*Ode to Mrs. Thrale*). Horses: *Tour*, p. 154 (unwillingly provided); From Macdonald, 26 Nov. 1785 (returned late). *Life*, v. 316 (15 Oct. 1773—"there is much want").

Views of Dr. Johnson] *Life*, v. 87 (22 Aug. 1773—giant), 261 (27 Sept. 1773—old buck), 146 (1 Sept. 1773—Rambler); *Tour*, pp. 244 (Orpheus), 127 (passage to Raasay).

p. 69

Raasay] Johnson to Mrs. Thrale, 15–21 Sept. 1773 (*Letters SJ*, i. 359–60—not ancient pastoral world); *Life*, v. 166 (8 Sept. 1773—"it entertained me"); *Tour*, pp. 137 and 422 ("cold mutton").

p. 70

The Highlands in transition] *Life*, v. 167 (9 Sept. 1773—"patriarchal life"); *Journey*, p. 57 ("a people"); Lord Archibald Campbell, *Records of Argyll*, 1885, p. 358 (ferrying of cattle); *Journey*, p. 152 (comforts of smoke); Johnson to Mrs. Thrale, 30 Sept. 1773 (*Letters SJ*, i. 367—plenty, civility, and cheerfulness). Johnson told Mrs. Thrale, "The hospitality of this remote region is like that of the golden age. We have found ourselves treated at every house as if we came to confer a benefit" (30 Sept. 1773—*Letters SJ*, i. 368).

Prince Charles Edward] *Life*, v. 187–205 (Boswell's account).

Johnson's investigations] Annait: *Life*, v. 220–21 (17 Sept. 1773); *Tour*, p. 179 n. 5. Second sight: Martin, pp. 321–48; *Life*, v. 163–64 (8 Sept. 1773—Macqueen's disbelief); *Journey*, p. 110 ("I never could advance"). *Journey*, p. 106 (Brownie).

p. 71
Macpherson] *Life*, v. 387 (10 Nov. 1773—Johnson's early scepticism), 164 (8 Sept. 1773—copy of *Fingal*), 242 (23 Sept. 1773—comparison of Gaelic and English); *Tour*, p. 205 (willow); *Life*, ii. 126 (1770—"unconnected rhapsody"), iv. 183 (after 30 Mar. 1783—"a man might write"); Wordsworth, "Essay Supplementary to the Preface" (of 1815); *Journey*, pp. 118–19 ("never existed in any other form").

p. 72
Journey to and arrival at Dunvegan] *Tour*, p. 155 ("nay, no wise man"): this scene is the subject of some fine, concise remarks by W. K. Wimsatt ("The Fact Imagined," p. 170). Johnson to Mrs. Thrale, 15–21 Sept. (*Letters SJ*, i. 360—"all the possible transpositions"), 30 Sept. 1773 (*Letters SJ*, i. 365—"very elegant of manners"); *Life*, v. 250 (23 Sept. 1773—"I would rather drink"); I. F. Grant, *The MacLeods*, 1959, pp. 501–18, 541–42 (Norman MacLeod).

p. 73
Johnsoniana at Dunvegan] *Life*, v. 209 (chastity), 210 (theory and practice), 211 (innate evil)—all 14 Sept. 1773; 214 (drinking), 215 (melancholy)—both 16 Sept. 1773.

Conversation at Dunvegan] *Tour*, p. 173 ("abundance of good things"); *Life*, v. 216–17 (16 Sept. 1773— seraglio); *Tour*, p. 177 (Boswell "properly prepared"); *Life*, v. 223 (18 Sept. 1773—"sea—islands," "Madam, rather than quit"), 249 (23 Sept. 1773—"how he would build"); *Journey*, p. 71 ("had tasted lotus").

p. 74
Boswell drunk] *Life*, v. 258–59 (25–26 Sept. 1773); *Tour*, p. 222.

p. 75
Copartnership] *Life*, v. 278 (2 Oct. 1773—copartnership, "immense fund"); *Journey*, p. 3 ("gaiety of conversation"); *Life*, v. 264 (28 Sept. 1773—Boswell "leads" Johnson); Johnson to Mrs. Thrale, 15–21 Sept. 1773 (*Letters SJ*, i. 356—troublesome kindness); *Tour*, p. 322 ("Inch Boswell").

Johnson among the Scots] *Life*, v. 278 (2 Oct. 1773—"say that to *him*," "roving among the Hebrides"), 341 (21 Oct. 1773—"*hogshead* of sense"); *Tour*, pp. 230–31 (" 'honest man' ").

p. 76
Boswell's narrative stance] *Life*, v. 282 (3 Oct. 1773—"disturbed by objections"); Swift: see, *inter alia*, H. W. Sams, "Swift's Satire of the Second Person," *ELH*, 26 (1959). Goldsmith: "An Essay on the Theatre."

Coll] *Journey*, p. 124 ("turnips will really grow"). The importation of turnips was the mark of the agricultural improver (Malcolm Gray, *The Highland Economy, 1750–1850*, 1957, pp. 76–86). *Tour*, p. 291 ("essential particular"); *Life*, v. 324–25 (17 Oct. 1773—"ancient Caledonian").

p. 77
Mull] *Life*, v. 377 n. 1 (rain), 295 (8 Oct. 1773—go on with existence), 318 (16 Oct. 1773—"most dolorous country"), 318–19 (16 Oct. 1773—stick "stolen").

Iona] *Tour*, p. 336 ("I warmed my soul"); *Journey*, p. 148 ("little to be envied").

p. 78
Lochbuie] On Lochbuie's attempt to exercise his heritable jurisdiction, see *Tour*, pp. 344, 435–36. *Tour* MS. pp. 637–38 ("bluff, hearty," "Johnstons of Glencoe"). Johnson describes Lochbuie as "rough and haughty and tenacious of his dignity" (*Journey*, p. 153). On reading "Glencoe" rather than "Glencroe," see Frank Brady, "Dr. Johnson and the Laird of Lochbuie" (letter), *Times Literary Supplement*, 27 Nov. 1970, p. 1391. *Tour*, p. 344 ("don't drink").

p. 79
Return to the mainland] Johnson to Mrs. Thrale, 30 Sept. (*Letters SJ*, i. 370—"shut up"), 24 Sept. 1773 (*Letters SJ*, i. 361—"every island"); *Life*, v. 154 (5 Sept. 1773—"when a man"). Johnson had compared Boswell to Antaeus when they landed on Mull (*Life*, v. 309—14 Oct. 1773).

Oban to Inveraray] Boswell stopped keeping a journal after their visit to Lochbuie. The notes from 22 October to 5 November read like this: "Friday 22 Oban/ Saturday 23 Ferry Lochaw Cowley—Inveraray/ Sunday 24 Ogden's Sermon Hervey. Duke's," etc. (J33.1). *Journey*, p. 158 ("nobler chorus"); *Life*, v. 368 (28 Oct. 1773—Johnson hates being thought an old man), 346 (23 Oct. 1773—drinks whisky).

Inveraray] *Tour*, p. 355 ("Methodist," "a fine picture"). Lady Betty, the Duchess's daughter by her first marriage, was descended from James II of Scotland through the Hamilton line. The religious fervour of the Methodists gave them the reputation of being credulous.

p. 80
The Lowlands] *Life*, v. 365 (27 Oct. 1773—"absurd visionaries"); Johnson to Mrs. Thrale, 3 Nov. 1773 (*Letters SJ*, i. 388—"she had lately"); *Life*, v. 375 (1 Nov. 1773—"my dear son").

Auchinleck] *Life*, v. 376 (2 Nov. 1773—"a *Jacobite fellow*"), 382 n. 2 ("a *dominie*"); To Temple, 30 Mar. 1767 (Morgan—library); *Life*, v. 377 (3 Nov. 1773—"who *can* like"); Ramsay, i. 166 (Lord Auchinleck as tree planter); *Journey*, p. 161 ("striking images"); *Tour*, p. 331 (landscapes defective without human figures); *Life*, i. 462 (30 July 1763—Johnson to visit Auchinleck).

p. 81
Quarrel between Johnson and Lord Auchinleck] *Life*, v. 382–84 (6 Nov. 1773—"they became exceedingly warm"); *Tour* MS. p. 706 ("intellectual," "a very capital scene"); *Tour*, p. 443 ("my father then had him," Malone's recollection); *Life*, v. 382 n. 2 (Scott's anecdote). *Durham on the Galatians* is a ghost, and J. W. Croker suggested that Lord Auchinleck meant Durham's *Commentary on the Book of Revelation* (*Life*, v. 383 n. 2).

p. 82
End of stay at Auchinleck] *Tour*, p. 444 ("pleasing satisfaction"); *Life*, v. 385 (8 Nov. 1773—"dignified courtesy").

Johnson in Edinburgh] *Life*, v. 395 (11–20 Nov. 1773—tea, harassed with invitations); From Johnson, 27 Nov. 1773 (*Life*, ii. 269 and n. 1—influences Boswell too much, candle grease); *Life*, v. 400 (11–20 Nov. 1773—"Areopagus"), 384 (6 Nov. 1773—Ursa Major). It was commonplace to compare Johnson to a bear (see *Life*, index, Johnson, I, s.v. bear). *Life*, v. 575 ("would not the *son*", which is Lady Anne's version of her *bon mot*; cf. Boswell's: *Life*, v. 401—11–20 Nov. 1773).

p. 83
Visit to Dalrymple] *Life*, v. 401–04 (20–21 Nov. 1773); the detail about moonlight comes from some of Boswell's notes on Johnson's visit printed in *Lond. Mag.* (43, 1774, 27). Boswell cites a parallel passage from Dalrymple's *Memoirs* to Johnson's parody: "Essex was at that time confined to the same chamber of the Tower from which his father Lord Capel had been led to death, and in which his wife's grandfather had inflicted a voluntary death upon himself. When he saw his friend carried to what he reckoned certain fate, their common enemies enjoying the spectacle, and reflected that it was he who had forced Lord Howard upon the confidence of Russell, he retired, and by a *Roman death* put an end to his misery" (*Life*, v. 403 n. 2—20 Nov. 1773). *Tour*, pp. xxvi (suave malice), 450–51 ("he was certain").

p. 84
Johnson on tour] *Life*, v. 405 (before From Hailes, 6 Feb. 1775—"pleasantest part"); *Journey*, p. 156 ("new scenes of nature"); *Life*, iii. app. B (projected jaunts).

"The transit of Johnson"] *Life*, v. 382 (6 Nov. 1773). The phrase, "more even in texture and more brilliant in finish," is taken from somewhere in F. A. Pottle's writings.

CHAPTER 5

p. 85

Kant] The passage quoted goes on: "The principle of *mutual love* admonishes men constantly to *come nearer* to each other; that of the *respect* which they owe each other, to keep themselves at a *distance* from one another" (*The Doctrine of Virtue*: Part 2 of *The Metaphysic of Morals*, trans. M. J. Gregor, 1964, p. 116).

p. 86.

Boswell on proper behaviour] Journ. 26 Nov. 1775 ("without reserve"), 4 Jan. 1776 (nothing secret), 28 Dec. 1762 ("I am too open"). Boswell defines *retenue* as "the power of suppressing what it is improper to utter" (*Hyp*. No. 23, "On Reserve"—Bailey, i. 284).

Intimacy between Boswell and Temple] From Temple, 2 Apr. 1778 ("the inexpressible satisfaction").

Temple's complaints] From Temple, 30 Mar. 1773 ("already dead," "sympathizing"), 26 Mar. ("solitary, cheerless"), 2–3 May 1772 ("your affection"), 21 Feb. 1773 (threatens to die). Later he wrote to Boswell: "As we have no reserve with one another, is it not very natural for us to complain when we meet with obstacles in our way, and do you think we love one another less or think less of one another upon that account? Certainly not; nay, far otherwise" (From Temple, 2 Apr. 1778).

p. 87

Boswell and the Temples] Journ. 7 May 1773 ("hurt a little"); Notes, 11–15 May 1773 (journey north). Quarrel papered over: From Temple, 21 June 1773; To Mrs. Temple, 31 Dec. 1774 (Morgan). Boswell was a poor prophet: one of Temple's sons, Frank, became an admiral; another, Octavius, became Governor of Sierra Leone. Octavius's son Frederick became Archbishop of Canterbury, and Frederick's son William also became Archbishop of Canterbury.

Literary Property case] *Lit. Car*. pp. 92–101; Murray, ii. 127–40. *New CBEL*, ii. 285 (Warburton).

Hinton v. Donaldson] From Temple, 30 July 1773 (Boswell speaks well). Campbell: Murray, ii. 135, citing *Caledonian Weekly Magazine*, i. 386–87 (28 July 1773). The Lord President voted only in the case of a tie, but he spoke in favour of Donaldson. Monboddo was the dissenting judge.

p. 88

Compilation of *Literary Property*] Add to sources listed two notes above, *Life*, v. 50 (17 Aug. 1773); Notes, 22, 23, 25 Dec. 1773; From Thomas Miller (Lord Justice Clerk), 5 Jan. 1774. A draft of the Lord President's speech, which Boswell rewrote from his dictation, survives (M75). Among the published speeches, Lord Hailes's looks conspicuously unrevised. *Scots Mag*. 36 (1774). 93 ("elegantly printed," distributed to peers).

Bonfires] Murray, ii. 139, citing Paton, iii. 294.

Gray] Notes, 26 July 1773; Murray, ii. 228–31, citing contemporary periodicals; letter from Sir James Fergusson to F. A. Pottle, 27 May 1959 (knife). If Gray had been hanged, his execution would probably have been reported in the *Scots Magazine*.

p. 89

Visitors] Notes, 5 July–10 Aug. 1773: 9 July (tea with Hume). From Temple, 20 July 1773. Boswell does not specify which Dilly visited him, but a letter from Edward Dilly to Benjamin Rush, 26 June 1773, shows that it was Charles (L. H. Butterfield, "The American

Interests of the Firm of E. and C. Dilly," *Papers* of the Bibliographical Society of America, 45, 1951, 310).

Masonic activities] Notes, 24 June 1773; Journ. 7 July 1774; Allan Mackenzie, *History of the Lodge Canongate Kilwinning, No.* 2, 1888, p. 97 ("the Lodge having met"). Murray summarizes Boswell's Masonic activities, citing *Cal. Mer.* 1 Dec. 1773, for Boswell's election as Joint Grand Warden. On examining the Lodge's records he noted the splash of wine (i. 229–34).

Boswell's spirits] To Langton, 14 Aug. 1773; From Temple, 30 Dec. 1773; Journ. Review of Winter Session, 1773–74.

On Boswell's going to London] To and From Johnson, 5 and c. 15 Mar. 1774 (*Life*, ii. 275–76).

Temple's *Essay*] From Temple, 15 Feb. 1774 (Hume's opinion); *Essay*, 1774, pp. 33–36 (Plato), 45–51 (sermon writers), 85 (farming). Leslie Stephen, *History of English Thought in the Eighteenth Century*, 3rd ed. 1902, bk. 12, sec. 99 (Wesley's remark). From Temple, 1–2 Feb. 1775 (hope for translation). In this letter Temple calls his *Essay* "trifling and superficial," but says that it has done him good.

p. 90
Boswell and Temple's *Essay*] From Temple, 15 Feb. (Boswell comments on), 31 May 1774 (exerts pressure on Dillys). Boswell also puffed the book in *Pub. Adv.* 16 Aug. 1774.

The Hebridean journal] From Edward Dilly, 23 Jan. 1775 (bring "observations"). Johnson on the journal: To Mrs. Thrale, 22 May ("I am not sorry"), 11—for ?12 ("one would think"), 19 June 1775 ("he moralized"): *Letters SJ*, ii. 31–32, 43, 47 respectively. Cannot be published: e.g. From Hailes, 9 Mar. 1775. Journ. 27 Mar. 1775 (Johnson's lack of enthusiasm); To Temple, 10 May 1775 (Morgan—might publish anyway).

p. 91
Book of Continental travels] Johnson on *Corsica*: *Life*, ii. 11 (before 15 Feb. 1766—encourages Boswell); From Johnson, 21 Aug. 1766 (*Life*, ii. 22—discourages Boswell), 9 Sept. 1769 (*Life*, ii. 70—praises *Corsica*). *Life*, iii. 300–01 (17 Apr. 1778—"can give an entertaining narrative"). A year later Dilly was still thinking of two volumes of Continental travels (Reg. Let. R. Dilly, 25 July 1776).

Periodical items] *Lond. Mag.* 43 (1774). 213–15 (Edinburgh theatre), 295 (Goldsmith's song), 388–91 and 429–31 (Bruce); Journ. 9 Aug. 1774 ("as from a flinty rock"). Bruce had actually explored the upper reaches of the Blue Nile.

Boswell on literary fame] Journ. 18 Feb. 1768 (author as mysterious); Preface to *Corsica* (most valuable of possessions).

Political ambitions] From Lord Auchinleck, 30 May 1763 (Parliament as objective); *Pol. Car.* pp. 21–22 (early ambition); Ginter, p. 114 and passim (Scottish hopes for family aggrandizement).

p. 92
Ayrshire election of 1774] *Pol. Car.* pp. 56–73: sources and material not identified in the present notes appear there. Journ. 5 Apr. 1773 (Kennedy); *Life*, v. 56 (18 Aug. 1773—influence in proportion to property); Journ. 15 Oct. 1774 ("democratical coalition"). Robert Warnock, "Boswell on the Grand Tour," *Studies in Philology*, 39 (1942). 661 ("peculiar turn of Boswell's mind"). *Pol. Car.* p. 14 n. 2 (resemblance between Boswell's and Burke's attitudes). Eglinton his "chief": Journ. 3 Jan. 1783, 17 Jan. 1784. Margaret's kinship to Eglinton: *LPS 85*, pp. 53–56; *Earlier Years*, p. 402.

p. 93
Boswell and his father] Boswell's later account: Journ. 18 Nov. 1775, 21 Nov. 1776. Lord Auchinleck's votes: he was credited with fourteen in a list of Jan. 1774 (Namier and

Brooke, i. 471–72), seems actually to have made ten votes (*Pol. Car.* p. 65 n. 1), and was credited with eight in a list of June 1774 (*Pol. Car.* p. 67). From Temple, 15 Feb. ("was ever anything"), 31 May 1774 (begs pardon); Namier and Brooke, i. 471–72 (Lord Auchinleck supports Kennedy, "annihilation of gentlemen's interest").

p. 94

Deeper issues] From William McQuhae, 26 Apr. 1763 ("greatest Whig"); To Oglethorpe, 2 Apr. 1774 ("High Tory"); Journ. 28 (entail), 17 July 1774 ("usual constraint"); *Pol. Car.* p. 65 n. 1 (earlier condemnation of nominal votes); Journ. 13 and 18 Nov. 1775 (mental failure). Ramsay confirms this failure, and implicitly the Lord President's undue influence (i. 176–77); earlier, he says, Lord Auchinleck condemned nominal and fictitious votes "as a vile evasion of the law and a temptation to perjury" (i. 163, corrected from the MS.—information from Sir James Fergusson).

Boswell and the Dundases] Journ. 16 Mar. 1777 (cipher), 6 Aug. 1774 (refuses to dine with President), 23 Feb. 1775 (not on speaking terms).

p. 95

Veronica's inoculation] From Pringle, 2 Feb. 1774.

Boswell as lawyer] Journ. Review Previous to the Summer Session, 1773–74 (business thin); From Temple, 31 May 1774 (success as lawyer, determined to improve knowledge); Journ. 12 Aug. 1774 (never so busy). Other lawyers: Ramsay, i. 131–35 (Lockhart), 380–83 (Macqueen); DNB (Campbell); Ramsay, i. 442–43 (Maclaurin). Ramsay says Maclaurin's practice was never lucrative (i. 448–49), but G. H. Ballantyne reports that a recent search through the Session Papers in the Signet Library shows he and Campbell attracted a disproportionate amount of business (Legal Calendar). Law college: To Langton, 10 Apr. 1774; Journ. 19 Aug.–16 Sept. 1774. Journ. 9 July 1774 (difficult legal point, conditional mood).

"Earl Fife's politics"] Summarized in Murray, ii. 146–74, and *Pol. Car.* p. 54. Boswell unimportant and consultations tedious: Journ. 20 June, 19 July 1774.

p. 96

"Ambition"] Journ. 27 Aug. 1774.

English bar] *Boswelliana*, p. 279 ("I always wished"). Wedderburn: Journ. 27 Mar. 1775; *Life*, i. 387 (before 16 May 1763). *Defence*, pp. 206–07 (Goldsmith's death); Journ. 6 July 1774 (talents only appreciated in London). Fear of disinheritance: e.g. Journ. 27 Mar. 1775.

Reid's trial in 1766] Summarized in *Earlier Years*, pp. 299, 308–09. *Defence*, p. 296 n. 4 (Miller's *obiter dictum*).

Reid's trial and aftermath, 1774] *Defence*, pp. 227–341, and app. A. Other than quotations, only material not found there is footnoted below. V. T. Murphy provides a valuable summary of the Reid affair in "The Miscellaneous Correspondence of James Boswell, 1774–75," Diss. City University of New York, 1981, pp. 129–46.

p. 97

"Crimes of a heinous nature"] *Defence*, p. 238.

"Infatuate"] *Defence*, p. 347.

Crosbie's refusal to take public part] He did, however, agree to give advice privately (Journ. 31 July 1774).

p. 98

"Only in the way," "I remember"] *Defence*, pp. 243–44.

Pitfour] Ramsay remarks on the smoothness of Pitfour's language and his "semblance of humility" (i. 184).

"Infamous and intestable"] *Defence*, p. 249.

p. 99
A hanging court] Journ. 22 Aug. 1778; Ramsay, i. 156 n. 1.

Reset capital if "habit and repute" proved] Murphy, p. 137.

Trial] *Defence*, p. 252 ("very masterly"), Nasmith to John Wilson Jr., 6 Sept. 1774 ("complained loudly").

"Much in liquor"] *Defence*, p. 253.

Sentence] *Defence*, pp. 254–55.

p. 100
Adam Smith] *Wealth of Nations*, bk. 5, ch. 1, pt. 2, para. 12.

Johnson on defending the guilty] *Life*, ii. 47–48 (spring 1768), v. 26–27 (15 Aug. 1773).

p. 101
Reprieve] The granting of the reprieve was subject to the Lord Justice Clerk's approval (Murphy, p. 141).

"While under sentence"] *Defence*, p. 290.

Thoughts about death] These questions are mainly suggested by *Hyp*. No. 68, "On Executions" (Bailey, ii. 276–85), most of which was originally published in *Pub. Adv.* 26 Apr. 1768. Journ. 19 Oct. 1769 (Johnson on death).

"I had wrought myself"] *Defence*, pp. 305–06.

p. 103
"Mournful case"] *Defence*, p. 308.

"To conciliate the lower populace"] *Defence*, p. 318.

Appeal to Queensberry] To Queensberry, 3 Sept. 1774.

"Bloody opinion"] To Crosbie, 6 Sept. 1774.

"Monstrously drunk"] *Defence*, p. 320.

p. 104
"He may curse you"] *Defence*, p. 327.

"Forenoon in particular"] *Lond. Chron.* 29 Sept. 1774.

Observer] Topham, pp. 59–61, cited in *Defence*, p. 333 n. 7. Reid was forty-eight.

"Take warning"] *Defence*, p. 335.

CHAPTER 6
p. 105
Sheriff-Depute of Ayrshire] Journ. 16 Nov. 1774. Johnson had earlier advised against taking the post (Journ. 18 Apr. 1772). The Sheriff-Depute acted as a judge, and two-thirds of the judges sitting on the Court of Session in 1774 had been sheriffs.

p. 106
Boswell's practice before his father] *Life*, ii. 510; *Earlier Years*, p. 330.

The Prestons] Journ. 24–27 Sept. 1774 (Valleyfield visit), 16 Oct. 1778 (other items).

William Miller] Journ. 6–18 Oct., 17 Nov. 1774. Quotations: Journ. 17 Nov. ("meridian of London," "I am resolved"), 7 ("assuring him"), 18 Oct. ("delirium," "spirited ideas"). *Trial of James Stuart of Dunearn*, 1822 (Alexander's death).

p. 107
Campbell's election] Journ. 11–31 Oct. 1774: 19 (delicate conscientiousness), 31 Oct. ("like a man relieved").

p. 108
Boswell's drinking] Journ. 4 Nov. (Advocates' Close), 24 (Irish officers), 31 Dec. (drams, distilling), 30 Sept. (drank hard), 9 Nov. 1774 (reform); *Life*, iii. 389 (24 Apr. 1779—"without skill"); From Temple, 14 June 1794 (gets drunk quickly).

p. 109
Boswell's mood and prospects] Journ. 15 Dec. 1774 (free will), 10 Jan. 1775 (hypochondria); To Oglethorpe, 25 Feb. 1775 (good spirits); Journ. 27 Mar. (£300 a year), 23 Feb. 1775 (President praises him); above, p. 90 (Johnson's compliment); To Johnson, 18 Feb. 1775 (*Life*, ii. 308—their names linked); Journ. 15 Feb. 1775 (Boswell summarizes situation).

Boswell and Margaret] Journ. 5 ("excellent sense"), 8 ("concubine"), 19 Mar. 1775 ("exuberance of amorous faculties"); To Temple, 18 Mar. 1775 (Morgan—"I am *too many*").

p. 110
Boswell arrives in London] Journ. 21 (Dillys'), 22 (Gerrard St.), 23 Mar. 1775 (Paoli's); *Life*, ii. 375–76 (12 May 1775—Johnson's); To Hailes, 1 Apr. 1775 (Newhailes MSS. 7,228—dinners).

Johnson's opinions] From Johnson, 7 Feb. 1775 (*Life*, ii. 297—"Scotch conspiracy"); *Life*, ii. 313 (after 21 Mar. 1775—*Taxation No Tyranny*), 319 (24 Mar. 1775—*Gulliver's Travels*), 327 (28 Mar. 1775—Gray), 340–42 (6 Apr. 1775—Cibber, George I), 365 (18 Apr. 1775—"extraordinary promptitude").

p. 111
References to Johnson] *Life*, ii. 325 (27 Mar. 1775—Garrick's prologues), 330 (1 Apr. 1775—orange peel); Journ. 1 Apr. 1775 (greatest pleasure). Boswell did not use Murphy's report, even in euphemized form, in the *Life*.

Remarks on biography] Journ. 27 Mar. ("Flemish painter"), 7 Apr. 1775 ("exact transcript").

Descriptions of Johnson] *Life*, ii. 378 (17 May 1775—laugh), 326 (27 Mar. 1775—"utterance"), 298–99 (lack of physical fear); Journ. 27 Mar. 1775 (interview with apprentice); *Life*, ii. 300 (beginning of 1775—Johnson's mind like ocean), 326 n. 5 (27 Mar. 1775—"*bow-wow way*"). "*Thralian* miscellany": Journ. 8 Apr. 1775; To Mrs. Thrale, 30 Aug. 1776; Hyde, *Friendship*, p. 29 n. 101. *Life*, ii. 326 (27 Mar. 1775—Garrick's mimicry); Journ. 10 Apr. 1775 ("when Boswell gets wine").

p. 112
Boswell's feelings, drinking] Journ. 26 Mar. ("I am a being"), 10 Apr. (man only happy when drunk), 27 ("drunk as *muck*"), 31 Mar. 1775 (Boswell drunk at Club).

Sex] Journ. 24 Mar. 1775 ("*vaga Venus*"); To Temple, 17 Apr. 1775 (Morgan—"too much claret"); Journ. 10 (Devonshire wench), 12 Apr. 1775 ("dalliance").

p. 113
Other feelings and activities] Journ. 14 ("heat of blood"), 2 Apr. 1775 (filling the day); To Temple, 19 June (Morgan—legal fees), 10 and 22 May 1775 (both Morgan—Inner Temple meals): in his letter of 22 May, Boswell wrote, "I *must* try to prevail with my father to consent to my trying my fortune at the English bar."

Wilton] To Pembroke, 2 and 22 Mar. 1775 (hints); Journ. 26 Mar. and 3 Apr. (invitation), 19–22 Apr. 1775 (visit). While at Wilton, Boswell was weighed by Lord Herbert, Pembroke's eldest son, who liked to weigh things, and a surviving note (M177) gives Boswell's weight as 11 st. 12 lbs. (166 lbs.). He seems to have been about 5'6" tall.

Mamhead] Journ. 23 Apr. 1775 (visit).   Pledge of sobriety: To Temple, 3 June 1775 (Morgan); Journ. 10 Feb. 1776.

Last weeks in London] *Life*, iii. 34–35 (11 Apr. 1776—living at Paoli's); To Temple, 17 and 22 May 1775 (both Morgan—other details); Johnson to Mrs. Thrale, 22 May 1775 (*Letters SJ*, ii. 31—present for stepmother).

Summer in Edinburgh] To Temple, 3 (Morgan—"unpleasing tone"), 19 June 1775 (Morgan—"coarse labourer"); Journ. Review of Summer Session, 1775 ("father's coldness," "notions of intercourse," "regular stock of knowledge," other details); To Temple, 12–14 Aug. 1775 (Morgan—"while afflicted with melancholy," "drunken manners").

p. 114
Difficulties with Lord Auchinleck] To Temple (all letters Morgan), 19 June (dissatisfaction with Boswell and Margaret), 12 Aug. (withholding of allowance, clouds recede), 2 Sept. ("it is hardly credible," though "I am doing"), 10 Oct. 1775 (rural beauties).   Boswell suspected Lady Auchinleck had persuaded her husband that Margaret was extravagant (Journ. 2 May 1780).

p. 115
Birth of Alexander] Journ. 9 Oct. 1775 (birth); To Temple, 10 Oct. 1775 ("supreme object"); From Oglethorpe, 1 Mar. 1776; From Pringle, 17 Oct. 1775.   Infant mortality: see, for example, the London Bills of Mortality in *Gent. Mag.* for 1774–76.

p. 116
Entail] Journ. 18 Nov. 1775 (Lord Auchinleck's proposal).   Lieutenant John, technically the next heir after Boswell, had again become irrational the year before, and Lord Auchinleck wanted to consign him quickly to a nearby madhouse with a bad reputation.   But Boswell, supported by Commissioner Cochrane, intervened, and Lord Auchinleck agreed to have John returned to his previous humane confinement in Newcastle (Journ. Dec. 1774, passim).   T.D., most like of the brothers to their father, was still in Valencia, and Lord Auchinleck said he should mind his business there (Journ. 21 Sept. 1777).

The despised David Boswell, dancing-master at Leith, was so remote a relation that he could hardly have been considered a possible heir, but descendants of the same Craigston branch of the family were to purchase and occupy Auchinleck House in the twentieth century. The dispute over the entail began at the time when both Boswell and his father were planning to marry (Journ. 13 Aug. 1769).   For further background to this quarrel, see *Earlier Years*, p. 80.

Boswell's views of entail] *Life* MS. Paper Apart for p. 495 (beginning of 1776—fervour for male succession from Lord Auchinleck); *Life*, ii. 412–15 (before 15 Jan. 1776—summary of dispute); Journ. 9 Jan. 1775 (cut his throat, the stone).

Agreement of 1762] *Earlier Years*, pp. 80–81; above, p. 40.

Threats of disinheritance] *Earlier Years*, pp. 80–81, 109, 280–81, 416–17; From Lord Auchinleck, 30 May 1763 (snuff out a candle); Journ. 16 and 27 Mar. 1775 (Boswell fears his father might sell the estate).

p. 117
Boswell's financial situation] Cf. Journ. 2 Jan. 1775 and 1 Jan. 1776.   Journ. 9 Jan. 1775 (no settlement on Margaret).

Other family members in dispute] Journ. 9 Jan. 1775 (Cochrane, "ancient barony"). T.D.: Journ. 17, 27 Oct., 19 Dec. 1775.   Journ. 30 Jan. 1776 (Claud).   Margaret: Journ. 17 (no feudal enthusiasm), 18 Nov. 1775 (violent).   Journ. 28 Jan. 1776 (Dr. John).

p. 118

Boswell and his ancestors] Like his grandfather: e.g. Journ. 10 Feb. 1776. *Life*, ii. 413 (before 15 Jan. 1776—Thomas Boswell).

Boswell's financial crisis] Journ. 8 and 23 Dec. 1775 (practice), 1 Jan. 1776, 17–18 Nov. 1775 (Lord Auchinleck agrees to pay £1,000, admonition; amount due), 18 Oct. 1776 (£200 from Boswell's allowance).

p. 119

Quarrel with Lord Auchinleck] Journ. 16 Oct. 1776 ("milder"), 27 Dec. 1775 (quarrel). "Wild speech": 29 Dec. 1775; the journal for 28–29 and part of 30 Dec. 1775 has been removed from the manuscript, but Boswell later dates this speech (Journ. 6 Feb. 1776).

p. 120

Boswell wavers about entail] Journ. 30 ("embarrassed circumstances"), 31 Dec. 1775 (investigation, entailing of Dalblair), 4 Jan. 1776 (Margaret writes to Johnson); From Johnson, 3 Feb. 1776 (*Life*, ii. 416–18); Journ. 7 Feb. (Margaret cries for joy), 24 (Hailes's opinion), 29 Jan. 1776 (further investigation); From Pringle, 6 Jan. 1776 ("not in my power").

p. 121

Boswell's feudal enthusiasm] Journ. 31 Dec. 1775; *Life*, ii. 412–15, esp. 414 n. 2 (before 15 Jan. 1776); Notes on Hailes's *Annals*, enclosed in To Hailes, 18 Jan. 1776.

Dalblair creditors] Journ. 10 Feb. 1776; Reg. Let. S. John McAdam, 10 Feb. 1776; Journ. 31 Dec. 1775 ("sacred trust").

Gambling] Journ. 21, 25, 31 Oct., 12 ("wizards"), 16, 26 Dec. 1775, 24 Feb., 7 Mar. 1776.

Drinking] Journ. 10 (smashes things), 13 Nov. 1775 ("constitution quite unfit").

Boswell's behaviour] Margaret criticizes Boswell: Journ. 9 May 1774, 31 Oct. 1775. Journ. 12 Dec. ("wonderfully easy"), 26 Nov. (renewed philandering), 4 Dec. 1775 ("she spoke to me"). Margaret waits up: Journ. 21, 31 Oct., 12 Dec. 1775, 24 Feb., 7 Mar. 1776.

p. 122

Boswell criticizes Margaret] Journ. 27 Nov. 1775 (lack of respect), 10 Feb. 1776 (insufficient attention to moods), 9 Dec. 1775 (throws egg).

Margaret supports Boswell against his father] E.g. Journ. 30 Dec. 1775, 10, 11, 12 Feb. 1776.

Self-denunciation] Journ. 12 Dec. ("good practice never long"), 7 Nov. ("deficient in judgement"), 22 Dec. 1775 ("imperfection in notions").

p. 123

Law practice] Journ. 23 Dec. 1775 (business better than last winter's), 12 and 15 (does a good job), 25 Jan. 1776 ("poor opinion," eight guineas).

McGraugh] Details from Journ. 25–26 Aug., 20 Dec. 1774; Papers in McGraugh's Case (Lg25:1—a terror); *Scots Mag.* 37 (1775). 732 (which says this is McGraugh's fourth offence). *Court of Session Garland* [ed. James Maidment] 1839 (*Patrick O'Connor's Advice*); Maidment cites *Edin. Eve. Cour.* 31 Aug. 1774, with a somewhat different account. Summaries of the case: *Defence*, p. 282 n. 8; *Ominous Years*, p. 47 n. 5.

Other legal cases] Most of these cases are reported in varying detail in Boswell's Legal Notebooks (Lg27, 29) and, for some, printed papers survive (Legal Calendar). *Life*, ii. 373–74 (after 6 May 1775—Paterson v. Alexander); the bond in this case is printed in *Scots Mag.* 37 (1775). 731–32. *Life*, iii. 58–64, with quotation on p. 58 (May 1776—Scotlands v. Thomson); ii. 372–73 (Dr. Memis); Papers in Gibson's Case (Lg28).

p. 124

Justiciary Opera] *Court of Session Garland*, pp. 31–42, taken from the 1816 version of

Alexander Boswell, the biographer's son. *Lit. Car.* pp. 270–73 (bibliographical details); Journ. 4 Mar. 1776 (other details).

p. 125
Boswell's schemes of improvement] Journ. 14 (pleased with existence), 11 Jan. (chemistry), 2 Feb. 1776 (Boswell and Erskine).

Writing projects] Journ. 20 and 26 (Covington), 19 Feb. (Kames), 17 (Hume), 13 Dec. 1775 (Dick); To Temple, 6 Nov. 1775 (Morgan—essay on the law); Notes on Hailes's *Annals*, enclosed in To Hailes, 18 Jan. 1776 (Ayrshire); From Temple, 25 June 1776 (Isle of Man); Journ. 9 Jan. 1776 ("Metaphysician"); To Temple, 18 Mar. 1775 (Morgan—cannot "fix").

p. 126
American Revolution] *Lond. Chron.* 23 July 1774 (*Boston Bill*), 21 Nov. 1776 (*Long Island Prisoners*); To Temple, 18 Mar. 1775 (Morgan—Britain and its Colonies); "Rampager," *Pub. Adv.* 9 Mar. 1776 (*"infantine dependence"*); *Lond. Chron.* 6 Aug. 1776 (Brant).

Agitation about entail] Journ. 6 (dream about father), 10 (swears at Margaret), 27 Jan.(throws guinea note in fire), 19 Feb. ("law business"), 6 Mar. (freed from scruples), 10 Feb. 1776 (postpones signing entail).

Fife election] Journ. 6–10 Mar. 1776: 6 ("indecently extravagant"), 10 Mar. (disconsolate situation).

p. 127
Departure from Edinburgh] Journ. 10–11 Mar. 1776 (all quotations).

Arrival in London] Journ. 12 (sunshine broke in), 16 Mar. 1776 ("happiness without alloy"). Duel: Journ. 15 (Pringle), 16 Mar. 1776 (Johnson). English bar: From Pringle, 6 Jan. 1776; Journ. 11 Jan. 1776; To Pringle, 26 Feb. 1776.

Mountstuart and the Militia Bill] *Pol. Car.* pp. 74–77; Journ. 17 Mar. 1776 ("noble Tory interest"); To Temple, 1 May 1776 (Morgan—"patronage"); Notes, 21 Apr. and 6 May 1776 (takes down, copies speech); Journ. 4 and 5 Jan. (pamphlet on Militia Bill), 17 Mar. 1776 ("Political State of Scotland").

p. 128
Independency] To Temple, 18 Mar. 1775 (Morgan); Notes, 10 May 1776.

Maule's sinecure] Journ. 29 Mar., 11 Apr. 1775, 17 Mar. 1776; Notes, 6 May 1776. The Clerkship was finally given to Andrew Stuart as part of the bargain by which Dundas became sole Keeper of the Signet (*Pol. Car.* p. 81).

Queensberry] Journ. 17 Mar. 1776 ("cold and indifferent"); Notes, 14 May 1776 (does not speak to North).

"Borax"] *Lond. Chron.* 25 Jan. 1776.

Mountstuart] Mountstuart to William Hamilton [1765] in F. L. Pleadwell, "Lord Mountstuart—Boswell's Maecenas," *American Collector*, 5 (1928). 235 (indolence); Sienese Reflections, No. 3 (quoted in *Grand Tour II*, p. 135—mirror). "Heraldic glories": William Beckford, *Liber Veritatis*, ed. Guy Chapman, 1930, p. 129; Beckford was writing as of 1824. Journ. 17 Mar. 1776 ("speaking in style of prince"). Portrait: Notes, 15 May 1776; Journ. 2 Dec. 1776. Dundas also had a hand in preparing the Militia Bill; for the struggle over it in the House of Commons, see Namier and Brooke, iii. 502–03.

p. 129
Douglas] Journ. 29–30 (made counsel), 31 Mar. 1776 ("much in liquor"). At unspecified times before 1 Jan. 1777, Boswell borrowed £250 from Douglas, £100 from Mountstuart, and £50 apiece from Paoli and Sir John Dick (Journ. 1 Jan. 1777).

"Pleasure"] Conversations with Johnson: Journ. 25 Mar., 5, 7 Apr. 1776. Journ. 22 ("occasional transient connections," course in concubinage), 23 Mar. 1776 ("crazy piety").

Women] Mrs. Stuart: e.g. 21, 31 Mar., 12 Apr. 1775, 14 Apr. 1776; Notes, 21 Apr. 1776. Confidante on adultery: Journ. 9 Mar. 1772, 21 Mar. 1775. Notes, 12 May 1776 (Countess of Eglinton). "No. 36": Journ. 17–29 Mar. 1776, passim; for her identity: *Ominous Years*, p. 263 n. 1; *Extremes*, p. 234 n. 2. Whores: 29–31 Mar., 1 Apr. 1776 ("license"). Journ. 31 Mar. ("cold and disturbed"), 10 ("irregularity of commerce"), 6 Apr. 1776 (*morbus*).

p. 130
Drinking] Journ. 30 Mar. 1776 (Paoli lectures him); To Temple, 28 Apr. 1776 (Morgan—gives up liquor, "I was really"); Notes, 10 May 1776 (Garrick).

Burns] F. A. Pottle points out that in Burns's case, unlike Boswell's, a tradition of sound criticism makes it necessary to treat Burns as a formidable literary artist: the critic "may speak of Burns's frailties of conduct as severely as he pleases, but he is bound to respect the qualities of his mind" ("The Life of Boswell," *Yale Review*, 35, 1945–46, 454–55).

Effect of London on Boswell] Journ. 18 Mar. ("insensibly overheated"), 14 Apr. 1776 ("it is hard"). In the latter passage Boswell refers to the narrowness of his social, rather than academic, education (*Earlier Years*, pp. 23–24). On the relationship among energy, desire, and restraint, see *Earlier Years*, p. 134. Journ. 17 Mar. 1776 ("live no more").

p. 131
Observes, tests, manipulates Johnson] *Life*, ii. 427 ("was kindly welcomed"). Mrs. Thrale wrote (Nov.–Dec. 1777): "Of all [Johnson's] intimates and friends, I think I never could find any who much loved him, Boswell and Burney excepted. . . . As to Burney, had they been more together, they would have liked each other less" (*Thraliana*, i. 182). *Life*, ii. 438–75, iii. 1–5 (19–29 Mar. 1776—Midlands), iii. 45–51 (26–29 Apr. 1776—Bath, Bristol); Journ. 25 Mar. 1776 (Harry Thrale); *Life*, iii. 39 (12 Apr. 1776—*Poetics*), 57 (May 1776—"two topics").

p. 132
Dinner at Dillys'] *Life*, iii. 65–78 (15 May 1776—dinner): *"visible signs"* (italics added). "The most famous": so R.W. Chapman wonders (*Letters SJ*, ii. 131 n.2). "Nice knowledge of character": *Hyp*. No. 58, "On Hospitality" (July 1782—Bailey, ii. 194). *Thraliana*, i. 62 n. 4 ("curiosity carried Boswell"); *Life*, v. 342 (22 Oct. 1773—"mischievous love"). Temptation as its own justification: e.g. To Johnson, 26 Apr. 1768 (*Life*, ii. 58): "Surely you have no reason to complain of my publishing a single paragraph of one of your letters; the temptation to it was so strong."

Boswell says in his Notes (15 May 1776) about Mrs. Williams: "Peevish a [little at first, managed her"]. The words in square brackets have been heavily crossed out in a recent ink.

p. 133
Mrs. Rudd's career] This summary is taken—some sentences and phrases verbatim—from *Ominous Years*, pp. 352–55.

Duchess of Kingston's trial] Journ. 15–16 Apr. 1776.

p. 134
First interview with Mrs. Rudd] Journ. 26 Mar. 1776 (extraordinary address). The interview took place on 22 Apr. 1776 (To Margaret, 23 Apr. 1776, which became To Temple, 28 Apr. 1776; the letter is endorsed: "To my wife—but not sent"). Goldsmith, *Retaliation*, l. 101 ("natural, simple, affecting").

p. 135
Further visits to Mrs. Rudd] Notes, 13, 14, 16 May 1776 (sings "Snake," "delirium," "like water"). "The Snake" has not been recovered. From Temple, 25 June 1776 (discourages correspondence).

Other farewells] Notes, 14 (Paoli), 8 May 1776 (Johnson welcomes to house). Takes leave of Johnson: Notes, 16 May 1776, with a couple of words supplied from *Life*, iii. 80 (16 May 1776). "Some great men" (14 May 1776—*Letters SJ*, ii. 130).

Scotland] Notes, 22 May–5 June 1776: 22 (poor indeed), 29 May ("black and indifferent"), 5 June ("you think too ill").

Relations and friends on entail] T.D.: e.g. Reg. Let. R. 4 Mar. 1776. Cochrane: Journ. 8 Aug. 1776; *Extremes*, p. 20 n. 3. From Pringle, 15 Mar. 1777. Temple had told Boswell that he and his family were absolutely in his father's power (From Temple, 16 July 1775).

p. 136
Signing of entail] Journ. 5–7 Aug. 1776. For the breaking of the entail seventy-five years later, see *Extremes*, p. 20 n. 2.

CHAPTER 7
p. 137
Belief in futurity] From Johnson, 3 July 1778 (*Life*, iii. 363—"the one solid basis"); Journ. 10 Dec. 1782 (hard that future state is unknown); *Life*, iii. 312 (17 Apr. 1778) and vi. 452–53 (Blair); *Hyp.* No. 42, "On Marriage" (Bailey, ii. 67–68—separation from spouse); *Life*, ii. 161–63 (28 Mar. 1772—too anthropomorphic a view), iii. 312–13 (17 Apr. 1778—copy of Shakespeare), v. 385 (8 Nov. 1773—no room for Whiggism). Boswell would have approved of Byron's

> For by many stories
> And true, we learn the angels all are Tories.
> *(Vision of Judgement*, ll. 207–08)

Johnson muttering] Arthur Murphy, "An Essay on the Life and Genius of Samuel Johnson" (1792) in *John. Misc.* i. 439. Murphy quotes only the first two lines.

p. 138
"I like to have more"] *Life*, iv. 299 (12 June 1784).

Boswell on immortality] *Life*, iii. 188 (22 Sept. 1777—"the great article"); Journ. 10 Aug. 1776 (soul identified with consciousness), 17 Dec. 1775 (doubts about eternity of punishment): see *Ominous Years*, p. 200 n. 3. Attitude towards disbelievers: e.g. *Life*, ii. 441–43 (20 Mar. 1776), iii. 10–12 (3 Apr. 1776). *Life*, iii. 380 (3 Apr. 1779—even one disbeliever). Boswell remarks: "But perhaps I considered as weakness that meek submission of reason to divine faith which religion requires, and from which I am too much estranged by being accustomed as a practical lawyer to continual close controversial reasoning" (Journ. 1 Nov. 1778). Voltaire: J. McManners, *Reflections at the Death Bed of Voltaire*, 1975.

Boswell's attitude towards Hume] Journ. 17 Dec. (Great Infidel), 13 Nov. 1775 ("in having pious faith").

Interview with Hume] The present narrative is made up from Boswell's accounts of his interview with Hume (*Extremes*, pp. 11–15). For Hume's reading of Locke and Clarke, see E. C. Mossner, *The Life of David Hume*, 1954, p. 51. Facts of an imaginative order: Boswell's beliefs were emotionally grounded. One of his arguments against those who endeavour "to sap the credit of our holy religion" is that they are so "forgetful of human comfort" as to give "countenance to . . . dreary infidelity" (*Life*, v. 30 n. 3—15 Aug. 1773). To Langton, 30 Aug. 1776 (Hume dies in great tranquillity).

p. 140
Effect of Hume's death] Journ. 10 and 29 Aug. 1776 (reads "worst" essays); To Mrs. Thrale, 30 Aug. 1776 ("considerable abilities"); Journ. 16 Sept. 1777 ("he lied"), 27 Dec.

1780 and 13 July 1781 (uneasy with sceptics), 21 (calls on Hume), 28 Aug. 1776 (has whore), 27 Feb. 1777 (mason's shed). Boswell may have taken another whore there the previous Dec. (Journ. 1 Dec. 1776). Journ. 10 Jan. 1784 (dream). For the present account of Boswell's reaction to Hume's dying, see *Extremes*, pp. xiv–xviii, from which some sentences are taken.

p. 141
Quotation from entail] *Boswelliana*, p. 108, corrected from the original warrant (SRO).

Margaret's illness] Journ. 11–27 Aug., 2 Sept. 1776.

Visit to Auchinleck] Journ. 10 Sept.–21 Oct. 1776: 20 Oct. ("in a little"), 16 (James Campbell), 24 Sept. (Lainshaw), 28 Sept.–4 Oct. (Galloway).

p. 142
Boswell and his father] Journ. 11 ("insensible attentions"), 20 Oct. ("*duty*"), 26 Sept. 1776 ("under parental awe"); To Oglethorpe, 20 Oct. 1776 ("romantic seat"); Journ. 18 Oct. 1776 (payment for Dalblair). Resentment against Lord Auchinleck: To Pringle, 2 Feb. 1777; To Johnson, 14 Feb. 1777 (not in *Life*). Lord Auchinleck's failure: e.g. Journ. 9, 13 Oct. 1776. Boswell fears being Head of Family: e.g. To Erskine, 9 May 1762; Journ. 13, 20 Oct. 1776. Journ. 27 May 1781 (tells George III he was pressed into law), 11 Mar. 1780 (feelings about practice of law), 20 Oct. 1776 (father bids farewell). Excitability: e.g. Journ. 22 Aug. 1780.

p. 144
Boswell's journal] The selective discussion here draws on the work of Geoffrey Scott and F. A. Pottle, but omits various points made in *Earlier Years*, pp. 86–94.

Motives] *Life*, iii. 228 (30 Mar. 1778—"a man loves to review"). Balancing books: just as the Muhammadans believe that two angels write down a person's good and bad actions so, Boswell says, a man should balance his books (Notes for *Hypochondriacks*—M119). *Life*, iii. 228 (30 Mar. 1778—"as a lady"), ii. 128 (1770—second marriages); Journ. 3 Feb. 1780 ("sickened"). A journal, according to a modern psychologist, Ira Progoff, allows one to "get rid of emotion without solving the problem. . . . It's like a pain-killer for a bad toothache—and later the abscess explodes": cited in Patrick Huyghe, "Diary Writing Turns a New Leaf," *New York Times*, Sunday Magazine, 8 Nov. 1981, p. 106. BP, ii. 182 ("Boswell kept resolutions").

Mirror] Georges May, *L'Autobiographie*, 1979, p. 184 n. 21 (Camus); Johnson, "Pope" (para. 273), *Lives*, iii. 207 ("very few can boast").

p. 145
Honesty and self-examination] Journ. 28 Dec. 1762 (wants to tell everything), 9 Mar. 1777 ("to mark real feelings"), 2 July 1782 ("a fair transcript"), 22 July 1781 ("comfortable Auchinleck frame"); *Boswelliana*, p. 286 ("few characters will bear"); *Earlier Years*, p. 16 ("habit of not thinking"); Journ. 22 Oct. 1782 ("I am lost"), 7 Mar. 1778 ("too concave a being"), 12 Sept. 1780 (studies others too closely), 11 May 1767 ("saw all things"); *Hyp*. No. 24 "On Censure" (Bailey, i. 297—skim pleasingly).

p. 146
"A consistent picture"] Journ. 27 Feb. 1763.

Journal *realizes* experience] BP, vi. 65 ("it is no exaggeration").

Preservation] Journ. 17 Mar. 1776 ("I should live"); *Hyp*. No. 66, "On Diaries" (Bailey, ii. 266, 262—a day unrecorded, Dutch journal); Journ. 29 Jan. 1780 ("it is unpleasing"); To Johnson, 29 Sept. 1777 (*Life*, iii. 209—greater satisfaction in recollection); Journ. 10 Apr. 1784 ("exceedingly rare"); *Life*, iv. 78 (30 Mar. 1781—"multiplication of felicity"). Boswell writes characteristically to Johnson that his Hebridean Journal, "which is so full and exact and minute, is really a treasure" (14 Feb. 1777—not in *Life*).

p. 147
Journal and life] Journ. 26 Sept. 1774 ("will go through almost anything"), 25 May

(Temple accuses of looking for adventures), 25 Jan. 1763 ("material period"), 8 May 1777 (dulness of life), 9 Oct. 1775 (Sandy's birth), 3 Feb. 1777 ("I had lately a thought"). James Jr.'s birth in 1778 similarly impelled Boswell to resolve to be more constant in keeping his journal (Journ. 15 Sept. 1778).

Journal as record] Entertaining narrative: e.g. Journ. 25 Oct. 1764, 14 June 1765. Collins, p. 18 (travel journal as snapshot album). Boswell planned from the beginning of his tour of the German courts to read his journal some day with Grange (To Grange, 10 Sept. 1764), and immediately showed some of his journal to Temple on his return from the Continent (Journ. 16 Feb. 1766). As mentioned earlier, Boswell hoped to extract an account of his travels from his Continental Journals (above, pp. 90–91).

Memoranda] On the memoranda, see *Grand Tour I*, p. 156 n. 3. Sometimes Boswell intermingled journal and instruction, as in much of the Italian Notes of 1765. For the effect of Boswell's Corsican experiences on his character, see Stanley Brodwin, " 'Old Plutarch at Auchinleck': Boswell's Muse of Corsica," *Philological Quarterly*, 62 (1983). 88.

p. 148
Journal as public and private] Boswell read from, or lent, his Hebridean Journal to Forbes (Journ. 1 Jan. 1775, 27 Mar. 1777), Mrs. Thrale (above, pp. 90–91), Reynolds (Journ. 27 Mar. 1775), Hailes (From Hailes, 9 Mar. 1775), and Grange (Journ. 2 Sept. 1777). Forbes also read his Ashbourne Journal (*Life*, iii. 208—after 24 Sept. 1777), as did Grange (below, p. 161). Boswell entertained Temple with part of his London Journal of 1775 (From Temple, 27 May 1775).

Boswell's care to explain incidents and to provide identifications (see comment in *Extremes*, p. 50 n. 6) suggests that he senses the (eventual?) reader over his shoulder; yet there are times when he baffles even those most intent readers, his editors.

On publishing journal] Journ. 31 July 1779 (on journal being published during lifetime), 3 Nov. 1775 ("my son would perhaps read").

"Pace of natural life"] Robert Latham in *The Diary of Samuel Pepys*, ed. Robert Latham and William Matthews, 1970–83, i. cxvi.

p. 149
Worry about being circumstantial] E.g. Journ. 14 Oct. 1774, 15 Nov. 1775, 28 Oct. 1776, 13 Jan. 1777.

Typical format of journal] See R. A. Fothergill, *Private Chronicles*, 1974, p. 58. This important study includes shrewd comments on Boswell's journal. Boswell's handling of dramatic scenes is discussed in *Earlier Years*, pp. 90–92.

p. 150
"Substantive level"] W. K. Wimsatt, "The Substantive Level," *The Verbal Icon*, 1954.

p. 152
Truth] *Life*, ii. 433 (16 Mar. 1776—"value of every story"); Journ. 24 Nov. 1775 (accuracy), 27 Feb. 1776 (exact states of mind).

Forbes] Slips stating "reprehensible passage" or the equivalent (C1305–08).

William Law] *Life*, iv. 294 (11 June 1784).

"Length of duration"] "Preface to Shakespeare," para. 3.

"That molecular whirlwind"] Cited in Béatrice Didier, *Le Journal intime*, 1976, p. 128.

p. 153
David] Journ. 15 Nov. 1776 (born, sickly child). Health improves: e.g. Journ. 3 Feb. 1777.

Annie Cuninghame] Journ. 7 (lazy and barren, Margaret uneasy), 16 Nov. 1776 ("little romping pleasure"); *Extremes*, p. 65 n. 1 (Veronica's comment); Journ. 8 Dec. 1776 ("when I saw her"), 20 Jan. 1777 ("shockingly harsh").

p. 154
"Man of her heart"] From Margaret, 22 July 1769.

Sexual wandering] Journ. 25 Nov. ("young slender slut"), 27 Nov. and 1 Dec. 1776 (Peggy Grant), 5 (Peggy Dundas), 27 Feb. ("big fat whore"), 7 Apr. ("old dallying companion"), 21 June ("Rubra"), 11 (Dolly), 15 July ("embarked"), 7 Apr. 1777 ("lesser lascivious sport").

Betty Montgomerie] Journ. 7 Apr. 1777 ("my fancy was pleased"). The Meadows is a park south of the Old Town. Journ. 21 July 1777 (dalliance). For Betty's marriage, see *Extremes*, p. 133 n. 3.

Return to the conjugal bed] Journ. 30 Nov. 1776.

Hypochondria] Journ. 15 (state of indifference), 24 Jan. (*"faintness of mind"*), 5 and 27 Feb. 1777 (confesses).

p. 155
Blames Lady Auchinleck] Journ. 29 Apr. 1777.

Boswell's character] From Temple, 25 June 1776 ("happy insinuation"). Life of every company: Journ. 18 Mar., 20 Oct. 1776, 19 Apr. 1777. Journ. 15 Dec. 1774 (not everyone likes him), 23 Nov. (too open), 11 Apr. 1776 (repeats things); Notes, 15 June 1777 (childish buffoonery); Journ. 18 Jan. 1775 and 9 Aug. 1776 (malevolent), 6 Feb. 1777 (almost despairs of acting properly), 2 and 27 Dec. 1776 (not a good father).

Forgiven, "was in remarkable vigour"] Journ. 11 Feb. 1777.

p. 156
Needs father's consent] Journ. 23 Mar. 1777.

Trip West] Journ. 6–11 Mar. 1777: 10 Mar. (funeral).

Ayrshire visits] Journ. 14–20 Mar. 1777: 16 Mar. (quotations).

Auchinleck] Journ. 20–25 Mar. 1777: 21 ("loved the country"), 23 ("pious duty"), 24 Mar. ("embraced me"); From Johnson, 21 Aug. 1766 (*Life*, ii. 22—"we all live").

David's death and aftermath] From Johnson, 3 May 1777 (*Life*, iii. 109—"to keep three"); Journ. 30 Mar. (Veronica and Effie, Boswell prays, gives up London trip), 20 Apr. 1777 (tests Veronica), 9 Jan. 1780 (evokes horrors of hell).

p. 157
Return to Auchinleck] Journ. 26 Apr.–8 May 1777: 3 May ("negative existence"). Reg. Let. S. Temple, 5 May 1777 (take a lead); Reg. Let. R. Lord Auchinleck, 6 June 1777 ("kindly letter"); Journ. 8 May 1777 (journal fails).

Rule v. Smith] The basic account appears in *Extremes*, pp. 122–26, 130 n. 7: 126 n. 7 (sources); and in *Scots Mag.* 39 (1777). 504–06. Smith's version of the affair is also drawn from David Rae's Information, 30 Dec. 1777, for the defendants (Edinburgh Central Library); Rule's version from Boswell's Information, 16 Dec. 1777, for the "prosecutor" (printed in *Extremes*, app. B). Rae, Information, p. 5 ("if he had been then"); William Roughead, "The Wandering Jurist," *In Queer Street*, 1932, pp. 132 ("kill him"), 142 ("merely a scuffle"); Notes, 17 May 1777 ("lively and well," "constitution to be unhappy"); *Scots Mag.* 39 (1777). 505 ("life is the first object").

p. 159
Boswell in May–June 1777] Notes, 11–12 ("presence of mind"), 14 (sexual relations), 26 May (General Assembly), 13 June 1777 (low spirits). House in Meadows: Notes, 28 May, 27 Sept. 1777; *Extremes*, p. 128 n. 7.

No kindliness between households] Notes, 27 July 1777; From Temple, 26 Aug. 1777.

Summer 1777] Notes, 29 ("depraved creature"), 26–27 June 1777 (Mountstuart). Margaret sick: Notes, 12, 13, 15 ("wandered"), 16 ("sunk and ill"), 29 July 1777 (miscarriage). Notes, 31 July ("must I rise"), 9 ("rising of session"), 13 ("sort of lightness"), 20 and 22 (wanders), 24–25 Aug. (kisses girl), 25 Aug.–4 Sept. 1777 (Bosville's visit).

p. 160
Ashbourne] Journ. 10–27 Sept. 1777. To Grange, 22 Sept. 1777 ("wisdom and wit"); Journ. 21 Sept. 1777 ("while I sat"); Mrs. Thrale to Johnson, 16 Sept. 1777 (*Letters SJ*, ii. 207—"will make Ashbourne alive"); From Johnson, 11 Sept. 1777 (*Life*, iii. 135—"a very high value"); To Johnson, 24 Feb. 1777 (*Life*, iii. 105—"my affection"); From Johnson, 24 Jan. 1778 (*Life*, iii. 216—"call for tenderness"); *Life*, iii. 198 (23 Sept. 1777—"my regard for you"). Boswell's notebook: *Boswell's Note Book, 1776–1777*, ed. R. W. Chapman, 1925, p. 23 left; Geoffrey Scott comments on the literal-mindedness (BP, vi. 157). An extended list of references in Johnson's letters to his love for Boswell appears in the index to *Letters SJ* (iii. 360).

p. 162
Boswell and Johnson at Ashbourne] Journ. 20 ("I really feel myself," talk of bullocks), 17 ("pitch of bellowing"), 18 ("dread of death," birthday), 16 (intimate thoughts), 23 (sitting up), 22 Sept. 1777 (Mrs. Macaulay). For Johnson and Mrs. Macaulay, see *Life*, i. 447–48 (21 July 1763). Much of this Ashbourne material also appears in the *Life* under the same dates.

p. 163
Thoughts of Johnson's death] E.g. Journ. 23 Sept. 1777, 17 Mar. 1778. From the beginning of their acquaintance, Boswell had been contemplating Johnson's death (e.g. Journ. 19 July 1763).

Johnson at Ashbourne] All dates 1777. *Life*, iii. 189 (22 Sept.—more uniformly social), 154–55 (17 Sept.—biography), 158–60 (18 Sept.—Warton), 167 (19 Sept.—hanging), 162 (19 Sept.—driving briskly), 178 (20 Sept.—tired of London), 138 (15 Sept.—curates), 184–85 (21 Sept.—actors), 190–91 (22 Sept.—waterfall), 199 (23 Sept.—"in calm conference").

Boswell at Ashbourne] Journ. 22 ("wretched changefulness"), 14 (meeting friend), 20 (Taylor's maids), 13 Sept. 1777 (attempting chambermaid).

p. 164
Boswell at Auchinleck] Journ. 17–28 Oct. 1777: 25 (Lord Auchinleck's memory), 24 ("disagreeable mutterings").

Margaret's illness and consequences] Journ. 28 Oct. 1777 (Boswell returns to Edinburgh); To Pembroke, 12 Jan. 1778 (Margaret housebound); Journ. 22 Jan. 1778 (Margaret goes out). Second marriage: Journ. 29 Oct. 1777, 19, 26 Jan. 1778. Journ. 2 and 12 Nov. ("rattled"), 14 Dec. 1777 ("*incapax*").

p. 165
Rule v. Smith] To sources listed above, n. to p. 157, add *Extremes*, pp. 195 n. 7, 207 n. 2 (general account). Journ. 22 Nov. 1777 (Gilkie a parody); Rae's Information, p. 17 (Rule in Berwick); Journ. 24 Nov. 1777 ("not warm as I have been"), 26 Jan. 1778 (quite indifferent); Roughead, pp. 164–66 (Gilkie gets last word). Roughead provides a full narrative of what is known of Gilkie's career.

Joseph Knight] *Extremes*, p. 183 n. 7 (general account); *Life*, iii. 200–05 (23 Sept.—Johnson's argument, "wild and dangerous attempt," Johnson's toast), 213 (Nov. 1777—"sooty stranger").

p. 166
Margaret spits blood] Journ. 5 Jan. 1778.

Lainshaw estate] *Extremes*, p. 205 n. 6 (general account); details in James Boswell, Petition of Sir Walter Montgomerie-Cuninghame, 3 Feb. 1778 (Houghton), and Court of Session Cases (Lg32, pp. 39–50, 71–72: 42—"ruinous deed"). Reg. Let. 1777–1778, passim (Cuninghames). T. C. Smout, *A History of the Scottish People, 1560–1830*, 1969, pp. 430–34 (colliers). Sir Walter sold out of the army to his brother David in 1778 (Reg. Let. R. David Cuninghame, 27 Sept. 1778).

p. 167
Margaret's health] To Johnson, 26 Feb. 1778 (*Life*, iii. 219—Margaret improved); Journ. 8 Mar. 1778 (pregnant).

Winter 1778] Journ. 24–25 Jan. 1778 (wench), 6 Oct. 1777 (plurality of women), 19 Feb. and 8 Mar. (*morbus*), 12 Mar. 1778 (cool relations). One or two leaves of the journal with the entries for 31 Jan.–12 Feb. 1778 have been removed, presumably as the result of family censorship. Journ. 7 (Court of Session as important enough sphere), 11 ("immediate business"), 12 Mar. 1778 (in agitation about London).

Preparations for London] Journ. 1 (start of year), 8 (lack of close cordiality), 13 Mar. 1778 (parting interview).

Activities in London] *Life*, iii. 324 (28 Apr. 1778—lives with Paoli); Journ. 21 Apr. (economy), 17 Mar. (London spirits without giddiness), 10 Apr. 1778 (loan from Mountstuart). Queensberry: Journ. 7 Apr. 1778; *Pol. Car.* p. 84. Reg. Let. S. Lord Auchinleck, Apr. 1778 ("that I have done well").

p. 168
Sex] Journ. 2–17 Apr. 1778 (*morbus*). No. 36: Journ. 3, 10 ("*balsamum femineum*"), 24, 25 ("vastly snug"), 26 Apr. 1778 ("*better* than formerly").

Water-drinking] E.g. Journ. 16 Mar. (ale), 14 (tokay), 24 (montepulciano), 30 (rhenish), 28 (Sir Joshua), 29 ("so awkward"), 8 Apr. ("doubts as to pleasure"), 19 May 1778 (best visit).

Boswell's responsiveness to London] Journ. 17 Mar. 1778 ("fully happy"). Pope: Journ. 17, 30 Mar. 1778 (two references); *Life*, ii. 350 (10 Apr. 1775—melancholy remark). Journ. 17 Mar. (on fixing happiness), 19 Apr. (unhappiness), 30 Mar. 1778 (London inexhaustible). A favourite: Journ. 7 Apr. 1778 (two references); From Temple, 21 Mar. 1777. Journ. 9 Apr. (Beauclerk), 18 May (born for England), 17 Apr. (cannot settle there), 22 Apr. and 18 May (must acquire a solid character), 30 Mar. 1778 ("*must* settle in London").

p. 169
Journal entries] Journ. 22 Mar. ("breakfast Burke"), 17 Apr. ("strong, fresh memory"), 17 and 21 Mar. (enough to gather experience), 26 (Cleland), 12 (Burke), 24 (Garrick), 3 (The Club), 9 Apr. 1778 (Reynolds's).

p. 170
Journalizing] Journ. 5 (Wilkes), 9 (Garrick), 10 Apr. (shorthand), 20 Mar. 1778 (memorabilia).

p. 171
Relations with Johnson] Journ. 10 Apr. 1778 ("don't be scribbling"); *Life*, iii. 260 (10 Apr. 1778—"secretly pleased"), v. 102 (24 Aug. 1773—Reynolds), iii. 300 (15 Apr. 1778—"a bright sun"); Journ. 30 Apr. (very polite man), 20 Mar. ("sort of regret"), 7 (travel well together), 15 (Boswell best travelling companion), 17 Apr. (Good Friday), 31 Mar. (fold his legs), 10 Apr. 1778 ("I will not be baited"); *Earlier Years*, p. 192 (Pottle's comment); *Life*, iii. 315 (18 Apr. 1778—horrible shock).

Quarrel, reconciliation] *Life*, iii. 337–38 (2 and 8 May 1778), 341–42 (9 May 1778—Mitre).

p. 173
Marchmont] Journ. 12 May 1778 ("I shall not be in town"); *Life*, iii. 345 (12 May 1778—humiliating application, "that unhappy temper").

Pennantian controversy] *Life*, iii. 271–78 (12 Apr. 1778).

Johnson's character] *Life*, iii. 238 (3 Apr. 1778—many particulars), 247 (7 Apr. 1778—"leaning and swinging"); Journ. 15 Apr. 1778 (book in lap).

p. 174
Johnson's conversation] Journ. 12 Apr. 1778 (£30 a year); *Life*, iii. 248 (7 Apr. 1778—Dodd's sermons), 289–90 (15 Apr. 1778—Mrs. Knowles); Journ. 22 Apr. 1778 (conversation all definitions); *Life*, iii. 319 (25 Apr. 1778—"his knowing clearly"), 317 (20 Apr. 1778—Percy's comparison).

Journal and *Life*] Journ. 28 Apr. 1778 ("inarticulate vociferation").   Garrick: Journ. 9 Apr. 1778; *Life*, iii. 258–59 (9 Apr. 1778).   Edwards: Journ. 17 Apr. 1778; *Life*, iii. 305 (17 Apr. 1778). *Life*, iii. 357 (19 May 1778—vow).

p. 175
Trip home] Journ. 23–28 May 1778.

CHAPTER 8
p. 177
The Rambler] *Life*, i. 215 (after 25 Sept. 1750—"in no writings whatever"), v. 154 (5 Sept. 1773—Johnson as rock).

Early thoughts of periodical papers] Journ. 14 Oct. 1762 ("well calculated"); *Hyp.* No. 10, "On Truth" (Bailey, i. 170—written in Milan).

Writing of *Hypochondriack*] *Hyp.* No. 70, "On Concluding" (Bailey, ii. 302—while "I had just time"); Journ. 22 Oct. 1778 (sentences as well-written as Johnson's).

Hypochondriac symptoms] See esp. *Hyp.* Nos. 6 and 39, both called "On Hypochondria"; *Earlier Years*, pp. 131–35.

p. 178
Causes of hypochondria] *Hyp.* No. 63, "On Hypochondria" (physical).   Hereditary: Boswell thought melancholy and insanity to be hereditary in his family (e.g. Journ. 22 July 1763, 3 Apr. 1780).   Evil spirits: *Hyp.* No. 63, "On Hypochondria" (Bailey, ii. 239); *Life*, iii. 176 n. 1 (20 Sept. 1777).   Boswell picked up this idea from Pringle, an eminent physician.   To Wilkes, 7 May 1765 (British Library—"if you would think justly").   For Boswell's remarks on "impotence of mind," see *Lond. Mag.* 44 (1775). 570–71, and 45 (1776). 593–94.

Boswell's style] For Addison as a model, see *Life*, i. 224–25 (near end of 1750).   Persona: *Hyp.* Nos. 7, "On Conscience"; 12, "On Love"; 30, "On Drinking" (Bailey, i. 154, 184, 330). "Easiness of expression" is Boswell's own early description of his style (Journ. 14 Oct. 1762).

Other essayists] Bacon, "Of Superstition"; Johnson, *Rambler*, No. 45.

p. 179
Content of *Hypochondriack*] From Temple, 24 Apr. 1779 ("more entertaining"); *Hyp.* No. 6, "On Hypochondria" (Bailey, i. 143–44—"strangely averse"); No. 37, "On Country Life" (Bailey, ii. 22—on examining physical world, daily living). No. 53, "On Words" (Bailey, ii. 150—"intense inquiry"); No. 22, "On Similarity among Authors" (Bailey, i. 277—"abstruse kind of speculation"); Journ. 1 Mar. 1784 ("sickened . . . perceptions").   Bailey gives many other references to Boswell's avoidance of minute examination (i. 152 n. 6, ii. 150 n. 2). *Hyp.* No. 53, "On Words" (Bailey, ii. 152—"cursory observations").

Quotations from *Hypochondriack*] *Hyp.* Nos. 33, "On Drinking" (Bailey, i. 353—"a dangerous pleasure"); 45, "On Parents and Children" (Bailey, ii. 90–91—"I knew a father"); 66, "On Diaries" (Bailey, ii. 262, 259—quotations).

p. 180
Boswell congratulates himself on writing essays] Journ. 13 Oct., 28 Dec. 1777, 28 Jan., 17 Sept. 1778, 17 June, 16 July 1779, 15 Jan., 16 Mar. 1780.

Johnson on selecting essays] Life, iv. 179–80 (following 30 Mar. 1783); To Temple, 6 July 1784 ("fine things"). Three incomplete sets of The Hypochondriack corrected for the press survive (P63–65), as well as some fifty pages of additional material for a collected edition (M119.1).

p. 181
Carlisle Assizes] Journ. 19–25 Aug. 1778: 24 Aug. ("easiest among strangers"), 22 Aug. (Lowther).

Birth of James, Jr.] Journ. 15 Sept. 1778.

p. 182
Seaforth Highlanders] Scots Mag. 40 (1778). 726–28 (summary); Pub. Adv. 29 Sept., 1 Oct. 1778; Journ. 28 Sept. 1778 (good spirits). John Prebble has reconstructed the mutiny in detail (Mutiny, 1975, pp. 89–144).

Sexual activities] Journ. Review, 11 Nov. 1778–1 Jan. 1779 ("strange countries"); Notes, 29–30 Jan., 19 Feb. 1779; To Johnson, 2 Feb. 1779 (Life, iii. 371—"solemn conversation").

Valleyfield, Auchinleck] Journ. 15 Oct.–11 Nov. 1778: 23 Oct. ("coldness"), 1 Nov. ("Auchinleck calm").

Legal practice] Journ. Review, 11 Nov. 1778–1 Jan. 1779 (scanty); Notes, 7 Mar. 1779 (Lawrie's warning). Campbell's Trustees v. Scotland: Scots Mag. 40 (1778). 721–22 (summary); Documents in Case (Lg34:1–3): Boswell's argument (Lg34:3—"beef and claret interest"); Legal Notebook (Lg32, pp. 73–90—judges' opinions).

p. 183
Anti-Catholic riot] Journ. 2–3 Feb. 1779; Laird, pp. 47 n. 4, 48 n. 6; E. C. Black, The Association, 1963, pp. 133–47 (summary). Wilkes wrote to Boswell: "Your kirk is an ill-natured, censorious, persecuting prude, and always at war with the flaunting prostitute of Babylon" (From Wilkes, 5 Mar. 1779).

p. 184
Tasker] Journ. 16 Mar. 1779 gives a more vivid account than Life, iii. 374–75, for the same date. So accurate was Boswell's description that some years later Isaac D'Israeli recognized Tasker at sight at a watering-place in Devon (Life, iii. 374 n. 1). Tasker seems to foreshadow Alfred Jingle, Esq.

Boswell neglects Johnson's sayings] Life, iii. 376 (26 Mar. 1779—"during my stay"); To Johnson, 29 Apr. 1779 (not in Life—"multiplicity of engagements"); Boswelliana, p. 318 (dated 27 May 1784—too much space).

Boswell's friends] To Temple, 3–8 May 1779 (Morgan—"am I not fortunate"); To Johnson, 22 Oct. 1779 (Life, iii. 412—"never left a house"); To Wilkes, 23 Mar. 1779 ("I believe I love").

p. 185
Mountstuart] Notes, 28 Mar. (angry), 5 Apr. 1779 (offers to assist). The next August, Mountstuart tried to help Boswell obtain the survivancy of the solicitorship to the Stamp Office in Scotland, but was unable to secure even this minor office for him (Reg. Let. S. and R. Mountstuart, 3 and 15 Aug. 1779).

Johnson, Langton, Paoli] Reg. Let. S. Johnson, 23 Feb. 1779 (great attraction); Journ.

15 Apr. 1779 (Langton as stick of umbrella); Notes, 1 Apr. 1779 (Langton presents book). Boswell's copy of *The Government of the Tongue* with his inscription about Langton's "delicate admonition" is in the Hyde Collection (*Laird*, p. 64 n. 8). Notes, 13 and 18 Apr. 1779 (Paoli's scolding); Journ. 30 May 1781 (Paoli's advice).

p. 186
Hackman] All material from *Laird*, pp. 72–100: 86–89 (account in *St. James's Chron.* 17 Apr. 1779). *Life*, iii. 384–85 (16 Apr. 1779—quarrel between Johnson and Beauclerk), 390 (24 Apr. 1779—Beauclerk's predominance). A bear and a polecat: Journ. 18 Apr. 1779, according to the conjectural reconstruction in *Laird*, p. 92. Johnson to Mrs. Thrale, 18 Sept. 1777 (*Letters SJ*, ii. 208—"age a very stubborn disease").

p. 187
Johnson and Marchmont] *Life*, iii. 392 (1 May 1779). Best suit and Parisian wig: Boswell noted these details on his copy of To Johnson, 29 Apr. 1779 (not in *Life*).

Father ill] To Johnson, 29 Apr. 1779 (not in *Life*).

Boswell stops at Southill] To Temple, 3–8 May 1779 (Morgan).

Lord Auchinleck] Notes, 11 May 1779 (Boswell's promise); Journ. 14 June 1779 (absents himself from Bench).

Summer 1779] Journ. 17 June ("resolved to be assiduous"), 11 Aug. 1779 (practice better); *Life*, iii. 394–98 (3 May–9 Sept. 1779—tests Johnson's affection); Journ. 14 July 1779 (summer insignificant).

Women] Journ. 1 July (♀), 25 Aug. (Portsburgh), 20 June 1779 ("evacuation").

p. 188
Spirits dwindle] Journ. 15 July (Lainshaw sold), 1 ("after having gone to bed"), 18 Sept. 1779 (coastal batteries).

Colonel Stuart] To Mrs. Stuart, 23 Mar. 1780 ("lovely, enchanting friend"); Journ. 24 (drinking until 7 a.m.), 21 (invitation), 17 Sept. ("nothing gave me satisfaction"), 25 June and 21–23 Sept. (hopes of preferment), 26 Sept. 1779 (Lord Auchinleck does not oppose journey).

London] To Johnson, 7 Nov. 1779 (*Life*, iii. 415—"log-book of felicity"); *Life*, iii. 399–400 (before 4 Oct. 1779—"second crop"). Marital infidelity: *Life* MS. 10 Oct. 1779, pp. 792–94, quoted in *Laird*, pp. 142–43; *Life*, iii. 407 (10 Oct. 1779—"Nay, Sir"); *Laird*, p. 143 n. 2 (deletion). Lord Newhaven: *Life*, iii. 408 (12 Oct. 1779); Journ. 7 May 1781 (Paoli's comment). To Johnson, 22 Oct. 1779 (*Life*, iii. 411—adieu to Mountstuart).

p. 189
Chester] Journ. Review, 9 Nov.–18 Dec. 1779 ("wonderful enthusiastic fondness"); To Johnson, 22 Oct. 1779 (*Life*, iii. 413—juvenile); To Temple, 4 Jan. 1780 (Morgan—"*great man*"); To Langton, 23 Dec. 1779 (Bishop, as happy as in London); To Johnson, 7 Nov. 1779 (*Life*, iii. 415—"avidity"); To Mrs. Stuart, 23 Mar. 1780 (recalls Chester).

Autumn and winter in Edinburgh, 1779–80] Journ. 11 Mar. 1780 ("judicious firmness"); Journ. Review, 9 Nov.–18 Dec. 1779 (more violent temper, "twice the number of pages").

Religious beliefs] Journ. 20 Apr. 1780 (Ogden on prayer), 19–20 Dec. 1779 (Veronica), 2 Jan. 1780 (Sandy). Lord Auchinleck: e.g. 23 Aug. 1780, 22 July 1781. In his review of *Laird*, John Updike points to Boswell's anxiety to ascertain his father's views (*New Yorker*, 6 Feb. 1978, p. 109).

p. 190
Family continuity] Journ. 8 (beats Sandy, father beat him), 6 Jan. 1780 (catechism, Margaret's objection), 24 Dec. 1779 ("will you ever say again"). Boswell's Family catechism is inaccurate (*Laird*, p. 160 n. 2).

p. 191
Society] "Dirt and gaiety": General Wolfe's phrase, quoted in G. B. Hill, *Footsteps of Dr. Johnson*, 1890, p. 47. *Hyp.* No. 58, "On Hospitality" (Bailey, ii. 191—"mark of a brutish disposition"); Journ. 17 June 1779 ("good social intercourse"); *Boswelliana*, p. 257 ("every jovial company"); Journ. 22 July 1774 (drinking makes ill-bred). Scottish manners: e.g. Journ. 15 Dec. 1764. Journ. 7 Mar. 1778 (rotation of mutual entertainment), 28 Dec. 1776 (abusive conversation, decline in invitations).

p. 192
Household] Journ. 8 May (Lawrie), 15 Feb. 1780 (Boswell does not hide hypochondria).

Relations] "Quite sunk": e.g. Journ. 11 Mar. 1780. Journ. 14 Jan. 1780 (captain of man-of-war); Ten Lines, 10 Jan. 1780 ("by me sits"). The Cuninghames were also Boswell's own first cousins once removed. Journ. 5 Apr. 1780 ("good clannish dinner"), 10 Jan. 1775 ("double satisfaction").

p. 193
Friends] Lady Colville: Journ. 27 Dec. 1779 (narrow), 22 Feb. 1781 (could tell mood). Prestonfield: e.g. Journ. 20 May 1780 (sheltie); Notes, 30 June 1780 ("foretaste of felicity").

Lords of Session] The Kames biographical project went back to 19 Feb. 1775 (above, p. 125). Boswell also continued to think of writing a life of Lord Covington (Journ. 11–12 Jan. 1780). Journ. 24 Apr. 1780 (dinner at Arniston).

p. 194
Friends] Hay: Journ. 25 Jan. ("flattery"), 12 July 1777 ("meanness"). Maclaurin's scepticism: e.g. Journ. 27 Dec. 1780 and 13 July 1781. *Life*, v. 476 (Scott on Nairne); Journ. 12 Feb. (gambling at Gordon's), 22 (Baillie willing to lend money), 6 Jan. 1780 (Forbes and Margaret appointed guardians), 28 July and 8 Aug. 1779 (Gillespie's stipend), 23 Sept. 1780 (Nicholls), 14 Sept. 1779 (Smith).

Finances] Journ. 1 Jan. 1780 (spent £100 less); To Temple, 4 Jan. 1780 (Morgan—Cuninghames); Ten Lines, 8 Jan. 1780 ("long have I struggled"). Loans refused: From Temple, 1–3 Feb. 1780; Journ. 12 Jan. 1780 (Eglinton); From Bosville, 22 Mar. 1780. Receives loans: Journ. 22 (Baillie), 24 Jan. (Dilly), 15 May 1780 (Wallace).

p. 195
No London, hopes to meet Johnson] *Life*, iii. 418 (beginning of 1780—cannot go to London); To Johnson, 2 May, and 24 Aug. to 1 Oct. 1780 combined (*Life*, iii. 424, 439—hopes to meet Johnson); From Johnson, 17 Oct. 1780 (*Life*, iii. 441–42—cannot meet this year).

Spirits] Journ. 24 ("could have cried"), 26 Feb. ("I exist in misery"), 12 (piety), 13–14 (writes to friends), 11 Mar. ("apprehended a failure"), 8 Apr. 1780 (spirits revive).

Braxfield] *Lit. Car.* pp. 101–05 (description, attribution); Journ. 27 Apr. ("if I had a pamphlet"), 15 (mystification, "plain style"), 22 May 1780 (Syme, "rights and privileges"); *Laird*, p. 216 n. 8 (*Cal. Mer.* letters). Juries were, in effect, hand-picked by the judges from a restricted list (H. W. Meikle, *Scotland and the French Revolution*, 1912, p. 132).

p. 196
T.D.'s early relations with Boswell] From T.D., 31 Oct. 1766; To Pasquale Paoli, 14 Mar. 1780.

Lord Auchinleck] Journ. 19 Mar. ("very old"), 8 Apr. 1780 ("good-night"), 6 Feb. (weary with failure), 21 Dec. 1779 (memory going), 16–17 May 1780 (indifferent to brother's death).

Home's remark] Journ. 2 June 1780.

Wandering] Notes, 20, 27 June, 14 July 1780. "Black" presumably refers to complexion, not skin colour.　Consequences: e.g. Notes, 17 July 1780; Journ. 14, 16 Aug., 17 Sept., 28 Dec. 1780; discussion in *Laird*, p. 281 n. 9.

p. 197

Arbiter] Journ. 12 Aug. 1780.　He had previously served as arbiter with Campbell in a case in 1776 (Journ. 3 Jan. 1776); in the same year he had been chosen to replace Macqueen as advocate in another case, a sign of his reputation (Journ. 28 Dec. 1776).

Lord Auchinleck's hobbies] *Life*, v. 376 (2 Nov. 1773—classics); Ramsay, i. 166 n. 1 (pruning trees); Journ. 31 Oct. 1778 (scrapes leaves), 21 Aug. 1780 (airing); To Pringle, 18 Mar. 1780 (tobacco); Journ. 1 Sept. (whist), 17–27 (Gillespie in attendance), 9 Aug. 1780 (protected by Lady Auchinleck).

Boswell at Auchinleck] Journ. 9 Sept. ("gowk"), 22 (Samson's burial), 24–28 Aug. (Sacrament Week), 4 Apr. 1772 ("descendants"): see I. S. Lustig, "Boswell and the Descendants of the Venerable Abraham," *Studies in English Literature*, 14 (1974).　Journ. 4 Sept. 1780 (Kames and Braxfield call); *Laird*, p. 239 n. 3 (Braxfield's advice).

p. 198

T.D. at Auchinleck] To Johnson, 29 Apr. 1780 (*Life*, iii. 433—"romantic family solemnity"); Journ. 17 Aug. 1780 ("heart, purse, and sword"); *Laird*, pp. 228–30 (oath and codicil).　"Provoking formality": cited in Sir Alexander Boswell, *Poetical Works*, ed. R. H. Smith, 1871, first issue, p. xli.　Journ. 13 Sept. 1780 ("David and I had disputed").

p. 199

Interview with Lord Auchinleck] Journ. 9 Aug. 1780 ("I hoped he was now").

Boswell remains a boy] Journ. 19 Aug. and 6 Sept. (thinks of childhood), 9 Sept. ("talked religiously"), 22 Aug. 1780 ("attending quietly").

Thoughts about Auchinleck and himself] Journ. 2 (living retired), 7 Sept. ("in independent tranquillity"), 21 Aug. ("a weak man"), 17 Sept. 1780 (almost recovered, "in perfect serenity").

CHAPTER 9

p. 201

Inviolable Plan] This document is printed in *Boswell in Holland*, ed. F. A. Pottle, 1952, app. I.

"The celebrated Mr. Boswell"] [?James Tytler] "An Account of Dr. Samuel Johnson" (1774), in *Early Biographies of Samuel Johnson*, ed. O M Brack, Jr., and R. E. Kelley, 1974, p. 11.

Rent-roll] Journ. 25 June 1779.

p. 202

Need to entertain] E.g. Journ. 12 Sept. 1780.

Boswell's attitude towards the military] E.g. Journ. 29 Mar. 1763; To Grange, 16 June 1763.

Making people feel pleased with themselves] Journ. 4 Nov. 1782.

p. 203

Boswell always wanting something] Journ. 2 June 1781.

p. 204

Penny-pinching moods] E.g. Journ. 5 June 1781.

"Gentleman of ancient blood"] *Life*, v. 51 (18 Aug. 1773).

"The Hypochondriack . . . has lately"] Sept. 1780: *Hyp.* No. 36, "On Country Life" (Bailey, ii. 19–20).

p. 205
FRIDAY 17 NOVEMBER] This and the two following entries from Journ.

"The Hypochondriack is himself"] Dec. 1780: *Hyp.* No. 39, "On Hypochondria" (Bailey, ii. 40–46). The lines quoted are from Edward Young's *Busiris*, act 3.

p. 206
Religious doubts] *Life*, ii. 106 (26 Oct. 1769—"his mind resembled"), iii. 154 (17 Feb. 1777—"unhappy uncertainty").

p. 207
Liberty and Necessity] *Life*, iii. 291 (15 Apr. 1778—"all theory"); Journ. 23 Aug. 1782 ("a *mere machine*").

Berkeley and Hume] Journ. 22 Sept. 1780. Boswell called Hume's *Dialogues Concerning Natural Religion* (1779) "posthumous poison" (Journ. 25 Jan. 1780). Yeats: *Blood and the Moon*.

p. 208
Fergusson] *Laird*, p. 236 n. 9 (background); Journ. 8 Sept. (Fergusson's visit, evasion), 30 Aug. ("case"); *Pol. Car.* pp. 42–43, 70–73 (Boswell's attitude towards Fergusson).

p. 209
"Rule our lords"] Cited in *LPS 85*, p. 60.

Ayrshire election of 1780] *Pol. Car.* pp. 87–89 (summary); Journ. 3 Mar. 1781 (keeps off melancholy). Quarrel with President: Journ. 6–10 Mar. 1781: all quotations from 6 and 10 Mar.

p. 210
Scene with Lord Auchinleck] Journ. 12 Mar. 1781.

First days in London] Journ. 21 Mar. 1781 (meets Johnson); From Johnson, 14 Mar. 1781 (*Life*, iv. 71—"hypocrisy of misery"); Journ. 28 Mar. 1781 ("I *must* allow").

The Thrales] Journ. 31 Mar., 1 Apr. 1781; Clifford, p. 173 (Thrales and Sophy Streatfeild); Johnson to Langton, 20 Mar. 1782 (*Life*, iv. 145—"whose eye for fifteen years"); *Life*, i. 491 (after July 1765—price of brewery).

p. 211
Ode] The first three stanzas and the last are taken from the manuscript, called "Epithalamium on Dr. J. and Mrs. T."; the fourth and fifth are taken from the printed version, 1788. All are quoted from *Laird*, pp. 319–21. Journ. 15 Apr. 1781 ("we both wished"). For the allusion to "*vain world*," see *Laird*, p. 324 n. 9.

p. 212
Johnson's and Boswell's sexuality] *Life*, v. 216 (16 Sept. 1773—"that majestic teacher"); To Temple, 18 Mar. 1775 (Morgan—"too many" for Margaret); Journ. Extraordinary Johnsoniana—*Tacenda* (20 Apr. 1783—too ugly); *Life*, iii. 341 (9 May 1778—talked about sexual intercourse); *Laird*, pp. 317–18 ("if Boswell's *Ode*").

p. 214
Fears about discovery of authorship] Journ. 13 (Good Friday), 15 Apr. 1781 (Easter Sunday); *Laird*, p. 318 (fear of Johnson's discovery). Mrs. Thrale's comment on the stanzas shows she did not suspect Boswell (Fletcher, iii. 439).

Charlotte Ann Burney's account] Quoted in *Laird*, pp. 309–12, from her diary in the British Library (Egerton MSS. 3700 B). Journ. 30 Apr. 1781 (calls on Dr. Burney). Boswell was to move into Hoole's house in 1786 (below, p. 336).

p. 215
Mrs. Garrick's] Journ. 20 Apr. 1781 ("I had said"); *Life*, iv. 99 (same date—"looking very serious").

Dissipation in London] Journ. 9 Apr. 1781 (widow); To Mrs. Stuart, 16 Apr. 1781; Notes, 1 ("ranged"), 6 May 1781 (ill after riot).   Names in journal: Journ. 12 (Dinah), 30 Apr. (No. 35, Madame de Wurtz), 2 and 5 May (Fanny Bates), 5 May 1781 (Lady Elgin, Mrs. Spencer). "No. 35" recalls Boswell's former dallying companion, "No. 36."

p. 216
Reproval, disease] Notes, 7 May 1781 (Paoli); Journ. 7 (Johnson), 7 and 14 May 1781 (gonorrhoea).

Miss Monckton's] *Life*, iv. 109–10 (shortly after 8 May 1781—date from Journ.); Piozzi, *Anecdotes* in *John. Misc.* i. 299 ("unaccountable volunteers").   This episode reveals a Boswellian undercurrent that he specifies elsewhere: "Boswell said when we see a man of eminence we desire nothing more than to be of his acquaintance.   We then wish to have him as a companion; and when we have attained that, we are impatient till we have gained a superiority over him. Such is the restless progress of man" (*Boswelliana* MS. p. 90).

p. 217
Happier occasions] Journ. 25–28 Apr. 1781 (Richmond, Royal Academy); *Life*, iv. 101–07 (8 May 1781—dinner at Dilly's): quotations on pp. 102, 103, 107.

Court] Visits: Journ. 16, 24, 30 (wishes to know King better), 27 May 1781 ("thought I could follow"); To Paoli, 27 July 1781; Journ. 7 Feb. 1763 (brightest wits).

Bute] To Bute, 3 May 1781; Journ. 16 Sept. 1773 ("let me value"), 5 ("nothing could induce you"), 13 ("living with people"), 31 May 1781 (sent for).   Mary Granville Delany, *Autobiography*, ed. Lady Llanover, 1861–62, v. 441 n. (Bute in rural retirement).

p. 218
Not recording Johnson] *Life*, iv. 100 (following 20 Apr. 1781—"I was at this time"), 491–92 (summary of Boswell's activities); Journ. 8 May 1781 ("dined Dilly's"); *Life*, iv. 108 (following 8 May 1781—"let us live double"); Journ. 16 (Rudd), 31 May 1781 (Macklin).

p. 219
Southill] Journ. 2–5 June 1781: 3 ("I'd fain be good"), 4 ("don't you be"), 5 June ("great circle").   Journ. 13 May 1781 (Graham's comment).

Return to Edinburgh] Journ. 2–3 June (can retain good spirits), 27 July ("insignificant"), 5 Aug. 1781 (too little authority over children); To Burke, 30 Apr. 1782 (Sheffield, Burke Papers, 1/623—"I am sure"); *Hyp.* Nos. 45, 46 (Bailey, ii. 89–91—quotations); Journ. 4 ("why keep a journal?"), 22 Aug. (thinks of suicide), 17 Nov. 1781 ("impotence of mind").

Pringle] Memoirs of Sir John Pringle (M217—weary and fretful, Boswell loves him); Journ. 30 June (Boswell's company does good), 9 Aug. ("I know not"), 22 July 1781 (Smith as caller); *Life*, iv. 24 n. 2 (1780—"flabby").   Pringle died on 18 Jan. 1782.

Auchinleck visit] Journ. 20 (coldness, venom), 30 Sept. 1781 (Boswell to report conditions).

p. 221
Autumn 1781] Journ. 5 Oct. (miscarriage), 3 (fat, swinishly sensual), 12 (busy practice), 13 Dec. 1781 ("preciseness and peremptoriness").   The six missing pages covered 16–29 Dec. 1781.

Winter 1782] Journ. 1 Jan. 1782 (lecture on exceeding income); From Johnson, 5 Jan. 1782 (*Life*, iv. 136—Margaret as anchor).   Political hopes: To Burke, 18 Mar. 1782 (Sheffield, Burke Papers, 1/534—"would the King"); *Pol. Car.* pp. 93–96 (Judge Advocate application, "serious conversation").

p. 222

Auchinleck visit] Journ. 13 ("pure as crystal"), 11 May 1782 ("prospect of being *Laird*").

Margaret] The special journal covers 22 June–11 Nov. 1782. BP, vi. 153 ("in the elaborate bookkeeping"); Journ. 4 ("I made a good many excerpts"), 2 July 1782 ("flights of fancy," "I put down").

p. 223

No hypochondria] Journ. 23 ("strong spirits"), 2 July 1782 (light diet).

Valleyfield] Journ. 20 ("grown a good deal"), 23 Aug. 1782 ("looked so genteel").

p. 224

Lord Auchinleck] Journ. 23 Nov. 1781 (catheter), 4 Feb. ("flashes of understanding"), 23 Jan. (house in New Town), 16 June (Lennox), 2 ("have you seen," "cold quarters"), 7 (makes Lady Auchinleck blush), 9 May ("he was mild"), 18 Aug. 1782 ("showed no more signs").

Sympathy of onlookers] Journ. 2 May (Gillespie), 22 July (Cochrane), 18 Aug. (Justice Clerk), 20 Feb. 1782 (Balbarton).

p. 225

Dialogue with Sandy] 16 June 1782 (M18).

Family quarrels] Journ. 1 ("contemptuous disgust"), 19 Aug. 1782 ("very disagreeable scene").

p. 226

Lord Auchinleck's death and funeral] Journ. 29 Aug.–1 Sept. 1782 (death). Funeral: Journ. 4 Sept. 1782; *Laird*, pp. 483–87. Long planned: e.g. Journ. 10 Mar. 1779. Scottish funerals were customarily costly (Ramsay, ii. 74).

p. 227

Family moves to Auchinleck] To Johnson, 1 Oct. 1782 (not in *Life*).

CHAPTER 10

p. 228

Auchinleck] *Life*, iii. 178 (20 Sept. 1777—"elegant house," 600 people). Boswell originally wrote 500, but changed the figure on counting families and computing five to a family (R. W. Chapman, "Boswell's Revises of the *Life of Johnson*," in D. N. Smith *et al. Johnson and Boswell Revised*, 1928, p. 28). The figure seems low, since 289 tenants "all fit to bear arms" signed the Address to the King in 1785 (*Jury*, pp. 313–14). Rent-roll: see eleventh note below ("income and expenses"). Journ. 14 Apr. 1782 ("old Scottish baron").

On going to London] Journ. 24–25, 27 Sept. 1782; From Johnson, c. 23 Sept. 1782 (*Life*, iv. 155—"prop and stay"); To Johnson, 1 Oct. 1782 (not in *Life*—"drawn irresistibly").

p. 229

Religious observances] Journ. 10 (family devotions), 13 Oct. 1782 (plans progress, Mauchline Church).

Activities at Auchinleck] Journ. 21 (arithmetic), 26–28 Oct. 1782 (Fairlie's visit); To Bruce, 13 Nov. 1782 (weekly journal); Book of Company, autumn 1782 (visits).

Speech at Quarter Sessions] *Cal. Mer.* 16 Nov. 1782 (Quarter Sessions speech); *Memoirs of the Late Mrs. Elizabeth Hamilton*, ed. E. Benger, 1818, i. 89 ("the concealed sentiments"); *Pol. Car.* pp. 97–98 (Boswell's views).

p. 230

New start in life] Journ. 10 ("rational and active"), 15 Oct. 1782 (Miss Peggie Montgomerie); Reg. Let. S. Dempster, 3 Nov. 1782 ("I am grown fond"); To Burke, 23 (altered to 26) Dec. 1782 (sixth sense).

p. 231
Lord Auchinleck's finances] Journ. 5 Mar. 1780 (pension); Ramsay, i. 165 ("abundantly economical").

Boswell's financial situation] State of My Affairs (A52—debts and assets). Boswell discovered the next spring that the *London Magazine* had suffered a considerable loss of capital (Journ. 2 Apr. 1783). He withdrew as a partner the following year (Reg. Let. S. Dilly, 7 Dec. 1784), and was eventually paid £44.1s. (Journ. 3 Dec. 1787).

Lord Auchinleck's trustees] *Pol. Car.* p. 156 (Dundas's promise); Disposition by Trustees of Lord Auchinleck, 25 Dec. 1784 (SRO—personal estate). The other trustees were Commissioner Cochrane, Claud Boswell, and Robert Boswell.

p. 232
Annuities] Lt. John, Dr. Boswell's daughters: Journ. 5 Oct. 1780; Bond of Aliment, 19 May 1780 (A4.6). Neither daughter married: Jasper John Boswell, MS. "History of the Boswells," vol. ii. part 6, p. 198 (Fondazione Sella, San Gerolamo, Biella). Journ. 28 July 1779 (Gillespie). Boswell's Expense Account for 1783 (A39) shows that Gillespie was paid £200 that year.

Lady Auchinleck] *Laird*, p. 257 n. 1 (settlements); To Johnson, 1 Oct. 1782 (not in *Life*—details of settlement); From Temple, 9 Sept. 1782 (£40 a year). It is hard to make sense of Dundas's comment that Lady Auchinleck "might have had more" (To Johnson, 1 Oct. 1782), unless he was referring to Lord Auchinleck's personal property.

Income and expenses] To Temple, 6–8 July 1784 (thought well-to-do); Journ. 12 Dec. 1784 (only £500 a year). The figure for estate improvements is a guess based on various statements; the other expenses are detailed in Boswell's Expense Accounts (A39). According to Fullarton, public burdens usually did not amount to more than 2% or 3% of the rental (p. 23), but that estimate seems to be low in Boswell's case. Boswell's share, as patron, of the minister's stipend alone seems to have been £44 a year (Expense Accounts for 1784—A39).

It is difficult to calculate Boswell's income from the estate at the time of his accession and for several years afterwards. In 1779, he estimated that he would succeed to an estate worth £1,500 a year. By the entail, no more than one-fourth of the estate could be burdened with annuities. Lord Auchinleck's annuities total £455, which means he must have valued the rent-roll at over £1,800. (In 1786, Boswell valued the annuities at £483; presumably his figure included an increased return on the locality lands: To Dundas, 10 July 1786). But in 1785, the "clear rent" (rent minus annuities, public burdens, and presumably debt interest) amounted to only £1,040 (Forbes to Veronica, 8 Aug. 1795—Somervell). Two years later James Bruce's rent-roll (everything except the locality lands) amounted to £1,240, with income from other sources on the estate of £430, for a total of £1,670 (information from N. P. Hankins). At the end of 1789, Boswell told Temple that his annual rent-roll exceeded £1,600 but that he had only £850 clear, and of that sum he had to spend £500 on his five children (To Temple, 28–30 Nov. 1789—Morgan). In the 1790s, the yearly rents increased rapidly, to £1,900 in 1795 (View of My Affairs, 1 Jan. 1795—A52). Apparently the tenants were always six months in arrears, and some much more than that (e.g. Journ. 30 Dec. 1784).

Gambled on his prospects] "Indeed," writes Fullarton, "considering the expense and inattention to affairs connected with the situation of a country gentleman, and natural tendency of counting upon imaginary rentals long before they become real ones; including too the prevailing course of entertaining, drinking, hunting, electioneering, show, equipage, and the concomitant attacks upon the purse and misapplication of the time," it is surprising that any unentailed estate survives, especially where it cannot be rescued by large sales of timber (p. 92).

Johnson's observation] From Johnson, 3 June 1782 (*Life*, iv. 152).

Resumes practice] Journ. 12 (practice better than expected), 3 Dec. (pleads with force, ease, and pleasure), 11 Nov. 1782 (Eglinton's agents).

Kames] Bruce Lenman, *An Economic History of Modern Scotland, 1660–1976*, 1977 ("feudal law"); *Boswelliana*, p. 279 (obstinacy of a mule). Life of Kames (M135—most of it is printed in *Jury*): 29 Nov. 1782 ("this is a good man"). Lord Hailes's Commonplace Book (NLS Acc. 7228/119—"addressed him thus"). Life of Kames: 10 Dec. ("an impenetrable veil"), 17 Feb. (several revelations), 10 ("pleasure of women," God has physical form), 20 Dec. 1782 ("nothing venerable"). Journ. 21 Dec. 1782 ("just saw him"); Chambers, ii. 171 ("fare ye a' weel").

p. 234
Good spirits] Journ. 5 Jan. 1783 ("I was just as I wished"). Not drinking: Journ. 3 Jan. (had drunk little), 23 Mar. 1783 (no credit), 2 Dec. 1782 (constitutional sobriety). Journ. 8 Jan. 1783 ("sound, cheerful spirits"); To Temple, 20 July 1784 ("local" mind).

p. 235
The crash] *Boswelliana*, p. 286 (Gulliver in Brobdingnag); Journ. 15–28 Jan. 1783 (depression). Body-mind: e.g. *Hyp.* No. 63, "On Hypochondria," and Bailey's list of references (ii. 237 n. 6). To Burke, 23 (altered to 26) Dec. 1782 (unhappy at Scots bar); *Life*, iii. 247 (7 Apr. 1778—can talk twice as much in London).

p. 236
Shadow of his father] Life of Kames (M135): 10 Dec. 1782 (father still present in mind); Journ. 29 Jan. 1783 ("tremulous awe"). In discussing a son's feelings about his dead father, Freud speaks of "the familiar phenomenon of 'deferred obedience,' " which expresses remorse and successful self-punishment ("A Seventeenth-Century Demonological Neurosis," *Standard Edition of the Complete Psychological Works*, trans. and ed. James Strachey, 1953–74, xix. 88).

Winter 1783] Journ. 8 (Johnson's letter), 26 ("a gentlemen of good fortune"), 13 ("I *must* believe"), 17 Feb. 1783 ("not in the least affected").

p. 237
London] Journ. 17 Mar. ("all human concerns"); *Life*, iv. 309 (15 June 1784—"very extensive acquaintance"); Journ. 22 Mar. 1783 ("hard exercise").

"Choice of life"] Phrase: Journ. 4 Apr. 1783; Mem. 21 Apr. 1783. Forbes to Langton, 9 Sept. 1782 ("very fair prospect"); To Temple, 6–8 July 1784 (declamatory powers); From Paoli, 31 Mar. 1780 (original in Italian—"you should expect"); *Boswelliana*, p. 225 (castles in the air); Journ. 19 Feb. 1783 ("the great difficulty"), 17 Apr. 1778 (timid restraint).

p. 238
Burke] Journ. 18 June (full satisfaction), 23 Aug. (greatest of minds), 19 Dec. 1782 ("Burkeish"); From Reynolds, 1 Oct. 1782 ("the pleasantest man"). Reynolds also mentioned this compliment to Langton (Reynolds to Langton, 12 Sept. 1782). Burke praised Boswell to General Conway as "a lawyer of ability and of general erudition, and the pleasantest and best-tempered man in the world" (Burke to Conway, 23 Apr. 1782, copy enclosed in From Burke, 23 Apr. 1782). Journ. 16 July 1782 (Dundas *knew* Burke wanted to help).

Visit to Gregories] Visit: Mem. 21 Apr. 1783; Journ. 21 Apr. 1783. *Jury*, pp. 116–17 (David Cuningham). Boswell wrote so hyperbolical an account of Gregories to Forbes that he burnt it (To Forbes, 5 May 1783—Somervell). Cuninghame recovered.

Mountstuart] Offends King of Sardinia: George III to C. J. Fox, 21 May 1782 (*Correspondence of George III*, ed. Sir John Fortescue, 1927–28, vi. 40). From Paoli, 24 Jan. 1783 (Mountstuart likes him); *Life*, iv. 209 (18 Apr. 1783—"noble-minded, generous, and princely"); Journ. 18 May 1783 ("there are but three ways").

p. 239
Dundas] To and From Dundas, 20 Apr. and 12 May 1782; Journ. 16 July 1782 (conversation in Parliament House), 3 Apr. ("open, frank, and hearty"), 18 May 1783 ("maintained ably").

p. 240
Johnson and Mrs. Thrale] Johnson to Malone, 27 Feb. 1782 (*Life*, iv. 141—"use all the freedom"). Clifford summarizes the changes in Johnson's relationship with Mrs. Thrale (Clifford, ch. 10).

Johnson and Boswell] Journ. 21 Mar. 1783 (first meeting); *Life*, i. 243 (after Mar. 1752—"obscure practiser"); Johnson to Robert Chambers, 19 Apr. 1783 (*Letters SJ*, iii. 18—"he is all"); Journ. 23 Mar. 1783 (second meeting); *Life*, iv. 201 (12 Apr. 1783—Wapping), 221 (15 May 1783—cant). Good Friday: *Life*, iv. 203–09; a fuller report from *Life* MS. appears in *Jury*, pp. 100–05. *Jury*, pp. 110–13 (*Tacenda*).

p. 243
Other activities in London] Nichols, *Anecdotes*, ii. 400 n. ("insinuating urbanity"); index to *Jury* (visits to Stuarts); Journ. 11–12 (Woodford), 8 May (Inglefield), 4 Apr. (master of his bottle), 18 May 1783 (Portuguese Chapel).

p. 244
Temple's situation] Reg. Let. S. Temple, 17 Apr. 1783 (friendship would wither); From Temple, 6 May 1784 (another baby); Bettany, pp. lxiv (eleven children), 114 (Octavius); Bettany, 27 Mar. 1783 ("notwithstanding the uniformity"). "Languid": Boswell's endorsement on From Temple, 11 Apr. 1783. From Temple, 20 Apr. 1783 ("unkind"); To Grange, 22–28 Apr. 1783 ("feeble spirits").

Temple in London] Bettany, 4–30 May 1783. Temple to Mrs. Temple, 29 May 1783 (Lewis Walpole—admires Paoli). Boswell breaks in drunk: Bettany, 24 May 1783; Journ. 23 May 1783 (see note in *Jury*, p. 149). Bettany, 25 May 1783 ("gave an account").

p. 245
Last conversations with Johnson] *Life*, iv. 223 (between 17 and 26 May 1783—hopes of preferment. For the date of that conversation, see *Jury*, p. 146.) Last interview that spring with Johnson: Journ. 29 May 1783, conflated with *Life*, iv. 225–26 and *Life* MS. pp. 910–11, all of the same date.

p. 246
London and departure] Journ. 29 May 1783 (Chelsea College); Mem. 30 May 1783 ("I am then to be steady").

Reconciliation with Temple] Temple to Mrs. Temple, 12 June 1783 (Beinecke—"both wrong and indiscreet"); From Temple, 13 June 1783 (vicar); Bettany, 15 June 1783 ("cannot go to Boswell"); From Temple, 27 May ("I shall be better pleased"), 8 July 1784 ("how pleasing it is to look").

p. 247
Mood in Edinburgh] Journ. 1 Aug. 1783 (miserable); To Paoli, 8 Aug. 1783 ("wasting my days"); Journ. 7 Aug. 1783 (Dundas's dismissal). Appeals to Burke: To and From Burke, 8 and 13 Aug. 1783.

Erskine's appointment] Namier and Brooke, ii. 365, 406; Kay, i. 125 (Advocate's gown).

Auchinleck] Journ. 11 ("uneasiness of low spirits"), 21 Sept. (entertaining company), 10 (anticipation of Johnson's death), 18 ("collecting ferns"), 30 Oct. 1783 ("paroxysm"). Elected preses: Journ. 28 Oct., 7 Nov. 1783. *Pol. Car.* p. 99 (petition against nominal votes); Journ. 10 Nov. 1783 ("I *must* submit").

p. 248
Anger at Coalition] To Burke, 20 Nov. 1783 ("choice of a Solicitor-General"); *Pol. Car.*

p. 103 n. 6 ("a fine fellow"); Journ. 21 Nov. 1783 (speaks to Erskine); *Pol. Car.* p. 100 (never approved of Coalition); Journ. 20 Dec. 1783 (proposed Faculty of Advocates' Address). The Address is printed in Buchanan, p. 350. *Pol. Car.* p. 103 (writes to Pembroke and Mountstuart); To Johnson, 8 Jan. 1784 (*Life*, iv. 259—"crisis of doubtful event"). The change of Ministry in 1783 produced a great clamour for a reduced number of places (Namier and Brooke, i. 124); Boswell's was only one voice among many.

p. 249

1783 *Letter*] Reg. Let. R. Dempster, 23 Jan. 1784 (best speech); *Parliamentary Register*, 12 (1783–84). 391 (Lee's remark), 515 (Dundas alludes to *Letter*); Boswell's original phrase (*LPS 83*, pp. 10–11) is quoted in the present text. *Pol. Car.* pp. 104–05 (reviews), 106 (private reactions). Mountstuart's "warm part": Thomas Coutts to Charles Stuart, 23 Dec. 1783 (*A Prime Minister and His Son*, ed. E. Stuart Wortley, 1925, p. 202). From Paoli, 20 Feb. 1784 (original in Italian—translated Foladare, p. 131); From Johnson, 24 Dec. 1783 (*Life*, iv. 249—"exaltations and depressions"), 27 Feb. 1784 (*Life*, iv. 261—"your paper").

Apparently Boswell never learned that Mountstuart, while at Turin, had upon his own initiative opened peace negotiations in 1780 with Jacques Necker, French Director of Finances. George III put an abrupt end to these overtures, but in spring 1782 with the connivance of Fox, now Foreign Minister, Mountstuart tried unsuccessfully to renew negotiations (Richard B. Morris, *The Peacemakers*, 1965, pp. 98–104, 108–11). At the time of this struggle between Pitt and Fox, Mountstuart must have thought his political future lay with Fox.

p. 250

Addresses, dissolution of Parliament] *Pol. Car.* pp. 106–08.

p. 251

Boswell's spirits rise] Journ. 7 (gonorrhoea), 21 Jan. (abstemiousness), 1 Mar. (thin), 10 Feb. 1784 ("decent show").

"Domestic disturbance"] Journ. 20 Feb., 12, 21 Mar., 2 Apr. 1784: see *Jury*, p. 256. That Miss Young was its motive is a guess: the disturbance was "domestic"; Boswell had a propensity for pursuing unattached women in his household; he had given Miss Young Italian lessons, a sign he had arranged to spend time with her (Journ. 13 Dec. 1783); and a letter from Mrs. Stuart to Margaret (19 July 1784), criticizing Miss Young for spending too much time and money on dress, suggests that the two women had been gossiping about her.

Letter's reception] Journ. 21 (gratifying), 1 (do him good), 10 Jan. 1784 ("to whom my congenial sentiments").

CHAPTER 11

p. 252

Ayrshire election of 1784] *Pol. Car.* pp. 99 and 108–14 (details); p. 59 (number of voters). Montgomerie to pass on seat: Reg. Let. R. Montgomerie, 2 Jan. 1784; To Temple, 20–22 July 1784.

p. 253

Eglinton-Dundas agreement] *Pol. Car.* pp. 111–13; K. G. Feiling, *The Second Tory Party, 1714–1832*, 1938, p. 167 ("common public bottom"); *LPS 85*, pp. 54–55 (reaction to agreement); Journ. 17–18 Mar. 1784 (Ayrshire Address, "I felt myself just").

p. 254

Burke] Journ. 10 Apr. 1784 (escapes death, "so great"); To Burke, 10 Apr. 1784.

p. 255

Johnson's health] Johnson to Taylor, 12 Apr. 1784 (*Life*, iv. 270); *Life*, iv. 259–64 (11 Feb.–7 Mar. 1784—medical correspondence); From Dick, 22 Feb. and 19 Mar. 1784; Dick to

Johnson, 22 Feb. 1784; From Cullen, 10 Mar. 1784 (*Life*, iv. 527–28); *Jury*, p. 191 n. 7 (summary).

Anna Seward] To and From Anna Seward, 18 May–23 June 1784 (several); *Pub. Adv.* 3 June 1784 (review).

p. 256
Johnson and Boswell, spring 1784] Johnson to Mrs. Thrale, 21 Apr. 1784 (*Letters SJ*, iii. 158—confined for four months); *Life* MS. p. 925 (15 May 1784—"copious and animated"); *Life*, iv. 280–81 (19 May 1784—"when I questioned"); *Jury*, pp. 228–29 (Mary Hamilton's account). Events at Oxford: *Life*, iv. 284–310 (3–15 June 1784): 308 (14 June—"pretty country place"), 301 (12 June—"no man would choose"), 294 (11 June—"in great agitation"), 299–300 (12 June—"I am afraid"); Journ. 11 June 1784 (when "I thought"); Mrs. Thrale to Johnson, ?c. 30 May 1773 (*Letters SJ*, i. 332—"dissipation is to you"); Johnson to Taylor, 23 June 1784 (*Letters SJ*, iii. 171—loves to travel with Boswell); Johnson to Mrs. Thrale, 17 June 1784 (*Letters SJ*, iii. 169—"as well as I could expect").

p. 258
The English bar] To Barnard, 14 May 1784; Reg. Let. S. Grange, 22 May 1784 (Dundas's opinion); *Life*, iv. 309–10 (15 June 1784—"you must take care"); From Johnson, 11 July (misdated June) 1784 (*Life*, iv. 351—"if after a few years"): the original letter, with the proper date, is printed by Buchanan, pp. 323–24. Memorabilia Paoli, 27 May 1784 (M211—"mankind as individuals").

p. 259
Boswell and advice] Journ. 5 Jan. 1763 (inclination the road to happiness), 26 Mar. 1777 ("immediate enjoyment").

Margaret's reaction] From Margaret, 26 May 1784 ("his sullen pride"), 22 July 1769 (£100 a year); Margaret to Robert Boswell, 3 July 1784; Mrs. Stuart to Margaret, 19 July 1784.

p. 260
Johnson's approval] *Life*, iii. 176 (20 Sept. 1777—*gust* for London); Johnson to Langton, 27 Mar.–13 Apr. 1784 (*Life*, iv. 267); Johnson to Mrs. Thrale (*Letters SJ*, iii. 165); Johnson to Forbes (Buchanan, pp. 325–26). Johnson does not mention the first of his two conditions in his letter to Boswell of 11 July 1784.

p. 261
Johnson's deteriorating health] *Life*, iv. 330–31 (25 June 1784—"alas!" said the General); *Life* MS. p. 966 (22 June 1784—"evident marks").

"Pious negotiation"] *Life*, iv. 328 (22 June 1784—"pious negotiation"), 337 (29 June 1784—"listened with attention"); To Thurlow, 24 June 1784 (*John. Misc.* ii. 459—Sastres); To Temple, 6–8 July 1784 ("choice dinner"); *Life*, iv. 338–39 (30 June 1784—"I accompanied him").

p. 262
Mrs. Thrale marries Piozzi] Johnson from and to Mrs. Thrale, 30 June–8 July 1784, and Johnson to Hester Maria Thrale, 1 July 1784 (*Letters SJ*, iii. 172–78—several); Clifford, pp. 228–31 (other details). "Same day" is a guess based on the supposition that Johnson wrote to Hester Maria Thrale immediately upon hearing from her.

Johnson's summer and autumn] *Life*, iv. 348–77 (26 July–16 Nov. 1784): From Johnson, 26 July (348—"they that have your kindness"), 348 (after From Johnson, 26 July—"mortgage"), Johnson to Brocklesby, 11 Sept. (357—"gloomy, frigid"), 374 (Nov. 1784—"I will be conquered").

p. 263
Boswell's report to Temple] To Temple, 6–8 July 1784. Anna Seward: Margaret Ashmun, *The Singing Swan*, 1931, pp. 178–87. Lord Chancellor's style: see, for example, Thur-

low's title as given in the *Universal British Directory of Trade*, 1791, i. 393. *Boswelliana* MS. p. 186 (9 May 1785—"il ne me manque").

p. 266
"All is sadly changed"] To Temple, 20–22 July 1784. Samuel Rogers recalled having been much offended as a young man by Blair's broad Scotch accent (*Recollections of the Table-Talk of Samuel Rogers* [ed. Alexander Dyce] 3rd ed. 1856, p. 46).

p. 267
Boswell's debts] View of My Affairs (A52). Forbes, Hunter: Financial Statements (A51); Journ. 23 Feb. 1785 (loan secured on house). Reg. Let. S. and R. Jan. and Dec. 1784 (several—loans from Treesbank's estate). Messenger deforced: Journ. 4 Dec. 1784; *Jury*, p. 267 n. 6.

p. 268
Edinburgh and London] *Boswelliana*, p. 287 ("they tear your hair"); *LPS 85*, p. 47 ("black, law black"); Journ. 6 May 1777 ("if I am not so solid"); *Life*, i. 422 (5 July 1763—"comprehending the whole of human life"), iii. 378–79 (1 Apr. 1779—free "from remark").

Correspondence with Johnson] To and From Johnson, July–Nov. 1784 (*Life*, iv. 379–80—several); Journ. 12 ("callous by reiteration"), 19 Nov. 1784 (hypochondria inexplicable). For the dating of Johnson's letters, see *Letters SJ*, iii. 187 n.

p. 269
Boswell feels neglected] Journ. 9 Dec. 1784 (all quotations).

p. 270
Reviving ambition] Journ. 9 ("Mr. Dundas said"), 12 Dec. 1784 (confidential conversation). In the House of Commons (5 Feb. 1784), Dundas said that if the House ceased to maintain its legislative function, "I must again return to the obscurity of a dull and laborious profession" (Namier and Brooke, i. 119).

p. 271
Johnson's death] Journ. 17–18 Dec. 1784; To Reynolds, 23 Dec. 1784 (Somervell).

Dilly and the *Hebrides*] Journ. Review of the Summer Session, 1775 ("great SUN"); Journ. 18 ("in the true spirit"), 28 Dec. 1784 ("in an honourable way"); Reg. Let. S. Dilly, 23 Dec. 1784; R. Dilly, 29 Jan. 1785.

p. 272
Boswell's dreams] *Jury*, pp. 276 n. 6, 284. The editors of *Jury* speculate plausibly that in the first dream the disordered library recalls Boswell's concern about not being willed a book, and the dream as a whole suggests his anxiety about his own mortality.

Collects Johnsoniana] Journ. 21 Jan. 1785.

p. 273
Winter 1785] Willockshill: Journ. 21 Mar. 1785; View of My Affairs (A52); To Robert Boswell, 10 June and 8 July 1784; *Jury*, p. 283 n. 8. Journ. 28 June 1779 ("rage for buying land"). Settlement on family: Journ. 19 Mar. 1785; *Jury*, p. 283 n. 9. Preparation of *Hebrides*: Journ. 21 Feb. 1785 (Gordon and Blair, to write in London); Reg. Let. S. Dilly, 11 Mar. 1785 (retirement).

Political developments] Montgomerie: *Pol. Car.* pp. 117–18; Journ. 21 Jan. 1785 ("I perceived"). *Pol. Car.* p. 118 (Knight Marshal's post); From Dundas, 30 Mar. 1785 ("you must be aware"); To Dundas, 13 Apr. 1785 ("as to fortune").

p. 274
Boswell's political strategy] Edward and A. G. Porritt explained Boswell's strategy long ago (*The Unreformed House of Commons*, 1903, ii. 137).

LPS 85] *Pol. Car.* pp. 119–29. Quotations from *LPS 85*: pp. 3 ("rage for *innovation*"),

44 ("it is *unjust*"), 9 ("the Stuarts"), 6 ("*Harry the Ninth*"), 9–10 ("the people of Scotland"), 62 ("I trust"), 94 and 101 n. (references to favourite couplet, which is Pope, *Satires*, II.i.51–52), 70 ("excuse my keeping company"), 90–91 ("Great Personage"). The only adequate discussion of the Diminishing Bill in its context is N. T. Phillipson, "Scottish Public Opinion and the Union in the Age of the Association," *Scotland in the Age of Improvement*, ed. N. T. Phillipson and Rosalind Mitchison, 1970.

p. 276
"Racy, full of good stories"] Phillipson, who continues, "Structurally it is rambling and incoherent, and wanders from one subject to another as the author's own inimitable train of consciousness directed it" (pp. 137–38).

More quotations] *LPS 85*, pp. 24 (Monboddo), 80 ("though not blessed"); *Pol. Car.* p. 120 ("the *mode* in which"); *LPS 85*, p. 92 ("hastily written").

p. 277
"Unpleasing uncertainty"] Journ. 10 May 1785. For bibliographical details, see I. S. Lustig, "The Manuscript as Biography: Boswell's *Letter to the People of Scotland*, 1785," *Papers of the Bibliographical Society of America*, 68 (1974). Dr. Lustig reaches the same general conclusions about Boswell's motives and methods as those advanced here.

Further quotations from *LPS 85*] Pp. 92 ("allow me"), 101 n. ("I wish").

p. 278
Advertisement] *Lond. Chron.* 3 June 1785, quoted here from *Lit. Car.* p. 111.

Reviews of *LPS 85*] *Pol. Car.* pp. 123–25.

p. 279
Progress of Diminishing Bill] Phillipson, pp. 128–37; *Pol. Car.* pp. 125–27.

Tenants' Address] *St. James's Chron.* 5 July 1785.

Answer to "An Ayrshireman"] Boswell thought so much of this answer that he had it reprinted as a broadside.

p. 280
Reactions to *LPS 85*] Phillipson, p. 139 (statue of gold); *Auld Reekie* (P4): the Fergusson referred to in the poem's title is Robert Fergusson, Burns's immediate predecessor. *Pol. Car.* pp. 127–29 (general reaction, fear of challenges). Erskine: quoted in a letter signed "Ximenes" (*Gent. Mag.* 55, 1785, 682). Journ. 10 July 1785 ("I, however, think"); From Malone, 5 Nov. 1785 ("you cannot imagine"); To Malone, 11 Nov. 1785 ("henceforth *to a certain degree*"). Apology in newspapers: *Edin. Eve. Cour.* 24 Dec. 1785; *Edin. Adv.* 27 Dec. 1785.

CHAPTER 12
p. 282
First month in London] Journ. 19–20 ("great day" and following), 28 Apr. 1785 (executions). "Swept round . . . girls": for phrasing, see BP, vi. 165–66; *Tour*, p. xiv. Girls: Expense Accounts (A39.1): 4 Apr. 1785 ("armour").

Social round] Journ. 13 and 28 Apr. (Richmond), 1–2 May (Woodford, "was brilliant"), 2 June 1785 (Lord Mayor's). The quotation about the gong comes from *St. James's Chron.* 14 June 1785, an account obviously written by Boswell himself. Further commemoration appeared in a newspaper *Ode on Mr. Boswell's Gong* (*Jury*, p. 306 n. 6). A "splendid old Canton gong, 21 in. dia." appears in an Auchinleck estate sale catalogue in 1906 (*Pride and Negligence*, p. 242).

p. 283

Starts on *Hebrides*] Journ. 29–30 Apr. ("full of bar scheme," "you must *feed* press"), 2 May 1785 (specimen).

Prostitutes] Polly Wilson: Journ. 25–26 Apr. 1785; *Jury*, p. 286 second n. 2.   Journ. 12–13 May 1785 (ys).

Pottle's summary] *Pride and Negligence*, p. 225; Journ. 13 May 1785.

p. 284

Betsy] Journ. 14 ("*three* then"), 16 May ("something not right"), 24–25 May and 1 June 1785 (St. Thomas's); Expense Accounts (A39.1—half-guinea fee).

Court] Journ. 20 May 1785.

Malone] *Gent. Mag.* 83. i (1813). 518 ("Memoir"); Mem. 29 May 1785 ("home and dress"); Journ. 30 May (will), 3 June 1785 ("almost all forenoon").

Malone's career] See P. S. Baker's Introduction to the Boswell–Malone correspondence forthcoming in the research series of the Yale Boswell Editions, which supplies references. Samuel Schoenbaum provides an informative account of Malone's Shakespearian interests in *Shakespeare's Lives*, 1970.   Schoenbaum, p. 780 n. 33 (*crede experto*); Farington, i. 88 (23 Jan. 1795—"too soft").

p. 285

Boswell and Malone collaborate] This account follows the Preface to the *Tour*, sometimes verbatim, and also owes some points to BP, vi. 161–73.   *Tour*, pp. 241–42 (turning journal into English).

p. 286

Malone's alterations] *Life*, v. 120 (27 Aug. 1773—"occasional excursions"), 104 (24 Aug. 1773—"urged drinking"), 180 (12 Sept. 1773—"in a boat"): the last of these changes was made as late as a revised proof (P84).   In quotations from the *Hebrides* the first edition is followed, though for the convenience of the reader references are given to the third edition (*Life*, v), when necessary.

Recasting indirect speech] See F. A. Pottle, "James Boswell, Journalist," in *The Age of Johnson*, ed. F. W. Hilles, 1949.

Cuts in *Hebrides*] *Life*, v. 259 n. 1 (26 Sept. 1773—focus on Johnson); *Tour*, pp. 220 ("description"), 101 n. 4 ("dinner"), 147 (privy in Raasay), 124 ("I observed tonight").

p. 287

Johnson's dignity] *Tour*, pp. 215 (Macaulay), 211 (punch), 201 (fishing).

Boswell's and Malone's alterations] All dates are 1785, unless otherwise noted.   From Malone, 5 Oct. ("it gave me pleasure"); To Malone, 13 Oct. ("I think 'I loved' "); *Life*, v. 40 (16 Aug. 1773—"I was pleased"); From Malone, 21 Oct. ("it is too colloquial"); *Life*, v. 48 (17 Aug. 1773—"but stay"); From Malone, 21 Oct. ("I wish the 'ha' "); To Malone, 27 Oct. ("I resign the 'ha' "): this passage, however, was left unchanged.   To Malone, 13 Oct. ("I like the passage").   On Malone's desire to spare Boswell derision, see P. S. Baker's forthcoming Introduction.   *Life*, v. 25–26 (15 Aug. 1773—"Johnson was pleased"); From Malone, 5 Oct. (Courtenay "wishes with me"); To Malone, 13 ("perhaps you and Courtenay"), 15 ("Veronica is herself"), 30 Oct. ("are you not"), 2 ("your kind attention"), 11 Nov. ("you have certainly").

p. 289

Garrick] *Tour*, pp. 211–12; *Life*, v. 249–50 (23 Sept. 1773).

Claims of authenticity] *Life*, v. 78 n. 5 (21 Aug. 1773—"my note of this"), 227 (19 Sept. 1773—"might be printed"), 279 (3 Oct. 1773—"very exact picture"), 312 n. 2 (14 Oct. 1773—Johnson's biography); To Malone, 13 Oct. 1785 ("*authenticity*").

p. 290
Boswell's recording of Johnson] To Malone, 13 Oct. 1785 ("I am determined"). For variations between Boswell's record of Johnson in the journal and in the *Hebrides*, see L. F. Powell, "Boswell's Original Journal of His Tour to the Hebrides and the Printed Version," *Essays and Studies*, 23 (1937). 62–63. The standard discussion of Boswell's recording of Johnson is Pottle, "Art and Authenticity," pp. 70–73.

p. 291
George III as collaborator] To George III, 6 June 1785; Journ. 15 June 1785 ("the trial"). Another account: a letter from Vice-Adm. Sir Alexander Cochrane to Sir J. C. Hippisley, 10 July 1819 (printed in *Jury*, pp. 311–12). *Life*, v. 185 (13 Sept. 1773—"grandson") and n. 4 ("I *know*"); Journ. 24 June 1785 ("a hint this"), 23 Apr. 1788 ("he asked me").

Reynolds's portrait] To Reynolds, 7 June 1785; *Jury*, pp. 309 first n. 6 (Reynolds's agreement), 308 n. 5 (a present).

p. 293
London, summer 1785] *Life*, Dedication (equal and placid temper). "The Gang": Philip Metcalfe's name for the four (Journ. 4 Jan. 1790). Journ. 13 Sept. (many pleasant days), 9 (great favourite), 6 Aug. 1785 ("such connections"). "Friends round the Globe": Journ. 27 July 1785; Expense Accounts (A39.1). Reg. Let. S. Temple, 30 Apr. 1785 (delicious life); To Robert Boswell, 26 Aug. 1785 (delightful metropolis); To Eglinton, 12 Sept. 1785 ("paradise"); Journ. 29 July 1785 (dinner at Courtenay's); *Pub. Adv.* 4 Aug. 1785 (list of company).

p. 294
Betsy] Journ. 6 (interview), 27 July 1785 (changed lodgings). Chelmsford: Journ. 17 Aug. and 9 Sept. 1785; *Jury*, p. 338 n. 4.

Mrs. Rudd] Journ. 9, 14 Aug. (second call), 10 Sept. ("told her honestly"), 24 Nov. 1785 ("had cravings"). Reynolds's lecture: Journ. 28 Aug. 1785 (the beginning of this entry is missing). Fanny Burney: her journal for 26 Feb. 1787.

p. 295
Account of execution] Journ. 6 July 1785. *Jury* reprints Boswell's account and the opening paragraph of "Execution Intelligence" (pp. 318–19). Fifer, pp. 199–200 (From Reynolds, 7 July 1785—defends public executions).

p. 296
London and Auchinleck] Journ. 21 (Court), 22 Sept. 1785 ("jury"); *Jury*, pp. 344–45 (Lee, Auchinleck).

Response to *Hebrides*] *Jury*, p. 345 (general account). All quotations from reviews appear in *Jury*, pp. 346–50. Knox, *Winter Evenings*, 2nd ed. 1790 (1st ed. 1788) i. 106–97 ("biography is every day").

Boswell on minutiae] Boswell talks of remarking particulars in *Corsica* (p. 352), presumably recalling Plutarch's stress on revealing detail (see *Life*, i. 31–32—introductory remarks), but he included only those of direct use in composing his heroic portrait of Paoli. *Tour*, p. 99 ("to see Mr. Johnson"); *Life*, v. 132 (30 Aug. 1773—"to see Dr. Johnson"), 19 (introductory remarks—"let me not"), 279 (3 Oct. 1773—"I must again").

p. 298
Courtenay's couplet] *Poetical Review of the Literary and Moral Character of the Late Samuel Johnson, LL. D.*, 1786, p. 33. In the poem as published, the first line is changed to "We love the writer, praise his happy vein." To Malone, 24 Jan. 1786 ("I cannot give"). "If I had lived": Montaigne, trans. W. Carew Hazlitt.

p. 299
"Johnsonophilus"] *Gent. Mag.* 55 (1785). 969.

Sterne] *Tristram Shandy*, I. xi.   Sterne took this definition from La Rochefoucauld.

p. 300
"Ravings of those absurd visionaries"] *Life*, v. 365 (27 Oct. 1773).

Writes to Garrick] 29 Aug. 1773 (*Life*, v. 347—23 Oct. 1773).

Opening character sketch of Johnson] *Life*, v. 18.

p. 301
Scene with Flora Macdonald] *Life*, v. 184 (12 Sept. 1773).

p. 302
"It is the same"] *Tour*, p. 288.

Johnson on the Scots] *Life*, v. 248–49 (23 Sept. 1773—"drunkenness"), 377 (3 Nov. 1773—opinion of Highlands).

p. 303
Individual animadversions] Blacklock: *Life*, v. 47 (17 Aug. 1773); From Blacklock, 12 Nov. 1785 (*Life*, v. 417–18).   Dun: *Life*, v. 382 (5 Nov. 1773); *Tour*, pp. 440, 442.   *Life*, v. 75 (21 Aug. 1773—Gardenstone), 105 (24 Aug. 1773—Slains), 403 (20 Nov. 1773—Dalrymple); Journ. 22 Jan. 1782 (Boswell despises Dalrymple).

Douglas] *Life*, v. 362 (26 Oct. 1773—"particularly complained"); Journ. 22 Mar. 1787 ("handsome letter").

p. 304
Mrs. Thrale] *Life*, v. 245 (23 Sept. 1773).

Burke] *Life*, v. 32 (15 Aug. 1773—"great variety") and n. 3; To Malone, 30 Oct. 1785 ("rich plumage"); From Burke, 4 Jan. 1786 ("I am extremely obliged").   The most concise summary of the flurry about the Burke footnote appears in *Life*, v. 32 and n. 3, 465.   The Boswell–Malone correspondence of Oct.–Nov. 1785 includes a continuing discussion of this footnote.   Burke was more open elsewhere in his dissatisfaction with the *Hebrides*: Michael Lort wrote to Mrs. Piozzi (31 Dec. 1785) that Burke had fallen "hard upon [Boswell] for the absurdities in that performance" (Clifford, p. 259 nn. 3–4).   And see More, ii. 101.

p. 305
Tytler] *Hebrides*, p. 486 (10 Nov. 1773—"did you observe").   This comment and Tytler's name were deleted in later editions.   In "James Boswell and Alexander Fraser Tytler," *The Biblioteck*, VI, i (1971). 1–16, Claire Lamont prints Tytler's first letter (31 Oct. 1785) and Boswell's response (6 Nov. 1785—"hasty expressions"), as well as some interesting excerpts from Tytler's Commonplace Book; but her account of the quarrel is somewhat misleading because it omits mention of six subsequent letters among Boswell, Tytler, and their intermediary, Dugald Stewart.   See this correspondence, 14 Oct.–1 Dec. 1785, and Journ. 18, 30 Nov. 1785.

p. 306
Macdonald] All material, sometimes verbatim, from F. A. Pottle's narrative (BP, xvi. 221–59), unless otherwise noted.   To Malone, 11 Nov. 1785 ("when you and I").

p. 309
Reaction in journal] Journ. 6 ("what mischief"), 8 ("my anxiety . . . sad agitation"), 9 ("awaked very ill . . . do I endure"), 10 ("had not slept"), 11 ("conscious that"), 12 Dec. 1785 ("the night . . . pious hope"); Lamont, p. 7 ("it is amazing").

p. 310
Aftermath of Macdonald affair] BP, xvi. 258–59 (F. A. Pottle's account).   In the *Life* MS.

(opp. p. 424—after 22 Nov. 1773), Boswell declared that Macdonald had not forced him to make changes in the *Hebrides*, but deleted the comment.

CHAPTER 13

p. 312
Lord Eglinton] *Tour*, pp. 416 (*savoir vivre*), 438 ("I lived").

p. 313
Holdsworth on Erskine] *History of English Law*, ed. A. L. Goodhart and H. G. Hanbury, 1938–72, xiii. 580.

Smell of a flambeau] *Life*, i. 461 (30 July 1763).

On removing to English bar] *Life*, v. 51 (18 Aug. 1773—"predominant passion"); To Malone, 8 Nov. 1785 (*grotta del cane*); Journ. 21 Nov. ("all seemed confused"), 25 Nov.–5 Dec. 1785 (various opinions). Dempster's early experience with Boswell's anxieties: To Grange, 23 Sept. 1763.

p. 315
Thurlow] *LPS 85*, p. 29 ("I bow the knee"); To Thurlow, 9 June 1785 (on Thurlow recognizing him); To and From Thurlow, 23 Sept. and 11 Oct. 1785 (copy of *Hebrides*); To Thurlow, 18 Dec. 1785 ("ambitious restlessness").

Barristers and Benchers] Sir F. D. MacKinnon, "The Law and the Lawyers," in *Johnson's England*, ed. A. S. Turberville, 1933, ii. 287 (barristers and King's Counsel). In February 1786, the seventeen Benchers of the Inner Temple included Thurlow himself (R. A. Roberts, *Calendar of the Inner Temple Records*, v, 1936, 474).

p. 316
Transfer to English bar] Journ. 20 Dec. ("*my wife's inclination*"), 26 Nov. 1785 (Margaret agrees to London); *LPS 85*, p. 55 ("a true Montgomerie").

Scotland] Journ. 28 Dec. 1785–27 Jan. 1786: 22 (Veronica spits blood), 19 ("very hearty day"), 20 Jan. ("I felt with disgust").

More on transfer to English bar] From Thurlow, 5 Jan. 1786 ("your succedaneum"); Journ. 9 Jan. 1786 (this letter); From Temple, 4 Jan. 1786 ("it is pity"); To Malone, 24 Jan. 1786 ("you speak philosophically"); Mem. 28 Jan. 1786 ("you felt *serenely*"); Journ. 27 Jan. 1786 ("the truth is").

p. 318
Called to the bar] Journ. 9, 13 Feb. 1786 ("a course of fish"). Expense Accounts (A57—cost of dinner).

Run-in with Burke] Journ. 7 Feb. 1786 ("calumny"); Boswell–Burke correspondence, 7–10 Feb. 1786 (several).

p. 319
Aggressiveness] *Life*, ii. 442 (20 Mar. 1776—exceedingly unwilling to be provoked to anger); Journ. 8 Feb. 1763 ("art for nettling people"); *Hyp.* No. 23, "On Reserve" (Bailey, i. 290—"slighter sort of uneasiness"); Journ. 17 Mar. 1776 ("usual fault"), 13 Oct. 1780 ("bad habit"); C. B. Tinker, *Young Boswell*, 1922, p. 166 (Boswell loved friction).

Mrs. Rudd] *Life*, iii. 79 (15 May 1776—"talents, address"); Journ. 4 Feb. 1786 ("wonderful"); M258 (the two descriptions of Mrs. Rudd).

p. 320
Boswell and Lee] *Pub. Adv.* 28, 29, 30 Sept. 1785; From Dilly, 5 Oct. 1785; From Lee, 3 Oct. 1785 ("your parts").

Squibs about Boswell at bar] E.g. *Pub. Adv.* 14, 27 Feb., 26 Apr., 3 May 1786; *Lond. Chron.* 4 Mar., 9 May 1786.   My knowledge of several periodical items, here and elsewhere, derives from an unpublished list of Boswelliana by Anthony E. Brown.

First experiences at the bar] To Malone, 14 Jan. 1786 (Blackstone); Legal Notebook (Lg40—Feb. 1786–20 July 1787); Thomas Ruggles, *The Barrister, or, Strictures on the Education Proper for the Bar*, 1792, ii. 75–76; Journ. 22 (first brief), 24 (Erskine's advice), 26–27 Feb. 1786 (interview with Thurlow, quarrel with Mrs. Rudd).

p. 322
Private reactions to the *Hebrides*] Pride of family: From Wilkes, 1 Oct. 1785; From Temple, 14 Oct. 1785.   Malone, writing as "Anti-Stiletto" in defence of Boswell, admitted that he put excessive emphasis on his ancestry (*Gent. Mag.* 56, 1786, 19).   Treatment of the living: From Forbes, 6 Dec. 1785; To Forbes, 20 Dec. 1785 (Somervell); From Drummond, 26 Dec. 1786, and Boswell's endorsement.   Sir Alexander Dick's widow and son also showed nervousness about Boswell's projected biography of him (To Margaret, 18 May 1786).

Praise: From Walker, 13 Nov. 1785; From Malone, 5 Oct. 1785 (Reynolds had read the book twice); Reynolds to Rutland, 26 Sept. 1785 (*Letters of Sir Joshua Reynolds*, ed. F. W. Hilles, 1929, p. 140).   Brydges, *Autobiography*, 1834, i. 134; Reg. Let. R. 3 Jan. 1786 ("anonymous fool"); From Malone, 19 Oct. 1785 (King); Journ. 2 Mar. 1786 (Queen); Fanny Burney's diary for 20 Dec. 1785; From Anna Seward, 12 Oct. 1785 ("good God"), 7 Mar. 1786 ("most extraordinary composition"); Reg. Let. R. 8 Mar. 1786 (Miss Seward flattering).

p. 324
Johnson on fame] *Life*, v. 400–01 (20 Nov. 1773).

Paper wars] E.g. items in *Gent. Mag.* 55 (1785) and 56 (1786) by Q, Johnsonophilus, Byblius, D.H., Anti-Stiletto, Gratian, Benvolio, T, Philanthropus, Pro Me, E.R.R., I.D.I., Bristolensis, and Boswell himself.   Anna Seward was Benvolio, and Richard Gough was Q, D.H., and Pro Me (Nichols, *Illustrations*, vii. 328–43).

Pindar] To Malone, 22 Mar. 1786 ("absurdly malignant").

p. 325
Parting from Lee and Mrs. Rudd] Journ. 9 Mar. 1786.

Larghan Clanbrassil] Printed in Alexander Boswell, *Songs Chiefly in the Scottish Dialect*, 1802. Somewhere I have read that it was sung to the tune of "Drunk at Night and Dry in the Morning."

On the circuit] From and To Malone, 27 and 31 Mar. 1786.

p. 326
Jokes on the Circuit] Lord Campbell, *Lives of the Lord Chancellors*, ed. J. A. Mallory, 1874–75, viii. 383 (Grand Court).   *Lord Eldon's Anecdote Book*, ed. A. L. J. Lincoln and R. L. McEwen, 1960, pp. 58–59 (Lee's feigned brief), 19–20 ("Boswell sent").

John Scott and feigned brief] J. C. Jeaffreson, *A Book about Lawyers*, 2nd ed. 1867 (Scott as ringleader); Horace Twiss, *Life of Eldon*, 1844, i. 130 (anecdote about Boswell).   The phrase *adhaesit pavimento*, from Psalm 119, appears in the Book of Common Prayer.   Sceptics about anecdote: Campbell, viii. 383; Jeaffreson, ii. 200; Pottle, BP, xvi. 182–84.   Possibly Eldon, in old age, confused two feigned briefs.   Lancaster Assizes: Feigned Brief (C1678).   Reg. Let. S. To John Boswell of Knockroon, 15 June 1787 (Scott "as shrewd and candid").   Many years later, Eldon spoke of having been a close friend of Boswell's (David Boyle to James Boswell, Jr., 4 Feb. 1811).

Another story about Boswell drunk in the streets appears in H. T. Cockburn, *Life of Lord Jeffrey*, 2nd ed. 1852, where Jeffrey, at the age of seventeen or eighteen, is said to have had "the honour of assisting to carry the biographer of Johnson, in a state of great intoxication, to bed.   For this he was rewarded the next morning by Mr. Boswell . . . clapping his head and telling him that he was a very promising lad, and that 'if you go on as you've begun you may live to be a Bozzy yourself yet' " (cited in *Life*, v. 24 n. 4). The only time Boswell visited Edinburgh after his departure in January 1786 was for ten days in 1793, when Jeffrey was nineteen years old and had already attended Oxford. It is hard to imagine Boswell clapping anyone of that age on the head, or referring to himself in conversation as "Bozzy."

p. 327
Two briefs] Legal Fees (Lg41).

Mrs. Piozzi's *Anecdotes*] The basic accounts are J. L. Clifford, "The Printing of Mrs. Piozzi's *Anecdotes of Dr. Johnson*," *Bulletin* of the John Rylands Library, 20 (1936); Clifford, ch. 12; J. C. Riely and Alvaro Ribeiro, " 'Mrs. Thrale' in the *Tour*: A Boswellian Puzzle," *Papers* of the Bibliographical Society of America, 69 (1975). Mary Hyde, in *The Impossible Friendship*, reviews the relationship between Boswell and Mrs. Thrale-Piozzi; I. S. Lustig discusses Boswell's attack on Mrs. Thrale-Piozzi in the *Life* and its background ("Boswell at Work: The 'Animadversions' on Mrs. Piozzi," *Modern Language Review*, 67, 1972). For the transformation of the material in *Thraliana* into the stories of the *Anecdotes*, see *Thraliana*, i. xviii–xxviii. Roy Pascal, *Design and Truth in Autobiography*, 1960, p. 70 (Maurois on memory). Mrs. Thrale herself said at one point that she did not care to trust either her memory or her veracity (Mrs. Thrale to Johnson, 18 July 1775—*Letters SJ*, ii. 69), and in response Johnson fretted at her forgetfulness (Johnson to Mrs. Thrale, 29 Aug. 1775—*Letters SJ*, ii. 84). More, ii. 16 (new-fashioned biography). Walpole's opinion: Walpole to Sir Horace Mann, 28 Mar. 1786 (*Letters HW*, xxv. 636). As W. K. Wimsatt remarks, Mrs. Thrale's Johnson "has little inner principle except that of savage neurosis" ("Images of Samuel Johnson," *ELH*, 41, 1974, 367).

p. 328
Mrs. Vesey on Piozzi] Blunt, ii. 275. For contrary opinions, see Clifford, pp. 307, 349.

Mrs. Thrale to Johnson] 21 Oct. 1781 (*Letters SJ*, ii. 441).

p. 329
Anonymous someone] *Anecdotes*, in *John. Misc.* i. 175 ("a trick"); *Life*, iv. 343 (after 1 July 1784—"they probably would"); To Mrs. Thrale, 9 July 1782 (Hyde—"I have invariably thought"); To Malone, 31 Mar. 1786 ("is *undoubtedly* levelled").

p. 330
Boswell's condensed notes] *Life*, iv. 343 (after 1 July 1784—"that anxious desire"). "Portable soup": Journ. 13 Sept. 1773; Life of Kames (M135—18 Nov. 1782); *Hyp*. No. 66, "On Diaries" (Mar. 1783—Bailey, ii. 259). Journ. 9 Jan. 1768 ("a hint"), 24 Mar. 1783 ("if I neglect"); *Tour*, p. 346 ("my journal cannot"); *Life*, iii. 270 (12 Apr. 1778—"slowly and distinctly"); Journ. 9 Apr. 1778 ("nonsense, as if"); *Life*, iv. 166 (21 Mar. 1783—"I was fixed"); Journ. 21 Mar. 1783 ("I have the substance"). Though occasionally incorrect in detail, Geoffrey Scott's discussion of Boswell's habits of recording as a whole is decisive (BP, vi. 15–30).

p. 331
Boswell's memory] The standard discussions, followed here, are two essays by F. A. Pottle: "The Power of Memory in Boswell and Scott," in *Essays on the Eighteenth Century Presented to David Nichol Smith*, 1945; and "Art and Authenticity." "Vigour of mind": the example is taken from Tinker, p. 205; the phrase occurs in *Life*, ii. 450 (20 Mar. 1776). "Naturally an excellent memory": French Themes, 29–30 Jan. 1764 (*Boswell in Holland*, ed. F. A. Pottle, 1952, p. 128). Brydges, i. 134 ("quickness of apprehension"); *Life*, v. 279 (3 Oct. 1773—"a very exact picture"); Boswell may have thought the wording of his journal, "a very exact picture of his life" (*Tour*, p. 245), was imprecise. Johnson mentions Boswell's journal many times in his letters to Mrs. Thrale; his references certainly imply its accuracy.

p. 332
Percy] A. C. C. Gaussen, *Percy: Prelate and Poet*, 1908, p. 217; Fifer, pp. lxxxiv–lxxxvii, 373 n. 12.

Pepys's letter] A. C. C. Gaussen, *A Later Pepys*, 1904, ii. 260.

p. 333
Boswell's anger at Mrs. Piozzi] To Malone, 31 Mar. ("malignant devil"), 3 Apr. 1786 (Hyde—"O brave we").

Mrs. Montagu on Boswell] To Mrs. Piozzi, 28 Mar. 1786 (*French Journals of Mrs. Thrale and Doctor Johnson*, ed. Moses Tyson and Henry Guppy, 1932, p. 43). Earlier, after Mrs. Thrale's remarriage, Mrs. Montagu conceded that she had "uncommon parts, but certainly never appeared a person of sound understanding; whoever possesses that blessing never is guilty of absurd conduct, or does anything which the world calls strange" (To Mrs. Vesey [?1784]—Blunt, ii. 275).

Boswell's newspaper response] *Gazetteer*, 17 Apr. 1786: for other listings, see *New CBEL*, ii. 1233. Johnson's profitability for his biographers was already a subject of newspaper comment (Werkmeister, p. 83). *Pub. Adv.*, 20–21 Apr. 1786 (*Piozzian Rhymes*, "Mr. Boswell's retort"). "Altius ibunt": this is the motto of at least two Scottish families, but I do not know why (or if) it is "celebrated." *Essay on Shakespeare*, 2nd ed. 1770, p. 214 ("galimatias"); Clifford, p. 273 n. 1 (*Essay* goes into another edition).

p. 334
No private quarrel] More, ii. 16 (topic spoiled conversation). Jenyns's *Epitaph* was widely reprinted; it is quoted here from *Gent. Mag.* 56 (May 1786). 428. *Bozzy and Piozzi*, ll. 533–46, 667–72; From Temple, 21 Apr. 1786 ("lying, scurrilous fellow"). F. A. Pottle, BP, xv. vii (talent to discriminate individual through speech).

p. 335
Mrs. Rudd] Reg. Let. S. Mrs. Rudd, 28 Mar. (confessed), R. 1 Apr. 1786 ("spirited"); Journ. 14 (resists seeing), 16 (Easter), 23 Apr. 1786 ("felt strangely"); From Temple, 14 July 1786 ("how can you"); Journ. 29 May 1787 (calls on Mrs. Rudd).

p. 336
Moving] House on Great Queen St.: Journ. 2 Feb. (old-fashioned, dark), 16 (moves), 26 May 1786 (rats). Margaret moves: From Margaret, 11 Apr. 1786 (furniture shipped); To Margaret, 18 May 1786 (Margaret to be at Auchinleck). The sale of the Edinburgh household belongings, 19 May 1786, fetched a little more than £23 (Roup-Roll of Household Furniture—A71.1).

Boswell's indecision] Journ. 29 Mar. 1786 (Bolton's advice). Margaret's illness: To Margaret, 18 May 1786 (Margaret ill); Journ. 26 May 1786 (on rack); Reg. Let. R. Bruce Campbell, 5 June 1786 (Margaret recovered). Journ. 3–4 (Malone, Courtenay, Paoli), 17 June (Forbeses), 5–8 Mar. (publicizes liaison), 22 (Mrs. Stuart), 23 ("all my English bar"), 27 June 1786 (Malone encourages); Mem. 27 June 1786 ("remember how well"); To Margaret, 3 July 1786 (should abandon English bar): "Dearest Life" was a common 18th-century salutation. Journ. 3 ("good plain dinner"), 4 July ("when I got"), 14 June 1786 (calls on Douglas); To Mountstuart, 15 July 1786.

p. 338
Appeal to Dundas] To Dundas, 10 July 1786; *Probationary Odes*, 1785, p. xxix ("but though *I* laugh"). Boswell also inserted a report in *Pub. Adv.* for 2 June 1786 that he had been offered the next vacancy on the Court of Session. Journ. 6 July 1786 (Paoli says past age of ambition).

p. 339
Starts work on *Life*] Journ. 24–25 Apr. 1786 (Scots appeal). This case, Cuninghame v. Cuninghame, involved the claims of the Cuninghame sons under their mother's settlements.

Journ. 27 Apr.–1 May (visits Oxford), 3 June 1786 (Malone stiffens his resolution). Marshall Waingrow has studied Boswell's gathering of materials in his thorough and valuable *Correspondence and Other Papers of James Boswell Relating to the Making of the "Life of Johnson,"* 1969. Other than direct quotations, only references not easily located or omitted in that volume are footnoted here. Attention is particularly called to the "Chronology of the Making of the *Life*" (pp. li–lxxviii).

p. 340
Conceptions of *Life*] *Life*, iv. 428 n. 2 (end of 1784—"immortal glory"); To William Bowles, 14 June 1785 ("monument"); To Anna Seward, 30 Apr. 1785 ("pyramid"); To Walker, 1 July 1785 ("mausoleum"); *Life*, Advertisement to the first edition (cairn); To Blair, 21 Apr. 1786 ("venture to promise"); Journ. 12 Oct. 1780 (*Life* in "scenes"); To Barnard, 20 Mar. 1785 ("valuable treasure"). The advertisement for the *Life* at the end of the *Hebrides* speaks both of a "literary monument" and of that "peculiar energy which marked every emanation of [Johnson's] mind."

Early work on *Life*] Journ. 9 ("make a skeleton"), 12 (skips dinner), 22 June ("sorted till stupefied"), 9–11 (milk and toast), 8 July 1786 ("delicate question"). For the interview with Hawkins, see F. A. Pottle, "The Dark Hints of Sir John Hawkins and Boswell," *New Light on Dr. Johnson*, ed. F. W. Hilles, 1959.

p. 341
Summer 1786] "My spirits were now so good that existence was a pleasure" (Reg. Let. S. Temple, 17 July 1786). Journ. 16 July (picnic), 26 July–2 Aug. (Home Circuit), 28 July 1786 (dinner at Wilkes's).

Grange's death] Walker summarizes Grange's last years and Boswell's efforts to help him (pp. xxxv–xxxvii). From Temple, 30 Nov. 1787 ("placid smile"). Boswell attempts to console and help: Reg. Let. S. Grange, 19 June 1784, 4, 30 Apr. 1785, 13 Feb., 7 June 1786. From Temple, 8 Aug. 1786 (martyr to sloth).

p. 342
Return to Auchinleck] To Malone, 19 Aug. 1786; Book of Company (date of arrival).

CHAPTER *14*
p. 343
Removal to London] Journ. Review, 20 Sept.–31 Oct. 1786 ("the knack of it"); Journ. 1–18 Nov. 1786: 13 ("always happy"), 7 ("one morning").

Dundas] To Dundas, 9 Nov. 1786 (SRO GD 51/5/400); From Dundas, 26 Nov. 1786 ("not the least disposition"). It must have irritated Dundas that Boswell had provided his enemies with ammunition (see *Pol. Car.* p. 139 n. 8).

p. 344
Asks to be made Recorder] The copy of Boswell's letter to Lonsdale, 9 Nov. 1786, is on the verso of the copy of his letter to Dundas of the same date. Repeatedly Boswell turns to both at the same time. Journ. 23 Nov. 1786 (doubts as to interference of peers).

Lonsdale] All references in *Pol. Car.* pp. 131–35, 139–41, or in Namier and Brooke, iii. 56–60, unless added here. Douglas Sutherland, *The Yellow Earl*, 1965, pp. 9–11 (sister, daughter of tenant farmer, offensive shopkeeper); *Rolliad*, 1785, part 2, p. 53; Journ. 3 June 1784 (Johnson on Lonsdale), 23 July 1786 (Eglinton). Boswell may not have asked Eglinton to introduce him to Lonsdale until after he had praised Lonsdale in print. *Life*, v. 113 n. 1 (26 Aug. 1773—"ancient family of Lowther").
In 1780 Lonsdale criticized duelling between M.P.'s in a speech in the House of Commons: "If free debate were to be interpreted into personal attack, and questions of a public nature

which came before either House were to be decided by the sword, Parliament would resemble a Polish diet" (quoted in A. S. Foord, *His Majesty's Opposition*, 1964, p. 358).   Later he boasted to Boswell that his threat of a challenge had made the Duke of Norfolk withdraw a petition in the House of Commons about the Westmorland militia, of which Lonsdale was Colonel (Journ. 5 Jan. 1788).

p. 347
Carlisle election of 1786] General accounts: Smith, "Mushroom Elections"; Ferguson, ch. 7; R. S. Ferguson and W. Nanson, *Some Municipal Records of the City of Carlisle*, 1887, pp. 36–40; *Pol. Car.* pp. 142–43 (Boswell's role); Namier and Brooke, i. 52 (Norfolk and five seats); "A Westmorland Freeholder" (P28.11—broadside).

p. 348
Carlisle's special significance] Journ. 30 Nov. (first sight), 4 (honoured father, melancholy), 1 Dec. 1786 ("real rise in dignity").

Lonsdale at Carlisle] Journ. 2 Dec. 1786 ("esempio"); *Life*, iii. 176 (20 Sept. 1777—madman); Journ. 25 Nov.–12 Dec. 1786: 3 Dec. ("solidity"), 29 Nov. ("quietissimi"), 2 ("such a noise"), 5 ("may have children," "shocking tyranny"), 6 ("no pleasure"), 4 ("you see who we are"), 7 ("load of weariness"), 9 ("strong dissertation"), 10 ("*forcible* Lord Macdonald"), 12 Dec. 1786 (*really* pleasant").   Reg. Let. Dec. 1786 (returns to London).   High spirits: Malone to Percy, 22 Dec. 1786 (*Correspondence of Thomas Percy and Edmond Malone*, ed. Arthur Tillotson, 1944, p. 50).   To Lonsdale, 3 Jan. 1787; Reg. Let. S. Lonsdale, 3 Jan. 1787 ("sincere compliment").   Fee: English Fees (Lg41); To Blair, 2 Aug. 1787 (extra 50 guineas).

p. 350
Congratulations] From Barnard, 23 Jan. 1787; From Percy, 6 Mar. 1787; From Blair, 25 Aug. 1787.   For a different interpretation of Percy's motives, see Fifer, p. lxxxiv.   Boswell himself certainly took the bishops at their word (Journ. 28 Dec. 1787).

p. 351
Lack of legal business] English Fees (Lg41) records only two fees (total 10 guineas) for the first six months of 1787.

Life "in great forwardness"] To Barnard, 6 Jan. 1787; *Pub. Adv.* 9 Feb. 1787; *St. James's Chron.* 15 May 1787.

Johnson on Hawkins] *Life*, i. 27 n. 2 ("degree of brutality").   Johnson, however, also described Hawkins to William Bowles, 5 Apr. 1784, as "a man of very diligent inquiry and very wide intelligence" (*Letters SJ*, iii. 150).   Pinches the diary: Hawkins, *Life of Johnson*, 2nd ed. 1787, p. 586; *Life*, iv. 406 n. 1 (Dec. 1784).

p. 352
Hawkins's knighthood] *Life*, i. 190 n. 4 (before May 1748—"upon occasion"); Bertram H. Davis, *A Proof of Eminence*, 1973, pp. 65 (wife's fortune), 240–46.

Hawkins's *Life of Johnson*] The first edition of Hawkins's *Johnson*, 1787, is cited here because it had by far the greater impact on Boswell's career, and because the second is comparatively rare: pp. 76 ("playhouse"), 164 ("outward deportment"), 327 ("garb"), 205 ("inertness and laxity"), 560 ("reading in bed"), 61 ("vulgar complaints"), 441 (poor edition of Shakespeare), 602 ("ostentatious bounty"), 224–31 (Dyer), 416–20 (Goldsmith), 218 ("men of loose principles"), 286 ("about five"), 589 ("you all pretend"), 205 ("no genuine impulse"), 219 ("false medium").

p. 353
Hawkins's reviewers] "Whereof, wherein": *Critical Review* (May 1787), cited in Davis, p. 353.   Porson: *Gent. Mag.* 57 (1787). 848 ("never omits an opportunity"), 652 ("compass of learning").

p. 354
Johnson's sexual irregularities] Hawkins, pp. 88, 545, 563–64; *Life*, iv. 395 (Dec. 1784—
"strange, dark manner").

Spring 1787] Journ. 30 (Malone keeps Boswell to *Life*), 5 and 6 (Margaret wants to return
to Auchinleck), 20 Mar. 1787 ("she with a high spirit"); To Malone, 14 Jan. 1786 ("command"
him); Journ. 22 Mar. ("if I should quit"), 9 (Sandy comforts), 14 Apr. (Lee, Burke), 11 May
1787 (King); To Forbes, 8 May 1787 (Somervell).

p. 356
Maxwell] To Maxwell, c. 10 June ("Johnsoniana"), 4 July 1787 ("I ought to apologize").

London, spring and summer 1787] Dundas: To Dundas, 19 May 1787 ("friendly conversation"); Notes, 20 June 1787 (calls on Dundas).   Lonsdale: To and From Lonsdale, 13
and 23 June 1787 ("I don't believe").   Home Circuit: Journ. or Notes, 10 July–9 Aug. 1787;
Legal Notebook (Lg40).   Notes, 20 Aug. 1787 (arrival at Auchinleck).

Sacrament Week] Notes, 23 Aug. 1787 ("Russel preached"); Burns, *The Holy Fair* (quotations); Burns, *Poetry*, ed. W. E. Henley and T. F. Henderson, 1896–97, i. 333 (Millar short).

p. 357
Millar] Boswells persuade Eglinton: From Fairlie, 20 Nov. and 23 Dec. 1786; Journ. 10
Apr. 1787.   From Millar, 23 May ("cutthroatlike fellows"), 5 ("I doubt not"), 2 Apr. 1787
("Mr. Russel, I am certain").   Settled in parish: Reg. Let. R. Millar, 13 Dec. 1787; *Fasti Scot.*
iii. 115.   *The Holy Fair* indeed was reprinted in the Edinburgh edition of Burns's poems,
1787.

p. 358
Auchinleck, 1787] To Forbes, 11 Oct. 1787 (Somervell—canvassing); *Pol. Car.* pp. 5–6
(Thurlow's decision); From Fairlie, 23 Dec. 1786 (votes, Sheriffship); Journ. 27 ("my worthy
friend Grange"), 24 Sept. 1787 (tenants lined up); From Malone, 14 Sept. 1787 ("we had
yesterday"); Journ. 29 Oct. 1787 (Burke's "shyness").

p. 359
Money difficulties] To Robert Boswell, 25 Sept. 1787 (Preston wants repayment); Journ.
26 Oct. 1787 (Dilly and Baldwin).   Bruce Boswell: Paoli had warned Boswell not to lend
Bruce fourpence (Journ. 9 Apr. 1781), but Boswell arranged the loan anyway (Journ. 31 May
1781).   He expressed his worry about the loan in a letter to Robert Boswell, Bruce's brother,
6 Oct. 1787.   Boswell was forced to pay off the loan in instalments in 1791 (BP, xviii. 100);
and it was not until after his death that Robert Boswell repaid the money (*Boswelliana*, p. 188;
Robert Boswell to Forbes, 3 July [?1795]—Somervell).   Gibb: View of My Affairs, 1 Jan. 1787
(A52—£200); Reg. Let. R. and S. Gibb, 7 and 10 Oct. 1786; From Gibb, 22 Dec. 1786; Reg.
Let. S. Gibb, 15 Oct. 1787.

Family problems] Journ. 18 Nov. (Margaret's complaint), 18 Oct. (Jamie's "vivacity," Sandy
unruly), 21 Mar. (testicle, hernia), 4 Nov. (Margaret unwilling to let Sandy go to boarding-
school), 3 Dec. 1787 ("elegance of manner").

Prospects] Dundas: Boswell–Dundas correspondence, July–Nov. 1787 (several); Reg. Let.
S. Temple, 10 Nov. 1787 (judge's place); Journ. 8 Nov. 1787 (Dundas dines).

Work on *Life*] Waingrow, pp. lx–lxi ("at *Life*"); Journ. 16 Nov. ("to attend laxly"), 28 Oct.
("went to Malone's"), 22 Nov. 1787 ("awaked very uneasy").

p. 360
Dinners] Journ. 22 Oct. (Boswell entertains), 11–12 Dec. 1787 ("most jovial meeting").
Malone had written the Prologue to *Julia*.   Jamie to Margaret, 5 Dec. 1788 ("Mrs. Buchanan
invited").

Recordership] To Lonsdale, 1 Dec. 1787 ("the office of Recorder").   Pay: Boswell's receipt, 9 July 1790 (Vouchers, 1789–90, in Chamberlain's Account Book, Carlisle—Cumbria County Record Office).   Journ. 20 Dec. 1787 ("I was agitated").

p. 361
The trip north] Journ. 23 ("his way was to call"), 21 Dec. (Lowther and Satterthwaite on Parliament).   "Independency": *Hyp*. No. 12, "On Love" (Sept. 1778—Bailey, i. 186).   Boswell would have had any doubts about Lonsdale's attitude towards his M.P.s resolved if he could have seen his letter to William Lowther, 26 Jan. 1782: "I would have you to know that the gentlemen who are brought into Parliament by me are not accountable to any person but myself for their conduct (when their constituents do not interfere)" (Namier and Brooke, iii. 59).

p. 362
The North and return] Journ. 24 ("told how a gentleman," *Alonzo*), 26 ("his camp *butcher*," "I thought I heard"), 28 ("viewed with wonder"), 30 Dec. 1787 ("felt myself very awkward"), 1 ("here is a room"), 5 ("I am *thinking*"), 14 Jan. 1788 (wife's appearance).

p. 365
Dissipation in London] Journ. 12 Feb. 1788 (Dilly's); Reg. Let. S. Rockville, 1 Feb. 1788 ("I would give up"); Journ. 17 Feb. 1788 ("it was wonderful"); To Mrs. Stuart, 23 July 1791 (neglect); Journ. 20 Feb. 1788 ("that if my living").

Progress on *Life*] To Percy, 9 Feb. 1788 (Berg); From Temple, 9 Feb. 1788; To Temple, 24–25 Feb. 1788 (Morgan—"Mason's *Life of Gray*"); Journ. 1 Mar. 1788 (52 pages); Waingrow, p. lxii (September publication).

p. 366
Letters to and from the Late Samuel Johnson] To Percy, 9 Feb. 1788 (Berg—"much entertainment"); *Life*, iv. 84 (4 Apr. 1781—"with respect"); *Letters*: 23 Nov. 1772 ("character of governess"), 3 Feb. (Thrale children), 3 Mar. 1775 ("I wish to live"), 7 May 1780 ("petticoat government").   Clifford, pp. 296–302 (*Letters* revised for publication); To Malone, 8 Mar. 1788 ("I am going on"); Journ. 12 Apr. 1788 (Lysons fills blanks—see comment in Clifford, p. 321).   Mrs. Piozzi's alterations of Johnson's letters: R. W. Chapman, "Mrs. Piozzi's Omissions from Johnson's Letters to Thrales," *Review of English Studies*, 22 (1946); Clifford, pp. 317–19.   As Chapman remarks, Mrs. Piozzi's malice in cooking the letters "was not strong enough to reach consistency" (*Letters SJ*, ii. 47 n. 6).   Boswell has possibly damaging letter: Mrs. Thrale to Johnson, 28 Apr. 1780 (*Life*, iii. 421–23, 536–37).   The letter is innocuous.

p. 368
Reaction to Piozzi *Letters*] Journ. 9 Mar. 1788 (Malone); Clifford, p. 310 (Taylor). For the transformation of the earlier version (the "Epithalamium") into the later *Ode*, see Hyde, *Friendship*, pp. 130–36.   Wit wasted on public: Boswell–Malone correspondence, June–July 1788 (several).

p. 369
Margaret's health] Journ. 9 ("severe fit"), 17 ("I fear I'm dying"), 28 Mar. 1788 ("being so much abroad"); Reg. Let. S. Lady Crawford, 10 Apr. 1788 ("my uneasiness"); Journ. 19 ("I am terrified"), 19–20 (stays out all night), 29–30 Apr. ("at night was much distressed"), 1 (recovers ring), 2 May 1788 (ankle sprained).

p. 370
Appeal to Temple] To Temple, 24–25 Feb. 1788 (Morgan—"*come, come*"); From Temple, 11 Mar. 1788 ("I long much"); Reg. Let. S. Temple, 15 Apr. 1788 ("relieve me").

Spring 1788] Journ. 27 (Scott), 22 (Burke), 25 Apr. 1788 (Walpole).

Taylor] *Records of My Life*, 1832, i. 216 ("universally well received"), 219 ("then quite a boy").   The most likely theatre dates fall in 1787–88.

p. 371
Boswell and Margaret] Journ. 3 ("inwardly shocked"), 1 (continous intoxication, Malone lectures), 5 (sexually restless), 10 May 1788 ("home, was asked").

Return to Auchinleck] Reg. Let. R. Wood, 21 Apr. 1788; Journ. 13 (Veronica at Mrs. Stevenson's), 15 (departure), 16 May 1788 (Stamford). Mrs. Stevenson's school was known as "the ladies' Eton" (H. B. Wheatley and Peter Cunningham, *London Past and Present*, 1891, iii. 132). Three of Mrs. Thrale-Piozzi's daughters were, or had been, at school there (Hyde, *Friendship*, p. 117).

CHAPTER 15
p. 373
Estate records] These are listed in N. P. Hankins's volume, "Boswell's Estate Correspondence," forthcoming in the Yale Boswell Editions. Mrs. Hankins provides detailed references to Auchinleck estate matters, and only those not included in her volume are given here.

p. 374
At Auchinleck] To Malone, 2 June 1788 (return trip, "sadly distressed"); To Forbes, 31 May 1788 (Somervell—"no man ever loved"); To James Bruce, 22 Apr. 1788 (wanted to be at Auchinleck); Reg. Let. S. Lady Crawford, 10 Apr. (his own inclinations), S. Malone, 5 June 1788 (sound spirits).

"Romantic rocks"] As early as 26 Sept. 1759, Boswell had written to Grange: "Auchinleck is a most sweet, romantic Place. There is a vast deal of wood and water, fine, retired, shady walks, and everything that can render the country agreeable to contemplative minds." James Paterson, *History of the Counties of Ayr and Wigton*, 1863, i. 186 (Old Castle); *Ordnance Gazetteer of Scotland*, ed. F. H. Groome, 1901 ("in a dream of the night," s.v. Airdsmoss); *New Statistical Account of Scotland by the Ministers of the Respective Parishes*, v (1845). 325 (eight others slain).

p. 375
View from Auchinleck House] Journ. 24 Aug. 1780 (prospect from roof), 23 Mar. 1777 ("I like that appearance").

First ambition] To Eglinton, 7 Feb. 1763.

Auchinleck House] *Life*, v. 379–81 (4 Nov. 1773): for another rendering of the motto, see *Earlier Years*, p. 10. *Journey*, p. 161 ("very stately"). A photograph of Auchinleck House appears in *Earlier Years*, following p. 102. Barony: Robert Bell, *Dictionary of the Law of Scotland*, 1807–08, s.v. baron.

p. 376
"Young laird"] When Boswell remarked to Sir Alexander Dick that a young laird was happier than an old one, Dick replied that the young laird lived in hope and the old one in fear (Journ. 11 Sept. 1783).

Bruce Campbell] Fullarton, p. 59.

Boswell instructs Bruce] To Bruce, 10 Dec. 1783.

Salaries] Schoolmaster's: a guess based on Boswell's Expense Accounts for 1785 (A39), and John Strawhorn, *Ayrshire*, 1975, pp. 147, 162–63. Minister's: *Stat. Acct.* xi. 433; and above, p. 232.

Hankins] From the Introduction to her forthcoming volume.

p. 377
Relations with tenants] Journ. 14 July 1788 (like Johnson); To Gibb, 4 June 1791 (*Letters JB*, ii. 483—no tenant "upon my estate"), 13 Nov. 1792 ("kindly remembrance"); Names of Tenants Holding Land in 17th Century (M10—Murdochs, etc). Boswell wrote in his will,

"I do beseech all the succeeding heirs of entail to be kind to the tenants and not to turn out old possessors to get a little more rent" (*Boswelliana*, p. 186).

Hypochondriack] No. 37, "On Country Life" (Oct. 1780—Bailey, ii. 24–25: "man of vivacity"; 26: "hypochondriac proprietor").

Johnson on country] *Life*, iv. 338 (30 June 1784).

To Malone] 12 July 1788 (Hyde—"very favourable remission," "dreary remonstrance," "I attend diligently").

p. 378
Forty or fifty counsel] Boswell listed them on a loose sheet enclosed in his Northern Circuit Journal, 1–29 July 1788 (J105.1).

Junior] Journ. 6–7 July 1788. Boswell reverted to his secretive Italian for part of this journal; F. A. Pottle's translation, occasionally modified, is used here.

Grand Night] Journ. 10 July 1788 ("din and foolishness"); To Richard Burke the Younger, 18 Mar. 1786 (Fifer, pp. 229–32—ceremony). For the verses, see *Grand Tour I*, p. 299.

Northern Circuit] Journ. 17 July 1788 ("getting over life"); *Life*, iv. 310 (15 June 1784— "by no means thought"). Lottery: e.g. To Malone, 10 Feb. 1791 (Hyde). Journ. 18 (Ambler), 23–25 (daily complaints), 5 (promoter of festivity), 16 (brief), 25 ("breastplate of ale"), 26–29 July 1788 (ill-judged experiment). Lancaster and return home: Expense Account, Northern Circuit, 1788 (A46); Reg. Let. Aug. 1788; Book of Company.

p. 379
Politics] Journ. 15 Mar. (encounters Pitt and Dundas), 19 Apr. 1788 ("had done the King's cause"); *Pub. Adv.* 12 May 1788 (withdraws candidacy); To Malone, 18 Sept. (rumour about Montgomerie), 12 July 1788 ("a declared candidate"). "Address to the Real Freeholders": Journ. 1 July 1788; *Edin. Adv.* 4 July 1788. Rides the county: To Malone, 18 Sept. 1788; Book of Company. *Pol. Car.* p. 153 (Whitefoord, Cathcart, Kilmarnock meeting); Ginter, p. 42 n. 2 (McDowall as stopgap); From James Cuninghame, 7 Sept. 1788 ("pass through life"); Recorder's Address, between 4 and 8 Oct. 1788 (Lg53).

p. 381
Return to London] To Malone, 18 Sept. 1788 (*Life*, on giving up wine, depressed, Margaret's anxiety). He and Malone miss each other: From Malone, Robert Jephson, and Courtenay, 29 Sept. 1788 ("make haste"); To Malone, 7 Oct. 1788 (Hyde). Book of Company (leaves Auchinleck); To Anna Seward, 24 Oct. 1788 (stops at Lichfield); From Lonsdale, 22 Oct. 1788, endorsement (arrives in London).

p. 382
Disclosure about Mrs. Rudd] This information comes from an odd source, Boswell's record of a flirtation with Wilhelmina Alexander, sister of a neighbouring laird. Under "Autumn 1787," Boswell wrote: "I told her confidentially of a romantic illicit connection and how I had owned it to wife. She informed me that it had been told—and others—which were not true" (M7).

Flees Cobham Park] To Malone, 17 Nov. 1788; To Margaret, 9–11 Nov. 1788.

p. 383
Burns's letter] At some point Bruce Campbell passed this letter on to Boswell, who endorsed it: "Mr. Robert Burns, *the poet*, expressing very high sentiments of me." The ballad and fugitive pieces have disappeared; presumably the ballad was *The Fête Champêtre*, composed to commemorate a festival held on the banks of the Ayr the previous July. In one stanza Burns mentions three of the Parliamentary candidates—Fergusson, Montgomerie, and Boswell:

Or will we send a man-o'-law?
Or will we send a sodger?
Or him wha led o'er Scotland a'
The meikle URSA MAJOR?   [great]

George III's madness] See, in particular, Ida Macalpine and Richard Hunter, *George III and the Mad-Business*, 1969; John Brooke, *King George III*, 1972, pp. 336–41. The King's interest in Lady Pembroke was persistent; when he went mad for the final time in 1810, he asserted firmly that he was married to her, an oblique but embarrassing riposte to the notorious infidelities of her late husband.

p. 384
Projected Regency pamphlet] To Temple, 10 Jan. 1789 (Morgan—"very warm popular pamphlets"); "Song for Carlton House" (M316—*studiously* composed").

"Coalition candidates"] Boswell means that both Fergusson and Cathcart had aligned themselves with Fox, who presumably was to head the Ministry when the Prince of Wales became Regent. See *Pol. Car.* pp. 154–56.

Lonsdale] Journ. 27 Mar. 1788 (strings); To Lonsdale, 23 Nov. 1788 ("very honourable distinction"); To Margaret, 28 ("business alluded to," "wonderfully well"), 24 Nov. 1788 ("Sandy did not hear").

p. 385
Hopes of practice] To Margaret, 5 Dec. 1788 ("visionary hopes," ignorance of forms, "*rank* of *barrister*"); From Malone, 12 Aug. 1788 ("you will never cease").

Moving] To Margaret, 9–11 Nov. 1788 (chambers in Temple).   "Neat, pretty, small house": To Euphemia, 19 Dec. 1788 (excerpt, Puttick and Simpson Sale Catalogue, 24 Dec. 1857).   To Temple, 10 Jan. 1789 (Morgan—camp lodging); Journ. 12 Dec. 1789 (Malone nearby).   Boswell asked Margaret to send any furniture she wanted to London "except *our own bed* (which I would not give for its weight in gold)" (To Margaret, 9–11 Nov. 1788).

Progress on *Life*] Waingrow, pp. lxiv–lxv; To Temple, 10 Jan. 1789 (Morgan).

p. 386
Correspondence with Temple] From Temple, 27 Nov. 1788 ("one ought to be something"); To Temple, 10 Jan. 1789 (Morgan—"in the country").

Work on *Life*] Journ. 17 Nov. 1774 ("keenness of temper"); *Life*, i. 463 (2 Aug. 1763—most indolent of men).

Correspondence with Margaret] To Margaret, 5 Dec. 1788 ("the *separation*"), 9 Feb. 1789 (Rosenbach—"how *can* you say").

p. 387
Dinner in Queen Anne Street] To Forbes, 27 Jan. 1789 (Somervell—"I can have"); *Life*, iv. 273 (15 May 1784—ever-cheerful Devaynes).   O'Reilly was probably a connection by marriage.

Reynolds's hospitality] Farington, "Memoirs of Reynolds," i. cciii–iv ("never more happy"), clxxxiv (£2,000 a year).   *Life*, Dedication ("enlarged hospitality").   Courtenay's description is quoted in James Northcote, *Life of Sir Joshua Reynolds*, 2nd ed. 1819, ii. 93–95.   Journ. 2 Apr. 1788 ("quite a hurly-burly").

p. 388
Boswell remains in London] Northern Circuit: To Margaret, 9 Feb. 1789 (Rosenbach); To Temple, 16 Feb. 1789 (Morgan); *Pol. Car.* pp. 156–57 (Pitt); From Temple, 26 Apr. 1789 ("person of your family").   Actually, people of much higher rank than Boswell solicited favours with great vehemence and persistence.   John Ehrman, *The Younger Pitt*, 1969, pp. 323–24 (Pitt not answering mail); To Temple, 31 Mar. 1789 (Lonsdale shows regard); Reg. Let. S. Blair, 13 Mar. 1789 (great lottery).

Margaret's illness] From James Bruce, 31 Jan. 1789 (too active); To Forbes, 23 May 1789 (Somervell—Sandy Wood); From John Campbell, 8 Mar. 1789 (would live only a month); To Margaret, 9 ("it pained me"), 24 Mar. 1789 ("truly kind").

p. 389
Doings in London] Details in To Margaret, 11 and 25 Mar. 1789; To Temple, 10 and 31 Mar. 1789 (both Morgan).

Boswell returns to Auchinleck] To Temple, 31 Mar. 1789 (Morgan—"my fever still continues"); Book of Company (date of arrival).

p. 390
Boswell's behaviour at Auchinleck] To Temple, 22 May 1789 (Morgan—"on purpose to soothe"); Journ. 16 Sept. 1776 (Treesbank's cancer); Book of Company (junkets about).

Address to Prince of Wales] *Pol. Car.* pp. 157–58; Record of Ayrshire Quarter Sessions (C52—fewer than 40 J.P.s sign); List of J.P.s (C53—140 J.P.s); J. W. Derry, *The Regency Crisis and the Whigs, 1788–9*, 1963, p. 93 (pro-Prince Addresses): examples are reported in *Edin. Adv.* 13, 17 Feb., 6 Mar. 1789. From Temple, 28 May 1789 ("generally thought"); Reg. Let. S. Lonsdale, 9 May 1789 (Address would please Lonsdale).

Summons to Lowther] To Temple, 22 May 1789 (Morgan—bruised shoulder, summons to Lowther); Book of Company (no immediate danger); Journ. 18–19 May 1789.

p. 391
Remorse] To Temple, 22 May 1789 (Morgan—"no man ever had"); From Temple, 8 Mar. ("nor can I explain"), 28 May 1789 ("how could you desert").

p. 392
Margaret dies] To Temple, 4 June 1789 (summons home); Book of Company (rapid journey); To Lonsdale, 8 June 1789 (time of death); To Temple, 3 July 1789 (Morgan—"I cried bitterly"). The first two sentences of the paragraph beginning "Boswell had been in London" are mainly taken from BP, xvii. 117. Boswell read the Anglican funeral service himself because the Church of Scotland strongly disapproved of funeral rites as redolent of popery.

CHAPTER 16
p. 393
Boswell's grief] From Temple, 20 June 1789 ("pour your griefs"); To Temple, 3 July (Morgan—"what distress"), 23 Aug. 1789 (Morgan—"my grief preys").

Dispersal of the family] To Temple, 28–30 Nov. 1789 (Morgan—Boswell feels helpless). Need to separate Veronica and Euphemia: To Mrs. Buchanan, 13 July 1789; From Lady Auchinleck, 16 July 1789. To Temple, 3 July 1789 (Morgan—Edinburgh-mannered girls); To Malone, 8 July 1789 (Sandy "a very determined"); To Temple, 28–30 Nov. 1789 (Morgan—Betsy pretty, clever; overindulgence); To Veronica, 2 July 1790 (true English miss).

p. 394
Feelings of guilt] To Lady Crawford, 13 June 1789 ("it is not often"); To Lonsdale, 8 June 1789 ("alas! my Lord"); To and From Penn, 3 and 10 July 1789; From Lonsdale, 20 July 1789 ("your friend, Lonsdale").

p. 395
Ayrshire politics] *Pol. Car.* pp. 160–61; Ginter, pp. 28, 68; To Temple, 2 Aug. 1789 (Morgan—"to own the truth").

Visit to Lowther] To Temple, 23 Aug. 1789 (Morgan) contains all details except the reappearance of the wig, which occurs in To Temple, 13–14 Oct. 1789 (Morgan).

p. 396

Return to London] Reg. Let. S. Lady Auchinleck, 19 Dec. 1789 ("what remains"); To Temple, 13–14 Oct. and 28–30 Nov. 1789 (both Morgan—financial situation, excessive drinking); Reg. Let. S. Campbell, 2 Dec. 1789 (will not let Auchinleck House); Journ. 13–20 ("C"), 15 Nov. 1789 ("wretched scene").

Progress on *Life*] To Temple, 13–14 Oct. 1789 (Morgan—first thirty pages); To Forbes, 7 Nov. 1789 (Somervell—May 1790 as publication date); To Temple, 28–30 Nov. 1789 (Morgan—"what labour").

p. 397

The Boswell children] To Euphemia, 5 Apr. 1790 (NLS MS. 2,521 f. 18–19v.—Euphemia unhappy); Veronica to Sandy, 21 Nov. ("squealing like a pig," Betsy scolds her father), 19 Oct. 1789 (Sandy miserable); To Sandy, 5 ("think and act"), 23 Nov. 1789 (writing from Utrecht); To Temple, 28–30 Nov. 1789 (Morgan—lack of authority, "extraordinary boy"). "Siege of Carthage": To Margaret, 11 Feb. 1789; BP, xvii. 149 n. 1. Journ. 19 Nov. 1789 ("such a group").

p. 398

Relationship with Lonsdale] Journ. 27 (never break engagement), 14 Nov. 1789 (Lonsdale knows Boswell wants to be M.P.); To Lonsdale, 26 Oct. 1789 ("may your steady friends"); Journ. 7 (honorary freemen victory), 10 (grand dinner), 18 ("absolutely easy"), 15 (loud and contradictory), 16 ("shocking ferocity"), 3 Dec. 1789 (Penn hopes to be Ambassador). Penn's hopes were never realized.

Mood in London] Journ. 19 ("cannot distinctly describe"), 30 Jan. ("vastly well"), 2 Feb. ("SOLID discursive flow"), 12–13 (calling the hours), 9 Jan. (strange in company of ladies), 28 July 1790 (essence of politeness).

p. 399

Matrimonial schemes] Journ. 9 Jan. 1790 (sensible, good-tempered woman). Lady Mary Lindsay: To Lady Mary, 23 Sept. and 16 Dec. 1789; Reg. Let. S. Lady Crawford, 8 Feb. 1790. Isabella Wilson: Journ. 22–23 July 1788; To and From Isabella Wilson, 9 and 19 Mar. 1790. Wilhelmina Alexander (M7). Miss Lister: Journ. 17 and 21 May 1790 ("singular character"). Jane Upton: Journ. 2–3 Mar. 1791, 31 Dec. 1792. Frances Bagnall: Journ. 10 June 1790, 7 Apr. 1791 (dinner).

Boswell not abstinent] Journ. 31 Jan. 1790 (sounded for stricture). "Enchantress": Account of Composition of "Verses to Lady Mary Lindsay" (M318): in the manuscript "seducing" replaces "disreputable." This figure, who stands in contrast to the virtuous Lady Mary, may be a Mrs. Fox mentioned in the journal (2–3, 14, 18 Apr. 1790). "Lovely Susanna": Drafts and Material for *No Abolition of Slavery* (M326), where Boswell also calls her Maria. "Angel" (M195). Reg. Let. S. Lady Crawford, 15 Apr. 1790 ("of my having"): "true as the dial" comes from Samuel Butler's *Hudibras* (III. ii. 175). From Lady Crawford, 19 Dec. 1790 (displeased by tone); Reg. Let. S. Temple, 13 Apr. 1790 ("Rousseaulike confession"); From Temple, 17 Apr. ("in love at fifty"), 13 Feb. 1790 ("the more you talk").

p. 400

Decision against Fergusson] *Whitehall Evening Post*, 2 Feb. 1790 (P118:2—terms of decision); To Robert Boswell, 1790–91 (several—on extracting money).

Ayrshire hopes] Abolition of nominal and fictitious votes: Journ. 19 Apr. 1790; *Pol. Car.* pp. 5–6. To Robert Boswell, 3 Apr. 1790 ("I shall make").

Queensberry] *Pol. Car.* pp. 164–65; To Queensberry, 9 Mar. 1790 ("silence . . . obloquy"). "Nasty old son": a Lady Hamilton, cited in Robert Burns, *Poems and Songs*, ed. James Kinsley, 1968, iii. 1344. Queensberry controlled seats for Dumfriesshire and Peeblesshire, and had a strong interest in the Dumfries burghs.

p. 401
Hastings] To Hastings, 27 Feb. 1790 ("enjoying the conversation"); Journ. 1 Mar. 1790 ("I view you").   Thurlow was one of Hastings's most vigorous supporters.

French Revolution] To Temple, 28–30 Nov. 1789 (Morgan—"intellectual earthquake"); Journ. 23 Jan. ("Irishly savage"), 2 Feb. 1790 ("really unpleasant").

"Death of Favras"] *Pol. Car.* pp. 174–75; Favras (M84:1—"has his head full"); *Pub. Adv.* 20 Mar. 1790 ("Death of Favras").   The starring role was to be designed for Kemble (M84:2).

p. 402
Paoli] BP, xviii. 29–30 (farewell dinner); From Temple, 27 Nov. 1788 ("uniformly and invariably good").   Foladare explains Paoli's attitude towards the Revolution (pp. 153–59).

Progress on the *Life*] Waingrow, pp. lxvii–lxviii; From Hailes, 24 Jan. 1790; From Percy, 19 Mar. 1790; To Percy, 9 Apr. 1790 (Berg); From Percy, 24 Apr. 1790.   Robinson's offer: To Langton, 9 Apr. 1790 ("a cool thousand"); Journ. 20 Feb. 1791 provides Robinson's name.

New schemes] Journ. 11 Apr. 1790 (history of Carlisle); From Temple, 24 Apr. 1790 ("what spirits").

Boswell's high spirits] From Courtenay [?between 26 and 29 May 1790] ("for God's sake"): this letter may belong to a later date.   Journ. 2 Apr. 1790 ("false spirits"); To Euphemia, 5 Apr. 1790 (NLS MS. 2,521 f. 18–19v.—"I was once").

p. 403
Burke] Journ. 23 Jan. 1790 ("you were not always").   As Foladare comments, Boswell, like the rest of us, did not so much reconcile contradictions as learn to live with them (p. 88). In his journal (2 Feb. 1790), Boswell records Burke as saying that he acted from circumstances, not principles: "*ex facto jus oritur*" (the law arises from facts)—an illuminating remark in relation to modern argument about the bases of Burke's political thought.

Attendance on Lonsdale] Quotations: Journ. 4, 10, 11 Apr. 1790.   The "dogs" may have been George Saul and Thomas Denton (Journ. 16 May 1790).   From Temple, 24 Apr. 1790 ("I do not like").

Temple and Lonsdale] Journ. 14 (Temple arrives), 15–17 May 1790 (weekend with Lonsdale).   Lonsdale's opinion about Reynolds may have been shared by others, because of the miscellaneous nature of his guests. But Boswell must have strongly resented the implied comparison between the tables where he most and least enjoyed dining.

Separate lodgings] From Temple, 24 Apr. and 10 May 1790; Journ. 14 May 1790 (Boswell insists).

p. 404
Reactions to Veronica] The extracts from Nancy's letters are printed in Bettany, pp. 70–71.   Her first letter can be dated from Boswell's journal as a little after 17 May 1790 (Veronica "is really vulgar"); she dates the second herself, 6 June 1790 ("you cannot conceive"); and the third ("I am vexed") seems to be dated sometime before 19 June 1790, on the basis of Temple's letter to Boswell of that date.   Veronica to Sandy, 18 June 1790 (sightseeing); other sights are mentioned in Boswell's and Temple's journals for the period.   Journ. 12 June (Veronica sensible and cheerful), 23 May 1790 (behaves well in company); From Temple, 19 June 1790 ("very good"), 7 July 1790 and 21 Mar. 1791 (conveys Nancy's love).

Boswell's spirits collapse] Journ. 29 May 1790 ("awaked sadly dejected");   Namier and Brooke, i. 110 (Westminster and Eton).

p. 405
Manic-depressive] The discussion here merely supplements that in *Earlier Years*, p. 134. When asked once at a lecture if he thought Boswell was a manic-depressive, F. A. Pottle

replied, "No, I can always tell when he is going to get depressed." Anyone who immerses himself in Boswell's journal acquires, I think, somewhat the same attitude, though the precise signals may be hard to specify. *Boswelliana*, p. 283 (spirits too high or too low): this remark is dated Feb. 1777. To Temple, 2–6 Apr. 1791 (Morgan—fluttering fancy).

Financial crisis] Journ. 20–21 May 1790; To Robert Boswell, 28 June 1790.

Jamie] Journ. 8 June (burgundy), 13 June and 5 July 1790 (morals). The vices Boswell feared were drinking, gambling, and eventually, whoring.

"Scarcely articulate"] Journ. 14 June 1790.

Temple in London] Quotations in Bettany, pp. 73–82. Journ. 14 (friendly and soothing), 15 June 1790 ("my dear friend"). Temple later forgot his irritation and wrote to Boswell of "the happy days we passed with you in St. Anne's [*sic*] St." (From Temple, 9 July 1792). He was to react very much the same way during a visit to Nicholls in Suffolk in 1795 (Bettany, pp. 128–46).

p. 406
Quarrel with Lonsdale] Quotations in Journ. 14–19 June 1790. Namier and Brooke, iii. 59 (Lonsdale initiates Parliamentary careers); To Penn, 26 June 1790 ("an ambitious hope").

p. 409
Boswell at Carlisle] To Temple, 21 July 1790 (Morgan—irksome captivity); Ferguson, p. 198 (Red-nosed Jerry); To Malone, 30 June 1790 ("such as might make," listless); To Veronica, 2 July 1790 ("think what"); Journ. 25 (good-humoured and obliging), 27 (devoured by hypochondria, inadequacies as parent), 24 June (rational, steady father), 5 July 1790 ("eager, vain stretchings").

p. 410
Correspondence with Temple] From Temple, 19 June 1790 ("I have nothing"); To Temple, 21 June 1790 (Morgan—"as to making"). No sooner had poor Temple got home than he felt wretched there too: Bettany, p. 83; From Temple, 7 July 1790.

Venereal disease] Journ. 5 July 1790 ("diseased mind"); To Malone, 30 June 1790 ("I am again unfortunate"); Journ. 29 June (walks with difficulty), 4–5 July (operates on sore), 28 June 1790 (quotes Ecclesiastes). For suggestions about Boswell's venereal career, see W. B. Ober, "*Boswell's Clap" and Other Essays*, 1979.

"What sunk me"] Journ. 7 July 1790.

Appeal for release] To Penn, 26 June 1790; Journ. 3 July 1790 ("most *cruel* man").

p. 411
Remainder of stay in Carlisle] Journ. 7 July 1790 ("would not be believed"). Attack on "Mushroom Hall": Journ. 10 July 1790; Smith, "Mushroom Elections," p. 117. To Veronica, 9 July 1790 ("gives me real concern"); To Robert Boswell, 24 June 1790 (resignation); Journ. 14 July 1790 ("again attacked me"); To Temple, 21 July 1790 (Morgan—"the Northern Tyrant").

p. 412
Boswell and Mountstuart] To Rousseau, 3 Oct. 1765 (original in French, trans. Frank Brady and Frederick A. Pottle).

Final reaction to Lonsdale] To Temple, 21 June 1790 (Morgan—"I deserve all"); To Forbes, 2–3 July 1790 (Somervell—"I always said"); Ehrman, p. 26 (Lonsdale's arrangement with Pitt); To Margaret, 28 Jan. 1789 ("Fortune, I trust"); Journ. 13 Aug. 1790 ("both L. and I").

Dempster's gloss on the break must have been delightful consolation: "It is in vain you assign the selfish and wise reason that nothing was to be expected from such a patron. . . .

Your real motive was, I am confident, some Whiggish independent spirit of peccant humour, hereditary, I own, and therefore the more excusable but also the more dangerous. Our edition of the story was that his Lordship intended bringing you into Parliament, that Lord Loughborough had got the Prince [of Wales] to ask the seat for Anstruther, and although it was obvious this favour, when so asked, could not be refused, yet you had taken pet and, as Aphra says in the play, 'dissolved the connection' " (From Dempster, 8 May 1791).

p. 413
Work on the *Life*] Journ. 8 June 1790 (Cornhill); To Forbes, 2–3 July (Somervell—"how tedious"), 11 Oct. 1790 (Somervell—"rich and various treasure"); Journ. 19 July (Malone's help), 8 Sept. 1790 (two volumes); From Temple, 8 Sept. 1790 ("a long book"); Journ. 10 Sept. 1790 (reproaches himself); From Langton, 2 Oct. 1790 (Malone delays departure); Fifer, p. 310 n. 11 (Malone leaves).

p. 414
Life in London] To Robert Boswell, 28 June 1790 ("*must* raise myself"); Journ. 21 June ("something fortunate"), 21 Aug. (drifts), 30 July 1790 (Piccadilly); To Robert Boswell, 28 Sept. 1790 ("this immense metropolis"); Journ. 19 (Old Burlington St.), 10 ("heat of the weather"), 7 (foolish), 11 and 12 Aug. 1790 (absurd), 22 Mar. 1768 ("sallied forth").

p. 415
Knockroon] To Sandy, 2 June 1790 ("ancient Family"); Journ. 13 Feb. 1794 (pretty little property, would do for Jamie); To Malone, 29 Jan. 1791 (Hyde—"ancient appanage"); To Sandy, 15 Oct. 1790 (MS. Arthur A. Houghton—bread and water); To Robert Boswell, 28 Sept. 1790 ("were I to have"); To Campbell, 16 Sept. 1790 (highest fair offer); To Malone, 29 Jan. 1791 (Hyde—price); To Lady Auchinleck, 4 June 1791 (exorbitant); To Robert Boswell, 15 Oct. 1790 (Fairlie lends money).   The negotiations for the purchase of Knockroon were more complicated than indicated here, but details will have to wait for volumes in the research edition.

Financial difficulties] BP, xviii. 100 (repaying Bruce Boswell's loan); Journ. 18 Mar. 1791 (selling copyright), 24 Nov. 1792 (Dilly and Baldwin lend money).

Boswell's social talents] Journ. 10 Sept. 1790 ("continual openings"); Farington, "Memoirs of Reynolds," i. cciii; Journ. 27 Feb. 1791 (Warren's remark); To Forbes, 11 Oct. 1790 (Somervell—dining with Reynolds); *Pub. Adv.* 9 Nov. 1790 ("two inseparable companions"). *General Eve. Post*, 1 Apr. 1790 (Humane Society dinner).

p. 416
Grocer of London] Accounts of the banquet appeared in various newspapers, e.g. *Pub. Adv.* 11 Nov. 1790.   The broadside is reproduced in BP, xviii. opp. p. 96.   *World*, 25 Nov. 1790 ("wasps of Opposition"), as quoted in [William Gifford] *The Baviad*, 1791, p. 3 n.

p. 417
Opening in Ayrshire] To Dundas, 16 Nov. 1790 (Hyde—"I assure you"), [?21–23 Nov. 1790] (NLS, Melville MS. 16, ff. 3–4—"as to your compliment").   "Tinged with convivial purple": Sir N. W. Wraxall, *Historical Memoirs of His Own Time*, 1836, ii. 221.

p. 418
Fanny Burney's account] *Diaries and Letters of Madame d'Arblay*, ed. Charlotte Barrett and Austin Dobson, 1904–05, iv. 432–33.

p. 419
Depression] To Sandy, 31 Jan. 1791 ("worse than I"); To Temple, 7 Feb. 1791 ("perpetually gnawed"); To Malone, 10 and 25 Feb. 1791 (both Hyde—asks for loan); From Malone, 24 Feb. 1791 (cannot lend money); To Malone, 10 Feb. (Hyde—80 pages, "concise though solemn," "strangely ill"), 29 Jan. ("indeed I go sluggishly"), 12 Mar. 1791 ("in this great metropolis").   On 25 Feb. 1791, Boswell wrote to Malone that he had not seen Reynolds for

a fortnight (Hyde).   Journ. 21–25 Feb. 1791 (Courtenay's repeated efforts); Courtenay to Malone, 22 Feb. 1791 (Osborn—"poor Boswell").   Boswell describes Seward's entertainment as "a pretty, little cold *souper*," which provided "a slight respite" (Journ. 17 Feb. 1791). From Malone, 5 Mar. 1791 ("without being"); From Temple, 21 Mar. 1791 ("makes my heart bleed").

p. 420
Boswell starts to recover] Journ. 1 Mar. 1791 ("distinctly pointed out"); To Malone, 4 Dec. 1790 (Hyde—promise to Courtenay); Journ. 27 Feb. 1791 (Warren's advice); To Malone, 8 Mar. 1791 (Hyde—Humane Society dinner). Journ. 15 May 1783 (*"vives secousses"*).

p. 421
No Abolition of Slavery] *Lit. Car.* pp. 144–48; Drafts and Material for *No Abolition* (M326). Journ. 15 Nov. 1762 (genius for poetry).   Quotations: ll. 187–88 ("From wise subordination's"), 249–50 ("of food, clothes"—italics added), 276 ("beauteous tyrant"), 282 ("between the decks"), 284 ("blessings"), 167 ("ancient Baron"), 172 ("Royal image").   Though Boswell's anonymity was easily penetrated, by convention he could deny authorship if challenged.

p. 422
Publication of *Life*] Waingrow, p. lxxv.

CHAPTER 17
p. 423
Studies of the *Life of Johnson*] This chapter draws in particular on the following: Thomas Carlyle, "Biography" and "Boswell's *Life of Johnson*," *Critical and Miscellaneous Essays*, 1869 (both originally 1832); Geoffrey Scott, *The Making of the "Life of Johnson*," BP, vi, 1929; F. A. Pottle's many essays on Boswell, especially "Art and Authenticity"; Joseph W. Reed, *English Biography in the Early Nineteenth Century, 1801–1838*, 1966; R. W. Rader, "Literary Form in Factual Narrative: The Example of Boswell's *Johnson*" in *Essays in Eighteenth-Century Biography*, ed. P. B. Daghlian, 1968; and Waingrow.   There are good brief comments in Harold Nicolson, *The Development of English Biography*, 1928.   In *The Boswellian Hero*, 1979, William C. Dowling develops a fresh view of Boswell as writer.   Other studies dealing with specific points are mentioned later in this chapter.   In a number of places it is necessary to repeat arguments and quotations used earlier in order to construct a coherent discussion.

"Delight and boast"] G. B. Hill's comment (*Life*, i. xli).

p. 424
"Memorial" and "imaginative" modes] A third category, "rational" modes (those based on reasoning), like the essay or treatise, fills out the typology.   This discussion is expanded in my *"Boswell's London Journal*: The Question of Memorial and Imaginative Modes," in *Literature and Society* (The Lawrence Henry Gipson Symposium, 1978), ed. Jan Fergus, 1981.

Johnson on biography] Johnson, "Milton" (para. 39), *Lives*, i. 100 ("we are perpetually moralists"); *Life*, v. 79 (21 Aug. 1773—"I esteem biography").

Xenophon's *Memorabilia*] Even if the *Memorabilia* are largely fictitious (see Arnaldo Momigliano, *The Development of Greek Biography*, 1971, p. 54).

p. 425
Gibbon] Arnaldo Momigliano, "Gibbon's Contribution to Historical Method," *Studies in Historiography*, 1966.

"A thousand . . . old women"] *Life*, iii. 172 (19 Sept. 1777).

Life as covert attack on Johnson] I may perhaps be forgiven for not having noted where this bizarrerie occurs.

p. 426

Fullness and exactness] *Life*, i. 30 (introductory remarks—"I will venture to say"); BP, vi. 16, based on Journ. 7 Apr. 1775 ("Boswell has an image"); *Life* MS. p. 446 (27 Mar. 1775—"I must be exact"); *Life*, iii. 191 (22 Sept. 1777—"Flemish picture").

p. 427

"In scenes"] Journ. 12 Oct. 1780. No doubt this decision accorded with Boswell's habit of perceiving his own life, in part, as a series of scenes (see Scott, BP, vi. 161; Reed, p. 134). This was an eighteenth-century commonplace.

Mode of presentation] *Life*, i. 29 (introductory remarks—"I have resolved"); To Temple, 24–25 Feb. 1788 (Morgan—"show us the *man*").

p. 428

Legal opinions] Johnson's legal opinions are an acquired taste, but they show his strength as a systematic reasoner in contrast to his talent as a debater in the short flights of conversation.

Memorable opinions] *Life*, ii. 231 (27 Apr. 1773—Garrick's), 66 (end of 1768—Goldsmith's), iii. 7 (3 Apr. 1776—Dr. Boswell's).

Note-taking] For Boswell's early account of note-taking, see Journ. 25 Oct. 1764, and F. A. Pottle's comment (*Grand Tour I*, p. 156 n. 3).

p. 429

Expansion of "Lit[erary] Prop[er]ty"] Notes, 9 May 1773; *Life*, ii. 259 (8—in mistake for 9—May 1773).

Boswell's recording] *Life*, iii. 294 (15 Apr. 1778—"standing upon the hearth"): the example comes from Collins, p. 36. Journ. 4 Nov. 1762 ("I have remembered"); *Life*, i. 421 (1 July 1763—"*strongly impregnated*"), ii. 326 n. 2 (Boswell's ability as a mimic). This discussion closely follows that in Pottle, "Art and Authenticity."

p. 430

"Great sand-drift"] Scott, BP, vi. 163.

Boswell and truth] Journ. 8 Jan. 1780 (father beat him), 1 Apr. 1781 ("carelessness as to the exactness"); *Boswelliana* MS. p. 207 ("one must clear head"). Boswell claimed that in writing the *Life* he almost never trusted to memory in cases of ascertainable fact (To Maclaurin, 22 Aug. 1791).

Johnson's pension] To Temple, 5 Mar. 1789 (Morgan—Johnson taught to cross-examine); *Life*, i. 373–74 (after 20 July 1762—"*Lord Bute* told me"): this example is taken from George Mallory, *Boswell the Biographer*, 1912, pp. 248–49, where italics were added. Some slight errors in Mallory's quotation are silently corrected. Boswell's anxiety about accuracy extended even into the final stage of revision (see examples given in R. W. Chapman, "Boswell's Revises of the *Life of Johnson*" in D. N. Smith *et al.*, *Johnson and Boswell Revised*, 1928, pp. 30–32).

Malone's share in *Life*] Boswell himself says that Malone helped with the proofs of "not more than one half" of the *Life* (Advertisement to the first edition). The figure seems closer to five-eighths, based on the chronology in Waingrow; To Hawkesbury, 1 Nov. 1790; To Malone, 4 Dec. 1790 (Hyde); and an examination of the revises. To Forbes, 2–3 July 1790 (Somervell—Malone taught him to go over a manuscript); From Malone, 23 Dec. 1790 ("pray take care"); To Malone, 18 Jan. 1791 (Hyde—visible difference in revision). It is easy to measure the gap between Boswell's genius and Malone's modest talent for biography by reading Malone's "Some Account of Sir Joshua Reynolds" in his edition of Reynolds's literary works, 2nd ed. 1798, a piece of clear, colourless scholarly prose, adequate but uninspired, and pulled out of shape by a footnote running under the text for eight pages, which labours a comparison between Reynolds and Laelius, a model of the cultivated Roman.

p. 431
Shaping of the Life] Waingrow, pp. xxviii ("every conceivable mode"), xliv ("*perfect* authenticity"); Pottle, "Art and Authenticity," p. 72 ("massively detailed conception"); Shaw, "Epistle Dedicatory," *Man and Superman*.

p. 432
Mechanical organization] See F. A. Pottle, "The Adequacy as Biography of Boswell's *Life of Johnson*," *Transactions* of the Johnson Society of Lichfield, 1974, p. 13.

" 'Live o'er each scene' "] *Life*, i. 30 (introductory remarks): Boswell is quoting Pope's *Prologue* to Addison's *Cato*, l. 4.

Lack of narrative urgency] See Pottle, "Adequacy as Biography," p. 9.

Reactions to the Life] Cumberland, ii. 228; Scott, "Samuel Johnson," *Miscellaneous Prose Works* [ed. J. G. Lockhart] 1834–36, iii. 261; Mallory, p. 145.

"Exuberant variety"] *Life*, i. 421 (5 July 1763).

Thematic repetition] The complications of the material also generate that interplay of patterns—theory vs. practice, past vs. present, expectation vs. experience, etc.—to be anticipated in any complex work.

Mitre] *Life*, iii. 341 (8 May 1778). Also, later, From Johnson, 14 Mar. 1781: "We will go again to the Mitre and talk old times over" (*Life*, iv. 71).

p. 433
Time and setting] *Life*, ii. 99 (26 Oct. 1769—"a pretty large circle"). On time, space, and aesthetic distance in the *Life*, see two thoughtful articles by P. K. Alkon, "Boswell's Control of Aesthetic Distance," *University of Toronto Quarterly*, 38 (1969); and "Boswellian Time," *Studies in Burke and His Time*, 14 (1973). Reed, p. 138 (props).

The boy is the man] *Life*, i. 47 (1719–25).

Johnson's characteristics] *Life*, i. 47 (1719–25—intellectual superiority), 213 (after 25 Sept. 1750—"astonishing force"), iii. 309 (17 Apr. 1778—"supereminent powers"), i. 39 (1712—"jealous independence"), 48 (1719–25—"dismal inertness"), 63 (beginning of 1729—"morbid melancholy"), iii. 401 (10 Oct. 1779—"vibration"). On Johnson's intellectual superiority, see Waingrow, pp. xlv–l.

Contradictions] Boswell makes this commonplace explicit in his final character sketch of Johnson (*Life*, iv. 426).

Johnson's failings] *Life*, iv. 325 (before 22 June 1784—"peculiarities and frailties"); Piozzi, *Anecdotes* in *John. Misc*. i. 313 ("blinking Sam"); *Life*, ii. 247 (7 May 1773—"a whore").

p. 434
Presentation] *Life*, ii. 111 (10 Nov. 1769—"full, fair, and distinct view"), 5 (beginning of 1766—"authentic precision").

Further characteristics] *Life*, v. 20 (introductory remarks—"oiliness and a gloss"), i. 286 (8 Apr. 1755—"politeness and urbanity"), iv. 170 (22 Mar. 1783—"fretfulness of his disease"); Waingrow, p. xlviii; Thomson, *Winter* (version of 1746), l. 674 ("vivid energy of sense"); Journ. 25 Apr. 1778 (Percy's remark).

p. 435
Boswell's image of Johnson] *Life*, iii. 80 (16 May 1776—"great and good man"), iv. 321 (June 1784—generous humanity).

Other Johnsonian incidents and traits] *Life*, iv. 284 (3 June 1784—roast mutton), ii. 465 (23 Mar. 1776—"if we may believe"), iii. 400 (4 Oct. 1779—"he sent for me"), 216 (24 Jan. 1778—"eager and unceasing curiosity"), iv. 36 n. 4 (beginning of 1781—"every fragment"), 191 (22 Sept. 1777—large dead cat).

p. 436
Johnson's conversation] *Life*, iii. 355 (16 May 1778—large treasure), i. 31 (introductory remarks—"peculiar value"), ii. 241–42 (30 Apr. 1773—main business), iv. 179 (after Mar. 1783—a man's intellectual ability), iii. 260 (10 Apr. 1778—"teemed with point"), iv. 112 (May 1781—"unexampled richness"), Dedication ("literary Colossus").

p. 437
Mind preying on itself] Reynolds pointed out that Johnson tried to escape from his own thoughts (*Life*, i. 144–45—end of 1739). *Life*, i. 72 (end of 1729—mind preying on itself). Murphy commented, "Indolence was the time of danger; it was then that his spirits, not employed abroad, turned with inward hostility against himself" (*John. Misc.* i. 409). Johnson himself wrote that "the greater part" of mankind, left to their own devices, "would prey upon the quiet of each other or, in the want of other objects, would prey upon themselves" (Johnson to George Staunton, 1 June 1762—*Life*, i. 367). *Life*, i. 250 (end of 1752—"you, you dogs"); Piozzi, *Anecdotes* in *John. Misc.* i. 234 (Johnson's fear of madness).

Black expressions] Johnson to Mme de Boufflers, 16 July 1771 (*Life*, ii. 405—"je ne cherche rien"); Johnson to Thomas Warton, 21 Dec. 1754 (*Life*, i. 277—"a solitary wanderer"); *Life*, i. 483 (spring 1764—"a limb amputated"), iii. 99 (beginning of 1777—"terror and anxiety"), ii. 190 (18 Apr. 1772—"private register"), 339 (5 Apr. 1775—courage the greatest virtue). Boswell omitted, however, in the *Life* "a striking anecdote" of Beattie's about Johnson's melancholy: Beattie "mentioned to Dr. Johnson his being troubled at times with shocking impious thoughts, of which he could not get rid. 'Sir,' said Dr. Johnson, 'if I was to divide my life in three parts, two of them have been filled with such thoughts' " (Journ. 12 Aug. 1782).

Johnson as teacher] *Life*, i. 201 (beginning of 1750—"majestic teacher"), iv. 65 (1781, before From Hastings, 2 Dec. 1790—"entrusted with a certain portion"), 155 (From Johnson, 7 Sept. 1782—"boundless importance"), ii. 10 (before 15 Feb. 1766—our first duty), 13 (15 Feb. 1766—subordination as favourite topic), 328–29 (28 Mar. 1775—"fair and comfortable order"). The last phrase is Boswell's generalization from Johnson's argument against unequal marriages.

p. 438
Johnson the moralist] Johnson to Baretti, 10 June 1761 (*Life*, i. 365—"supported with impatience"); *Life*, iii. 53 (beginning of May 1776—"progress from want to want"), 58 (middle of May 1776—"every man is to take"), ii. 110 (10 Nov. 1769—"do not expect more"), 475 (26 Mar. 1776—observations "deep and sure"), iv. 428 (end of 1784—"attentive and minute survey"), 50 (1781, on "Life of Pope"—"conversation perhaps more admirable"). Years earlier Boswell had asserted that many people thought Johnson's conversation excelled his writings ("On the Profession of a Player," *Lond. Mag.* 39, 1770, 469). Burke also thought Johnson "showed more powers of mind in company than in his writings" (*Life*, iv. 316 n. 1). *Life*, iv. 300–03 (12 June 1784—existence far more miserable than happy), 221 (15 May 1783—"clear your *mind* of cant").

p. 439
Johnson's last days] *Life*, ii. 297 (after 7 Feb. 1775—"the venerable sage"); From Johnson, 24 Dec. 1783 (*Life*, iv. 249—sickness and solitude); Johnson to Reynolds, 19 Aug. 1784 (*Life*, iv. 366—mortality's frown); Pottle, "Adequacy as Biography," p. 17 ("fallen lip"); *Life*, iv. 374 (Nov. 1784—"a new acquaintance," "animated and lofty"), 415 (Dec. 1784—refuses opiates).

Light and shade] *Life*, i. 30 (introductory remarks).

Boswell as author] *Life*, i. 328 (after 8 Mar. 1758—"I love to exhibit sketches"). "Easy and delighted comprehension": "The Life of Boswell," *Yale Review*, 35 (1945). 456. Journ. 16 Sept. 1769 ("how small a speck"). Ruskin's comment: *Praeterita*, ed. Kenneth Clark, 1949, p. 211. *Life*, ii. 82–83 (16 Oct. 1769—"Garrick played round").

p. 441

Hugh Blair] *Lectures on Rhetoric and Belles Lettres*, ed. H. F. Harding, 1965, i. 391. Boswell may actually have absorbed this lesson from Adam Smith's lectures (see my "Boswell's Self-Presentation and His Critics," *Studies in English Literature*, 12, 1972, 553–54).

p. 442

Boswell the character] Insatiably curious: e.g. Journ. 8 May 1783; *Life*, iv. 380 (Nov. 1784—"peculiar plan"), v. 211 (14 Sept. 1773—"there is something noble"). No sense of shame: e.g. Journ. 31 Jan. 1784. Geoffrey Scott instances a couple of cases where Boswell suppressed mention of his weaknesses (BP, vi. 192). Great authors: I have repeated F. A. Pottle's point (*Earlier Years*, pp. 366–67), because of its importance.

Boswell's vision] To Temple, 13 Feb. 1790 (Morgan—"surely have the art"). "That rare faculty": *Early History of Charles James Fox*, 1880, p. 154 n. 1. Proust's insight: *À la recherche du temps perdu*, Pléiade ed. 1954, iii. 895. *Life*, iv. 97 (20 Apr. 1781—"whispered to Mrs. Boscawen"). Realization vs. invention: see F. A. Pottle, ed., *Boswell's London Journal, 1762–1763*, 1950, pp. 13–14. Carlyle, *Critical and Miscellaneous Essays*, iv. 18 ("open loving heart"). "Visionary of the real": "Images of Samuel Johnson," *ELH*, 41 (1974). 359. *Life* (Advertisement to the second edition—Johnsonized the land); Charles Lamb, "Grace before Meat," *Essays of Elia* ("author of *The Rambler*"); Carlyle, iv. 39 ("best possible resemblance").

p. 445

Reception of the *Life*] "Memoirs" in *Lit. Car.* p. xliv ("received by the world"); Daily Sales of the First Edition of the *Life* (A60—888 copies sold): Boswell's arithmetic, however, is uncertain. Parodies: some are listed in *New CBEL*, ii. 1237–38; P101 collects a number of them. *Critical Review*, II. iii (July 1791). 268 ("brutal severity," "insensibility"), 258 ("affected self-importance"). Johnson's weaknesses: e.g. Fanny Burney to Mrs. Phillips, June 1792 (*Journals of Fanny Burney*, ed. Joyce Hemlow *et al.*, 1972–82, i. 181–82). *Life*, i. 30 (introductory remarks—writing life not panegyric) and n. 4 ("begged he would mitigate"). Dr. Burney to Malone, 10 Oct. 1798: Roger Lonsdale, *Dr. Charles Burney*, 1965, p. 359 ("he was equally careless").

Percy's reaction] Fifer, pp. lxxxvi–lxxxvii. For the Pennantian controversy, see above, p. 173. *Life*, ii. 455 (21 Mar. 1776—Hanover rat). That Percy continued implacable appears from the notes he wrote about Boswell in 1805, which were printed in Robert Anderson's *Life of Johnson*, 3rd ed. 1815.

p. 446

Hurd] Francis Kilvert, *Memoirs of Richard Hurd*, 1860, p. 254 ("a striking likeness"); *Life*, iv. 47 n. 2 (1781, on the "Life of Pope"—when "well-advanced in life"). Elsewhere Boswell described Hurd as "a learned and polite prelate" (*Life*, iv. 290 n. 4—10 June 1784).

Wilkes] To Wilkes, 25 June 1791 (British Library—"a wonderful book"); John Wilkes, *Letters to His Daughter*, 1804, iv. 5 ("earth is as thirsty"): Wilkes's letter is dated there 1 June 1789, but his reference to two quarto volumes shows that the *Life* is meant. *Life*, iv. 107 n. 2 (8 May 1781—lion and goat); From Wilkes, 1 Oct. 1785 (objections to the *Hebrides*).

Criticism of Johnson and Boswell] *Private Correspondence of David Garrick* [ed. James Boaden] 1831–32, ii. 68 (John Hoadly to Garrick, 25 July 1775—"puffy pensioner"); Werkmeister, p. 89, citing a letter by "Quante," in *Morn. Post*, 1 Aug. 1786 ("insolent bigotry"); *Life*, iv. 314 n. 3 ("with a lumber of learning"); Nicholls to Temple, 21 July 1791 (Beinecke—"I have run through").

Goldsmith] James Prior, *Life of Oliver Goldsmith*, 1837, i. 444–46 (criticism of Boswell's depiction); *Portraits by Sir Joshua Reynolds*, ed. F. W. Hilles, 1952, p. 48 ("sing, stand upon his head"). The most recent study of Boswell's treatment of Goldsmith finds it accurate and fair (Lee Morgan, "Boswell's Portrait of Goldsmith," in *Studies in Honor of John C. Hodges and Alwin Thaler*, 1961).

p. 447
Boswell's criticism of others] Of those attacked, Hawkins had died in 1789. Mrs. Piozzi, who lived until 1821, confined her response to marginalia, which have been reproduced in E. G. Fletcher's edition of the *Life*, 1938. To give Mrs. Piozzi a hearing, she says of a remark Boswell credited to Baretti: "Baretti excelled in a malicious lie: he beat Boswell himself in *courage* of coining untruths; I know not whether his *skill* was superior" (Fletcher, ii. 324 n.). What appears to be Gibbon's only response is oblique: "I have always condemned the practice of transforming a private memorial into a vehicle of satire and praise" (*Autobiographies*, ed. John Murray, 1896, p. 307 n. 28). Boswell is conspicuously absent from Gibbon's list of outstanding members of The Club (ibid. p. 307 n. 27).

Gentleman's Magazine] 61 (May 1791). 466 ("received by the public"). That Nichols was the reviewer is a guess, but as editor of the *Gentleman's Magazine* it seems unlikely he would have permitted anyone else to review the *Life*, since he was proud of his acquaintance both with Johnson and Boswell.

Griffiths] *Monthly Review*, II. vii (Jan. 1792). 5 ("astonished at Mr. B.'s"), viii (May 1792). 72 ("in his mind's undress"), vii (Jan. 1792). 4 ("give us *all*").

English Review] 18 (July 1791). 1 ("airy garrulity").

Serious readers] Among the sermons, political tracts, and travel books the *Monthly Review* focused on, it gave most attention at the time to de Fleurieu's *Discoveries of the French in 1768 and 1769 to the South-East of New Guinea*. The *Critical Review* devoted considerable space to travel books, but also featured Necker's *Historical Review of His Administration* and Robertson's *Historical Disquisition Concerning India*. All the reviews of the other still-remembered book of the year, Paine's *Rights of Man*, were hostile.

Life lacked dignity] See Scott, BP, vi. 17.

Other estimates of the *Life*] *Works of the British Poets*, ed. Robert Anderson, 1795, xi. 780 ("with some venial exceptions"); *Gent. Mag.* 65 (June 1795). 472 (Malone's letter); James Northcote, *Memoirs of Sir Joshua Reynolds*, 1813, p. 183 ("very few books"); Macaulay, "Boswell's Life of Johnson," *Critical and Miscellaneous Essays*, 1841–43, ii. 26 ("Eclipse is first"): Eclipse was a famous racehorse. BP, xviii. 339–41 (Sandy's and Jamie's verses): "adveniit" is an impossible form. To Burke, 16 July 1791 ("Mr. Burke told me").

p. 449
Errors] Most of Boswell's errors came from trusting second-hand reports. The most important, his statement that Johnson spent three years at Oxford instead of the actual one (*Life*, i. 78—1731), was based on Adams's apparently authoritative information (From Adams, 17 Feb. 1785; see Waingrow, p. 57, n. 11-11). Boswell anticipated his critics: "I shall not be surprised if omissions or mistakes be pointed out with invidious severity" (*Life*, Advertisement to the first edition). The minuteness of the points on which modern scholars triumph over Boswell's accuracy testifies to the general unassailability of his account.

Johnson the conversationalist] *Life*, i. 10 n. 1 (Burke's comment); Journ. 17 Jan. 1776 (food of his soul). A recent comment by the historian A. J. P. Taylor illustrates the persistence with which the ordinary reader has continued to value Johnson the person more than Johnson the writer. In rating Johnson as the greatest of Englishmen, Taylor says, "Many qualities can be educed to justify this assertion. Johnson composed the first great dictionary of the English language. *Lives of the Poets* is a model of biographies on a small scale and I wish I had the gifts to write something comparable. These writings, though admirable, are irrelevant to his greatness. This was based on his character, on what he did and on what he said. Johnson was profound. He was moral. Above all, he was human. Indeed he carried English human nature to the highest point of which we have knowledge" (quoted in *Johnsonian News Letter*, Dec. 1982, p. 3). This view of Johnson, of course, derives primarily from Boswell's depiction of him.

Boswell as commentator] *Life*, iv. 284–85 (3 June 1784—"bore the journey"). For the complaint, see Donald Greene, "The Uses of Autobiography in the Eighteenth Century," in *Essays in Eighteenth-Century Biography*, ed. P. B. Daghlian, 1968, p. 45. It will sufficiently discredit such uninformed conjecture to recall that Johnson said Boswell was "the best travelling companion in the world" (Journ. 15 Apr. 1778) and remarked to Taylor about Boswell a week after this Oxford jaunt, "I love to travel with him" (above, p. 258).

Contemporary testimony to the *Life*'s accuracy] Adams: *Life*, Advertisement to the first edition. Malone's testimony is, of course, implicit in the help he gave Boswell; and his comments on the inaccuracies of Hawkins and Mrs. Piozzi are harsher than Boswell's own: e.g. *Life*, i. 481 n. 3. Reynolds: *R. B. Adam Library*, 1929, iii. 23, as corrected ("every word in it"); and see *Life*, Dedication.

Damage to credibility] See Ian Jack, "Two Biographers: Lockhart and Boswell" in *Johnson, Boswell, and Their Circle*, 1965, pp. 283–85.

Boswell's acquaintance with Johnson] 425 days: this is the rough estimate of P. A. W. Collins, "Boswell's Contact with Johnson," *Notes and Queries*, 201 (1956). 164. Mrs. Thrale herself admitted that Boswell "really knows ten times more anecdotes of [Johnson's] life than I do who see so much more of him" (*Thraliana*, i. 195—Dec. 1777). Journ. 13 Feb. 1766 (hugged to Johnson like a sack).

CHAPTER 18

p. 451

Percy's letter] Percy to the Rev. Thomas Stedman, 22 May 1798, quoted here from the draft as given in Fifer, pp. lxxxvi–lxxxvii; a shorter version of the letter as sent is quoted in A. C. C. Gaussen, *Percy: Prelate and Poet*, 1908, p. 217. Fifer, p. lxxxvii ("it is to be feared").

"Memoirs"] As printed in *Lit. Car.* Quotations: pp. xxix n. 1 ("certain peculiarity"), xxxi ("almost enthusiastic notion"), xxxvii–xxxviii ("from their earliest years"), xxxviii ("excellent judgement"), xl ("admirable sense"), xli ("so well known"), xlii ("it was generally supposed"), xliii ("downright Shippen"), xxxii ("egotism and self-applause"), xliii–xliv ("this melancholy event"). *Les Égarements du cœur et de l'esprit* is a tale by Crébillon *fils*.

p. 453

Life publicity campaign] Unidentified newspaper (P100:14—Mrs. Piozzi's attempt); *St. James's Chron.* 28 May 1791 (P100:25—*Life* sold more copies than *Reflections*); *Pub. Adv.* 16 (P100.1:3—union of matter and spirit), 21 May 1791 (P100.1:6—"LION's *marrow*"); unidentified newspaper, c. July 1791 (P100:34—more durable monument): Boswell has written "Seward" on the clipping. *Pub. Adv.* 1 (P100:27—Langton), 18 June 1791 (P100:32—Boswell's portrait, an *opera*).

Invitations] *Pub. Adv.* 27 May 1791 (P100:24).

p. 454

Correspondence with Scott] To and From Scott, 2–9 Aug. 1791 (several). Scott himself had "remonstrated sharply" with Boswell about an anecdote concerning Blackstone, the great legal commentator, which he had supplied (Fifer, p. 348 n. 1). The present disagreement caused no permanent breach. Scott wrote to Malone after Boswell's death: "I regret with you most heartily that we have lost a companion in poor Bozzy whose place is never to be supplied. Poor fellow! I lament our loss of him beyond measure" (?24 May 1795).

Correspondence with Burke] To Burke, 16 July 1791 ("it is long since"); From Malone, 14 Sept. 1787 (Burke's coldness); From Burke, 20 July 1791 ("we shall, I trust").

p. 455
Reporting conversation] Journ. 1 Jan. 1793 (had lost the faculty of recording); To Sandy,
7 Feb. 1794 ("you must be very cautious"); Fifer, p. lxxxvii ("continued to the end").

p. 456
Mlle Divry] To and From Mlle Divry, June–Aug. 1791 (several), with her French translated without specification. Other references: To Lord Eliot, 1 July 1791 ("gay little *Parisienne*"); Journ. 3 Sept. 1792 ("mercenary and base creature").

Miss Milles] To Temple, 22 Aug. 1791 (Morgan—"daughter of the late Dean"). To and
From Miss Milles, July 1791 (several): here and elsewhere Boswell's French is left uncorrected.
Later Boswell's estimate of Miss Milles's fortune declined to £7,000 (From Temple, 11 Mar.
1792). *Earlier Years*, pp. 144–45 and 209 (Zélide).

p. 457
Home Circuit] Unidentified newspaper, c. 8 Aug. 1791 (P121:3—Prodigal Son); To
Temple, 22 Aug. 1791 (Morgan—circuit); *Pub. Adv.* 23 Aug. 1791 (P121:4—Grand Fleet).
Daily Sales of the First Edition of the *Life* (A60—1,200 copies).

Auchinleck] Book of Company (journey there and movements around Ayrshire); To
Forbes, 27 Sept. 1791 (Somervell—description of Sandy); To Temple, 22 Nov. 1791 (Mor-
gan—languor and gloom, "I visited a good deal"); *Pol. Car.* p. 168 (triumph over Fergusson).
Ironically, the elimination of nominal and fictitious votes led in 1796 to the election of Col.
William Fullarton, that member of the Opposition whose projected candidacy Boswell had
violently opposed earlier; above, p. 417. From Sandy, 30 Oct. 1791 (return trip).

Depression in London] To Robert Boswell, 1 Nov. 1791 ("scanty and difficult subsistence"); To and From Harriet Milles, 26 and 30 Nov. 1791; To Temple, 22 Nov. 1791 (Morgan—
Reynolds's situation); To Paoli, 10 Dec. 1791 (Reynolds moping, "alternate agitation"); To
Barnard, 12–15 Feb. 1792 ("does not wish to see his friends"); To Forbes, 24 Oct. 1793
(Somervell—"no man feels it"); Forbes to Barnard, 19 Apr. 1792 (Somervell—"a point of
concentration"); Foladare, pp. 169–70 (Paoli's problems); From Temple, 6 Dec. 1791 ("ever
dissatisfied"); "Hope travels through": e.g. To Forbes, 29 May 1794 (Somervell). *Life*, i. 344
(after Apr. 1759—imperfect present and the hereafter); To T.D., 13 Oct. 1794 (Hyde—"I
am conscious").

p. 459
Family life] To Lady Auchinleck, 4 June 1791. Dislikes dining at home: e.g. Journ. 20
Nov. 1793. Obituarist: *Oracle*, 25 May 1795, cited in Werkmeister, p. 184.

Clubs] *Life*, iv. 252 n. 2 (Boswell clubbable, Essex Head Club); Fifer, p. 352 nn. 4, 5
(Boswell elected to Royal Academy); To Barnard, 16 Aug. 1792 (select number). Apparently
the Royal Academy Club had about 25–30 members, but no list of them seems to have been
published, and some of those mentioned here may not have been members at the same time
as Boswell. (For the membership, see scattered references in Farington, and John T. Smith,
Nollekens and His Time, ed. Wilfred Whitten, 2nd ed. 1929, i. 187.) Boswell resigned from
the Free and Easy Club in 1793 because of its expense and late hours (Journ. 12 Aug. and
15 Oct. 1793). A list of members of the Eumelian Club appears in H. J. Rose, *New General
Biographical Dictionary*, 1857, ii. 240.

p. 460
Boswell's social talents] Satisfaction in eating and drinking: *LPS 85*, quoted in "Memoirs"
(*Lit. Car.* p. xliii). Journ. 3 Sept. 1792 (no man "so universally easy"); *Life*, v. 76 (21 Aug.
1773—so much good humour), iii. 362 n. 2 ("a man might as well assume"). Defining good
humour as "only the good humour necessary to conversation," Mrs. Thrale—no great admirer—gave Boswell 19 points out of a possible 20; Reynolds got 10 points, and Johnson
zero. (*Thraliana*, i. 329–30—July 1778). *Anecdotes and Egotisms of Henry Mackenzie*, ed.
H. W. Thompson, 1927, p. 112 ("wit always evaporated"); *John. Misc.* ii. 425 (Stewart).

Opinions about Boswell] Farington, i. 96 (28 Sept. 1806—"in removing reserve"): the hostess was Lady Thomond, earlier Lady Inchiquin. Malone in *Gent. Mag.* 65 (June 1795). 471 ("convivial without being *social*"); Whitley, ii. 173 (Lady Lucan): Boswell paid Lord and Lady Lucan an elaborate compliment in the *Life* (iv. 326—before 22 June 1784). Fife to Edward Jerningham, 14 Oct. 1795 (Huntington MSS. JE 358—"but the voice"). Fife goes on, "He had a good heart, well informed, and much humour." Boswell and Seward agreed that Fife's prosing would have been intolerable were it not for his good nature and good dinners (Boswelliana—M57). Cumberland, ii. 228 ("I loved the man"); Fanny Burney to Mrs. Phillips, June 1792 (Burney, *Journals*, ed. Hemlow, i. 181–82—"how many starts").

p. 462
Boswell's friends] Windham: e.g. From Windham, 9 Aug. 1791; From Malone, 1 Sept. 1793. Journ. 11 Nov. 1793 (Seward); From Inchiquin, 9 June 1791 ("certain pleasure"); Journ. 3–6 Aug. 1793 (Chambers); From Cator, 16 Dec. 1791 (Christmas holidays): in the *Life*, Boswell called Cator's country seat "one of the finest places at which I ever was a guest" (iv. 313—after 16 June 1784). Lettsom: e.g. Journ. 21 Aug. 1790. From Lettsom, 18 June 1791 (advice about drinking). Ode celebrating Lettsom: *Ode to Mr. Charles Dilly* (*Gent. Mag.* 61, 1791, 367, 564). Taylor, i. 215 ("I must keep in"); Nichols, *Anec.* iii. 190 n. ("tried the strength").

Curtis] Mock-epitaph: E. B. Impey, *Memoirs of Sir Elijah Impey*, 1846, p. 370: the couplet-writer was Samuel Tolfrey. *Pub. Adv.* 29 June 1791 (P121.1:1—song "loudly applauded"); Werkmeister, pp. 112–13 (called City Laureate); *Pub. Adv.* 28 June 1792 (P122:3—universal approbation); *Morn. Chron.* shortly after 26 June 1792 (P115—"chaunted some miserable doggerel"); *Diary*, 27 June 1792 (cited in Werkmeister, pp. 169–73, which gives attendance); *Pub. Adv.* 7 July 1792 (P122:7—"Old Stingo"); *Song for the Glorious 26th of June* (P160—broadside); *St. James's Chron.* 26 June 1792 (P124:2—"*notoriety*"). Dr. Werkmeister reports the incident in detail (pp. 169–79), but her inferences are unreliable.

p. 463
Boswell helps his relations] To Treesbank, Reg. Let. S. 5 July 1786 (cornetcy); To Barnard, 19 Feb. 1794 (Webster); *Pol. Car.* pp. 115 n. 2 and 178 ("Young Knockroon"); To Robert Boswell, 30 June 1793 (Montgomery Boswell); From Bruce Boswell, 6 Sept. 1792 (storekeeper in Calcutta). T.D.: *Pol. Car.* p. 169 (appointment); almanacs, 1792–1812 (career); *Boswelliana*, pp. 196–97 (Col. Bruce Boswell).

p. 464
Boswell helps others] *Pol. Car.* pp. 169 n. 8 (Frank Temple), 172 (Dawson). Supposedly the hardest naval promotion to obtain was that from midshipman to lieutenant (To Temple, 22 Aug. 1791—Morgan). Pickpocket, whose name was Daniel Merchant: Journ. 25 Feb. 1786; From T.D. 24 Mar. 1786. Apprentice, whose name was John Constantin: Journ. 9 Dec. 1793. To Temple, 15 Sept. 1790 (Morgan—Ross). Janet Little: From and To Janet Little, 11 and 22 Oct. 1791; Janet Little, *Poetical Works*, 1792 (dedication, a dozen copies).

Mary Broad] Prison "a paradise": *Lond. Chron.* 12 July 1792, quoted in F. A. Pottle, *Boswell and the Girl from Botany Bay*, 1938, p. 24. Unless otherwise indicated, Mary Broad's story is taken from this narrative. Further details of the voyage to Timor appear in two accounts included in *True Patriots All*, ed. G. C. Ingleton, 1952.

p. 465
Boswell's spirits pick up] To Sandy, 25 Feb. 1792; To Temple, 29 Mar. 1792 (Morgan).

Efforts on behalf of Mary Broad] From Francis Chalie, 30 Apr. 1793, verso (collects subscriptions); From Temple, 18 July 1793 (family eminent for sheep-stealing).

Mary Broad's annuity] The Yale Boswell Collection contains Mary's semi-annual receipts, and a small packet endorsed by Boswell, "leaves from Botany Bay used as tea," which holds a handful of heavily veined brown leaves.

Parson's poem] *Heroic Epistle from Mary Broad in Cornwall to James Boswell, Esq. in London* (C2188.4). The poem is modelled on Pope's *Mary Gulliver to Captain Lemuel Gulliver*, with a touch of his *Eloisa to Abelard*. For the innocence of Boswell's relationship with Mary, see Pottle, *Botany Bay*, p. 43.

p. 466

1792 uneventful] To Barnard, 16 Aug. 1792 (asks to join Macartney). Veronica as harpsichordist: e.g. Journ. 28 Aug. 1781. Inventories of Auchinleck House show that her harpsichord was moved, over the years, from dining-room to library to lumber room (A2.6: 2, 5, 6). Veronica to Margaret, 7 Dec. 1788 (Euphemia as singer). Euphemia later composed a never-performed opera for Drury Lane (*Boswelliana*, pp. 195–96). Haydn comes to dinner: To and From Lord Exeter, 25 and 26 June 1792, and Boswell's endorsement on the latter. Margate Infirmary: From the Margate Infirmary Committee, 15 June 1792 ("rock of benevolence"); Fifer, p. 366 n. 4. From Temple, 9 July 1792 ("in a perpetual hurry"); To Robert Boswell, 13 June 1792 ("I *cannot* forget").

Hatfield House] To Lord Salisbury, 2 Aug. 1792 ("I am exceedingly hurt"); From Lady Salisbury, c. 17 May 1793 (apology accepted).

Life] To Paoli, 16 Aug. 1792 (1,660 copies sold); Journ. 24 Nov. 1792 (profit). The remaining 61 copies were deposited for copyright purposes or given away: Sale of the First Edition of the *Life* (A59:4,5).

Biography of Reynolds] To Barnard, 16 Aug. 1792. Boswell later told Farington that he was afraid of offending Lady Inchiquin by what he would have to say about Reynolds's well-known dispute with other members of the Royal Academy (Farington, i. 95—27 Mar. 1795).

Sandy at Auchinleck] To Claud Alexander, 9 June 1792 (*Letters JB*, ii. 488).

p. 467

Miss Williams] Journ. 17 Aug. 1792 ("it seems after dinner"): Boswell inked over this passage. Betsy was twelve at the time. Notes, 5 May 1776 (seraglio).

Trip to Devon and Cornwall] Journ. 17 Aug.–16 Sept. 1792; To Malone, 16 Sept. 1792 ("would to GOD"); Journ. 3 ("my mind *rusts*," "warmth of heart"), 9 Sept. 1792 ("as my friend"); To Sandy, 29 Aug. 1792 (daughters not enjoying trip); Nancy Temple to Padgy Peters, 8 Sept. 1792 (Powlett—"boisterous and unpleasant").

p. 469

Visit at parsonage] Mrs. Temple shows dislike of Boswell: Nancy Temple to Charles Powlett, 14 Sept. 1796 (Bettany, p. lxx). Journ. 11 Sept. 1792 (Boswell disgusted with Mrs. Temple). Boswell and Temple admire each other's offspring: e.g. From Temple, 9 July 1792 ("you are very partial to Nancy"), 18 Oct. 1793 (Veronica and Euphemia "have great discernment, good humour, and pleasantry. Delight more in their company, and you will make them whatever you please").

Depression again] To Blair, 3 Nov. 1792 (languishes out of London); Journ. 10 Dec. (depression struck after return), 31 Oct. ("I had no hope"), 6 Nov. (indignant in Westminster Hall), 8 ("as he had been"), 21 Dec. 1792 ("during all this fit").

p. 470

Sexual encounters] Quotations, in order: Journ. 26, 27, 12 Nov. 1792.

Drinking] Journ. 31 Oct. and 30 Dec. 1792 (not drinking). The heavy drinking is mentioned often.

CHAPTER 19

p. 471

Choice of minister] From William Fullarton, 12 Oct. 1792 ("many trumpeters"); John Strawhorn, *Ayrshire*, 1975, p. 135 (Mrs. Buchan); To Robert Findlay, 13 Nov. 1792 (preacher of revelation); Burns, *Holy Fair* ("cauld harangues"); To Blair, 3 Nov. 1792 ("their edification"). The minister's duties are well sketched in John Galt's *Annals of the Parish*, 1821. Forty-three letters: the last letter Boswell docketed was to [?William Dalrymple] 23 July 1793. Marion S. Pottle tells me that 59 letters about the appointment survive in the Yale Boswell Collection.

p. 472

Boswell visits Edinburgh] To Forbes, 11 May 1793 (Somervell—"my wonder"). Boswell reached Edinburgh on 23 Mar. 1793 (Book of Company).

Louis XVI's execution] F. O'Gorman, *The Whig Party and the French Revolution*, 1967, p. 117 (news arrives in London); *Pol. Car.* p. 172 (subscription); From Barnard, after 14 July 1791 ("real and genuine brick"). The brick is missing, but the letter looks as if it had been wrapped around it (see Fifer, pp. xxxvi, 341 nn. 1, 2).

Thurlow] Journ. 24 Dec. 1793 ("very good speech," interview). The interview had taken place in May.

p. 473

The *Life*] From Erskine, 14 Jan. 1793 ("with infinite avidity"); *Life*, iv. 190 (1783—"such was the heat"), 391 n. 1 (Nov.–Dec. 1784—Knox), iii. 243 n. 4 (7 Apr. 1778—"lover of wine"), 271 n. 5 (12 Apr. 1778—Duchess of Northumberland), 179 n. 1 (20 Sept. 1777—Westminster Hall); To Blair, 3 Nov. 1792 ("I am sure"). On Boswell's footnotes, see F. A. Pottle, "The Life of Boswell," *Yale Review*, 35 (1945). 453, from which my comment is adapted.

Boswell's critics] Percy: Waingrow, pp. 597–99; Fifer, pp. lxxxvi–lxxxvii. *Life*, ii. 148 n. 2 (21 Mar. 1772—Beattie's "extreme sensibility"); *New CBEL*, ii. 1238 (Anna Seward's and other letters in *Gent. Mag.*); *Gent. Mag.* 63 (Dec. 1793). 1101 ("defenceless female"). Waingrow summarizes the Seward dispute and its ironies (pp. 439 n. 2, 576 n. 6).

p. 474

"I have an ardent ambition"] *Life*, ii. 69 n. 3 (before 9 Sept. 1769).

Quarrel with Malone] From Malone, 13 May 1793 ("wild rhodomontade"); Proof (P102); To Malone, 17 May 1793 ("I assured him"); Malone to Forbes, 5 July 1798 (Somervell— "having afterwards"); To Sandy, 20 Dec. 1793 (gave as good as he got).

p. 475

Other projects] To Thomas Stedman, 19 Dec. 1793 (Blair, Walton, Webster); From Sandy, 13 July 1792 (Family memoirs); Nichols, *Anec.* ii. 400 n. (*Beggar's Opera*); Journ. 15 Feb. 1794 (Steele). *Lit. Car.*'s list of projects (pp. 301–09) is far from complete. Journ. 4 Apr. 1794 ("dined at Mr. Cator's"), 29 Aug. 1792 (fear of book on Cornish tour).

p. 476

"Travels"] To Forbes, 11 May (Somervell—"your travels afford"), 24 Oct. 1793 (Somervell—"although I should"); From Temple, 31 ("I don't think"), 26 May 1794 ("strange that you").

Temple's "characters"] *Lond. Mag.* 41 (1772). 140 (Temple's sketch of Gray). Temple had offered his sketch of Johnson immediately after his death (From Temple, 6 Jan. 1785) but, when Boswell rejected it, admitted that any such character sketch would be based on "only casual and superficial observation" (From Temple, 4 Jan. 1786). Still, Temple wrote to Edward Jerningham (14 Apr. 1785) offering to show him a sketch of Johnson "that I believe you will allow to be a true likeness; but Boswell must not see it, nor know who drew it" (Lewis Bettany, *Edward Jerningham and His Friends*, 1919, p. 309). Presumably this, or a modified version of it, is the sketch included in the anonymous *Character of Dr. Johnson with Illustrations from Mrs. Piozzi, Sir John Hawkins, and Mr. Boswell*, which Dilly published in 1792. The author describes Johnson as "shutting or turning up the whites of his eyes in a most disagreeable manner" (p. 1); "pawing his meat with his great, coarse, sooty hands" (p. 2); swallowing lemonade "to a nauseous excess" (p. 3); and "taking up a knife or fork and looking along it as if it were a spying glass" (p. 5). The author concludes that Johnson was "a man undoubtedly of merit, learning, and talents, but all of them overrated by his partial admirers." On the other hand, he praises Boswell: "Where is he not received with pleasure?" (p. 22). Nicholls wrote to Temple (11 Mar. 1793): "I am glad the swollen and bloated reputation of Johnson owes to your pen a very fair and just pruning and reduction" (Beinecke). It is difficult to believe that since Dilly published this piece Boswell did not know who wrote it. But he shows no signs of even having heard of it.

p. 477
Boswell's papers] In his will, dated 28 May 1785, Boswell left the proceeds from any publishable material that could be extracted from his papers to his younger children (*Pride and Negligence*, pp. 8–9). "Younger children" is a legal term designating all the children except Sandy, Boswell's heir.

Boswell plans trip] To Gibb, 31 May 1793 (trip). Robbery: Sandy to Forbes, 11 June 1793 (Somervell); *Lond. Chron.* 11 June 1793. From Temple, 15 June 1793 (admonishes Boswell); To Temple, 21 June 1793 (Morgan—"this shall be a *crisis*"). Later Pughe asked for help because he had made an imprudent marriage, his family had cut him off, his wife had been brought to bed, and he hadn't a guinea. Boswell assisted him (From and To J. Pughe, Oct.–Nov. 1793, several). To Langton, 24 July 1793 (Hyde—"I was sorry").

Second edition of the *Life*] To Langton, 24 July 1793 (Hyde—400 copies sold). Boswell's record of sales of the second edition (A62) actually shows some 360 copies sold in the first week and over 400 in the first three weeks. *Lit. Car.* pp. 168–69 (description of second edition).

p. 478
Principal Additions] Journ. 6 Aug. 1793 (only occupation); *Lit. Car.* p. 212 (description); *Critical Review*, new arr. 9 (Nov. 1793). 313. The *Principal Additions* had been printed by early November when Boswell sent Sir William Scott a copy (From Scott, 2 Nov. 1793).

Third edition of the *Life*] Dilly to Forbes, 12 July 1798 (Somervell); Advertisement to the third edition.

Boswell's summer, 1793] *Gent. Mag.* 63 (1793). 774 (Bosville's death); Journ. 22 Aug. 1793 (gives up tour); From James Jr., 3 Aug. 1793 (boys at Auchinleck); Journ. 6 Sept. (Malone at Stratford), 10 Aug. (departed friends), 4–5 Sept. 1793 (meeting with Inchiquins).

Nancy Temple and Charles Powlett Jr.] Most of the story appears in Temple's diary (Bettany), in the Boswell–Temple correspondence, and in manuscripts in the Powlett Collection; it will be documented in detail in the research edition of the Boswell–Temple correspondence, edited by Thomas Crawford, to whom I am grateful for making me acquainted with vital parts of this material. From Temple, 6 Sept. 1793 (£300 a year). Impedimenta: Powlett spoke of 18 boxes of his own, which "will take up immense room," and further boxes of his mother's (Powlett to Nancy Temple, 25 July 1793—Powlett). From Temple, 7 Sept. 1793 (Powletts get on his nerves).

p. 479
Temple's story] Mrs. Temple's disposition: e.g. From Temple, 16 Aug. 1790. From Temple, 11 July 1792 ("she hardly knows"). An angel: e.g. From Temple, 28 Dec. 1793. From Temple, 6 Sept. 1793 (Sukey's age). A delusion: e.g. From Temple, 18 July 1793. To Temple, 21 June 1793 (Morgan—diversion or escape).

Temple's mission a success] From Temple, 5 Nov. 1793.

Powlett and Sukey] From Temple, 6 Oct. 1793 (quarrel with Powlett): Nancy Temple's "Diary," 8 Oct. 1793 (Powlett—most violent dispute); From Temple, 19 (Sukey denies story), 31 Dec. 1793 ("six-and-thirty years!"); Powlett spreads story: e.g. From Temple, 10 Feb. 1794. Frank was about 23 at this time (Bettany, p. 114).

Temple forbids marriage] From Temple, 19 Dec. (Powlett "diabolical"), 11 July 1793 (Powlett Sr. remarries); From Nancy Temple to Mrs. Percy Powlett, 12 Dec. 1792 (Powlett—utterly selfish); From Temple, 18 Oct. 1793 (Powlett's debts).   Debauchery at Cambridge: Lord Stawell to Charles Powlett Jr., ?after 11 Nov. 1793 (Powlett); From Temple, 18 Dec. 1793.   From Temple, 5 Nov. (Nancy "indelicate"), 7 Sept. 1793 (no notion of economy).   To Temple, 14 Oct. 1793 (Morgan—Boswell sympathizes with anger).   On reading some letters from Boswell to her father after their deaths, Nancy wrote to Powlett that if Boswell were not dead, "I fear I could not forgive the cruel, unfeeling, unjust, and illiberal manner [in which] he expresses himself not only of me and my poor Frank but of my excellent and beloved mother.   O my friend, what virtue can screen us from malevolent sarcasm if hers was unable to defend her. . . .   What can excuse him from endeavouring to sow dissension in the family of his friend, for exasperating a father against his children by filling him with suspicions which he must have known were base and unworthy both of him and us!" (14 Sept. 1796—Powlett).

p. 480

Boswell's amorous adventures] Journ. 19 and 20 Aug. and 13 Oct. ("old acquaintance"), 16 and 17 Dec. ("C"), 15 and 16 Mar. 1794 (〰): 〰 recurs on 2 Apr. 1794 (Journ.). Presumably this "C" is not the one mentioned in 1789.   Journ. 15 Feb. (fear of impregnation), 2 and 5 Apr. 1794 (fear of infection); From Temple, 6 Feb. 1793 ("the lovely Maria!"); Journ. 19 May 1790 and 9 Feb. 1794 (marriage out of the question): he did tell Temple once that if he could find "a proper object" he would not let his children stand in the way (To Temple, 14 Oct. 1794—Morgan).

Boswell's illusions] Chambers in Temple: lease (M124); Journ. 5 Nov. 1792: they cost him about £40 a year.   Journ. 12 Nov. 1793 (Westminster Hall appearance).   Home Circuit: Home Circuit Sessions (Lg62, 64, 66–67, 69–70); Expense Accounts, Home Circuit, 1792–94 (A47–50).   Journ. 9 Nov. 1793 (gave his life variety), 16 Jan. 1794 (resolves to go on circuit only from time to time).

Health] Bumps: From Temple, 20 Dec. 1793, 10 Feb and 7 Mar. 1794.   From Sandy, 1 July 1792 ("that can stand the labour").   Dance's and Lawrence's sketches appear as nos. 103 and 100 in John Kerslake's catalogue, Mr. Boswell, 1967.   Farington, i. 6 (6 Oct. 1793—"much altered for the worse").   But at the same period Farington also records that Boswell made "a very good speech" at the Royal Academy Club which was "very well received" (i. 22—3 Dec. 1793).

p. 481

"I was incessantly thinking"] Journ. 25 Oct. 1793.

Dining out] These dinners occurred respectively on 12 Feb., 2, 3, 6, 29, 30 Mar., and 10 Apr. 1794 (Journ.).   From Windham, 13 Mar. 1794 ("for one day"); Journ. 4 Feb. (Bleaden), 25 Mar. (Townshend), 22 Feb. 1794 (Robert Boswell).

Financial difficulties] To Sandy, 10 May ("rich day," narrowest manner), 3 Mar. 1794 (improvements); From T.D., 7 Dec. 1793 (C. B. Tinker's typescript; original not traced—rents in arrears); Audit of Household Expenditures (A68:6—"the two young ladies"); Journ. 18 Feb. 1794 (stays away from Club).

p. 482
Corsica] Foladare, pp. 180–224 (historical situation); To Dundas, 17 Mar. 1794 (wishes to be made Minister); Journ. 26 Mar. 1794 ("cold, ministerial" response).

Temple on Boswell] From Temple, 18 Apr. ("I tenderly sympathize"), 5 June 1794 ("unless you correct").

p. 483
Temple on Temple] From Temple, 18 July 1793 ("even healthier"), 15 ("it is very odd"), 25 and 26 Feb., 7 and 13 Mar. (insipid poems), 30 Jan. ("whining folly"), 7 Mar. ("it never seems to enter"), 4 May 1794 (wants his wife again), 18 July 1793 ("are all my ambitions"), 30 Jan. 1794 ("a little deranged"); Bettany, pp. lxiii–lxiv (falling off horse); From Temple, 20 Oct. 1794 ("let us be gay"). Frank continued to assert, and Sukey to deny, that they had had sexual relations (From Temple, 3 Nov. 1794).

Nancy and Powlett] Nancy Temple's "Diary," 30 Aug. 1794 (Powlett—Nicholls's intervention, £400 a year). Nancy and Powlett were married in 1796, a few months after Temple's death. Two years later Jane Austen described Nancy as "silly and cross as well as extravagant" (Jane Austen to Cassandra Austen, 18 Dec. 1798—Jane Austen, *Letters*, ed. R. W. Chapman, 1932, i. 39).

"Your drinking is owing"] From Temple, 3 and 5 June 1794.

p. 484
Second edition of *Life*] To Sandy, 17 Mar. 1794 (800 copies). Farington says that during his lifetime Boswell made about £2,500 from the *Life*. After his death, Cadell bought the copyright for £300, which proved to be a very good bargain for him (iii. 52—31 Jan. 1805). If Farington's figure is correct, then Boswell's profit on the second edition was about £950. Boswell calculated that he cleared about £9.9s on every twelve copies (Profits of Second Edition of *Life*—A63), but some copies were sold at a discount (Settlements between Boswell and Dilly—A64). At a tentative guess, 1,200 copies of the second edition were printed.

On going to Auchinleck] To Sandy, 13 Mar. ("spoiled by variety"), 10 May (on taking the girls), 26 Feb. 1794 (cannot introduce Sandy).

Boswell's stay at Auchinleck] To James Jr., 30 June ("wonderfully good spirits"), 14 July (dulness and vulgarity), 22 Aug. (girls take to country doings), 21 July 1794 (applies to estate affairs, Windham's appointment); From James Jr., 25 July 1794 (Lord High Chancellor); To James Jr., 11 Aug. 1794 (newspapers welcome to their fun).

Depression at Auchinleck] To James Jr., 27 Oct. 1794 ("country does not at all"); To Malone, 18 Nov. 1794 ("I have been uncommonly moderate"); To James Jr., 12 Sept. 1794 ("I still indulge"); From James Jr., 18 Oct. ("read and write," abridgement of *Corsica*), 10 Nov. 1794 ("any little pamphlet"); From T.D., 5 Dec. 1794 (new edition of *Corsica*); To James Jr., 21 Nov. 1794 ("try to avoid repining"); From Temple, 3 Nov. 1794 ("you complain of your ill success").

p. 485
Boswell's sense of himself] Journ. 13 Feb. 1794 ("my constant cause"); To Temple, 10 Jan. 1789 (Morgan—"has ever raged"); Johnson, "Roscommon" (para. 23—"thus it is"), *Lives*, i. 235; Journ. 10 Apr. 1772 ("I just sat"); To Forbes, 29 May 1794 (Somervell—"is still at my heart").

p. 486
Boswell and his children] From Temple, 18 July 1793 ("how eccentric soever"); To James Jr., 14 July ("loud familiarity"), 12 Sept. 1794 ("the old man"); To Sandy, 26 Nov. 1794 ("veins of classical quotation"); To James Jr., 15 Dec. 1794 (hopes for Sandy as lawyer); To Sandy, 6 Dec. 1794 (studies too hard); To James Jr., 21 July (quarrels less with girls), 29 Sept. 1794 (their running into company); From Temple, 20 Oct. 1794 (fiddlers and singers); From James

Jr., 10 Nov. 1794 (leechlike emigrés).   But Boswell came to the rescue of two emigrés when they were imprisoned for debt (Journ. 8 Feb. 1794).   Journ. 20 Aug. 1792 (apologizes to Pembroke).

p. 487
Children's love for Boswell] Sandy's "Journal of His Travels," 28 Apr. 1796 (C277.5— "I was now at the court").   Betsy: From Temple, 5 June 1794 (a favourite); From T.D., 16 Oct. 1794 (jumps for joy).   Farington, i. 325–26 (25 Sept. 1801—Euphemia).

Boswell and James Jr.] To James Jr., 22 Aug. 1794 (companions); From Lady Auchinleck, 6 July 1793 ("really a fine boy").   James thought her very kind, and even said that old battleaxe, Miss Peggie, was "as good natured as can be" (From James Jr., 6 July 1793).   From James Jr., c. 24 Dec. 1794 (long, dreary separation), 6 July 1793 ("I remain again and again").

Last days at Auchinleck] The Book of Company records the movements of the family at Auchinleck.   To James Jr., 29 (the girls' giggle), 15 ("quite overcome"), 21 Nov. 1794 ("day of excessive vitality"); To Sandy, 26 Nov. 1794 ("can *fight a battle*"); "Pathetic Song" (M342). Comfortable hours: From T.D., 20 Dec. 1794; To Sandy, 23 Feb. 1795.   To James Jr., 15 Nov. 1794 ("weather it out"); To Forbes, 15 Dec. 1794 (Somervell—"I have good reasons"). The previous spring before leaving London, he had told Forbes, "Practice at the English bar seems unattainable by me" (29 May 1794—Somervell); To James Jr., 3 Jan. 1795 (spirits fully revived); From James Jr., 5 Jan. 1795 ("Oh, Sir"); To James Jr., 13 Jan. 1795 (return trip).

p. 488
Winter in London] *Pol. Car.* pp. 172–73 (Eamer); William Henry Ireland, *Confessions*, 1805, p. 96 (Boswell kisses manuscript).   Malone knocked this forgery on the head with *An Inquiry into the Authenticity of Certain Papers Attributed to Shakespeare*, 1796.   To Lady Orkney, 22 Mar. 1795 (flirts); To Paoli, (?Mar. 1795—"Ministry of this country").   Wynyard: General Note Following L1311 in the forthcoming *Catalogue* of the Yale Boswell Collection.   Major Semple: Joseph W. Reed provides the details in "Boswell and the Major," *Kenyon Review*, 28 (1966). 161–84.

Bequest to Veronica] F. A. Pottle, "Notes on the Importance of Private Legal Documents for the Writing of Biography and Literary History," *Proceedings* of the American Philosophical Society, 106 (1962). 328–30: 328 ("the two great affections").

p. 489
Boswell's last days] Journ. 9 Mar. 1795 (existence exhilarates); From Temple, 5 Mar. 1795 (Dundas more favourable).

p. 35
Last illness and death] James Jr., to Temple, 17 Apr. 1795 (Morgan—Boswell taken ill); To Hastings, 24 Apr. 1795 (British Library—congratulations); T.D. to Temple, 4 May 1795 (Morgan—swelling in bladder); Farington, i. 267 (31 Mar. 1799—"fell upon *those parts*"); From Boswell and James Jr. to Temple, 8 May 1795 (Morgan—"I would fain write"); Malone to Forbes, 25 Apr. 1796 (Somervell—"he seemed to think himself").   T.D. to Temple, 13 May 1795 (Morgan—"good hopes are entertained"); James Jr. to Temple, 16 (Morgan), 18 May 1795 (Morgan—"since I wrote last"); T.D. to Temple, 19 May 1795 (Morgan—time of death). Modern diagnosis: W. B. Ober, *"Boswell's Clap" and Other Essays*, 1979, p. 28.   It seems to have been no more than coincidence that Boswell's grandfather, "Old James," had also died of a strangury at about the age of 75 (Jasper John Boswell, MS. "History of the Boswells," vol. 2, part 4, p. 122—Fondazione Sella, San Gerolamo, Biella), and Lord Auchinleck at 58 had been stricken with the same illness.

Veronica, who nursed her father during his last illness, shortly afterwards fell sick herself, according to Sandy because of the fatigue she had undergone; specifically, "her affection exceeded her strength and she . . . strained herself in attempting to lift him" (Alexander

Boswell to Forbes, 18 Aug. 1795—Somervell).   She died that September, aged 22, actually from the rapid onslaught of consumption.

Final opinions] Malone to Windham, 21 May 1795 (*The Windham Papers* [ed. Lewis Melville] 1913, i. 297–98).   Forbes to Malone, 30 June 1796 (Hyde—"most striking memorials").

p. 491
Burial] Forbes to Veronica, 13 June 1795 (Somervell).

INDEX

This is principally an index of proper names, but includes a few subject headings (e.g. Bible, London, Parliament, Scotland and Scots). Sources are not indexed. Sovereigns and members of British royal families are entered under their first names, and all others under their surnames. Titles of books are entered under their authors. A hyphen between page numbers (e.g. Percy, 310–12) does not necessarily indicate continuous discussion, but just that Percy is mentioned on all three pages. The following abbreviations are used: D. (Duke), M. (Marquess), E. (Earl), V. (Viscount), B. (Baron), Bt. (Baronet), Kt. (Knight), Archbp. (Archbishop), Bp. (Bishop), W.S. (Writer to the Signet), LA (Lord Auchinleck), JB (James Boswell), SJ (Samuel Johnson), MM (Margaret Montgomerie Boswell), WJT (William Johnson Temple).

BOSWELL, JAMES (JB), (*cont.*):

own excuse, 523; loves confrontation, 132, 319; dutiful (submissive), 141–43, 155, 157, 163, 199, 204, 220, on company that awes him, 162, 172, 182, 208, 348, 350, loves authority over him, 208, 346, 348; honesty (openness, exhibitionism), 145, 155, 223, 249, 277–78, 302, 387, 394, 441–42, 445, 475; fear of nothingness (annihilation), 146–48, 179, 206, 235; lazy (barren, indolent), 153, 205, 269, 271, on impotence of mind, 178, 199–200, 220, 276–77, 419, thinks of retirement, 199, 246, 396, insignificant (feeble, paralysed), 220, 235, 393, timid, unfit for employment, 393, 482; too jocular, 155, 270; tests people's affections, 157, 161, 187; literal–minded, 162, 177; likes theatre, 163, attends theatre, 371; resentful, 163–64, 203, 248; thoughts of second marriage, 165, 223, 399, 456–57, 480, 576; "rattles," 165, loves to talk, 236, talks well, 460; on slavery, 165–66, 421–22; loves pomp, 181; fond of military life, 189, 194, 202; respect for truth, 190, 430; attentive to old connections, 194; always wants something, 203; perceptive about self, 203, lacks self-knowledge, 236; wants employment from King, 217, 221, 254, 265–67, 312, 458; likes to study great characters, 218, 348, 401; feels he is very good, 219; warmth of imagination, 222, 468; rational and active, 231; aggressive, 232; has "local" mind, 235; seeks advice, 238, 240, 314–15, 339, 406, does not act on, 259, 317, lacks power of decision, 238, lacks self-control, 259, does not take responsibility for self, 314, 379, 413; feels life loses vividness, 248, thinks no man would live life over, 257; identifies himself with London, 268; indulges in discontent, 269; and ticket in "lottery" of life, 273, 275, 277, 378–79, 388; vanity (egotism), 277–78, 281, 451, 468, 475; sense of humour, 278, 452; careless about reputation, 295, has deficient sense of shame, 442; has milk of human kindness, 306; has high notions of dignity, 327, 379, cannot preserve uniform dignity, 474; has excellent memory, 332, 429, 455; wants to be conspicuous, 364, 381, 386, 390, 405, 421; poor at imposed tasks, 369; thinks variety of ideas (images) removes uneasiness, 371; lacks interest in landscape, 375; fears loneliness, 405; feels fortune should favour him, 413–15; has dark complexion, 422; tolerant, 444, 452; fears future, 458–59; loves eating and drinking, 460, wants to be superior to others, 536; sees life as series of "scenes," 565; attitude towards London (about forty-five, mostly favourable, references)

III. *Health, spirits.* Early illness, 2; has (suspects) venereal infection, 5, 41, 130, 167–68, 197, 216, 284, 326, 336, 410, 480, 490; has cold, 87, 164, 235; good spirits (about thirty references); drinks (gets drunk—about forty references), attitude towards drinking, 108–09, 113, 162, 179–80, 234–35, 371, 384, 406, 467, 477, 489–90, sobriety (water-drink-

ing), 179–80, 222–23, 227, 234–35, 355, 421, 470, 472, 485; sprains ankle, 120, 370; headaches, 135, 343, 412; thoughts of suicide, 135, 220; bruised knee, 136; depression (about forty references), melancholy (hypochondria), 162, 177–78, 204–06, 223, 530, alternate agitation and depression, 458, not manic-depressive, 561–62; enjoys good health, 201, 265, 369; grows fat, 221, 480, grows thin, 251, weight and height, 519; influenza, 222, 234; bruised shoulder, 390–91; urethral stricture, 400; "scorbutic" eruptions, 469; bad cut, 477; "bumps" on head, 480; health deteriorates, 480–81; last illness, 489–91, 578

IV. *As Lawyer, and Law cases.*

a. *At Scots bar.* Passes advocate, 4; practice, 13–14, 43–44, 95, 108–09, 149, 182, 187, 189, 195, 197, 204, 232, 236, 251, 502; fees, 13, 19, 43, 109, 113–14, 123, 187, 231, 502, 553; in General Assembly, 14, 21, 39, 159, 196, 502; in House of Lords, 26, 29–30, 168, 210, 245, 339–40, 471–72, 551–52; on speaking in court, 26, 29–30, 95, 109, 196, 202, 237, 245, 264, 471–72; does well in legal argument, 39, 95, 246, 508; pressed into law, 40, 143; Faculty examiner, 43; likes, 49, bored by practice, 87–88, 126, 155, 195, 235; studies law, 95; deficient as lawyer, 95, 123, 198, 202; conflict in attitude towards being lawyer, 95–96, 105; advocates trial by jury in civil causes, 99, 196, 280; sense of justice, 100; ready to give up practice, 159; arbiter in causes, 197, 534; reputation, 534

b. *At English bar.* On going to English bar, 96, 127, 162, 202–04, 221, 237–38, 258–60, 263–66, 310–18, 337; on study for, 263–66, 319–21, 336–37, 378; called, 318; law cases, 321–22, 327; in London law courts, 321–22, 343, 351, 359, 370, 480, 576; and Northern Circuit, 325–27, 335, 339, 341, 361, 363, 370, 378–80, 388, 395, as junior counsel on, 325–26, 378, given feigned brief, 326–27; thinks of abandoning bar, 336–40, 363, 370; and Home Circuit, 341–42, 356, 358, 457, 480; Mayor's Counsel, Carlisle, 347–50; (wants to be) Recorder, Carlisle, 356, 360–61, 363–64, 378–81, 407–12, 452, addresses grand jury, 381; on chambers in Inner Temple, 385, 396, 480, 576; *misc.*, 385, 409, 452, 459, 469, 472, 487, 578

c. *Law cases.* Reid, 4, 96–106, 123; Douglas Cause, 4, 9, 29, 79, 88, 129, 157, 201, 346, 452; Harris, 13–14, 502; St. Ninians, 14–15, 21, 502–03; Miller v. Angelo, 19, 503; McMaster, 21; Burnett v. Clark, 26, 504; Candacraig, 26; George McDonald, 26; Wilson v. Smith and Armour, 26; Campbell v. Hastie, 26, 29–31, 505; People of Marykirk v. Brymer, 39–40; Fullarton v. Dalrymple, 43–44; Grieve v. Borland, 44–45; Richard Robertson, 45; Cameron v. Tosh, 45, 508; Hinton v. Donaldson, 87–88, 515; Thomas Gray, 88–89, 515; Earl Fife's politics, 95–96; McGraugh, 123, 521; Rickson v. Bird, 123; Jack v. Copland, 123; Dick v. His Creditors, 124;